A SURVEY OF HINDUISM

A SURVEY OF HINDUISM

KLAUS K. KLOSTERMAIER

State University of New York Press

Published by
State University of New York Press, Albany

Printed in the United States of America

For information, address State University of New York
Press, State University Plaza, Albany, N.Y., 12246

Library of Congress Cataloging-in-Publication Data

Klostermaier, Klaus K., 1933-
A survey of Hinduism/Klaus K. Klostermaier.
p. cm.
Bibliography: p.
Includes index.
ISBN 0-88706-807-3. ISBN 0-88706-809-X (pbk.)
1. Hinduism. I. Title
BL 1202.K56 1989
294.5—dc 19 87-32918
CIP

10 9 8 7 6 5 4 3 2

For Doris, Sonja, Cornelia and Evelyn.

Contents

PART III: THE STRUCTURAL SUPPORTS OF HINDUISM

List of Drawings

List of Photographs

Preface

A Survey of Hinduism is intended as an introduction to the fascinating and multifaceted religions of India commonly referred to as Hinduism. No previous knowledge of any detail is presupposed but also readers with some background are hoped to profit from the study of the work and the literature referred to. While there are several reliable treatments of Hinduism from historical and literary perspectives, an understanding of what Hinduism means to its followers seemed to be better conveyed through a topical treatment as is done here.

During the many years of preparation of the book many friends and colleagues, in India, Europe, Australia and North-America have made contributions by either providing information or helping editorially. For this I wish to thank them all, in particular Antonia Fonseca, Eric Sharpe and Brenda Cantelo. For diligently typing and retyping the extensive manuscript I wish to thank Shelley Bozyk. I am much obliged to Gnomi Schrift Gouldin who did so much as copy-editor to improve the quality of the work. Finally I wish to thank the Research Administration of the University of Manitoba for various grants to prepare the manuscript and the illustrations.

Winnipeg, February 1988

Klaus K. Klostermaier

Acknowledgments

Acknowledgment is made to *Indian and Foreign Review* for the reproduction of drawing No. 2; to *Hindu Viśva* for the reproduction of drawings 1, 3-17 and 19-21; to Annemarie Steggles for drawing No. 22; to Otto Hederer for assisting in photographs No. 23, and 25 to 34, and to the Ramanashram in Tiruvannamalai for photograph No. 35.

Note on Pronunciation and Use of Sanskrit words

As a rule the Sanskrit vowels have the same value as Italian vowels; a dash above a vowel means a length: ā - aa. Consonants correspond, with few exceptions, to the English consonants. Among the more notable differences are aspirate consonants: e.g. *th* is not pronounced like the English *th* in *the*, but it is a double consonant like ho*th*ouse. C (and its aspirate) is pronounced like dsh. ś and ṣ are pronounced sh. As a rule Sanskrit words are quoted in the text in their uninflected stem-form. In some cases, where Indian words have become part of the English vocabulary, the English form of writing has been retained. Names have usually been quoted as they appear in the documents referred to, and no attempt has been made to correctly transliterate them or to provide them with diacritical marks. In the bibliography Indian names have been usually dealt with as if they were European names. While this is technically not always correct (Śastri, Iyer, Iyengar, etc. are really titles and not proper names) it makes it easier to identify authors.

A SURVEY OF HINDUISM

Figure 1 Śiva *Trimūrti* from Elephanta

Introduction

> Among all the great religions of the world there is none more catholic, more assimilative, than the mass of beliefs which go to make up what is popularly known as Hinduism.
>
> —*W. Crooke*[1]

MOST OF INDIA'S 800 million people call themselves Hindus. In addition, some 20 million Hindus are settled all over the world, substantial numbers of them in North America. Hindu gurus have become very visible in the West during the past few decades as promoters of a faith that many young Westerners adopted as their own. Hinduism is the oldest living major tradition on earth, with roots reaching back into the prehistory of humankind. It has preserved beliefs and practices from times immemorial and it has developed under the influence of many other traditions. For many centuries, India was a distant and mysterious land to Westerners. Since the Age of Discovery—and it is an interesting coincidence that the discovery of America took place as the result of Europe's search for India—India has become increasingly accessible to the West. The West realized that India had more to offer than spices and markets, and in turn, India gave up its initial reserve opening up its treasures of literature and culture to Western scholars. India's heritage is readily accessible today. Hinduism is also a vibrant living tradition. It is about this tradition that the present work intends to inform and for which it wishes to create some understanding.

Hinduism, while offering many striking parallels to other great religions, nevertheless cannot be compared with any of them. That has as much to do with its history as with its present adherents, with the way religion has been conceived in India and the way it is understood today in the West. Considering the growth of Hinduism and the great variety of its expressions, one is tempted to see not so much a parallel between Hinduism and other religions but between Hinduism and what one could call, for the moment, Europeanism or Americanism. Hinduism, while

1. Govindajī Temple, Vṛndāvan

certainly circumscribing Indian religiosity, has many other dimensions of a historico-cultural and socio-political nature. Hinduism both represented and always found itself in a situation of cultural and religious pluralism. Hinduism has aroused the curiosity not only of scholars of religion but equally that of sociologists and anthropologists, political scientists and archeologists, philosophers and historians, as well as the philologists who were the first to become seriously interested in Hindu literature. We must remind ourselves, however, that Hinduism was created by its sages and saints not to provide material for doctoral dissertations for Western scholars or to enable anthropologists and sociologists to do their field work but for the physical and spiritual sustenance of its population. Hinduism is intended to interpret reality to Hindus, to make life more meaningful to them, to provide them with a theoretical and practical framework for their individual and corporate existence, to educate them intellectually and morally, and finally, to fulfill their longing for ultimate freedom and salvation.

In contrast to Ancient Greece and Rome, whose classical literatures and traditions have been the major inspiration of Western humanities but whose modern successor nations have little in common with them, India is a modern country in which much of the classical tradition is still alive. It is alive not only in the age-old rituals that continue to be performed or in the popular stories from epics and *Purāṇas* that are still enjoyed by contemporary audiences in theaters and films but also in the structure of its society and many of its laws, in its institutions and in its popular customs. It would be wrong, however, to portray Hinduism as a specimen of fossilized past, a tradition unable to change, a museum exhibit that must not be touched. Quite the contrary, Hinduism has undergone many changes, is rapidly adapting to modern times, and is constantly bringing forth new movements and taking new directions. Hinduism has always been more than mere religion in the modern Western sense, and it aims at being a comprehensive way of life as well today, a tradition by which people can live.

Many Westerners who come to India experience a culture shock, that has not so much to do with the difference in living standards between India and the West—a difference that is rapidly diminishing—but with the different kind of logic of life. Hinduism is built on assumptions different from those of the West. Once these are accepted, Hinduism appears as logical and as consistent as any other tradition.

J. K. Galbraith, the former U.S. ambassador to India and a great friend of India, once described India as a "functioning anarchy." Anybody who has lived in the country for any length of time will agree. However, the emphasis is on *functioning*, somehow everything works in the end. There may not be a grand design, a model that can be rationalized, a theory that is followed through, but the many small solutions to small problems somehow come together to make it work. Bibhuti S. Yadav, a Hindu teaching at a U.S. college and an articulate defender of Vaiṣṇavism's *puṣṭimārga*, once wrote:

> "The socalled Hinduism is a rolling conference of conceptual spaces, all of them facing all, and all of them requiring all. Each claims loyalty to the *śrutis*, each showing how its claims are decisively true, and charging the rival schools with perpetuating the confusion of tongue in the *dharmakṣetra*. . . . A lay Hindu . . . is a living contradiction, unsynthetic and logically incomplete to any and all. "Synthetic unity" has never existed in Hinduism, neither in conceptual space nor in lived time. Hinduism is a moving form of life whose predicament is to be incomplete to its own logics; it is a history of contradictions in flesh, fortunately demanding that their resolution be constantly postponed.[2]

Not to leave a wrong impression at this point, within its own framework, presupposing its own presuppositions, each school of Hinduism is logical and consistent. By being what it is, a quite easily noticeable "living contradiction" if looked at from the standpoint of any one system, it probably is truer to life than other major religions, which claim to follow one authority, to have one faith and one center.

Because of its nature as a "rolling conference of conceptual spaces" and the constant interaction among all its facets, it is important for us to gain first an overall view, to provide a survey rather than an in-depth study of one system or one set of concepts that can conveniently be called *Hinduism.*

The bewilderment of westerners who come into contact with living Hinduism may also have to do with the available literature on Hinduism. Much of it is devoted to some kind of orchid-collecting not to a description of the real landscape. Much popular writing about India either attempts to shock the reader by describing bizarre happenings and sinister characters or to romanticize a country and civilization so delightfully different from our own. Much scholarly writing focusses on the past of India, the literature and architectural monuments, the practices and institutions of classical India. A great amount has been written, and continues to be written, on Vedic ritual and ancient Indian kingship, topics no doubt of great historic significance but of very marginal relevance today. Similarly, many a book on Hindu mythology, on the gods and goddesses of India, more often than not makes no attempt to tell the reader how contemporary Hindus understand these deities, how and why they worship them, but frequently tries to prove a Freudian, a Jungian, or other psychological or anthropological thesis, playing around with theoretical models that are clever and appear plausible to western intellectuals but explain little and often distort a great deal of Hindu reality. Given the enormous mass of writings connected with Hinduism, it is very easy to find supportive quotes for any thesis. It is another question whether the thesis would be acceptable to Hindus and whether it fits the context in India.

In this book, the attempt is made to describe Hinduism as the living tradition of the Hindus, a tradition with its own logic and with a purpose of its own. The intention is to portray Hinduism in such a way that contemporary Hindus would be able to recognize themselves in it and outsiders would be helped to understand something of this tradition, which is alien to them but about which they are curious, the tradtion they encounter on a visit to India.

The intention of this survey of Hinduism is to offer correct information on Hinduism as a whole and also to make a modern westerner understand some of its meaning. To do so, the information has to be selective. Hinduism is simply too large a subject to be dealt with exhaustively in a volume this size, and too much has been written about it that need not be repeated but can be referred to. Understanding, obviously, can be communicated only to the extent that it is available. Understanding usually takes the form of translating something unknown into known categories. The choice of the categories into which one translates is crucial and cannot be totally arbitrary. Understanding in a nonelementary sense happens within certain systematic contexts, operating with certain presuppositions and identifying certain structures.[3] Thus, an interpretation of a phenomenon like Hinduism in modern western categories takes place within a given philosophical, theological, sociological, anthropological, historical, or political framework. These frameworks facilitate the integration of information but they also may hinder us from seeing the specifics and those aspects for which there is no parallel. As L. Dumont has remarked, "Hindu religion, or philosophy is at least as all-embracing in its own way as any sociological theory may be."[4] The same is true, of course, for Indian attempts to understand the West. Learning apparently entails a certain amount of tension, it requires the working out of alternative viewpoints, it aims at the recognition of unresolved problems. Learning about Hinduism is no exception to this.

Intentionally, I did not choose the framework of any one particular contemporary Western academic discipline.[5] This made my task at once easier and more difficult. Easier because it removes the need to justify with the concepts of a particular discipline what obviously does not fit into its schema.[6] More difficult because the range of phenomena to be dealt with becomes so much larger, the choice of vocabulary more problematic, the risk of transgressing beyond one's competence so much greater.

The study of other cultures is no longer just the hobby of a few leisured academics, it has or should become a major component of general education. The modern world is connected through networks of trade and commerce, political and military alliances, and through large scale migrations of populations. If we consider each other as belonging to one humankind, we cannot consider cultures and races as eternally immovable barriers—nor can we ignore them. We can penetrate them and can enter into an exchange. L. Dumont has emphatically expressed the conviction that "cultures not only *can* be made to communicate, they *must*."[7] Through that communication we will doubtlessly also become capable of sharing other cultures' viewpoints, seeing their logic from within, and valuing as precious what was merely exotic to us before. In this case we will not only learn *about* Hinduism, but also learn *from* Hinduism.

Hinduism, as a way of life embraces all aspects of culture. Here, I am concentrating on those aspects of Hinduism that are "religious" in a more specific sense, without either leaving out or completely separating from it, other aspects of life that in the West are no longer connected with religion. In spite of its all-inclusive character, Hindu religion has a metaphysical core and there is no denying the fact that it gave a religious interpretation to the whole of "secular life." The degree to which secular life was given a religious meaning varied, of course, from person to person and from age to age. Hinduism has always left its adherents much freedom to choose among many options and, except in matters that had to do with caste rules, exerted little pressure on its followers. India has always held a great variety of races and cultures within its boundaries, varieties of languages, traditions, gods, and cults. In spite of the emergence of all-India denominations within Hinduism, such as Vaiṣṇavism and Śaivism, the regional roots of particular branches of sects are very much in evidence and local practices vary markedly from one region to another. One can neither presume uniformity of belief and worship on the basis of adherence to one of the major all-India Hindu *sampradāyas* nor can one postulate a norm for such behavior on the basis of a particular local practice. At all times, the flexibility of Hinduism also showed in the very obvious difference between theory and practice, a difference that makes it all the more unlikely to understand Hinduism by merely paying attention to its verbalized theory without having observed it living practice.

Serious Western study of India began as Sanskrit philology with the establishment of chairs for Sanskrit in major European universities. It concentrated on classical drama and epics; on Vedānta, *Veda*, and grammar; and eventually on the Prākrits, which were part of the Sanskrit dramas and also the canonical languages of the Buddhists and Jains. The study of modern Indian languages and especially the study of Tamil and other South Indian languages developed only very recently in the West and, with it, the interest in "folk-religion," the *Purāṇas*, and mediaeval literature in Indian vernaculars. Few Indianists today would doubt the importance of these languages and literatures for an understanding of almost all aspects of Indian culture, but work is still scarce. Many more Western scholars know Sanskrit than Tamil, and many more translations are available of ancient Pāli and Ardhamāgadhī works than of medieval or modern Hindī, Marathī, or Bengālī texts. The situation is slowly changing but a balance is far from being achieved.

Nobody will deny the importance of knowing Sanskrit and the intrinsic value of Sanskrit literature. After all, Sanskrit was the language of Brahmin scholarship for more than two thousand years and Sanskrit literature constitutes an irreplaceable treasure house of the literary achievements of many generations of Indian poets, scholars, and thinkers. One must not forget however, that several times in Indian history successful attempts were made to break the monopoly of Sanskrit by expressing important ideas and lofty thoughts in other languages.

An impressive vernacular literature has developed, which embodies and further develops the ancient culture and, by virute of being vernacular, reaches much larger strata of the population. Thus, the Hindī re-creation of the *Rāmāyaṇa*, Tulasīdāsa's free rerendering of Vālmīki's Sanskrit work in the mediaeval Hindī *Rāmcaritmānas*, has become immensely more popular than the Sanskrit original, and it has influenced the thoughts and values of a much larger number of people. Contemporary translations of epics and *Purāṇas* in Indian vernaculars and religious journals in Hindī, Marāthī, Gujarātī, Bengālī, Tamiḷ, etc. reach a much wider audience than the classical Sanskrit treatises that form the bulk of studies of western Indological scholarship. To some extent, modern vernacular religious literature keeps repeating and exposing the content of the classical texts, but it is not *mere* repetition and exposition. A popular religious journal in modern Hindī like *Kalyāṇ*, which has a monthly circulation of over 160,000, also deals with contemporary problems and offers a fairly faithful mirror of recent developments within Hinduism. Not only simple folk write letters and express their religious sentiments in journals like this, they also provide a medium through which scholars and religious leaders address a large readership. Reading such literature with some regularity is, next to living in India and being in touch with religiously interested Hindus, perhaps the best means to survey contemporary Hinduism.

As a young man and as a student of Indian religions at a European university, I made a quite deliberate decision not to publish anything on Hinduism unless I had seen Indian reality for myself and experienced Hinduism in loco. So I looked for an opportunity to immerse myself in a Hindu milieu. I eventually found this through an invitation from the late Swami Bon Maharaj to join his Institute of Indian Philosophy in Vrindaban, Uttar Pradesh. Vrindaban meanwhile has become quite well-known due to the spread of the Hare Krishna movement and their preaching of Caitanya Vaiṣṇavism. The sojourn in Vrindaban, the daily experience of a vibrant and intense Hinduism, the many contacts with pious and learned Hindus, and the increased motivation to read and study the sources has shaped my perception and my representation of Hinduism found in this book.[8]

Vrindaban was a small town and surrounded by numerous villages, which then were largely untouched by modern developments. I moved from there to Bombay, a modern metropolis, the most westernized of India's big cities. Hinduism flourished in Bombay as well, and I learned to appreciate the new ways in which it appeared and the appeal it had for sophisticated modern people.[9] A year spent in Madras opened my eyes to the quite distinct Dravidian tradition within Hinduism, a tradition whose distinctiveness is emphasized also through contemporary political developments.

Life in India, for most people, is quite unromantic. For the majority of Indians, to provide for the daily necessities, be it in the villages or in the big cities, is an exhausting, competitive task. There is real poverty in India, unemployment, disillusionment among the youth; there are natural calamities and social tensions, language riots and religious confrontations. To experience all this for ten years has a sobering effect on one's youthful enthusiasm and prevents one from unduly romanticising India, present or past. But living in India, nevertheless, also makes one aware of the reality of a magnificent old civilization, of the influence of great figures and movements from the past and the present, the pervasive presence of religion in all aspects of daily life, for better or worse. No amount of reading can replace the immediacy of recognition from an encounter with a *saṁnyāsi* who has spent a lifetime in pursuit of *mokṣa.* No theory of art can do what a visit to a place like Elephanta or Ajanta does to a sensitive person. No description can adequately express the sensation of participation in a major temple feast in a place like Madurai.

Over 80 percent of India's population is Hindu. With an estimated 800 million Indians, that leaves a considerable number of non-Hindus who in some way or other interact with the Hindu majority.[10] The largest group, no doubt, are the Muslims. Even after partition, which was intended to give to Indian Muslims a homeland of their own in Pakistan, some 80 million Muslims still live in India. The coexistence of this large minority with the Hindu majority is an uneasy one. Centuries of conflict have created a permanent, latent tension that, at the slightest provocation, can flare up into a riot, often with great loss of life and property on both sides. The Sikhs, for long counted as part of Hinduism, are now asserting their own religio-cultural identity. They constitute only about 2 percent

2. Scene on the *ghāṭs* of Benares

of India's population but are strongly concentrated in the Punjab, where they claim to have a (slight) majority. Not all Sikhs are convinced that they need a separate Khalistān, but the more extremist faction does not shy away from terrorism and murder to press the claim. About the same number of Indians are Christians, around 14 million, followers of a great many different churches and denominations.

The tribals, officially now called *ādivāsīs*, the original inhabitants of the country, make up a sizeable minority of over 45 million. They compose hundreds of different groups, strongly concentrated in Central India but found throughout the subcontinent. They are in varying degrees influenced by Hindu culture and often have lost their own languages but they, in turn, have greatly contributed to the development of Hinduism. Many castes, especially among the lower ones, were formed by assimilating tribes to Hinduism. Much of the local tradition of Hinduism can be linked to tribal origins: tribal forms of deities merged into larger Hindu gods, tribal places of worship and sacred spots taken over by Hinduism as *tīrthas* and places where Hindu temples were built.[11]

In a countermove to the so-called Sanskritization, a term coined by M. N. Srinivas to describe the trend among low castes and tribals to heighten their status by employing brahmin priests and by adopting high-caste rituals, a reassertion of tribal culture is taking place in India. To some extent, this results from a deliberate policy encouraged by the central government to protect the cultures of the tribes. It also is a reaction against what tribals perceived to be Hindu aggressiveness and exploitation.

Furthermore, an estimated 100 million Indians are and are not Hindus. These are the people whom Gandhi had called *Harijans* (God's people) and who were otherwise known as outcastes. Strictly speaking, they had no right within traditional Hindu society, but they lived with and functioned at the margins of it.[12] They even patterned their own society along caste structures, observing higher and lower, clean and unclean among themselves. Under Dr. Ambedkar, himself a Māhār, a member of a scheduled caste, several million abandoned Hinduism and adopted Buddhism as their religion, but most stayed within Hinduism. The Indian government made special provisions for the scheduled castes by reserving places in schools and positions in government for them. Some have done fairly well economically, but the majority still lives on the margins of Hindu society—quite literally so. Atrocities against Harijans are still quite commonplace and a caste-Hindu backlash is noticeable against what is seen as "pampering" of the scheduled castes by the government.

A writer on the history of Hinduism can choose an agreed upon periodization of Indian history as basic plan. Someone dealing with Hindu philosophy has a convenient traditional schema to follow. Similarly, someone studying Hinduism from a sociological point may either choose to follow the topicalization of a particular school of thought or adopt the traditional Hindu categorization. If one entertains the ambition to deal with Hinduism as a whole, comprehensively, historically and topically, philosophically and sociologically, one has to find one's own disposition and must justify it before one's readers. The brief introductions to each of the three parts of the book are designed to provide a rationale for what that part contains.

The first part of the book attempts to lay the groundwork by briefly describing the history of the relation between India and the West, the development of Hinduism, the criteria by which Hinduism defines itself relative to other traditions, the basic writings that possess canonical value, and the common world view and the accepted theology underlying Hinduism. The second part deals with Hindu religion in the most specific sense and adopts the time-honored *trimārga* scheme describing the path of work, of knowledge, and of loving devotion. The most salient features of each are described in some detail, features that are prominent in contemporary Hindu practice and theory. The third part attempts to identify the structural supports of Hinduism, supports that include the physical reality of India, sacred time and space, the fixation of thought in recognized systems, and social order and reform. While necessarily not complete, the sketch of Hinduism offered within this survey aims at being a recognizable likeness. The chronology is designed to highlight certain events and persons and also to allow the reader to retrace the historic sequence and locate dates mentioned in the book itself. The glossary serves as a condensed dictionary for Indian terms used in describing Hinduism. The bibliography aims at providing both more detailed and more advanced reading in the area; it is not intended to be exhaustive in any area, and the lack of mention of a work should not be interpreted as a value judgement.

India is a large country in which a considerable portion of humanity lives. India's civilization in all its aspects—material, intellectual, artistic, spiritual—is a major component of world civilization and has been so for at least five thousand years. Learning about it widens one's horizons and makes one better understand what it means to be human. The world civilization now forming would be much the poorer if it left out the contributions India has made and continues to make. As A. Bharati wrote some time ago, "In time academic Indology must become as important and as pervasive in the West as the related and more widely known, because older, classical academic disciplines. Sanskrit must become as familiar to the west as Greek, and the Vedānta, Buddhism and Jainism must become as well known as the works of Plato, Hume and Russell."[13]

There are many good reasons for Westerners to study Hinduism, theoretical as well as practical. Hinduism already forms a large and important part of the human heritage and, as such, is of intrinsic interest to all who care to learn about humanity. It is, more specifically, also the tradition that has molded the thought of hundreds of millions of people, inhabiting a country that is rapidly becoming a modern power and a major factor in world affairs. For our sake as well as for the sake of the others, we should make every effort to understand these people and enter into a fruitful dialogue with them.

Indian books often end with a *kṣamā prārthana*, a statement in which the writer requests the readers' indulgence for the shortcomings of the book. It may be appropriate to begin with such a *kṣamā prārthana*, directed not so much toward those who look for information about Hinduism in this book but toward those about whom the book is written, although I never intended to offend them nor would I knowingly distort what they have said about themselves. The very idea of writing, as an outsider, about the life and religion of a people as large and as ancient as the Hindus, requires, I believe, an apology. Others have done it before, of course, but that says nothing about its appropriateness.

Quite articulate critique of Western "orientalism" has been voiced by orientals and westerners alike. Orientalist constructions of India[14] have, of course, much to do with constructions of reality in general that were attempted by the systematizing western mind. Sociological, psychological, economical, historical constructions of Europe or America fall into the same category. It is an attitude communicated with the very idea of "science" or "scientific" and it consists basically in the assumption that the "scientist" knows better and, eventually, will know it all.

No matter what a citizen thinks and says, the political scientist has the last word. For the psychologist, the words the subject uses to describe his or her state of mind are only so much raw material to be worked over. In the end, it is the psychologist who really knows the patient's mind and not the person on the couch. For the average social scientist, a people's self-expressions are just a mass of data. It is the social scientist, not the people, who brings order into the chaos, gives meaning to the data—the social scientists's meaning, of course.

Hindus are quite capable of speaking for themselves. This is acknowledged in this book by letting Hindu voices speak for Hinduism and keeping outsiders' voices and interpretations to a minimum. If one thinks that one can be scholarly only by reducing everything to preconceived notions and preexisting schemata, then the intention of this book has not been "scholarly." If, on the other hand, one concedes that the positivistic model of understanding (a model that implies that the one who knows dominates what is known, controls it, and by implication directs it toward his or her

3. Ancient Śiva-sanctuary beneath old Pīpal-tree

purposes) seriously distorts what it pretends to explain, we may be ready for another, truer, possibly more Indian kind of scholarship.[15] Instead of adopting functionalism, structuralism, or some other mechanical-statistical approach to Hinduism, I intend to identify with the issues as articulated by Hindus themselves. If the words had not been burdened with so many unacceptable overtones and associations, I would call it a *concerned method* or a *humanistic approach;* that is, a method that takes its cues from the articulations of those described, an approach that respects the personalities of the "object of study." For me, Hinduism is not a "case" to be studied and to be brought within preformed, preset categories (taken from Western culture) but an expression of human nature and culture every bit as original and to be accepted on its own terms, as I expect my own culture to be.

Part I

Hinduism: Development And Essence

The vastness and heterogeneity of Hinduism offers enormous challenges to anyone attempting to describe it. Before venturing to provide a survey of Hinduism to readers seeking an initiation into the subject, a writer has to decide what to include and what to leave out, how to qualify statements in order not to make them appear unjustifiedly dogmatic, and how to arrange the material that is to be presented as the "essentials" of Hinduism. While a great many questions are still open regarding the history and development of Hinduism, and the traditional Hindu neglect of chronology makes it often impossible to date persons or literary works within less than a five hundred year margin, the chapter dealing with these matters was one of the easier ones to write. After all, one can get hold of names and books, coins and monuments, noticeable periods and styles, which are, essentially, factual. It is more difficult to present the essentials of Hinduism in a noncontroversial manner.

The question What are the essentials of Hinduism? will receive as many different answers as one asks people. Many Hindus presume that whatever their thoughts on God, the world, and humankind are must be Hinduism. Others draw the boundaries so narrowly on the basis of caste and ritual purity that relatively few would qualify. Questions of orthodoxy had to be answered by those who were responsible for maintaining a distinct Hindu tradition vis-á-vis breakaway movements from within and assaults from without. The answers given here to the questions of who is orthodox and who is heretic may not be acceptable to all, but they represent authoritative opinions and should convince the reader that, contrary to some popular assumptions shared by some liberal Hindus and non-Hindus, Hinduism is not simply the sumtotal of all other religions and that the tolerance of Hinduism has definite limits.

The identity of Hinduism rests on the particular revelation on which the Hindu tradition believes itself to be grounded. A revelation, by its very nature, is specific and cannot be derived from general principles or from commonly accessible facts. The Vedas and the other books that are held sacred as scriptures by Hindus differentiate Hinduism from other religions that possess their own specific holy books, and they permit us, at least in a negative way, to define the essentials of Hinduism against what is not Hinduism.

Although acceptance of the Veda as revealed scripture is certainly the most basic criterion for anyone to declare himself a Hindu (the preferred self-designation of Hinduism in Indian languages is *Vaidik dharma*, the religion of the *Veda*), another genre of literature has shaped the minds and hearts of present day Hindus much more profoundly: the two great epics, *Mahābhārata* and *Rāmāyaṇa*, and the voluminous *Purāṇas*, the true bibles of Hinduism. It is typical for Hinduism to have not one but eighteen such scriptures, accepted by the followers of the various great sects. They exalt Viṣṇu, Śiva, Devī to the highest position, they contain the colorful myths for which Hinduism is famous, they instruct their readers in matters of worship and hygiene, and promise health, wealth, and eternal salvation to all who recite them. The *itihāsa-purāṇa* literature is enormous; it has hardly any parallel in another culture. Not all Hindus can be expected to be fully acquainted with it, though many know surprisingly much from it.

There is one book, however, that virtually all Hindus know and from which many recite daily by heart: the *Bhagavadgītā*, the Song of the Lord. It has become a classic also in the West; scores of translations are available in English and other European languages. It is a Kṛṣṇa book, but it articulates much that is typical for all of Hinduism and contains advice and opinion that most Hindus accept as expressing their own aspirations.

The relative geographic isolation of the Indian subcontinent facilitated the development over long periods of time of a civilization that was little influenced from the outside. Cosmological and other ideas developed and found fairly universal acceptance throughout India, which together could be termed the *Hindu world picture.* The Hindu world view appears in many variants but it also shows a surprisingly large number of common features, features distinctive enough to set it off against the world views of other civilizations.

All observers, including Hindus themselves, would describe Hinduism as polytheistic. Nowhere else in the world do we find such a profusion of gods and goddesses, of divine beings and demons, ramifications of genealogies of gods, and manifestations of the divinity in human and animal forms. But that is only the surface of Hinduism, the colorful appearance of a tradition that has enormous depths. While Hinduism could never be conceived as a parallel to biblical or Islamic monotheism, it has developed its own sophisticated notions of the unity of the highest principle, and many forms of Vaiṣṇavism, Śaivism, or Śāktism have theologies in which One Supreme Being is given the title and role of Lord, or Mistress, the creator, sustainer and destroyer of the whole universe, and the savior of those who believe in him or her.

1. India and the West

India has created a special momentum in world history as a country to be searched for.

—*G. W. F. Hegel*[1]

SINCE THE BEGINNING of recorded history, the West has been fascinated by India.[2] From Classical Antiquity, countless fanciful tales and amusing fables circulated throughout Europe, concerning India's peoples, its animals and plants, its sun and rains, its mountains and rivers, and these continued to be retold until the late Middle Ages. But not all was fancy and fable. Accurate descriptions of certain parts of India were given in ancient times by writers who had either accompanied western adventurers or who had travelled there on their own initiative, for purposes of trade or simply out of curiosity.

EARLY CONTACTS BETWEEN EAST AND WEST

The greatest single impetus in this direction in Antiquity was the invasion of India by the armies of Alexander the Great in 327-6 B.C.E. More than one eyewitness described the battles Alexander fought, the rivers he crossed and the cities he conquered, the allies he won and the kings he defeated. The newcomers were awed by the heat of the Indian plains, the great numbers of war elephants, the enormous size of the population, and the curiosity of their customs and manners. Even then, the wisdom of Indian holy men was proverbial. Accordingly, one of the first things Alexander did on entering India was to converse with some of these "gymnosophists", in spite of the fact that they were instrumental in encouraging Indian resistance against the Macedonian invasion.[3] The Greeks seem to have admired the brusque and incisive manner of these men, and so famous did they become that eventually Alexander asked one of them (whom the Greeks called Kálanos) to succeed his preceptor Aristotle as his constant companion and counsellor. This "naked wise man" seems to have been a Jain *muni* of the *Digaṁbara* sect. He was to end his life voluntarily on a pyre, having discovered that he was suffering from an incurable disease.[4]

The early mediaeval Alexander romance contains an exchange of letters between Alexander and an Indian king, Dindimus, in which Alexander asks for, and receives information about the Brahmins. "We Brahmins," the king writes, "lead a pure and simple life; we commit no sins; we do not want to have more than what is reasonable. We suffer and sustain everything." In short, the Brahmins lead an ideal life, they can teach wisdom and renunciation. In his reply to Dindimus, Alexander recognizes that "only the Brahmins are good people."[5] This high opinion of Brahmins is still noticeable in the eighteenth century, when Lessing in his *Nathan* proclaims that only at the Ganges one can find morally perfect people.

For several centuries, a lively commerce developed between the ancient Mediterranean world and India, particularly the ports on the western coast. The most famous of these ports was Sopāra, not far from modern Bombay, which was recently renamed Mumbāī. Present-day Cranganore in Kerala, identified with the ancient Muziris, claims to have had trade contacts with ancient Egypt under Queen Hatsheput, who sent five ships to obtain spices, as well as with ancient Israel during King Solomon's reign. Apparently, the contact did not break off after Egypt was conquered by Greece and later by Rome. According to I. K. K. Menon "there is evidence of a temple of Augustus near Muziris and a force of 1200 Roman soldiers stationed in the town for the protection of Roman commerce."[6] Large hoards of Roman coins were found also on the east coast, near today's Mahābalipuram, a sign of commerce with Roman traders, who must have rounded the southern tip of India to reach that place. Taprobane, identified with today's Srī Laṅka, plays a major role in ancient accounts of India. The island is described to be even more wonderful and exotic than India herself. The kings of Magadha and Malwa exchanged ambassadors with Greece. A Maurya ruler invited one of the Greek Sophists to join his court. One of the greatest of the Indo-Greek kings became famous as the dialogue partner of the great Buddhist sage Nāgasena,[7] while in the opposite direction, Buddhist missionaries are known to have settled in Alexandria and other cities of the ancient West. These early contacts were not limited to the exchange of pleasantries. One Greek ambassador went so far as to erect a Garuḍa column in honor of Vasudeva, while Greek epic poetry was translated into Indian languages and heard with appreciation in the court of Broach. The celebrated collection of Indian animal fables, the *Pañcatantra,* found its way into the West in a variety of translations and adaptations, including a version of the life of Buddha that resulted in the creation of the legend of Saint Josaphat.[8]

It is evident, then, that Indian thought was present in the fashionable intellectual circuit of ancient Athens, and there is every reason to suppose that Indian religious and philosophical ideas exercized some influence on early and classical Greek philosophy.[9]

Interest in India increased considerably during the time of the Roman Emperors. During the time between the reign of Augustus and that of Caracalla, East-West commerce flourished. A colony of Indian merchants is known to have existed in Alexandria, and under Augustus, Claudius, and Antoninus Pius, Indian embassies visited Rome. At least one celebrated Greek philosopher, the neo-Pythagorean Apollonius of Tyana (first century C.E.), is reputed to have visited India in order to improve his knowledge of Indian wisdom.

Both Greeks and Romans habitually tried to understand the religions of India by trying to fit them as far as possible into Greco-Roman categories. Deities in particular were spoken of not in Indian but in Greek terms and called by Greek names. Thus, Śiva was identified as "Diónysos", Kṛṣṇa (or perhaps Indra) as "Héracles." The great Indian epics were compared to those of Homer. Doctrinally, the Indian concept of transmigration had its counterpart in the *metempsychósis* taught by Pythagoras and Plato; nor was Indian asceticism altogether foreign to a people who remembered Diogenes and his followers.[10] According to one persistent legend, Jesus Christ even spent the time between the twelfth and thirtieth years, a period of his life about which the Gospels are silent, in India, studying with Buddhist *bhikkus* and Vedāntin *ācāryas.*[11]

Towards the end of the second century, Tertullian, a Christian writer, defended his fellow believers from the accusation that they were "useless and should therefore be exterminated" by stating that the Christians were "neither Brahmins, or Indian gymnosophists, forest-dwellers or withdrawn from life," but that they participated fully in the public and economic activities of Rome.[12] Some centuries later, the writer of the treatise *De moribus brachmanorum* (originally thought to have been written by Ambrose of Milan, now considered to be the work of Prosper of Aquitania) had high praise for the Brahmins who could serve, he says, as exemplars to Christians.[13]

With the victory of Christianity in the West and the simultaneous decline of the Roman Empire, and still more with the Arab conquest of the Near and Middle East, the West lost contact with India. All that remained were faint and often distorted memories of India as a land of fabulous riches, of exotic creatures and a fantastic religion. However, the Arab conquest of India once more intensified exchange between India and the West, a West over which Arab influence was also now becoming more deeply felt.[14] Alberuni, a Muslim traveller who visited India between 1017 and 1030, gave an admirably comprehensive account of many aspects of India's culture, including a fairly detailed summary of some important works of religious literature, unknown to the West until then.[15] It was through the Arabs that Indian learning reached the West, particularly in the fields of medicine, mathematics, and astrology. Indeed, the Indian decimal system and its symbols became known in the West as Arabic numerals.

The great merchant-adventurer Marco Polo (1254-1324) visited and described a number of places in India, but his accounts were not usually taken seriously by his contemporaries, who considered him to be something of a storyteller rather than a serious topographer.[16] It was the search for India that led Christopher Columbus to the discovery of the New World in 1493. To this very day, we call the original inhabitants of America Indians and find it often awkward to specify whether we mean American Indians or Indian Indians. The West's contact with India intensified after Vasco da Gama's historic voyage around the cape of Good Hope in 1498, which led to an increased interest in India by the European powers. Together with the generals and the merchants, Christian missionaries came to the subcontinent. Some of them became interested in India's local religions and, though frequently showing a heavy apologetic bias, some seventeenth and eighteenth century missionaries produced works that provided much useful material about India.[17]

BEGINNING SCHOLARLY INTEREST IN INDIA

By the middle of the eighteenth century, European scholars were starting to get interested in India's literature, but initially they were severely handicapped by the Brahmin's reluctance to teach Sanskrit to *mlecchas* (foreigners) or to allow them to read their scriptures. The German romantic philosopher Arthur Schopenhauer (1788-1860), whose enthusiastic praises of the Upaniṣads are frequently cited, had to rely on a Latin translation by Anquetil du Perron from a Persian version by Prince Dara Shikoh of the original Sanskrit text!

During the first half of the eighteenth century, J. E. Hanxleden wrote the first Sanskrit grammar, under the title *Grammatica Granthamia seu Samscrdumica.*[18] It was never printed but was put to use by J. P. Wessdin (Fra Paolino de St. Bartolomeo) who wrote two Sanskrit grammars and some quite informative works on India toward the end of the eighteenth century.[19] The greatest incentive to the scholarly study of India's history and culture, however, was provided by the British administration, which encouraged research and the publication of materials pertinent to its own purposes.[20] Typically, the first Sanskrit works to be translated into English were the Hindu law codes, which the British officials needed to know. The British East India Company commissioned a group of Indian *paṇḍits* to compile a compendium of current Hindu law from the numerous original sources. The resulting work, *Vivādārṇavasetu*, had first to be translated into Persian before an English translation could be made by an Englishman. It was published in 1776 by the East India Company under the title *A Code of Gentoo Law*.

The first Englishman to have a good knowledge of Sanskrit was Charles Wilkins, whom Warren Hastings (then governor general of Bengal) had encouraged to study with the Brahmins in Benares. In 1785, he published an English translation of the *Bhagavadgītā*, followed two years later by a translation of the *Hitopadeśa*. His Sanskrit grammar, which appeared in 1808, became the basis for all later work.

One of the most important figures in European Indology was Sir William Jones (1746-1794), who had acquired a good command of Persian and Arabic before coming to India in 1783, where he immediately took up the study of Sanskrit. One year later, he founded the Asiatic Society of Bengal, which was soon to become the leading center for the publication of text editions and translations of important Hindu writings. Jones translated the *Manusmṛti* and published it in 1794 under the title *Institutes of Hindu Law, or the Ordinances of Manu*. After Jones' death, the work was continued by Thomas Colebrook, who edited and translated numerous Sanskrit works. As professor of Sanskrit at Fort William College, Calcutta, he published in 1798 a four volume series, *A Digest of Hindu Law on Contracts and Successions*, which consisted of translations of legal materials collected by a group of Indian *paṇḍits*. Less interested in literature and poetry than in more scholarly Hindu works on law, arithmetics, astronomy, grammar, philosophy, and religion, he was the first Western scholar to provide correct and precise information about the Veda, in "On the Vedas, or Sacred Writings of the Hindus"; Roberto de Nobili's *Ezour Vedam* being exposed as a fraud.[21]

Another Englishman, Alexander Hamilton, had studied Sanskrit in India and was detained in Paris on his way back to England on account of Anglo-French hostilities. He became instructor to the first generation of French and German Sanskritists, for whom university chairs were established in the first half of the nineteenth century. While thus far those in continental Europe who wished to study Indian culture had had to rely on French and German translations of English versions and monographs, they now could draw upon the resources of their own, scholars who began to produce text editions and original versions. August Wilhelm von Schlegel, the brother of the poet Friedrich Schlegel, became the first professor of Sanskrit at the newly established university of Bonn in 1818. A. L. Chézy, the first French Sanskrit scholar, held the chair at the Collège de France in Paris.[22] Franz Bopp, a fellow student of Schlegel at Paris, became the founder of comparative philology and linguistics.[23]

Though the East India Company at first did not allow Christian missionaries into its territories and maintained a policy of religious non-interference, Western Christians considered India as a mission field and tried to employ Indian studies for this purpose. Missionary activities on East India Company territory began in 1813, though William Carey had been at work in Serampore, a Danish settlement near Calcutta, since 1800. A further step was taken in 1830, with the opening of Scottish missionary Alexander Duff's school in Calcutta. In the same year, the famous Sanskritist H. H. Wilson became the first holder of the Boden Professorship in Oxford, founded in order "to promote the translation of the Scriptures into Sanskrit, so as to enable his countrymen to proceed in the conversion of the natives of India to the Christian religion." Both H. H. Wilson (1832-1860) and his successor to the chair, M. Monier-Williams (1860-1888), engaged in lexicographic work in order to lay the foundations for Bible translations, which were soon made into the main languages of India.[24]

Following the historical trend that dominated European scholarship in the nineteenth century, French and German scholars examined the *Vedas*, the oldest document of Indian religious literature. Some of the students taught by Eugène Burnouf at the Collège de France later attained lasting eminence as Vedic scholars. One of these was Rudolph Roth, who together with Otto Böthlingk edited the seven volume *St. Petersburg Wörterbuch* (1852-1875), which remains unsurpassed. Friedrich Max Müller became the most famous of them all. The son of the poet Wilhelm Müller, he earned fame through his monumental edition of the *Ṛgveda with Sāyana's Commentary* (1849-1874). Of even greater significance than his Indological work is that, due to his wide general education and interests, he became the founder of comparative religion as a scholarly discipline. Perhaps the crowning achievement of his life's work was his editorship of the fifty volumes of the *Sacred Books of the East* (1876-1904).[25]

Müller did not find in his native Germany the support for his studies offered by England, which subsequently became the main center of Indian studies and libraries. An astonishingly large number of brilliant scholars devoted themselves to the study of India's past in the decades that followed. Indology became a respected discipline at most major European universities and scholars published a steady stream of critical text editions, translations, monographs, and dictionaries.[26] They even impressed the traditional Indian *paṇḍits* by their learning, and soon the first Hindu scholars arrived to study in European departments of Sanskrit and to familiarize themselves with the scholarly methods developed in the West. Recognized Indian scholars, especially those proficient in English, were invited on lecture tours through the West and were thus given opportunity to explain authentically the traditions of India to an attentive but often misinformed audience.[27]

In the United States, the popular philosophers Ralph Waldo Emerson (1803-1882) and Henry David Thoreau (1817-1862) were the first to show some serious interest in Indian thought, especially in Vedānta. The first to teach courses in Sanskrit was Isaac Nordheimer, who offered a course at the City University of New York as early as 1836. Edward Eldridge Salisbury introduced Sanskrit at Yale in 1841, and the prestigious American Oriental Society was founded in 1842. Though Indologists form only part of its membership, its journal and its monograph series are the major organs for classical Indian studies in the United States. Since the latter half of the nineteenth century, several outstanding Sanskritists have taught and worked in the United States. Charles Rockwell Lanman (1850-1941), one of Rudolph Roth's students, became the founder-editor of the Harvard Oriental Series; his *Sanskrit Reader* is still in use. J. H. Wood's (1864-1935) translation of the major commentaries and glosses to Patañjalis *Yogasūtra* is still widely referred to. Maurice Bloomfield (1885-1928) emerged as one of the major Vedic scholars of his time; his *Vedic Concordance*, a monumental work, has been recently reprinted. Edward Washburn Hopkins' (1857-1932) books on the *Mahābhārata* are still authoritative on many points. Robert Ernest Hume (1877-1948) has deservedly gained fame for his translation of the *Thirteen Principal Upaniṣads*, which has seen many reprints. Franklin Edgerton's (1885-1963) *Bhagavadgītā* has been acknowledged as the most scholarly translation to date.[28]

Today all Western countries have university departments and research institutes undertaking advanced studies in Indology, including religious and philosophical Hinduism. An impressive percentage of scholars referred to in this book are native Indians who enjoy the added advantage of working with materials from their own living traditions. It almost goes without saying that India is today once more the leading country in Indian studies, both in the traditional way of learning as represented by the *paṇḍit* schools and in the modern methods initiated by Western scholars and continued and refined by Indian academicians. Indian universities publish numerous scholarly journals in English and in this way contribute to the West's understanding of the Indian tradition.

SCHOLARLY AND EXISTENTIAL INTERESTS

Early Western interest in Indian studies was kindled, on the one hand, by the requirements of the British administration in India and, on the other, by the predominantly historical and philological interests of Western scholars, trained in their own classical Greek and Latin traditions. More recently, the accent has shifted to the content of Indian philosophical and religious literature. The attitude of classical Western Indology had centered on strictly objective scholarly research; the professionals often frowned upon people who tried to identify themselves with certain positions of the Indian tradition on which they worked. The great works of this period, like Christian Larssen's monumental *Indische Altertumskunde* or Friedrich Bühler's *Grundriss der indoarischen Philologie und Altertumskunde*, dealt with India as the established classical scholars had dealt with Ancient Greece and Rome. For all their enthusiasm in their professional studies, which centered on India's classical past, these scholars did not give up their typically Western way of thinking. By their own choice, they remained outsiders, fulfilling their calling as scholars according to the Western ideal, sometimes even refusing, as Max Müller did, to pay a visit to India.

The social and spiritual convulsions of our time, beginning with World War I, together with the renewed self-consciousness of the generation that had experienced the Indian Renaissance, have made many of our contemporaries more ready to listen to what India has (and always had) to say. There was a remarkable growth of interest in Buddhism in the early 1920s. On a more scholarly level, a great stimulus for Indian studies was provided by the first East-West Philosophers' Conference, organized by Charles A. Moore (1901-1967) in Honolulu in 1949. Subsequent meetings have been attended by a considerable number of eminent scholars from India.[29]

It is not easy to analyze the reasons for this new development. The contemporary West no longer has a unifying world view, a commonly accepted religion or philosophy of life that could serve as basis for the solution of its social or psychological problems and that could be used as sustenance in times of crisis. The experiences of the last fifty years undermined the naive optimism that had grown from a faith in unlimited technological progress. Having witnessed a complete breakdown of much that was taken for granted in former times, we are now faced with a deep-rooted insecurity and probably the irreparable loss of the authority of those institutions that for centuries had provided Westerners with a firm framework for their life and thought. An increasing number of people are opening to the suggestion that they might replace some traditional Western values and attitudes, which have proved short lived and self-destructive, with Eastern modes of thought, which have nourished cultures that have endured for thousands of years.[30] Slowly, however, the realization is also dawning that a mere replacement of one set of ideas and values by another would help us as little as did the timid or arrogant aloofness of former times.

Patterns of partnership are beginning to dominate in international relations, a partnership that includes dialogue on all levels, allowing differences even of a basic nature to coexist without interrupting communication. Much of what we find in Hinduism has no counterpart in the West. Hindu thinkers have anticipated ideas and developed theories in many areas that have only recently begun to be explored in the West. In the analysis of language, in the technicalities of hermeneutics, in the methods of psychosomatic activation, and in philosophical and religious speculation and spiritual training—in all these areas Hindu India is centuries ahead of the West. Western thinkers, through their study of Indian philosophies and religions, have "discovered a new technical philosophy of undreamed-of complexity and ingenuity" and this contact has "expanded the imagination, increased the number of categories, made possible new studies in the history of logic, revealed new sensations and has driven the mind back to its origin and out to its possibilities."[31]

INTERPRETING HINDUISM IN WESTERN TERMS

Early Western Indologists used to deal with everything that concerned India. Meanwhile, the field has grown to such an extent that specialization has become necessary both for the sake of the integrity of research and for the sake of students interested in Indian studies. Even within the specialized field of Hinduism, one has to narrow one's inquiry to either a particular school of thought, a period, or even a single person. Nevertheless, in order to assign the correct place of one's particular research within the larger framework of Hindu culture, one must familiarize oneself with other aspects and the history of the total phenomenon.

There is a certain temptation for Westerners who study Hinduism to follow through vaguely familiar thoughts and to complete them according to their own thought models. This temptation must be resisted, because all further interpretation would then be based upon principles that had been borrowed from elsewhere. The historicity of each tradition must be taken seriously, not only in the vaguely idealistic (and ultimately unhistorical) Hegelian sense but in its own exact and precise historical factuality. Hinduism is what it is today because it has developed that way through its own history. It is not necessarily what we would like or wish it to be.

History always offers several alternatives for the development of each idea; this development depends on circumstances and unforeseeable factors that translate one of these possibilities into historical fact. Western approaches to reality—the compartmentalization of knowledge into such categories as science and arts, philosophy and theology, sociology and psychology—do not coincide with Indian approaches and their specific avenues of inquiry.[32] Despite more than 150 years of diligent work by a handful of devoted scholars, on many essential points, we have not yet reached a verbal understanding. Western languages have no adequate translations for many of the key terms in philosophical and religious Sanskrit texts. Ananda Coomaraswamy, who must have suffered quite acutely under this situation, stated: "Asiatic thought has hardly been, can hardly be presented in European phraseology without distortion and what is called the appreciation of Asiatic art is mainly based on categorical misinterpretations."[33] Misunderstandings are thus bound to happen even with the best of intentions, and even good intention cannot always be taken for granted. To try to avoid some misunderstandings, the representation of Hinduism in this book uses original terms wherever practicable.

At some later state, we may be able to discover for ourselves that Hinduism and Western religions do not differ so much in the answers they give to similar problems but in the problems they consider relevant. Problems that never occur to the Westerner may be of the utmost significance for the Hindu. Hinduism is not a variant of Western religion, the very structure of Hinduism is different. Scholars like Betty Heimann,[34] Heinrich Zimmer,[35] Maryla Falk,[36] René Guénon,[37] Stella Kramrisch,[38] and Wendy O'Flaherty,[39]—Westerners well grounded in their own traditions—have made structural studies of Hinduism that presuppose not only specialized Indological expertise but also a comprehensive general knowledge and a great deal of empathy. We must not expect everything we find in Hinduism to fit into the frame of our present knowledge. Modern science cannot be adequately explained in the terminology of mediaeval philosophy of nature; equally, Indian philosophical and religious thought cannot be satisfactorily reproduced using our current Western idiom. Translations of authoritative Hindu literature are always interpretations, for better or for worse, according to the insight of the translator. This is true for the translations of many a European philologist with an insufficient philosophical background—not to mention those "translators" who, ignorant of the original languages, simply restyle an existing translation in the fashion and idiom of the day. This applies still more to some Indian translators who are unfamiliar with the real meaning of the Western terminology they frequently use. And occasionally a translation can be more tendentious than an original work, if it is meant to support the particular viewpoint of a particular proselytizer.

In those points that are really crucial, the meaning of a text cannot be found without a thorough study of the sources in the original languages within their original context. The literary sources of Indian philosophy and religion, moreover, are quite frequently written in such a concise and condensed style that a student cannot even understand them grammatically without oral instruction and commentary. Furthermore, the same terms are used in different senses by different systems. There are also frequent indirect quotations from and references to writings with which the Indian expert is familiar but that a Western reader without a competent guide would overlook.[40] A Western student of Hinduism has to learn how to read and to understand Hindu sources from learned Hindus: the premises they work with, the axioms they take for granted, the problems they consider relevant.

Although India and the West quite obviously differ from each other, as every casual visitor of India will notice, one ought to be leery of the dichotomisation of East and West along the lines of spiritual versus materialistic, collective versus individualistic, or archaic versus modern. Whether it has to do with more recent developments or with a better knowledge of both East and West than previously available, it appears that all these characteristics are distributed fairly evenly throughout East and West, and one will, in all likelihood, have to choose others, if one wishes to insist that the "East is East and West is West" and so forth. Indians have made some major contributions to contemporary modern science and technology and Westerners have been recognized by their Indian colleagues as specialists in Sanskrit learning and commended for their genuine understanding of Hindu culture. It is, in all likelihood, less a problem of fundamental differences than of mutual recognition and learning from each other in the interest of developing a truly cosmopolitan civilization.

ENCOUNTERING HINDUS AND HINDUISM

A book can never replace the experience of the living encounter, but it can prepare the ground for it. Thorough familiarization with the background of the dialogue partner is the first requirement for a meaningful encounter. It goes without saying that no claim can be made to an exhaustive treatment or to an interpretation that would not show shortcomings due to personal limitations. There are, even now, subtle and highly competent Hindu philosophers whose Hinduism is virtually inaccessible to those who have not undertaken the necessary training. And there are millions of Hindus who practice diverse archaic cults and ceremonies, rationalizing in their own peculiar ways the effectiveness and meaning of what they are doing. If we are to understand Hinduism as it is and not to construct to our own purposes an artificial Hindu religion that we are able to manipulate, we have to be open to the whole panorama of phenomena that together constitute the living tradition of Hindu India.

More and more Hindu gurus and swāmīs in ochre robes are coming to Europe and to America to lecture, to collect funds, to establish centers, and to launch religious movements adapted to the Western mind. The quite phenomenal expansion of Mahesh Yogi Maharishi's Transcendental Meditation Society, the success of Swami Bhaktivedanta's International Society for Krishna Consciousness, and the mass pilgrimages of plane loads of Americans to Balyogeshwar Guruji's camp were not merely the result of smart organization and cleverly manipulated publicity; they also reflect an obvious need on the part of many people in the West, especially among the young. In the new Hindu movements, they hope to find what they have missed in their synagogues and churches: practical guidance in self-discovery, an integrated world view, systematic training of psychic powers, emotional satisfaction, and perhaps, true mystical experience. It would be very sad if Hindu propaganda in the West were to lead only to the establishment of a few Hindu sects, missing the great opportunity for the growth of new, genuinely modern forms of spirituality by entering into dialogue with the still living Western religious tradition. Such an encounter would certainly prove beneficial to both partners; it may even be necessary for them if they are to survive as interpreters of the meaning of life in a time of confused, disintegrating local traditions.

2. The History and Development of Hinduism

> Thus I saw the moving drama of the Indian people in the present, and could often trace the threads which bound their lives to the past, even while their eyes were turned to the future. Everywhere I found a cultural background which had exerted a powerful influence on their lives.
>
> —*J. Nehru*[1]

EVERY LIVING TRADITION, and the Hindu tradition perhaps more than others, is profoundly shaped by its own history. Through that history even those features the tradition itself considers to be nonhistorical are strongly affected. Attempts to describe the "essence" of Hinduism in terms of absolute doctrinal formulations must fail simply because they neglect the historical dimension and the development that has led to those beliefs. As J. C. Heesterman has said,

> Tradition is characterized by the inner conflict of atemporal order and temporal shift rather than by resiliance and adaptiveness. It is this unresolved conflict that provides the motive force we perceive as the flexibility of tradition. Indian civilization offers a particularly clear case of this dynamic inner conflict. The conflict is not just handled surreptitiously by way of situational compromise. Once we look beyond the hard surface of the projected absolute order, it appears subtly, but no less effectively, to be expressed by the same scriptures that so impressively expound the *dharma*'s absoluteness.[2]

ORIGINS OF HINDUISM

It is impossible to give a precise definition of Hinduism or to point out the exact place and time of its origin. The very name *Hinduism* owes its origin to chance; foreigners in the West extended the name of the province of Sindh to the whole country lying across the Indus river and simply called all its inhabitants *Hindus* and their religion *Hinduism.* Contemporary Hinduism preserves many elements from various sources, differently emphasized in various parts of the country and by individual groups of people. Roughly speaking we may identity four main streams of tradition that have coalesced to form Hinduism:

- the traditions of the original inhabitants of India, whose stone-age culture has been traced back about half a million years[3] and some of whose practices and beliefs may still be alive among the numerous tribes of *ādivāsis;*[4]
- influences from the so-called Indus civilization, which was rediscovered only half a century ago and which apparently extended over a vast area of northwestern and northern India;[5]
- the very old and highly developed Dravidian culture, represented by the Tamils today and possibly preserving certain features of the Indus civilization;[6]
- Vedic religion, brought into India by Āryan invaders and settlers and spread throughout the greater part of India by conquests and missionary movements.[7]

Later invasions, and contacts with the Muslims and the modern world, again contributed to the development of certain ideas within Hinduism. Despite the frequency with which Indian patterns of life have been disrupted, India nevertheless is "a country of enduring survivals,"[8] an open-air museum of the history of religion and culture. A continuing Indian tradition underlies the attempts to define the Hindu identity in terms of religion.

The most common description which Hindus give to their religion is *sanātana dharma,* "eternal religion," a term that has several overtones.[9] It presupposes that the Vedic Sanskritic tradition is *the* religion; it also gave rise to exclusivist tendencies with Hinduism. In the ninth century, Śaṅkara reestablished *sanātana dharma* against the heresies of Buddhism and Jainism in India and sent out his missionaries to spread the pure doctrine all over India. The claim to be defenders of *sanātana dharma* was also made by schools of thought hostile to Śaṅkara. In modern times, movements like the *Ārya Samāj,* which considered popular *purāṇic* Hinduism to be a corrupt form of the true religion, tried to reintroduce a purely Vedic *sanātana dharma.* In contemporary Hinduism, we find attempts to widen

4. Nāga, Khajurāho 12th ct.

the circle of *sanātana dharma*, or Hinduism, to embrace also the Jainas, Buddhists, Sikhs, and all the sects of Hinduism.

Most Hindus prefer even now to define their religion in a more restricted fashion and they call themselves *Śaivas, Vaiṣṇavas, Śāktas*, or whatever group they belong to. There are others who feel the need to define the unity underlying the nationhood of India in terms that would allow Hindus to transcend sectarian boundaries within India and at the same time distinguish them from the followers of other traditions. A collection of statements on the topic Essentials of Hinduism by some thiry prominent Hindus, which appeared about fifty years ago, shows as many different standpoints without allowing one to single out any specific characteristics of Hinduism.[10] V. D. Savarkar, for many years the chief ideologue of the Hindu Mahāsabhā, distinguished *Hindudharma*, Hinduism that defies definition, from *Hindutva*, Hindudom, a more inclusive term. Thus he wrote:

> A Hindu is one who feels attachment to the land that extends from *Sindhu* to *Sindhu* (sea) as the land of his forefathers—as his Fatherland; who inherits the blood of the great race whose first and discernible source could be traced by the Himālāyan altitudes of the Vedic *Saptasindhus* and which, assimilating all that was incorporated and ennobling all that was assimilated, has grown into and come to be known as the Hindu people; and who, as a consequence of the foregoing attributes, has inherited and claims as his own the Hindu *sanskṛti*, the Hindu civilization, as represented in a common history, common heroes, a common literature, a common art, a common law and a common jurisprudence, common fairs and festivals, rites and rituals, ceremonies and sacraments.[11]

Even less modest is the description of the "indefinable Hindu" given by the former R. S. S. leader M. S. Golwalkar.

> We, the Hindus, have based our whole existence on God. . . . In a way, we are *anādi*, without a beginning. To define such a people is impossible, just as we cannot express or define Reality because words came into existence after Reality. Similar is the case with the Hindu people. We existed when there was no necessity for any name. We were the good, the enlightened people. We were the people who knew the laws of nature and the laws of the Spirit. We built a great civilization, a great culture and a unique social order. We had brought into actual life almost every thing that was beneficial to mankind. Then the rest of humanity was just bipeds and so no distinctive name was given to us. Sometimes in trying to distinguish our people from others we were called the "enlightened," the *Āryas* and the rest, the *Mlecchas*. When different faiths arose in foreign lands in the course of time and those alien faiths came in contact with us, then the necessity for naming was felt.[12]

More specific is the definition given to Hinduism by the *Viśva Hindu*

Figure 2.1 Prehistoric Rockpaintings and Drawings from Bhimbhetka

Pariṣad, the World Council of Hindus, which was founded in 1964 and which held "a historic assembly" during the *Kumbha Melā* at Prayāga (Allahābad) in January 1966. There the attempt was made to formulate something like a basic creed to which all Hindus could subscribe, to devise some common rites, and to develop a canon of holy books, in order to give visible unity to Hinduism.[13]

Definitions of Hinduism, even in a very vague form, have usually taken their inspiration from Vedic religion. Recently, however, the great importance of the other streams of Indian tradition have gained more attention. Thus, D. D. Kosambi remarks:

> It is still not possible to establish a general sequence of development from the stone age down in the most densely settled areas, namely the Punjab, the Gangetic basin, the coastal strip of the peninsula. There were notable intrusions in each of these regions. Yet India shows extraordinary continuity of culture. The violent breaks known to have occurred in the political and theological superstructure have not prevented long survivals of observances that have no sanction in the official Brahmin works, hence can only have originated in the most primitive stages of human society; moreover the Hindu scriptures and even more the observances sanctified in practice by Brahmanism show adoption of non-brahmanic local rites. That is, the process of assimilation was mutual, a peculiar characteristic of India.[14]

Nobody has as yet interpreted the religious significance of the prehistoric cave paintings at Bhimbetka (ca. 30,000 B.C.E.), which were discovered only in 1967 (see Figure 2.1); and we do not know whether or how the people who created them are related to the present-day populations of India.[15] The religions of most of the Indian *ādivāsis* show strong Hindu influences; but some more or less universal Hindu beliefs like rebirth and transmigration of the *jīva* from animal to human existence probably originated among the autochthonous populations. Our knowledge of the Indus civilization is still very fragmentary; the script has not yet been deciphered and most descriptions of the nonmaterial culture of its people are based on little more than guesswork.[16] Certain seals and terracotta figurines have been connected with the origins of Śiva and Śakti cults (see Figure 2.2). From skeletal finds we can infer that the population was racially mixed and that some of the cities must have met with a sudden, violent end.[17] For quite some time this has been associated with the invasion of the Āryan tribes, in whose holy book, the *Ṛgveda*, frequent mention is made of the destruction of powerful centers and irrigation schemes.[18] Recently the opinion has gained ground that the cities there died out slowly due to the dessication of the lower Indus basin and that the Āryans destroyed only minor remnants of it. Another opinion links the ancestors of the

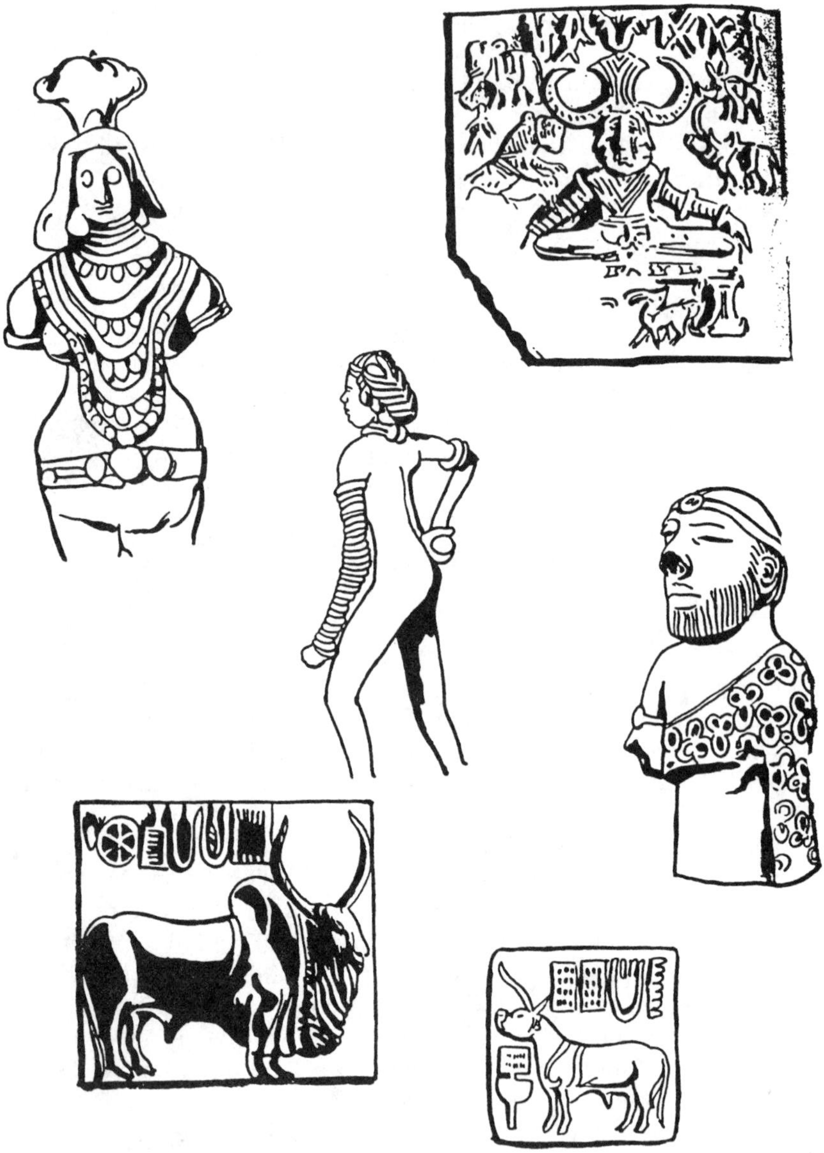

Figure 2.2 Seals and Figurines from the Indus Civilization

Tamils to Mohenjo-Daro and Harappa: the ancient Dravidians are supposed to have migrated south and settled in today's Tamiḷnadu, preserving the heritage of the Indus culture, its myths and its gods, which again found their way back into the Brahmanic religion through the *Purāṇas, Saṁhitas*, and *Āgamas.*[19]

THE ĀRYAN COMPONENT IN HINDUISM

The Āryan immigration, whatever its importance in the long history of the Indian subcontinent, strongly shaped India's religion. By no means had the immigrants a homogenous religion, but there were common features that linked the basic five clans. They called themselves *ārya*, the noble ones, people of rank and quality, showing a good measure of arrogance toward the darker skinned, "ignoble" natives. About the origin of these *Āryans*, many partly imaginative theories have been advanced.[20] B. G. Tilak suggested that they came from the northern polar region and migrated into India as early as 6000 B.C.E. F. E. Pargiter, a great Puranic scholar, identifying the Vedic Āryans with the Puranic Ailas, thinks that they originally came into India about 2050 B.C.E. from the mid-Himālāyas and first settled in the area of Prāyāga, from where they started their expansion toward the northwest.[21] Though Pargiter's case is quite strong, Indologists in general continue to hold the theory that the Āryans came into India from the northwest, either from southern Russia or from Iran, after separating from the Iranians.[22] They arrived, so the commonly held opinion goes, between 1500 and 1200 B.C.E. in several waves, pushing east and south. Ancient Indian chronology is such a difficult field of study, with many radically different methods developed by a variety of scholars, that it would be highly premature to opt arbitrarily for one set of dates, thereby explicitly or implicitly rejecting the research of other competent scholars.[23] Western scholars who were initially inclined to disregard traditional Indian history, quite often had to admit that they had underestimated the strength and exactness of it. Archaeology has often confirmed statements contained in ancient Indian literature that seemed either unbelievable or distorted to Western scholars who had grown up in the tradition of Western classical history.[24]

In contrast to the highly developed urban culture of the Harappan civilization, the Āryans brought with them a relatively simple village culture and a patriarchal style of life. Though there is a strong probability that the institution of Brahmanism and the core of the *Ṛg-Veda* itself antedate the Āryan invasion of India,[25] both were associated with them so closely and at such an early date that for all practical purposes, we may safely identify the Vedic religion with the early official worship of the Āryans. Since epic and Puranic literature may be of equal age, representing the more popular aspects of religion in ancient India, we have to consider it from the very beginning as complementary to the *Vedas.*[26]

Āryan society appears at a very early stage to have had a hierarchial structure with *brahmins* and *kṣatriyas* competing for the first place; *vaiśyas* constituting the bulk of independent farmers, cattle breeders, artisans, and traders; while the *śūdras* provided services of all kinds. Outside this structure there existed the indigenous tribal population, which became partly assimilated in the course of time. Also, slavery seems to have been known in ancient India.[27]

The Brahmins were the custodians of the *yajña*, the all-powerful sacrifice. The hymns and rites connected with it were handed down orally from generation to generation, jealously guarded from outsiders. Whereas Brahmanic religion knew neither temple nor image, the religious tradition preserved in the epics and Purāṇas, with its *mūrtis* and *maṇḍirs*, its miracles and myths, became more popular, assimilating, transforming, and often replacing Vedic religion. The Vedic sacrifices continue to this day in one form or another, and Vedic ritual is observed by most Hindus on ceremonial occasions.[28] But, on the whole, the epic and Puranic forms of Hinduism, often with a strongly local accent, prevail and dominate the Indian religious landscape.

Puranic accounts mention Ṛṣi Agastya, an Āryan missionary who was responsible for the Hinduization of South India. Hindu influence spread further to Southeast Asia and Indonesia during the "Golden Age" of India.[29] Although, for several centuries, Buddhism and Jainism claimed most followers and enjoyed the patronage of the most powerful rulers, a Hindu renaissance, under the Guptas in North India and the Pallavas in the South, all but swept away these "heretical" movements and established Hindu supremacy both in cultic form and in religious speculation.[30] The Brahmins, while upholding Vedic tradition, especially in Vedāntic philosophy, successfully catered to the people by assuming the lead in the various great sects of the Śaivas, the Vaiṣṇavas, and later the Śāktas. There were regular missionary movements within India, and books like the *Bhagavadgītā*, the *Rāmāyaṇa* (especially in *Tulasīdāsa*'s version), and the *Bhāgavata Purāṇa* were widely disseminated. Geographically, Śaivism predominates in South India; Vaiṣṇavism prevails in the North; while Bengal, Assam, and Orissa are strongly Śākta. But in most places followers of different Hindu traditions live side by side.

However, frictions among different groups of Hindus were not unknown, and Indian history knows of Śaiva kings persecuting Vaiṣṇavas and Vaiṣṇava rulers exiling followers of other faiths.[31] Indeed, some of

5. Platform for *rasa-līlā* dance in Sevākuñj, Vṛndāvan

the sectarian scriptures are venomous and malicious in their abuse of countersects,[32] and quite often regional and local differences are also very marked.[33]

In trying to take account of the factors that helped shape Hinduism, we must not forget the physical and geographical reality of India![34] For the Hindu, the very concrete land of *Bhārata* is Holy Land, and certainly the landscape has for thousands of years been the fountainhead of religious inspiration, too. The mighty mountain ranges of the Himālāyas, unconquered for thousands of years, its peaks clad in eternal snow; the powerful rivers that nourish and quite often ravage the country; the vast seas surrounding it; the immense plains with their murderous heat in summer; the huge bright stars and a moon almost as luminous as the sun; the abundant species of plants and animals; the hot, dusty summers and the cloud-heavy monsoons—all these have fired the spirit of a multiracial population, gifted with a vivid imagination, active emotions, and sharp intelligence and combined to produce the multicolored flowergarden of Hinduism.

Hinduism is very much tied to specific places and local traditions. The towns and districts associated with certain *avatārs* are the holy lands for the followers of particular sects and the destination of countless pilgrims.[35] The great rivers are also holy rivers, since their waters purify those who bathe in them from all their sins.[36] All over India certain trees receive worship, either as manifestations of Viṣṇu or Śiva in the form of the *tulasī* or *uḍumbara*, after being sanctified through ceremonies like the marriage of trees, or by having shrines established beneath them.[37] Other local sanctuaries, certain images, the tomb of a renowned *yogi*, or the memorial of an especially conspicuous occurence (often a stone with a peculiar shape or with some strange imprints) form centers for pilgrimages in smaller provinces. Some mountains and hills, foremost amongst them Kailāsa and Aruṇācala, have been considered sacred from time immemorial. As a geographic entity, India offers the occasions of sanctification: only in India are cows, snakes, rats, and vultures sacred; only in India do ascetic and religious practices lead to salvation. Ancient India singled out *Madhyadeśa*, the heartland of India, as the really holy land; beyond its boundaries salvation could not be gained.

This feature must be borne in mind if we wish to understand the real Hinduism. The attempted universalization of Hinduism as we find it in Vivekananda or Radhakrishnan is largely the result of their Western Christian training.

CHANGE AND DEVELOPMENT WITHIN HINDUISM

New ideas and problems continually stimulated the growth of new developments within Hinduism. In recent times, the most powerful of these new ideas has been nationalism, which has become an integral part of modern Hinduism. The great national philosophers proclaim an identity of nationalism and Hinduism: Hinduism, they say, is the raison d'être of India.[38] Hinduism is becoming an ideology of Indian nationhood for a variety of groups, the common bond of the culturally and linguistically divergent parts of India. Even those secular politicians of India who dissociate themselves from the Hinduism of the temples and the pilgrimages, from *paṇḍas* and *sādhus*, give their nationalism a religious halo. The idea of India as *Bhārat-Mātā* stands for the sanctity and inviolability of the territory of India. Jawaharlal Nehru, the great humanist and sometimes caustic critic of Hinduism, wrote in his will that he did not want any religious ceremonies to be performed after his death; he did wish, however, that part of his ashes be scattered over India and into the Ganges. Hinduism traditionally does not recognize the borderlines within which religion in the West has been confined for some centuries. Politics, social structures, hygiene, science—everything is assimilated and considered as part of the divine reality.

The intrusion of the West into traditional India has also created enormous problems for Hinduism. There are those who want to turn the clock back and purge India of all it has learned from the West in the last two hundred years. Others naively fail to see any problem at all and simply identify Marx, Freud, and Einstein with some *avatāra* of Viṣṇu. But there are also intelligent, sensitive people in India, who suffer under the cultural schizophrenia and who try to find ways to a new sanity. A. D. Moddie in *Brahmanical Culture and Modernity* seems to offer a good analysis, when he writes

> Ours is the problem of a painful transition, made more painful by resistances to a modern aesthetic and industrial culture by Brahmanical minds, smug with a moral and hierarchical superiority of the past and out of touch with the practical and attitudinal needs of the present . . . we are striving today for the most strategic thing in our time, a new identity for ourselves and the world . . . it is no less than an identity with the spirit of the age, the fulfillment of a new *karma*.

More concretely, he pinpoints the areas of tension between the "Brahmanical" and the "modern" mind thus:

> The Brahmanical attributes in this context are of the old society, traditional, caste-dominated, hierarchical, authoritarian, village and land-based. That culture is status-oriented and it inherently shuns change, social and technological. . . . What is written on the *patra* is naively to be assumed law, life and

> reality. The modern or industrial culture is essentially international, not village or caste-based in its social motivations. It is scientific, rational, it is achievement-oriented and it acknowledges not a hard hierarchy but a mobile elite of intellects, skills, and, yes—wealth.

Moddie thinks that the Hindus are held back from readily and freely accepting the modern culture by their religious traditions, which have become instincts.

> The formidable law of Karma and the theory of re-incarnation induce little sense of obligation and achievement this side of death. Generations of belief in a long cycle of existences produces a degree of fatalism, a deep belief in *bhāg* . . . this life is dismissed as *māyā* or *līlā*, a play of the gods, or a *jāl* in which one is entrapped. Why strive in an illusion?[39]

A Westerner who has had occasion to witness the rise of the new castes in industrial societies, of status-oriented thinking, and of bureaucratic hierarchies would not, perhaps, follow Moddie in his praise of the modern or industrial culture. Perhaps, this is a stage that all mature societies reach once technological innovation has ceased to be the primary force of social transformation. Our society, dominated by management hierarchies and trade-union conservatism, may in many ways become more rigid within the next generation than we would like it to be.

Hindus are quite often diametrically opposed to one another on very basic issues. But in an almost indefinable way they remain Hindus, in spite of the complexity of their peculiarities and prejudices, which as a people they will hardly be able to shed or to radically alter.[40] Much of Hinduism may be mere tradition and many Hindus may disown conventions they have been brought up with, yet Hinduism as a whole shows amazing life and vigor. It is and remains one of the world's great living religions, undoubtedly challenged by modernity but also reinforced by it. If Hinduism follows the path outlined by S. Radhakrishnan, shedding its sectarian and narrowly dogmatic aspects, it may become even more appealing to modern people, not only in India but also in the West. It may, at the same time, become even more difficult to define than even before.[41]

Whereas many Indians, especially those in the big cities and in professions that demand a modern "Western" orientation, may be secularized and largely Westernized, one should not believe that only the backward traditionalists, the small-town businessmen and *paṇḍits* keep Hinduism alive in our time. Among the spokespersons for contemporary Hinduism are extraordinarily intelligent, highly educated, and politically astute men and women who are nonetheless modern for being Hindu.

The great strength of Hinduism at all times has been its capacity to absorb and assimilate ideas from many different sources without giving up its own peculiar fundamental orientation. Though Jainism and Buddhism originally broke away from the Brahmanic-Vedic community, the religion that finally emerged as Hinduism during the Gupta restoration showed features of Buddhism and Jainism and was thus able to exert an almost universal appeal to the people of India. This quite often implied a somewhat radical reorientation. Despite the practice of animal sacrifice and meat eating in the Vedic religion, the new Hinduism that emerged as Vaiṣṇavism adopted the Jain principles of the rejection of animal sacrifice and dietary vegetarianism, and the Buddhists are considered to have been instrumental in providing it with the doctrinal superstructure of repeated *avatāras*.

Also, it is not unlikely that Judeo-Christian influences were at work during the first centuries of the Christian era, molding certain aspects of Hinduism. During the time of the Roman Emperors, when anti-Semitic laws forced Jews from the heartlands of the Roman Empire to emigrate, a considerable number settled on the West coast of India. There is a group of black Jews in South India, who must have intermarried with the local population. In addition, the Bene Israel, a group of white Jews who preserved their racial purity, are established in several major centers, including Bombay, where they have two synagogues.[42] It is impossible to determine to what extent these long-time residents, belonging to a different religion, have influenced Hinduism in the localities where they have been in contact. According to an old tradition of the Christians in Kerala, Thomas, one of the Twelve Apostles of Jesus, preached his faith along the Malabar coast in South India and was martyred close to the modern city of Madras.[43] The Mar Thoma Christians maintain that he preached the Gospel in Northern India, too, even in the famous university town of Taxila, and that he established several churches on the banks of the river Yamunā. Despite strong arguments that suggest a link between the Syrian Christians of India and Nestorian communities in Asia Minor in the fourth century, it is not impossible that some Christians were already living in Malabar before then. These South Indian Christians maintained their numbers largely unchanged throughout the centuries. They lived in peace with their Hindu neighbors and had their own caste structure. Some scholars have attempted to link certain forms of Vaiṣṇavism to Christian influences:[44] the worship of the infant Kṛṣṇa and certain peculiarities of Madhva's theology, for example, his belief in being Vāyu's, the "spirit's," incarnation and his doctrine of predestination.

There had always been a quite lively exchange between Greece and northern India, and the commerce in ideas must have been mutual. Indians not only gave of their religion and philosophy but also received. Those channels of communication did not break when the Arabs conquered the Middle East. Settlements of Arab merchants in Indian seaports were common in pre-Muslim times. It is again a quite well-founded suggestion that, during the first centuries of the Muslim era, an Arabic version of the Gospel stories was brought to India and was assimilated by various groups.[45]

The contact between Hindus and Islam resulted not only in a relatively large number of (sometimes forced) conversions but also in a friendly and fruitful exchange on a broad level. Several of the Muslim rulers were impressed by, and sympathetic to, the Hindu sages and scholars. Some, like Akbar, went so far as to provoke a reaction from a Muslim orthodoxy, afraid that the Muslim faith might suffer through the acceptance of Hindu ideas. A considerable number of Hindus, however, found Islamic ideas worth adopting, and new movements sprang up in which Hindus and Muslims felt equally at home. Kabīr, the Muslim weaver, attracted Hindus into his *panth;* and Gurū Nānak, the Hindu, wanted his Sikhism to be a universal religion, embodying the best of both the Hindu and Muslim traditions. Direct links to influences from Islam may be found in the development of *bhakti*, especially in North India, with its emphasis on the oneness of God and exclusive love of Him, the equality of all worshippers before Him, and its insistence that basic human virtues rather than wealth or status are the signs of true religiosity.

The European invasion, beginning with the Portuguese occupation of Goa, also had its religious impact on Hinduism. The first Portuguese missionaries not only succeeded in getting legislation passed that forced non-Christians either to become Christians or to emigrate and had Hindu temples destroyed, but they also rebaptized thousands of (in their opinion) schismatic Christians, thereby splitting the Indian Christian community into feuding Latin and Syrian factions.[46] Protestant missions under the Danish Lutherans, the British Anglicans, the American Baptists and Methodists, and numerous others set out to shepherd Indians into their different churches, in the process sometimes implanting into their proselytes not only an aversion to their Hindu past but also a hatred of rival Christian factions. Except for a few courageous attempts by individuals, who often enough had to defend themselves against attacks from within their own churches, the Christian missions in India tragically ignored India's indigenous religion. Hindus like Rājā Rām Mohan Roy, Keshub Chunder Sen, Swāmi Vivekānanda, and to a certain degree Mahātmā Gāndhi and Sarvepalli Rādhākrishnan tried to integrate what they found most attractive in Christianity into their own vision of Hinduism.[47] It was mainly the ethics of the Gospels and the social concern of the Christian missionaries that found the approval of modern Hindus and evoked in them the desire to develop their own religion in these areas. Swami Vivekānanda, one of the most influential Hindus around the turn of the century, attempted to reawaken the pride of Hindus in their own tradition, institutionalizing these new features in his Ramakrishna Mission. Although the Ramakrishna movement is not considered an orthodox *sampradāya* by the more conservative Hindus, it has nevertheless captured the imagination of a great many modern and progressive Hindus and is held to be a nonsectarian and universal expression of a new, reformed Hinduism, which at the same time preserves the best of the ancient tradition.

Recent attempts, beginning with Brahmabhandav Upadhyay, to articulate a "Hindu-Christianity," to introduce Hindu rites and scriptures into Christian worship and daily life, may result in a new form of Hinduism as well as a new Christianity.[48]

Despite its openness to many influences and the considerable changes that it has undergone throughout the ages, there is a distinct character, an unbroken tradition, and a unifying principle that allows Hinduism to be faithful to itself while inviting others to share whatever treasures they may possess. In all the historic encounters between Hinduism and other religions, Hinduism has always emerged stronger and richer and has succeeded in absorbing the other elements.

3. Hindu *Dharma:* Orthodoxy And Heresy In Hinduism

All those traditions and all those despicable systems of philosophy which are not based on the Veda produce no reward after death; for they are declared to be founded on darkness. All those [doctrines] differing from [the Veda] which spring up and [soon] perish, are worthless and false, because they are of modern date.

—Manusmṛti *XII, 95*

TRANSLATIONS CAN SOMETIMES be quite revealing. If we try to find an Indian synonym for the term *religion*—admittedly difficult to define even within the Western tradition!—we have to choose from a variety of terms, none of which coincides precisely with our word. The most common and most general term is *dharma*, usually translated as "religion." Another important aspect of religion is expressed by the term *sādhana*, frequently rendered in English as "realization." In its sociological sense, *religion* may often have to be understood as *sampradāya*, mostly (and erroneously) translated as "sect," which describes the great Hindu traditions like Vaiṣṇavism, Śaivism, and Śāktism and their subdivisions. The *ṣaddarśanas*, the "six viewpoints" that have been accepted within Hindu tradition as orthodox (religious) systems, must also be included, as must the *trimārga* scheme, which organizes the entire range of religious affiliations into *karmamārga, bhaktimārga*, and *jñānamārga*, the path of works, the path of loving devotion, and the path of knowledge, respectively. The representation of Hindu religion will differ again according to the affiliation of the writer with regard to caste or position in society; thus, a Brahmin householder will offer a different presentation of religion from that of a *saṁnyāsin*, who has given up all caste affiliation and all ritual. It may help to explain some of these terms in more detail.

THE MEANING OF HINDU *DHARMA*

Dharma (etymologically from the root *dhṛ-*, "to sustain" or "to uphold") has been given diverse meanings in various Indian schools of thought. At one end of the spectrum, we have the Buddhist interpretation, in which *dharma* is merely a logical element of a proposition. Generally, however, it is used with reference to religion in the specific sense of socio-ethical laws and obligations. *Manusmṛti*, the most important authority on the subject, explains the root of *dharma* as "the Veda in its entirety, the traditions (*smṛtis*) fixed by men conversant with the Vedas, the customs of righteous people and self-contentment (*ātmanastuṣṭi*)."[1] The promise is held out to the man who follows all the rules laid down in Manu's law book that "he will obtain fame here on earth and supreme bliss beyond."[2] The same book also excommunicates as *nāstikas* those who place their own reasoning above the authority of tradition.[3] *Nāstika* is normally translated as "atheist," though it does not quite correspond to its English equivalent. In India, followers of atheistic systems like that of the Sāṁkhya are *āstikas* or orthodox, because they do not explicitly question or reject the Vedas; whereas Buddhists and Jains or the followers of any non-Vedic religions are *nāstikas*, including also the solidly materialistic and hedonistic Lokāyatas. The *dharma* of the *Manusmṛti* is also geographically defined:

> The land between the two sacred rivers Sarasvatī and Dṛṣadvatī, this land created by divine powers is the Brahmāvarta. The customs prevailing in this country, passed on from generation to generation, that is called the right behavior (*sadācāra*). From a Brahmin born and raised in this country, all men should learn their ways. The country where the black antelope naturally moves about is the one that is fit for sacrifice—beyond is that of the *mlecchas* [the barbarians, the unclean!]. A twiceborn [viz., a Brahmin, a Kṣatriya, a Vaiṣya] should resort to this country and dwell in it; a Śūdra, however, may for the sake of gaining his livelihood live anywhere.[4]

From the point of view of content, this *dharma* comprises social classification and the division of society into four *varṇas*, each with its particular functions and rights; the whole complex of sacrifices and rituals; the *saṁskāras*, performed at the critical periods of life; marriage laws, right of succession, and the regulation of the relationships between men and women, parents and children, teachers and pupils; and the definition of sin and atonement, pilgrimages and vows, feasts and celebrations, including the myths concerning the creation of the universe, transmigration and final emancipation.[5]

Since, according to Hindu tradition, Manu is the mythical ancestor of all of humankind, his ordinances are *mānava dharma*, "the law of mankind," and *sanātana dharma*, "eternal" and "natural" religion. Modern Hindu scholars try to justify this claim in terms of the many religions and systems of law prevailing in the world as well as to specify how it relates to Hindu law. Thus, Śrī Nārāyaṇjī Puruṣottama Sāngaṇī explains:

> Upon which as a fundament everything is built and which gives to the whole world its order, that which provides man in this world with blessed peace and in the next with supreme bliss and helps to attain to complete emancipation, that is *sanātana dharma*, the eternal religion. It is of the nature of God, because it has developed through God himself. As God has no beginning, middle, or end, so the *sanātana dharma* has no beginning or end. It is beginningless, of hoary antiquity, always the same, in it there is no development or change. This religion is from God and therefore God is its Lord.[6]

He continues to state in detail that this religion of mankind exists in a general form, comprising the duties of firmness, forgiveness, restraint, abstention from stealing, purity, control over the senses, forbearance, knowledge, truth, and freedom from hatred and anger and in a specific form as absolute truth "revealed only to Hindus, different according to the *caturvarṇāśrama* scheme of life". The concept of *svadharma* is a very crucial one: *dharma* is right conduct not in a general sense but specified for each caste and for each situation in life. Time and again, the rule laid down in the *Bhagavadgītā* is quoted: "It is better to fulfil one's own duties (*dharma*), however imperfectly, than to do that of another, however perfect it may be."[7]

Thus, *dharma* presupposes a social order in which all functions and duties are assigned to separate classes whose smooth interaction guarantees the well-being of society as a whole and, beyond this, maintains the harmony of the whole universe. *Dharma* has its roots in the structure of the cosmos, and the socio-ethical law of humanity is but one facet of an all-embracing law encompassing all beings. For this reason, we can also appreciate the frequently quoted maxim: "The 'law' when violated destroys—when preserved protects: therefore *dharma* should not be violated lest the violated *dharma* destroy us."[8] *Dharma*, at least theoretically, is its own justification: *dharma* does not depend on a personal authority that could also make exceptions and pardon a transgressor; it is inherent in nature and does not allow modifications. *Dharma* guarantees the continued existence of India; the *avatāras* appear in order to rescue *dharma* from corruption and thus restore the country. In the strictest and fullest sense, *dharma* coincides with Hinduism. This did not prevent certain developments from taking place within what was considered "law" in Indian history nor did it exclude the treatment of many moral questions on a rational and universal basis.

Though from an absolutist, Vedāntist standpoint good and evil are relative, the two sides of one coin as it were, the *dharmaśāstra* tradition of India has labored continuously to sharply separate *dharma* from *adharma*, to spell out quite unambiguously what is meant by "righteousness" and "unrighteousness," and what they lead to.

The fourth-century logician Vātsyāyana analyzed the elements of both in the following manner: *adharma* as well as *dharma* depend either on body, speech, or mind. Unrighteousness related to the body is threefold: *hiṁsā* (violence), *steya* (theft), and *pratisiddha maithuna* (unlawful sexual indulgence). Correspondingly, righteousness connected with the body consists in *dāna* (charity), *paritrāṇa* (succor of the distressed), and *paricaraṇa* (rendering service). The vices originating from speech are *mithyā* (falsehood), *paruṣa* (caustic talk), *sūcanā* (calumny), and *asaṁbaddha* (absurd talk). The corresponding virtues of speech are *satya* (veracity), *hitavācana* (talking with good intention), *priyavācana* (gentle talk), and *svādhyāya* (recitation of scriptures). *Adharma* connected with the mind is threefold: *paradroha* (ill will), *paradravyābhīpsā* (covetousness), and *nāstikya* (irreligiosity). *Dharma* originating in the mind is *dayā* (compassion), *aspṛhā* (disinterestedness), and *śraddhā* (faith or piety).[9]

Patañjali's *Yogasūtras* offer a less systematic but more popular series of virtues necessary for the attainment of peace of mind and are an exposition of *dharma* under the two categories of *yama* and *niyama* (restraints and observances). The *yama* comprise nonviolence, veracity, abstinence from theft, continence, and abstinence from avariciousness; the *niyama* purity, contentment, ritual actions, study, and "making the Lord the motive of all action."[10] Through these and similar analyses of *dharma*, the universal validity of *dharma* emerges quite clearly, though its motivation and particular application may be typically Hindu. A voluminous *dharmaśāstra* literature has developed over the centuries containing, as well as casuistry and local law, much that has been at the center of ethical reflection in the West, too.[11] As liberal forces in the West fought to change laws, which were defended by conservative institutions as divine or natural laws, so modern Hindus have often found the custodians of *dharma* obstructing the path toward social justice and progress.[12] The defenders of the traditional law allowed the burning of widows, the frequently inhuman ways in which the upper castes treated the outcastes, the superstitions and vices of the past. For this reason, many of those who fought for a better lot for the masses became bitter enemies of the established order. In recent times, voices could be heard from within the tradition advocating reform without overthrowing the entire structure. "Hinduism is not a static structure, but a dynamic force" wrote A. S. Altekar, adding

> Unfortunately, the truth of this proposition is not sufficiently realized by the Hindus themselves. The orthodox Hindu believes that Hinduism is once and for all time fashioned by the pristine *śāstras* of hoary antiquity; the educated Hindu is not sufficiently acquainted with the history of his culture and religion to know their true nature. It was a dark day when the non-official change-sanctioning authority, the Daśāvarā Pariṣad of the Smṛti, was replaced by a government department presided over by the Minister for Religion. For, when Hindu rule came to an end in the thirteenth century, this department also disappeared, and during the last six hundred years Hinduism has remained more or less static. With no authoritative and intelligent agency to guide him, the average Hindu believes that religious beliefs, philosophical theories and social practices current in the twelfth century comprise the whole of this tradition and it is his conviction that these beliefs and practices are sanctioned by the scriptures (which he does not understand), and that to depart from them is an unpardonable sin. This utter and pitiable ignorance of the real nature of Hinduism is at the root of the amazing opposition which measures like the Hindu Code have evoked in the recent past even in educated circles.[13]

There is no doubt that "modernity" has made inroads into traditional Indian *dharma*, and a respected authority like Laxman Shastri Joshi finds that "the moral foundations of Indian society appear to be crumbling rapidly."[14] He sees, to his distress, that "nationalism appears to be taking the place of the old socio-religious consciousness" which he considers "not a healthy product of the new human civilization." He takes a bold stance, however, when he declares: "The need has arisen today for laying the foundations of a new ethics without invoking the aid of collectivity, God or any supernatural or transcendental principle. We need an ethics that will give man the confidence in his powers of creating his own social existence. . . . Morality is the beauty of human existence, it is the rhythm of human life."

Reflections about *dharma*, however, do not remain in the sphere of ethical theory, they enter into very practical issues: laws for the new Indian republic that would be binding on all the diverse groups of Hindus, who so far had been following a multitude of traditional laws sanctioned by various *śāstras*, and "codes of conduct" for all those who engage in public activities. India in fact abrogated traditional law in certain sectors, when it declared "untouchability" to be abolished and discrimination on account of caste to be punishable. As daily life shows in countless instances, the transition is not easy and can by no means be considered to have been completed.[15]

We shall have constant need to refer to *dharma* when describing the various aspects of Hindu life and doctrine. A few other key concepts for the understanding of religion in the Indian sense will be introduced at this juncture.

REACHING INDIVIDUAL PERFECTION THROUGH *SĀDHANA*

Sādhana (derived from the root *sādh-*, "to finish" or "to accomplish") denotes the "means of realization." One who practices a *sādhana* is a *sādhaka*, a word closely related to the word *sādhu*, the "just man" or "saint." While *dharma* is imposed on persons by nature or by society, they are free to choose their own *sādhana*. Therefore, there is basically only one *dharma*, but there are countless *sādhanas*, which differ considerably. They are connected insofar as, according to the classical *caturvarṇāśrama* scheme, the last stage in the life of a Brahmin was to be that of *saṁnyāsa*, a wandering ascetic, wholly dedicated to *sādhana*, the pursuit of complete emancipation. The scheme has been departed from quite frequently, even in former times; in fact, any man or woman can become a member of a *sampradāya* (a religious order) and practice the *sādhana* that agrees with his or her condition.[16] Though the classical schema of the three ways is usually applied, there are many more ways, and almost every sect and subsect has its own ideas about *sādhana*. All agree, however, in the basic conviction that human beings are not born free but must liberate themselves through discipline.

The analysis of the nature of bondage determines also the nature of the *sādhana:* for the followers of Śaṅkara, bondage consists in an illusion about the real nature of the Self; for the followers of Rāmānuja, it is forgetfulness of the Lord; for many *bhakti* schools, it is a wrong emotional attitude toward world and God; and for the *śakti* schools, a separation from the Mother. *Sādhana* entails bodily as well as mental and spiritual practices. It is usually practiced under the guidance of a guru, through whom the disciple has to search and whom he or she has to serve. The general name for the ascetic practices is *tapas*, literally "heat." Some of those practices must go back to prehistoric times. Ancient Vedic texts already used the term, and sometimes the creation of the universe itself is ascribed to *tapas*. *Tapas* may mean anything, from real self-torture and record-breaking austerity to the recitation of sacred syllables and the chanting of melodies. Fasting, *prāṇayama* (breath control), *japa* (repetition of a name of God or a short *mantra*), and study of scriptures are among the most common practices. At the *melās*, one can observe other varieties of *tapas:* lying on a bed of thorns or nails, prolonged standing on one leg, lifting one arm for years until it is withered, looking straight into the glaring sun for long hours, and similar feats. Many ascetics keep silence for years. This is one of the most powerful means of storing up spiritual energy.

Although, perhaps under Christian influence, the practices associated with *sādhanas* are often associated with theistic ideas not very different from the ideas of the value of voluntary suffering and self-mortification,

6. Temple scene in Mathurā

originally they had nothing to do with either ethical perfection or pleasing God. *Tapas* used to be seen as psycho-physical energy, the accumulation of which determined one's position in the universe. The aim, therefore, was to reach a higher position with greater power through *tapas*.

There are numerous stories in Indian literature about forest hermits who had accumulated so much *tapas*, that the gods, and even the highest among them, Indra, became afraid of losing their positions. As their ultimate weapon, the gods usually sent to the ascetic a bewitchingly beautiful heavenly damsel to confuse his thoughts or a rude fellow to make him lose his temper in an outburst of anger, thereby burning up all his stored up *tapas* energy. The ascetic would then have to start afresh, unless he decided to embrace another vocation. If a man had gathered enough *tapas*, he could compel a *deva* to appear before him who would have to offer him an absolutely effective boon, opening up infinite possibilities for the imagination of authors and poets. The boons are limited by the power of the god, and the *tapasvin* has to make the right choice. If the god is not quick witted enough, the ascetic who called him can also turn the boon against the god. The gods, therefore, usually grant boons with built-in precautions, stipulating the conditions under which the boon would be effective.

A telling story is that of Vikra. After practicing severe *tapas* for many years, he called Śiva, asking him to grant the boon, that whosoever's head he would touch, that man should die instantly. Śiva laughingly granted the boon, realizing his folly only when Vikra chased his wife and him, to try out the new art. Śiva in his despair sought refuge with Viṣṇu, asking for advice. Viṣṇu, cunningly, induced doubt in Vikra. Śiva, he told Vikra, cannot always be taken seriously. He might have been joking or lying, so try it first on yourself. Vikra did so and thus killed himself with the boon he had received. The story has as its main theme the superiority of Viṣṇu over Śiva, who has to appeal to Viṣṇu to save his life.

ORTHODOXY BATTLING HERESY

This incident reveals something of the rivalry that exists between the different *sampradāyas*, the various sects of Hinduism. The great majority of Hindus belong to Vaiṣṇavism, Śaivism, or Śāktism; all of which have countless subdivisions, springing from local traditions, cults, and a great many religious teachers.[17] Among them there had often been competition for the dominance of Viṣṇu, Śiva, or Devī and not seldom intolerance and fanatical zeal as well. In the nineteenth century, the *kumbha-melās*, when a large number of *sādhus* of all *sampradāyas* congregated, witnessed regular battles between Śaivas and Vaiṣṇavas in which many lost their lives.[18] The immediate reason for the quarrels was usually a question of precedence in the ritual bath at the most auspicious time, but there always lurked a much larger and more important issue—the right belief! Vaiṣṇavas are absolutely sure that Viṣṇu alone is the Lord and that placing Śiva above Viṣṇu is the grossest heresy and disbelief. And Śaivas, of course, know that only Śiva is the Great Lord, whom all must adore and serve and for whose glory they spend themselves. The *Liṅgapurāṇa* promises Śiva's heaven to one who kills or tears out the tongue of someone who reviles Śiva.[19] The Vaiṣṇava scriptures contain not only barbed stories, such as the one about Vikra, but also venomous invectives against all who do not follow Viṣṇu.[20] Considerable friction also existed between the followers of these Puranic traditions and the orthodox Vedic Brahmins. The Pañcarātrins, one of the prominent sects of Vaiṣṇavas, were labelled great sinners, whose existence was the result of killing cows in some former birth. They were accused of being absolutely non-Vedic; further, it was held by the orthodox, that the literatures of the Śāktas, Śaivas, and Pañcarātras were for the delusion of humankind.[21]

Both Śaivas and Vaiṣṇavas considered the "atheistic" Buddhists and Jains their common enemy.[22] Numerous are the historical instances of persecution of people who refused to conform to the idea of orthodoxy that demanded the acknowledgment of Brahmanic authority and Vedic revelation.[23]

Some authors seem to think that, among the *avatāras* of Viṣṇu, Buddha would have been received in a spirit of tolerance. But the way in which this Buddha-*avatāra* is described in the *Viṣṇupurāṇa* and the general Hindu attitude of considering both good and evil as coming from the same Supreme Being would suggest that we have here an early and unmistakably hostile Hindu text dealing with Buddhism.[24]

Buddha is introduced as one of many forms of the *māyāmoha* (delusive power) of Viṣṇu. He engages in what may be called psychological warfare against the *daityas* on behalf of the *devas*, who have come to take refuge with him. He is sent to destroy the enemies of the Vaiṣṇavas from within. He is characterized as *raktāmbara*, dressed in a red garment, as *mṛdvalpamadhurākṣara*, speaking gently, calmly, and sweetly. The teachings, which he communicates for the self-destruction of the *daityas*, considered as pernicious and heretical by the Hindus, are

1. the killing of animals for sacrifices should be discontinued;
2. the whole world is *vijñānamaya*, a product of the mind;
3. the world is *anādhāram*, without support; and
4. the world is engaged in pursuit of error that it mistakes for knowledge.

As a result of this teaching, the *daityas* abandon the *dharma* of the Vedas and the *smṛtis*, and they induce others to do the same. The same *māyāmoha* of Viṣṇu had appeared before Buddha as "a naked mendicant with shaven head and a bunch of peacock feathers in his hands," and he is to appear again as the preacher of the Cārvāka doctrines.

The *Viṣṇupurāṇa* calls the Ṛk, Yajus, and Sāmaveda the "garments" of a man: a man is naked if he goes without them. The *daityas*, seduced by Buddha are in such a position. Whereas the *devas* were unable to dislodge the *daityas* before, they now defeat them: "The armour of *dharma*, which had formerly protected the *daityas* had been discarded by them and upon its abandonment followed their destruction."

The *Viṣṇupurāṇa* follows up the story of the defeat of the *daityas* by establishing general rules concerning the treatment of heretics. The text calls them *nagna*, "naked," in tune with the aforementioned idea, and *pāpakṛt*, "sinners." The criterion of orthodoxy is behavior in conformity with the rules laid down for each one of the four *āśramas*. There is no fifth *āśrama*, the text categorically states. Our Purāṇa shows special concern for the conscientious performance of the daily rites prescribed for the householder, the most prominent feature of Buddhists being the neglect of them. A neglect of the daily rites for a year is considered so grave a sin that there is no expiation for it: "There is no sinner upon earth more culpable than one in whose dwelling the *devas*, the *ṛṣis*, the *pitṛs* and the *bhūtas* are left to sigh without an oblation."

The *Viṣṇupurāṇa* suggests complete excommunication of the Buddhists: all social contact must be broken, even looking at a heretic necessitates lengthy expiations. The Hindu who dines with a Buddhist goes to hell. Buddhists are to be considered as unclean, whatever their caste affiliation may have been. Not only is the Hindu told to have nothing to do with the Buddhist, he must discourage the Buddhist from associating with him: if a heretic observes a faithful one in his rituals, these remain without fruit.

To illustrate its teaching, the *Viṣṇupurāṇa* tells the story of King Śatadhanu and his pious wife. The mere conversation of the king with a *pāṣaṇḍa* suffices to let him be reborn as a dog, a wolf, a vulture, a crow, and a peacock before assuming a human body again. The instrument of his salvation is his wife, who looked away from the heretic when the king conversed with him and thus remained undefiled.

According to an old tradition, Śaṅkarācārya tried to reconcile the rival Hindu sects in the eighth century by introducing the so-called *pañcāyatanapūjā*, the simultaneous worship of Gaṇeṣa, Sūrya, Viṣṇu, Śiva, and Devī, explaining that all deities were but different forms of the one Brahman, the invisible Supreme Being.[25] That this attempt was not well received by all those who clung to the idea of one God is illustrated by a story in which the followers of Madhva, the "Hammer of the Jainas," explain their master's negative relationship to Śaṅkara and his followers:

> The demon Manimat was born as the illegitimate child of a widow and was therefore called Śaṅkara. He studied the *śāstras* with Śiva's blessings and the depraved welcomed him. He really taught Buddhism under the guise of Vedānta. He seduced the wife of his brahmin host and used to make converts by his magic arts. When he died, he asked his disciples to kill Satyaprajñā, the true teacher of Vedānta; the followers of Śaṅkara were tyrannical people who burnt down monasteries, destroyed cattle and killed women and children. They converted Prajñātīrtha, their chief opponent, by force. The disciples of Prajñātīrtha, however, were secretly attached to the true Vedāntic doctrine and they made one of their disciples thoroughly learned in the Vedic scriptures. Acutyaprekṣa, the teacher of Madhva, was a disciple of this true type of teacher, who originated from Satyaprajñā. Madhva was an incarnation of Vāyu for the purpose of destroying the false doctrines of Śaṅkara, which were like the doctrines of the Lokāyatas, Jainas and Pāśupatas, but were more obnoxious and injurious.[26]

The same Śaṅkara is said to have had the Kārpātikas whipped because they were not Vedic. He founded the Daśanāmi order and established *maṭhas* at four strategic points in India, allocating to each a quarter of India for missionary purposes. Śaṅkara, as described in the *Digvijaya*, "the conquest of space," conformed to the current idea of the *ācārya*, the "master" who had to be able to defend his own position against all objections and to defeat his opponents in public debate.

Though quite often the existence of "six viewpoints," accepted as orthodox, is taken as a sign of doctrinal tolerance within Hinduism, each author necessarily identifies himself with one system and tries to prove the others either wrong or defective. The decision to call a system orthodox or heretical is often based on subjective criteria and sectarian affiliations. Thus Mādhava, a fourteenth century Advaitin, arranges his *Sarvadarśana-saṁgraha*, the summary of all systems, in such a way that each following system cancels out the preceding one. In the end, Advaita Vedānta, as expounded by Śaṅkara, emerges as the only truth.[27] Thus, the Cārvākas, unabashed materialists and hedonists and enemies of the Vedic-Brahmanic religion, are defeated by the Buddhists, who in turn are proved wrong by the Jainas. These have to give way to the Rāmānujists, who in turn are superseded by the followers of Madhva. Four schools of Śaivism, the Pāśupata, the Śaiva, the Pratyābhijñā, and the Raseśvara systems, cancel each other out successively. The truth of the next, the Vaiśeṣika system, is overthrown by the Naiyāyikās, who suffer defeat at the hands of the Mīmāṁsakas. These in turn have to give way to the followers of Pāṇini, who are ousted by the Sāṁkhya system. The Yoga system finally comes closest to the truth, which is fully present in Śaṅkara's Advaita Vedānta.

The *Brahma-sūtra*, as understood by Śaṅkara, is largely a refutation of non-Vedāntic systems of thought. Not only does it reject the four major schools of Buddhism but also Sāṁkhya and Bhāgavatism. Śaṅkara explains the need for the exposition of Brahma knowledge by stating that "there are many various opinions, partly based on sound arguments and scriptural texts and partly on fallacious arguments and scriptural texts misunderstood. If a man would embrace one of these opinions without previous consideration, he would bar himself from the highest beatitude and incur grievous loss."[28]

Synopses of the various systems from other standpoints will choose a different sequence in order to prove their views right. The accusation hurled against rival sects of not being Vedic or being ignorant of the correct methods of interpretation of texts results either in the insinuation that the doctrines in question reveal crypto-*nāstikas*, or in the "tolerant" opinion that the others have some glimpses of truth mixed with untruth, while the system held by the writer is the whole and sole truth.

Religious Hinduism is unanimous, however, in rejecting, besides Buddhism and Jainism, the system known as Cārvāka or Lokāyata, a solidly materialistic system that, as part of India's "realistic" philosophical tradition, has also engaged the attention of Western scholars more recently.[29] Mādhava wrote that he thought most of his contemporaries in fourteenth century India to be Cārvākas, regarding wealth and pleasure as the only aim in life and living according to the motto: "As long as you live enjoy yourself—nobody can escape from death. Once this body is consumed by fire—how will you ever return?" The only reality they acknowledge is material: the four elements—earth, water, air and fire, together with their combinations. The so-called spirit of man is only a byproduct of these, similar to the emergence of alcohol in the fermentation of certain substances. Man's soul dies with the body. They even quote scripture to corroborate their theories: "Arising from out of these elements, one also re-enters into them. When one has departed, there is no more knowledge," says the *Bṛhadāraṇyaka-Upaniṣad.*[30] Wisdom consists in aiming at the maximum enjoyment with the least trouble and in avoiding grief. To their more pious contemporaries who ask why one should go to such lengths in organizing sacrifices and religious celebrations, they coolly reply: religion is only of use for the priests as their means of livelihood; the Vedas are full of untruth and contradictions. The Vedic paṇḍits defeat each other, and the authority of the way of knowledge is cancelled by those who advocate the way of works. The Vedas are nothing but the incoherent rhapsodies of swindlers and impostors. It is difficult to surpass the cynicism of the

Cārvākas, as illustrated in the following quotation from an otherwise lost work by a certain Bṛhaspati:

> There is no heaven, no spiritual liberation, nor any soul in another world. The good deeds of the various classes do not leave any trace. The *agnihotra*, the three Vedas, the *saṃnyāsin*'s three staffs, the ashes on one's body are all inventions, made for gaining a livelihood by those who lack vigour and intelligence. If an animal slaughtered in the *jyotiṣṭoma* goes to heaven, why does the sacrificer not immediately kill his father? If *śrāddha*, the sacrifice for the deceased, does profit the dead, then the traveller does not need to take any provisions on his journey. If sacrifice nourishes the beings in heaven, why not those who stand on a rooftop? Let a man enjoy his life and let him eat *ghī* even if he has debts. Once the body is burnt, how should he return? Why does one who leaves his body not return for the sake of his relations? I tell you why: all these ceremonies are without value, they have been introduced by the Brahmins for the sake of gain. The authors of the three Vedas were frauds and humbugs. The well-known formulae of pandits, priests and their like, the obscene ritual prescribed for the queen in the *aśvamedha* were all invented by rogues and demons.[31]

As almost everything else in Hinduism, so also the dichotomy between orthodox and heretics operates differently on different levels. On one level, the level of caste-regulated behavior, the distinction between *āstika* and *nāstika* is quite clear; *āstikas* are excommunicated. On another level, the level of personal religiosity and devotion, the distinction is blurred; as caste is not observed in the gatherings of *bhaktas*, so *bhakti* religion offers salvation also to those who are *nāstikas*. It introduces, however, its own criteria for excommunication: sins against the name are unforgivable.

The two levels on which Hinduism moves, not only the level of the absolute and the relative, are in constant interaction. The observation of caste rules and Vedic propriety alone would not qualify a person for salvation by Viṣṇu—the person must be elected by Him, an election that must be earned through acts of devotion and service—such behavior also is insisted upon by Vaiṣṇava writers. However—and here we again switch levels—the perfect one, the saint, the guru, can take liberties with rules and regulations: divine licence suspends human law. And again, in a devotional context, a person may be considered a saint, a soul close to God, and still may be denied those rights that come from observing caste regulations.

Hindus, of course, are used to compartmentalizing society and to accepting a corresponding compartmentalization of right and wrong behavior. The devotee, in *satsaṅg*, moves temporarily into another society, the group of the believers that operates under its own laws. The termination of the *satsaṅg* brings about the termination of this status, and the person moves back into the caste he or she was born into.

Though it may be impossible to establish criteria of orthodoxy that would find acceptance by all Hindus, it would not be correct to conclude that such an idea is absent from Hinduism and that, instead we have to substitute for it an idea of "orthopraxy."[32] Doctrinal issues have been discussed by Hindus throughout the ages with tenacity and with the understanding that there is always an aspect of absolute truth reflected in any particular religious doctrine. Although there has never been one central authority in Hinduism strong enough to decide the issue categorically, the numerous heads of the various Hindu churches have nevertheless established very rigorous canons from within which their understanding of orthodoxy is defined.[33] Thus, they clearly determine which books have to be considered as revelation, which authors may be used as commentators, and which line of tradition must be followed. Students of religion in traditional institutions were not supposed to read other books or to listen to any other teacher. This often made them incapable of appreciating or understanding any version of Hinduism that differed from their own. Even today, the debates between pandits of different schools are often quite acrimonious and filled with narrow-minded attempts to "defeat" each other. It is somewhat amusing to hear American Hare Kṛṣṇa followers repeat the traditional Caitanyite arguments against Advaita, of which they probably know very little. The more recent history of Hinduism is also fraught with intolerance. The *Ārya Samāj* and its offspring, the *Hindu Mahāsabhā* and the *Rāṣṭrīya Svayamsevak Sangh*, have intimidated and often provoked non-Hindus. They have been responsible for numerous Hindu-Muslim riots, for atrocities in the name of the true religion, and finally, for the assassination of Mahātmā Gandhi, whom they considered an enemy of Hinduism.

In a nonviolent but nevertheless very effective way, the caste *pañcāyats* and the leaders of *sampradāyas* have always exercized control over their members, carefully watching them and enforcing their views of orthodoxy, if necessary through imposition of penances or expulsion from the community. Hinduism may appear to be very vague and extremely tolerant to the outsider, but the insider must conform to very precise regulations of life within the group. *Svadharma*, each person's peculiar set of duties and obligations, orders and restricts that person's life. Those who have achieved freedom from social duties by choosing *saṁnyāsa* must conform to the precise rules of their own particular *sampradāya*, if they do not want to risk being reprimanded by zealous colleagues. When *sādhus* meet, they first ask about each other's *sampradāya* and guru; quite often they remonstrate with one another, pointing out violations of rules and customs.

Someone who lives with a guru has to serve her or him conscientiously and loyally, without showing any sign of an independent opinion. For many, the guru represents God; to contradict him or her would be blasphemy; blind faith and unquestioning service are considered to be the way to eternal bliss; and the attitude of certain gurus toward the rest of humanity consists, at an advanced age, of a mixture of limitless arrogance, naive self-deceit, and megalomania, not unfrequently supported by European and American admirers.

In our time, rivalries between different denominations of Hinduism often acquire political overtones. Thus, a recent takeover of the Vaiṣṇā Devī shrine by an independent board supported by the governor of Kashmir resulted in a bitter exchange between Karan Singh, the president of the *Virāt Hindu Samāj* and the governor, Jagmohan. Karan Singh accused Jagmohan of being an Ārya Samājist and, as such, being against image worship, whereas he himself defended the rights of the Dharmarth Trust, which is "responsible for the advancement and promotion of *Sanātana Dharma.*"[34]

4. Revelation and Scripture in Hinduism

> Let Scripture be your standard for laying down what should be done and what should not. Knowing what the rules of Scripture have determined, do your work in this world.
>
> —Bhagavadgītā *XVI, 24*

NO OTHER LIVING tradition can claim scriptures as numerous or as ancient as Hinduism; none can boast an unbroken tradition preserved as faithfully as the Hindu tradition. The sources of Hinduism are not only historical materials to be studied by the scholar of antiquity, they have been recited and studied by the faithful throughout the ages. Today the reading of a Hindu religious scripture is always carried out with some kind of solemnity. In order to ward off all unfavorable influences and to create an auspicious disposition, a so-called *maṅgalaśloka* is recited before the text proper begins, hymns of praise and devotion to a number of deities, to the guru, and to the text to be read. Time, place, and the external circumstances of the recitation are regulated, and the reading itself is usually done in a prescribed recitative.[1] It is essential to observe all these rules in order to obtain the fruits of the reading, which are quite often spelled out concretely at the end of the book itself.[2] The reading is not terminated abruptly either. The last sentence is read twice, thus indicating the end of the reading. The gods who were addressed in the beginning are now implored to forgive all inattention, disrespect, and incorrect or imperfect reading; this is the so-called *aparādhakṣamāpañca stotra*, marking the conclusion of the recitation.

The book of scripture itself is always treated with reverence; it is never laid on the bare floor and is carefully guarded against all disrespect. In former times, Hindus did not allow people from low castes or foreigners to read or to possess their sacred books. Nowadays, anyone can buy printed copies, and quite often translations as well, of the Hindu scriptures in a bookstore. Though secular Western scholars have begun to analyze and dissect the Hindu scriptures, Hindus continue to regard them as revelations,[3] given to their ancestors as a special privilege, and they resent the secularist view that sees in them only ancient literature. Before the sacred lore was written down, it existed for untold centuries as an oral tradition handed down from generation to generation.[4] It was committed to writing only at a relatively late period in its history—and even now the proper study consists in memorizing the texts. The authentic Hindu tradition consists of that chain of authorities in which the oral tradition has been kept alive.[5]

The various sacred books of the Hindus are not all considered to hold the same degree of revelation. At an early age, the Indians developed a precise, widely accepted theological epistemology, according to which all authoritative literature is categorized. The *prasthāna trayī*, the triad of instruments for the attainment of religious knowledge, consists of *śruti, smṛti*, and *nyāya* or *pramāṇa*. From Śaṅkara (eighth century C.E.) onward, these were identified by the Vedāntins with the *Upaniṣads*, the *Bhagavadgītā*, and the *Brahmasūtra*. Other schools, for example, the Mīmāṁsakas, would not agree with this. As the different sects and schools of Hinduism differ in their ideas concerning orthodoxy and heresy, so they differ also in the recognition of certain classes of scriptures and their relative position in this scheme.

REVELATION PROPER: *ŚRUTI*

Śruti literally means that which has been perceived through hearing; it is "revelation" in the most literal sense. As a technical term, it comprises the scriptures with the highest theological value, containing supreme and undebatable authority. *Śruti* may be commented upon but can never be questioned. In theological debates, discussion is carried on only for the purpose of establishing the meaning of *śruti*. Hārīta, an author of an early *dharmasūtra*,[6] holds the opinion that *śruti* is of two kinds, the Vedic and the Tantric or Āgamic. He thereby acknowledges that in his time the non-Vedic traditions had become powerful enough to claim a position equal to that of the *Veda*, which originally had held this title exclusively. Even now the *sanātanists*, the followers of the Vedic *dharma*, refuse to acknowledge the *Āgamas*, the scriptures of the Vaiṣṇavas, Śaivas, and Śāktas as *śruti*. This is a rather unrealistic position, since for more than a thousand years Hindu religion has been influenced much more by the

Āgamas than by the *Vedas*, and even the acknowledged *ācāryas* of Vedānta accepted the Āgamas and shaped their interpretation of Vedic texts accordingly.[7]

For all practical purposes, then, we have to accept two mainstreams of *śruti*, though no Hindu will allow that all the scriptures accepted by the one or the other Hindu sect are revelation and therefore are of any consequence to him.

The *Veda*, sacred knowledge, comprises several categories of literature.[8] The oldest part, the Veda in the strict sense, is divided into four *saṁhitās* or collections: *Ṛgveda*,[9] a collection of more than a thousand hymns to various gods; *Sāmaveda*,[10] a collection of extracts from the former with the appropriate musical instructions for recitation; *Yajurveda*,[11] the book of Vedic ceremonies; and *Atharvaveda*,[12] a heterogeneous collection of hymns and spells. The four *Vedas* are neither sacred history nor doctrine; they are the instruments for the performance of the *yajña*, the sacrifice that stood at the center of Vedic religion.[13]

Traditional scholars correlate the secular learning of the Hindus as *Upavedas* or supplementary knowledge with the four *Vedas: Arthaveda*, the science of statecraft and politics with the *Ṛgveda; Gandharvaveda*, music and the fine arts with the *Sāmaveda; Dhanuṣveda*, the art of archery (and warfare in general) with *Yajurveda;* and *Āyurveda*, medicine and biology, with the *Atharvaveda.*[14]

Despite the existence of four *Vedas*, the *Ṛgveda* occupies a special position as *śruti.* Because of the importance given to the exact wording, to the very sounds and syllables of the text itself, a series of auxiliary sciences for the study of the Veda, the *Vedāṅgas*, came into existence early as an essential part of the Brahmin's training.[15] Among them *Śīkṣa* handles precise and faultless pronunciation; *Kalpa* discusses the details of ritual; *Vyākaraṇa* is the study of grammar, including some linguistics and philology; *Nirukta* deals with the etymology of unusual and rare words; *Chaṇḍa* specializes in the explanation and practice of verse meters; and *Jyotiṣa* teaches planetary science, astronomy and astrology together, which was (and is) the instrument for determining the right moment for religious acts.[16] Though the *Vedāṅgas* are not part of the *śruti*, they are indispensable for those who have to perform Vedic rituals.

The thoroughness of these auxiliary sciences is quite extraordinary. In order to hand down the text of the hymns of the *Ṛgveda* orthologically, special mnemonic and reading techniques were developed. The student had to learn each verse in eleven different ways: forwards and backwards, with combinations and retro-combinations of letters, omitting certain letters and doubling others. The hymns were never simply read but had to be recited in an exactly prescribed pitch. The recitation had to be accompanied by precisely studied movements of the right arm and of the fingers according to accent and pitch. A young Brahmin had to go through many years of intensive training before he was qualified to officiate at a sacrifice. Since it was believed that a single mispronounced syllable could spoil the entire costly arrangement, extreme care was taken to perfect the Brahmin's training. Harsh punishment awaited the offender: a Brahmin who read the Veda without the correct movements of the hand faced expulsion from his caste; one who did not pay attention to the exact length of the syllables, to cadences and tunes, was threatened with being reduced to ashes and being reborn as a vile animal. The effect of the *mantra* was supposed to depend on its correct pronunciation rather than on the meaning of a sentence or the action of a deity. The *Śatapatha Brāhmaṇa* carries a telling myth. Tvaṣṭṛ, whose son Viśvarūpa had been killed by Indra, is about to conjure up, with a soma libation, *Vṛtra indraśatruḥ*, the one who cannot fail to kill Indra because in him all the powers of the *devas* are combined. Because of a wrong accent in the infallible *mantra*, the one who was destined to kill Indra is destined, unfailingly, to be killed by Indra.[17] This belief in the literal efficacy of the mantra has been analyzed and systematized in one of the recognized orthodox schools, the *Pūrva Mīmāṁsā*.

The *Brāhmaṇas*, a voluminous collection of ancient writings dealing mainly with explanations of the sacrifice, are also considered to be part of *śruti*, though they are less in the foreground than the *Āraṇyakas*, the forest treatises, and the *Upaniṣads*. The two latter classes of writings are sometimes intermingled[18] and they contain similar materials. The *Upaniṣads* are also called the *Vedānta*, the end of the Veda. They mark the latest part of the *Veda*, and they are regarded as its end and aim. With the *Upaniṣads*, *śruti* comes to its end, according to the *Smārtas*. Within *śruti* is a twofold division, *Karmakāṇḍa* and *Jñānakāṇḍa*. The Vedic *Saṁhitās* and the *Brāhmaṇas*, which center around the sacrifice, make up the "part of action" brought into a system by *Pūrva Mīmāṁsā;* the *Āraṇyakas* and the *Upaniṣads*, with their emphasis on speculation and intuitive knowledge, form the *Jñānakaṇḍa*, the part of wisdom. It has found its systematic development in the numerous schools of Vedānta philosophy. The most authoritative Vedāntins quote from about 15 *Upaniṣads* in their references to scripture; the popular editions contain 108 *Upaniṣads*.[19] Besides these, at least 100 more *Upaniṣads* have been composed in recent centuries; even today, certain sects and schools mold their teachings in the form of an *Upaniṣad* to lend it greater authority with the orthodox.[20]

Each of the *Upaniṣads* belongs to one of the Vedic *Saṁhitās;* thus there are *Ṛgveda Upaniṣads, Sāmaveda Upaniṣads*, and so on. Among the *Saṁhitās* again, different traditions are distinguished, pointing out that Vedic religion developed within, and was handed over by, a number of families, each of which kept its own particular traditions and rites within the general frame of Vedic religion.[21] The *Upaniṣads* in their imagery show quite clearly the specific family relationship. The *Bṛhadāraṇyaka Upaniṣad*, belonging to the white *Yajurveda*, begins its cosmogonic and soteriological speculations with a metaphorical explanation of the horse sacrifice that is the specific symbol of the white *Yajurveda* and treated prominently in the *Śatapatha Brāhmaṇa*, which belongs to the same school. The *Upaniṣads* contain a good deal of "mystical" practice and theory, but they have also numerous allusions to the rites and ceremonies of the Vedas.

The later *Upaniṣads* are compendia of doctrines of various schools of Hinduism and really belong to the *Āgamas*, a class of literature considered as authoritative and as ancient as the Vedas by the followers of Vaiṣṇavism, Śaivism, and Śāktism; that is, by the majority of Hindus.

The term *āgama*, "scripture," is often used to denote all writings considered revealed by the Hindus. More specifically, the term is used in connection with non-Vedic scriptures considered to be revelation by particular Hindu sects. Thus, we have traditional lists of 108 *Pañcarātra* or *Vaiṣṇava Āgamas* (also called *Saṁhitās*), 28 *Śaiva Āgamas*, and 77

7. Houses on the Ganges waterfront in Benares

Śākta Āgamas (also called *Tantras*). Each of these sects has numerous subsects, and the recognition of a scripture depends on one's affiliation with them.[22] In the most specific sense, the scriptures of the Śaivites are called *āgamas*. They normally consist of four parts: *jñāna* or knowledge, *yoga* or concentration, *kriyā* or rituals, and *caryā* or rules for daily life. The latter two parts are considered to be the most important and are usually the most extensive, since they affect worship and life in a major way. This class of scriptures had been neglected by Western scholars for a long time. After the pioneering work of R. O. Schrader,[23] others followed and a steady stream of text editions and translations has appeared lately. The *Āgamas* have been found important not only as sources for the beliefs and practices of the sects by which they have been adopted as scriptures but also for the study of the cultural history of India. They often contain detailed information on temple building, image making, and performance of public festivals. According to G. S. Murti

> The *Āgama* is fundamentally a *Sādhana Śāstra* . . . it prescribes a particular way of life and a practical course of self-discipline in conformity with the theoretical teachings of its philosophy. It also governs, to a considerable degree, the forms of worship performed in the temples and the forms of rituals performed in the homes. . . . For the past hundreds of years the Vedic sacrifices or *yajñas* have largely given place—specially in South India—to resplendent rituals of temple-worship based on the *Āgamas*.[24]

The *Purāṇas*, another large class of sacred books of Hinduism, to be examined in more detail in another chapter, also are considered scripture by some Hindu sects. Thus, Vaiṣṇavas would quote the *Viṣṇu Purāṇa* and the *Bhāgavata Purāṇa* side by side with the *Upaniṣads* as equal in authority. *Purāṇas* as well as *Āgamas* make claims to be direct revelations of the god with whom they are affiliated and contain numerous passages in which the Supreme God is the speaker and promulgator of commands. The more general Hindu practice would assign them a place within *smṛti*.[25]

The *Bhagavadgītā* has acquired a special position within Hinduism, it calls itself an *Upaniṣad*, claiming the authority of the *śruti*. It no doubt comes from the Vedānta tradition, but it also shows strongly *Āgama* influences. Traditional authorities of Vedānta philosophy consider it as the *smṛti-prasthāna*.

In between *śruti* and *smṛti* come the numerous *sūtras*, short compendia summarizing the rules concerning public sacrifices (*Śrautasūtras*), domestic rites (*Gṛhyasūtras*) and general religious law (*Dharmasūtras*)—collectively, these are called the *Kalpasūtras*. Since they do not usually contain new revelation, they are not quoted in doctrinal arguments.[26]

SACRED TRADITION: *SMṚTI*

Smṛti (literally, "that which has been remembered") tradition, constitutes the second authority. The term is used in either a narrower sense (comprising only the *Dharmaśāstras*) or in a wider sense (including *Itihāsa* and *Purāṇa*). The *smṛti* in the narrow sense are associated with family traditions within Vedic religion and as the works belonging to *śruti*. Their rules are therefore not always identical, and in case of doubt, each Brahmin was bound to follow his own *smṛti* rather than any other authority. The *smṛtis* as we have them today must have been preceded by centuries of development; the many references to former lawgivers and scholars again establish an unbroken succession of *dharma*.[27]

Among the *smṛtis* the *Manusmṛti* occupies a special place and has been accepted more widely than any other such code. Manu is considered to have been the ancestor of the entire human race and the lawgiver for all men; he did not make the law but promulgated the revealed *dharma* as it applied to different classes of society. The castes and the regulation of life according to the *caturvarnāśrama* scheme are connected with creation itself, the description of which forms the first part of the book. After dealing with what one expects from a law book—rules for castes, duties of individual classes of people, civil and criminal law, sacrifices and atonements—the book concludes with an excursus on transmigration and supreme bliss.[28] Although it certainly allows us glimpses of social life in ancient India, we must bear in mind that such books often do not reflect the actual conditions but an ideal aimed at by the authorities.[29]

Among the numerous other *smṛtis, Yājñavalkyasmṛti* and *Viṣṇusmṛti* deserve special mention. The latter already includes a Vaiṣṇava interpretation of *dharma*.[30]

For daily life, *smṛti* is often of greater importance than *śruti;* it affects the life of every Hindu in many details. The most orthodox Hindus are called the *smārtas,* followers of tradition, which still influences Indian society to a very large degree.[31]

A good deal of the material of both *śruti* (in the Vedic sense) and *smṛti* has been incorporated into *Itihāsa-Purāṇa* (literally, "ancient history"). It comprises the two great epics, the *Mahābhārata* (Figure 4.1) and the *Rāmāyaṇa*, and the eighteen *Mahāpurāṇas;* some schools also claim the title for a large number of so-called *Upapurāṇas*.[32] Since these books are written in a more popular style, containing many stories and examples, they have found a place in the heart of the Indian masses and even today probably exert a much greater influence on the mind and imagination of the majority of the Indian people than any other literature. The *Mahābhārata* and the eighteen *Mahāpurāṇas* are said to have been composed by Vyāsa Kṛṣṇadvaipayana, the same *Ṛṣi*, who according to tradition, compiled the Veda in response to revelation. This enhances the authority of these books as sources of religion and law. In the *Purāṇas*, however, the split between the various sects and schools of Hinduism becomes most pronounced and many chapters are narrowly sectarian in character.[33] The core of the *Purāṇas* may well be as old as the Vedas; we read in some *Upaniṣads* that *Purāṇas* were narrated during the protracted sacrifical sessions. The *Purāṇas* quite frequently contain the full or expanded versions of myths alluded to in the Vedic hymns, and tales of heroes and gods even antedating the Veda may have been preserved in them. Attempts to reconstruct the *Ur-Purāṇa*, the original *Purāṇa Saṁhitā*, have not been very successful, and therefore scholars have concentrated on studies of the *Vāyu Purāṇa*, as most probably containing most of its ancient form.[34]

The text of the epics and *Purāṇas* that we have in our printed editions has been fixed only between the fourth and the tenth centuries C.E., but the materials contained in them very often belong to a much earlier period. Not long ago a monumental critical edition of the *Mahābhārata* was completed in Poona; the analyses and notes in the twenty-two volumes allow a more accurate historical study of this immense storehouse of Indian cultural and religious tradition than was possible with the various traditional

Figure 4.1 Sage Vyāsa Dictating the *Mahābhārata* to Gaṇeśa

recensions.[35] The *Rāmāyaṇa*, ascribed to Vālmīki, has a less universal scope; but its appeal to large groups of Hindus, especially in its numerous reworkings in vernaculars, has also given it the status of a scripture. The Oriental Institute in Baroda has recently completed a critical edition.[36]

Several attempts have been made to bring out critical editions of the *Purāṇas;* but it is an enormous task and requires a large amount of preliminary work.[37] The *Purāṇas* have been long neglected by modern scholars; only recently has their value as sources of historical and geographical information been vindicated. For a knowledge of popular Hinduism as it is and has been for some centuries, they are indispensable. All the stories about God and gods, about saints and demons, heavens and hells, creation and annihilation, incarnation and release that have shaped the Indian religious mind are to be found in the many thousands of pages of the *Purāṇas.*

Itihāsa and *Purāṇa* have, in the course of time, absorbed almost the entire religious literature, including the philosophical speculation of the *darśanas,* so that the average pious Hindu could claim to have *śruti, smṛti,* and *nyāya,* the whole religion, while reading his *Purāṇa.*[38]

THE INTERPRETATION OF THE REVEALED WORD: PRAMĀṆA

Nyāya, or *pramāṇa,* logical argument or rational proof, is the third avenue of religious knowledge in Hinduism. The term *nyāya* also is used in the general sense of logical proof and as the specific name of a school of thought that specialized in logic and epistemology.[39] All Hindu theologians clarify at the beginning of their treatises their evaluation of the traditional six modes of knowing, determining which of them they consider as means for religious knowledge. These modes are *pratyakṣa,* sense perception; *anumāna,* inference; *śabda,* authority, especially of scriptures; *upamāna,* analogy; *arthāpatti,* hypothetical supposition; and *abhāva,* nonperception. Religious knowledge derives mostly from *śabda,* the Word.

Centuries before the West had developed its own brand of linguistic analytical philosophy, Indian theologians had evolved the most subtle philosophy of language, in whose controversies many interesting problems of a theological nature are raised. As T. R. V. Murti says: "Indian philosophy has rightly considered language and thought as intimately related. The *Nyāya-Vaiśeṣika* is essentially a philosophy of *padārtha,* the meaning of words. As in Aristotle, here also categories of language are categories of Being. . . . Both the *Pūrva* and *Uttara Mīmāṁsā* do not profess to be anything more than an exegesis of the Revealed Word (the Veda)."[40]

The most important contributions to the elucidation of the Word have been made by the *Pūrva Mīmāṁsā* and the grammarians. For the Brahmanic tradition, language itself is of divine origin, the Spirit descending and embodying itself in phenomena, assuming various guises and disclosing its real nature to the sensitive soul.[41] The *Mīmāṁsakas* analyze the problem What makes a word meaningful? They found that it is the connection of the word with *akṛti*, the Uncreated Idea, which as such is incomprehensible and never exhausted by the individual word. *Śabda* is ever present and eternal in this form. We do not always perceive it, because its perception depends on its manifestation through the physical word sound. If it were not eternal, the word could not be understood every time it is uttered. The word that we speak and hear is only a partial manifestation of an eternal, meaningful reality; it is not produced by our utterance. Since the word is not an effect, it is not perishable either.[42]

The school of Pāṇini, the grammarian, developed this *śabda* philosophy further in the theory of *sphoṭa*. Etymologically, *sphoṭa* means a boil that, when opened, suddenly ejects its contents. Similarly, the meaning of a word appears suddenly after the syllables have been pronounced; none of the individual syllables convey either a part or the whole of the meaning. Thus, they say: "The eternal word, called *sphoṭa*, without parts and the cause of the world, is verily Brahman. Thus it has been declared by Bhartṛhari: 'Brahman without beginning or end is the indestructible essence of speech—it shines forth in the meaning of all things and out of it comes the whole world'!"[43]

Ultimately, according to this school, all words denote the Supreme Brahman and they maintain that "he who is well-versed in the Word-Brahman attains to the Supreme Brahman."[44] Language had been one of the main concerns of Indians throughout the ages. Pāṇiṇi, in the fourth century B.C.E., wrote "the first scientific grammar," unsurpassed as a single-handed achievement even today. His *Aṣṭādhyāyī*[45] introduces a perfect phonetic system of the Sanskrit alphabet, offers an astonishingly complete analysis of the contemporary linguistic materials, and is the first work to trace words to a limited number of verbal roots.[46] There were grammarians before him, as his references reveal, and there followed others, notably Kātyāyana and Patañjali,[47] to complete and develop the work. Similarly, the Dravidians occupied themselves with linguistic studies of which the *Tolkāppiam* is particularly renowned for its age and its perception.[48] Language itself, not only the scriptures, was considered "divine," an attribute that even extended to the characters in which it was written.[49] Sanskrit, the "refined language" of scholarship became the repository of all knowledge. It became a treasury not only of the symbolic world of ideas and experiences, but also of law and logic. As medium of communication it became the instrument for the precise expression of a great many logical connections. Learning the language, especially studying grammar, was considered a spiritual discipline.

THE POWER OF THE REVEALED WORD

Words of blessing and curses were always taken seriously by the Hindus; an almost material substantiality was attached to them, that would bring about their realization almost automatically. The *mantra*, used in connection with the Vedic sacrifice, works without fail. The word is a power that makes the gods subject to the will of man. "Brahman is the word," and the Brahmin is the keeper and lord of it. Speech itself was addressed as a deity as early as in the time of the *Ṛgveda.*[50] In later Hinduism, the body of a divinity was considered to consist of *mantras*, which are identical with cosmic processes. No sacrifice could be performed without words. The *Atharvaveda* has *mantras* for and against everything: *mantras* to cure fever and illness, to awaken love and affection, to raise enmity and hatred, and to make sick and kill an enemy. Tantric Hinduism operated with esoteric syllables that were meaningless for the noninitiate but full of significance and power for the one who had received *dīkṣā.*[51]

The most famous, most powerful and most mysterious of all *mantras* is OM, (or AUM), also called *praṇava*, the *ur-mantra.* Many expositions have been brought forward, none of them fully convincing.[52] The texts that speak of OM suggest that it has to be understood from within the context of the *mantra* theory. A *mantra* need not have an intelligible word meaning; it is the sound equivalent of some reality and, at the same time, the medium by which this otherwise transcendent reality is reached. OM is not a concept of something but the *śabda-Brahman*, the Supreme Being in the form of sound. It is the primeval sound, the medium between pure, spiritual *Brahman* and the concrete material world. The *Chāṇḍogya Upaniṣad* calls OM the "all-word."[53] Through the identification of important concepts and beings, the *mantra* OM, otherwise empty, is filled with concepts and meaning. The recitation of OM, on the one hand, reduces all beings into the nothing of OM, "the image of the supreme reality." On the other hand, the recitation makes OM itself meaningful without, however, identifying it with any particular being.

The *Māṇḍukya Upaniṣad* identified AUM with the four stages of consciousness: *A* stands for the waking state, *U* for dream, *M* for deep sleep. AUM in its totality corresponds to *turīya*, the transcendent state. There is no logical proof for the statement "Om is Brahman,"[54] it is *śruti*, revelation! "OM—this syllable is the whole world. Its further explanation is: the past, the present and the future—everything is just the word OM. And whatever else that transcends threefold time—that too is just the word OM. . . . OM is the *ātman.*"[55] OM stands at the beginning of every hymn and every religious action, as well as of every recitation of a sacred text. With OM everything comes to a conclusion.

Since the sacred texts themselves have the quality of *mantras*, the opinion could develop that it is ultimately unimportant whether their meaning is understood or not. Many Brahmins who traditionally function at the occasions where the recitation of Vedic *mantras* is required do not really understand their meaning. The blessing derived from scripture does not depend on its comprehension, as the example of the *Śrīmad Bhāgavata Māhātmya* explains:

> He who daily recites the *Bhāgavata*, with the uttering of every single letter gathers as much merit as he would get by the gift of a brown cow. He who daily listens to half or even a quarter of a verse from the *Bhāgavata* gathers merit as from the gift of a thousand cows. It is better to keep half or quarter of a verse from the *Bhāgavata* in one's house than a collection of hundreds and thousands of other holy books. The glorious and holy *Bhāgavata* confers long life, freedom from disease and good health. He who recites it or listens to it is freed from all sins. To the man who prostrates before a copy of the *Bhāgavata* I give wealth.[56]

True to this interpretation, rich merchants arrange frequently for the reading of holy books over loudspeaker systems. Hired Brahmins recite the whole book without interruption. Hardly anyone listens; it is enough to recite the text faithfully in order to gain merit.

The whole life of a Hindu is enveloped in *mantras*. According to the most orthodox rules, the conception of a child is supposed to be accompanied by the recitation of *mantras*. *Mantras* are spoken over the expectant mother before birth; birth itself, name giving, initiation and marriage, purification and temple visits, death and cremation—all these have to be performed with *mantras*. At the time of initiation an ascetic receives his or her personal *mantra*, whispered into the ear by the *guru*. This will be the *daimónion* through which each distinguishes himself or herself from others. It is a name that nobody knows but the initiate and his or her master. The initiate is not permitted to divulge this secret word unless personally required to give *dīkṣā* to a disciple. Many Hindus carry *mantras* written on tiny pieces of paper in small capsules of copper, silver, or gold fastened to an arm, leg, or neck to protect themselves from certain illnesses or as a safeguard against the evil eye.

Time and again, this faith in the effectiveness of the *mantras* leads to scurrilous happenings. Some years ago a businessman had lodged a complaint with the police against a *sādhu* who had boasted of a miraculous *mantra* through which he could double any given amount of money. With great expectations, the businessman gave the holy man 2000 rupees. The *sādhu*, however, disappeared with the amount before he had doubled it.[57]

The understanding of Scripture as *mantra*, however, should obscure neither the importance of its understandable content nor the tremendous effort of countless generations of Hindus to derive meaning from it and to build up a coherent system of philosophico-religious thought. The desire for comprehension led at a very early stage to the elaboration of the *sūtras*, in which the essentials of certain branches of knowledge are condensed and systematized. One of the most important works of this kind are the *Brahmasūtras*, also called *Vedāntasūtras*, a compendium of 550 short statements that purports to render pithily the rich content of the main *Upaniṣads*. In it, the attempt is made to expurgate the contradictions among different *Upaniṣadic* doctrines.[58] The voluminous commentaries upon this text, written in the course of centuries, are the main works of Vedānta. Similarly, there are *sūtras* and *bhāṣyas* in all the other areas of Hindu thought. The desire to understand and to grasp the meaning of revealed truths has helped to produce some of the most penetrating works of philosophical theology. But all debate has to stop before the revealed word itself, which cannot be altered or cancelled. Thus, the devout Hindu scholar will often break off a discussion at the point at which it gets interesting to the outsider: the discussion of the theological presuppositions of all argumentation, the central and basic ideas and doctrines. Hindus will normally quote their favorite scripture and explain it; they may quote it again to make their point, but they will not engage in discussion about it. They are convinced that all questioning has definite limits; to question too much is to destroy the foundation upon which one stands and which alone allows one to engage in meaningful conversation.

5. *Itihāsa* and *Purāṇa*: The Heart of Hinduism

Śruti and *smṛti* are the two eyes of *dharma*, but the *Purāṇa* is its heart—on no other foundation does it rest but these three.

—Devībhāgavata Purāṇa *XI, 1, 21*

*I*TIHĀSA, HISTORY, IS the collective term for the *Rāmāyaṇa* and the *Mahābhārata*, in Western publications usually called the *Great Epics.*[1] Related to them in character and importance are the *Purāṇas*, ancient books, of which usually eighteen are accepted as *Mahāpurāṇas*, scriptures of the major Hindu churches. The *Itihāsa-Purāṇa* are often called the fifth *Veda*, the Holy Book of the mass of people who were not entitled to study the four Vedas. For a long time, Western scholarship has played down the importance of the *Itihāsa-Purāṇa*, partly because of its largely mythological content, partly also because the existing texts and editions offered such a bewildering variety of readings, claiming ancient origins for obviously very recent interpolations and on the whole lacking the unity of theme and structure of epic or historical works in the Western sense. Indian tradition has always claimed great antiquity and authority for these writings, and though the more critical approach of modern Indian scholars[2] has had to dismantle some of the cherished legends surrounding these books, it has tended on the whole to reinforce the traditional view and lend it greater importance.[3] As has been the case in several areas studied earlier, in the field of *Itihāsa-Purāṇa* studies, one has to respect the Indianness of the literature and its subject matter in order not to approach it with models of epics or history taken from elsewhere. The *Itihāsa-Purāṇa* are in a very real sense the heart of Hinduism, with all its strengths and weaknesses. Although the core of the *Itihāsa-Purāṇa* may go back to perhaps the seventh century B.C.E., it is much more popular and much more alive today in India than any folk epic in Europe.

Indian languages are strongly influenced by the vocabulary and the imagery of the *Itihāsa-Purāṇa;* the numerous rewritings of these texts in the Indian vernaculars are quite often the first major literary works in those languages. If one wishes to understand Hindu religious and theological terminology, one has to turn to these books constantly. They have become the medium of imparting secular knowledge as well: they are the sources for much of Indian sociology, politics, medicine, astrology, geography, and so on. Reading the *Itihāsa-Purāṇa* today one can still discover in these texts the character of the Indian people, enlarged, typified, idealized—and true in an uncanny sense. The personalities described, their wishes and fantasies, their joys and sorrows, their emotions and ideas are much closer to the India of our own time than the venerable age of the books would suggest. Many Indians bear the names of the heroes and heroines of the *Itihāsa-Purāṇa;* most are familiar from early childhood with the stories contained in them, stories that combine entertainment with moral education. School readers in the Indian vernaculars are full of tales from them. Countless films and dramas take their subjects, often with very little modification, from these ancient books. Even simple people in the villages can speak with such enthusiasm and earnestness about Rāma and Sītā, about Kṛṣṇa and Arjuna, Hanuman and Rāvaṇa, Bharata and Lakṣmana that one realizes that contemporary India also identifies with the tradition expressed in the *Itihāsa-Purāṇa.* Broadcasting, printing presses, films, and musicals keep this "true history of India" alive, a "history not of events, but of the urges and aspirations, strivings and purposes of the nation."[4] Whatever critical literary scholars may find out about the texts and their history, Hinduism without them would not be what it is. Anyone interested in the real religion of the Indian people today would find the *Itihāsa-Purāṇa* the best source for all aspects of the contemporary living religion of the masses.

THE GREAT EPIC

> The *Mahābhārata* represents a whole literature rather than a single homogeneous work; it constitutes a veritable treasure-house of Indian lore, both secular and religious. No other single work gives such insight into the innermost depths of the soul of the people. It is a "Song of Victory," commemorating the deeds of heroism in a war fought to avenge insults to womanhood and to maintain the just rights of a dynasty that extended the heritage of Bharata and knit together the North, East, West and South of India into one empire. It is a *purāṇa-saṁhitā* containing diverse stories of seers and sages, of beautiful maids and dutiful wives, of valiant warriors and saintly kings. It is also a magnificent poem describing in inimitable language the

> fury of the battle field, the stillness of the forest-hermitage, the majesty of the roaring sea dancing with billows and laughing with foam, the just indignation of a true daughter of a warrior line, and the lament of the aged mother of dead heroes. It is an authoritative book of law, morality, and social and political philosophy, laying down rules for the attainment of *dharma, artha* and *kāma*, called *trivarga*, and also showing the way of liberation expounding the highest religious philosophy of India.[5]

Since the sixth century C.E., the *Mahābhārata* has been called *śata-sāhasrī saṁhitā*, the collection of 100,000 stanzas. In Western terms, this means that this huge work is four times as voluminous as the Bible or eight times the text of the *Iliad* and the *Odyssey*, the greatest Greek epics, together. A work of this magnitude has its history. Generations of scholars have been busy trying to find the *Ur-Mahābhārata* within the huge mass of literature of the great epic. Attempts to strip away the various layers of narrative and arrive at the original saga have had as little success as the endeavour to explain the whole work as an invention designed to illustrate maxims of law.[6] The *Mahābhārata, Critical Edition*, one of the greatest literary enterprises of any time in any language, did not even try to reconstruct the "original Mahābhārata" but aimed at constituting an "accepted text" by retaining all that was common to the numerous recensions, relegating to notes and appendices those portions that, on account of their weaker textual evidence, could be supposed to have been added after the final redaction around 400 C.E.[7]

On the whole, the traditional view has gained strength through the failure of the modern criticism regarding the origin and development of the *Mahābhārata.* Thus, many scholars today accept the view that the *Mahābhārata* underwent two major recensions: it began as *Jāya*, a poem about the victory of the Pāṇḍavas over the Kauravas, of about 7000 *ślokas.* This is supposed to have been the work of Vyāsa, also known as Kṛṣṇa Dvaipayana, the son of Parāsara and Satyavatī. It was augmented to about three times its former length in the *Bhārata* by Vaiśampayana, who recited it at the snake sacrifice of Janamejaya. The *Sūta*, who heard it there, related it as *Mahābhārata* of 100,000 verses to the assembly of sages in the Naimiṣa forest during the sacrifice performed by Śaunaka.

The present edition of the *Mahābhārata* itself speaks of three beginnings:[8] *manvādi*, beginning from Manu, corresponding to the first twelve *parvans* ("chapters") of the present work; *āstikādi*, beginning with Astika, comprising *parvans* 13 to 53; *uparicarādi*, from *parvan* 54 onward.

The text of the *Mahābhārata* that emerges in the critical edition is in the form the work took after the editing by the Bhārgavas, a family of learned Brahmans claiming descent from the Vedic sage Bhṛgu, who had specialized in *dharma* and *nīti.* This family rewrote the text completely, making it primarily into a source book of instruction on religious law. The new didactic materials were incorporated mainly in the *Śānti* and *Anuśāsana Parvans*, which now cover almost one-fourth of the whole *Mahābhārata*, raising the work to the rank of a *smṛti.* After this, *Bhārgava-Mahābhārata* became popular in India, and the different regions developed their own recensions of it, incorporating material that seemed to be of local importance. The so-called northern and southern recensions are the principal ones, differing by as much as a third of the full text.

At some point, as yet unknown, the *Mahābhārata* was subdivided into 18 *parvans* of varying length: the smallest is the *Mahāprasthānika, parvan* 17, with only 120 stanzas; the longest the *Śānti, parvan* 12, with 14,525 stanzas. Of greater importance is the subdivision into ninety-eight sub-*parvans*, that divide the work topically into more congruous sections. As *khila-bhāga*, supplement to the *Mahābhārata*, the *Harivaṃśa*, a Kṛṣṇaite work is very often added in the editions. In itself, it is a rather voluminous work of some 16,000 *ślokas.*[9]

The *Mahābhārata* consequently became a veritable encyclopedia, and it carries this verse about its own scope: "Whatever is written here,

8. Gopuram (entrance-tower) to a South Indian temple

may also be found elsewhere; but what is not found here, cannot be found anywhere else either."[10]

Not content with the sheer mass of writing contained in it, which covers all possible aspects of secular and religious culture, traditional Hindu interpreters have widened the scope of its teaching exponentially by explaining the *Mahābhārata* to have three different layers of meaning in each of its words. Thus Madhvācārya, commenting on the verse of the three beginnings, writes:

> The meaning of the *Bhārata*, in so far as it is a relation of the facts and events with which Śrī Kṛṣṇa and the Paṇḍavas are connected, is *āstikādi*, or historical. That interpretation by which we find lessons on virtue, divine love, and the other ten qualities, on sacred duty and righteous practices, on character and training, on Brahmā and the other gods, is called *manvādi*, or religious and moral. Thirdly, the interpretation by which every sentence, word or syllable is shown to be the significant name, or to be the declaration of the glories, of the Almighty Ruler of the universe, is called *auparicara* or transcendental.[11]

A modern scholar, the initiator of the *Mahābhārata, Critical Edition*, took up this idea to explain the three planes on which it must be understood in its complete meaning. On the mundane plane, the story deals with the realistic account of a fierce fratricidal war of annihilation with its interest centered on the epic characters. On the ethical plane, the war is seen as a conflict between *dharma* and *adharma*, good and evil, justice and injustice, with the final victory of *dharma*. On the transcendental plane, the war is fought between the higher and the lower self of humanity.

> Arjuna, the superman under the guidance of Kṛṣṇa, the Super-self, emerges successful in this conflict, after he has destroyed with the sword of knowledge the ignorance embodied in his illegitimate desires and passions symbolized by his relatives, teachers, elders and friends ranged on the other side. In this interpretation Śrī Kṛṣṇa is the *Paramātman*, and Arjuna the *Jīvātman*. Dhṛtarāṣṭra is a symbol of the vacillating ego-centric self, while his sons symbolize in their aggregate the brood of ego-centric desires and passions. Vidura stands for *Buddhi*, the one-pointed reason, and Bhīṣma is tradition, the time-bound element in human life and society.[12]

The main story of the *Mahābhārata* can be sketched out in a few lines.[13] Vicitravīrya, a king of the lunar dynasty, has two sons: Dhṛtarāṣṭra and Paṇḍu. According to custom Dhṛtarāṣṭra, the elder son is to succeed his father; but as he was born blind, his younger brother, Paṇḍu, is made king instead. Paṇḍu dies after a brief reign, leaving behind five minor sons from his two wives. Thus, the blind Dhṛtarāṣṭra assumes kingship.

His hundred sons, the Kauravas, grow up with the five Pāṇḍavas, whom Dhṛtarāṣṭra appears to consider the rightful heirs.

Duryodhana, the eldest among the Kauravas, however, claims the throne and attempts to eliminate the Pāṇḍavas through a series of criminal tricks. He points out that his father had been the eldest son and rightful heir to the throne and succeeds in exiling the Pāṇḍavas together with their common wife, Draupadī. Duryodhana, thinking them to be dead, takes over the kingdom from his father. During their sojourn in the forest, however, the Pāṇḍavas win allies and challenge Duryodhana to battle. In order to avoid a war, blind old Dhṛtarāṣṭra divides the kingdom into two parts, leaving half to his own sons and giving the other half to the Pāṇḍavas. Yudhiṣṭhira, the eldest Pāṇḍava, is installed as king of Indraprāṣṭa, identified with the later Delhi, whereas Duryodhana remains king of Hastinapūra, the Elephant fortress some sixty miles to the north.

An uneasy peace prevails, riddled with quarrels and fights. During a visit to Indraprāṣṭa, Duryodhana falls into a pond. Draupadī finds the situation absurdly comical and breaks out in laughter. This loss of face has fatal consequences: Duryodhana challenges Yudhiṣṭhira to a game of dice where the winner takes all. Yudhiṣṭhira is carried away by his passion for gambling and loses everything to the Kauravas: his kingdom, his private possessions, his elephants, his brothers, himself, and finally Draupadī. Draupadī, on being called into the gambling den, refuses to come. The Kauravas rudely pull her in by the hair and tear her clothes off to humiliate her. Bhīma on seeing this takes a terrible oath: "May I never enter the resting place of my fathers unless I have torn open the breast of this stupid dog of a Bhārata in battle and drunk his blood!" Again, blind old Dhṛtarāṣṭra intervenes and prevails upon Duryodhana to return the kingdom to the Pāṇḍavas.

This time Duryodhana does not give in. He demands that another round of dice be played with the imposition that the losers would have to go into the jungle for twelve years, remain incognito for one more year in the country, and only then be allowed to return openly. If, during the thirteenth year, they were found out, they would have to go back into exile for another twelve years. The Pāṇḍavas again lose the game and have to leave for the forest. The *Mahābhārata* fills the twelve years in the forest with beautiful stories through which the numerous hermits living there edify the refugees. They manage, in the thirteenth year, to get employment in the very court of Duryodhana, without being recognized and appear at the beginning of the fourteenth year before the king to reclaim their kingdom. But Duryodhana is no longer willing to give up his empire. Thus, both parties prepare for an all-out war.

The Great War, lasting for eighteen days, is described in six hundred chapters. Using means both fair and foul, the Pāṇḍavas emerge as the victors. Very few of those who entered the war on either side are still alive, and the survivors' weeping and lamenting overshadows any joy that might accompany this hard-won victory. The Pāṇḍavas, although victorious, leave the kingdom in the hands of a younger relation and start toward the Himālayas to go to Indra's heaven. Four of the five brothers die on their way, only Yudhiṣṭhira reaches the goal. According to Indian tradition, the Great War marks the beginning of the *Kaliyuga*, the Age of Strife: the age in which righteousness has given way to unrighteousness, where *dharma* is only one footed and humankind goes toward its inevitable doom. For example, a story typical of those that abound in the *Mahābhārata*, about when the Pāṇḍavas dwelt in the forest, may be related here.[14]

Towards the close of the Pāṇḍavas' exile, a deer carried away the fire-stone of a devout hermit. The man began to lament, "How shall I now offer my fire sacrifice, unable to light a fire?" He approached the Pāṇḍavas for help. They pursued the deer but could not catch it, because it was not an ordinary deer. Exhausted and miserable, they sat under a banyan tree and bewailed their fate: "So helpless and weak have we become; we cannot even render a small service to a Brahmin." Bhīma said: "Yes, it is true. We should have killed those scoundrels when they dragged Draupadī into the hall by her hair. Because we have not done it, we have been reduced to such weakness!" Arjuna agreed with him: "I watched in silence while the vulgar creature insulted her. We have deserved our fate."

Since Yudhiṣṭhira felt great thirst, he asked Nakula to climb a tree to see whether a river or a pond was close by. Nakula saw cranes and water plants in not too great a distance, so he went to fetch water. When he reached the pond, he at once lay down to drink. No sooner had he dipped his hand into the water than he heard a voice: "Do not hurry! This pond is mine. Answer first my questions, then you may drink!" Nakula's thirst was too strong, he drank at once; immediately he dropped down lifeless. When Nakula did not return for a long time, Yudhiṣṭhira sent Sahadeva to fetch water. He met with the same fate as Nakula. Arjuna and Bhīma, sent after Sahadeva, also did not return.

Finally, Yudhiṣṭhira had to go by himself. Seeing his four brothers dead beside the water, he began to lament: "Is this to be the end? You have been taken away just when our exile was coming to its end! The gods themselves have forsaken me in my unhappy state!" Still grieving, he stepped into the pond to drink. The voice was heard again: "Your brothers died, because they would not listen to me. First give an answer to my questions, then drink, for this pond is mine!" Yudhiṣṭhira asked for the questions. The *yakṣa* said: "What makes the sun shine each day?" Yudhiṣṭhira replied: "The power of Brahman."

9. Keśighāṭ in Vṛndāvan where Kṛṣṇa subdued the demon Keśi

"What saves a man from every danger?"

"Courage saves a man from all dangers!"

"Studying which science does a man become wise?"

"Not through the study of any science but by living in the company of wise men does a man become wise!"

"Who is a more noble protector than the earth?"

"The mother who brings up the children she has given birth to, she is a more noble protector than the earth."

"Who is higher than heaven?"

"The father."

"Who is swifter than wind?"

"The mind!"

"Who is more miserable than a straw blown about the wind?"

"A careworn heart!"

"Who is the traveller's friend?"

"The willingness to learn!"

"Who is the husband's friend?"

"The wife."

"Who is man's companion in death?"

"*Dharma* alone accompanies a man on his lonely journey after death!"

"Which is the largest vessel?"

"The earth, for it contains all other vessels!"

"What is happiness?"

"Happiness is the result of proper conduct!"

"What makes a man popular by abandoning it?"

"Pride! Because if a man renounces it, he will be loved by all!"

"Which loss brings joy and not mourning?"

"Anger! If we give up anger we are no longer subject to suffering."

"What makes a person rich if he loses it?"

"Desire! If we give it up we shall be rich!"

"What makes a man a Brahmin? Is it birth, good conduct, or erudition? Answer rightly!"

"Birth and erudition do not make a man a Brahmin, only good conduct does. No matter how erudite a man may be, if he is the slave of bad habits he is no Brahmin. Even if he is well versed in the four Vedas, if he has bad habits he belongs to a low class!"

"Which is the most surprising thing in this world?"

"Every day people see other creatures leave for the abode of Yama, yet those that remain behind behave as if they were going to live forever. This really is the most astonishing thing in this world."

In this manner, the *yakṣa* asked many questions and Yudhiṣṭhira replied to them. In the end, the *yakṣa* addressed him thus: "O King! One of your brothers will return to life. Which one do you want?"

Yudhiṣṭhira thought for a while and then said: "May Nakula, he who is of the color of a dark cloud, lotus eyed, broad shouldered, long armed, he who lies here like a felled oak tree, may he return to life!"

The *yakṣa* was content and asked: "Why did you prefer Nakula to Bhīma, who has the strength of 16,000 elephants? I have heard that Bhīma is your favorite! And why not Arjuna, whose skill with weapons is your protection? Tell me, why did you chose Nakula and not these two?"

Yudhiṣṭhira replied: "*Dharma* is the only protection of man, not Bhīma and not Arjuna. If *dharma* is violated man will be annihilated. Kuntī and Mādrī were my father's two wives. I am a son of Kuntī, she is not entirely bereft of children. To fulfill the law of righteousness I pray that Mādrī's son Nakula be returned to life!"

The *yakṣa* liked Yudhiṣṭhira's sense of justice and returned all his brothers to life. He was in fact Yama in disguise, the lord of death who had adopted the form of the deer and the *yakṣa* to test his son Yudhiṣṭhira, whom he now embraced and blessed: "Only a few days and the twelve years will be over. The thirteenth year will also pass and your enemies will not find you out. Your undertaking will be brought to a happy end!"

The story ends with a familiar promise, showing a moralizing Brahmin's mind: "Those who listen to the story of Yudhiṣṭhira's meeting with his father, Yama, will never tread on evil paths. They will never seek discord with their friends nor envy others for their wealth. They will never be victims of lust and will never set their hearts on things that pass away."

THE HINDU'S FAVORITE BOOK

The *Rāmāyaṇa*, since ancient times considered to be the composition of Vālmīki,[15] is shorter, more unified, more appealing, and even more popular than the *Mahābhārata*. In its present form it constitutes about one-quarter of the volume of the *Mahābhārata*, about 24,000 *ślokas*. A good deal of textual criticism has been done by Western scholars. Some assumed that the original core of the book was identical with the Buddhist *Daśaratha Jātaka*,[16] a theory that was given up when it was proved that this *Jātaka* is a much later work. Again, the traditional Indian view seems to emerge as substantially correct historically. Before being reduced to writing, the story of Rāma, the Prince of Ayodhyā, was sung as a ballad by wandering bards in the courts of kings. The *Rāmāyaṇa* itself says that the first recitation took place in the forest before a gathering of sages, the second in the streets of Ayodhyā, and the third and final one in the palace of Rāma, after the horse sacrifice, through which Rāma confirmed his

10. Pavilions on the Yamunā erected on the spot where Kṛṣṇa subdued Kaliyanāga

enthronement. It is not difficult to discern in the present *Rāmāyaṇa* text interpolations that often interrupt the flow of the narrative: Purāṇic stories, genealogical lists, imitations of motifs from the *Mahābhārata*, repetitions, and perhaps again under Bhārgava influence, additions of ethical, philosophical, and other didactic materials.[17]

In its numerous reworkings in the vernaculars, the *Rāmāyaṇa* has become a kind of a family bible for millions of Hindus. Mahātmā Gāndhī praised the *Rāmacaritamānasa* of the sixteenth century poet Tulasīdāsa[18] as the greatest work in the entire religious literature of the world. Countless Indian villagers know a large number of its *dohas*, summarizing not only the story of Rāma but also epigrammatically expressing the accumulated wisdom of India. Scholars have hailed it as "the perfect example of the perfect book."

The *Vālmīki Rāmāyaṇa*, also called *Ādikāvya*, or first epic poem, has also recently appeared in a critical edition. Work on this edition brought to light a great number of recensions in various parts of the country, which can be grouped into a northern and a southern family of texts, with considerable differences. The southern text, which is less smooth and polished than the northern one, seems to be the older one.[19] The hypothesis of an *Ur-Rāmāyaṇa*, from which both recensions stem, has been considered quite valid. The present text is divided into seven *kāṇḍas* of fairly equal length.[20] Most scholars assume that the first and the last *kāṇḍas* are later additions to the core of the story. As regards the interpretation of the Rāma story, most Western scholars consider the original tale as a ballad about a human hero, later made into an *avatāra* of Viṣṇu when the *avatāra* doctrine became popular. Indians are inclined to consider Rāma as a historical figure as well as to assume that Vālmīki from the very beginning considered Rāma as a divine being.[21] In view of the rather fluid use of the divine attribute in Hindu writings, this would be an acceptable position.

The basic Rāma story as told by Vālmīki is quite brief.[22] In the *Bālakāṇḍa*, we hear about the birth and childhood of Rāma, son of King Daśaratha and queen Kauśalyā, one of the king's three wives. The other wives were Kaikeyī, who bore Bharata, and Sumitrā, whose sons were Lakṣmana and Śatrughna. The marriage of Rāma with Sītā, the lovely daughter of King Janaka of Videha, is narrated at great length. Janaka had offered his daughter in marriage to any hero who would be able to bend the bow of Rudra, which was in his possession. The bow, which no previous suitor was even able to lift from the floor, becomes a willing instrument in Rāma's hand.[23] Rāma and Sītā spend a brief happy time at Ayodhyā after their marriage. Daśaratha, feeling the burden of his age, intends to crown Rāma king and retire.

Everything is prepared and there is general rejoicing among the people of Ayodhyā, for Rāma has been a very popular prince. In the very night before the *abhiṣeka*, however, Mantharā, the hunchbacked evil-minded servant of Kaikeyī, Daśaratha's favorite wife, succeeds in poisoning Kaikeyī's mind by suggesting that if Rāma became king, he would try to kill his potential rivals—the first of whom would be Bharata, Kaikeyī's only son. Worried, Kaikeyī looks for means to prevent the coronation, and Mantharā comes up with some devilish advice. A long time ago, Kaikeyī had carried the unconscious Daśaratha from the battlefield, thus saving his life. Daśaratha, recovered, promised to fulfill any two wishes that Kaikeyī would utter. Kaikeyī had stored up this credit; now she wants to make use of it. Rāma should be banned for fourteen years into forest exile and her own son, Bharata, should be crowned king.

Daśaratha pleads and threatens, entreats and curses Kaikeyī, to no avail. He must keep his word. Bharata is not in Ayodhyā at the time of this tragic happening, he has no hand in it. Rāma receives the bad news with a manly spirit; he consoles his father and expresses his willingness to go into the forest exile in order to help his father keep his promise. He even visits Kaikeyī to show that he does not bear a grudge against her. Sītā and Lakṣmaṇa ask to be allowed to share Rāma's exile. When the three of them leave, the whole town of Ayodhyā is plunged into grief and Daśaratha dies soon afterwards of a broken heart.

On his return to Ayodhyā, Bharata learns what has happened. He refuses to accept the kingship and proceeds with Śatrughna into the forest to persuade Rāma to return as king. Rāma refuses; his father's word is sacred to him. Bharata then places Rāma's sandals upon the throne, considering himself as his trustee till the time of Rāma's return.

Rāma's sojourn in the forest is filled with many incidents similar to those narrated in the *Mahābhārata* about the Pāṇḍava's exile. Fights against the *rakṣasas*, the hobgoblins and forest spirits of Indian folklore, interpreted by many Western scholars as the dark-skinned aboriginals; entertaining and edifying stories from forest-hermits; and a variety of other adventures fill the *Āraṇyakāṇḍa*. Vālmīki is a master of poetic painting in his descriptions of the beauty of the forests. Because Rāma kills many of the *rakṣasas*, making the forest a safe and peaceful place to live in for pious hermits, he befriends many Brahmins and becomes the enemy of the *rakṣasas*.

One day, Śurpaṇakhī ("Ears-like-winnowing-fans"), the sister of Rāvaṇa, the powerful king of the *rakṣasas*, comes to Rāma's dwelling place. She is infatuated with Rāma and has turned herself into a beautiful woman. She asks Rāma to marry her. Rāma tells her that he is already married and counsels her to try her luck with his brother, Lakṣmaṇa. When he, too, refuses her, she returns to Rāma, which makes Sītā burst out laughing.

Śurpaṇakhī is enraged, assumes a terrible form, and threatens to devour Sītā. Lakṣmaṇa cuts off her ears and nose and sends her home in disgrace.

Rāvaṇa is infuriated and bent on vengeance. On his insistence, the demon Marica transforms himself into a gold-spotted deer, appearing before Rāma's hut, so beautiful and enticing that Sītā pleads and weeps, threatens and curses Rāma to get the deer for her. Rāma, suspecting an evil trick of a *rakṣasa*, prevails on Lakṣmaṇa to guard Sītā and not to leave her alone under any circumstances. Rāma meanwhile pursues the elusive gold-spotted deer, at last killing it with an arrow. Dying, the demon cries out, "O Lakṣmaṇa, O Sītā," sounding as if Rāma was in mortal danger. True to Rāma's word Lakṣmana does not want to leave Sītā. But Sītā, quite mad with fear for Rāma, accuses Lakṣmaṇa of evil intentions and threatens to kill herself. Lakṣmaṇa now goes in search of Rāma, finds him quite unharmed, and returns with him to the hermitage only to find Sītā gone.

Rāvaṇa, disguised as a pious hermit, had invaded the place in Lakṣmana's absence and had carried her off to Laṅka, his kingdom.[24] Rāma and Lakṣmaṇa begin their search for Sītā. Many animals and trees give them clues. Jaṭayu, an aged vulture who has been mortally wounded in his fight against Rāvaṇa, informs them about the identity of the abductor. They win numerous allies, the most important of which is Hanuman, the monkey king, with his numerous troops. Hanuman's magic tricks are ultimately responsible for the success of the search. He can jump for miles and has the power to make himself as small as a mouse or as tall as a mountain. He finds out that Sītā is kept prisoner in Rāvaṇa's palace at Laṅka. Rāvaṇa, in a not ungentlemanly manner, tries to woo her with flatteries, promises, and threats; at one time, he even produces a cut-off head that looks like Rāma's. Sītā is unimpressed and remains faithful to Rāma. Hanuman visits Sītā, comforts her, and carries messages between Rāma and his wife.

At last, Rāma prepares for war against Rāvaṇa. The monkeys build a bridge between Cape Kaṇyākumārī and Śrī Laṅka (the line of islands is even now called Hanumansetu, "Hanuman bridge") across which the entire army invades Laṅka. A long, bloody battle ensues, in which both sides suffer heavy losses. Rāvaṇa has many powerful magic weapons at his disposal, and if it were not for Hanuman who fetches healing herbs from the Himālayas, Rāma and his friends all would be dead. Finally, the monkey army storms Rāvaṇa's fortress city. Laṅka goes up in flames and Sītā is reunited with Rāma.

When the fourteen years of exile are over, Rāma triumphantly reenters Ayodhyā as king. But the happy end of the story, at which every reader rejoices, is not the real end after all. Because people entertain gossipy suspicions about Sītā's fidelity, since she spent a long time in another man's house, Rāma asks Sītā to undergo a fire ordeal in order to prove her innocence. Sītā submits to it and passes the test but, despite her proven fidelity, nevertheless is sent off to the forest. After a long time, she returns from the forest with her two sons and takes a final oath of purification: "I have never thought of another man but Rāma; may the earth receive me to confirm this! I have always worshipped only him in words, thoughts, and deeds; may mother earth receive me to confirm this! I have never known any man but Rāma; may the goddess earth accept me!" After these words, the earth opens up and Sītā disappears in her.

The last chapters of the *Rāmāyaṇa* relate how Rāma, Bharata, Śatrughna, and all the citizens of Ayodhyā leave the city and go to the river Sarayu. There, Rāma and his brothers physically enter the body of Viṣṇu, thus proving their divine origin.

The beautiful language and the poetry of the *Rāmāyaṇa* would suffice to make it a favorite of the Indians; but they also admire Rāma's obedience toward his father, his generosity toward Kaikeyī, Sītā's fidelity in following Rāma into the jungle and during her captivity, Bharata's and Lakṣmana's brotherly loyalty, and the greatness and strength of Rāma. If ever an ancient literary work remains alive in our time, it is the *Rāmāyaṇa*! It is read and sung every day by numberless Hindus, humble and high; it is worshipped and held sacred and performed in *Rāma-Līlās* every year in small towns and big cities. After the monsoon rains are over, at the time of the Dasserah festival, people in villages and cities gather to reenact the drama of Rāma and Sītā. The killing of Rāvaṇa and his retinue is the main attraction. Depending on their means, each community erects tall figures on bamboo sticks, fills them with straw and covers them with colored paper, stuffing the limbs with firecrackers. At nightfall, these demons are lit and explode to the delight of all; the forces of good, embodied in Rāma, have again proved victorious over the forces of evil, symbolized in Rāvaṇa.

"The *Rāmāyaṇa* will be read in this country of Bharata as long as its rivers continue to flow and its mountains remain in their place" reads one verse, and the Hindu, who cherishes the *Rāmāyaṇa*, also does so in order to gain the award promised in one of its concluding *ślokas:* "Whoever reads this noble work that tells of Rāma's deeds, he will be free from all his faults and sins; with all his kin and relatives he will go to heaven."[25]

The *Mahābhārata* and the *Rāmāyaṇa* have much in common. Certain sections were borrowed from the *Rāmāyaṇa* and transposed into the *Mahābhārata* or vice versa, and they also reveal a common fund of mythology and a common mentality.[26]

11. Outer hall in a South Indian Temple

THE *PURĀṆAS:* THE BIBLES OF HINDUISM

The *Purāṇas*, neglected and rejected by the rationalistic nineteenth century as representing a corruption of Vedic religion and childish fabulation,[27] have regained, among Indological scholars as well, the central place that they have always occupied in living Hinduism.[28] According to Puranic tradition, Brahmā uttered the *Purāṇas* as the first of all the scriptures; only later did he communicate the *Vedas.* As we have seen, some major schools of Hinduism accord the status of *śruti* to several of the *Purāṇas*, attributing equal age and authority to both *Purāṇas* and *Vedas.*

According to the greatest authority in the field, R. C. Hazra, "it is difficult to say definitely how and when the *Purāṇas* first came into being, though their claim to great antiquity next only to that of the Vedas cannot be denied."[29] The word *purāṇa*, perhaps not yet in the precise sense of later time, occurs already in the *Atharva Veda*, the *Śatapatha Brāhmaṇa*, the *Bṛhadāraṇyaka Upaniṣad*, and other early works.[30] According to Hazra,

> The way in which the *Purāṇa* has been connected with sacrifice as well as with the *yajus* in the *Atharvaveda*, the theory of the origin of the universe from sacrifice as expounded in the *Puruṣa-sūkta* of the *Ṛg-Veda* and the topics constituting the *pāriplava ākhyānas* or recurring narrations in the *aśvamedha* sacrifice, tend to indicate that the *Purāṇa*, as a branch of learning, had its beginning in the Vedic period and originated in the narrative portion (*ākhyāna bhāga*) of the Vedic sacrifice, which, in the *Brāhmaṇas*, is repeatedly identified with the god Prajāpati, the precursor of the later Brahmā, the creator.[31]

All the extant *Mahāpurāṇas*, eighteen in number, as tradition has it, with 400,000 *ślokas* altogether, are said to have Vyāsa as their author. Textual criticism of the *Purāṇas* is even more complicated than that of the great epics. The sheer mass of material, the sectarian claims connected with quite a few of them, and the great liberty taken by writers of all ages of interpolating passages into the *Purāṇas* make any serious study of the *Purāṇas* at the present stage seem an almost hopeless undertaking.

The *Purāṇas*, representing the popular religious traditions, were never subject to codification as were the Vedic *sūktas*, who were the official text at official functions of state and had to be uniform. Having existed for centuries in oral versions, with many local variants, and reduced to writing at very different times with no strict rules, they probably cannot be brought out in any meaningful critical edition. Written *Purāṇa* texts, with many variants, have been around for many centuries, and a sort of received text has developed, which is often available in several printed editions. Motilal Banarsidass recently reprinted all *Mahā-Purāṇas* in parallel to its fifty volume English translation. The undertaking of the Kashiraj Trust to bring out critical editions of the *Purāṇas* must be understood as an attempt to collate existing manuscripts and editions and establish some sort of accepted version, embodying wht most texts have in common. L. Rocher's argument against the possibility of critical editions is quite convincing: the *Purāṇas* were not meant to be books.

There is a widely shared opinion among Indian scholars that centuries before the beginning of the Christian era, there was an "original *Purāṇa Saṁhitā*." According to V. S. Agrawala, Lomaharṣana, the original teacher of the *Purāṇa*, taught the *Mūlasaṁhitā* to six pupils, the authors of the *Parasaṁhitās* of 4000 to 6000 *ślokas* each, dealing with essentially the same four topics, each constituting a *pāda: sarga* or creation of the world, *pratisarga* or dissolution, *manvantara* or world ages, and *vaṁśa* or genealogies. This original *catur-pāda* form is preserved in the extant *Vāyu Purāṇa* and the *Brahmāṇḍa Purāṇa.* The *Vāyu* is usually considered to come closest to the *Ur-Purāṇa*, and Agrawala thought he could recover the *Mūlasaṁhitā* from the present text of the *Vāyu Purāṇa* by eliminating some eighty spurious, interpolated chapters.

The *Amarakośa*, an ancient Sanskrit lexicon,[32] defines *purāṇam* as *pañcalakṣanam*, having five characteristic topics, namely, the four just mentioned plus *vaṁśānucarita*, or stories about the deeds of the descendants of the dynasties glorified in it.

The *Viṣṇu Purāṇa*, one of the oldest, conforms best to this pattern; but even here quite a number of additional topics are dealt with. In many other *Purāṇas*, the "five topics" are barely touched; altogether the material illustrating *pañcalakṣana* constitutes only about one-fortieth of the present texts. Important topics in addition to those already mentioned are the *puruṣārthas*, the four aims of life—*artha* or wealth, *kāma* or enjoyment, *dharma* or rules for life, and *mokṣa* or spirituality—the *vratas* or religious observances, *śrāddha* or rites for departed ancestors, *tīrtha* or description of places of pilgrimage, *dāna* or gifts, *vṛtti* or means of subsistence, *rakṣa* or manifestations of higher beings, *mukti* or release, *hetu* or the potential *jīva*, and *apāśraya* or Brahman as the "support."

R. C. Hazra thinks that, from the third to the fifth century, those matters were added to the *Ur-Purāṇa* that formed the subject matter of the early *smṛtis;* whereas, from the sixth century onward, new topics were added dealing with holy places, image worship, astrology, etc. that now form the bulk of the Puranic lore. The oldest and most original parts of the *Purāṇas* seem to be their mythology and history. Quite a few scholars are inclined to consider the Puranic lists of dynasties as of considerable historical value. F. E. Pargiter spent the better part of his life in a reconstruction of the ancient Indian historical tradition[33] according to Puranic records. He has come up with some very interesting suggestions as regards the expansion of the Āryans in India, which would go a long way in explaining many puzzles of the Āryan origins but which also overturns almost the whole of established Vedic historical scholarship.[34] According to one theory, the various *Purāṇas* came into existence as a consequence of the attempt to provide each of the Vedic *śākhās* with a *Purāṇa* of its own. Another theory, no less plausible, especially in view of the numerous *sthāla-purāṇas* or local chronicles, connects the various *Purāṇas* with different parts of India: "The *Brahmā Purāṇa* may represent the Orissan version of the original work, just as the *Padma Purāṇa* may give that of Puṣkara, the *Agni* that of Gāyā, the *Varāha* that of Mathurā, the *Vāmana* that of Thaneśvar, the *Kūrma* that of Benares and the *Matsya* that of the Brahmans on the Narmadā."[35]

A Vaiṣṇava schema divides the eighteen *Mahāpurāṇas* according to the three *guṇas* into *sāttvika* or Viṣṇu, composed of the *Viṣṇu, Bhāgavata, Nāradīya, Garuḍa, Padma*, and *Varāha; rājasa* or Brahmā, composed of the *Brahmā, Brahmāṇḍa, Brahmavaivarta, Mārkaṇḍeya, Bhaviśya*, and *Vāmana;* and *tāmasa* or Śiva, composed of the *Śiva, Liṅga, Skanda, Agni, Matsya*, and *Kūrma.* That this schema is entirely inadequate becomes apparent when one considers the fact, quite evident in the present texts, that several *Purāṇas* have been reworked more than once from different sectarian standpoints, combining Vaiṣṇava, Śaiva, and Śākta features. The *Upapurāṇas* lend themselves even less than the *Mahāpurāṇas* to a satisfactory classification. Not even their number can be determined exactly. A few of them claim to be, and have the status of, *Mahāpurāṇas*, that is, they are *śruti* for the followers of the particular group in question.[36]

For the results of Puranic research, the reader must look to specialized works. In a general way, one can state that the texts of the *Mahāpurāṇas*, as they have been printed, have been fixed between the time of 400 C.E. and 1000 C.E., the *Viṣṇu Purāṇa* being closest to the earlier date and the *Bhāgavata Purāṇa* nearest to the latter. But, as said before, it is not possible to assign any specific date to one of these works, containing as they do materials from hoary antiquity together with quite recent chapters, among other things dealing with Akbar's court and the British in India.[37] Most of the *Purāṇas* have been translated into English, and it is quite easy for anyone interested in this literature to get acquainted with the contents and style of this class of writings "whose importance for the development of Hinduism can never be overrated."[38]

The *Purāṇas*, like all Hindu scriptures, give at the end the succession of sages and saints through which they have been transmitted, concluding with a *phalaśloka*, the promise of reward for reading them:

> Whoever hears this great mystery which removes the contamination of the Kali age, shall be freed from all his sins. He who hears it every day redeems his obligations towards *devas, pitṛs* and men. The great and rarely attainable merit that a man acquires by the gift of a brown cow, he derives from hearing ten chapters of this *Purāṇa.* He who hears the entire *Purāṇa* obtains assuredly the reward that attends the uninterrupted celebration of the *Aśvamedha.* He who reads and retains with faith this *Purāṇa* acquires such purity as exists not in the world, the eternal state of perfection.[39]

Apart from the texts in the *Purāṇas* that extol the merits of reading them, there are *Māhātmyas*, praises of the greatness of each *Purāṇa*, very often printed with the texts in the available editions. They pour lavish praise on the texts themselves and promise untold happiness and reward to all who even recite as little as a fraction of a verse or keep a part of the book in their dwellings. As the *Śrīmad Bhāgavata Māhātmya* says:

> It is better to preserve in one's house one half or even one quarter verse copies from *Śrīmad Bhāgavata* than a collection of hundred and thousands of other scriptures. There is no deliverance at any time from the noose of Yama for him whose house does not contain a copy of the *Śrīmad Bhāgavata* in the Kali age. I, the Lord, take up my abode in the house of a person, that contains a verse, one half of a verse or even a quarter verse of the *Śrīmad Bhāgavata* written by hand. I never forsake the person who daily narrates my stories and is intent on hearing them and whose mind delights in them.[40]

Itihāsa-Purāṇa is great literature, and as more adequate translations become available, these books may become quite popular in Western countries, too. They contain fantasies that delight Western as well as Indian children, and they offer entertainment also to the more sophisticated lover of literature. Dealing as they do with timeless human experiences, the joys and tragedies of humankind anywhere, they speak to a Western audience as well as an Indian one.[41]

Students of myths and symbols will find them an inexhaustible source not only of materials but also of interpretations and theories, students of comparative law and ethics will find some of the most interesting resources in them. Their vastness and their overall lack of a specific ideology make them very adaptable to changing circumstances and provide them with great strength and resilience—which is the sign of vigorous life.

6. The *Bhagavadgītā*

> He who reads this sacred dialogue of ours, by him I consider myself worshipped through the sacrifice of knowledge.
> And the man who listens to it with faith and without scoffing, liberated, he shall attain to the happy realm of the righteous.
>
> —Bhagavadgītā *XVIII, 70f.*

THROUGHOUT THE LONG history of Hinduism, the popularity and authority of the *Bhagavadgītā*, the Song of the Lord, has been and still is unrivalled.[1] It was accepted by Vedāntins as the second of the *prasthānas*, and it has been received by the masses as a book of spiritual guidance and comfort. Whoever reads it for the first time will be struck by its beauty and depth; countless Hindus know it by heart and quote it on many occasions as an expression of their faith and of their own insights. All over India, and also in many places of the Western hemisphere, *Gītā* lectures attract large numbers of people. Many are convinced that the *Bhagavadgītā* is the key book for the respiritualization of humankind in our age. A careful study of the *Gītā*, however, will very soon reveal the need for a key to this key book. Simple as the tale may seem and popular as the work has become, it is by no means an easy book, and some of the greatest Indian scholars have grappled with the historical and philosophical problems it presents.

The *Bhagavadgītā* in its present form constitutes Chapters 23-40 in the *Bhīṣmaparvan* of the *Mahābhārata*, one of the numerous philosophico-theological interpolations in the Great Epic.[2] Since we possess Śaṅkarācārya's commentary on the *Bhagavadgītā*, and this presupposes the same text that we possess,[3] we know with certainty that the *Gītā* has not been changed in the last 1200 years or more. The very fact that Śaṅkara commented upon it, despite its obvious theistic and Kṛṣṇaitic bias would permit the conclusion that, at the time, it already enjoyed a very high standing among both philosophers and ordinary people. Little is known about the text before that date, and this is why we find the most extraordinary range of views among scholars, both as regards the age and the original form of this poem.

R. D. Ranade, one of India's great religious scholars of the recent past, in a study entitled *The Bhagavadgītā as a Philosophy of God-Realization, Being a Clue Through the Labyrinth of Modern Interpretations*,[4] offered a critique of dozens of different opinions on the date and message of the *Bhagavadgītā*. Numerous Western scholars have tried to explain the obvious inconsistencies of the present text by stripping the *Ur-Gītā* from later additions and interpolations. According to Holtzmann, the original *Gītā* was Vedāntic in character and the unorthodox *bhakti* doctrines were grafted onto it. According to Garbe, the original *Gītā* was a devotional and sectarian (Kṛṣṇaite) tract, to which the Vedāntic portions were tacked on under the influence of Brahmanism. Hopkins thought that the *Gītā* was a Kṛṣṇaite version of an older Viṣṇuite poem, and this in turn was at first a nonsectarian work, perhaps a late Upanishad.[5] W. Garbe proceeded, on philological grounds, to sift out what he considered the additions and kept only 530 of the 700 *ślokas* as genuine, all of them non-Vedāntic.[6] H. Oldenberg, a reputable Sanskritist in his time, thought that the original *Gītā* comprised only the first twelve of the present eighteen chapters, the last six being added later. R. Otto came to the conclusion that the original *Gītā* consisted of only 133 stanzas; the rest, added and interpolated later. The original text did not contain any doctrinal matter, whereas the eight tracts that were added brought in sectarian dogma. Several Western scholars, bitterly opposed by Indians, maintained that the *Gītā* betrayed a Christian influence.[7] The most articulate of these was probably F. Lorinser, who in 1869 wrote a metrical version of the *Bhagavadgītā*. He tried to prove that the author of the *Gītā* had used the New Testament, especially the Pauline epistles, weaving Christian ideas and conceptions into his system. A. Weber, another Sanskrit scholar, saw in the *Nārāyaṇīya* section of the *Mahābhārata* a report of an Indian's visit to a Western, Christian country and attributed the *Gītā* to the authorship of such Brahmins, who had familiarized themselves with Christianity in Alexandria. Necessarily, these authors had to give to the *Bhagavadgītā* a fairly recent date, usually around 200 C.E. In the opinion of most scholars today, the *Bhagavadgītā* in its major portions antedates the Christian era. Some decades ago, a Kashmiri Buddhist tried to prove that the *Gītā* was a Buddhist work or at least that it borrowed heavily from Buddhism.[8]

In our day, numerous practical interpretations of the *Bhagavadgītā* have been given. The one that attracted most attention and criticism may have been B. G. Tilak's *Gītā Rahasya*, in which the *Gītā* is interpreted as "a Gospel of action."[9] Mahātmā Gāndhī spoke quite frequently on the *Bhagavadgītā*, which he called his mother; and his secretary published a *Gītā* translation-cum-interpretation that reflects Gāndhī's own thoughts.[10] Mahātmā Gāndhī saw in the *Bhagavadgītā* an allegory of human life that has to fight out the dilemma between divinely ordained duty and personal preference. Śrī Aurobindo Ghose finds in the *Bhagavadgītā* all the major points of his own philosophy: the ascending grades of consciousness, the gnostic ideal, the superman, and the transformation of matter into spirit.[11] S. Radhakrishnan, whose edition tries to synthesize all the great classical interpretations of the *Bhagavadgītā* into a modern philosophy of life, eventually comes up with a modernized version of Advaita Vedānta as the original purport of the *Bhagavadgītā*.[12]

Without claiming to be able to solve all the questions raised by the many scholars who have written the most contradictory comments on the *Bhagavadgītā*, we may briefly summarize the views of S. K. Belvalkar, the editor of the *Bhīṣmaparvan* in the *Mahābhārata, Critical Edition*, who on other occasions as well has demonstrated his thorough knowledge of the problems related to the *Gītā*. Belvalkar assumes that, as the *Mahābhārata* underwent at least two recensions before it was fixed in the "modern" form, the *Gītā* also underwent a certain degree of rewriting. On the other hand, he maintains that the *Gītā*, in its main contents, has always been what it is today, that is, there has never been an original *Gītā* to which foreign and substantially different elements were added. He explains, quite plausibly, that the *Gītā* is a pre-Buddhistic work, representing a heroic Brahmanic effort to reunite people exposed to the most radical and most diverse religious ideas.[13] This reunion had to include all the still acceptable streams of religiosity of the time—Brahmanic ritual, Upanishadic knowledge and devotional forms of cult and worship, with the firm frame of *varṇāśrama dharma* as the unifying bond—a concept also found in modern times, when all could call themselves Hindus, regardless of the particular religious beliefs or rituals they followed, as long as they remain within the caste structure. Belvalkar calls the *Bhagavadgītā* the "Swan-song of the centuries of Śrauta religion" and thinks that

> the peculiar achievement of the *Bhagavadgītā* as a philosophical poem consisted precisely in having successfully gathered together under one banner the Brahmanic ritualists and the Upanishadic Vedāntists, the Sāṁkhya pacifists and the Yoga activists, the devotees of Kṛṣṇa and the free-thinking recluses, as also the majority of the average adherents of established institutions—not excluding women and the depressed classes, whom Brahmanism had denied the right of Vedic sacraments—requiring each of its constituents to give up or modify a part of his dogma in the interest of a compromise on a common platform with the other constituents. The ultimate position reached was philo-

> sophically quite self-consistent, special efforts being made to modulate the current opposition between *Jñāna* and *Bhakti*, between *Karman* and *Saṁnyāsa*, and between Ritualism and the Ātmanism.[14]

It may be easier for an Indian scholar, who has grown up in the thought patterns of his own tradition, to see harmony where the Westerner, trained in analytical thinking, sees contradiction. Since the *Bhagavadgītā* is very much an Indian book, we should respect the traditional Indian attitude toward it and read it as a scripture rather than dissect it as a philosophical treatise.

Notwithstanding the critical approach of many Western Indologists, the *Bhagavadgītā* has become a favorite book of many Westerners as well. Wilkins made the *Gītā* known in Europe through his English translation, which appeared in 1785. August von Schlegel produced a critical text edition and a Latin translation in 1823. Wilhelm von Humboldt, who read this Latin version, was so enthusiastic that he declared that "this episode of the *Mahābhārata* is the most beautiful, nay perhaps even the only true philosophical poem which we can find in all the literatures known to us."[15] Several good English translations have appeared in the last few decades, and one can say without exaggeration that the *Bhagavadgītā* should be read by everyone who claims to have more than just a provincial education. W. Callewaert and S. Hemraj, in their *Bhagavadgītānuvāda*,[16] not only try to trace the original text of the *Bhagavadgītā* but also mention scores of commentaries and hundreds of translations into virtually all the major, and some minor, languages of the world. The *Bhagavadgītā* was one of the texts that every Vedāntācārya had to comment upon. In addition, many others wrote commentaries in Sanskrit and in Indian vernaculars as well as in European languages. New translations into English keep appearing almost every year—apparently none of the existing versions is satisfactory to all of those who use it and study it.

In the narrative of the *Mahābhārata*, the *Bhagavadgītā* is inserted just before the outbreak of the actual battle between the Kauravas and the Pāṇḍavas. The two related clans are fighting for their kingdom; the Kauravas, who have usurped the reign, are defending their claim against the Pāṇḍavas, the rightful heirs, who have been cheated out of their possession. Arjuna, the hero of the *Bhagavadgītā*, is the leader of the rightful claimants. With him is Kṛṣṇa as his charioteer, a befriended king of Dwāraka, whose divine character is to become manifest only during the narration of the *Gītā* itself. Kṛṣṇa has sent his army to help the Kauravas, who are also his friends. Just when both armies are fully arrayed against each other, Arjuna realizes what he is going to do. He is about to fight and kill his relations, teachers, friends—and realizing that, he is ready to give up the war altogether, telling Kṛṣṇa: "I would not kill these, though killed myself, not for the rule over the three worlds—how much less for the sake of this earthly kingdom? What pleasure should we have after having slain the sons of Dhṛtarāṣṭra, our brothers? Only sin will we reap if we kill them!"

He repeats the tenets of the traditional *dharma*, which teaches that killing members of one's own family leads to the destruction of the whole family and to punishment in hell. "Far better would it be for me if the sons of Dhṛtarāṣṭra, with weapons in hand, should slay me in battle, while I remain unresisting and unarmed." Arjuna then throws away his bow and arrow, depressed and overwhelmed by grief.

In the second chapter, Kṛṣṇa begins to speak. The message itself is quite brief: "You have to fight, Arjuna!" Kṛṣṇa, however, persuades Arjuna with arguments taken from the various established viewpoints, appearing in the process not only as the charioteer of Arjuna but as the great teacher of wisdom, nay, as the Supreme revealing himself and his plans. He begins by telling Arjuna that his attitude is *anārya*, not noble, that it is not conducive to *svarga*, the old Vedic heaven, and that it leads to dishonor; it is unmanly not to fight here and now! Since Arjuna is familiar with these thoughts they do not impress him as a solution to his problem; he plainly admits his confusion and asks Kṛṣṇa to teach him as a guru teaches his disciple, and he again declares: "I will not fight!" Slowly Kṛṣṇa comes out with the New Philosophy that is able not only to solve the moral dilemma but to leave behind the Old Morality: Wisdom, he says, consists in realizing that the *ātman* is permanent, while the body by its very nature is doomed to die: there is no reason to grieve for either the dead or the living.

> Never was there a time when I was not, nor you, nor these lords of men, nor will there ever be a time hereafter when we shall cease to be. . . .
> He who thinks that this slays and he who thinks that this is slain, both of them fail to perceive the truth; this one neither slays nor is slain.
> He is never born nor does he die at any time, nor having once come to be does he again cease to be.
> He is unborn, eternal, permanent and primeaval. He is not slain when the body is slain.
> Just as a person casts off worn-out garments and puts on others that are new, even so does the embodied soul cast off worn-out bodies and take on others that are new.

This philosophical argument by itself would not be sufficient to justify fighting a war; it just helps eventually to get rid of feelings of guilt over the action itself by suggesting that it does not involve the *ātman*, neither actively

12. Wayside shrine in Vṛndāvan

nor passively, but remains on the periphery of reality, in the sphere of change and inevitable death. The motivation to fight is supposed to come from the appeal to the *kṣatriya-dharma*, the iron rule that tells every one what is right and wrong. As Kṛṣṇa puts it: "There exists no greater good for a *kṣatriya* than a war enjoined by *dharma;* happy the *kṣatriyas*, for whom such a war comes of itself as an open door to heaven." A violation of this duty would be sinful and would bring shame, because it would make people think he is a coward—the worst that could happen to a professional warrior! Both the possibilities that the risk of war entails are preferable to the abstention from war: "If you are killed you will go to heaven; if you win, you will enjoy the earth; treating alike pleasure and pain, gain and loss, victory and defeat, get ready for battle; thus you will not incur any sin!"

Kṛṣṇa calls the teaching he has given so far, Sāṁkhya, and he is now ready to teach also the wisdom of *yoga*, which, if accepted, frees from the bondage that *karma* imposes. And he speaks words that are really the gist of the whole *Bhagavadgītā* and that have influenced practical ethics in India throughout the centuries: "Your rightful claim[17] extends to actions only, not to the results; the fruits of action should not be your motive but also do not cling to inaction. Established in Yoga, do your work after abandoning attachment, unmoved by success or failure."

In order to drive away the idea of renouncing, which has fascinated Arjuna so far and appeared to him as a solution of the dilemma, Kṛṣṇa tells Arjuna that *yoga* is neither inaction nor mere action but *karmasu kauśalam*, skill in action, action with understanding. He then describes the "wise man," the true Yogi, as one who has given up all desires and whose *ātman* is content in the *ātman*. Untroubled in the midst of sorrows and free from lust amidst pleasures; free from passion, fear, and anger; without attachment of any kind, neither rejoicing in the good nor dejected by evil; drawing away the senses from the objects of sense as a tortoise draws its limbs under its shell; acting free from self-interest—this is the "divine state" that brings supreme happiness.

The basic message is thus given in the second chapter; most of the rest is a further explanation of the main points. Arjuna asks for a motivation of action, when Kṛṣṇa explains the insight of Yoga as the highest way of life. Kṛṣṇa clarifies the matter by pointing out that of yore he had been the teacher of two different ways of salvation: a way of knowledge for the contemplatives and a way of works for the actives. Nature, so he says, depends on continued work: "Do your alloted work, for action is better than inaction; even bodily life cannot go on without action. All work, except sacrificial action, causes bondage: therefore do your work as a *yajña*, free from all attachment." The work of the perfect man is not done with a view to further his own interests but in the interest of *lokasaṅgraha*, the good of the world. Kṛṣṇa points to his own example. He has no desire unfulfilled and yet he continually engages in action in order to give an example to humankind: "If I should cease to work, these worlds would fall in ruin and I should be the creator of disordered life and destroy these peoples."

Kṛṣṇa's teaching is not absolutely new at the time of the discourse with Arjuna. He refers back to Īkṣvāku, who taught it and who had received it from Manu via Vivasvān—Kṛṣṇa had taught it to him! Arjuna does not quite understand how Kṛṣṇa, who is about his own age, could possibly have been the teacher of mythical ancestors! Kṛṣṇa now explains his repeated coming into the world:

> Many are my lives that are past. . . . Though I am unborn and my Self is imperishable, the Lord of all creatures, establishing myself in my own nature I become embodied through my *māyā.*
>
> Whenever *dharma* declines and *adharma* rises up, I create myself [a body]; for the protection of the good, for the destruction of the wicked and for the establishment of *dharma* I come into being in every age.

Kṛṣṇa is the creator of the *caturvarṇāśramadharma:* though himself unchangeable, he has ordained action to men, an action, however, that is not what ordinary people usually understand by that word.

"He who in action sees inaction and in inaction action, he is the wise, the *yogi*, the one who has fulfilled his duty." Doing one's duty because of duty, *niṣkāma karma,* desireless action, is the ideal; and this activity does not entangle people in further karma but is in itself liberating because it is centered on Kṛṣṇa, who is free from *karma* and who destroys it.

The *Bhagavadgītā* explains Yoga in several chapters in very much the same way, often with the same words, as Patañjali in his *Yogasūtra.* It also describes the origin of the world in the Sāṁkhya style, repeating the traditional two-way theory of the soul's course after death. It reaches its religious peak, however, in Chapters 9-11, where Kṛṣṇa pronounces his divine self-revelation, the *rājavidyā,* the royal knowledge, *rājaguhyam,* the royal secret, *pavitram idam uttamam,* this most holy subject, open to realization and, within the traditional religion, the only way to escape from rebirth.[18] Kṛṣṇa says:

> By me this whole universe is permeated through my unmanifested form (*avyakta mūrti*). All beings are established in me but I am not established in them. My *ātman* sustains all things but is not established in them. As the air moves everywhere in space, thus are all things established in me because I support them. At the end of each *kalpa* all beings return into my *prakṛti,* from where I send them forth again at the beginning of the *kalpa.* Under my instructions *prakṛti* gives birth to all things and thus the world revolves.[19]

It is foolishness to despise God in a human body and wisdom to recognize him in all things:

> I am the ritual action, I am the sacrifice, I am the ancestral oblation, I am the medicinal herb, I am the sacred hymn, I am the *ghī*, the fire and the offering. I am the father of this world, the mother and the support. I am the object of knowledge, the sanctifier. I am the Om, the *ṛk*, the *sāma* and the *yajus*. I am the goal, the support, the lord, the inner witness, the secret abode, the refuge, the friend. I am the origin and the dissolution, the ground, the resting place and the imperishable seed. I give heat, I withhold and I send forth the rain. I am immortality and also death, I am *sat* and *asat*.[20]

Since Kṛṣṇa is the all-pervading and omnipresent Supreme, he is also the recipient of all devotion and offering. In the instructions for worship, the *bhakti*-character of the *Gītā* appears most clearly:

> Whosoever offers me with *bhakti* [devotion], a leaf, a flower, a fruit or water, that offering of *bhakti*, of the pure-hearted I accept. Whatever you do, eat, offer, give, suffer, dedicate, it as a *tarpaṇa* [libation, offering] to me. Thus you will be freed from the good and evil results that accompany actions. I am alike to all beings, none is hateful to me, none a favorite. But those who worship me with *bhakti* are in me and I in them. Those who take refuge in me, be they low-born, women, *vaiṣyas* or *śūdras*, attain the highest abode. On me fix your mind, be devoted to me, worship me and revere me; having yoked yourself to my self you will attain me.[21]

The entire tenth chapter deals with the *vibhutivistarayoga*,[22] the description of the manifestations of God in things—important for the time in which it was written because here Kṛṣṇa explains himself as the core and essence of Vedic religion and life. The eleventh chapter, called *viśvarūpa-darśana*, the vision of the cosmic form of God, is the most powerful and quite overwhelming.

Arjuna, impressed by the oral revelation of God's greatness has one great desire: *draṣṭumicchāmi te rūpamaiśvaram puruṣottama* ("I wish to see your divine body, O greatest of all beings!")[23] Kṛṣṇa is willing to fulfill this wish, but Arjuna is unable to see God with his natural vision; Kṛṣṇa has to endow him with divine eyes to see the divinity. What Arjuna then sees, terrifies him: "In your body, O Lord, I see all the *devas* and the hosts of beings, Brahmā seated on the lotus-throne and the *ṛṣis* and *nāgas*. I behold you, infinite in form on all sides, with numberless arms, bellies, faces and eyes, but I do not see your end or your middle or your beginning." More relevant for the concrete situation of the war into which Arjuna is about to enter, he sees how all the warriors whom he knows

13. Lakṣman Jhūlā in Rishikesh

> are rushing into your flaming mouths as torrents rushing into the ocean. As moths rush swiftly into a blazing fire to perish there, so do these men rush into yours mouths with great speed to their own destruction. Devouring all the world on every side with your flaming mouths you lick them up. Your fiery rays fill this whole universe and scorch it with their fierce radiance, O Viṣṇu!"

Kṛṣṇa responds with a profound revelation of the relativity of time:

> *Kālo'smi*, time am I, world-destroying, come to the end to subdue the world. Even without you all the warriors arrayed in the opposing armies shall not live on. Therefore arise and fight and win glory. Conquering your enemies enjoy a prosperous kingdom. They have been slain by me already, you be the instrument alone. Slay Drona, Bhīṣma, Jayadratha, Karṇa and the other heroes who are doomed by me. Be not afraid. Fight! You will conquer your enemies in battle!

Arjuna then falls prostrate and praises Viṣṇu under many titles, asking him at the end of his prayer to assume his familiar form again, because he is terrified by the *viśvarūpa*, the all form.

The twelfth chapter contains a brief discourse on the superiority of *bhakti* to *jñāna* and a description of the true *bhakta*, which repeats what had been said before. The thirteenth chapter, entitled *kṣetrakṣetrajñā-vibhāgayoga*, the discrimination between the "field" and the "knower of the field," develops a *puruṣa-prakṛti* theory that agrees in many points with Sāṁkhya, assuming however that there is only one *puruṣa*, Viṣṇu-Kṛṣṇa.

All the following chapters are occupied with demonstrating the applicability of the *triguṇa* scheme to various spheres of life and describing consequently three kinds of faith, of food, of sacrifice, of austerities, of gifts, of knowledge, of work, of doers, of understanding, of steadiness and of happiness—implying always that the follower of Kṛṣṇa partakes of the *sattvaguṇa*, the nature of Viṣṇu. This, incidentally, is good āgamic-paurāṇic Vaiṣṇavism. From these chapters emerges the picture of the true Kṛṣṇaite as being fearless, pure of mind, steadfast in knowledge and concentration, charitable, devoted to the study of scriptures, dedicated to austerities, upright, nonviolent, truthful, free from anger, peaceful, forgiving, compassionate, gentle, modest, and humble. There is a touch of Advaita in the last passages, where Kṛṣṇa describes the blessed state of the perfect sage:

> Endowed with a pure understanding, firmly restraining himself, turning away from sound and other objects of sense and casting aside affection and aversion, dwelling in solitude, eating but little, controlling speech, body and mind, and ever engaged in meditation and concentration and taking refuge in renunciation,

casting aside egoism, violence, arrogance, desire, anger, avarice, tranquil in mind, he becomes worthy to become one with *brahman.* Having become one with *brahman,* tranquil in spirit, he neither grieves nor desires. Regarding all beings as alike, he attains supreme *bhakti* to me. Through *bhakti* he gains knowledge of me, having gained knowledge of me in truth he enters into me.[24]

The *Bhagavadgītā* ends with a renewed injunction of Kṛṣṇa for Arjuna to fight, promising him final liberation:

You are dear to me, I shall tell you what is good for you: Fix your mind on me, be devoted to me, sacrifice to me, prostrate yourself before me, thus you will come to me. I promise you truly, for you are dear to me. Abandon all reliance on [traditional] *dharma* and take your refuge (*śaraṇam*) alone to me. Do not worry, I shall release you from all sins![25]

The *Gītā* attaches the customary blessings for all those who read it, an untold number of Hindus over twenty-five centuries. Many Indians, and increasingly many non-Indians, too, have considered the *Gītā* not only a book to be read and studied but a guide to living. A need for such guidance is felt, especially in times of crises and confusion like ours, when the institutions are no longer able to provide orientation and when there are no longer commonly accepted values and standards. Clearly, the *Gītā* is a book of crisis. Without referring to the *Gītā,* a modern writer describes the symptoms of the manifestation of crisis—and he clearly means our own time—in terms that could be taken straight from the *Gītā* as "loss of meaning, withdrawal of legitimation, confusion of orientations, anomie, destabilization of collective identities, alienation, psychopathologies, breakdowns in tradition, withdrawal of motivation."[26] A direct modern Western reference to the *Bhagavadgītā* occurred in a context, in which to call it historical is almost an understatement—it may better be called apocalyptic. In the course of his trial, J. Robert Oppenheimer, who was accused of passing atomic secrets to the Soviet Union, described the thoughts that passed through his mind when he witnessed the first atomic test explosion in the desert of New Mexico.

In the stage version by Heiner Kipphart, which closely follows the official protocol, the conversation between State Prosecutor Evans and defendant Oppenheimer reads like this:[27]

Evans: I am addressing myself to the moral scruples, the contradiction that, on the one hand, you were prepared to go ahead with the matter of which you were, on the other hand, afraid of. When did you experience this contradiction for the first time?

Oppenheimer: When we ignited the first atomic bomb in the desert of Alamogordo.
Evans: Could you be more precise?
Oppenheimer: On the sight of the fireball two ancient verses came to my mind. The one: "Of a thousand suns in the sky if suddenly should burst forth the light, it would be like unto the light of that Exalted One." (*BG* XI, 12) The other: "Death am I, cause of destruction of the worlds, matured and set out to gather in the worlds there" (*BG* XI, 32).
Evans: How do you know that a new idea is really important?
Oppenheimer: By the sense of a deep horror gripping me.

While the prophetic dimension of the *Bhagavadgītā* can be clearly perceived as applicable to our own time—a time of crisis, a time of disorientation, a time of foreboding of universal doom—it is not so easy to establish the universal applicability of its ethics. Although everybody can understand and even to a degree practice desirelessness and selfless action, the promised effect can only be had within the *varṇāśramadharma:* only by selflessly following one's *svadharma* can one be united with the creator of *dharma* and the rewarder of self-surrender. *Dharma*, as the *Gītā* understands it, is irrevocably tied up with *varṇāśramadharma*. *Varṇāśramadharma* as the eternal world order has ontological, built-in sanctions that simply do not apply to those who were not born to it. The mutuality of *éthos* and *pólis*, of ethics and society, demands that there first be an embodiment of an *éthos* before there can be an articulation of ethics.

India, too, has built its atom bomb and the prospect of another fratricidal war of infinitely larger proportions than that described by the *Gītā* looms large, not only over India but over the whole world. The modern world is not following *varṇāśramadharma*, its major decisions are not preceded by dialogues between the main actors and their God. Questions of ethics, of religious right and moral wrong, do not enter into the power calculations of today's mighty. Rewriting the *Gītā* from such a perspective, Rikhi Jaipaul, a contemporary Indian poet, has composed a kind of *Upagītā* that no longer offers transcendental hope in the face of a universal cataclysm. The new apocalypse is short:[28]

Kurukshetra Revisited

Clear-eyed Arjuna scanning the ruin ahead
his heart overcome with sorrow asked
which will be worse—to win or lose,

will the few with limitless power
condemn the many to karmas not their own,
will the mind that moves the soul prevail?
Pondering deep into the darkening night
of the long journey of man to his doom,
the silent Krishna had reason to lament
and washed his hands in innocence divine.
Soldiers and airmen will not fall with glory
like autumn leaves to sprout again in spring,
souls of sailors will not return as sea gulls,
warmongers will no longer sit on moonbeams
reaching to the stars for their profits;
no more the chivalries and virtues of war
nor hopes of living to fight another day,
foes and friends and neutrals alike
will perish together in the white nuclear night,
their fathers' souls will rise to die again.
Nevermore the ways of our fathers, nevermore,
for in one mad act man can outwit his God
and attain the nirvana of his own oblivion;
in his final fling of self-defense there lies
the destruction of his world to make a legal point
of supervening sovereignty in pursuit of security;
helpless in the iron grip of cause and effect
his means shape his end, baring the moral flaw
and epic pride that feed the fires of his pyre;
alas that which may save him will die with him.

7. The World of the Hindu

I wish to hear from you how this world was, and how in future it will be. What is its substance, and whence proceeded animate and inanimate things? Into what has it been resolved and into what will its dissolution again occur? How were the elements manifested?

—*Maitreya in* Viṣṇupurāṇa *I, 1*

THE HINDU VIEW of the world, like all ancient world views, is a mythologico-religious one. It does not derive from experimentally verifiable scientific data but superimposes a mythical or religious pattern on the visible world, a pattern that stems from a different layer of consciousness. It is a representation of the universe within and reflects the psychological, metaphysical, and religious structure of the ideas of the people rather than describes the factual conditions in the objective cosmos. Whatever its source may have been, the world picture a civilization accepts becomes the basis of its morals and its aspirations, its ideas of real and unreal, right and wrong. An examination of the world view of the Hindu cannot compare Hindu writings with modern scientific cosmology or geo-history, instead it must study information about the mind and religion of Hindus throughout the ages.

VEDIC CREATION MYTHS

In the *Ṛgveda, pṛthivī-dyaus*, Earth and Heaven, are divinities. India shares this heaven-earth division and religion with a good many other peoples,[1] who similarly explain the world as originating from a pair of world parents. "Which was the former, which of them the later? How born? O sages, who discerns? They bear of themselves all that has existence.

Day and Night revolve as on a wheel."[2] But this simple scheme could not accommodate the numerous new developments in Vedic religion, which uses a basic partition of the universe into *triloka*, "three worlds," which combine the places for gods, ancestors, and humans. To each of the worlds, eleven *devas* were assigned, with various functions. As S. Kramrisch explains:

> Heaven and earth, as dyadic monad, are a closed unit. It must be violated, split into its components, and these must be separated, lest they fall together and the world-to-be collapses. The act of creative violation and the power of keeping apart the pair so that they become Father Heaven and Mother Earth between whom all life is engendered is the test by which a creator god establishes his supremacy. He makes the Dyad into Two. He is the One and at the same time the Third, who plays the leading part in the cosmic drama. He is hero and artist in one.[3]

Speculation about the origin of the world is one of the staples of almost all religions, and quite frequently much of the rest of their philosophy is derived from this starting point. The earlier Vedic hymns have many scattered references to the origin of the world, involving a variety of gods; only in the later hymns does anything like a definite doctrine emerge. One hymn is addressed to *Viśvakarman*, the One who makes all.[4] He is called mighty in mind and power, maker, disposer and most lofty presence, the Father who made us, the One beyond the seven *ṛṣis*. He is described as not to be found, "another thing has risen up among you."[5]

The two best-known Vedic descriptions of creation, however, are the so-called *puruṣa sūkta* and the *nāsadīya sūkta*. The former, true to the basic Vedic philosophy, derives everything from a ritual sacrifice. Thus, it goes, "Thousand-headed was the *puruṣa*, thousand-eyed, thousand-footed. He embraced the earth on all sides, and stood beyond the breadth of ten fingers. The *puruṣa* is this all, that which was and which shall be. He is Lord of immortality, which he outgrows through [sacrificial] food. One-fourth of him is all beings. The three-fourths of him is the immortal in heaven."

This *puruṣa* begets *virāj*, the "widespread," and together both bring forth *puruṣa* the son, who becomes the sacrificial victim of the great sacrifice of the gods. From this great sacrifice originate the verses of the Vedas, horses, cattle, goats, and sheep. The four castes, also, have their origin in him, the sacrificial victim. The *Brahmin* was his mouth, out of his two arms were made the *kṣatriyas*, his two thighs became the *vaiṣyas*, and from his feet the *śūdras* were born.[6] From his mind was born the moon, from his eye the sun, from his mouth Indra and Agni, from his breath Vāyu, from his navel the sky, from his head the heaven, from his feet the earth, and from his ears the quarters.

Yajñena yajñam ayajanta devāḥ,[7] "the gods offered the sacrifice through the sacrifice." The *yajña* is the great creative force. We find here the germ of the later *Pāñcarātra* system, the idea that Viṣṇu is also the material cause of the universe, out of which everything is fashioned.

A more speculative treatment of the topic of creation is found in the *nāsadīya sūkta*, in the last book of the Veda:

> Neither being, nor nonbeing existed: there was no air, no sky that is beyond it. What was concealed? Wherein? In whose protection? And was there deep unfathomable water? Death then existed not, nor life immortal, of neither night nor day was there any token. By its inherent force the One breathed windless: no other thing existed beyond that. There was at first darkness, by darkness hidden; without distinctive marks, this all was water. That which, becoming, was covered by the void, that One by force of heat came into being. Desire entered the One in the beginning: it was the earliest seed, the product of thought. The sages searching in their hearts with wisdom, found the kin of being in nonbeing. . . . Who knows for certain? Who shall declare it? Whence was it born, and whence came this creation? The gods were born after this world's creation: then who can know from whence it has arisen? None can know from whence creation has arisen and whether he has or has not produced it: he who surveys it in the highest heaven, he only knows, or, perhaps.[8]

Several key words of Vedic religion are employed here: *tapas*, heat, the power of the *yogi*, is said to be responsible for the first stirring of creation; *kāma*, desire or lust, is the cause of both the multiplicity and the inherent impermanence of things. The terms *asat*, "nonbeing," and *sat*, "being," do not have the Greek meaning we connect with them but the Indian one, which differs considerably: *asat* is an entity without determination, akin to chaos, unstructured matter in the modern sense. The asymmetry of *sat* and *asat*, which is, as it were, complementary, is of a similarly fundamental nature as that between chaos and order, entropy and negentropy, as understood by modern science. *Sat* and *asat* are positive and negative poles, complementary, whose tension produces and maintains the many things.

As will become still clearer from later accounts, the Hindu idea of creation presupposes some kind of uncreated substratum, and the account is concerned more with the molding and ordering of this basic material than with its absolute beginning. As S. Kramrisch sees it:

> The three ontological moments in the relation of *sat* and *asat* correspond to different levels in the structure of creation. The dark Un-create on high has for its lower limit the first streak of the dawn of creation in the highest heaven. . . . Sunk below creation, the non-existent is negativity; the existent is

> the cosmos, the ordered world, the world of *ṛta*, a work of art. The non-existent is chaos, decomposition, the absence of *ṛta*, the domain of *nirriti.* It is the counterpart, *apud principium*, by the act of creation and separation, of the Darkness that was—and is—before the beginning of things.[9]

The Upanishads have a great variety of theories to explain both the beginning of the universe and its structure. According to the *Bṛhadāraṇyaka Upaniṣad*, in the beginning the *ātman*, the Self, was alone, in the form of a *puruṣa*, a male being. He looked around and saw nothing besides himself. He said, "I am." He was afraid and he had no joy; he longed for another being. He was as large as a man and woman embracing. He divided himself into two: husband and wife. Thus, human beings were created. She turned into a cow, he became a bull. She turned into a mare, he became a stallion. And thus the various kinds of animals came into existence.[10] The account given here reveals the first traces of the *Sāṁkhya* system, in which everything owes its origin to the interaction between *puruṣa* and *prakṛti*, the uncreated principles, one male and the other female, spirit and matter, passivity and activity.

Another ancient motif is that of the world-egg, which floats on the primordial ocean and from which spring the many creatures on earth.[11] According to some texts, the first being to come forth from the primeval egg was Viśvakarman, the Vedic creator-god. The world-egg, and the origination of the universe from it, is a favorite theme of many later Hindu works, notably the *Purāṇas.*

Manu's account of creation is informed by his endeavor to derive the socio-ethical law of *dharma* from the nature and structure of the universe itself. In the beginning, the world was in chaos (*tamas*), without distinguishable forms and attributes, as if in sleep. Then appeared the *svayambhu bhagavān*, the Lord who is of Himself, invisible and without distinguishing characteristics. He removed the darkness. This *paramātman* was filled with a desire to create beings. He created water and put the seed *śaktirūpi*, power form, into it. This seed shone with the splendor of a thousand suns. It then became an egg, as bright as gold, and from it issued Brahmā, who shaped all the worlds. He, who is the origin of everything, eternal, of the form of *sat* and *asat, puruṣa* who issued from it, he is called Brahmā. For a whole year, he remained in the form of an egg, and then, through concentrated thought (*dhyāna*), divided himself into two.

From the two halves were created heaven and earth and space in between them: the eight points of the compass, the place of water and the sea. From the Self, he produced mind (*manas*),[12] containing in him both *sat* and *asat;* from this came individuality (*ahaṁkāra*),[13] with pride and dominion.[14] The following chapters in *Manusmṛti* enumerate the successive creation of the twenty-four principles from which, according to the Sāṁkhya system, everything is made. *Mahat*, the Great Principle, all that contains the three *guṇas* in themselves, the five sense organs, and so on was created first. The various celestial beings were then created, along with *yajña*, the sacrifice. For it *Ṛk, Yajur*, and *Sāmaveda* were produced out of Agni, Vāyu, and Sūrya. *Tapas*, heat power; as well as *rati*, erotic pleasure; *icchhā*, desire; and *krodha*, anger, were created. *Dharma* and *adharma* and all other pairs of opposites like *hiṁsā* and *ahiṁsā*, cruelty and kindness, were apportioned to the various beings by Brahmā himself.

The origin of the four castes is explained in the same terms as the account in the *puruṣa-sūkta*. Brahmā divides his body into two parts. Out of their union springs up the first human being, Virāj. Virāj practices *tapas* in order to create Prajāpati, who brings forth ten *maharṣis* as well as seven Manus, *devas*, and the various kinds of good and evil spirits: the *Yakṣas* and *Piśācas, Gandharvas* and *Āpsaras, Nāgas* and *Garuḍas.*

In the *Manusmṛti*, we already find the idea of a periodical creation and destruction of the world, as well as all the divisions of time from the winking of an eye to the world ages.[15] One day and night are made up of thirty *muhūrtas*, each *muhūrta* of thirty *kalās*, each *kalā* of thirty *kāṣṭās*, and each *kāṣṭā* of eighteen *nimeṣās*.

> The sun divides days and nights, both human and divine; the night is for the repose and the day for work. A month is a day and night of the departed ancestors; the dark fortnight is their day of work, the bright fortnight their time of sleep. A year is the day and night of the *devas;* the half year during which the sun progresses to the north will be their day, that during which the sun goes southward, the night.

There follows a description of the day and night of Brahmā and of the world ages: the *Kṛta-yuga* consists of 4000 years of the *devas;* the twilight preceding it consists of as many hundreds and the twilight following it of the same number. In the other three *yugas* with their twilights preceding and following, the thousands and hundreds are diminished by one each. "These twelve thousand years are called one age of the *devas.* One thousand ages of the gods make one day of Brahman, and his night has the same length. . . . At the end of that day and night he who was asleep awakes and, after awaking, creates."[16]

The *Manusmṛti* as well as the *Purāṇas* make use of the term *Manvantara*, an age of Manu or age of humankind, calculated as seventy-one ages of the *devas.* "The *Manvantaras*, the creations and destructions of the world, are numberless; sporting as it were, Brahman repeats this again and again." Throughout we find what we might term historical pessimism: the world is in constant moral decline.

> In the *Kṛta* age *dharma* is four-footed and complete; and so is truth (*satya*), nor does any gain accrue to men by unrighteousness. In the other three ages *dharma* is successively deprived of one foot, and through theft, falsehood and fraud the merit is diminished by one fourth. Men are free from disease, accomplish all their aims, and live four hundred years in the *Kṛta* age, but in the *Treta* and the succeeding ages their life is lessened by one quarter.

Dharma too is different according to the ages. In the *Kṛta* age, *tapas* is the chief virtue; in the *Treta* age, wisdom; in the *Dvāpara*, the performance of sacrifices; and in the *Kali* age, in which we now live, *dāna* or liberality.[17]

In all the *Purāṇas*, our present age is described as being close to universal chaos and final destruction. The laws that governed and upheld humankind in former ages have broken down, humankind has become weak, oppressed by numerous calamities, and short lived.

PURANIC COSMOGRAPHY

Before dealing with details of traditional history, which almost exclusively concerns the *Kali* age, it may be worthwhile to mention some features of the traditional world description offered mainly in the *Purāṇas* and presupposed in all historical or mythical narrations.[18] The Hindus certainly had a quite accurate knowledge of those parts of India in which they lived, and at certain times, they also ventured forth across the seas. Not content with their experiences, they constructed a complete world model in which everything found its exact place. Though the descriptions of these models in various texts differ in a number of substantial details, all of them begin with Mount Meru as the center of the world, around which Jambudvīpa, the known world (mainly India), is situated.

The *Mahābhārata* has preserved an older version of the world model in which four *dvīpas*, or continents, were arranged around Mount Meru, with the Ocean of Salt as the southern border of the world, and the Ocean of Milk as the northern.[19] The fully developed Puranic model is much more complex. It includes seven *dvīpas* surrounded by and surrounding seven concentric oceans. In the center of this world stands Mount Meru, forming with *Jambu-Dvīpa* the innermost circle. Its boundary is formed by a vast ring of salt water, the *lavana-sāgara*, followed by another concentric ring of land and so on.[20] This model is illustrated in Figure 7.1.

Aṇḍakaṭaha Tamas	128	Shell of the World Egg Darkness
Lokālokaśaila Kañcanībhūmī	128	World-No-World Mountains Land of Gold
Jalasāgara Puṣkaradvīpa	64 64	Sea of Sweet Water Blue-Lotus Land
Kṣirasāgara Śākadvīpa	32 32	Milk Ocean Teak Tree Land
Dadhisamūdra Krauñcadvīpa	16 16	Buttermilk Ocean Heron Land
Sarpisamūdra Kuśadvīpa	8 7	Melted-Butter Ocean Kuśa Land
Surāsamūdra Śālmaladvīpa	4 4	Wine Ocean Silk-Cotton-Tree Land
Ikṣurasasamūdra Plakṣadvīpa	2 2	Sugar-Cane-Juice Ocean Fig-Tree Land
Lāvaṇasamūdra Jambudvīpa	1 1	Salt-Water Ocean Roseapple-Tree Land
	510	Mount Meru

Figure 7.1 Purāṇic World Model

The middle column of Figure 7.1 indicates the width of each ring of sea or land, using the diameter of *jambudvīpa* (given as 100,000 *yojanas*)[21] as the basic unit. The whole map has to be imagined as consisting of concentric circles, whose center is Mount Meru, the pivot of *Jambudvīpa.*[22] The parts of *Jambudvīpa* are illustrated in detail in Figure 7.2.

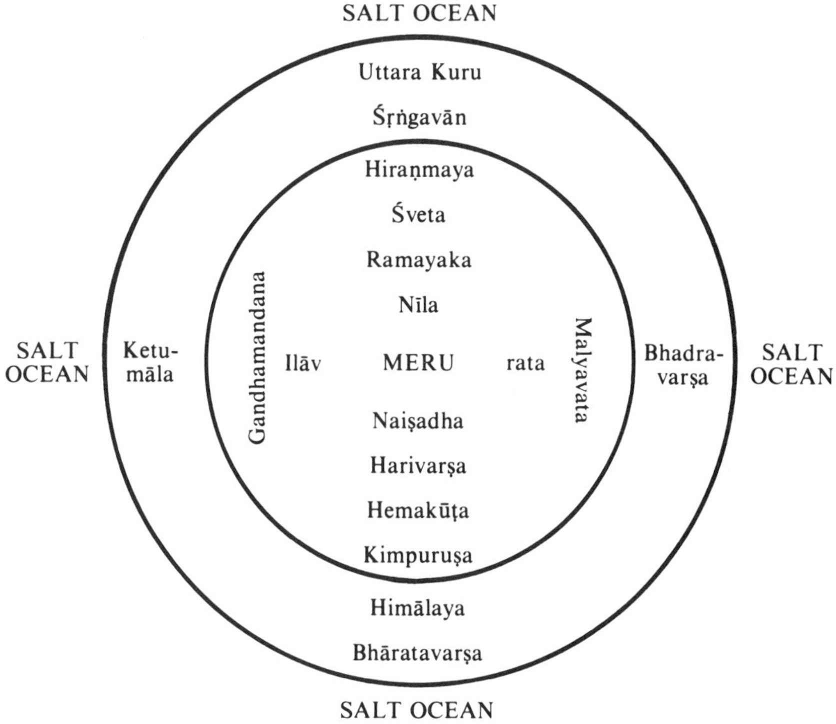

Figure 7.2 The Map of the Purāṇic World Model

Bhāratavarṣa (India) again is divided into nine parts, ruled over by kings from the dynasties descended from Satājit.[23] This king can be traced back through various illustrious rulers to Pṛthu, from whom the earth (*pṛthvi*) took her name, since he "subdued the earth," levelling it and beginning to cultivate it. Whereas the other eight parts of *Jambudvīpa* are described as "places of perfect enjoyment, where happiness is spontaneous and uninterrupted, without vicissitude, without age and death, without distinction of virtue or vice, without any change brought about by the cycle of sages," *Bhāratavarṣa* is subject to the deterioration brought about by the succession of the four *yugas;* it knows suffering and death. But it is praised nevertheless as "the best of the divisions of *Jambudvīpa*, because it is the land of works," which enables people to gain heaven or even final emancipation. The gods themselves praise the good fortune of those born in *Bhāratavarṣa.*[24] We leave out the details of the description of the several parts of *Jambudvīpa*, which contain much valuable information about the geography and ethnology of ancient India.

A few words about Mount Meru, the Golden Mountain in the center of *Jambudvīpa* may be of value for an understanding of Indian mythology, however. Its height is given as 84,000 *yojanas*, its depth below the surface of the earth as 16,000. Its diameter at the summit is 32,000 *yojanas* and at the base, 16,000 *yojanas;* "so that this mountain is like the seed-cup of the lotus of the earth." From the base of Mount Meru extend mighty mountain ridges; on its summit the vast city of Brahmā extends 14,000 *yojanas*. And around it, at the cardinal points and in the intermediate quarters, is situated the stately city of Indra and the cities of the other regents of the spheres. The capital of Brahmā is enclosed by the river Ganges that, issuing from the foot of Viṣṇu[25] and washing the lunar orb, falls here from the skies and, after encircling the city, divides into four mighty rivers.

The *Purāṇas* describe in detail not only *Jambudvīpa* but also the other continents with their geography and history. In the five continents outside *Jambudvīpa*, the lives of men last for 5000 years; they are happy, sinless, and enjoy uninterrupted bliss. They have their own system of classes, corresponding to the four castes in *Bhāratavarṣa*, but this division does not result in any friction or deprivation of one group relative to another. In *Puṣkaradvīpa* men live a thousand years, free from sickness and sorrow and unruffled by anger and affection. There is neither virtue nor vice, neither killer nor slain; there is no jealousy, envy, fear, hatred; neither is there truth or falsehood. Food is produced spontaneously there. There is no distinction of caste and order, there are no fixed institutes, nor are rites performed for the sake of merit. The three *Vedas*, the *Purāṇas*, ethics, policy, and the laws of service are unknown. It is, in fact, a terrestrial paradise where time yields happiness to all its inhabitants, who are exempt from sickness and decay. A *Nyāgrodha*-tree grows on this land, which is the special abode of Brahmā, and he resides in it, adored by *devas* and *asuras.*[26]

> Beyond the sea of fresh water is a region of twice its extent, where the land is of gold and where no living beings reside. Thence extends the *Lokāloka* mountain, which is 10,000 *yojanas* in breadth and as many in height; and beyond it perpetual darkness invests the mountain all around; which darkness is again encompassed by the shell of the world-egg. Thus the universe with its exterior shell is 500 million *yojanas* in extent. It is the mother and nurse of all creatures, the foundation of all worlds, and the principal element.[27]

The universe as described in Hindu cosmology is geocentric: the earth is the center of the entire universe, though not its best part as regards enjoyment. It is, however, best suited for "work," for the possibilities that it opens to gain the supreme end, liberation. The Hindu world, however, is less ethnocentric than, for instance, the world view of the ancient Near Eastern peoples, in particular those of ancient Israel. Mount Meru, the center of the Hindu world, is far away from *Bhāratavarṣa.* Only later Hindu sects identify the center of the world with their centers of worship. Thus, Śaivites consider Cidāmbaram as the world center, Vaiṣṇavas identify Vrindābana with the pivot of the world. The Purāṇic accounts are also quite modest when comparing their own country with other countries. The people in other countries are described as materially much better off, and they are free from most of the hazards that beset the people of Bhārat.

A vertical section produces the following "layers" or sheaths of the world-egg, the *brahmāṇḍa:*[28]

Satyaloka	
Tapoloka	
Janaloka	
Maharloka	
Svarloka (planets)	Regions of the consequences of work
Bhuvarloka (sky)	
Bhurloka (earth)	
Atala (white)	Netherworlds
Vitala (black)	
Nitala (purple)	
Gabhastimat (yellow)	
Mahātala (sandy)	
Sutala (stony)	
Pātāla (golden)	
Śeṣa (the world-snake)	
Raurava, etc. (28 *narakas* or hells)	

Beginning with the earth as the center, the *Purāṇa* explains the netherworlds, which are not to be confused with hells or with the idea of netherworlds in the West. Each of the seven netherworlds extends 10,000 *yojanas* below the surface of the one preceding it. "They are embellished with magnificent palaces in which dwell numerous *Dānavas, Daityas, Yakṣas* and great *Nāgas.* The Muni Nārada after his return from those regions to the skies declared amongst the celestials that *Pātāla* was much more delightful than Indra's heaven."[29]

Below these is *Śeṣa,* the "form of Viṣṇu proceeding from the quality of darkness," also called *Ananta,* the endless one, with a thousand heads, embellished with the *svāstika. Śeṣa* bears the entire world like a diadem upon his head. When *Ananta,* his eyes rolling with intoxication, yawns, the earth, with all her woods and mountains, seas and rivers, trembles. The hells "beneath the earth and beneath the waters" are the place of punishment for sinners, specified according to their crimes.[30]

The sphere of the earth (moving upwards) "extends as far as it is illuminated by the rays of the sun and moon; and to the same extent the sphere of the sky extends upwards, till the beginning of the sphere of the planets." The solar orb is situated 100,000 *yojanas* from the earth and that of the moon an equal distance from the sun. At the same interval above the moon are the orbits of all lunar constellations. *Budha* (Mercury) is 200,000 *yojanas* above the lunar mansions; *Śukra* (Venus) is at the same distance from *Budha. Aṅgāraka* (Mars) is as far above *Śukra; Bṛhaspati* (Jupiter) as far from *Aṅgāraka,* while *Śani* (Saturn) is 250,000 leagues beyond *Bṛhaspati.* The sphere of the *Seven Ṛṣis* is 100,000 *yojanas* above *Śani;* and at a similar height above these is the *Dhruva* (Pole Star), the pivot of the whole planetary circle. *Bhur, Bhuvar,* and *Svar* form "the region of the consequence of works"; the region of the works that bring merit is *Bhāratavarṣa* alone.[31]

Above *Dhruva,* at the distance of 10 million *yojanas,* lies *Maharloka,* whose inhabitants dwell in it for a *Kalpa* or a day of Brahmā. At twice that distance is *Janaloka,* where *Sanāndana* and other pure-minded sons of Brahmā reside. At four times the distance, between the last two, lies the *Tapoloka,* inhabited by the *devas* called *Vaibhrajas,* whom fire cannot harm. At six times the distance lies *Satyaloka,* the sphere of truth, whose inhabitants will never know death again. *Satyaloka* is also called *Brahmāloka.* Above this, some of the sectarian texts add *Viṣṇuloka* (or *Vaikuṇṭha*), and *Śivaloka* (or *Kailāsa*), assigning the supreme place to the deity of their choice.[32]

The world-egg (with its seven *dvīpas* and *samudras,* its seven *lokas,* and its seven netherworlds; *Śeṣa* and the hells beneath—all within the shell of *brahmāṇḍa*) is but the center of a greater universe, which is stratified according to the following scheme:

- *Pradhāna-Puruṣa* (primaeval matter and spirit)
    - *mahat* (the first principle)
    - *bhutādi* (the gross elements)
    - *nabhas* (ether)
    - *vāyu* (wind)
    - *vahni* (fire)
    - *ambu* (water)
- World-Egg (earth)

The *Viṣṇu Purāṇa* explains this in detail.[33] The world is encompassed on all sides and above and below by the shell of the egg of Brahman, in the same manner as the seed of the wood-apple is encircled by its rind. Around the outer surface of the shell flows water, for a space equal to ten times the diameter of the world. The waters are encompassed by fire, fire by air, air by ether, ether by the gross elements, these by the first principle. Each of these extends in breadth ten times that layer which it encloses, and the last is enveloped by *pradhāna*, which is infinite and its extent cannot be enumerated. It is therefore called the boundless, the illimitable cause of all existing things, supreme nature or *prakṛti*, the cause of all world-eggs of which there are thousands and tens of thousands, millions and thousands of millions. Within *pradhāna* resides *puman*, diffusive, conscious, and self-irradiating, as fire is inherent in flint. Both are encompassed by the energy of Viṣṇu (*viṣṇuśakti*), which causes the separation of the two at the period of dissolution, and causes their continued existence, as well as their recombination at the time of creation.

PAST AND FUTURE WORLD RULERS

The universe of the Hindu is peopled by all possible degrees of being: inanimate objects, plants, animals, demons, *devas*, semidivine beings, humans, etc. The *Purāṇas* contain poetic genealogies of all of them. For our purposes it will be of interest to outline briefly the history of the human race, as reported in traditional Hindu literature. Several scholars have tried to reconstruct ancient Indian history with the names and dates supplied in epics and *Purāṇas*. So far, they have come to no agreement as regards the most important dates, especially that of the Bhārata War, which is considered the central landmark in ancient Indian history.[34] Since we are not directly concerned with history in the modern Western sense, we may content ourselves with a summary of the opinion of one authority in this area.[35] Without necessarily accepting his chronology, we nevertheless get an idea of a historically probable calculation and gain some familiarity with the more prominent names in Indian history and mythology.

From Brahmā, the creator, was born Manu Svayambhuva,[36] who divided into a male and a female and produced two sons, Priyavrata and Uttānapāda, and two daughters, Prasūti and Ākūti. From these were born *Dharma* and *Adharma* and their progeny: *Śraddhā* (faith), *Lakṣmī* (good fortune), *Kriyā* (action), *Buddhi* (intelligence), *Śānti* (peace); as well as *Hiṁsā* (violence), *Anṛta* (falsehood), *Nikṛti* (immorality), *Bhaya* (fear), *Māyā* (deceit), *Mṛtyu* (death), *Duḥkha* (pain), *Śoka* (sorrow), *Tṛṣṇa* (greed), *Krodha* (anger), etc.

We move into the realm of protohistory with the story of Vena, the grandson of Cakṣusa, in the line of the sixth Manu.[37] Apparently, Vena offended the religious feelings of his subjects by proclaiming himself to be God and forbidding all other cults. The *ṛṣis*, who were worshippers of Hari, did not accept his claim to divine kingship and killed Vena, who left no heir. In the period following the death of the king, anarchy spread terror among the people, who clamoured for a ruler. The *ṛṣis* drilled the left thigh of the dead king; out of it came a dwarfish black being, whom they called Niṣāda and who became the ancestor of the Niṣādas in the Vindhya mountains. They drilled the right arm of the dead king and produced Pṛthu, at whose birth heaven and earth rejoiced. His consecration is described at great length; he is celebrated as the initiator of agriculture, road construction, and city building.

From his line sprang Manu Vaivasvata, the savior of humanity at the time of the Great Flood. We have several accounts of the deluge, which also plays a great role in the popular traditions of other cultures.[38] Pusalker accepts the flood as historical event that took place around 3100 B.C.E. In Hindu mythology, it is connected with the *Matsya-avatāra* of Viṣṇu. A small fish swam into Manu's hands when he was taking his morning bath and asked for protection. Manu put it first into a jar, then into a pond, and, when it was fully grown, back into the sea. The fish gave Manu a warning about the coming flood and advised him to prepare a ship and enter it at an appointed time. Manu did so, and when the flood finally came, the fish appeared again and pulled Manu's boat to the northern mountains. After the water had subsided, Manu was ordered to disembark and descend from the mountain, whose slope therefore is called *Manoravatāraṇam*, Manu's descent.

He was the only human being saved—and with him humankind took a new beginning. He was also the first lawgiver and first tax collector. His eldest offspring had a double personality, as the male Ila and the female Ilā. Ilā, who married Budha, gave birth to Pururavas, the originator of the Aila or Lunar dynasty. From Ila's eldest son, Īkṣvāku, who had his capital at Ayodhyā, sprang the Aikṣvaka or Solar dynasty. The other eight sons of Manu also became founders of peoples and dynasties, whose lines are recorded.

According to the most famous kings in the lists, Pusalker divides the history after Manu into a *Yayāti* period (3000-2750 B.C.E.), a *Māndhātṛ* period (2750-2550 B.C.E.), a *Paraśurāma* period (2550-2350 B.C.E.), a *Rāmacandra* period (2350-1950 B.C.E.), a *Kṛṣṇa* period (1950-1400 B.C.E.). The end of this era coincides with the great Bhārata War, which according to Indian tradition marks the beginning of the *Kali-yuga*, the last and most evil of all the ages of humankind.[39]

The *Purāṇas* have lists of dynasties of kingdoms that flourished at the end of the Bhārata War and continued until they were absorbed by the great Nanda Empire of Magadha in the fourth century B.C.E.[40] One of the prominent figures in the *Purāṇas* is Parīkṣit, a Kaurava king who lived after the great war. Largely from Buddhist accounts, we are informed about the kingdoms of Kośala and Kāśī. The kings ruling over Magadha gradually extended their influence, until they were the only great power in northern India.

Between Manu, the savior of humankind, and the Bhārata War, the *Purāṇas* list ninety-five generations of kings, on whom they report in the past tense. From Parīkṣit, "the ruling king,"[41] onwards, they use the future tense, thus giving these genealogies the character of prophecies and enhancing their authority. They offer quite precise information regarding names and important details of the kings' lives and deaths up to the time of the Guptas in the fourth century C.E. Then, again, the names and stories become fanciful, further developing the idea of a constant deterioration of the quality of life during the *Kaliyuga*, which lasts for 360,000 years from the death of Kṛṣṇa.[42] After enumerating a large number of names, the *Purāṇa* states:

> These will all be contemporary monarchs, reigning over the earth; kings of churlish spirit, violent temper, and ever addicted to falsehood and wickedness. They will inflict death on women, children and cows; they will seize upon the property of their subjects; they will be of limited power, and will, for the most part, rise and fall rapidly. Their lives will be short, their desires insatiable, and they will display but little piety. The people of the various countries will follow their example. . . . Wealth and piety will decrease day by day, until the world will be wholly depraved. Then property alone will confer rank; wealth will be the only source of devotion; passion will be the sole bond of union between the sexes; falsehood will be the only means of success in litigation; and women

> will be objects merely of sensual gratification. Earth will be venerated but for its mineral treasures, dishonesty will be a universal means of subsistence, presumption will be substituted for learning. No man's life will exceed three and twenty years. Thus in the Kali age shall decay constantly proceed, until the human race approaches its annihilation.

At the end of these times, *Kalki*, a divine incarnation, will arise, who

> will destroy all the *mlecchas* and thieves, and all whose minds are devoted to iniquity. He will then re-establish *dharma* on earth, and the minds of those who live at the end of the Kali age shall be awakened. . . . The men who are thus changed by virtue of that peculiar time shall be as the seeds of human beings and shall give birth to a race who shall follow the laws of the *Kṛta* age.

The *Purāṇa* adds some astronomical information from which the end of the times can be foretold; also included is the prophecy that Devapī, of the race of Puru and Maru of the family of Īkṣvāku, will outlive all others and constitute the germ of the renewal of the *Kṛta* age, after 1200 years of Brahmā's night have elapsed.[43]

In more recent times, Hindus have also become acquainted with geography and history in the modern sense, which in many details is in conflict with traditional teaching. There are some who tenaciously cling to the literal truth of the scriptures and reject modern scholarship as biased and ignorant. In a number of cases, recent scholarship has vindicated the ancient traditions over the rash assumptions of former generations of historians. Some Hindus also try to harmonize the scriptural accounts with modern scientific ideas in geology or biology, often in a somewhat forced way.[44] Others have found a compromise between tradition and modernity, sometimes demythologizing and allegorizing the scriptures so as to uphold their truth and sound modern at the same time.

In a manner typical of modern enlightened Hinduism, S. Radhakrishnan demythologised Hinduism in a speech before the *Viśva Hindu Sammelan* in New Delhi,[45] stating that there was nothing sectarian or dogmatic about Hinduism, which was but the reconciliation of all paths to God. The Hindu myth of the creation of the world, he continued, implies that life came out of matter, animal life out of plant life, and gave rise in time to human reason. The famous myth of the churning of the Milk Ocean (see Figure 7.3) out of which the gods derived *amṛta*, the nectar of immortality, he interprets as the "churning of the spirit" out of which comes purity of heart.

Hinduism has shown throughout its long history an ambivalent relationship to the physical universe. This ambivalence probably is articulated most clearly in the positions assumed by Śaṅkara and Rāmānuja, authors from the Indian Middle Ages but holding opinions that connect with Upanishadic texts. For Śaṅkara as well as Rāmānuja, the visible world has its origin in *Brahman*, the Absolute. But while for Śaṅkara the world is *māyā*, a kind of illusion or appearance and an alienation of the Self, for Rāmānuja it is the body of God, sharing some of the qualities ascribed to the Supreme, real and sacramentally necessary.

In opposition to the One Supreme, the world is characterized by duality: the opposites of *dharma* and *adharma*, of good and evil, of hot and cold, of gods and demons are possible only in the world and the world is constituted by them. This fundamental structure is articulated in the popular creation stories of the *Purāṇas* as well as in the sophisticated cosmological speculation of the *Darśanas*. It appears in the self-partition of *Brahman* in the Upanishads and in the *sura-asura* contest of the Churning of the Milk Ocean, in the *puruṣa-prakṛti* dualism of Sāṁkhya, and in the *vyavahāra-paramārtha* distinction of Śaṅkara. Within the dualism, a tripartite schema supplies the dynamics of development. The Pṛthvi-Dyaus polarity of the Veda becomes sacrificially relevant as *triloka*, three worlds. The *puruṣa-prakṛti* polarity is actualized toward liberation through the *tri-guṇa* dynamics. The *vyavahāra-paramārtha* dichotomy includes the

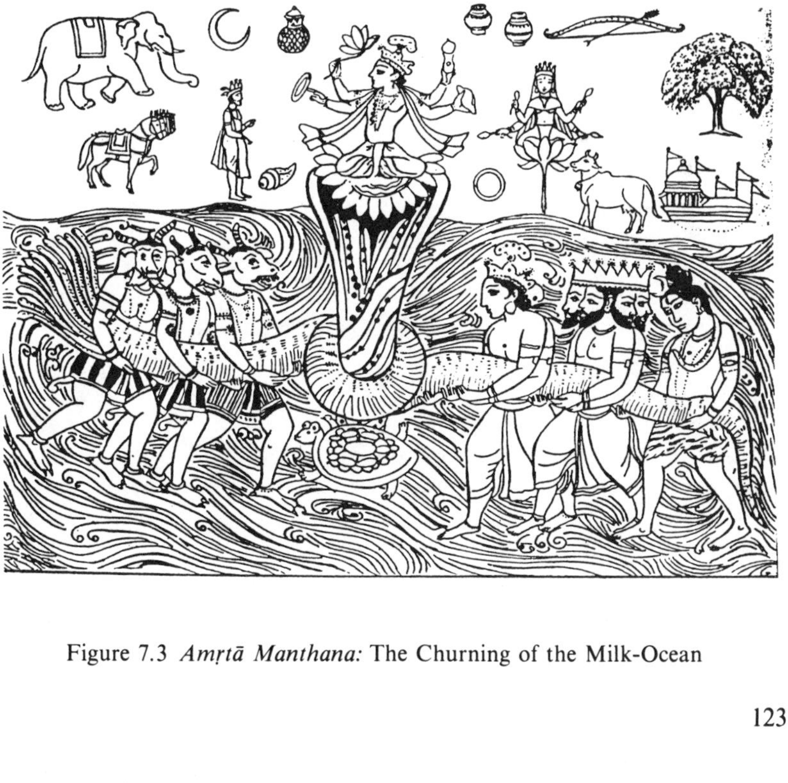

Figure 7.3 *Amṛtā Manthana:* The Churning of the Milk-Ocean

active pursuit of the triad of the *puruṣārthas.* Behind the colorful and seemingly naive stories in which the traditional Hindu world view is often described, there are profound ideas and structural insights that could well be expressed in modern abstract mathematical terms, as has been done.

8. The Many Gods and the One God of Hinduism

"Yes, said he, "but just how many gods are there Yājñavalkya?"

"Thirty-three." . . .

"Yes," said he, "but just how many gods are there, Yājñavalkya?"

"One . . ."

—Bṛhadāraṇyaka Upaniṣad *III, IX, 1*

ABOUT A SCORE of different Sanskrit words are rendered by the one English word *god.* We have to look at some of them in order to find out how Hindus can at one and the same time have many gods and believe in One God.

VEDIC *DEVAS*

When English publications on Vedic religion speak about gods, they use this term as translation for the Vedic word *deva* or *devatā.*[1] Thus, they enumerate faithfully the eleven celestial gods, the eleven atmospheric gods, and the eleven terrestrial gods. F. Max Müller was struck by the evident fact that in a number of hymns the god to whom the song was addressed was praised as the only one, the supreme, the greatest, and that praise was not restricted to one and the same god, but given to various gods in various hymns. This did not conform to the classical notion of *polytheism*, so Müller coined the new term *henotheism* (from the Greek term *henos*, = "one") to distinguish this religion from *monotheism*, the revealed biblical religion. The Hindu *deva* is not God. At the most, *deva* could be loosely translated as a "divine being." Etymologically, it means

14. Agni, Khajurāho 12th ct.

"shiny", "exalted." Thus, we find that the term *deva* covers everything that has to do with the supernatural: all figures, forms, processes and emotions, melodies, books and verse meters—whatever needs the explanation of a superior origin or status—are called *devas* or *devatā* in one place or another.[2] The functions of different parts of the body, symbols, and syllables are explained as *deva.* In Vedic religion, the term is used in a relatively restricted way; even there, however, it is not equated with *God,* but with *supernatural powers* in a general sense.

Anthropologists have become aware of the importance of the idea of "power" in tribal religions. R. N. Dandekar has shown quite convincingly that behind the Vedic *deva* worship lies the idea of an all-pervading ultimate power, of which the *devas* partake without being quite identical with it. According to him, most of the Ṛgvedic *devas* are created for the myths and not the myths for the *devas.* Mythology is thus primary and the *devas* are secondary. The Vedic *ṛṣis* had a message that they conveyed in images for which they created the concrete figures of the *devas.* Thus, Vedic mythology is evolutionary, implying a change of the character of a *deva* according to changed circumstances.

Much more important than the variable figure of the *deva* was the basic underlying potency of which the individual *devas* were only expressions and manifestations; the Vedic counterpart to the *mana* power is the *asura* power, which is shared by all beings, especially the *devas.* This is also the explanation for the highly variable and flexible anthropomorphism of the Vedic *devas.* There is, strictly speaking, no Vedic pantheon in the sense in which there is a Greek or a Roman one.[3]

The Vedic seer did not share the outlook of modern people. Though *agni* is the term for "fire" in the most general sense, to the Vedic religious mind the reality of *agni* is not simply the chemical process of carbonization of organic matter that a modern scientist would associate with the term *fire.* In fire is seen a *deva,* a transcendent aspect that makes *agni* fit to be used as an expression that hints at a something beyond the material reality investigated by modern chemistry. *Agni* is a *deva,* not a "personification of a natural phenomenon," as nineteenth century Western scholarship would describe it, but the manifestation of a transcendent power. The physical reality of fire is so obvious and so necessary that the Hindu does not think of spiritualizing it away; but there is more to it than meets the senses, the *ṛṣi* is inspired to "see" and express the mystery behind all visible reality. Objective natural science never found *devas* nor will it find God in the physical universe. It requires the sensibilities of a *kavi,* poet and prophet, to discover divine reality.

Granting that the hymns of the *Ṛgveda* in their present form are an ancient revision of a still more ancient text[4] and keeping in mind what has already been said about the evolutionary character of Vedic mythology, it is quite reasonable that at different stages different *devas* were at the center of Vedic religion. Our present Veda text is dominated by Indra, a rather late arrival in Vedic religion who is difficult to circumscribe because he assumes at least three different roles: Indra the cosmic power, Indra the warlike leader of the Āryans, and Indra the ancient mythical dragon-killing hero.[5] Popular books on Indian religion still carry the nineteenth century cliché of Indra as the "personification of the rain storm" or the "weather god." Quite apart from the misunderstanding of the nature of a *deva* we must also reject this idea, because "most of the descriptions of Indra are centered round the war with, and subsequent victory over, Vṛtra. A proper understanding of this point, would, therefore, serve as an adequate starting point for a critical study of Indra's personality and character."[6] A study of this myth reveals that Indra, contradictory as many of his single features may be, is the manifestation of the saving divine power defeating the opposing demonic power.[7]

Of the more than 1000 hymns in the *Ṛgveda*,[8] about a quarter are addressed to Indra alone. While not dealing exhaustively with all the questions surrounding the nature of God Indra, an impression of the nature of Vedic devotion to Indra can be achieved by quoting one of them expressing Indra's greatness. The titles given to Indra in this hymn—*maghavān, mahāvīra, deva eka, rāja,* etc.—are essential attributes of the High God, titles that are given to the Savior God in later developments of Indian religion. The hymns indeed allude to historical events and historic personalities when describing the personality of Indra, but the sum total of attributes given to him is more than just the apotheosis of a warrior hero. That the slaying of Vṛtra by Indra is more than the victory of a warrior over his enemy seems to suggest itself to us, when we read that the effect was that Indra "raised the Sun for all to see."

It is the work of the High God to "chase away the humbled brood of demons," to "encompass the worlds from all sides," and to "divide day and night." It is the High God alone "before whom even the Heaven and Earth bow down," "without whose help our people never conquer," who is "the bestower of food and wealth," "man's helper from old, not disappointing hope, friend of our friends, rich in mighty deeds." Indra's authority as High God is finally established through his victory over the demon, whom no human being would be able to defeat. Only if Indra is understood as a symbol and manifestation of the High God do the attributes given to him make sense, especially since the same attributes are given to other *devas*, the same deeds are ascribed to Agni, to Soma, to Varuṇa and others. "They call him Indra, Mitra, Varuṇa, Agni and he is heavenly-winged Garutman. To what is One, sages give many a title."[9] Indra is only one of the names given to the Savior God. The Supreme was first, and only under specific circumstances did he receive the name of Indra. The Supreme is nameless; men give names to him, variously describing him in categories taken from cosmic events, from history, or from their own experience.

> He, who as soon as he was born became the first among the high-souled *devas*, their protector on acount of his power and might, he who made the worlds tremble before his breath on account of his valour, he, O men, is Indra!
>
> He who fixed fast and firm the earth that staggered, and set at rest the agitated mountains, who measured out the air's wide middle region and gave the heaven support, he, O men, is Indra!
>
> Who slew the dragon, freed the seven rivers and drove the cattle forth from Vala's cave, who generated fire between two stones, the spoiler in warriors' battle, he, O men, is Indra!
>
> By whom the universe was made to tremble, who chased away the defeated host of dark-skins, and like a gambler gathering his winnings, seized the foe's riches, he, O men, is Indra!
>
> Of him the terrible, they ask: Where is he? They also say: He is not. He sweeps away like birds, the enemies' possessions. Have faith in him, for he, O men, is Indra.
>
> Inciter to action of the poor and humble, of the priest and the suppliant singer, fair-faced he gives his favours to the one who pressed Soma between two stones, he, O men, is Indra!
>
> He under whose supreme control are horses, all chariots, the villages and cattle, he who gave being to sun and dawn, who leads the water, he, O men, is Indra!
>
> To whom two armies cry in close encounter, both enemies, the stronger and the weaker, whom two invoke upon one chariot mounted, each for himself, he, O men, is Indra.
>
> Without whose help our people never conquer, whom, battling, they invoke to give them succour, who became the universe's likeness, who shook the unmovable [mountains], he, O men, is Indra.
>
> He who struck before they knew the danger, with his weapon many a sinner, who does not give pardon to one who provokes him, who slays the *dasyu*, he, O men, is Indra.
>
> Even the Heaven and the Earth bow down before him, before his breath the mountains tremble. Known as the Soma-drinker, armed with thunder, who wields the bolt, he, O men, is Indra![10]

Indra emerges as the power, which increases even more through the sacrifice and the *mantras.* The *devas* themselves depend on the mortals, religion is a two-way street to power!

Next to Indra, Agni is the *deva* most often addressed in the Vedic hymns. He is indispensable in the all-important business of sacrifice! The very first hymn of the *Ṛgveda Saṁhitā* and some two hundred more are addressed to him. "I praise Agni, the *purohit* [priest], the divine *ṛtvik* [another class of Vedic priests], the *hotar* [a third class of Vedic priests], lavisher of wealth. Worthy is Agni to be praised by the living as by the ancient *ṛṣis*. He shall conduct the *devas* to this place. Through Agni man obtains wealth."[11]

Agni-fire is the medium through which the material gift of the sacrifice is transformed into the spiritual substance of which the gods can partake and from which they draw their strength!

One of the most impressive and beautiful hymns is addressed to Savitṛ, the "inspirer," sun, light, intelligence, the luster of beauty.

> Agni I first invoke for prosperity, I call on Mitra and Varuṇa to come to help, I call on night who gives rest to all moving life, I call on Savitṛ, the divine helper. Throughout the dusky firmament advancing, laying to rest the mortal and the immortal, borne in his golden chariot he cometh, the divine Savitṛ who looks upon every creature. The *deva* moves by the upward path, the downward, with two bright bays, adorable he journeys. Savitṛ comes, the helper from afar, and chases away all distress and sorrow.[12]

Heaven and Earth are hymned as *devas*. Aditi, "Mother Earth", is also mentioned separately. The Maruts, the storm winds, are a group of *devas* frequently mentioned. Rivers and waters appear as divinities. The *soma* juice and the *kuśa* grass, both indispensable for the sacrifice, are variously referred to as *devas*.

The *devas* are not the moral ideals for men to follow nor are they considered as lawgivers. The hymns speak of *ṛta*, "the law," as independent of the *devas*, standing apart and above them as an impersonal and infallibly effective power. The word *ṛta* is connected with *ṛtu*, the seasons, the regular round of spring, summer, rain, autumn, and winter. Beyond that we can understand *ṛta* as the principle of order behind all things and events. In a way, *ṛta* foreshadows both the later *karman* and *brahman*. Several *devas*, especially Mitra and Varuṇa, are invoked as the guardians of *ṛta* but never as its creators. Both are also thought to reward good and punish evil.[13]

The fact that our Western culture has lost the ability to appreciate nature as a manifestation of the divine makes many of us unable to appreciate Vedic *deva* worship without using categories drawn from a mechanized world. It is not just a superstitious remnant if today Hindus offer praises and prayers to the rising sun at the time of their morning prayer. Many a modern Indian among those sun worshippers knows about the physical properties of the sun, its surface temperature, and its chemical composition. Worship is not addressed to the astronomical body, not to a symbolic idea, but to the *sūrya-deva*, the metaphysical reality through which an aspect of the supreme reality becomes relevant for people. Quite frequently, one

15. Kubera, Khajurāho 12th ct.

may observe a pious person worshipfully saluting the electric light after switching it on in the evening. Indian peasants regard the cow as the seat of many *devas* and worship it; factory workers offer worship to their machines on certain days, to the *deva* of technology by whose operations they live. They may grasp in their own way what many of us have not yet quite understood—that all things, whether made by humans or not, manifest a power that is beyond humans.

UPANIṢADIC *BRAHMAN* AND PURĀNIC *ĪŚVARA*

In a dialogue in the *Bṛhadāraṇyaka-Upaniṣad*, Yājñavalkya is asked the crucial question, *kati devāḥ*, How many are the *devas*? His first answer is a quotation from a Vedic text, "Three hundred and three and three thousand and three." Pressed on, he reduces the number first to thirty-three, then to six, then to three, to two, to one and a half and finally to one. Asked Which is the one *deva*? he answers, "The *prāṇa* [breath, life]. The Brahman. He is called *tyat* [that]."[14]

Though the *devas* still figure in sacrificial practice and religious debate, the question Who is God? is answered here in terms that have remained the Hindu answer ever since. *Brahman*, untranslatable, identified with the revealed word uttered by the Brahmins, with the soul of everything, with the creator and maintainer of the world, with the inner principle of the universe—*brahman* becomes the term around which the loftiest religious speculation has revolved for thousands of years, and it is still the term used to designate the supreme being. *Brahman* has always retained an aura of the not quite concrete, the spiritual, that escaped the grasp of the ordinary worshipper. The terms used to express the Supreme in its concreteness are equally old: *īśa* or *īśvara*, the lord, or *bhagavān*, the Exalted One, are titles given to the Supreme Being by Hindus even now. The name associated with this title now becomes rather crucial. Whereas the Vedic *ṛṣi* was casual in associating names with the title *deva*, because a plurality of *devas* seemed quite natural and even necessary to grasp different facets of the nameless one, to the new theologians a plurality of Lords seems intrinsically impossible and they insist that the One, with whom they associate the title *īśvara* or *bhagavān*, is the only One, as *Brahman* is by necessity one only, ultimately identical with the Lord.

The exclusive association of the title *Lord* with one particular name has led to the development of mutually exclusive religions whose worship and mythology centred around the One God, dismissing in this process the gods of the others as minor beings. Later attempts to unify different sects, at least theoretically, and to consider their rival Lords as equal sharers of one divine power in the *trimūrti* have sometimes led to wrong conclusions among Western students of Hinduism. Hindu texts do indeed speak of the triad of Brahmā as creator, Viṣṇu as preserver, and Śiva as destroyer, fulfilling the functions of the One God, but all those texts belong to one of the traditions in which the Supreme is identical with one of those names and the three separate names are but different aspects of the same being.[15] Some of the famous *trimūrtis* are quite clearly recognizable as artistic expressions of different modalities of one and the same *īśvara.*[16]

Brahmā, the first of the three, has no following worth mentioning today; only a few temples in India offer worship to him. Several sectarian accounts try to explain why he has receded into obscurity. According to an ancient Śaivite myth he was born with five heads. When he became interested in Pārvatī, the wife of Śiva, the latter chopped off one of Brahmā's heads. Since that time he has been shown with only four heads. In his four hands, he carries the Vedas, a water-vessel, a ladle, and a *mālā.* In the *Mahābhārata,* he is addressed as *pitāmahā,* the grandfather, who instructs the *ṛṣis* on religious matters. In Vaiṣṇava mythology, he has the role of the demiurge: enthroned on the lotus that grows out from Viṣṇu's navel, he shapes the world. The Śaivite tale that Brahmā was deprived of worship because of a lie may be understood as blackmail of the Brahmins, whose special Lord he must have been and who did not recognize the Śaivites as orthodox.[17]

Within the present-day practice of the *pañcāyatanapūjā* among non-sectarian Hindus, Sūrya, Śiva, Viṣṇu, Devī, and Gaṇeśa are worshipped. Sūrya (Figure 8.1) is possibly the most Vedic of the five; we find his worship already in the *Ṛgveda,* under the title of Sāvitrī. As the source of life, light, and warmth, he is the natural "Lord of creation." He is also the source of inner enlightenment, as the famous *Gāyatrīmantra* suggests.[18] Purāṇic accounts associate Manu, the ancestor of humankind, and Yama and Yamī, the god and goddess of the netherworlds and death, with Sūrya as his children.[19] The same Purāṇa has given him four wives: *samjñā* (knowledge), *rājñī* (splendor), *prabhā* (light), and *chāyā* (shade). At certain times, there had been a strong movement of worshippers of Sūrya as Lord, as evidenced by Sūrya temples and *Saura-purāṇas.*[20]

Śiva figures as the One God and the Lord for many millions of Hindus today. Śaivism may indeed be the most ancient of India's religions. Several soapstone seals found in excavated sites of the Indus civilization have been interpreted as part of the Śaivite tradition, depicting Śiva Paśupati (the Lord of the animals), Śiva Trimukha (the three-faced Śiva), and Śiva Mahāyogi (Śiva the ascetic).[21] Numerous *liṅgas* have been found in these sites, too, a further link with present-day Śaivism, in which the *liṅga* is the main object of worship.[22]

Viṣṇu

Garuḍa

Durgā

Sūrya

Figure 8.1 Some Hindu *devas*

A second important source for the development of Śaivism is the ancient Draviḍa culture. The name *Śiva*, the benevolent or gracious one, may be but a Sanskritization of an old Tamil name, *Śivan*, the red one.[23] The mythology and basic philosophy of Śaivism seems to have grown in the Draviḍa country; Tamilnādu is still the center of Śaivism.

Tribal religions may also have had their share in the development of Śaivism. According to various scholars, the Śibi in northwest Punjab show in their very name an association with Śaivism.[24] Some of the Austric and proto-Australoid tribes in northeastern India are thought to have been responsible for the development of *liṅga* worship; the very word *liṅga* is thought to derive from Mon-Khmer languages.[25]

Vedic religion, in which the numerous fearsome Rudras played a great role, may have added another dimension to Śiva worship. Despite his name, his prominent feature is wrath, and terror and destruction are associated with him much more prominently than grace. One of the most interesting texts, the *Śatarudrīya* of the *Yajurveda*, uses titles and epithets for Śiva that are still in common use. He is called *Nīlakaṇṭha*, the blue-throated;[26] *Paśupati*, the lord of the animals; *Śārva; Bhava;* and *Śobhya.* His divinity is affirmed when he is described as the one who stretched out the earth, as the one who is immanent in places and objects, in stones, plants, and animals. Also the paradoxical ascription of contradictory attributes is used: after being praised as the great lord of all beings, he is called cheat and Lord of thieves, a dwarf and a giant, fierce and terrible, and the source of happiness and delight.

The main sources of Śaivism, however, are found in later texts, which are considered as revelations by the followers of Śiva. The *Śvetāśvatara Upaniṣad* has for Śaivas the same importance as the better known *Bhagavad-gītā* has for the Vaiṣṇavas. Then there are several *Śaiva-Purāṇas* and *Śaiva-Āgamas* as well as Śaivite sections in the *Mahābhārata.* The *Svetāśva-tara Upaniṣad* quite openly identifies *Brahman* with Śiva when it says, "The immortal and imperishable Hara exercises complete control over the perishable *prakṛti* and the powerless *jīva:* this radiant Hara is the One Alone."[27]

The *Rāmāyaṇa* contains some very old versions of Śiva myths. The *Mahābhārata* has a catalogue of 1000 names of Śiva, a litany that still occupies a central place in Śaivite devotion. It mentions all the salvific deeds of Śiva, from whom most of his popular names are derived; he is identified with the sun; he is called the artificer of the universe, the Master and Lord of all creatures. He gives boons, he destroys and creates again, he smites and heals. He is the *Maheśvara*, the Great Lord.[28] Some of the great myths of Śiva found in the *Purāṇas* still stand in the center of Śaivite liturgy and theology.

The worshippers of *Bhairava*, the fearsome form of Śiva, who are quite numerous in Mahārāṣṭra, derive their motivation from the myth of Dakṣa. By Śiva's forceful intervention in the form of *Bhairava*, Dakṣa was converted from being an enemy of Śiva into a devotee, reciting with his goat head the thousand names in praise of Śiva.[29]

Śaiva-siddhāntins, a large group of sophisticated Śiva worshippers in South India, see in *Śiva Nīlakaṇṭha* the most convincing proof of God's love for humankind. According to the myth, Śiva was prepared to drink the poison that threatened to destroy all life, when *devas* and *asuras* churned the Ocean of Milk to obtain *amṛta*, the nectar of immortality. The poison was so powerful that it left a blue stain on Śiva's throat; for the pious, the stain is the sign of Śiva's self-sacrificing love and vicarious suffering.[30]

The most celebrated Śiva motif is that of the *Naṭarāja*, the King of the Dance. The Purāṇas mention a *taṇḍava*, a dance of world destruction, and a *līlā*, the dance of the enamoured Śiva. A South Indian text records the following details of the myth. Followers of the orthodox Brahmin school of Mīmāṁsā tried to destroy Śiva by creating in succession a fierce tiger, a serpent, and an elephant, whom Śiva killed. Finally, they sent the embodiment of evil, in the form of the dwarf *muyalahan* to overthrow Śiva, but Śiva began his cosmic dance, subduing the dwarf and thereby liberating the world.

Śiva Naṭarāja has been immortalized in this pose in countless beautiful sculptures, especially in South India. Śaivite theology has invested each and every detail of this image with meaning. Thus, it symbolizes for the pious the divine activities of God: "Creation arises from the drum, protection proceeds from the hand of hope, from fire proceeds destruction, from the foot that is planted upon *muyalahan* proceeds the destruction of evil, the foot held aloft gives deliverance."[31] His smile shows his uninvolved transcendence, the three eyes are interpreted either as sun, moon, and fire or as the three powers of Śiva: will, knowledge, and action. The garland of skulls around his neck identifies him as time and the death of all beings. The single skull on his chest is that of Brahmā, the creator of the world—all beings are mortal, only Śiva is eternal.[32]

Śiva also appears in twenty-eight *avatāras*, said to be the revealers of the twenty-eight *Śaiva Āgamas*, the scriptures held sacred by the Śaivites. Quite often one finds representations of Śiva with five heads. The famous *Śivāṣṭamūrti* combines eight forms of Śiva. Those combinations may be the reflection of amalgamations of individual local or tribal cults that were unified into Śaivism in historical times. A frequent representation shows *Śiva ardhanārī*, half man-half woman in one figure, symbolizing the inseparable unity of Śiva and Śakti.[33]

Śiva's abode and paradise is *Kailāsa*, open to all who worship Śiva, irrespective of caste or sex.[34] *Śaivapurāṇas* abound in descriptions of hells and the means to escape from them. The famous *mṛtyuñjayakavacam*,[35] the armor giving victory over death, is believed to have been provided by Śiva himself to his devotees so that they might overcome the fear of death.

The most important manifestation of Śiva, his presence and the object of worship for his devotees, is the *liṅga*. This is the only "image" of Śiva, the formless absolute Being, to be found in the innermost sanctuary of a Śiva temple. The most ancient *liṅga* that still receives public worship is found in Guḍimally, South India, and dates from the second century B.C.E. Its phallic origin is established beyond doubt, but it also can be safely said that it does not evoke any phallic associations in the minds of the worshippers. Many local myths describe the Śiva *liṅgodbhava*, Śiva's appearance from within an icon of this kind. The twelve famous *Jyotirliṅgas*, liṅgas made of light, each the center of a pilgrimage, are said to have come into existence by themselves, without human hand, and thus manifest special potency. Many miraculous events are reported from those places.[36] An ancient custom associated with Śaivism is wearing a garland of *rudrākṣa* beads, used for *Śiva-japa*, the repetition of the bliss-giving name of Śiva, and a sign of belonging to Śiva. Also numerous Śaivites smear their bodies with white ashes; Śiva is said to have a white body!

One of the great Śiva centers is Cidāmbaram, a town not far from Madras. For the devotees, it is the very center of the world. In its thousand-pillared hall, daily festivals are arranged for the worship of Śiva, splendid and awesome spectacles. In Cidāmbaram, Śiva is said to dance his cosmic drama—but, as the Śiva mystics say: Cidāmbaram is everywhere! Thus, speaks Tirunāvukkaraśu Swāmi: "He is difficult to find, but he lives in the heart of the good. He is the innermost secret of the scriptures, inscrutable and unrecognized. He is honey and milk and the bright light. He is the king of the gods, within Viṣṇu and Brahmā, in flame and wind, in the roaring seas and in the towering mountains."[37]

In front of Śiva temples, one usually finds the image of *nandi*, a bull, quite often of huge proportions. The bull is Śiva's mount, associated with Śiva from time immemorial. This again may be one of the remnants of a formerly independent animal worship that became part of Śaivism.

Numerically, Viṣṇu commands the largest following. Vaiṣṇavas are split into numerous sects and schools of thought.

Viṣṇu is one of the *devas* of the *Ṛgveda;* certain passages in the *Brāhmaṇas* suggest that Viṣṇu is of solar origin.[38] But here, too, the name Viṣṇu, translated as the "all-pervading one," may be only a Sanskritization of an older Dravidian name (*viñ*, "the blue sky"), an opinion confirmed by the tradition, even now, of always painting Viṣṇu a dark blue color.[39]

The totemism of tribal cults may have led to the development of the

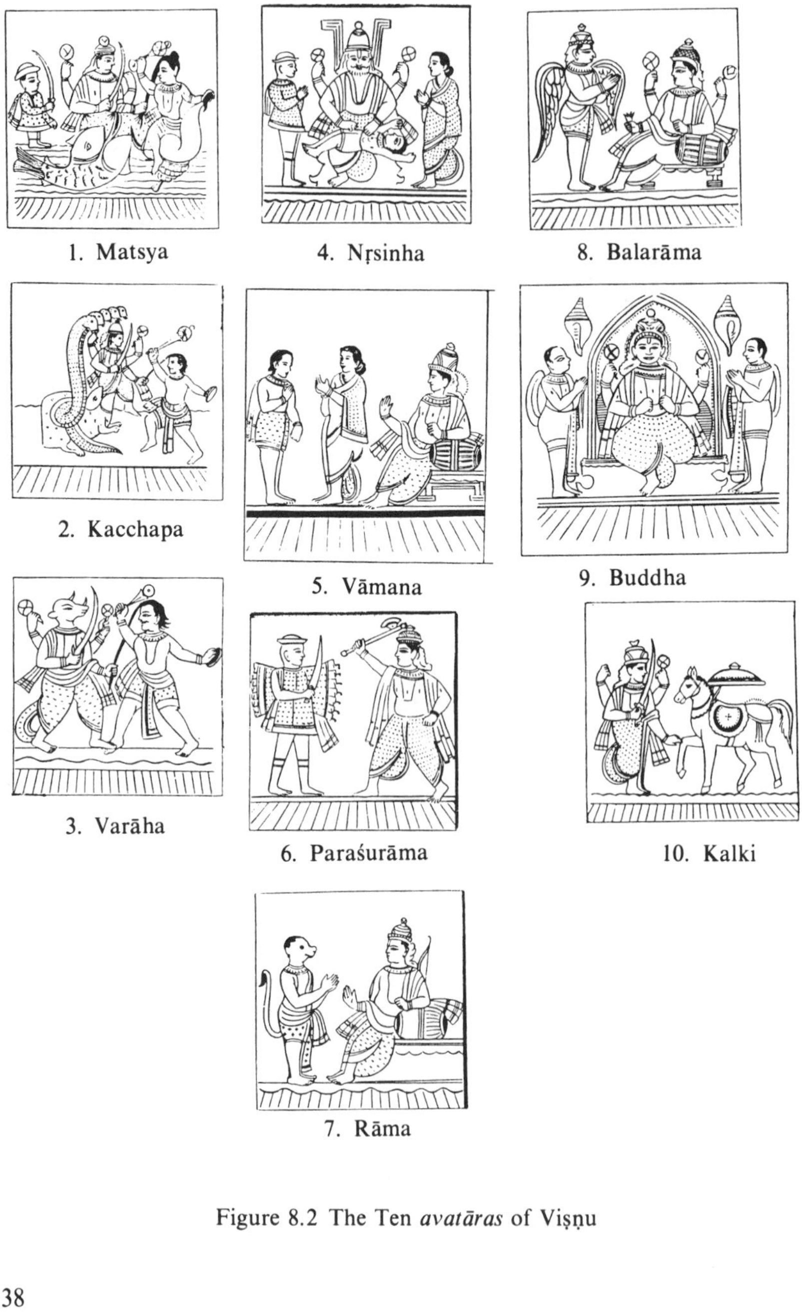

Figure 8.2 The Ten *avatāras* of Viṣṇu

doctrine of the *avatāras*, the descents of Viṣṇu (Figure 8.2), as may also the Buddhist teaching of the *bodhisattvas*, appearing at different ages. The *Nārāyaṇa* and the *Vāsudeva Kṛṣṇa* cult merged into Vaiṣṇavism in pre-Christian times and gave it perhaps the most powerful stimulus for further development. It seems fairly certain that the basis for the latter was a historical Kṛṣṇa, a hero from the Vṛṣṇi clan of the Yādava tribe in and around Mathurā, one of the oldest cities of India. Pāṇini mentions "*bhakti* to Vasudeva," and we have the testimony of Megasthenes that Kṛṣṇa worship was established already in the fourth century B.C.E. in that region. Possibly, this Kṛṣṇa is also the founder of Bhāgavatism, which found its literary expression in some of the favorite scriptures of the Hindus, especially the *Bhāgavata Purāṇa.*

The Viṣṇu tradition is perhaps the most typical of all the forms of Hinduism and the greatest books of Indian literature reflect it strongly. The *Mahābhārata* is primarily a Vaiṣṇava book; the *Rāmāyaṇa* tells of Rāma, the *avatāra* of Viṣṇu. One of the most ancient of the Purāṇas is the *Viṣṇu Purāṇa*, and the numerous *Vaiṣṇava Saṁhitās* have been the models on which the sectarian books of other religions have been based. The most popular book of the entire Hindu literature, the *Bhagavadgītā*, is a Kṛṣṇa scripture. Throughout the ages, countless inspired devotees of Viṣṇu have composed an incomparable store of *bhakti* hymns that live in the literally incessant *bhajans* and *kīrtans* throughout India even today.[40] *Viṣṇu-bhakti* knows all shades of love, from the respectful devotion of servants to masters through the affectionate relationship between parent and child to the passionate eroticism of Kṛṣṇa and Rādhā.

The most important Viṣṇu-myth is that of *Viṣṇu trivikrama.* Viṣṇu, appearing as a small boy at the feet of Bali, the ruler of the earth, asks for as much land as he can cover with three strides. His first stride conquers the earth, his second the sky, and for the third step Bali offers his own head as support. In this way, he established himself as the ruler of the world.

In Vaiṣṇava mythology, the myths connected with the *avatāras* occupy the foremost place both in the imagination of the people and in the scriptures.[41] Besides the ten most common ones—Matsya, Kūrma, Varāha, Vāmana, Nārasinha, Paraśurāma, Rāmacandra, Kṛṣṇa, Balarāma, and Kalki, who will come at the end of the *Kali-yuga*—some scriptures list a score of others, including Buddha and Kapila, for example. Rāma and Kṛṣṇa enjoy particular favor and an immense literature has grown around them. Ayodhyā and Mathurā-Vṛndāvana are *the* centers of pilgrimage, where their presence is still alive in many ways. The images of Viṣṇu are of particular importance; they are the real and physical presence of the god who has the earth and the individual souls as his body. Viṣṇu, too, is praised by his devotees in a litany of thousand names, which glorify his mythical exploits and enumerate his divine qualities.[42] *Hari* is the most common name under which he is invoked. *Nārāyaṇa, Keśava, Puruṣottama* are other favorite names that are not only signs of identification but also powerful spells in themselves.

Ekanāṭha, a sixteenth century Mahratta poet, sings:

> How sweet is the curdling of liquid *ghī.* So blissful is the seeker, when the hidden one reveals his form. Dark is he, dark is the totally unknown and locked is the way to thoughts and words: the scriptures are silent, the Vedas do not utter a word. Not so the revealed one. How bright! How near! Our thirst is quenched if only he appears, who is so dear to our heart. The ever perfect one, eternal bliss, being and thought—see, it is Govinda, source of ecstasy and rapture. Strength, courage, honour and exalted spirit—see, we witness our God sharing all this. If I but catch a glimpse of God, my eye-sight is restored. I have escaped the net of life, the guilt of my senses is cancelled. In the light of the lamp all hidden things are made apparent—so it is when I think of my God; the God from faraway is here![43]

Viṣṇu's heaven is called *Vaikuṇṭha;* but the various subdivisions of Vaiṣṇavism have also introduced new heavens as, for example, Kṛṣṇa's celestial Vṛndābana or Goloka and Rāma's heavenly Ayodhyā. Viṣṇu's *vahana* is the winged Garuḍa; a special landing post is available for him in South Indian temples.

Usually Śiva and Viṣṇu are represented together with their wives, Pārvatī and Śrī, around whom the *Purāṇas* have also woven a rich mythology. In Śāktism, however, it is the Goddess who assumes the role of the Supreme Being, whether depicted without a male consort or as superior to him.

Śakti means "power" personified in the Goddess, the Divine Mother to whom are ascribed all the functions that Viṣṇu has for the Vaiṣṇavas or Śiva for the Śaivas: creation, maintenance and destruction of the world, illusion and liberation. The female terracotta figures found in many sites of the Indus civilization so much resemble the *devī*-images kept in the homes of today's Indian villages that one may safely infer that they bear witness to a cult of the goddess. The Indus cvilization again may be considered part of a larger culture, spreading from the Mediterranean in the west to Central India in the east, in which the Great Mother was the creator; the lady of humans, beasts, and plants; the liberator; and the symbol of transcendent spiritual transformation.[44] The very name *Umā*, as well as her association with a mountain and the lion, seems to connect her with Babylonia, Accad, and the Dravidian cultures.[45] Another important current of Devī religion comes from indigenous village cults, "the

1. Brāhmī 2. Māheśvarī 3. Kaumārī

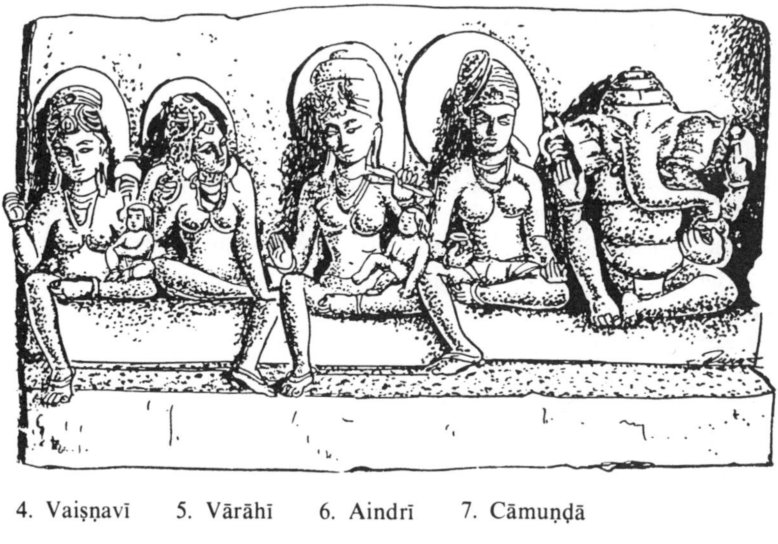

4. Vaiṣṇavī 5. Vārāhī 6. Aindrī 7. Cāmuṇḍā

Figure 8.3 The Seven Mothers

most ancient form of Indian religion."[46] The Goddess is implored to drive away the evil spirits that cause diseases and asked to help grow vegetables.

Many ancient Indian (non-*āryan*) tribes also had goddesses, whose worship coalesced in the course of time with that of the Great Mother. Figure 8.3. shows some of these goddesses. The forms of worship practiced by the tribes—bloody, including human, sacrifices—are still associated with Devī worship. Very often the worship of deceased women of a village merges with the worship of the Great Mother, a process of "making religion" that can still be observed in Indian villages. Many of the names of the Goddess, found in the litany of thousand names, are probably the names of these local village goddesses. Also many of her functions are taken unmistakably from village religion.

Generally, the Āryans must have been hostile toward the cult of the Mother, but in the *Mahābhārata* we find Durgā established as a war goddess, superseding Indra in this function.[47] The goddess of war also played a major role in Tamiḷnādu.[48] There are, no doubt, also Vedic elements in Devī religion: the worship of the Earth (*pṛthvī*) as a goddess for instance, or the worship of *Vāk*, the Word, as pointed out. But, it is in the *Purāṇas* and *Tantras*, which perhaps already show influences from Inner Asia, that Śāktism becomes fully developed in its mythology and cult. In Śāktism, *prakṛti* or *māyā* becomes the active principle of the universe, both as a metaphysical principle and a concrete personality. The most important center of Śakti-worship was and still is Kāmarūpa in today's Assam. Also, the great rivers of India, principally the Gaṅgā and the Yamunā, have been worshipped as goddesses since ancient times.[49] The most important Devī myth, her killing of *mahiṣāsura*, the embodiment of evil in a buffalo form, is the focus of the immensely popular *Durgā-pūjā* celebrations, which are still held in Bengal. Devī is represented figuratively in many forms, particular depictions usually alluding to one of her mythological exploits. A peculiar feature of Tantricism, however, are the *yantras*, symbolic diagrams considered by Śāktas to be representations of Devī.[50]

Śiva mythology associates Gaṇeśa, another popular deity, with Śiva's family.[51] But it seems that the elephant-headed, pot-bellied patron-god of businessmen and scholars (Figure 8.4) comes from an older stratum of religion, in which animal worship was predominant. This may also be the case with Hanuman, the monkey god, who in the *Rāmāyaṇa* is made the chief ally of Rāma and thus comes to be associated with Viṣṇu worship. The genealogies and family trees of the main deities so frequent in the Purāṇas are attempts, not always successful, to coordinate the various popular deities and to make them appear, if not as manifestations of the one God, then at least as his children or servants.[52]

God is not dead in India and not a mere memory of the past. There are

Pārvatī

Gaṇapati

Kārtikeya

Sarasvatī

Figure 8.4 Śiva's Family

numerous "living gods" and "incarnations," everywhere in India today. Some of them claim to continue the ancient line of Viṣṇu, Śiva, or Devī *avatāras*, while others simply assume that they are the Supreme in a human body. It is not uncommon in India to get an invitation "to meet God the Father in person," to listen to the latest revelation through an *avatāra* of God, or to be confronted by someone who utters the word of God in the first person singular.

Many Hindu homes are lavishly decorated with color prints of a great many Hindu gods and goddesses, often joined by the gods and goddesses of other religions and the pictures of contemporary heroes. Thus, side by side with Śiva, Viṣṇu, and Devī one can see Jesus and Zoroaster, Gautama Buddha and Jīna Mahavīra, Mahātmā Gāndhī and Jawaharlal Nehru, and many others. But, if questioned about the many gods, even illiterate villagers will answer: *bhagvān ek hai*, the Lord is One. They may not be able to figure out in theological terms how the many gods and the One God hang together and they may not be sure about the hierarchy among the many manifestations, but they know that ultimately there is only One and that the many somehow merge into the One.

Hindu theology has many ways of explaining the unity of *Brahman* in the diversity of *iṣṭadevatās:* different psychological needs of people must be satisfied differently, local traditions and specific revelations must be accommodated, the ineffable can only be predicated in, quite literally, thousands of forms. Among the *sahasranāmas*, the litanies of thousand names that are recited in honor of each of the great gods, the overlap is considerable: each one would be named creator, preserver, destroyer of the universe; each one would be called Truth,[53] Grace, and Deliverance. Each one, in the end, is the same: One.[54]

Part II

Trimārga: The Three Hindu Paths To Liberation

One of the oldest, most popular and most important divisions of Hinduism is into the three paths: *karmamārga*, the path of works; *jñānamārga*, the path of knowledge; and *bhaktimārga*, the path of loving devotion. Some conceive of these as representing a kind of evolution of Hinduism, the sequence depending on which of the paths one considers the highest.

While it is a historically established fact that the prevalence and full recognition of *bhaktimārga* took place after that of *jñānamārga* and that Vedic religion placed a major emphasis on *karma* or sacrificial ritual, the three paths coexisted for a long time, and they mix and merge at many points. The practice of the average Hindu contains elements of all of them with particular emphasis given to one according to personal preference.

The idea of "religion" as a "path" is found in other cultures, too, but the idea of a plurality of equivalent paths is fairly unique to Hinduism. True, there is also rivalry between adherents of different Hindu paths and some suggest that only one of them is the true path, the others being lower or incomplete, but the general understanding is that of equally valid options.

Within each *mārga*, the latitude varies. *Karmamārga* is a discipline that has to be followed fairly uniformly, allowing only for minor local variants. *Jñānamārga* comes in various shapes, the *Upaniṣads* specify thirty-two different *vidyās*. However, the need to have a teacher and the requirement of absolute loyalty toward the guru restrict individual choices once a guru has been selected. *Bhaktimārga* leaves personal choices widely open. Not only can one choose one's *īṣṭadevatā* and call oneself a devotee of Viṣṇu, Śiva, Devī, or another *deva*, within each sect one can also choose a variety of interpretations and practices. It is especially the *bhaktimārga* that constantly brings forth new developments and movements.

In spite of what has been said about the options among and within the different paths, Hindu religion is highly structured and tends to embrace a person's entire life with its regulations. Hinduism is basically very conservative, and many of the regulations going back to Vedic times are still effective in shaping the daily routine of millions of Hindus. Some of this routine is described in Chapter 9, "The Path of Works: *Karmamārga*." Hinduism, like all traditional religions, was always aware of the ethical dimension of life and that the moral universe is fragile and in need not only of being preserved but also of being constantly restored. Notions of guilt and sin play a great role in Hinduism, and devices for righting wrongs and atoning for sins occupy a large place in the life of many Hindus. Rites of passage are fairly universal. Hinduism has designed elaborate rituals in its *saṁskāras* not only to accompany its members into the next stage of life but also to augment their spiritual powers and to ensure personal fulfillment.

More than anything else, *jñānamārga*, the path of knowledge, attracts non-Hindus, who admire the deep wisdom and spiritual insights of the Hindu sages. The *Upaniṣads* and the literature based on them deal with human universals, the discovery of one's true self and the soul of the world, liberating knowledge and the final emancipation.

While the *karmamārga* presupposes high-caste standing, and the *jñānamārga* is largely for an intellectual elite, the *bhaktimārga*, the path of loving devotion, has universal appeal. It promises salvation and heaven also to low-caste people, to women and children, and even to animals. Great waves of God love have swept over India periodically and have left behind large congregations of devotees, an enormous treasure of inspired poetry, thousands of beautiful temples, and millions of images in which the deities are physically present to their worshippers. Only some moments of this history of God intoxication can be recalled in the chapters on Viṣṇu, Śiva, and Devī; only a small amount of literature can be referred to; and only very inadequately can the fervor be described that animates Hindus who celebrate the great feasts in honor of their deities in the major centers of devotion. Even though, in the course of the last 3000 or more years, all of India has come under the influence first of Vedic and then Purāṇic and Tāntric Hinduism and even though all regions of India have preserved some of their own local traditions in temple architecture, festivals, and songs, one region stands out for its distinct culture and its independent tradition: Tamiḷnādu, the land of the Tamils in South India. Tamil belongs to a family of languages totally different from Sanskrit and the other North-

Indian languages. Tamilians claim that both their language and their culture are older than that of the North. There is no doubt that, in spite of the extensive Sanskritization that took place and that resulted in most of the Tamils today being Śaivites or Vaiṣṇavas, recognizing the same sacred books and traditions as the rest of India, Dravidian elements are strong and distinctive enough to warrant a special chapter on the gods of the Tamils. This, too, of course, is an incomplete sketch of a rich and colorful tradition within Hinduism. It may serve as a first introduction to a large subject and as a further reminder that, besides its Vedic and Sanskritic heritage, traditional Hinduism has important non-Vedic and non-Sanskritic components.

9. The Path of Works: *Karmamārga*

In ancient days the Lord of creatures created men along with sacrifice and said: "By this shall you bring forth and this shall be unto you that which will yield the milk of your desires."

—Bhagavadgītā *III, 10*

IN FEBRUARY 1962, Indian newspapers carried numerous articles describing measures to meet a predicted *aṣṭāgraha*, an astronomical conjunction of earth, sun, moon, and five planets. The astrologers were unanimous in considering it an extremely evil omen, possibly the harbinger of the end of the world. Some journalists were serious; others tried to joke a little; none dared to call the whole thing a humbug. Despite the fact that, astronomically speaking, the *aṣṭāgraha* was not quite accurate, millions of Hindus were frankly worried, expecting a ghastly catastrophe. Many sold all their belongings and went to Prayāga, Kāśī, or some other holy place, from which one goes directly to heaven at the time of death or one can attain *mokṣa.* The rich engaged thousands of paṇḍits and Brahmins to organize Vedic *yajñas* that would go on for weeks, reciting millions of Vedic *mantras.* The dreaded event passed without a major disaster. What had happened? The world had been saved through the creation of the auspicious *karma* produced in the ritual appropriate for the occasion.

Ritual is one of the most prominent and most important features of Hinduism, and it has two main sources: the Vedic and the Āgamic traditions.[1] For the sake of a more methodical presentation a separate treatment of Vedic ritual, as it emerges from the classical texts, will be given here before describing other forms that are more popular today. The rationale of both of these forms of ritual, as expressed in the Pūrva-Mīmāṁsā system and the Āgamic treatises is quite different, too, as shall be seen.

THE VEDIC WAY TO HEAVEN

Quite early in the Veda, the distinction was drawn between the *karmakāṇḍa* and the *jñānakāṇḍa*, the part dealing with "works" and the part dealing with "knowledge," different not only in their contents but also in their ultimate aims. The aim of the *karmakāṇḍa* lies within *triloka*, the tripartite universe of heaven, earth, and netherworlds. It promises bliss and wealth and a sojourn in *svarga*, a heaven with earthly pleasure, as the highest goal after death. *Jñānakāṇḍa* is not interested in things of this earth nor those in heaven; it wants insight into, and communion with, a reality that is nonsensual and not transient, *Brahman*. It is meant for those who have given up all worldly liabilities, with interests that go beyond spouse and children, house and property, business and entertainment. The householders living within their family circle had to choose *karmamārga* to secure what they needed and wished for and also to conform to the social pattern established upon a firm basis of ritual. Later theorists try to demonstrate that the two elements, the life of the householder and the life of the ascetic, constituted the even balance of an ideal social order. In reality, there was and is considerable friction and competition between the two. Some texts praise the householder, who provides nourishment for all, and other texts speak of the spiritual merit that the whole society derives from the *saṁnyāsins*' efforts; but there is also ample evidence of householders' polemics against *saṁnyāsa*, which was considered by many an exaggeration, said to go against the *śāstras* and to be a violation of the basic duties ordained by the Vedas.[2]

Householders knew that everything depended on their work; what was true for food and drink and shelter was assumed to be true of sunshine and rain, of happiness and ill-luck, too. Religion for them was work that, when properly done, produced its fruits. From that basic consideration developed an intricate system and a theology of sacrifice that explained everything as being the result of ritual, *yajña*, including the creation of the universe.[3] As the importance of the proper performance of religious work rose, so did the importance of the Brahmins, the professionals of ritual sacrifice.

An explanation may be required to prevent a possible misunderstanding of the term *sacrifice.* In the fully developed Vedic system, it had little to do with the devotion with which Hindus today offer their *pūjā.* *Yajña* in Vedic tradition is an act that has its own intrinsic power and "exercises compulsion not only over the gods but also over natural phenomena without requiring the cooperation of the gods"[4] (Figure 9.1). When we understand the nature of the *devas* as manifestations of a power greater than themselves and not wholly identical with any of them, we may also appreciate the Vedic analysis of the *yajña* as requiring four components: *dravya*, or sacrificial matter; *tyāga*, or the relinquishing of the object sacrificed; a *devatā*, to be addressed as the recipient, and a *mantra*, or effective word—none of which may be omitted. As a reality, the *yajña* is more comprehensive than a *deva:* it has power over the *deva.*[5] There is a businesslike atmosphere prevailing in Vedic sacrificial religion. Every desired object has its specified sacrifice, every sacrifice has its price. Since the *devas* are believed to depend on the *yajña*, the Vedic sacrificer can tell them quite openly: "If you give me what I want, I shall give to you. If you don't give me, I shall not give to you. If you take something away from me, I shall take away from you."[6]

Offering sacrifices was part of *dharma*, of the established world order and the particular social order. Kings had to arrange for public *yajñas* for

Figure 9.1 Vedic Firesacrifice

the welfare of their people; householders had to maintain domestic sacrifices for the well-being of their families. Public sacrifices were splendid and costly events in former ages; they have become relatively rare but they are still performed occasionally. At the occasion of the *aṣṭāgraha* mentioned earlier, quite a number of such public Vedic sacrifices were performed by thousands of Brahmins, paid by rich businesspeople and industrialists, who alone were able to afford the hundreds of thousands of rupees required. On November 27, 1957, under the headline "*Sādhus* Perform *Mahā Yajña* to Fight Menace of H-Bombs," the *Times of India* reported a public sacrifice arranged by a former governor of Bombay. More than 500 *sādhus* and *paṇḍits* gathered in Bombay for a *Mahā Yajña* to reconcile the *devas* and to increase the spiritual strength of humankind, "to purify the evil, morbid and dangerous atmosphere pervading the world because of atom bombs and H-bombs."[7] The Indian weekly *Blitz* carried a report about a Vedic sacrifice ordered by Jana Sangh politicians with the intent to kill Indira Gandhi through spells.[8]

In 1975, Dutch-American Indologist Frits Staal had Kerala Brahmins perform an ancient Vedic sacrifice, the *Agnicayana*. The whole procedure, the preparations including burning and laying the bricks for the fire altar, putting up the *paṇḍal*, performance of the *yajña* itself, and demolition of the fire altar after its use, are shown on an hour-long film, which was made by the experts, who also set down their observations and reflexions in an impressive two-tome study.[9] The subsequent controversy arising around the performance, the challenge to the claim that what was filmed is exactly what Vedic Brahmins did 3000 years ago need not be dealt with here. The points that Staal proved are that Vedic traditions are preserved in some parts of India, that the detail laid down in ancient ritual works is observed on occasions like this, and that such grand sacrifices are enormously expensive.[10]

According to an Upaniṣadic teaching, humanity owes its existence to the "five fire sacrifices,"[11] and the classical *śāstras* circumscribe, with the term *pañca mahāyajña*, five great sacrifices, the routine of daily duties of the Brahmin. When the Brahmin had no other obligations, the execution of these occupied all of his time; under the pressure of changing circumstances, the five sacrifices were reduced to mere symbolic gestures. Thus, *deva-yajña*, the sacrifice to the gods, could be performed by throwing a stick of wood into the fire; *pitṛ-yajña*, the sacrifice to the ancestors, could be fulfilled by pouring a glass of water onto the floor; *bhūta-yajña*, sacrifice to all creatures, can be reduced to throwing out a small ball of rice; *manuṣya-yajña*, the sacrifice to men or hospitality in the widest sense, is fulfilled by giving a mouthful of rice to a Brahmin; *brahma-yajña*, the *mantra* sacrifice or study of the *Veda*, may consist in the recitation of one single line of scripture. Those, however, who can afford the time, frequently perform the elaborate ceremonies detailed in the *śāstras* and fill their days with holy ritual and sacred chant. The ideal daily routine of the Brahmin as outlined in the law books may be followed in its entirety by very few people in India today. But, surprisingly, many practice part of it quite regularly.

THE VEDIC WAY OF LIFE

Vedic tradition also endows the biological facts and necessities of hygiene with a religious meaning and provides for a detailed regulation of everyday life.[12] The Hindu householder is enjoined by his *śāstras* to rise at dawn. The first word he speaks should be the name of his *iṣṭadevatā*, the chosen deity. He should direct his eyes toward the palms of his hands, to behold an auspicious object as the first thing every morning. Then, he is to touch the floor to perform as the first work of the day an auspicious action and then to bow before the images of gods in his room. The *mantras* and prayers vary according to denomination and family tradition. Various scriptures enjoin the householder to begin the day by thinking what he is going to do today to increase *dharma* and *artha*, righteousness and wealth, and about the efforts he will take toward this end.

The scriptures provide very detailed rules for daily hygiene. In an age concerned about environmental pollution, we can appreciate the great subtlety of the ancient Hindus in promoting physical cleanliness, when we see how they surrounded the vital functions with many religious thoughts and rules. The daily bath is a necessity in India as well as a religious precept. While pouring water with the *loṭha* (brass vessel) over himself the pious Hindu is supposed to recite a *mantra*, such as the following:

> O you waters, in the manner that makes you the source of our fortune, pour strength into us so that our vision may be wide and beautiful. This your essence, which is so auspicious, let us enjoy here, you who are like loving mothers. Be our refuge for the removal of evil, wherewith you delight us. O waters, truly you have created us."

Tarpaṇa as part of the morning ablutions must be specially mentioned. The bather folds his hands to hold some water and lets it flow back into the river while reciting *mantras* to *devas* and *pitṛs*. Each day after the bath, clean clothes are put on.. The sacred thread, called *yajñopavīta* or *janëu* is never removed at the bath but, according to the different occasions, worn differently. After sipping some water from the hollow of his hand the Hindu, if he belongs to one of the more recent *saṁpradāyas*, applies the specific marks of his denomination to his body. This spiritual make-up is done very lovingly and carefully: vertical lines on the forehead for the Śaivas, horizontal lines for the Vaiṣṇavas, with many variations according to the particular subsect. Many write the name of their God or short *mantras* with white paste on their skins. According to many religious books, all ceremonies and prayers are fruitless if the devotee does not carry the signs of his God on his body.

The Śaivite *Bhasmajābalopaniṣad* is exclusively concerned with the preparation and significance of the *tripuṇḍra*, the three lines in honor of Śiva. It describes how the sacred ashes are to be prepared from the dung of a brown cow and how the markings are to be applied.

> For Brahmins the wearing of *bhasma* [ashes] alone is the right conduct. Without wearing the sign one should not drink nor do anything else. He who has given up the sign out of negligence should neither recite the *gāyatrī-mantra* nor put offerings into the sacred fire, nor worship the gods, the *ṛṣis* or the *pitṛs*. That alone is the right path to destroy all sin and attain the means of salvation. . . . He who makes use of this sign of ashes in the early morning is delivered of the sin he may have committed during the night and of the sin that originates in the stealing of gold. He who resorts to this at midday and looks, meditating, into the sun, is freed from the sin of drinking intoxicating beverages, the stealing of gold, the killing of Brahmins, the killing of a cow, the slaying of a horse, the murder of his *guru*, his mother and his father. By taking his refuge to the sign of ashes three times a day, he attains the fruit of vedic studies, he attains the merits of ablutions in all the three and a half crores of sacred waters; he attains the fullness of life.[13]

The morning prayer that follows, called *saṁdhyā*, is still observed by millions of Hindus every day. It is to take place before sunrise and to end when the sun's disk is fully above the horizon. The main text is the *gāyatrī mantra*, which is to be repeated several times; the scriptures recommend to the faithful to prolong it as much as possible because the ancestors had attained long life, understanding, honor, and glory by this means. One of the strangest rites still practiced is the daily "driving out of evil." The Brahmin takes water into the hollow of his right hand, brings it close to his nose, blows onto the water through the right and the left nostrils, repeats the *mantra* three times, and pours the water out. The *saṁdhyā*-rites have been lengthened in later schools by the inclusion of many texts from *Purāṇas*, but very few people use those long versions.

The orthodox *smārta* is enjoined to proceed to *agniṣṭoma* after his *saṁdhyā* is completed, to redeem the first of his debts, with which everyone is born. Most ordinary Hindus will perform *japa* instead, the repetition of a brief *mantra* or of one of the names of God. These vary according to the religious affiliation; but all believe that the name of their own God, if recited often, would confer blessing and ultimate redemption. If *japa* is to be effective, the recitation has to be done with the help of a *mālā*, a string of beads, different again according to the different sects. Vaiṣṇavas use a *mālā* made up of beads from the wood of the *tulasī* tree; Śaivites are obliged to put their faith in the *Rudrākṣa-mālā* made from the seeds of a shrub. Usually the *mālās* have 16, 32, 64, or 108 beads. Numerous treatises explain the merits of the *mālās* and recommend their use through an account of their divine origin. Thus, the Śaivite *Rudrākṣajabalopaniṣad* writes:

> Thus spoke the Lord Kālāgnirudra: "To bring about the destruction of Tripura, I had to close my eyes. From my eyes fell waterdrops. These drops turned into *rudrākṣas*. For the sake of the deliverance of all living beings I have disposed that by the mere uttering of their names as much merit is gathered as by the gift of ten cows, and by looking at them and touching them twice as much. . . . If worn by the pious the *rudrākṣas* absolve of all sins committed by day or by night . . ."

Precise instructions follow, how many of these beads to wear, what kind of beads to choose, and so on.[14]

Every morning, All India Radio broadcasts *śahnai*-music, not because the oboelike instrument is a favorite with the program director but because its sounds are traditionally considered auspicious and the Hindu who listens to such is ensured a happy day. The radio morning program also includes recitations from the *Mahābhārata* or the *Rāmāyaṇa.* Hindus devote much care to the separation of auspicious from inauspicious objects, sights, sounds, and times. Hindu newspapers contain a daily extract from the *pañcāṅga*, with an indication of the astrological data, lists of auspicious and inauspicious colors and directions. There are differences of opinion on many of these, but some are universally recognized typifications. A brahmin, a cow, fire, gold, *ghī*, the sun, water and a courtesan, for instance, are considered to be auspicious objects to behold, and one may look forward to a good day if any of them is seen first thing in the morning. Quite serious people delay a long-planned journey or postpone an important decision if they happen to meet a cripple, a madman, a drunkard, a bald-headed man, or a *saṁnyāsin*, considered to be inauspicious sights.

A BRAHMIN'S DUTIES

The orthodox Brahmin is supposed to fill the first part of his day with these religious exercises. After that, he is to study or to read his Veda, do his *svādhyāya*, to gather firewood, flowers, and grass for worship. The third part of the day should be devoted to earning money. In the olden days, there were strict rules for it, a distinction between permitted and forbidden occupations. Formerly, the nonobservance of such rules entailed punishment like expulsion from the caste; today, especially in big cities, much of this has been forgotten.

Since ancient times, the teaching of the Veda had been the Brahmin's privilege. He was not allowed to ask for payment, but the student was bound to give regularly to his guru presents according to the wealth of his family. "Receiving gifts" is the Brahmins' privilege even today, and many insist on it. The common expression "to honor a Brahmin" means to make a gift to him. Today, Brahmins are found in a great many different professions. They are farmers, government officials, lawyers, and teachers; but cooks, soldiers, and employees, too, are found among them. Since, by tradition, Brahmins had an educational privilege, even in modern times they have been able to occupy relatively more influential posts, and to some extent, today's India is still Brahmin dominated.[15]

After midday, the orthodox Brahmin was instructed to take another bath and to offer an elaborate *tarpaṇa* to the *devas*, the *pitṛs*, and *ṛṣis:* "May the *devas, ṛṣis, pitṛs*, the human beings, all beings from Brahmā right down to the blade of grass be satiated, likewise all ancestors, the mother, the maternal grandfather and the rest, may this water do good to the millions of families of bygone days who live in the seven *dvīpas*."[16] The longer formula takes up a great deal of time, enumerates thirty-one *devatās* singly, mentions a long list of *ṛṣis* and relations. At the mention of each single name water is sprinkled, with the word *tṛpyatu*, "may he be pleased with it."

The *deva-yajña* used to be an elaborate ritual. As regards the domestic rites, it has been largely replaced by *pūjā*, the worship of an image according to Āgamic scriptures. Official Vedic worship did not make use of images, as far as we know, but popular religion was certainly not totally identical with Vedic orthodoxy, as the *Atharva Veda* shows. *Purāṇas, Saṁhitās, Āgamas*, and *Tantras* have taken over a good deal of Vedic terminology and regulations and combined them with material from other traditions. Thus, we find countless chapters detailing the obligatory daily domestic rites that are followed by many households. The average Hindu family has its *mūrti*, before which daily worship is offered quite formally several times a day. The particulars—vessels to be used, materials to be employed, color of flowers, etc.—vary from sect to sect. In its elaborate form, *pūjā* consists of sixty-four individual ceremonies; in daily ceremonies at home usually only part of them are performed. These are *āvāhana*, invitation of the *Iṣṭadevatā; āsana*, offering a seat to the deity; *pādya*, offering water to wash the feet; *arghya*, offering water for washing the hands; *ācamanīya*, offering water to rinse the mouth; *snānīya*, water for a bath; *vastra*, leaves for clothing the deity; *yajñopavīta*, offering a sacred thread; *candana*, sandalwood paste; *puṣpa*, flowers; *dhūpa*, incense; *dīpa*, a lighted lamp; *naivedya*, offering cooked food; *tāmbūla*, a betel nut; *dakṣiṇā*, some money; *nāmaskāra*, a solemn greeting; *pradakṣiṇā*, circumambulation; and *mantra-puṣpa*, scattering a handful of blossoms before the image, reciting some honorific *mantras*. Each individual gesture is accompanied by appropriate *mantras*, varying from sect to sect. Many of the ancient *śāstras* give explicit order to distribute food to different deities in various parts of the house, to gods and to *caṇḍālas*, the outcastes,[17] to lepers and cripples, to crows and insects. Eating is considered to be a "sacrifice to the gods who dwell in the body."

Almost all nations consider hospitality a virtue. *Manuṣya-yajña*, one of the basic duties of the Brahmin, is interpreted by Manu as "honoring guests." There is a possibility of understanding it in an allegorical sense, too. *Agni*, the fire, is the "guest of the householder" and whatever is thrown into the fire is considered to be an offering of food "to the guest." On the other hand, there are also Hindus who retain the literal meaning of the precept and make it a point to invite at least one guest to every major meal. The interpretation of *atithi* (guest), given in the *śāstras* says that only a Brahmin can be, properly speaking, a guest, that hospitality is restricted to one meal and one overnight stay if the guest arrives late in the evening and cannot return home. A guest who has been disappointed or turned away can unload all his sins upon the householder and can take away from him his *puṇya*, his merit.[18]

If a *saṁnyāsi* turns up as a guest, according to Hindu theory, the host has to consider himself lucky; it is not the guest who should be grateful for hospitality but the host must thank the *saṁnyāsi* for the opportunity to earn merit. The practice, at least today, is less than ideal though, and few *saṁnyāsis* would approach an unknown family for hospitality. However, the invited guest, especially if he is a *swāmī*, is showered with effusive attention. India still has a tradition of hospitality that has no parallel in the contemporary West. Wealthy pious Hindus of the past and the present have established numerous guest houses in places of pilgrimage; those *dharmaśālas* offer usually free shelter and quite frequently also free food to travellers and pilgrims, irrespective of their creed or color.

"He who goes to a meal without having performed the various sacrifices consumes only sin, he does not really eat," says an old proverb. Only one who fulfills the rules of *dharma* gains strength from his food. "All beings live by food. The Veda explains: 'Food is life; therefore one should give food!, eating is the supreme sacrifice!'" say the *Upaniṣads*.[19] *Anna*, food, and *bhojana*, eating, occupy first place among the topics of conversation of the average Hindu. Mahātmā Gāndhī's writings convey some impression of the solicitude and anxiety the Hindus bestow on their daily meals, on diet and preparation. There is good reason behind it, of course. India has known famines and times of scarcity throughout recorded history, and the Indian climate makes it necessary to take care of one's health far more than in moderate zones. Many a Hindu knows hundreds of health rules from home, and it is common for religious books to give instruction also with regard to food and meals. The traditional Indian housewife spends most of her time in the kitchen preparing the meals. The reputation of Indian cuisine is not undeserved, although the majority of the population has to be satisfied with a somewhat monotonous routine. The *Upaniṣads* even offer a theology of food: "If food is pure, the mind becomes pure. When understanding is pure it allows strong concentration [on the Self]. If this is safeguarded, all the knots [that fetter the Self to the world] are loosened."[20]

Next to the treatment of marriage, food in all its aspects takes up the broadest space in the *dharmaśāstras.* Caste rules concern primarily intermarrying and interdining, specifying who may receive food from whom and who may not, thereby drawing very close social borderlines between different groups of people. Whereas the ancient Vedic Indians seem to have had few food taboos, according to available documents they were meat eaters not excluding beef, under Buddhist and Jain influence meat eating became considered irreligious. Several Hindu rulers, and even some Muslims, forbade the slaughter of animals. Animal sacrifices were replaced by flower *pūjās*, meat dishes by vegetarian food. The majority of Hindus today are vegetarians for religious reasons, which are frequently fortified by hygienic arguments.

The religious books specify the kinds of food that may be taken by particular groups of people. The rules also have regional variations. The Brahmins of Uttar Pradesh avoid all meat, fish, eggs, and many other things; the Brahmins of Bengal and South India must have a piece of fish with their rice and they also often eat eggs. The strictest rules have been devised by the Vaiṣṇavas, who classify all foods into *rājasik*, "exciting," *tāmasik*, "foul," and *sāttvik*, "pure." Only the last category is permitted, excluding thereby not only all meat and fish but also onions, garlic, red fruits like tomatoes, and many other things. Special rules obtain for the frequent days of fast observed by different groups at different times.[21]

THE THEORY OF VEDIC *YAJÑA*

The understanding of Hinduism as a whole calls for a somewhat more thorough study of the Vedic public sacrifices, though most of them belong irrevocably to the past. Indological scholars have done an enormous amount of work in this area, editing and translating virtually all the preserved texts and making detailed studies of many historical problems.[22] The Vedic *saṁhitās* were exclusively meant for use at the public sacrifices and official rituals; the highly technical *śrauta-sūtras* lay down with great precision the details of the public sacrifices. Hindu literature reports on *yajñas* to which thousands of Brahmins were invited and at which hundreds of sacrificial animals were slaughtered; *yajñas* lasting for months, even years, that cost so much that they could impoverish the richest man.[23] Since the effect of the Vedic sacrifice depended on the correct pronunciation of the *mantra*, the precision of the ritual and the observance of hundreds of minute circumstances, it very soon became the exclusive domain of sacrificial specialists, the Brahmin priests. The significance of Brahmanic priesthood increased in proportion as the sacrifice became more complicated. Even for the humblest of Vedic sacrifices, four or five Brahmin specialists were required, hundreds for the major ones.

The efficacy of the Vedic sacrifice was supposed to depend on the offering: several remarks in Vedic works give some reason to assume that the most noble and most efficacious sacrifice was the *puruṣamedha*, the human sacrifice.[24] It made the sacrificer equal to Prajāpati, the creator. The accounts we have give the impression that this was a real sacrifice according to an elaborate ritual, not just a symbolic ceremony.[25]

Animal sacrifices were very common; one proof of this is the opposition to them by early religious reformers like Buddha and Mahāvīra. The greatest was the *aśvamedha*, the horse sacrifice, to be performed by kings as part of their assuming "universal power."[26] So highly was it regarded, even in later times when its performance had become extremely rare,[27] that the *Bhāgavata Purāṇa* can declare that the extermination of the whole of humankind could be atoned for by one single *aśvamedha*. It was also taken as the highest unit for religious merit in describing the *puṇya* accruing from pilgrimage to certain holy places. The Daśāśvamedha Ghāṭ in Vāraṇāsī has been so named because a bath in the Ganges at this particular spot is supposed to bring as much merit as the performance of ten horse sacrifices. The animal most often sacrificed, however, was the goat. The *Brāhmaṇas* give the following explanation for it:

> When the *devas* had killed a man for their sacrifice, that part of him which was fit to be made an offering went out and entered a horse. Thence the horse became an animal fit to be sacrificed. From the horse it went into the ox, from there into the goat. In the goat it remained for the longest time, therefore the goat is best fitted to be sacrificed.[28]

The goat contains the most *medha*, "sacrificial substance," which is required for ensuring the proper result from the sacrifice.

The common daily oblation consisted of rice, barley cakes, butter, curds, and milk, in short the *devas* were supposed to have the same taste as humans. A very important ingredient of most sacrifices was *soma*, the intoxicating sap of a plant.[29] It is often called *amṛta*, "nectar of immortality"; an entire hymn collection of the *Ṛgveda* consists of nothing but *soma* hymns. According to tradition an eagle brought it to Indra; by partaking of it the *devas* gained immortality. *Soma* is called child of heaven and is supposed to have healing powers, to drive away blindness and lameness. One hymn reads: "We have drunk *soma*, we have become immortal; we have gone to the light, we have found the *devas*. What can hostility now do to us, and what the malice of mortal men, O immortal one!"[30]

The Vedic sacrifices are intimately connected with the course of time and with the movement of the heavenly bodies. They are an expression of an awareness that human existence is precarious and time bound. Over and over, the sacrifice is equated with the year, the month, the day, or the various seasons; and the sacrifice itself is considered essential for maintaining the flow of time. The full-moon and new-moon sacrifices have always been, and still are, of fundamental importance; their ritual became the model for all the other *iṣṭis*. If the new-moon sacrifice were not offered, there would be no more moon. Even today, the religious calendar of the Hindus is a lunar calendar, with all the complications and difficulties that result from it. The lunar month is divided into thirty *tithis*, fifteen *tithis* of the dark half and fifteen *tithis* of the bright half, which do not coincide at all with the "days" of our calendar and have to be learned from the indispensable *pañcāṅga*. Since the "auspicious time" in which important events must take place—marriage ceremonies, the opening of great buildings, the beginning of the parliamentary sessions, etc.—is calculated according to *muhūrtas*, subdivisions of the lunar *tithis* (there are thirty *muhūrtas* in each *tithi* of approximately 45 minutes duration), the specialists acquainted with the *pañcāṅga*, who sit on the pavements of small towns and big cities, are never without a clientele in need of their services.

NEW MEANINGS OF SACRIFICE

Whereas the Vedic sacrifice gives the impression of a transaction in which little or no emotion is invested, the *devas* do not have to be won over through any sign of affection or love, in later times the emotional content of the sacrifice became predominant. The value of the gift offered may be insignificant, the sacrificer may be ignorant of Vedic *mantras* and ceremony; what counts is devotion to the God, whose grace is sought and who only considers the heart. As Kṛṣṇa tells Arjuna in the *Bhagavadgītā:*

"Whosoever offers to me with devotion (*bhakti*) a leaf, a fruit, a flower, a cup of water—that offering of love, of the pure of heart, I accept."[31] The *Purāṇas* compete with each other in telling the masses, who could never hope to participate in a Vedic public ceremony, that devotion alone counts. This devotion may be expressed in a symbolic gesture, perhaps the repetition of the name of God or the offering of an incense stick or a flower.

But, inevitably, the formalism at work in the Vedic religion also entered the *Āgamas*. They abound in detailed regulations for worship, ordering and forbidding certain acts and words as firmly as the Vedic *sūtras* did.[32] Worship at the major temples follows a very strict ritual that, according to tradition, usually had been instituted by the God through a revelation to a leading *ācārya*, who codified it.[33] The basic pattern of worship follows the pattern of personal attention devoted to an honored guest or a king.[34] Whereas the *deva* in the Veda is but a transitory symbolic fixation of the ultimate power, the *īśvara* of the *Purāṇas* is the Ultimate in person, present in his image, ready to give his personal grace to the one who worships him. The rationalization of *karma*, the ritual act, in this "new devotion" is quite different from that of the Vedic sacrificial religion.

According to the *Pūrva Mīmāṁsā*, the school of orthodox Vedic interpretation, each Vedic sacrifice, duly performed, produced an incorruptible substance called *apūrva*, independent of *devas*, which was at the sacrificer's disposal after death. Whatever else the sacrificers might have done, having the *apūrva* from a sacrifice ensured a sojourn in heaven; they would come to heaven, whether or not the *devas* were willing. In the "new religion," the devotees had to be constantly on the alert to remain in their God's favor; eternal salvation could be gained or lost even in the last moment of life. Popular stories tell of great sinners, who according to all the Vedic rules would be condemned to the lowest hells, winning immediate eternal bliss through an even inadvertent utterance of the name of Hari or Śiva.[35] The *Purāṇas* insist on regular worship of God as means to win God's grace and a good deal of the activity of the pious is directed toward gaining *puṇya* by performing actions that are described in the holy books as ordained by God for this end: *japa*, the repetition of the name of God; singing the praises of God; reading holy books; attending temple services; worshipping the image; going on pilgrimages; and so on. Though there are constant reminders of the affection and emotion with which a devotee has to do the daily worship in order to "fulfill the law"; quite frequently these actions are performed mechanically, as if they could become effective automatically and magically.

Comparative studies of ritual have pointed out a great many parallels between notions of sacrifice and cult of the Vedic Indian and that of other people.[36] Anthropologists and ethologists speak of "ritual behavior" even in animals, assuming that not only human societies but also animals feel an urge to perform acts that among humans are called ritual. The implications are farreaching. For one, the beginnings of ritual would not lay in rational deliberation and conscious reflection but in the subconscious psyche, perhaps even in the biological sphere. The other conclusion to be drawn would be that rituals are likely to continue, in spite of periodic major enlightenments that belittle and ridicule them as meaningless and unable to achieve their purpose. Meaningless they may be, as F. Staal has tried to prove,[37] but not purposeless. Cārvākas and Buddhists derided Vedic ritual and succeeded to some extent in interrupting Vedic sacrificial tradition. New forms of ritual developed, also among the Buddhists. Nineteenth century reformers debunked old as well as new forms of ritual and sacrifice. And, again, other forms developed and have found acceptance among contemporary Hindus.

10. Purity and Merit: The Twin Concerns of *Karmamārga*

> Pure, Maruts, pure yourselves, are your oblations; to you, the pure, pure sacrifice I offer.
> By Law they came to truth, the Law's observers, bright by their birth, and pure, and sanctifying.
>
> —Ṛgveda *VI, 56, 12*

WHILE CERTAIN ASPECTS of purity in Hinduism certainly have to do with bodily fluids and their discharge (menstruating women are considered ritually impure, to mention the most obvious of such instances), it would be wrong to identify the issue of purity in Hinduism totally with this aspect, as some Indologists, under the influence of a certain school of anthropology, seem to do. In addition to materially conditioned purity, there is a very sophisticated notion of a higher purity, partly ethical, partly spiritual. Thus, purity of mind is the central theme of the teaching of the present Śaṅkarācāryas, the *jagadgurus*, or "world teachers," whose words carry authority and are listened to with great seriousness by a great many Hindus.[1] "Purity of mind is thought to bring the mind to greater understanding. Purity of mind, requisite for devotion and meditation, leads on to religious knowledge. Two classic qualifications for self-knowledge are freedom from desires and purity of mind." To some extent the notion of auspicious-inauspicious central to Hinduism runs parallel to that of purity-impurity. Here, as in most other cases, Hindu practice and belief does not simply follow from a logical extension of one basic idea but a plurality of basic notions from which, quite logically but not always in mutually compatible fashion, specific beliefs and practices flow.

The Hindu notion of merit is also multidimensional. Besides the Vedic idea of *apūrva*, the merit accruing from a sacrifice that can be stored up for later use in heaven, we find Purāṇic ideas of gaining merit by either reciting the names of a deity or by performing *pūjā*. Quite different but not unrelated is the idea, also very widespread among Hindus, that *tapas*, self-mortification, self-imposed and voluntary, both purifies and confers merit. Equally, the idea of gaining purity and merit, not only for oneself but also for ancestors and others, by going on pilgrimage and bathing in a *tīrtha* is accepted fairly universally by Hindus.[2] It is not really a Vedic idea but combines with Vedic ideas in the pratical life of Hindus. More on this will be said in a later chapter, which explains how gaining of purity and merit is tied to specific times and places.

The inextricable conjunction of the rather impersonal Vedic and the highly personal Purāṇic traditions make it impossible to clearly differentiate in the activities of traditional Hindus among acts done to obtain ritual purity, to gain merit, or to win the grace of God, which, in a certain sense, obviates everything else.

Hinduism is not a primitive magico-ritualistic tribal cult—if such exist—in which purely externalized and quite mechanical criteria would be used to decide who was to participate in the tribal rites; it is a very complex and a very sophisticated tradition. Certainly, it preserved archaic and magical elements, but it integrated those with ethical reflection and theological thought. For a fuller understanding of this tradition, it is not enough to observe what can be seen by way of ritual action but also to read, or listen to, reflections on ethical issues by learned and thoughtful Hindus, past and present. The *Upaniṣads* already throw doubt on the efficacy of Vedic ritual: they recommend asceticism and introspection as means to gain purity and earn merit.

Throughout the history of Hinduism, on the one hand, there is an insistence of performing the prescribed ritual to achieve and maintain one's status within the *varṇāśramadharma* and, on the other hand, the clearly expressed conviction that rituals alone are not sufficient and the purity they effect is not enough to reach the ultimate aim of life, *mokṣa*. Numerous Hindu saints and singers denounced ritualism and ridiculed the belief that ritual purity would win a person entry to the realm of God. Personal virtues as well as social engagement, genuine devotion and service to God are stressed as means to reach purity and to gain merit.

The majority of today's Hindus would agree. The equivocal nature of the Hindu notions of purity and merit is underscored by the fact that most Hindus make use of all available means offered to earn merit and to purify themselves, regardless of the source from which they come. Devout Hindus will accept the blessing of a Christian priest as well as the *aśīrvādams* of Hindu *pūjāris*, they will visit places of pilgrimage regardless of which religion they belong to, and they will participate in all forms of worship that appeal to them. They will, however, follow their own traditional Vedic practices where religion intersects with their standing in society and will undergo the prescribed *saṁskāras.*

ETHICAL STANDARDS OF HINDUISM

Hindu tradition has devoted a great deal of intellectual work to the clarification of moral and ethical issues. In the context of this book, it is impossible even to mention all the important authors and views.[3] As the brief discussion of *dharma* has shown, religion and the morality connected with it are defined within the framework of the *varṇāśrama* scheme as *svadharma,* morality appropriate to each class and to each stage in life. But certain moral precepts are supposed to be common to all humankind. The so-called *sādhāraṇadharma* has a number of features in common with the Ten Commandments of the Bible or the natural law of the Western classical philosophical tradition. Hindu ethics as a whole, however, shows so many peculiar features that it would be misleading to represent it in Western terminology. Nor is the Hindu tradition united in the articulation of its ethical thought. Numerous schools have produced sometimes radically different views on important matters. Only some of these will be described here; for others more specialized works will have to be consulted.[4]

Hindu ethics, generally speaking, is strongly "scriptural," that is, oriented to the mandates given in recognized *śruti.* The Vedic tradition was largely replaced and absorbed by the Purāṇic-Āgamic tradition, which in addition to general rules and precepts has numerous special provisions for the followers of each individual sect and group. Combined with what we would call moral and ethical principles we find rules relating to forms of worship, ritual purity, and also items of practical wisdom and hygiene.

The supreme ideal of most branches of Hinduism is the sage, who is imperturbable, free from affection and hatred, not influenced by good or bad luck. For him there is, strictly speaking, no more morality. He is "beyond good and evil" in a literal sense, because *pravṛtti,* "volition," the spring of action, has dried up. This is the situation of the fully realized person, as the *Vedānta* describes it. Not too well-informed people derive from such statements the impression that Hinduism as a whole does not care for ethics. Good and evil are relative according to the teaching of the *Upaniṣads;* relative to the whole world of *karma.* As long as people actively participate in it are they bound by it as by an absolute rule!

A discussion has gone on in India for many centuries whether righteousness affects the innermost self or whether it is just accidental to it. Many

Indians consider morality a quality of the *ātman*, a subjective category that also depends on the intentions of the doer.[5] In order that a moral rule may qualify as a precept apart from its scriptural basis, its inherent goodness must usually also be proved. Since scriptural precepts, which also include rituals, are of such great importance, Hindu thinkers have devoted much thought to finding the reasons for their validity. According to the orthodox *Mīmāṁsā* school, the scriptural laws express something like a universal moral imperative, which produces *ātmākūta*, an impulse in the self to do what has been prescribed, together with an insight into the rightness of the precept.[6]

According to the Naiyāyikas, the professional logicians,

> whatever the Lord commands is good and is good *because* the Lord commands it. Similarly, whatever the Lord forbids is evil and is evil because the Lord forbids it. The authority of the scriptural prescriptions on the will of the agent is such a *vyāpāra* or process in the agent himself: it is the desire for the good and aversion towards the evil involved in the injunctions and prohibitions of scripture as the Lord's commands. It is these desires and aversions in the agent that are the real operative forces, and moral authority is the operation of good and evil through the agent's subjective desires and aversions.[7]

Many authors operate with a basic distinction of *sukha*, "agreeable," *duḥkha*, "painful," or *hita* ("wholesome")-*ahita* ("unwholesome"), which may be considered a rule of thumb for moral decisions in concrete situations. Thus, for instance, the precept of truthfulness has to be realized within this situational ethics, as expressed by a leading contemporary Indian thinker: "The final standard of truth is the amount of good that is rendered to people by one's words. Even a mistatement or a false statement, if beneficial to all beings, should be regarded as preferable to a rigorous truthful statement."[8] That this is not just the isolated opinion of an avant garde thinker is proved by numerous sayings and proverbs in popular scriptures.

A different, absolute, standard is introduced by the *Bhagavadgītā* with *niṣkāma karma*, the disinterested pursuit of the Lord's command as duty for duty's sake.[9]

VICE AND VIRTUE IN HINDUISM

Both popular and scholarly books describe *moha, lobha, krodha* (delusion, greed, and anger) as the root of all vices, "the gates to hell," as the *Bhagavadgītā* says.[10] Some authors try to reduce the first two into one, but all are unanimous in considering the deeds performed under the influence of these passions as sinful.

Jayanta specifies the three roots further[11] and identifies with their help the most common vices. *Moha* is given the title *pāpatama*, "head sin," because without delusion, he says, there cannot be greed and anger. The direct consequences of delusion are misjudgement, perplexity, conceit, and heedlessness. The consequences of desire are sexual craving, extreme niggardliness, worldliness, thirst for pleasure, and greed. Aversion produces anger, envy, jealousy, malevolence, and malice.

Before proceeding with a detailed description of the system of vices in the classical *śāstras*, it may help to quote some popular scriptures, the source of the common Hindu's ethical education, to see what a Hindu considers to be the life a good person should live. Since a great deal of traditional Hinduism is quite patently patriarchal, it is no use to apply inclusive language. Many of the texts speak of men only and highlight male ideas and ideals, virtues and vices of men rather than of all humans. The *Viṣṇu Purāṇa* enjoins the respectable man to worship gods, cows, Brahmans, *sādhus*, elders, and teachers. He should dress in neat garments, use delicate herbs and flowers, wear emeralds and other precious stones, keep his hair smooth and neat, scent his person with agreeable perfumes, and always go handsomely attired, decorated with garlands of white flowers.

He should never appropriate another's belongings nor address anyone in an unkindly way. He should speak amiably and truthfully and never make public another's faults. He should not mount a dangerous vehicle nor seek shade along the bank of a river. He should not associate with ill-famed people, sinners, or drunkards, with one who has many enemies, with a harlot or her pimp, with a pauper or a liar, with a slanderer or a knave. He should not swim against the current of a rapid stream, enter a house on fire, or climb to the top of a tree.

When together with others, he should not grind his teeth, blow his nose, or yawn with an uncovered mouth; he should not clear his throat noisily, cough or laugh loudly, or break wind noisily; he should not bite his nails or scratch the ground nor put his beard into his mouth.

He should avoid going by night to a place where four roads meet, to the village tree, to the cemetery, or to an ill-famed woman's house. He should not cross the shadow of a venerable person, of the image of a deity, of a flag, or of a heavenly body. He should not travel alone through the forest nor sleep by himself in an empty house. He should stay away from hair, bones, thorns, filth, remnants of offerings, ashes, chaff, and the bathing place of someone else. He should not go near a beast of prey and should rise from his bed as soon as he awakens. He should avoid exposure to frost, wind, sunshine. He should not bathe, sleep, or rinse his mouth when naked. He should not offer any oblations or greetings with only one garment on. He should not engage in a dispute with superiors or inferiors because, the text says "controversy and marriage are to be permitted only between equals." He must never circumambulate the temple in such a way, that it is on his left side[12] nor spit in front of the moon, fire, the sun, water, wind, or any respectable person. He must not urinate while standing or upon a highway. He must not treat women with disrespect nor trust them completely. He is to be generous toward the poor. He should carry an umbrella for protection against sun and rain, a staff when walking by night, and wear shoes. He should speak wisely, moderately, and kindly.

> The earth is upheld by the truthfulness of those who have subdued their passions and are never contaminated by desire, delusion and anger. Let therefore a wise man ever speak the truth when it is agreeable, and when the truth would inflict pain let him hold his peace. Let him not utter that which, though acceptable, would be detrimental; for it would be better to speak that which would be salutary. A considerate man will always cultivate, in act, thought and speech, that which is good for living beings, both in this world and the next.[13]

Detailed instructions are given for each activity and situation in life, giving guidance in a very practical form interspersed with religious precepts. A very similar list is provided in the *Cārakasaṁhitā*, a classical text on medicine, which combines technical medical matters with general rules for a good and healthy life.[14] That health and religion go hand in hand is commonly accepted among Hindus. There attaches, therefore, a moral stigma to people afflicted with leprosy or other deforming diseases, which makes their lot still more miserable. But, generally, the Hindu has a quite sound moral sense—old-fashioned, perhaps, and tinged with sectarian over-emphasis on ritual in some cases but practical and sure in the essentials.

To introduce also sources in languages other than Sanskrit, a few verses from the *Tirukkuṛaḷ*, the sacred book of the Tamilians, which the Hindus in South India treasure as the "Tamilveda," may be quoted here.

> People without love think only of themselves; people who have love free themselves of the self for the sake of others.
>
> Heaven and earth are not enough reward for a friendly service that is given without any thought of gain.
>
> The joy of the revengeful lasts but a single day, but the peace-lover's joy lasts forever.
>
> Those who fast and mortify themselves are great, but greater are they who forgive wrongdoing.
>
> This is wisdom supreme: do not repay with evil, evil done to you.[15]

GREAT SINS AND LESSER SINS

The classic *dharmaśāstra* developed a fairly comprehensive casuistry, classifying and cataloging sins and their appropriate penances. Sins have their special consequences and, thus, social sanctions as well as religious ones. It is worth noting that the digests of Hindu law treat *prayaścittas*, penances and atonement for sins, after dealing with purity and impurity.[16] The principal division of sin in the *śāstras* is between *mahāpātakas*, great sins, and *upapātakas*, minor sins. The former are generally given as five, interpreted differently by various authors.

Brāhmaṇahatyā, the killing of a Brahmin, was considered the most grievous of all offences, unforgivable and expiated only by death. Some paṇḍits hold that it includes all members of the upper castes who have studied the Vedas. The killing of an unborn child and of a pregnant woman was considered equally vile. The killing of a man of a lower caste or of an outcaste is treated by some law books only as a minor offence, a far lesser crime than the killing of a cow. The *śāstras* provide also for non-Brahmins by saying that it would be a *mahāpātaka* for a *kṣatriya* to flee from the battlefield or to mete out, as a ruler, unjust punishment; for a *vaiśya* to use false scales and false weights; for a *śūdra* to sell meat, to injure a Brahmin, to have sexual intercourse with a Brahmin woman, or to drink milk from a *kapilā* (brownish) cow, reserved for the Brahmins. There is no *dharma* proper for the casteless. From the orthodox point of view they are on a level with the animals as far as religious merit is concerned. Accordingly, offenses committed by them against caste people were punished with disproportionate harshness and crimes against them by people from higher castes were absolved very easily with a merely formal penance.

The second *mahāpātakam* is *surāpāna*, drinking of intoxicating beverages. It is the object of long treatises, classifications, restrictions and excuses, to find out what exactly was meant by *surā*. Strict interpreters forbid all alcoholic drinks and all drugs. Most paṇḍits allow the *śūdras* to drink their toddy and liquor without incurring sin. Among *sādhus*, especially the uneducated ones, it was common practice to improve their capacity for meditating by using drugs.

Steyam, stealing, is the third grave sin; but this is a qualified theft defined as "stealing a large amount of gold from a Brahmin." Long treatises specify quantity, persons, and circumstances. Generally speaking, traditional India did not know the capitalist idolization of personal property and even the *śāstras* formally allow theft of food for cows, of materials for sacrifice, or of modest quantities of food for one's personal use. Again, almost daily occurrences of brutal punishment meted out to Harijans for minor theft show that the law was written by, and for the benefit of, the higher castes.

The fourth *mahāpātakam* is *guruvaṅganāgama*, relations with the preceptor's wife. Some authorities interpret guru in this context as father and not as religious master and the prohibition would relate to incest, applicable also to the spiritual father.

The last of the great sins is *mahāpātakasaṁsārga*, association with a great sinner. The law forbids one to eat with him, live with him, ride with him, or accept him as friend or pupil.

Some of the later texts broaden the concept of "great sin" and add a series of offenses that they consider equivalent: kidnapping; horse stealing; theft of diamonds or land; sexual relations with members of the lowest castes, relatives, or a holy person.

All the *mahāpātakas* are technically unpardonable and there is no penance that would make a person who incurred one of these sins acceptable again in his caste. From the religious point of view, some *śāstras* say that such sinners could expiate through their death the offenses they have committed. The sectarian texts of the *Purāṇas*, however, handle such cases quite easily, by recommending some religious practice associated with the Lord, who if worshipped forgives and condones everything.

As regards the *upapātakas*, the minor offences, there is wide discrepancy and a lack of an accepted classification. One authority mentions five: relinquishing the sacred fire, offending the guru, atheism (*nāstikya*, disregard for the traditional religion), gaining one's livelihood from an unbeliever, and sale of the *soma* plant. Others add forgetting the Veda, neglecting the Veda study, violation of *brahmacarya*, the vow of celibacy. Longer lists enumerate more than fifty minor sins, many of them quite serious offenses that can, however, be made good by performing the prescribed penance. Thus, offenses like the preparation of salt (the breaking of a state monopoly), accepting money for teaching the Veda, the study of false *śāstras*, killing a woman, marrying off a younger son before his elder brother, installation of devices that kill living organisms or cause injury (like an oil press), and the sale of one's wife are mentioned together with common theft, adultery, cruelty toward parents, unrestrained pleasure-seeking, and the usurpation of the priestly office.[17]

PENANCE AND ATONEMENT

Manu decrees that he who causes pain to a Brahmin, steals, cheats, and commits unnatural sexual acts loses caste. One who kills a donkey, horse, deer, elephant, snake, or buffalo is transferred to a mixed caste.

The *śāstras* stress the importance of undergoing the prescribed penances by pointing out the evil consequences a sin may have in another rebirth, if it has not been washed away through *prayaścitta*. Thus, according to Manu, stealing gold shows in diseased nails and drinking spirits in black teeth; murder of a Brahmin in consumption; violation of the guru's wife in skin disease; calumny in stinking breath; stealing of cloth in leprosy: "Thus, in consequence of a remnant of the guilt are born idiots, dumb, deaf and deformed men, despised by the virtuous."[18]

In addition to possible consequences in rebirth, Hindu scriptures quite frequently give detailed descriptions of the hells in which individual sinners are punished for their sins. People who have injured living beings have to suffer being cut with sharp blades for ages; people who have committed adultery are punished by being tied to a red-hot image that they have to embrace for many years; liars are hung with their mouth in pools of foul matter.[19] The ancient *śāstras*, which belong to a period in which religious and secular authority were one, however, have quite precise rules in their criminal code; for the sake of preserving society they could be neither as extravagant nor as lenient as the *Purāṇas*. They distinguish between unintentional and intentional acts; the former are usually expiated by reciting Vedic texts, the latter demand special penances.[20] Those special penances in fact constitute the criminal code of ancient India and are still of great importance in traditional jurisprudence. Some of the modes of atonement have gone out of practice, others still apply.

Manu, for instance prescribes for unintentional *brāhmaṇahatyā* "to make a hut in the forest and dwell in it for twelve years, subsisting on alms and making the skull of a dead man his flag" or to try to expose himself in a battle to archers or to surrender his whole property to a Brahmin or to sacrifice his life for the sake of Brahmins or cows—or verbal absolution from three Brahmins.[21] Austerities, recitation of Vedic texts, performance of special sacrifices, breath control, gifts, pilgrimages, ablutions, and rituals are among the means imposed by religious authorities even now for offenses. If performed properly, they are supposed to take away the sins and their consequences in this and future births. Thus Manu says: "By confession, by repentance, by austerity and by reciting the Veda a sinner is freed from guilt, as also by liberality. . . . In so far as his heart loathes his evil deed, so far is his body freed from that guilt. He who has committed a sin and has repented is freed from that sin, but only by ceasing with the promise: 'I will do so no more'."[22]

Normally, in addition to repentance, an actual atonement is demanded. One of the most widely practiced penances is *prāṇayama*, breath control. The "man of sin" is "burnt" by regular controlled inhalation and retention and exhalation of air.

Tapas, literally "heat," designating all sorts of austerities, is the general means for making reparation for wrong doing. It may include sexual continence, truthfulness, frequent bathing, wearing wet clothes, sleeping on the floor, and fasting for a specific length of time. "*Tapas* quickly consumes all sins" goes the proverbial saying. Under certain circumstances *tapas* can also be won by proxy: devout widows perform penances that are meant to profit their deceased husbands; the rich pay the poor to perform *tapas* on their behalf. Merit bestowed upon another is lost to oneself; therefore, one can read in popular books moving stories of the ultimate penance somebody performs by giving away as a gift the whole store of *tapas* acquired in many years of hard work.

Agniṣṭoma, a gift consumed by fire, is another traditionally accepted means of atonement. It is to be accompanied by shaving one's head and beard, bathing in holy water muttering *mantras*, pouring *ghī* into the fire, abstinence, and truthfulness in speech. The sin is thrown into the fire and burnt along with the offering.

Japa may be the most common and widespread means of atonement for Hindus today. It can be of three kinds: *vācika*, audible murmuring, is the lowest; *upāmṣu*, inaudible lisping, confers ten times more merit; *mānasa*, mental recitation, is worth a hundred times as much. For the purpose of atonement, the books prescribe a high number of recitations of certain formulas or names. In ancient times, *japa* was accessible only to the upper castes, who had the right to recite the *Veda*. It was forbidden to the *śūdras* and outcastes; if they practiced it nevertheless, it remained without effect. Later, a special kind of *japa* was created for *śūdras* and women. The *Purāṇas* again are full of *mantras* and *stotras* that carry with them the promise of expiating all sins if recited even once by anyone. The mere utterance of the revealed name of God frees many generations from hells and punishments.

Dāna, the offering of gifts to Brahmins, is among the acts most often recommended in the *śāstras* to atone for crimes. The gift of gold is especially effective, as is the gift of a cow, a horse, or land. Gifts are even potent enough to annihilate the accumulated guilt of former lives. Numerous copperplates have been preserved that document the gift of land for the purpose of gaining religious merit for the donor and his ancestors. Even today, industrialists build temples and rest houses for pilgrims for the same purpose; hundreds of beggars and cripples give to the pious Hindus who visit a temple ample opportunity to rid themselves of their sins by distributing money, food, and cloth.

Upavāsa, fasting, is another popular form of penance. In its strict sense, it entails total abstinence from food and drink, and even at present, numerous Indians keep a total fast on a good number of days in a year. For the more sophisticated and theologically astute Hindus, *upavāsa* often means nothing more than observing certain restrictions in the kind of food they eat, with the same religious merit attached to it. Thus, the Vaiṣṇavas, who are strict vegetarians, fast on *ekādaśī*, every eleventh day in each half of the lunar month. On those days, they are not supposed to eat cereals grown above the ground: rice, wheat, barley, *dāl.* Whatever grows below the ground, all roots and tubers, as well as milk and dairy products may be eaten.

Tīrthayātra, pilgrimage to holy places, is another popular penance. The *Mahābhārata* already mentions the "seven holy cities": Kāśī, Prayāga, Mathurā, Ujjainī, Haridvāra, Ayodhyā, and Gāyā. Each one is the goal of millions of Hindu pilgrims seeking to atone for their own sins and the sins of their ancestors. The *Purāṇas* carry numerous *māhātmyas*, praises of those holy places, in which the merits of visiting the sacred spots are described in detail. Even in the modern India of steel combines, jet travel, and political parties, millions of people are constantly on the move to wash away their sins. Many people retire to one of the holy cities in their old age, and quite a few arrange to be brought to Banaras to die, because then one does not have to fear punishment or rebirth.

Many Hindus undertake these penances of their own accord; others are told to do so, often by the caste *pañcāyat*, which oversees the affairs of its members and interferes, if necessary. Crimes of social relevance were punished by the secular authority. According to Manu, the Brahmins could, however, take the law into their own hands, because they were superior to the *kṣatriya.* But that they, too, had in reality to abide by the decisions of the ruler, becomes clear when we hear that they may "punish through their own weapon, which is the word of the Veda" and use the spells of the *Atharvaveda* against those who have offended them.[23]

THE IDEAL OF HOLINESS

It is only natural that the more aware a person is of the holiness of the Lord, the more conscious he or she is of sin. Thus, texts meant for the more exclusive circles of religious professionals contain a far more scrupulous determination of sins and a greater urgency for acts of atonement. The Vaiṣṇavas, considering *sevā* or service of the Lord Viṣṇu the sole aim of life, have special lists of "sins against service." These include entering the temple on a car or with shoes on, neglecting to celebrate the feasts of Viṣṇu, greeting the image of Viṣṇu with one hand only, turning one's back toward it, stretching one's feet toward the image, laying down or eating before the image, gossiping before the image, eating one's food without first having offered it to Viṣṇu, etc. All signs of disrespect or negligence before the bodily presence of the Lord in his image are thus considered sins, to be atoned for through the repetition of the name of Viṣṇu. The "sins against the name," however, cannot be atoned for. They are ten, according to the authorities: offending a Vaiṣṇava by scolding him; thinking that both Viṣṇu and Śiva are Lord; thinking that the guru is a mere human being; reproaching the *Vedas, Purāṇas,* and other scriptures; interpreting the name; speaking or thinking ill of the name; committing sins on the strength of the name; considering other good works as equal to the recitation of the name; teaching the name to people who have no faith; and disliking the name even after having heard about its greatness.[24]

NEW DEPARTURES ON THE PATH OF WORKS

A new understanding of the Path of Works developed since the late eighteenth century, possibly under the influence of contact with the British and a socially-conscious Christianity. The eagerness with which Ram Mohan Roy responded to New Testament ethics and with which he successfully fought against cruel traditions like *satī* and infanticide did not lead to a large-scale Hindu conversion to Christianity but to a Hindu Renaissance with clearly social and ethical overtones. The call to action of Kṛṣṇa in the *Bhagavadgītā* was interpreted as a call to remedy the social ills of Hindu society, and eventually as a call to liberate the homeland of the Hindus from foreign domination. B. G. Tilak's commentary on the *Gītā*, "the Gospel of Action," gives an explicitly socio-political slant to the old notion of *karmamārga.* So did Mahātmā Gāndhī and many others in his footsteps.

Age-old notions of purity still are of importance to groups of traditional high-caste Hindus, and the idea of holiness, as the *bhakti* prophets of the late Middle Ages preached it, is still meaningful to large numbers of devotees. But, increasingly, Hinduism understands its mission as a secular, cultural, political one: the mission to form a strong modern nation-state on the basis of *Hindutva,* a distinct tradition grown from older forms of Hinduism and capable of sustaining a modern society.

1. *Annaprāśana:* First Feeding of Solid Food

2. *Cuḍākarma:* Tonsure Before Receiving Sacred Thread

3. *Vivāha:* Marriage

4. *Nāmakāraṇa:* Name Giving

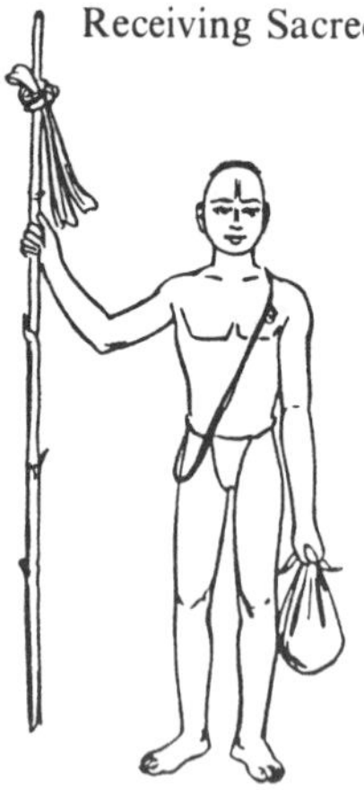

5. *Saṁnyāsa:* Renouncing

Figure 11.1 Some *saṁskāras*

11. The Hindu Sacraments: The *Saṁskāras*

With holy rites, prescribed by the Veda, must the ceremony of conception and other sacraments be performed for twice-born men, which sanctify the body and purify in this life and after death.

—Manusmṛti *II, 26*

THE *SAṀSKĀRAS*, USUALLY described as the sacraments of Hinduism, are rites by means of which a Hindu becomes a full member of the socio-religious community.[1] They begin with conception and end with cremation, "sanctifying the body and purifying it in this life and after death."[2] The classical *śāstras* list a great number of *saṁskāras* that apparently were in use in former times; nowadays, only a few are practiced, but an immense importance attaches to these in the practical life of Hindus (see Figure 11.1).

Manu explains the effect of the different *saṁskāras* thus:

> In the case of the twice-born[3] the sins that come from seed and womb are redeemed through *homas* during pregnancy, through *jātakarma*, the ritual performed at birth, through *cauḍa*, the tonsure of the whole head leaving only one lock at the crown of the head, and the girdling with *muñja*-grass. This body is made fit for the attainment of Brahma through *svādhyāya*, the study of scripture, by observance of *vratas*, holy vows, through the so-called *traividyā*, by worshipping the *devas*, *pitṛs* and *ṛṣis*, by begetting a son and through the daily performance of the *pañca mahāyajñas* as well as public *yajñas*.[4]

Hindus associate great significance with the ceremonies surrounding the birth of a child and the name giving. Popular works like the *Viṣṇu Purāṇa* offer instructions like these:

> When a son is born, let his father perform the ceremonies proper on the birth of a child. . . . Let him feed a couple of Brahmans and according to his means offer sacrifices to the *devas* and *pitṛs*. . . . On the tenth day after birth[5] let the father give a name to his child; the first term of which shall be the appellation of a god, the second of a man as Śarma for a *brahmin*, Varma for a *kṣatriya*, Gupta for a *vaiśya* and Dāsa for a *śūdra*. A name should not be void of meaning: it should not be indecent, nor absurd, nor ill-omened, nor fearful, it should consist of an even number of syllables, it should not be too long or too short, nor too full of long vowels, but contain a due proportion of short vowels and be easily articulated.[6]

Manu adds that the names of women should be easy to pronounce, not imply anything dreadful, possess a plain meaning, be auspicious, end in long vowels, and contain a word of blessing (*āśīrvāda*).[7] In the fourth month, the "leaving of the house" ceremony should be celebrated; in the sixth, the first feeding with rice, and other family customs. In the first or third year, all boys of the three upper castes are supposed to get *cauḍa* or tonsure.

THE SECOND BIRTH

Upanayana, the initiation, is among the most important *saṁskāras* still in fairly universal use, even in liberal Hindu families. According to the *śāstras*, it is to take place in the eighth year for a *Brahmin* boy, in the eleventh for a *Kṣatriya* boy, and in the twelfth for a *Vaiśya* boy.[8] The investiture with the *yajñopavīta* or *janëu*, the sacred thread, marks the end of the young twice-born's childhood and innocence, as he enters studentship, the first of the four *āśramas* or stages of his life. From now on he is held responsible for his actions. As a child, he had no duties and could incur no guilt; he did not have to observe restrictions regarding permitted and prohibited food; he was free in his speech and his lies were not punished. In ancient times, the young *brahmacari* took up residence with his guru to be taught in the Vedas; nowadays, the boys normally remain with their families and continue attending the same school as before. Nevertheless, it marks an important occasion in the life of a Hindu boy, since it is often the first personal and conscious encounter with his religion as part of his own life. Most families keep contact with their traditional paṇḍit, who instructs the boys in their *dharma*.

The exact time for the ceremony of *upanayana* is determined by the family astrologer. The occasion still retains something of an initiation ceremony; a crucial rite of passage that in olden times could result in the death of the candidate. The boy is given a wooden staff and dressed with a belt of *muñja* grass. His head is shaved, except for the *śikha.* The Brahmin who performs the ceremony recites *mantras* to Savitri, asking him not to let the boy die.

Then the sacred thread is put on for the first time, henceforth to be worn day and night. It consists of three times three single threads about two yards long and normally is worn over the right shoulder. The origin of the *janëu* has not been explained as yet. Many believe it to be the remnant of a garment. Neglect of the *janëu* can lead to expulsion from the caste, and good works without the *janëu* bring no fruit. Traditionally, also the *gāyatrī-mantra* was imparted to the young Brahmin at this occasion; its repetition was meant to be the common means of expiation for sins.

The ancient *śāstras* contain a complete *brahmacari-dharma* for the boys, to be observed from the time of initiation till marriage. The reformist Ārya Samāj attempts to revive it in its *gurukulas*, where young boys and girls are kept under strict discipline from the age of four to twenty. There are also still a few Vedic schools in India where young boys spend several years in the manner prescribed by the *śāstras:* mornings and evenings the boys chant Vedic hymns in chorus; the daytime is devoted to memorizing the *Veda*, studying the *Vedāṅgas*, and collecting firewood. Quite strict rules must be observed with regard to food. The boys have to be very respectful toward the guru, never addressing him without certain honorific titles. Complete sexual continence is of the essence; the very name of this mode of life was synonymous with chastity. A *brahmacari* who failed in this respect had to submit to very humiliating, painful, and lengthy penances. Manu says he must go around clad in the skin of a donkey for a whole year, beg food in seven houses while confessing his sin, eat only once a day, and bath three times daily. Usually, this stage of life ended with marriage at the age of around twenty. But there had always been *naiṣṭhika brahmacarins* who continued to live as *brahmacaris* without ever marrying.[9]

THE SACRAMENT FOR MEN AND WOMEN

The most important *saṁskāra* had always been and still is *vivāha*, marriage. Hindu law knew eight forms of marriage, of which it recognized four as legal, though not all of them equally worthy.[10] Besides the normal case of arrangement through the parents, Hinduism also legalized forms of love marriage. Monogamy is the rule today, though traditional Hindu law permitted a man to marry up to four wives. After many years of work—and against the opposition of many traditional Hindus—the government of India passed *The Hindu Marriage Act* in 1955, which, with several amendments, became the official marriage law for Hindus in 1976, replacing earlier legislation. It unified Hindu marriage law, which had existed in a number of regional variants, and also brought it closer to modern Western law by recognising civil marriage and allowing divorce, also at the request of the wife. Its enactment was not universally welcomed, not even among Western experts in Hindu law.[11]

The *Mahābhārata* describes a society in which polyandry was practiced; Draupadī is the wife of the five Pāṇḍava brothers. A few tribes in the hills around Tehrī Garhwal practice it even today.

Popular books and *śāstras* alike give advice about the "auspicious" and "inauspicious" signs to look for in one's marriage partner. Thus, we read that a man should select a maiden "who has neither too much nor too little hair, is neither black nor yellow complexioned, neither a cripple, nor deformed." He must nor marry a girl who is vicious or unhealthy, of low origin, ill-educated, with a disease inherited from father or mother, of a masculine appearance, with a croaky voice, a harsh skin, with white nails, red eyes, fat hands, too short, or too tall. She also should be "in kin at least five degrees removed from his mother and seven from his father."[12]

The actual ceremonies of the marriage culminate in a feast very often so sumptuous that poor families take up ruinous loans in order to meet the expenses and provide food for all those who expect to be invited. Depending on status, a richly decorated horse or an elephant must be hired, dancers and musicians must entertain the numerous guests, paṇḍits and Brahmins must be paid their *dakṣiṇās*. The ceremonies differ from one region to another, but everywhere they follow a certain pattern that is meaningful and rests on ancient traditions.[13]

One of the texts details the following ritual. To the west of the fire altar, there is to be placed a grinding stone; to the northeast, a water jug. The bridegroom sacrifices while the bride holds his hand. He faces west and she looks toward the east, while he says: "I take thy hand in mine for happy fortune."[14] He takes her thumb only if he wishes only for sons, the other fingers only if he wishes only for daughters, the whole hand if he wants both boys and girls. Three times the bridegroom leads the bride around the fire, murmuring: "I am *amā* [this], you are *sā* [she]; I am heaven, you are earth; I am *sāma*, you are *ṛk*. Let us marry each other, let us beget sons and daughters. Kind to each other, friendly, with well-meaning mind may we live a hundred years." Each time he makes her step onto a stone with the words: "Step on this stone, be firm as stone, overcome the enemies, trample down the adversary." Then the bridegroom pours *ghī* over the bride's hands, and the bride's brother sprinkles grains of rice over their hands, this repeated three times.

The bridegroom loosens the hairband of the bride with the words: "I deliver you from the bonds of Varuṇa." He asks her to take seven steps to the north, saying: "May you take a step for power, a step for strength, one for wealth, one for fortune, one for descendants, one for good times. May you be my friend with the seventh step. May you be faithful to me. Let us have many sons. May they reach a ripe old age." The officiating paṇḍit brings the heads of bride and bridegroom close together and sprinkles them with water.

The bride is supposed to spend the three nights following the wedding ceremony in the house of an older Brahmin woman whose husband and children are still living. When the bride has seen the pole-star, the star *arundhatī*, and the seven *ṛṣis*,[15] she must break her silence by saying: "May my husband live long and may I bear him children." When entering her own house she is to say: "May your happiness increase here through your sons and daughters." The bridegroom then kindles their own sacred fire. The bride sits on a bull's hide and is first given curds to eat with the *mantra:* "May all gods unite our hearts."

There are countless variations and additions to the ceremony just described. Some prescribed that the couple should look into the sun, that the bridegroom should carry the bride over the threshold, that he should touch her heart with *mantras*, that he should offer silver and gold before the statues of Śiva and Gaurī. Also, the patriarchal or matriarchal tradition prevailing in the area is expressed in the relative importance of bride or bridegroom in the wedding ceremonies and the entrance to their home.

According to the *Ṛgveda* the goal of marriage is to enable a man to sacrifice to the devas and to beget a son who will ensure the continuity of the sacrifice. Woman was called "half of man" and the domestic sacrifice could only be performed by husband and wife jointly. The son, *putra*, is so called, the scriptures say, because he pulls his parents out (*tra*) from hell (*pu*). He is necessary not only for the pride of the family to continue its line but also for its spiritual welfare in the next world. *Śrāddha*, the last rites, could be properly performed only by a male descendent. Without *śrāddha*, the deceased remains forever a *preta*, a ghost.[16]

There are special sections in Hindu law, called *strīdharma*, that regulate the rights and obligations of married women, who even in traditional, patriarchal Hindu India were not simply the slaves of men. Manu has some flattering remarks about the mother being the goddess of the house and the gods showering happiness on the house where the woman is honored.[17] To underline this, he says:

> The house, in which female relations, not being duly honoured, pronounce a curse, perishes completely as if destroyed by magic. Hence men who seek happiness should always honour women on holidays and festivals with gifts of jewelry, clothes and good food. In that family where the husband is pleased

with his wife and the wife with her husband happiness will assuredly be lasting.[18]

On the other hand, Manu also warns men against woman, the perpetual temptress,[19] and decrees that she should never be independent: "In childhood a female must be subject to her father, in youth to her husband, when her lord is dead to her sons. She is not to separate from her husband. Though destitute of virtue, seeking pleasure or devoid of good qualities, a husband must be constantly worshipped as a god by a faithful wife."[20]

She must always be cheerful, clever in her household affairs, careful in cleaning her utensils, economical in expenditure, and faithful to her husband not only as long as he lives but until her own death.[21] In former times, the highest test of fidelity was the voluntary self-immolation on the husband's funeral pyre; occasionally it is said that this is still performed, though it has long been forbidden by law. In places of pilgrimage numerous widows spend the rest of their lives attached to temples and religios establishments, singing *bhajans* for some wealthy donor, who provides them with food and shelter.

PROVIDING FOR THE BEYOND

Antyeṣṭi, the last rites, also called *mṛtyusaṁskāra*, the sacrament of death is still performed today by practically all Hindus, orthodox as well as liberal. Hindus usually burn their dead, except in times of great disasters. Some sects like the Vīraśaivas practice burial. Also small children and *saṁnyāsis* are buried; poor people, for whom nobody is willing to pay the expenditure of cremation, are often unceremoniously thrown into the nearest river. But, ordinarily, a Hindu will provide during his lifetime for a *śrāddha* to be performed according to the *śāstras*. Details of the rites vary greatly according to the status of the departed, but there is a basic pattern followed by most.

After the hair and nails of the dead person have been cut off, the body is washed, the *tilaka* applied to the forehead, and it is wrapped in a new piece of cloth and garlanded with flowers. The one who performs the rites, normally the eldest son, washes his feet, sips water, does *prāṇayama*, and prays to the earth.

Then the litter is carried by some men or on a cart drawn by cows to the *smāsana*, the cremation grounds. The eldest son then circumambulates the place prepared for cremation and sprinkles water over it. With an iron rod, he draws three lines on the floor, saying: "I draw a line for Yama, the lord of cremation; I draw a line for *kāla*, time, the lord of cremation, I draw a line for *mṛtyu*, death, the lord of cremation." Some sesame seeds are put into the mouth of the deceased and the body is put upon the funeral pyre. His wife, if still alive, lays down beside him and is "called back to life" by her brother-in-law. After several minor rituals, during which five little balls made of flour are placed on different parts of the dead body, the pyre is lit by the eldest son. Rich people burn their dead with sandalwood which spreads a powerful and pleasant scent, strong enough to cover up the smell that is so typical of the cremation grounds.

While the pyre is burning, lengthy sections from the "hymns for the dead" are recited.[22] Yama is called upon to give the deceased a good place among the ancestors. The *pitṛs* are invoked as patrons of the living. Agni is invited not to harm the deceased but to carry him safely across with his body into the kingdom of the fathers. Pūṣan, the creator, the life of the universe, is besought to keep the departed in safety. Finally, the earth is besought to be good to the dead. One of the mourners is appointed to lift a filled earthen water jug onto his left shoulder, make a hole in the back of the jug, and walk three times around the burning corpse. The jug is knocked three times and then completely broken. The relatives—no other people are allowed to participate—then turn to the left and leave the cremation grounds without looking back, the youngest child in front.

Old taboos attach to the last rites; dealing with corpses causes ritual impurity, and thus the relations first go to a brook or river, immerse themselves three times, facing south (the direction of Yama, the god of the netherworlds), sip some water, and deposit the stone used for breaking the jug on the shore. They then sacrifice water mixed with sesame, saying: "O departed one, may this water, mixed with sesame, reach you". On the threshold of the house, they sip water and touch auspicious objects like fire, cow dung, and water before entering. The burning place is cooled with a mixture of milk and water under recitation of Ṛgvedic verses. On one of the following days, the skull is shattered and the remnants of the bones are gathered into an earthenware jar that, after some time, is either thrown into a holy river, preferably the Gaṅgā or Yamunā, at some *tīrtha*, to ensure the felicity of the departed, or buried with some ritual on a piece of land set apart for that purpose.

Saṁnyāsis, those who have received *dīkṣā* that anticipates cremation, are buried in a yoga posture. Frequently, a chapellike memorial, called *samādhī*, is erected over the tomb of famous and popular *sādhus*, and people keep coming to those places, seeking advice and assistance from the heavenly master.

Cremation rites are only the first part of *antyeṣṭi*. For ten days after the burning, water mixed with sesame is offered every day together with the leaves of certain trees. On the tenth day, the eldest son, who officiated at the cremation, goes to the cremation ground and offers a *piṇḍa*, a small ball of rice, saying: "May this *piṇḍa* benefit the *preta* of so-and-so of this family so that his ghost may not feel hunger and thirst." According to the belief of many Hindus it is important that crows should come and peck at the *piṇḍas*. If they do not come the relatives believe that the deceased has left the world with wishes unfulfilled. Often they try to attract the crows for hours, with promises to fulfill the wish of the departed. The stone upon which the sacrifice was offered is anointed and thrown into the water. A handful of water is then offered to the *preta*.

There is a popular belief that a man for whom the proper *śrāddha* ceremonies have not been performed has to remain forever a *piśāca*, an evil ghost, even if numerous sacrifices are offered on his behalf at some later date. According to the *Purāṇas*, immediately after cremation, every person receives a *yatanīya-śarīra*, a body that will be subject to tortures and suffering in relation to the sins committed; the *bhaktas* of Viṣṇu, however, receive an incorruptible body like Viṣṇu's, with four arms, in which to enjoy forever the presence of Viṣṇu and serve him eternally. The subtle body of the deceased, so another story goes, in which the dead person lives until the next rebirth in another body, is built up by means of the funerary rites.

Present Hindu practice seems to rest on an imperfect synthesis of various strands of belief relating to the afterlife. On the one hand, the *Purāṇas* faithfully describe the Vedic cremation ritual without adding anything sectarian.[23] On the other hand, they abound in descriptions of rebirths, heavens, and hells that are quite obviously irreconcilable with the Vedic conception,[24] which aims at transforming the dead soul into a venerated ancestor, without any hint at rebirth or sectarian heaven and hell.

According to the *sūtras* the admission of the *preta* into the circle of the *pitṛs* is obtained through the *sapiṇḍīkaraṇa*, which normally takes place one year after death. On every new-moon day until then, a special *śrāddha* called *ekoddiṣṭa* is performed for the benefit of the deceased. Four earthen vessels are filled with a mixture of water, sesame seeds, and scents: one for the *preta*, and one each for his father, grandfather, and great-grandfather. The contents of the pot for the *preta* is poured into the other three pots while *mantras* are recited. From now on the new *preta* ranks as the first of the *pitṛs;* his great-grandfather drops from the list according to the Vedic rule "There can be no fourth *piṇḍa*." Now the "ghost" has become a "father," regularly mentioned in the numerous ancestor libations throughout the year. Hindu scriptures contain numerous chapters detailing the *śrāddha* ceremonies that form one of the most important parts of Hindu cult.

Thus, through the last sacrament, the meaning of the *saṁskāras* is fulfilled: the Brahmin, transformed into a twice-born being through *upanayana*, attaining the fullness of manhood in *vivāha*, becomes a "complete being," worthy of worship, through *śrāddha*, and is thus able to provide blessings for his descendants.

Through the performance of *saṁskāras*, all Hindus practice the *karmakāṇḍa*, the Path of Works, though as far as their beliefs and intellectual convictions are concerned, they may choose to follow the *bhaktimārga* or the *jñānamārga*, the ways of devotion and knowledge. We have to remember this before dealing with the Path of Devotion and the Path of Knowledge. Although theological polemics of representatives of one path often may create the impression of exclusivity and a rejection of "wrong paths," in actual life the Hindu participates in all three ways and would not risk the condemnation associated with missing out on any of them.

12. The Path of Knowledge: *Jñānamārga*

He who knows Brahman as the real, as knowledge, as the infinite,
Set down in the secret place [of the heart] and in the highest heaven,
He obtains all desires,
Together with the allknowing Brahman.

—Taittirīya Upaniṣad *II, 1*

THE *UPANIṢADS*, ALSO called *Vedānta* or "the end of the *Veda*," are the basis for mainstream Indian philosophical and mystical tradition, which refers to them as to its source and ultimate authority. Today, the hymns from the Vedic *saṁhitās* mainly serve a practical purpose, as part of the ritual; very few draw their personal religion and beliefs from them. The *Upaniṣads*, however, are studied, quoted, and used even now in arguments and in attempts to build up a contemporary spirituality.

Chronologically, the *Upaniṣads* constitute the last part of *śruti*, connected via specific *brāhmaṇas* and *āraṇyakas* to the *saṁhitās*.[1] It has become customary, however, to consider them as a class of texts by themselves and to publish them independent of the rest of *śruti*.[2] They are treated by some authors as a kind of protestant countercurrent to the prevailing Vedic sacrificial religion; by others, as a plain continuation of the same tradition. Both views have their merits and their evident shortcomings. The *Upaniṣads* quote the *Vedas* quite frequently and make use of Vedic ideas; they also contain anti-Vedic polemics and represent unorthodox viewpoints.[3] There is, however, a difference between the *saṁhitās* and the *Upaniṣads*, recognized since early times by the Hindu interpreters. The *Vedas* and *brāhmaṇas* center around the sacrificial ritual whose ultimate goal is *svarga* or heaven; *the Upaniṣads* proclaim an esoteric teaching, the dispensability of ritual, and the attainment of freedom and immortality through a process of concentration and spiritual interiorization. This difference prompted ancient writers to classify the religion of the *Upaniṣads* as *jñānamārga*, "the way of knowledge" in contrast to the *karmamārga*, "the way of works" propounded by *saṁhitās* and *brāhmaṇas*. The *Upaniṣads* vary considerably in length; among the thirteen *Upaniṣads*, normally considered the authentic or principal ones, the longest amounts to about a hundred printed pages and the shortest to only about three pages.

THE PRINCIPAL UPANIṢADS: THEIR AUTHORS AND THEIR TEACHINGS

The following chronology has been accepted fairly commonly by scholars: *Bṛhadāraṇyaka* and *Chāṇḍogya* form the oldest group, then come *Īśa* and *Kena;* the third group is made up of *Aitareya, Taittirīya*, and *Kauśītakī;* the fourth of *Kaṭha, Muṇḍaka*, and *Śvetāśvatara;* with *Praśna, Maitrī*, and *Māṇḍūkya* concluding the "principal *Upaniṣads*."[4] This chronology does not take into account the different strata in each of the more lengthy texts, pertaining to different eras. The rest of the 108 Upaniṣads that are commonly considered as canonical in one way or other belong partly to much later times and normally represent sectarian teachings of various groups, which would preclude their universal acceptance.

Quite frequently, the *Īśā(vāsya) Upaniṣad* is described as the most important one, the essence of all the Upaniṣadic teaching. This may be due partly to its brevity, partly to its concentrated contents; but the *Upaniṣads* mentioned earlier contain much that differs in content from the *Īśa* and much that adds to it.

The designation *Upaniṣad* is usually explained as derived from *upa* ("close by") *ni* ("down") *ṣad* ("sit"), implying a form of teaching from the teacher's mouth to the pupil's ear, a secret doctrine, or at least a teaching that was not common knowledge of the people. Since the date given to the principal *Upaniṣads* varies between 4000 B.C.E.[5] and 600 B.C.E.,[6] no precise information about the authors' identities can be given. The *Upaniṣads* do mention a great number of names, both in the texts and in the lists of *guruparaṁparā* at the end of the texts, and we must assume that many of those names refer to actual historical persons that might be called Upaniṣadic philosophers.[7]

In certain parts of the *Upaniṣads*, intended to convey a teaching through hyperbole or metaphor, the names of *devas* and *ṛṣis* are mentioned as authors of certain doctrines or practices, an ascription that does not allow any historical verification. Over the centuries, other parts of the

Upaniṣads have been transmitted anonymously. Numerous individual theories and exercises, however, are connected with definite names, most probably representing eminent historical persons. Maitrī, after whom one entire *Upaniṣad* is called, must have been a great mystic who lived and taught things laid down in his *Upaniṣad.* Kauśītaki, another name connected with an entire *Upaniṣad,* could have been the author of the doctrine of the three meditations and the first to have identified *prāṇa,* "life breath," with *Brahman.* Jaivali can well be considered the author of the *pañcāgni vidyā,* the understanding of the entire cosmic process as a symbol of and model for sacrifice in the Vedic sense.[8] Uddalaka can be identified from the *Chāṇḍogya Upaniṣad* as the author of a quite interesting cosmology, differing in his views from other early cosmologists whose names are mentioned as well.[9] Kauśala Aśvalāyana is an early psychologist whose teachings are recorded briefly in the *Praśna Upaniṣad.*[10] He is superseded by the psycho-metaphysician Pippalāda, who developed the doctrine of *rayī* and *prāṇa,* the Indian equivalent of the Aristotelian *hyle* and *morphe* (matter and form) dualism. A Vāmadeva appears as a master theoretician of the doctrine of rebirth, who held that man is born three times: at the time of his conception, at the time of the birth of his own child, and at the time of rebirth after death.

The most important group of Upaniṣadic philosophers are those connected with spirituality, the real core of Upaniṣadic teaching. The teaching of Śaṇḍilya is preserved in a section of the *Chāṇḍogya,*[11] that of Dadyac in a section of the *Bṛhadāraṇyaka* expounding the *madhuvidyā*[12] and the interdependence of all things. Another famous philosopher is Sanatkumāra, introduced as the preceptor of Nārada in the *Chāṇḍogya;* for him happiness, *ānanda,* is the center of all human effort.[13] Aruṇi and Yājñavalkya, his pupil, emerge as the two most frequently mentioned and most important Upaniṣadic teachers. Both develop what might be called a metaphysical psychology, a rigorous method of realization and an appropriate theory of its process. Gārgī, one of the two wives of Yājñavalkya, plays a major role in a section of the *Bṛhadāraṇyaka Upaniṣad.* She is the first Indian woman philosopher we know of.[14]

Before reading any of the *Upaniṣad* texts, it is necessary to familiarize oneself with the method of teaching used by them, which is often so different from our current philosophical or theological presentation as to bar any true understanding of it. The *Upaniṣads* are fond of riddles and enigmatic comparisons,[15] employing images and illustrations drawn from ancient Indian experiences and theories rather than from present ones. Often one must be familiar with a great deal of background before being able to follow the argument of the *Upaniṣads.*

Sometimes, the *Upaniṣads* also employ the aphoristic method, condensing an entire world view into one sentence or even one syllable.[16] Closely connected is the apophatic method, the way in which Socrates preferred to teach. Instead of a positive answer, the student is given a question or a piece of purely negative information about what is *not* truth, thus compelling him or her to transcend verbal, conceptual understanding and see that the proper answer to truly important questions consists of silence rather than of talk.[17] Quite often, the *Upaniṣads* derive certain teachings from an etymology of key words; those etymologies, too, do not always follow the paths of contemporary Sanskrit scholarship but employ certain models that demand some study of the historical background beyond mere linguistics.

Myths are quite frequently employed, and these often constitute, in literary terms, the most beautiful portions of the *Upaniṣads.*[18] Analogies are utilized to lead the student gradually to the level of insight required to understand the teacher's perception of reality. Monologues are not absent, though they are much less frequent than in later philosophical and theological teaching.

The most interesting and potentially most valuable method is the dialectics employed in some of the major *Upaniṣads.* The ancient Indians certainly were great debaters, as we know from other sources. They sharpened their dialectical skills in protracted controversies with exponents of other views, as the accounts in the Pāli canon, for instance, show. Buddhists were largely responsible for the refinement of dialectical skills used by the Hindus to overthrow them. It was an ancient Indian practice to challenge an adversary to a public debate, which had to end with the defeat of one of the two contestants. The loser of the argument, at the same time, usually lost all of his disciples, who went over to the conqueror. Thus, the biographer of the great Śaṅkara entitles his work the *Digvijāya*, the conquest of the four quarters by his hero, who was successful in debate after debate against his rivals.

With regard to the contents of the *Upaniṣads*, they do not contain a systematic treatise of philosophy but a string of more or less developed insights, theories, and principles.

The *Vedāntasūtra*, also called *Brahmasūtra*, ascribed to Badarāyaṇa, attempts to summarize and systematize the basic philosophy of the *Upaniṣads* in four *adhyāyas* or treatises, containing altogether 550 aphorisms. It has become the basic text of all the schools of Vedānta philosophy, and the *bhāṣyas*, or commentaries, written upon it constitute the main works of the different systems, often offering diametrically opposed interpretations of the same brief *sūtra.* As research has shown quite convincingly, this *Vedāntasūtra* represents largely the position taken by the *Chāṇḍogya Upaniṣad*, with a few additions here and there. It leaves out much of the contents of the other *Upaniṣads*, which can hardly be brought together under one system.

MAJOR THEMES IN THE UPANIṢADS

The problems raised by the *Upaniṣads* do not coincide with the approaches developed by recent Western academic disciplines. They deal with physics, biology, psychology, religion, and philosophy as well as with mythology and astrology.

One of the threads that runs through much of the Upaniṣadic quest is the enquiry into the hidden ground of being and the root of one's existence, the essence of things and the bond that keeps them together. This search concerns as much the physical structure of material things as the spiritual dimension of human existence. Like the philosophizing of the pre-Socratics of ancient Greece, the Upaniṣadic approach is neither purely physical nor purely metaphysical, neither purely psychological nor purely logical according to modern categories. Instead, it is a holistic approach that allows us to put the elements of knowledge acquired through different methods into one mosaic of the world, rough in its details but impressive in its totality.

We have mentioned earlier some of the Upaniṣadic ideas concerning the origin of the universe. The search for the substratum common to all beings and its origin is one of the main themes dealt with in different *Upaniṣads*. Along with attempts to understand water, air, fire or *ākāśa*, ether or space as the *Urelement* is the interesting theory of the *Taittirīya*, which assumes five basic elements: fire, water, earth, wind, and space. The whole universe is structured in pentads, corresponding to the elementary pentad, resulting in an ontic interrelationship, a true cosmic harmony: "Five-fold verily, is this all, with the fivefold indeed does one win the fivefold."[19]

This theory gains importance in connection with rebirth. At the time of death, the faculties and organs of the body return to their respective places in the cosmos: the eye to the sun, the vital breath to the wind, the flesh to the earth, the fluids to the water, thought to space. We cannot overlook here the relevance of the *pañcāgni vidyā*, the doctrine of the five fires that explains the entire creation as an interlocking succession of five sacrifices. This connection again gains importance in yoga philosophy, where an attempt is made to establish real connections between the corresponding parts of the microcosm and the macrocosm, ideas that, incidentally, are not foreign to the Western tradition either.[20]

Imagined contests between the individual organs of the body and the various functions, concerning their relative importance for the others, look like entertaining children's stories. In fact, they are quite serious philosophy, attempting to reduce the fivefold reality of the microcosm to the One, which in its turn must be the principal element of the universe itself, sustaining all being. The conclusion that *prāṇa*, the breath of life, supports the life of all the other functions brings us very close indeed to the central *ātman-brahman* speculation, which we shall examine more closely in the next chapter.[21]

An other Upaniṣadic seer derives the existence of all beings from hunger, the equivalent of death.[22] Knowing means controlling; thus the *Upaniṣad* sets out to teach the conquest of death. It cannot take place in the sphere of phenomena, where rebirth and redeath are necessarily part of nature, it must reach beyond. The conquest of the inner space, the opening of the seemingly closed world of nature, constitutes the most precious portion of the *Upaniṣads* for us today. The "ultimate," the "point of rest," the "immutable," the Upaniṣads find, is the inner core of all things, the reason for their existence. Though invisible, it is more powerful than the visible. It is delicate and subtle, impervious to the senses but "self-evident." It cannot be made into the object of objective reasoning but exists only as the identity found in introspection. The ultimate, to be sure, is unborn, unchanging, and immortal. Its abode is "the abode of the heart"—seemingly manifold but in fact one. It is not identical with any thing, it is no-thing; it is neither the object seen nor the faculty of seeing: it is the seeing of the seeing, the hearing of the hearing, the thinking of thinking. As such it is inscrutable, and yet it is present in everything and realizable in all situations. It is the truth and the reality of things, not only *satya* but *satyasya satya*.[23]

THE QUEST FOR REALITY BEYOND APPEARANCE

Reality is the term that stands at the center of all the endeavor of Indian philosophy; the differentiation between the obvious and the real, the conditional and the essential, the apparent and the true. The quest for reality finally leads to the discovery that reality cannot be found outside but only inside. Thus the *jñānamārga*, the Path of Knowledge, does not constitute a system of objective conceptual statements but a way toward self-discovery. The ground of the universe and the ground of our own existence are identical.

This self-discovery takes place in stages, of which the Upaniṣads usually enumerate four. The most systematic exposition of this four-step process of cognition is given in the *Māṇḍūkya*.[24]

The first and lowest stage of awareness is *jāgarita-sthāna*, the normal state of being awake and, hence, open to sense perception and rational thought. The spirit of a person is poured out into a multitude of objective things, bound to space and time and to the laws of the physical universe.

Svapna-sthāna, the dreaming state, "in which one cognizes internal objects" is already higher, because the spirit is no longer subject to the laws of the physical world or bound to space and time. The person now creates the world in which he or she moves and steps out of the limitations of physical nature by creating whatever the mind conceives.

Suṣupti, profound and dreamless sleep, is the third state, higher again than dream. It is a "blissful state," a state of unification in which the spirit is no longer scattered over a profusion of objective and subjective things, but there is no consciousness of this unification and bliss.

Turīya, the fourth state, is beyond all that: it is perception of neither external nor internal objects, neither knowledge nor ignorance; it is without describable qualities; it is supreme consciousness of consciousness, a cessation of all movement and all multiplicity, complete freedom. It is the self; and it is the knowledge of the self, which is the same, because the self, as the Upaniṣad understands it, is pure knowledge, being, bliss.

The knowledge we ordinarily possess is a knowledge of something. The knowledge of *turīya* is a knowledge of nothing in particular but of the ground of all things and all knowing. It is the self knowing itself as the self, not the function of an isolated capacity of the mind but an awareness, lighting up the subject itself as pure perception. Thus, *jñāna* is not a conceptual synthesis of a subject-object polarity but the experience of the subject in reality as such. The aporia of the coexistence of the finite and infinite, the real and unreal, the temporal and eternal, the subjective and objective is not resolved but seen as nonexistent. *Jñāna* is the self-enlightenment of reality as such, the self-consciousness of reality. In *jñāna* consciousness rests in itself, knowing nothing beyond this self-consciousness that has no objective content.

The difficulty lies in interpreting and communicating this knowledge through concepts whose validity is negated by this very knowledge. The concepts are all taken from the sphere of objective knowledge, in which *jñāna* cannot happen. On the level of the perception of the ultimate as reality, there cannot be any concepts, because there is no more multiplicity, no thing with which this knowledge could be identified. It is not possible to have some of this knowledge; one either has it fully or not at all. Perception of *ātman* is indivisible. There is, however, scope for growth: the knowledge may be dimly perceived before becoming overwhelmingly clear. The *Muṇḍaka Upaniṣad* distinguishes between a *para*, a higher, and an *apara*, a lower knowledge. The lower is the knowledge of the *Vedas* and *Vedāṅgas*, traditional knowledge. The higher is that "wherewith the imperishable is grasped." Thus, it says:

> That which is invisible, incomprehensible, without family or caste, without eye and ear, without hand or foot, eternal, all-permeating, omnipresent, extremely subtle: that is the imperishable recognized by the wise as the source of all beings. Just as the spider emits a thread and absorbs it again, or as grass sprouts from the earth or as hair grows on a living body, thus everything has its roots in the imperishable.[25]

THE UNIQUENESS OF VEDĀNTIC KNOWLEDGE

It is very difficult to express the knowledge, or the way leading to it, in Western terminology, which is heavily dependent on Greek thought.[26] Knowledge and way in the Indian understanding have stages, not set side by side but within each other, in depth, within consciousness itself. Its aim is to reach reality itself, not to abstract a concept from it. This means not only training the mind but developing a life-style of inwardness, from within which life then develops in a new way, whose knowledge is simply incommensurable with the knowledge achieved through sense perception and abstraction from it. The closer this knowledge comes to reality, the less can concepts express it adequately. It is possible to make statements about this knowledge—as well as about the *ātman* and about *turīya*, all ultimately identical!—statements that are to be understood only as dialectical approximations: it is immanent and transcendent at the same time and neither immanent nor transcendent nor a combination of both. Every concept employed must at once be negated. Affirmation and negation at the same time, the *neti neti*, not thus, not thus, leads to a higher level of consciousness, where there is neither affirmation nor negation.

Human existence has not only a horizontal, historical dimension, but a vertical, non historical one as well. To cope with actual human existence, this movement toward the center, the attainment of a level of consciousness of the self, is indispensable. In our age of popularized technology, all problems seem to be understood as questions concerning quantifiable material entities. Our "soul science" declares all ultimate questioning as sickness because it presupposes the negation of a transcendent reality. Upaniṣadic thinking "rests" and is static as far as the outward movement and change in topic is concerned; for people unused to probing the depths, this vertical movement does not "lead further" and is considered uninteresting. There is no visible progress, and one needs time and patience.

There are signs that some of our contemporaries have realized that technological toys cannot serve as substitutes for the soul and that technical progress does not equal happiness. They have taken up ideas developed 3000 years ago in a materially far less developed culture in which, nevertheless, dissatisfaction with things could be strong enough to come to understand the no-thing as supreme bliss and fulfillment.

In the *Upaniṣads*, the specific knowledge is always emphasized as being new and different, *brahmavidyā* is considered to be much higher and incomparably better than sacrifical knowledge. In the light of *jñāna-mārga*, Vedic ritual religion is ignorance and darkness, a shaky raft unable to cross the ocean of existence. But, the *Upaniṣads* know well that a knowledge boasted of becomes an expression of ignorance, worse even than plain and naive not knowing. Thus, the *Īśa Upaniṣad* says: "Into blind darkness enter they that worship ignorance; into darkness greater than that, as it were, they that delight in knowledge."[27]

Compared to the Path of Work and its solid factual knowledge of the mechanism of sacrifices, the Path of Knowledge means turning toward the subject and the realization that the subject can never be understood as part of something else but only as a self-contained totality; it cannot be grasped in a concept but only in a realization. The realization is not *of* the ultimate but *is* itself the ultimate. Who knows himself or herself knows reality. The *method* of knowing reality is what the *Upaniṣads* can teach. They cannot teach reality. Everyone has to find it for himself or herself, using the method taught.

There are outward conditions to be fulfilled, too. According to some *Upaniṣads*, membership in the Brahmin caste is absolutely required and the disciple must have gone through the Vedic *saṁskāras*, especially the *upanayana*, before taking up the *jñānamārga* with a reputed teacher. Then the student has to undergo a long process of physical, mental, and moral preparation before being led to the formulas of knowledge. The preparation seems to be the more impressive part—the realization may be imparted in a sentence, a word, even in silence at the very end of the period of training. It is not the acquisition of some outward knowledge but an awareness of actual reality, the removal of so many layers of nonreality. Basically, nothing new is made known in realization; it is a subjective change to see everyday things and happenings as manifestations of the absolute; to see the self not as the individual "I" with physical needs and demands but as reality in the ultimate sense.

The imparting of *jñāna* does not have the characteristics of an instruction but of a revelation. Therefore, it is important not only to approach a scholar of all the traditional sciences but someone who has received revelation through a chain of bearers of this same light, a guru standing in the *guru paraṁparā*. The teacher does not choose his students, the students ask the teacher for admittance. The students must serve their master faithfully and submit to strict discipline; little of the long time is spent in oral instruction, most of it is *tapasya*, ascetical training, which sharpens the energies of the intellect, especially the power of discrimination, which is most essential.

A person must learn to distinguish the self from what is not the self, reality from appearance, and must be strong enough to reject all that is nonessential and nonreal. Through this, the students gain access to new depth and to new horizons that enable them to understand the true meaning of the words used to express the higher knowledge. Self-realization can be neither gained nor taught vicariously; everyone has to gain it personally. The guru points the way, supervises the training, clarifies doubts. As is written in the *Method of Enlightening the Disciple:*

> The *guru* is one who is endowed with the power of furnishing arguments pro and con, of understanding questions and remembering them, one who possesses tranquillity, self-control, compassion and a desire to help others, who is versed in the scriptures and unattached to enjoyments both seen and unseen, who has renounced the means to all kinds of actions, is a knower of Brahman and established in it and who is devoid of shortcomings such as ostentation, pride, deceit, cunning, jugglery, falsehood, egotism and attachment.[28]

The discussions between master and pupil, as recorded in the *Upaniṣads*, are very often a Socratic kind of questioning, to bring to light truth from within the disciple. Words are imperfect instruments through which to discover the unspeakable. They can be understood only when realization has already taken place; and by then, they are redundant. They serve to repudiate wrong conceptions and to prevent false identifications. The common method of logic, to arrive at conclusions from certain premises by way of syllogisms, is considered to be inadequate. It can only provide particular and finite object knowledge, never an all-encompassing subject realization. The means therefore for finding truth is not discursive reasoning but meditation. The *Upaniṣads* differ in their methods of meditation; some begin with gradually widening cosmic contemplations, others utilize the Vedic religious symbolism, still others employ *mantras* like the *OM.* From the audible sound, the aspirant reaches out to the soundless until he or she can finally say: "*Om* is Brahman, *Om* is the universe."

The *Upaniṣads* are not only records of ancient India, they are part of the living Hindu tradition. Quite often, they are recited as other scriptures are, memorized and quoted by people who do not spend their time as disciples of a guru. The recitations are quite frequently begun by the following *śloka*, which in itself sums up the essential teaching of the *Upaniṣads:*

> *pūrṇam adaḥ pūrṇam idam pūrṇāt pūrṇam udacyate pūrṇasya pūrṇam ādāya pūrṇam evāvaśiṣyate*
>
> "Fullness is this, fullness is that. Fullness proceeds from fullness. Having taken fullness from fullness, fullness itself remains."

The conclusion of the *Upaniṣad*, again recited, is often a promise of liberation as the following:

> This Brahmā told to Prajāpati, Prajāpati to Manu, Manu to mankind. He who has learned the Veda from the family of a teacher according to rule, in the time left over from serving his teacher, he who, after having returned to his family, settled down in a home of his own, continued to study what he has learned and has virtuous sons, he who concentrates all his senses in the self, who practices kindness towards all creatures, he who behaves thus throughout his life reaches the Brahmā-world, does not return hither again, verily he does not return hither again.[29]

The *Upaniṣads* are the great book of principles, India's *prote gnosis*, its basic philosophy, from which branch out the many systems of Vedānta of all later centuries.

13. *Ātman* and *Brahman*: Self and All

> Verily, this body (*śarīra*) is mortal. It has been appropriated by Death. But it is the standing ground of the deathless, bodiless Self (*ātman*).
>
> —Chāṇḍogya Upaniṣad *VIII, XII, 1*

DESPITE THE GREAT number of interesting topics dealt with in the *Upaniṣads*, their central concern is undoubtedly the knowledge of and path to *ātman* and *brahman*. It is impossible, however, to synthesize all the statements of even the principal *Upaniṣads* and to expound its *ātman-brahman* philosophy, what can be done is to indicate certain main trends of thought. One of these very obvious tendencies is the repeated attempt to arrange the seemingly infinite plurality of things in a limited number of categories, coordinating macrocosm and microcosm, and to understand manifold reality as a combination of relatively few primordial elements. By means of a progressive reduction one can finally arrive at the One, which is further reduced to an immaterial essence pervading everything without being identical with any one object. One could initially express it thus: the wise men of the Upaniṣads seek to grasp the real as the ultimate support of all phenomena.

They follow, in the main, two distinct paths. One begins with the outside world and the manifold objects, reducing them to five elements, to three, and finally to one. The other begins with a person's subjective consciousness and discovers in its depths the real, which proves to be the source of everything. Finally, the realization dawns that the immanent *ātman* is identical with the transcendent *brahman: ātman* is *brahman*. We have simplified things to establish a pattern; from the texts themselves we shall see that *Upaniṣadic* thought is much more complex and subtle.

In a lively discussion between the great philosopher Yājñavalkya and his wife, Gārgī Vācaknavī, the first of those two ways is demonstrated.

"Yājñavalkya", said Gārgī, "since all this world is woven, warp and woof, on water, on what, pray, is the water woven, warp and woof?"

"On wind, O Gārgī!"

"On what is the wind woven?"

"On the sky, O Gārgī."

The questioning goes on, and Yājñavalkya explains the "warp and woof" of each world within the cosmology of the time, as discussed earlier: the sky is "woven" on the world of the *gandharvas*, this on the sphere of the sun, this on the sphere of the moon, this on the world of the planets, this on the world of the *devas*, this on the realm of *Indra*, this again on the *prajāpati-loka*, the world of the creator of all beings.

"On what then is the world of the Lord of Creation woven?"

"On the world of *Brahman* says Yājñavalkya.

Gārgī tries to press on, wanting to know what comes after *Brahman*, as its substratum, but Yājñavalkya rejects the question: "Gārgī, do not question too much lest your head fall off. Verily you are asking too much about the divine being, about which we are not to question too much. Do not, Gārgī, question too much." Thereupon, Gārgī Vācaknavī kept silent.[1]

Before proceeding with texts, a brief etymological explanation of *ātman* and *brahman* may be of some help, though an understanding of both terms emerges, better perhaps, from the texts themselves, because there we can appreciate their deep ambiguity, the impossibility of really defining them.

Ātman is the grammatical form of the reflexive personal pronoun in Sanskrit; according to context it can mean the body, anything that one considers belonging to or a part of oneself, a meaning that leads to the probing question of what really constitutes one's "self", the subject of all feelings, thought, and wishes.

Brahman has many meanings. It is derived from the verbal root *bṛh-*, "to grow," to become great. In the Vedas, *brahman* means sacred utterance, that through which the *devas* become great. Later, it came to be used as a term denoting ritual and also those who were in charge of it, the *Brāhmaṇas*. The *Upaniṣads*, finally, use it as a designation for the ultimate reality, to be understood as the life breath of the universe and everything in it.[2]

But it is also used more loosely, in an analogous way; the word, the eye, the ear, the heart, the sun, space are all called *brahman*. Elsewhere every identification with any concrete object is denied, and *brahman* becomes a synonym for the unfathomable, the unthinkable, the mysterious that has no name. The popular Hindu sects equate *brahman* with Viṣṇu, Śiva, or Devī, respectively, giving it the qualities and attributes of the creator, the preserver, and the destroyer, seeing in it a "supreme person" with qualities that are described in detail. Advaita Vedānta has refused to identify *brahman* with any activity or quality and rather prefers to draw a distinction within *brahman* to express the conviction that the ultimate ground of all being is without any qualities or activities, since that would denote change. It is therefore *nirguṇa.*

A word of caution may be appropriate here. It would be misleading to translate *ātman* as "soul" and *brahman* as "supreme being," as we find quite frequently in popular books. Both words have a Western background and already reveal a specific solution to a problem that is left open in the *Upaniṣads*, namely, the question of the oneness and the plurality of reality. We shall avoid a wrong identification of *ātman* and *brahman* with foreign concepts if we consider in detail how the *Upaniṣads* arrive at their *ātman-brahman* realization.

> Om. The brahman-knower obtains the supreme. As has been said: One who knows *brahman* as the real [*satya*, which also means truth], as knowledge (*jñāna*) and then as the infinite (*ananta*), placed in the secret cave of the heart and in the highest heaven realizes all desires along with *brahman.* From this *ātman*, verily arose *ākāśa*, which means space or ether, a fine and subtle substance permeating the universe; from this came air, from air fire, from fire water, from water the earth, from the earth herbs, from herbs food, from food *puruṣa*, the "person." . . . From food (*anna*) verily are produced whatsoever creatures dwell on the earth. By food alone they live. And at the end they pass into it. Food is verily the first-born of the being. . . . Verily those who worship *brahman* as food obtain all food.
>
> Different from, and within that sphere that consists of food (*annarasamaya*) is the self that consists of life-breath (*ātma prāṇamaya*) by which it is filled. This has the form of a *puruṣa.* . . . The *devas* breathe this life-breath (*prāṇa*), as also do men and beasts; *prāṇa* is the life (*ayus*) of all. They who worship *brahman* as *prāṇa* attain a full life . . . this is the *ātman* of the former. Different from it and within the *prāṇa*-sphere is the self made of mind (*ātma manomaya*), by which it is filled. This [again] has the form of a *puruṣa* . . . Different from and within it, is the self that consists of understanding (*ātma vijñānamaya*), by which it is filled. This too has the form of a *puruṣa.* Faith (*śraddhā*) is its head, order (*ṛta*) its southern side, truth (*satya*) its northern side, yoga its soul (*ātma*) and the great one (*maha*) its foundation. Understanding directs the sacrifice and the actions. All *devas* worship the *brahman* which is understanding as the foremost. . . . Different from and within that which consists of understanding is the self consisting of bliss (*ātma ānandamaya*), by which it is filled. This too has the form of a *puruṣa* . . . his body is the bliss (*ānanda ātma*), *brahman* the foundation. . . . He who is here in the *puruṣa* and yonder in the sun, he is one. He who knows this, on departing from this world, reaches the *ātman* consisting of food, of life-breath, of mind,

> of understanding, of bliss. Where words do not reach and the mind cannot grasp, there is the *brahman* full of bliss; who knows it does not fear anything.[3]

We can learn from this one text, among other things, the rather complex meaning of the term *ātman;* a meaning that would not allow us to equate it with the term *soul*, as it is normally used in the West.

The distinction of the five strata of *ātman*, corresponding to five different *brahman* realities is quite instructive: each reality is the inner core of the one preceding it, till we reach the very heart of being, which is *ānanda*, bliss, and which cannot be further qualified as having an "exterior" and an "interior." The self of a person needs nourishment, which builds up a material self; it requires life breath, which builds up a subtle material self; it requires mind, which develops the intellectual self; further on, it requires understanding, developing the sphere of deep insight. The core and the heart of reality, finally, is the sphere of bliss, where *ātman* is seen as consisting of and resting on *brahman*. For each sphere of the self, there is a corresponding ultimate, to be realized as relative, step by step, till the true ultimate is reached.

What is *brahman?* We have seen one answer to the question. Another approach is given in the *Chāṇḍogya Upaniṣad*. A father, whose son has just returned from his guru full of pride in his knowledge, questions him about the *brahman*. The son has to admit his ignorance and has to hear from his father that unless he knows *brahman*, he knows nothing at all.

The father tries to teach him by way of practical experiments: "Bring a fig," says the father. Śvetaketu, the son, brings it. "Divide it. What do you see?"

"Tiny seeds," is the son's answer.

"Divide one of the seeds. What do you see?"

"Nothing."

Now follows the essential teaching: "My dear, that subtle essence which you do not perceive, that is the source of this mighty Nyagrodha tree. That which is so tiny (*aṇimā*) is the *ātman* of all. This is the true, the self, that you are, Śvetaketu!"[4]

The teaching drawn from the next experiment is the same. Śvetaketu is asked to throw a handful of salt into a vessel filled with water, to taste it in different places, and then to try to separate salt again from water. The salt is one with the water, it cannot be separated, though Śvetaketu knows that it is different from it. This is the *ātman*, all-pervading, inseparable from objects, not identical with them. And his father concludes this lesson with the same formula: *Tat tvam asi*, that you are! The invisible substance that makes the Nyagrodha tree grow is the life of humans too, even more—the one who knows it, is it!

The same *Upaniṣad* has another well-known instruction on *brahman:* Prajāpati, the Father of all that is born, announces:

> The *ātman* who is free from all evil, free from old age, free from death, free from worry, free from hunger and thirst, whose desire is *satya*, truth and reality, whose purpose is *satya*, he should be sought, him one must strive to understand. One who has found this *ātman* and understands him attains all worlds and the fulfillment of all desires.

The *devas* and *asuras* hear this; they too are without this ultimate fulfillment, they too have everything to learn. Indra, the king of the *devas*, and Virocana, the chief of the *asuras*, approach Prajāpati for instruction. For thirty-two years, they live as *brahmacaris;* they serve their guru without hearing a word about *ātman.* After the time is up, Prajāpati asks them for what purpose they had originally come. They repeat the words that Prajāpati had used and state that they were seeking the sorrowless, deathless *ātman.*

Now Prajāpati instructs them. They are told to look at themselves in the mirror of a sheet of water and to report their impressions. They find that they see themselves (*ātmānam*), "a picture even to the very hairs and nails." Prajāpati asks them to put on their best clothes, adorn themselves, look again into the mirror, and to report about it. The two say that they see themselves well-dressed and neat. And Prajāpati concludes: "That is the immortal, fearless *brahman*". The two leave, satisfied that they got what they wanted. Prajāpati looked after them and said to himself: "They go away, without having perceived, without having known the self. All who follow such a doctrine will perish."

Virocana declares to the *asuras* that bodily happiness is the one and all there is. Indra, however, before returning to the *devas*, realizes an objection: if the *ātman* is identical with the bodily reality, it will suffer as the body suffers, become blind, lame, crippled as the body, perish together within the body. "I see no good in this", he concludes and returns to Prajāpati. He serves him another thirty-two years and, at the end of this long term, is asked the same question but gets a different answer: "The one who happily moves about in a dream is the *ātman*, the immortal fearless *brahman.*" At first Indra is satisfied and takes leave; before reaching his heaven he discovers the fault in this answer, too: someone who dreams of being chased and tortured, of mourning and dying, suffers sorrow and cannot be called happy.

Back he goes to serve again for thirty-two years. Now Prajāpati comes up with a new secret: "He who dwells in deep, dreamless sleep is the *ātman*, the immortal fearless *brahman.*" Indra, after a brief satisfaction with this answer, again becomes skeptical: One who sleeps is not aware of himself and his bliss. It is as if he did not exist at all. Prajāpati commends Indra's sharp mind and tells him to serve him for only another five years, after which time he will really impart the ultimate secret to him. When the time has come, he instructs him as follows:

> Mortal, indeed, is this body. It is held by death; but it is the support of his deathless bodiless *ātman*. Verily with a body one cannot have freedom from pleasure and pain. But pleasure and pain do not touch the bodiless. Bodiless are air, clouds, lightning, thunder. . . . Even so that serene one, when rising up from this body and reaching the highest light, appears in his own form. Such is the Supreme Person. . . . He who finds this *ātman* obtains all worlds and the fulfillment of his wishes.[5]

Indra, the king of heaven, had to wait for 101 years before he was given the full insight; a human should not desist, therefore, from his effort, even if realization is not reached at the first attempt.

A fairly systematic treatment of the *ātman-brahman* theme is provided by the *Muṇḍaka Upaniṣad.* After demonstrating the social and secular necessity of Vedic rites and sacrifices and their intrinsic inadequacy to save one from repeated old age and death, it develops the exigencies and methods of *brahman* knowledge. Realization of *brahman*, the imperishable, the *puruṣa*, the true, the real, can only be attained through a guru.

> That is the truth: as from a fire, blazing, sparks like fire issue forth by the thousands, so many kinds of beings issue forth from the imperishable and they return to it. Splendid and without a bodily form is this *puruṣa*, without and within, unborn, without life breath and without mind, higher than the supreme element. From him are born life breath and mind, all the sense organs, also space, air, light, water and earth, the support of all. Fire is his head, his eyes are the sun and the moon, the regions are his ears, the revealed *Vedas* are his speech, air is his life breath and his heart is the universe. Out of his feet the earth is born, indeed he is the soul of all beings.

One by one, the text explains how everything issues out of this *brahman.* He must be known both as being (*sat*) and nonbeing (*asat*), as the support of everything, upon whom the sky, the earth and space is woven.

> In the highest sphere, made of gold, is *brahman* without stain, without parts, pure, the light of lights. The sun shines not there, nor the moon nor the stars, nor the lightning either, whence then this fire? Everything has its shine from this shining one, his shine illumines the world. *Brahman*, indeed is immortal, in front, behind, to the right and left is *brahman.* It spreads forth below and above. *Brahman*, indeed is this all, the greatest. . . . When a seer sees the creator

> of golden color, the Lord, the *puruṣa*, the womb of *brahman*, then he becomes a knower, freed from good and evil.[6]

The *Bṛhadāraṇyaka Upaniṣad* explains the immanence of *brahman* in all things as the result of its entering into them after creating them. "He entered into them even to the tips of the nails, as a razor is hidden in the razor case. They do not see him. When breathing, he is called *prāṇa*, breath, when speaking he is called *vāk*, speech, when seeing he is called *cakṣus*, eye, when hearing he is called *śrotra*, ear, when thinking he is called *manas*, mind."

The *Upaniṣad* also instructs that by meditating on the *ātman* one realizes all things to be one, and oneself to be one with it: "Whosoever knows thus, *aham brahmāsmi*, I am Brahman, becomes this all. Even the *devas* cannot prevent him from becoming thus, for he becomes their *ātman*."[7]

Here we have one of the four *mahāvākyas*, the Great Sayings, that are supposed to express the gist of the Upaniṣadic teaching in one word. Earlier, we saw another one, *tat tvam asi*, the that-you-are teaching of Uddālaka.[8] Elsewhere we read *ayam ātma brahman*, this self is the *brahman*,[9] and *prajñānam brahman*, wisdom is *brahman*.[10] The *mahāvākyas* cannot be applied to the three lower stages of consciousness, they are true only of *turīya*.

If one were to attempt an understanding of the *ātman-brahman* from a Western perspective it would be difficult to find the right categories of interpretation. Some have chosen an easy way by just labelling the *Upaniṣads pantheistic* and thus have done with it. This is, however, no longer possible. The *Upaniṣads* never state that objects, as they are and as they are normally perceived, are simply identical with the absolute. The *Upaniṣads* demand, first of all, a transcendence into another level of being and consciousness. It would be wrong to compare the *Upaniṣads* with rationalist theology; comparisons, if any are legitimate, can be valid only on the level of what is commonly and vaguely called mysticism. The *Upaniṣads* do not present a fully developed theological system, they offer experiences and visions.

The Upanisadic *ātman* is not simply and unequivocally identical with *brahman* under all circumstances, only in *turīya*, the real consciousness of the *Upaniṣads*, which is not easily accessible. Only persistent effort opens up the depths of the self. Reality, once discovered, appears as "self-evident," but to come to this conclusion requires going through a long and time-consuming process of *neti, neti*, of physical and spiritual discipline. Recognition of the self and the absolute, *ātman* and *brahman*, as one and the same reality, comes only after penetration to the state of being wherein the person is stripped of all qualities. To follow the steps outlined in the *Kena* and *Bṛhadāraṇyaka*, to realize the *satyasa satya*, the reality of reality, means being led into an aporia, a perfect darkness, a last portal, impossible to pass unless it be opened from within.

14. *Karma, Vidyā, Mokṣa:* Liberation from Rebirth

> From the unreal lead me to the Real,
> From darkness lead me to light,
> From ignorance lead me to knowledge,
> From death lead me to immortality.
>
> —Aitareya Brāhmaṇa *II, 1*

THE *BṚHADĀRAṆYAKA UPANIṢAD* describes the death of a man thus:

> Just as a heavily loaded cart moves creaking, so the *ātman* of the body with the *ātman* of wisdom on it moves creaking, when breathing becomes small through old age or disease then just as a mango or some other fruit loosens itself so this *puruṣa* frees himself from these limbs and returns again to the womb. . . . When this *ātman* becomes weak and confused, as it were, all the *prāṇas*, the life-breaths gather round him. He takes into himself those sparks of light and recedes into the heart. When the eye-*puruṣa* departs, he cannot recognizes forms any more. "He is becoming one, he does not see" so they say; "he is becoming one, he cannot smell," they say; "he is becoming one, he does not taste," they say; "he is becoming one, he does not speak," they say; "he is becoming one, he does not hear," they say; "he is becoming one, he does not think," they say; "he is becoming one, he does not feel," they say; "he is becoming one, he does not know," they say. The point of his heart becomes lighted up and by that light the *ātman* departs either through the eye or through the head or through other apertures of the body. And when he thus departs, the *prāṇas* depart after him. He becomes understanding, he follows after understanding. His knowledge and his deeds follow him as does also his previous wisdom.
>
> Just as a caterpillar, when it has come to the end of one blade of grass, and after having made its approach to another one, draws itself together towards it, so this *ātman*, after having thrown away this body and after having dispelled ignorance, draws itself together. And as the goldsmith, taking a

> piece of gold, turns it into another, newer and more beautiful shape, even so does this *ātman*, after having thrown away this body, make unto himself newer and more beautiful shapes like that of the *pitṛs*, the *gandharvas*, the *devas*, of *Prajāpati*, of *Brahmā* or some other being. This *ātman* indeed is *brahman* consisting of understanding, mind, life, sight, hearing, earth, water, air, space, light and darkness, desire and desirelessness, anger and freedom from anger, righteousness and unrighteousness and all things. This is what is meant by saying: "It consists of this and consists of that." As one acts and as one behaves so one becomes. The one who does good becomes good; the one who does evil becomes evil. One becomes righteous by righteous action, unrighteous by unrighteous action. Others, however, say: a *puruṣa* consists of desire (*kāma*). As his desire is, so is his determination (*kratur*); as his determination is, such deed he commits; whatever deed he commits, that he attains.
>
> On this there is the following verse: The object to which the mind (*manas*) is attached, the subtle self (*liṅga*) goes together with the deed, being attached to it alone. Exhausting the results of whatever works he did in this world he comes again from that world to this world for work. This is true for the mind with desires. The mind who is free from desire, whose desire is satisfied, whose desire is the *ātman*, his *prāṇas* do not depart. Since he is *brahman*, he goes into *brahman*.
>
> On this there is the following verse: "When all the desires that dwell in the heart are cast away, then does the mortal become immortal, then he attains *brahman* here."[1]

Death is a theme that looms large in the *Upaniṣads*. Death is the creator and the destroyer of all that is. Death, especially in the form of redeath (*punarmṛtyu*),[2] is the greatest evil that threatens the existence of man. Faith in rebirth seems to be accepted in the *Upaniṣads* without further argument. Scholars generally assume that it formed part of the religion of the indigenous peoples of India, which influenced Vedic religion quite heavily. According to the *Upaniṣads*, the Vedic *yajña* cannot save from repeated death, to which even the *devas* are subjected in one way or another. At the root of the Upaniṣadic search for the liberation, which goes beyond the attainment of the status of *devas*, there is a certain skepticism with regard to the nature of the *devas*. For the *Upaniṣads*, they are in the sphere of sense experience and, therefore, in the lower ranges of consciousness and reality. Thus, the process of liberation does not depend on any intervention from the side of the *devas*. The *Upaniṣads* do not deny a Supreme God; certain texts quite clearly speak of the *Puruṣottama*, of grace and election as essential for liberation,[3] but their concern is the immanent process of liberation in the subjective consciousness. Death is a happening on the periphery of external consciousness, as are all physical and psychical ills, and so one is affected by these only so long as one is caught up in the lower stages of consciousness. Reality and consciousness are identical, a unity of bliss and immortality, freedom from change, freedom from rebirth and redeath.[4]

The most important synonym for death in the *Upaniṣads* is *kāla*, time. Everything created by time must also find its end in time: *manas, apas, arka, prithvī, tejas*, the body and the senses, sun, earth and water—everything must die. Only that which is not born from death-time, the *ātman*, is not liable to die. The dialogue between Naciketas and death in the *Kaṭha Upaniṣad*, a most beautiful and profound passage, makes it quite evident that the basic aim of the *Upaniṣads* is to show a way of escape from repeated death.[5]

Fundamental to the Upaniṣadic understanding of death and liberation is the metaphysical anthropology presupposed in it, which differs substantially from both popular and academic philosophic understanding in the West. As discussed earlier, the five different *ātman* correspond to five different components or "sheaths" of human existence. Barring more detailed subdivisions, Vedāntic anthropology considers the human person to be composed of *sthūla śarīra, sūkṣma śarīra*, and *ātman-brahman*. The gross body is destined to disintegrate at the time of death. The subtle body, with all the imprints of deeds and thoughts of the previous life, is preserved and clings to its *ātman;* this results in intermediate existences in heaven or hell, depending on the quality of the deeds, and finally in an earthly rebirth. *Karma* keeps in motion the vicious circle of action, desire, reward, and new action. The *karma* of former births is worked out in the present birth; and *karma* acquired in this birth, good or bad, works toward a future birth. The *Upaniṣads* have several similar accounts of the route that the dead take before they are reborn as human beings; these texts, often elaborated, have found a place also in the *Purāṇas* and other popular Hindu scriptures. The *Upaniṣads* generally describe a *devayāna* and a *pitṛyāna*, the former leading to no return, the latter leading to relatively enjoyable rebirths on earth. Those who go neither way are reborn as animals or demons, before slowly ascending the ladder of being again.

Thus says the *Bṛhadāraṇyaka Upaniṣad:*

> Those who meditate on the truth in the forest with faith, pass into the light, from the light into the day, from the day into the half-month of the waxing moon, from the half-month of the waxing moon into the six months which the sun travels northward, from these months into the world of the *devas*, from the world of the *devas* into the sun, from the sun into the lightning. Then one of the mind-born goes to the sphere of lightning and leads them to the *brahmā-loka*.
>
> In the *brahmā-loka* they live for a long time. For these there is no return. Those who, through *yajñas*, gifts and austerities, conquer the worlds, pass into the smoke, from the smoke into the night, from the night into the half-month

of the waning moon, from the half-month of the waning moon into the six months during which the sun travels southward, from these months into the world of the fathers, from the world of the fathers into the moon. Reaching the moon they become food. There the *devas*, as they say to King Soma, increase, decrease even to feed upon them there.

When that is over, they pass into space, from space into wind, from wind into rain, from rain into the earth. Reaching the earth they become food. Again they are offered in the fire of man.[6] Thence they are born in the fire of woman with a view to going to other worlds. Thus do they go round. But those who do not know these two ways, become insects, moths and whatever there is here that bites.[7]

Other texts describe rebirth as the search for a womb of the *puruṣa*, the thumb-sized homunculus made up of subtle body and *ātman*.

The cause of rebirth is *karma*, inherent in the subtle body. The cause of liberation from rebirth is the cutting of the bond that ties *ātman* to the subtle body and with it to *karma*.

Though it is easy to give a correct etymology of *karma* from the verbal root *kṛ-*, "to do," "to act," and although the word has become one of the favorite terms of the present generation, its meaning is difficult to explain.[8] Literally, it is simply the deed done, work performed. But the deed is not terminated when a certain action comes to an end. The accomplished deed is a new entity that, as such, continues to exert its own influence, even without the will and activity of the doer. The whole *karmamārga* is based on this teaching of the objective efficacy of the accomplished deed. The *apūrva* of the Mīmāṁsakas, the suspended latent causality of ritual actions is quite an ingenious invention in this direction; it allows substantiated causality to accumulate like a bank account for later use in heaven.

Karma is neither material nor spiritual in the usual sense of those terms. It can be produced and annihilated, it can lead to good and to evil consequences, but it is always finite, however powerful its influence may be. It is, in a sense, the law of nature; universal, because it applies to all of nature, but finite, because nature itself is finite. *Karma* is often understood as fate, especially by Westerners;[9] they might then also relate it to the Greek *moîra*. But we must take note of a very important difference: the *moîra* of the Greeks cannot be influenced; *karma* can! To the Greek mind, this helplessness makes tragedy possible, tragedy being the ultimate and inevitably fatal clash of man's will with fate. Indian literature does not know tragedy; *karma* can be influenced or even totally neutralized through religion! The aspect of life, so prominent in Western thought, that decisions once made cannot be revoked, that the "laws of being" cannot even be changed by the Supreme, himself a being—this aspect is absent from Indian thought. The possibility of rebirths, of world creations and destructions in an endless series, offers the possibility of ever new changes in decisions made, of ever new developments, so that no being's downfall is final and irredeemable. *Karma* does not cancel free will and genuinely free decisions, nor do free will and one's own decisions neutralize *karma.* *Karma* has been called scientific by many modern Indians, and psychologists are investigating experimentally the memories of former births in such people who claim to have them.

The *Upaniṣads* maintain that they have found a way to deal with *karma* that is better than that of the Vedas: not to produce good *karma* as counterbalance for bad *karma*, but to eliminate *karma* altogether!

> Unsteady, verily, are these boats of the eighteen sacrificial formulas, which are said to be the lower *karma.* The deluded, who delight in these as leading to good, fall again into old age and death. Abiding in the midst of ignorance, wise in their own esteem, thinking themselves to be learned, fools, afflicted with troubles, they go about like blind men led by one who is himself blind. The immature, living variously in ignorance, think "we have accomplished our aim." Since those who perform sacrifices do not understand because of their attachment, they sink down, wretched, when their *lokas* are exhausted. These deluded men, regarding sacrifices and works of merit as most important, do not know any other good. Having enjoyed heaven won by good *karma* they enter this world again, or a lower one. But those who practise *tapas* and *śraddhā* in the forest, the *śānta*, the tranquil and peaceful ones, knowers, who live the life of a mendicant, depart free from sin, through the door of the sun to the place where dwells the immortal, imperishable *ātman.*[10]

The *Upaniṣads* contain a sacred teaching that does what Vedic work could not do. The *Vedas* give to the *āryas* the means to influence *karma*, and they are far above the *mlecchas* who are excluded from it; but the knowledge contained in the *Upaniṣads* grants a degree of happiness, freedom, and light that makes the *Vedas* look like a fetter, like night and unhappiness. Far from providing only a temporary relief from the ills of the world, the knowledge of the *Upaniṣads* uproots the weed called *karma* and deprives it of its soil, the body. The body is where *karma* operates and from whence it comes. At the level of the *dvandvas*, the pairs of opposites that make up the world—heat and cold, pleasure and suffering, birth and death—it is impossible to obtain pure and eternal bliss and life. The body cannot be redeemed, because it is part of the world of the *dvandvas* itself. Freedom implies freedom from the pairs of opposites, from the body. The one who is completely free is "beyond good and evil" in an ontological sense. "As water does not cling to the lotus leaf, so evil deeds do not cling to one who knows *brahman.*"[11] There is no transformation of the finite into the infinite, of the mortal into the immortal; there is only the separation of the finite and the infinite, of the mortal from immortal, of the subtle body with its *karma* from the *ātman* that is by nature free, infinite, immortal. "The knot of the heart is cut, all the doubts are dispelled and *karma* comes to an end when He is seen."[12]

The path of the *Upaniṣads* was and is that of an élite that could afford to cut all ties with society and devote itself to the spirit. For the majority of Hindus, in ancient as well as in contemporary India, religion is understood to be the path of works. Pilgrimages, almsgiving, recitation of prayers, and other good works are supposed to create *puṇya*, which allows one to dwell for some time in heaven and attain a good rebirth. The *Purāṇas*, however, in an attempt to assimilate Vedāntic teaching as well as popular practices, promise "enlightenment" as the result of the uttering of the name of God or of devotional worship of the image, and assure the devotee that the Supreme God will take upon himself all the *karma* of his devotees. The *bhakta* is freed from rebirth, not so much through the process of gradual sublimation, as through the grace of God.[13]

There is no longer any meaning in ritual actions if one has wholly transcended the sphere of *karma*. But the *Brahmasūtras* enjoin the one who has knowledge to continue performing the usual rituals, lest he be considered an irreligious man. *Nitya karma*, the daily obligatory ritual does not result in *karma* for one who performs it with wisdom but augments *vidyā*. Work done in a disinterested way, as *niṣkāma karma*, does not entangle in this world but is a symbol of freedom to act without considering the results of one's action. The *Upaniṣads* have the notion of a *jīvanmukta*, the one who is completely free while still living in a body: like a potter's wheel that turns for some time after the pot has been shaped, due to the impetus given to it by the potter, so the physical life of the free person is carried on without any connection to the *ātman*, which has found its meaning in itself.

Mokṣa or *mukti*, "liberation," the key term of Vedāntic philosophy, is hardly ever used by the *Upaniṣads* to describe the ultimate condition; they prefer expressions like immortality, bliss, becoming *brahman*.[14] This freedom is "not a new acquisition, a product, an effect or result of any action, but it always existed as the Truth of our nature; we are always emancipated and always free."[15] In the Upaniṣadic doctrines, a person is given the means to remove the obstacles, the wrong notions; liberation itself is an event that comes from the *ātman*'s own interiority. This is the deeper truth beneath apparently paradoxical statements. The *Upaniṣads* say that release from old age and death, bliss and immortality, consists in "knowing the unknowable *brahman*."[16] It entails both a separation of consciousness from sense-object knowledge and an extension of consciousness until it finally includes everything.

The *Upaniṣads* say "the liberated becomes everything."[17] The statement "*ātman* is *brahman*" is the liberating truth itself, and as such, it is immortality. From the standpoint of objective knowledge, the ultimate knowledge is a negation of knowledge: *brahman* is not to be seen, not be heard, not to be thought, but those who understand the seeing of the seeing, the hearing of the hearing, the innermost principle underlying all, know *brahman* also in a positive way. The very differentiation between the Self and the not Self is enlightenment about the Self; there is no further need to prove the nonexistence of not being.

The supreme condition of humanity, its true freedom, is identical with Truth-Reality being bliss: it is "self-awareness" that has no object-subject polarity but is everything as pure consciousness.[18] There is no further need to cleanse the *ātman* from sin and to make it perfect: being free from sin, incapable of sin, incapable of being perfected, is a result of the fact that it *is*. "Deathlessness," then, consists in becoming conscious of the innermost support of the personality, in gaining unity with the Ultimate.[19] Whatever has been created goes back to its source, the body with all its parts and faculties is dissolved into the elements from which it was derived. The *ātman* withdraws its support from these its own creations, and thus, they fall back into their nonexistence, into their difference from *ātman* that proves them to be nothing by themselves. By leaving everything, it gains the whole, and by reducing its consciousness to the barest subject awareness, it becomes all-consciousness.[20]

Mokṣa is but the recognition of a situation that always existed as such; it is a psychological breakthrough not an ontological change. It is not a quickening of the dead, not a resurrection and transfiguration of the body but its rejection. It is not heaven but the overcoming of heaven, making all objective bliss redundant.

Liberation is beyond happiness and unhappiness, beyond heaven and hell. Whoever wants something must take its opposite into the bargain. Whoever seeks redemption as a positive reality must accept bondage with it. For the *Upaniṣads*, the way out of the tragic hopelessness, which sees human life as a constant frustration, is given by the insight that sorrow and death do not touch the innermost core of man. The way of knowledge, strictly speaking, is therefore not a path to salvation but a method of discrimination; the *jīvanmukta* is not a saint but a sage. As the *Upaniṣad* says: "Such a one, verily, the thought does not torment: Why have I not done the right? Why have I committed sin? One who knows this, saves oneself from these. Truly, from both of these one saves oneself—one who knows this."[21]

However, it would be a mistake to conclude that the *Upaniṣads* are amoral. On the contrary, they contain many passages with rigorous ethical commands. Thus, the *Taittirīya Upaniṣad* contains the following instruction to a pupil: "Speak the truth! Practise *dharma*! Do not neglect the study of the Veda! Be one to whom mother, father, teacher and guest are like *devas!* Do not do what others find reproachable!"[22] The very prerequisite for being accepted as a student was a high moral standard, and the life of the student demanded a more rigorous self-discipline than would normally be considered necessary. But morality is only a prerequisite; it is a matter of course for the one whose interests are no longer in sense gratification and possession of material goods. There comes a point when a person realizes that real goodness is not to be found in the accidental quality of a finite act but in the heart of being itself, of being at one with the ultimate reality. Although several other ideas are at work in the *karmamārga*, as we have seen earlier, and in the *bhaktimārga*, which will be described in the following chapters, the *Upaniṣads* as the basis of the *jñānamārga* had, and have, a tremendous impact on Hinduism as such and are representative of one of the major themes of Eastern religion: the acceptance of the aloneness of human existence not only as inevitable but as fulfilling, the overcoming of suffering and sorrow by realizing their nonreality, liberation through insight into one's true nature, the negation of redemption because of a profound recognition of its intrinsic impossibility. It is useless to try to save a human—all are saved, if they would only see it! "Just as the flowing rivers disappear in the ocean casting off shape and name, even so the knower, freed from name and shape, attains to the divine *puruṣa*, higher than the high. One, indeed, who knows the Supreme *brahman* becomes *brahman* himself."[23]

15. The Path of Loving Devotion: *Bhaktimārga*

> Fix thy mind on Me; be devoted to Me, sacrifice to Me; prostrate thyself before me; so shalt thou come to Me. I promise thee truly, for thou art dear to Me.
>
> —Bhagavadgītā *XIII, 65*

THE MAJORITY OF Hindus are followers of the *bhaktimārga*, whose exterior manifestation in temples, images, processions, feasts, and popular gurus characterizes so much of present-day India. The term *bhakti*, used so frequently as the key word in this form of religion, defies an exact and adequate translation.[1] In addition to the general difficulty of translating crucial words from Sanskrit into English, the problem is compounded by two quite peculiar handicaps. First, the etymology of the word is not clear. *Bhakti* as a past participle, according to its grammatical form, can be derived from two different verbal roots. If derived from the root *bhañj-*, "to separate," *bhakti* would have to be translated as separation. That makes sense insofar as *bhakti* systems presuppose the Supreme, Absolute Being to be unidentical with, and separated from, the individual human being. In this view, inner longing for reunion is characteristic of human life, and the *bhakta* is aware of the painful separation between himself or herself and God and tries to overcome it. The majority of Indian scholars, however, derive *bhakti* from the root *bhaj-*, "to worship," "to be devoted to." This, too, makes sense, since *bhakti* religion consists of acts of worship and loving devotion toward God. The second problem in trying to find an English equivalent for *bhakti* is the diversity of definitions given to *bhakti* by the numerous different schools of thought and groups of worshippers, providing many subtle specifications and subdivisions of *bhakti*, considered by the respective believers to be of the very essence of *bhakti*. We shall examine a few of them.

There are two classical texts that call themselves *Bhaktisūtras*, purporting to present the authoritative definition of *bhakti* and quite openly imitating the style of the *Vedāntasūtras* in order to impress those for whom these were the supreme authority.[2] Thus, Śāṇḍilya begins: *athātobhaktijijñāsa*, "now, then, an enquiry into *bhakti*." He continues defining it as *sāparānuraktirīśvare*, "passionate longing for the Lord from one's whole heart," and he says that in it a person finds immortality. In it is contained the knowledge of God; but since haters of God also have this knowledge, only loving devotion combined with knowledge can save a person.[3]

Nārada, the author of the other *Bhaktisūtra*, defines *bhakti* as *parama premā*, highest affection for the Lord, possessing immortality in itself, "gaining which a person becomes perfect, immortal and satisfied, attaining which a person does not desire anything, does not hate, does not exult, does not exert himself or herself [in furtherance of self-interest]. Having known that, a person becomes intoxicated, becomes motionless, becomes one who enjoys the self."[4]

The *Bhagavadgītā*, probably the best known *bhakti*-scripture, sees the essence of *bhakti* in fixing one's mind on Kṛṣṇa and worshipping him; this description probably would cover most of the general features of the different kinds of *bhakti*.[5]

DEVELOPMENT OF *BHAKTI*

In its full development and almost complete domination of the Indian religious scene, historically, the *bhaktimārga* comes as the last path for the attainment of salvation, after *karmamārga* and *jñānamārga*. However, it would be wrong to set the three paths into some sort of evolutionary sequence. In all probability all three *mārgas* were present throughout Indian religious history, though their official recognition and preference varied. P. V. Kane sees in many hymns of the *Ṛgveda* evidence of *Indra-bhakti* or *Varuṇa-bhakti*. The fact that Varuṇa is in many respects the Vedic equivalent of the Puranic Viṣṇu may be understood as a first stage of *Viṣṇubhakti*, which later became so prominent.[6]

We do not find the word *bhakti* in the principal *Upaniṣads*, but the *Kaṭha Upaniṣad* and the *Muṇḍaka Upaniṣad* have a doctrine of grace typical for *bhakti:* "This *ātman* cannot be reached through insight or much learning nor through explanation. It can only be comprehended by one who is chosen by the supreme *ātman*—to such a person He reveals His form."[7] Similarly, the frequent use of the word *puruṣa uttama*, the supreme person, to describe the *Brahman* in the *Upaniṣads*, a term that became a proper name of Viṣṇu in *bhakti* religion, would indicate the presence of *bhakti* ideas in Vedic times.[8]

The *Śvetāśvatara Upaniṣad*, which is a fairly early text, expounds a fully developed *Śiva-bhakti;* certainly this attitude took time to mature into such a systematic treatise. The later *Upaniṣads* are mostly *bhakti* treatises, quite close in terminology to the *Saṁhitās* and *Āgamas*, the recognized scriptures of Vaiṣṇavism and Śaivism. The most popular class of literature in India, the *Mahābhārata*, the *Rāmāyaṇa*, and the *Purāṇas*, are the sources from which *bhakti* religions have drawn their inspiration for centuries. These books frequently constitute encyclopedic summaries of the entire religious heritage of India, seen from the viewpoint of a *bhakta.*

Bhakti movements have produced inner-Indian missionary thrusts and are now also reaching out for Western converts. The best known and most numerous, but not the only, *bhakti*-movement in the West is the Hare Krishna movement (International Society for Kṛṣṇa Consciousness), which has done much to translate and distribute classical *bhakti*-literature and especially the literature of the Caitanya school of Bengal Vaiṣṇavism, to which it is affiliated. *Bhakti* has inspired thousands of Indian poets and singer-saints, whose hymns are still popular with large masses of Hindus. Even illiterate Indian villagers are familiar with the songs of the Āḷvārs and Nāyanmārs in South India or with couplets from Tulsīdās, Kabīr, Sūrdās, Tukārām, Rāmprasād, and many others from the North, whose stanzas they chant and quote as summaries of their own religious wisdom.[9]

Bhakti had a wide appeal from the very beginning, not only because it recognized the emotional approach to God as fully valid but also because it broke down all the barriers of privilege, which had kept large groups of the population from *karmamārga* and *jñānamārga. Bhakti* became the way of salvation for everyone: women and children, low castes and outcastes, could become fully recognized members of the *bhakti* movement. Some of the great *bhaktas* are saints for Hindus, Muslims, and Sikhs alike. Even Christians in India are beginning to accept them as theirs and are finding the religiosity of these *bhaktas* to be deep and genuine. Some of the universally revered *bhaktas* were outcastes, like Nanda and Cokamela, some were women, like Mīrābāī and Āṇḍāl, others were great sinners for whom orthodoxy could not find means of salvation. Kabīr, one of the finest Hindī poets of mediaeval India, reputedly was a Muslim weaver. His songs are favorites with countless Hindus in northern India even today. He says in one of them:

> It is foolish to ask a saint his caste. The *Brahman*, the *Kṣatriya*, the *Vaiṣya*, and the *Śūdra*, all seek but God. The barber has looked for God, too, and so has the washerman and the carpenter; even Raidās was a seeker after God.

Ṛṣi Svapaca was a tanner. Hindus and Muslims have equally realized God, there is no scope of distinction in the ultimate aim.

Saints like Kabīr may be considered as even transcending *bhakti* in its more specific sense when he sings:

> My true guru has shown me the way: I have given up all rites and ceremonies, I bathe no more in holy rivers. I then became aware that I alone was mad, the whole world sane. I had been disturbing those intelligent people! No longer could I live in the dust of subservience; no longer do I ring the temple-bells, nor do I enthrone a divine image. I no longer offer flowers. Mortification does not please the Lord; we do not reach Him by going about naked and torturing ourselves. They who are kind and righteous, who do not get entangled in this world's dealings, who consider all creatures on earth as their own self, they attain to the Immortal, the true God is with them forever. Kabīr says: Those attain the true name[10] whose words are pure, who are devoid of pride and self-deceit.

THE PRACTICE OF THE *BHAKTIMĀRGA*

Most of what Kabīr rejects here constitutes the routine of the average *bhakta*, and it must be illustrated in some detail in order to draw a sketch of a follower of the path of devotion. *Bhaktas* are organized into a large number of *sampradāyas*, denominations or sects. Certain features are common to them. Thus, the most popular *Stotraratnas*, the prayer books, contain hymns to all the main deities, who form the objects of loving devotion and adoration of many groups of *bhaktas;* included are prayers to Ganeṣa, Viṣṇu, Śiva, Sūrya, Devī, Datta, Rāma, Kṛṣṇa, as well as hymns to Gaṅgā and Yamunā, the planets, and various less popular *avatāras* of the main deities.[11] Numerically, the Viṣṇu-*bhaktas*, with their many subdivisions, are the most important group. Śiva-*bhaktas* come second and Devī-*bhaktas* or *Śāktas* rank third, followed by the rest. Though there are enough differences among the various groups to make mutual vilification, or even persecution, far from uncommon in Indian religious history, they all have so much in common with regard to practices and beliefs that it is possible to describe *bhakti* in general without specifying in each instance to which particular *saṁpradāya* one is referring.

The promise of salvation for all resulted in a tendency to simplify the requirements for it, so that all might be able to fulfill the essence of righteousness, however poor and unlearned they might be. This has led practically all the *bhakti* schools to teaching that the name of God is sufficient to bring salvation to everyone who utters it.

1. Śravaṇa: Listening

2. Kīrtana: Singing

3. Smaraṇa: Remembering

4. Arcana: Worshipping

5. Pādasevana: Serving

Figure 15.1 The Nine Degrees of Devotion

The story of saint Ajamila, very popular with *Viṣṇubhaktas*, is typical. Ajamila was a Brahmin who had married a woman of his own caste according to the proper rites. After some time, he fell in love with a low-caste woman, repudiated his rightful wife, and had ten sons from the concubine. He wasted his whole life in gambling and thieving. When he reached the age of eighty, he felt that he was going to die. Before his death, he wanted to see his youngest son and called out with a loud voice, "Nārāyaṇa!" Nārāyaṇa also happens to be one of the names of Lord Viṣṇu, and though Ajamila had not thought of Him, the utterance of the name wiped out all his sins and he was given a place of honor in Viṣṇu's heaven.[12]

In several places the *Bhāgavata Purāṇa* underlines this belief when it teaches: "The utterance of the Lord's Name completely destroys all sin, even when it is due to the Name being associated with something else, or is done jocularly, or as a result of involuntary sound or in derision."[13]

A contemporary magazine, in an *Appeal for Japa of the Divine Name*, exhorts its readers to recite the "*mantra* of the sixteen Names," which is "Great Mantra" for the *japa* of Kṛṣṇa-*bhaktas:*

> *Hare Rām Hare Rām Rām Hare Hare*
> *Hare Kṛṣṇa Hare Kṛṣṇa Kṛṣṇa Kṛṣṇa Hare Hare.*

It carries the following message.

> The whole world is groaning inwardly at present. Tyranny, persecution, immorality, disputes, sin, war, and destruction are on the increase everywhere. The mounting irreverence toward religion and God is turning humanity into a race of cannibals. As a result natural calamities have also multiplied. Earthquakes, floods, drought, famine, food scarcity, and epidemics have become alarmingly frequent. No one knows where they will lead us. Under such circumstances, resorting to God is the only way out of this inferno of calamities. Taking to the repetition of the Divine Name is essential for complete self-surrender to God. There is no calamity which will not yield to the Divine Name and there is nothing which cannot be achieved by the Divine Name. Powerful counterforces might delay the achievement, but the Divine Name is infallible in bringing its reward. In this dark age of Kali, the Divine Name is our only resort. Therefore, for the good of India and the world at large, everybody should repeat and sing the Divine Name both for worldly gains and otherworldly peace and happiness, nay even for reaching the ultimate goal of our existence, viz. God-Realization.

There follows an appeal to the readers of the magazine to make a vow to perform *japa* and to send in an account of the number of times the complete *mantra* has been recited, aiming at twenty crores of repetitions.[14] "Persons of all castes and communities and of every age and sex can undertake this *japa*. Everyone should repeat the *mantra* at least 108 times every day. Intimation of the *japa* should be sent to the *nāma-japa* section of *Kalyāṇ*-office, Gorakhpur, U.P."[15]

Equal power is attributed to the name of Śiva or Devī by the Śaivites and Śāktas, though usually the wearing of certain marks and signs also is considered essential in order to benefit from *japa*. The great devotion to the Name has led to the composition of litanies of the thousand names of God, the *sahasranāmas;* a large number of the names given in these to Viṣṇu, Śiva, and Devī by their followers are identical. Apart from the great popularity of the practice among the masses of Hindus, the theologians of the *bhaktimārga* have developed theological arguments for it, too. In order to be effective, the *nāma-japa* must be undertaken with a name that God himself has revealed in the Scriptures. God is identical with such a self-revealed name, God's *śabda*, and that lends power to the sound of the Name itself. Repetition of the Name is the most powerful remedy against all sins and faults. The sins against the Name itself, however, are unpardonable and exclude a person from the community of *bhaktas* as a heretic.[16]

However generous the *bhaktimārga* might be toward the traditionally unorthodox, it has created its own divisions between orthodox and heretics. The *Varāha Purāṇa*, a Vaiṣṇava scripture, declares that at Viṣṇu's instance Śiva proclaimed the *Śaivasiddhānta* in order to lead astray those who should not be saved.[17] The *Padma Purāṇa*, another Vaiṣṇava scripture, declares all non-Vaiṣṇavite doctrines to be paths leading to hell. Thus it says:

> Hear, O Goddess, I declare now the *tāmasaśāstras*, the scriptures of darkness, through which a wise man becomes a sinner even if he only thinks of them. At first I declared through my *moha-māyā*, my deluding form, the Śaiva teachings such as the *Paśupata* system. The following doctrines were laid down by brahmins who were deluded by my illusionary power: Kaṇāda proclaimed the great *Vaiśeṣika* system; the *Nyāya* and *Sāṁkhya* systems were taught by Gautama and Kapila; the much maligned Cārvāka system was explained by Bṛhaspati, while Viṣṇu took on the form of Buddha to destroy the *daityas* who proclaim the false teachings of the Buddhists and go about naked or in blue garments. I myself, O goddess, took on the body of a brahmin and in *Kaliyuga* proclaimed the wrong *śāstras* of the *māyā*-doctrine [i.e., Śaṅkara's *Advaita Vedānta*], which is but Buddhism in disguise. The brahmin Jaimini composed the great system of *Pūrvamīmāṁsā* which is worthless because it advocates atheistic doctrines.[18]

Bhakti means not only love for God, but also enmity toward those who do not love him in the same way. Even a saint like Tulsīdās, whose verses generally exude a very humane form of religiosity, teaches the *Rāmabhaktas:*

16. Playing Kṛṣṇa's flute in Sevakuñj

> Avoid those who do not love Rāma and Sītā, as your most bitter enemies, no matter how near of kin they may be. Prahlāda resisted his father, Vibhiṣāna left his brother, and Bharata his mother. Bali dispossessed his guru and the *gopīs* left their husbands in order to come to the Lord, and their mode of conduct became a source of joy and happiness for the whole world. Only insofar as they are related to God are children and relations worthy of one's love.

So, too, the *Bhagavadgītā*, often quoted as a document of Hindu tolerance, condemns the people who are not Kṛṣṇa-*bhaktas* as evildoers and bewildered fools.[19]

THE THEORY OF DEVOTION

The extreme conclusions drawn from a dogmatic understanding of *bhaktimārga* should not make us blind to the very great contribution that *bhaktas* have made to religious thought and practice. They represent a way that has recently been gaining great popularity in the West: the activation of emotions as a genuine path to God and to personal fulfillment. The teachers of *bhakti* have developed systems that reveal a good deal of psychological insight. They usually distinguish different degrees in *bhakti;* perfect love has to grow and mature over the years and gradually permeate the whole life of the *bhakta.*

Thus, Nārada in his *Bhaktisūtras* enumerates eleven degrees of *bhakti. Bhakti* begins with the glorification of Kṛṣṇa's greatness; then the *bhakta* proceeds to the love of Kṛṣṇa's beauty, to worship him according to the rules of his religion, he remembers him constantly, considers himself first as the Lord's slave, then as his companion, as his parent; finally he evokes the love a wife has toward her husband, surrenders completely to him, feels completely absorbed in him, and feels nothing else but the pain of separation from the Lord! It is quite remarkable that Nārada considers the pain lovers experience when they are separated from each other as the highest form of love.[20]

The *Bhāgavata Purāṇa* has a more popular enumeration of nine steps of *bhakti* (see Figure 15.1), which begins with listening to talks about Viṣṇu, continues with the recitation of his name, remembrance and veneration of his feet, offering *pūjā* before his image, prostrating oneself before him, considering oneself a slave of Viṣṇu, a friend, and finally to surrender completely to him.[21]

Rāmānuja, the greatest *bhakti* theologian so far, enumerates six prerequisites for someone embarking on the *bhaktimārga:* a *bhakta* has to observe certain dietary rules, show complete disregard for worldly objects,

6. Vandana: Praising

8. Sakhya: Companionship

7. Dāsya: Servitude

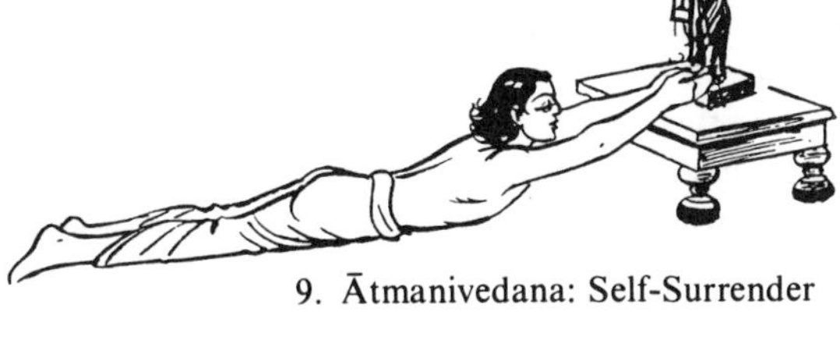

9. Ātmanivedana: Self-Surrender

Figure 15.2 The Nine degrees of Devotion

continue faithfully all religious activities, perform *pūjā*, behave virtuously, and be free from depression.[22]

The central act of *bhakti* is *prapatti*, self-surrender, which consists of five individual components: the intention of submitting to the Lord; giving up resistance to the Lord; the belief in the protection of the Lord; the prayer that the Lord may save his devotees; the consciousness of utter helplessness.

Taking refuge in the Lord, the *śaraṇāgatī* of both popular and theological *bhakti* writings, is considered the act that makes the person a *bhakta*. Some, like Madhva, wish the devotees to proclaim their surrender to God outwardly, too, by branding themselves with the *cakra*, the sign of Viṣṇu, or by stamping their bodies with his name.[23]

In its Gauḍīa-Vaiṣṇavism, Bengal has produced the most emotional and also the most subtle form of *bhakti*-teaching.[24] It makes use of the concept of *rasa*, a key term in literary criticism, in which a scale of emotions and their conditions have been developed.[25] Nine basic *rasas* are usually given, corresponding to as many fundamental "feelings." The most intense of these is *śṛṅgāra;* erotic love. Then come *hāsya*, laughter, derision; followed by *karuṇa*, compassion and pain. *Krodha*, anger, and *bibhatsā*, vexation, are important as well as firmness and steadfastness (*vīrya*). *Bhayanakā*, fearfulness; *adbhuta*, admiration; and *śānta*, tranquillity, conclude the classical scheme. For the Caitanyites, Kṛṣṇa is the *akhilarasāmṛtamūrti*, the embodiment of the essence of all sentiments. Their method of realization is a gradual development of feeling to such a high pitch that only Kṛṣṇa and Kṛṣṇa alone can be its object. Even more, the devotee realizes that ultimately the love one has for Kṛṣṇa is just a sharing of Kṛṣṇa's own *hlādinīśakti*, Kṛṣṇa's power of joyful love.

The fully developed teaching of this school distinguishes between three grades of *bhakti*, each again subdivided several times. *Sādhanabhakti*, the first stage, contains *vaidhibhakti*, ritualistic devotion, and *rāgānugā*, passionate following. It begins with having faith in Kṛṣṇa, enjoins association with good people, participation in worship, avoidance of the worthless, steadfast devotion, and a real liking of the Lord, which results in attachment and love. The next major stage is *bhāvanabhakti*, emotional devotion, in which the theory of *rasas* finds a masterful application. Beginning with the sentiment of peacefulness, continuing through servitude, companionship, parental love, and culminating in *madhurasa*, sweet love, the authors expound a complex system of religious psychology, at the center of which is Kṛṣṇa's divine bodily presence.

When emotional devotion has fully matured, it develops into the third stage of *bhakti, premā*, which is simply love at its highest level. This is considered to be permanent and cannot be taken away from the devotee under any circumstances.[26] One who has reached this stage may be called an ideal *bhakta* according to the description in the *Caitanyacaritāmṛta:*

> In pure love the devotee renounces all desire, all ritual, all knowledge and all actions and is attached to Kṛṣṇa with all powers. The true *bhakta* wants nothing from the Lord, but is content with loving him. A Kṛṣṇabhakta is kind and truthful, treats all people alike, hurts no one and is generous, tactful, pure, unselfish, at peace with himself and others. A *bhakta* does good to others and clings to Kṛṣṇa as only support. A *bhakta* has no wishes, makes no efforts except to honour Kṛṣṇa, is constant and controls all passions. A *bhakta* is always ready to give honour to others, humble, and willing to bear grief without a complaint. A *bhakta* seeks the company of the truly pious and gives up association with those who do not adhere to Kṛṣṇa.[27]

The same text describes the true Vaiṣṇava as "more humble than a blade of grass, more patient than a tree, honouring others without seeking honour" and says: "such a one is worthy of uttering Kṛṣṇa's name."

The ethical overflow of the loving devotion to God is stressed by Puruṣottamācārya, a teacher of the Śrī Vaiṣṇava school of South India, who considers the six constituents of *bhakti* to be treating everyone with good will and friendliness and discarding what is contrary to it; refraining from all malice, backbiting, falsehood, and violence; having strong faith in the protection of the Lord; praying to the Lord; discarding all false pride and egotism; completely entrusting oneself and whatever belongs to oneself to the Lord, being convinced that such complete resignation earns God's grace and mercy.[28]

Śaiva and Śākta schools have developed systems of Śiva and Devī *bhakti.* These are often quite similar to the Vaiṣṇava *bhakti* that we have briefly discussed. Thus, the *Paśupatas* prescribe certain activities designed to express and augment a person's love for Śiva. One is told to repeat the name of Śiva, to meditate on Śiva's nature, to bathe in ashes, to behave like a madman, to sing, to laugh, and to shake.[29]

The most sophisticated system of Śiva *bhakti,* however, is known as *Śaivasiddhānta;* a living faith for millions of Hindus in Tamiḷnādu to this very day. According to its main texts, *bhakti* to Śiva develops in four stages. *Dāsamārga,* the slave's way consists of practices such as cleaning a Śiva temple, smearing its floor with cow-dung, weaving garlands of different kinds of flowers for the decoration of the image of Śiva, uttering the praises of the Lord, lighting the temple lamps, maintaining flower gardens and offering one's services to any devotee of Śiva. This is the beginner's form of Śiva-*bhakti.* The next stage, *satputramārga,* the true son's way, prescribes the preparation of the articles necessary for Śiva *pūjā* (Figure 15.2) and meditation on Śiva as of the form of light. The third

Figure 15.3 Implements Used for Daily *pūjā*

stage is called *sahamārga*, the associate's way, and consists of *yoga:* withdrawal of the senses from their objects, breath control, suspension of mental activities, recitation of *mantras*, and direction of vital breaths through the six body centers. The last and highest stage is called *sanmārga*, the way of truth and reality: *bhakti* in the form of Śiva knowledge has now been fully developed and is identical with liberation and bliss.[30]

As just one example of devotion to the goddess, a hymn by the famous Bengali Śākta poet Rāmprasād may be given here:

> Mind, worship Her who saves on the other side of the Ocean of the World. Know once and for all what worth is in the trash of wealth. Vain is hope in men or money, this was said of old. Where wast thou, whence hast thou come, and whither, O whither wilt thou go? The world is glass, and ever amid its snares delusion makes men dance. Thou art in the lap of an enchantress, held fast in thy prison. Pride, malice, anger, attachment to thy lovers, by what wisdom of judgment was it that thou didst divide the kingdom of thy body among these? The day is nearly done: think therefore in thy heart, the resting place of Kālī, that island filled with jewels, think upon the things that day has brought thee. Prasād says: the name of Durgā is my promised Land of Salvation, fields flowing with nectar. Tell thy tongue evermore to utter Her name.[31]

THE IMPORTANCE OF GOD'S NAME

"Taking the Name" is perhaps the most essential step in the process of becoming a *bhakta.* Since *bhakti* teachers do not lay stress on traditional scholarship or ascetic practices, which require long training and above average strength of will and intellect, they have developed an entire *sādhana* around the name, and individual *japa* as well as congregational *saṁkīrtan* have become the most typical expressions of *bhakti.* At the centers of *bhakti* religion, hundreds of people, often paid, chant day and night in *bhajan-āśramas* the names that spell merit and salvation. One of the better known saints of our time, Swami Rāma Tīrtha says:

> As creation owes its origin to the "word" (OM) so the sacred names of Rāma, Kṛṣṇa, Hari are the vehicle that brings the individual back to him. Keep to them and you can obtain *sākṣātkāra*, or vision, of the *iṣṭadevatā*, your chosen deity, whose name or *mantra* you have chosen, as well as his *dhāma*, his sphere. The chanting of OM goes on in all eternity in the tiniest atom of creation and it acts instrumentally in *pravṛtti*, the expansion, and in *nivṛtti*, the contraction of the worlds. If we would trace back the steps and catch the sound and precede *nivṛtti* on its return, we would arrive at the eternal *Vaikunṭha*, Viṣṇu's heaven. It is our aim to reach this world of divine bliss where all rebirth ends, and this we hope to attain through *saṁkīrtan.*[32]

Bhaktas attribute an infallible effect to *saṁkīrtan:* the great saints Caitanya, Mīrābāī, Kabīr, and Tukārāma entered Viṣṇu's body without leaving behind their physical bodies on earth. They find effusive praise for the practice of the singing of the name: "The Name of the Lord is truly a drop of nectar, a heavenly taste in my mouth. My guru has taught me the greatness of the Name; today I have experienced its power."[33]

Traditionally, five rules have to be followed in the recitation of the name. The name must express the supreme divinity, it must be given by a guru at the time of initiation, it must be practiced in a spirit of devotion, and it must be accompanied by a saintly life. The name must also be sung melodiously with a heart full of love and longing. The various tunes correspond to various spheres and it is necessary to choose the appropriate melody.

The guru has been mentioned repeatedly in connection with the name—for the *bhakti* schools he or she is of the utmost importance. *Bhaktas* see in the guru the personal representative of the Supreme Lord; and contrary to the *saṁnyāsis*, they keep a lifelong connection with and dependence upon the guru. Quite often the guru is considered an incarnation of God, already during lifetime receiving formal worship. More frequently still, he or she is worshipped after death in a sanctuary built over the tomb. One school of thought is inclined to put the guru even above the transcendent God. A text says: "The *guru* must always be worshipped, the *guru* is exalted because the *guru* is one with the *mantra.* Hari is pleased if the *guru* is pleased. Millions of acts of worship are otherwise rejected. If Hari is angry, the *guru* is our defence; but from the *guru*'s wrath there is no protection."

Gurus in the *bhakti* schools are usually surrounded by a group of devotees, who serve and worship them as their guides and gods. Often, this is quite beautiful and one can meet really religious families around spiritual fathers or mothers; but quite frequently, if the guru is an unbalanced, moody, capricious person, the resulting forms of religious life are grotesque and edify little. Devotees then are told that they have to consider the whims and temper tantrums of their gurus as Kṛṣṇa's own *līlā*, His play that cannot be rationalized but has to be accepted as divine manifestation. Since according to the *bhaktas'* understanding serving God, *sevā*, is the essence of religion, the service offered to the gurus—cooking, sweeping, obeying orders, etc.—forms the exercise of religion in an immediate sense.

True and genuine religion, beginning with a fascination for God, who is Truth, Goodness and Beauty, results in genuine humility, joy and contentment. In the words of Nārada:

Attaining love of God a person has no more desire for anything, is free from grief and hatred, does not get excited over anything, does not make exertions in the furtherance of self-interest. Such a person becomes intoxicated and fascinated, as it were, being completely immersed in the enjoyment of the bliss of *ātman.*[34]

16. Lord Viṣṇu and His Devotees

Viṣṇu is the instructor of the whole world: what else should anyone learn or teach, save Him, the Supreme Spirit?

—Viṣṇu Purāṇa *I, 17*

Homage to thee, O lotus-eyed, homage to thee, O Supreme Being! Homage to thee, the soul of all worlds, homage to thee, armed with the sharp discus. Homage to thee, who created the universe as Brahmā, supports it as Viṣṇu and destroys it as Rudra at the end of times. Homage to thee O trinity, the one who exists in three forms. Devas, Yakṣas, Asuras, Siddhas, Nāgas, Gandharvas, Kinnaras, Piśācas, Rakṣasas, humans and beasts, birds, immovable things, ants and reptiles; earth, water, fire, ether and air, sound, touch and taste, sight, smell, mind, intellect, ego, time and the qualities of primaeval matter—of all these thou art the underlying reality; thou art the universe, changeless one! Knowledge and ignorance, truth and untruth, poison as well as nectar, art thou. Thou art action leading to bondage and also action leading to freedom taught by the Vedas. The enjoyer, the means and the fruits of all actions art thou, O Viṣṇu. The Yogis meditate on thee and to thee the sacrificers sacrifice. It is thou who accepts the sacrificial oblations to *devas* and the food offered to the *pitṛs*, who assumes the form of *devas* and *pitṛs*. The universe before us is thy mighty form, a smaller form of thine is this world of ours. Still smaller forms of thine are the different kinds of beings and what is called their inner self is an exceedingly subtle form of thine. Om, homage without end to the Bhagavān Vasudeva, whom no one transcends but who transcends all![1]

In those and similar words, countless pious Hindus praise Viṣṇu, whom they have accepted as their only and supreme Lord. The prayer mentions a few of the fundamental tenets of Vaiṣṇava faith, especially the immanence of Viṣṇu in all beings and his transcendence, and we shall consider a few more, without claiming to be able to exhaust the wealth

17. Viṣṇu Upendra, Khajurāho 12th ct.

of imagery and speculation produced in the long history of the various schools of Vaiṣṇavism.

Contemporary Vaiṣṇavism, the largest among the Hindu sects, has its sources not only in Vedic religion but also in Dravidian traditions and in tribal and local cults. The earliest of these worshipped Nārāyana and Vāsudeva Kṛṣṇa, as described in some portions of the *Mahābhārata* and the *Pāñcarātra* cults of Bhāgavatism, records of which still exist in the early Viṣṇu *Purāṇas* and the Vaiṣṇava *saṁhitās*.[2]

Vaiṣṇavism has developed the most variegated and richest mythology of all the schools of Hinduism. At the core of Vaiṣṇavism, however, is Lord Viṣṇu as savior, a belief that, again, has found expression in countless myths. The oldest, and perhaps most basic, myth of this kind is that of Viṣṇu *trivikrama*, Viṣṇu who took the three steps; later, it was combined with a myth of one of the *avatāras, vāmana*, the dwarf. Allusions to it are found in the *Ṛgveda*,[3] establishing a connection between a Viṣṇu cult and the worship of the sun in the morning, at noon, and in the evening. It is embellished in the epics and *Purāṇas* and is designed to give a basis to the claim that Viṣṇu's is the whole universe!

Another Vedic hymn[4] has become the basis of all later Vaiṣṇava speculation about Viṣṇu as the material cause of all beings. The very important, and most probably very old, *Nārāyaṇīya* section of the *Mahābhārata*[5] tells about a revelation of a religion of salvation given to two sages, Nāra and Nārada in *Śvetadvīpa*, the White Island, situated to the north and inhabited by a race of white wise beings, all of them worshippers of Nārāyaṇa. Around the turn of the century, this interesting text prompted some scholars to suspect a Christian influence in Vaiṣṇavism.[6]

VIṢṆU *AVATĀRAS*

The most popular, and consequently the most important, part of Viṣṇu mythology centers around the *avatāras*, the bodily descents of Viṣṇu exercizing his function as savior of the world.[7] The *Bhagavadgītā* explains that the Supreme One comes down to earth whenever *dharma* is in danger, to save the good and to destroy the wicked.[8]

Generally, one speaks nowadays of the *daśāvatāras*, ten embodiments of Visnu, though some texts mention a large number, including a good many historical figures like Buddha and Kapila, the founder of the *Sāṁkhya* system. In all probability the systematization of the *avatāras* belongs to a relatively late period. The animal forms, such as *matsya*, the fish, *kūrma*, the tortoise, and *varāha*, the boar, are possibly Vedic Prajāpati transformations and reminiscences of old tribal totems; the human forms,

Figure 16.1 Viṣṇu in Human Form

like Rāma and Kṛṣṇa (Figure 16.1), could represent deifications of historical persons, tribal heroes, and founders of sects; while other forms may go back to local gods and tribal deities.[9]

Vaiṣṇavism, taken as a more or less unified religion, represents the constant effort to bring the growing mass of mythology together under one principle and to harmonize the heterogeneous elements from various local traditions. The ten most widely recognized *avatāras* are described in so many texts that it will suffice to merely mention them and some features of the myths connected with them without going into details.[10]

Matsya, the fish, defeated the *asuras* who had stolen the Vedas and returned them to the Brahmins. *Ekaśriṅga*, the unicorn, saved Manu from the flood in which the rest of humankind perished. *Kūrma*, the tortoise, supported the mountain Maṇḍara, which was used by the gods to churn *amṛta*, nectar, from the Milk Ocean. *Varāha*, the boar, lifted the earth from the waters into which she had sunk and thus saved her. *Nṛsiṅha*, the man-lion, saved the *bhakta* Prahlāda from his father and persecutor, Hiraṇya-kaśīpu, and in doing so he saved the whole world. *Vāmana*, the dwarf, defeated Bali, the king of the Earth, and regained the three worlds for the *devas*, who had been exiled from it. From his feet arose the Ganges. *Paraśu-rāma*, Rāma with the battle-axe, saved the Brahmins by annihilating the Kṣatriyas. The *Rāma* and *Kṛṣṇa avatāras* are the most popular and occupy a category by themselves. They are the universal saviors not limited to a particular epoch, as the others are; they save all who surrender to them. *Balarāma*, the brother of Kṛṣṇa, is remembered as the killer of Pralamba and a host of other demons. *Kalki* is the only *avatāra* to come in the future: as the eschatological manifestation of Viṣṇu on a white horse, he is to be the final liberator of the world from *kali*, the embodiment of strife, and all his evil influences. Apart from these, a number of other *avatāras* play a certain role in some of the Vaiṣṇava scriptures and cult centers.[11]

The *Bhāgavata Purāṇa* teaches the famous *Nārāyaṇakāvaca*, the prayer called the "protective shield of Viṣṇu," in which all the *avatāras* of Viṣṇu are invoked, remembering their salvific deeds in the past as a guarantee for present and future salvation.[12]

Rāma was worshipped locally as a hero and a divine king probably long before he came to be considered as an *avatāra* of Viṣṇu,[13] and he is certainly older than the *Vālmīki Rāmāyaṇa*, the celebrated epic narrating his adventures. His worship as a Viṣṇu *avatāra* must be comparatively late, certainly later than that of Vāsudeva Kṛṣṇa. Even now the human features of Rāma and Sītā, his consort, seem to be more in the foreground of popular religious consciousness than his divinity. A late work, the so-called *Adhyātma Rāmāyaṇa*, explains Rāma and his exploits as manifestations of the supreme Viṣṇu in the following manner:

> The Lord of Jānakī, who is intelligence itself and, though immutable, being requested by the *devas* to remove the afflictions of the world, took the illusory form of a man and was apparently born in the solar dynasty. After attaining to fame eternal, capable of destroying sins by killing the foremost of the demons, he again took up his real nature as *brahman.*[14]

Ayodhyā, the city of Rāma, has become the center of the *Rāma-bhaktas*, with millions of devotees flocking to the sacred sites each year.

The most popular among the Viṣṇu *avatāras* is, undoubtedly, Kṛṣṇa, the black one, also called Śyāma.[15] Many of his worshippers consider him not only an *avatāra* in the usual sense, namely Viṣṇu accepting a human disguise in which he appears, but as *svayam bhagavān*, the Lord Himself in His eternal body. The many scriptures inspired by the Kṛṣṇa cult do not tire of emphasizing that Kṛṣṇa is the savior, the ultimate and definite manifestation of Viṣṇu, for the benefit of all who choose to become his devotees.

Present-day Kṛṣṇa worship is an amalgam of various elements.[16] According to historical testimonies, Kṛṣṇa-Vāsudeva worship already flourished in and around Mathurā several centuries before Christ. A second important element is the cult of Kṛṣṇa Govinda, perhaps the tribal deity of the Ahīrs. Still later is the worship of the Divine Child Kṛṣṇa, a quite prominent feature of modern Kṛṣṇaism. The last element seems to have been Kṛṣṇa, the lover of the *gopīs*, among whom Rādhā occupies a special position. It is possible that this latter element developed under Tantric influence. In some books, Kṛṣṇa is considered to be the founder and first teacher of the Bhāgavata religion. The question of Kṛṣṇa's historicity is being studied quite seriously.[17]

The numerous myths reveal a faith in Kṛṣṇa as a manifestation of God, capable of liberating humankind. His birth is surrounded by miracles. As a little baby, he gave proof of his divine power. As a young man, he lifted up Govardhana and defied Indra. He is the object of passionate love that inspired some of India's greatest poets to unrivalled masterpieces, like Jayadeva, who wrote the immortal *Gītāgovinda.* He also is the teacher of the way of salvation in the *Bhagavadgītā* and the *Bhāgavata Purāṇa*, certainly the most popular religious books in the whole of India.[18]

Not only was Kṛṣṇaism influenced by the identification of Kṛṣṇa with Viṣṇu, but also Vaiṣṇavism as a whole was partly transformed and reinterpreted in the light of the popular and powerful Kṛṣṇa religion. Bhāgavatism may have brought an element of cosmic religion into Kṛṣṇa worship; but Kṛṣṇa mythology has certainly brought a strongly human element into Bhāgavatism. Kṛṣṇa is not a God enthroned in majesty, inaccessible to humanity, but he is a sweet child, a naughty boy, a comrade in youthful adventures, an ardent lover—and thus a savior! The center of Kṛṣṇa

18. Varāha *avatāra*, Khajurāho 12th ct.

worship was always *Brājbhūmi*, the district of Mathurā, with Vrindābana, Govardhāna, and Gokula associated with Kṛṣṇa from time immemorial. Millions of *Kṛṣṇa-bhaktas* visit these places every year and participate in the numerous festivities that reenact scenes from Kṛṣṇa's life on earth.[19]

Though, in the earlier sources, there is no mention of Śrī, the consort of Viṣṇu; in later Vaiṣṇavism, Śrī becomes part and parcel of Viṣṇu religion. Apparently, Śrī also was worshipped independently before her cult was integrated into Vaiṣṇavism. Now she is considered inseparable from Viṣṇu: Viṣṇu has on his body a mark called *śrīvatsa*, representing his consort. In later Vaiṣṇavism, she is identified with Rādhā; and Caitanya, the sixteenth-century Bengali Kṛṣṇa mystic, is held by his followers to be an *avatāra* of Kṛṣṇa and Rādhā together. The most prominent form of South Indian Vaiṣṇavism is called Śrī-Vaiṣṇavism because of its strong emphasis on the role of Śrī. It draws heavily on the popular *bhakti* religion of the Āḷvārs, so that we can see in Śrī worship an element of popular Indian religion, in which the worship of goddesses always occupied a prominent place.[20]

VIṢṆU THEOLOGY

Vaiṣṇavism is intimately connected with image worship. Its rationale is provided in the *Pāñcarātra*[21] theology, which has been fairly commonly accepted by all groups of Vaiṣṇavas. Following the description in a widely acknowledged handbook, here is a short sketch of it.

Īśvara, the Lord Viṣṇu, is the ruler of all, the giver of all gifts, the preserver of all, the cause of all effects; and he has everything, except himself and his own consciousness, as his body. *Īśvara* is thus the material cause of the universe, becoming through the act of creation the efficient cause as well as the concomitant cause of all things, insofar as he is immanent in time. *Īśvara*, who animates the whole world, is not touched by its imperfections. He is omnipresent through his form, through his knowledge of all things and events, and through his body. He is free from the limitations of space, time, and objects. He is *sat-cit-ānanda*, being, consciousness, and bliss; and he is free from sin. He is the refuge and the protector of all beings, having the qualities of gentleness and mercy.

Īśvara exists in five different forms: as *para, vyūha, vibhava, antaryāmin* and *ārcāvatāra*. Viṣṇu in his own supreme and transcendent form is called *para*, expressed in names like *Parabrahman, Paravasudeva*. He is endowed with a divine body having four arms and adorned by the insignia of his supreme lordship, seated on *śeṣa*, the infinite world-snake, residing in *Vaikuṇṭha*.

He manifests his powers severally in four *vyūhas*, whose names are

Vāsudeva, Saṁkarṣana, Pradyumna, and Aniruddha, and who exist for the purpose of creation and worship. Vāsudeva is filled with the six divine qualities; the others have two each, namely *jñāna* and *bala*, knowledge and strength; *aiśvarya* and *vīrya*, lordship and heroism; *śakti* and *tejas*, power and splendor. Each of them descends into three sub-*vyūhas*, such as Keśava, etc., who are the presiding deities of the twelve months, each having special insignia and powers. Keśava shines like gold, and he carries four *cakras* or discusses. The dark-skinned Nārāyaṇa carries four *śaṅkhas*, conches. Madhva, who is bright like sapphire, holds four *gaḍas*, or clubs. Govinda who shines as the moon, carries four *śārṅgas*, or bows. Viṣṇu, of the color of the blue lotus, has four *halas*, or ploughs. Madhusūdana, who is like a bright-hued lotus, carries four *muśalas*, or hammers. The fire-colored Trivikrama bears four *khadgas*, or swords. Vāmana, radiant like the dawn, holds four *vajras*, or thunderbolts. Śrīdhāra, like a white lotus, bears four *paṭṭisas*, or spears. Hṛṣikeśa, brilliant as the lightning, carries four *mudgaras*, or axes; Padmanābha, effulgent as the midday sun, bears five *audhas*, or shields. Damodāra, red-white like an Indra-gopa beetle, holds four *pāśas*, or nooses.

Under the category *vibhava* come the *avatāras*, which were mentioned earlier. The text distinguishes between full and partial *avatāras*. It also teaches that "The cause for the descent of an *avatāra* is only the free will of *Īśvara* and not *karma*. Its fruit is the protection of the good people and the destruction of the wicked."

Antaryāmin is the form of *Īśvara* that resides in the human heart. He stays with the *jīvātman* as a friend in the experiences of heaven and hell and is recognizable by the Yogi. For practical religious purposes, the *ārcāvatāra*, the visible image of God, is the most important. The text describes it as follows:

> The *ārcāvatāra* is that special form which accepts as body, without intervention of spatial or temporal distance, any kind of matter which the *bhakta* might wish to choose, descending into it with an *aprākṛtaśarīra*, a non-material body; he then depends on the devotee concerning bathing, eating, sitting, sleeping, etc. He is filled with divine qualities and tolerates everything, being present thus in houses, villages, towns, holy places, hills and so forth. He is fourfold on the basis of the difference as *svayamvyakta*, self-manifest, *daiva*, manifest through *devas*, *saiddha* manifest through saints and *manuṣa* manifest through ordinary human beings.[22]

Images, understood as a physical presence of Viṣṇu, are a very important part of Vaiṣṇavism. The fame of a temple depends on the power of its *mūrti*, and each devout Vaiṣṇava family maintains at least one figure of Viṣṇu or of one of the *avatāras* in the house, which receives regular worship.

Apart from the anthropomorphic images also the *tulasī* plant, usually kept in a pot in the yard of the house, and the *śālagrāma*, an ammonite from the Gaṇḍaka River (in Nepal), are worshipped as embodiments of Viṣṇu.

Vaiṣṇavism has also a highly developed temple architecture. Some of the most impressive buildings in the world, such as the Śrīraṅgam temple near Tiruchirapaḷḷi, are consecrated to Viṣṇu. In most images, Viṣṇu is represented either standing upright or lying on his couch, the world-snake *śeṣa*, and usually accompanied by Śrī. The *avatāras* have been represented, quite frequently, in the poses described in the myths. Feasts observed in honor of Viṣṇu are so numerous that it is impossible to mention them all; a few will be described in a later chapter. Today, the feasts of the *avatāras* are in the foreground, especially the birthdays of Kṛṣṇa and Rāma.

Despite the prevalence of a highly emotional *bhakti* and often quite unstructured forms of worship, we must not overlook the very rich systematic theological heritage of Vaiṣṇavism and its compendious, minutely ordered liturgies.

Vaiṣṇavas generally insist that *their* interpretation of the great classics, which are universally accepted by Hindus, is the only correct one, rejecting for instance Śaṅkara's Advaitic interpretation of the *Upaniṣads* as heretical. There is good reason to assume that the first commentary on the *Brahmasūtras*, the lost gloss by Bodhāyana, had indeed been theistic. Vaiṣṇavas, then, interpret many passages in the Vedas and the *Upaniṣads* in a Vaiṣṇava way. According to Rāmānuja, for instance, all words in the *Veda*, like *power, form, splendor, body*, and similar expressions, mean Viṣṇu, and similarly, Viṣṇu is intended by the *Upaniṣads* when they mention "the soul of all," "the highest *Brahman*," the "supreme reality," and so on. The earliest attempts to systematize Vaiṣṇavism seem to rely upon the Sāṁkhya system, as testified to by the *Pāñcarātra Āgamas*. The difference of Vaiṣṇava Sāṁkhya lies in its attributing to Viṣṇu the authorship of *prakṛti* and of liberation. The *Bhāgavata Purāṇa*, which considers Kapila an *avatāra* of Viṣṇu, contains the fullest account of Vaiṣṇava Sāṁkhya, concluding with the exhortation: "Therefore through devotion, dispassion and spiritual wisdom acquired through a concentrated mind one should contemplate the Inner Controller as present in this very body, though apart from it."[23]

VAIṢṆAVA VEDĀNTA

More prominent today in Vaiṣṇava theology are the systems deriving from *Vedānta* and developing from the tenth century onwards. They begin with the *ācāryas* of Śrīraṅgam, who combined the fervor of the popular

Figure 16.2 Nammāḷvār

religious literature of the Āḷvārs with Upaniṣadic *jñāna.* Nāṭha Muni, the first of them, was the son of the great *Pāñcarātra* master Īśvara Muni. He gave to the Tamiḷ *Prabandham* of the Āḷvārs the status of *śruti* in Śrīraṅgam and established himself as the supreme teaching authority. His successor, Yamunācārya, was a great Vedāntin who left several systematic works. According to a legend, he kept three fingers bent on his death-bed, interpreted by Rāmānuja, his successor, as three unfulfilled wishes that he was going to redeem; namely, to give to the Vaiṣṇavas a commentary on the *Brahmasūtra,* to perpetuate the memory of Parāśara, the author of the *Viṣṇu Purāṇa,* and to spread the glory of Nammāḷvār (Figure 16.2), considered to be the greatest among the Āḷvārs.[24]

Rāmānuja proved to be a great organizer and a great writer. He made the most successful attempt to establish a theistic Vedānta interpretation in contrast to Śaṅkara's Advaita. In addition to the commentary on the *Brahmasūtra,* called *Śrībhāṣya,* Rāmānuja wrote a commentary on the *Bhagavadgītā,* as well as several minor independent and valuable works. Perhaps the best known of these is the *Vedārthasaṁgraha,* a veritable compendium of Vaiṣṇava Vedānta, written in beautiful language.[25] In Rāmānuja's theology, *brahman* is identical with Viṣṇu, who is described as *rakṣaka,* the Redeemer.

Viṣṇu comes down from his heavenly throne to enter *saṁsāra* for the sake of assisting the struggling *jīvas* to attain salvation; he suffers and endures pain with them and leads them by the hand like a friend. This guidance is given through the medium of the *avatāras* and the guru, the "fully trust-worthy person" who tells the lost *jīvas* about their real identity and returns them to their father.[26] Though in their original nature, the *jīvas* are particles of the divine nature, due to certain limitations, described as "heedlessness," they become entangled in *saṁsāra* and thereby are unhappy. The lord remains with the *jīvas* as *antaryāmi* to guide them, without taking away the *jīvas'* freedom to follow their own ways. "The Lord then, recognizing those who perform good actions as devotees who obey His commands, blesses them with piety, riches, worldly pleasures and final release, while those who transgress His commands He causes to experience the opposite of all this."[27] Viṣṇu himself is the *mukti-dātā,* the giver of salvation, and the role of humans is to prepare the way for God to meet them, to dispose themselves for God's grace. The central act is *prapatti,* self-surrender.

The following text, in Rāmānuja's words, gives in a nutshell the way to salvation:

> The pathway through which the supreme brahman is to be attained is as follows. By an accumulation of great merit the sins of the past lives are destroyed. Thus

19. Vittal/Vithobha (Viṣṇu) Mahārāṣṭra, Heras Institute Bombay

> liberated, a person will seek refuge at the feet of the Puruṣottama. Such self-surrender begets an inclination toward Him. Then the aspirant acquires knowledge of reality from the scriptures aided by the instruction of holy teachers. Then, by a steady effort, the *bhakta* develops in an ever-increasing measure the qualities of soul, like the control of mind, sense control, austerity, purity, forgiveness, sincerity, fearlessness, mercy, and nonviolence. The *bhaktas* continue with the ritual duties and offer their very own self at the lotuslike feet of the Puruṣottama. They ceaselessly worship Him with dedication. The Puruṣottama, who is overflowing with compassion, being pleased with such love, showers His grace on the aspirants, which destroys all inner darkness. In such devotees, there develops *bhakti,* which is valued for its own sake, which is uninterrupted, an absolute delight in itself, and which is meditation that has taken on the character of the most vivid and immediate vision. Through such *bhakti* is the Supreme attained.[28]

Rāmānuja underscores the importance of the guru with the beautiful parable of a young prince, who in the course of boyish play loses his way in the forest. He is reared by a good Brahmin, who knows nothing about the boy's background. When the boy has reached his sixteenth year, a "fully trustworthy person" tells him who his father is and that he longs to see him. The boy is exceedingly happy and starts on his way to his real home; his father has gone out from his palace to meet him halfway. Rāmānuja sees in the "fully trustworthy person" a model of the true guru. The first among the gurus is Śrī, mediating between God and *bhakta.* She is the embodiment of divine grace and mercy whose entreaties win the forgiveness of Viṣṇu for the *jīva.* The human guru should be like her: entirely free from egotism, always desirous of the welfare of others, not swayed by the love of fame or profit.[29]

Shortly after Rāmānuja's death the unity of Śrīvaiṣṇavism was disrupted and two major schools developed, based on differing dogmatic as well as linguistic tenets. The *Vaḍagalais*, or Northerners, whose main teacher was Vedāntadeśika, maintained that Sanskrit scriptures were the only true ones; whereas the *Teṅgalais*, or Southerners, whose principal master was Lokācārya Pillai, preferred the Tamiḷ scriptures. They are also known as the monkey school and the cat school, respectively, because the Northerners likened the process of salvation to the activity of a young monkey, who must cling to his mother if he is to be carried away from a fire, whereas the southerners saw the best illustration of the process of salvation in a young kitten, whose mother picks it up and carries it out.[30]

One of the most colorful of all Vaiṣṇava *ācāryas* was Madhva, the exponent of Dvaita Vedānta, who became known as "hammer of the Jains." He demanded stigmatization of the *Viṣṇu-bhakta* with a *cakra* as prerequisite for salvation. Madhva considered himself the third *avatāra* of Vāyu, a mediator between Viṣṇu and humankind. According to him, the *jīva* is an image of Viṣṇu, like a reflection in a mirror; and the relationship between God and person is described as *biṁba-pratibiṁba*, splendor and its reflection. His doctrine of predestination is quite unique in Indian religion. According to his understanding, certain persons are destined never to become liberated and must remain in eternal bondage. He also assumed that there would be differences in the bliss experienced by those who have reached heaven. He described the oneness of the perfect *bhakta* with Viṣṇu in a beautiful image: "The released takes everything with the hand of Hari, sees through the eye of Hari only, walks with the feet of Hari." The perfectly free ones even enter into Viṣṇu at will and issue out from him.[31]

Another great master of the Vaiṣṇava tradition is Nimbārka, for whom the role of the guru becomes all-important. "Surrender to the guru" is the central act of saving faith, and the disciple makes a statement to the effect that the guru is considered the only savior from mundane existence.[32]

Vallabha, another Vaiṣṇava Vedāntin, emphasizes the role of Śrī, a theme that becomes prominent again in Gauḍīa-Vaiṣṇavism, showing perhaps some Tantric influence.[33]

VAIṢṆAVA SAINTS AND SINGERS

Caitanya is one of the most renowned figures in modern Vaiṣṇavism. He has become known to many Westerners as the *Mahāprabhu*, the Great Lord of the Hare Kṛṣṇa movement.[34] Though he is not really the author of the emotionally refined Gauḍīa-Vaiṣṇavism, he and his learned disciples made it into an important religious movement, influential far beyond the boundaries of Bengal. He knew the *Bhāgavata Purāṇa;* he had read the Kṛṣṇa poetry of Caṇḍīdāsa and Vidyāpati; he was familiar with Bilvamaṅgala's *Kṛṣṇakarṇāmṛta* and Jayadeva's *Gītāgovinda;* and the practice of *kīrtana* was already widespread in his time. Caitanya never wrote a book,[35] but among his disciples he had very able men who formulated the theology of the movement that Caitanya initiated. Rūpa Goswāmi's *Haribhaktirasāmṛtasindhu* is the authentic summa theologica of the Caitanyites, and Gopala Bhaṭṭa's *Haribhaktivilāsa* codifies the accepted form of their ritual.

Caitanya's is a pure Kṛṣṇa religion. At its center stands Kṛṣṇa as the full manifestation of God and the continued presence of Kṛṣṇa in Brāja, more specifically the Kṛṣṇa of Vṛndāvana, the great lover of the *gopīs*, the perfect partners in this love. According to the Caitanyites, the *Bhāgavata Purāṇa* is *śruti* as well as the only authentic commentary on the *Brahmasūtra.* Nevertheless, another Caitanyite, Baladeva Vidyābhuṣana, felt impelled to write a formal *bhāṣya* on the *Brahmasūtra* as well, called *Govinda Bhāṣya.*[36]

The real source of the continued vitality and popularity of Vaiṣṇavism seems to lie in its poets and singers, who for centuries travelled up and down the subcontinent to kindle *bhakti* to Viṣṇu in the hearts of their compatriots. Their concern is not with theology or liturgy but *bhakti* for the sake of liberation. Their main topic is the misery of this life and the glory of the life of God. A very striking feature is their insistence on the cultivation of a high moral standard: purity, truthfulness, patience, forbearance, love, renunciation, giving up of all selfishness, contentment with one's state of life, self-control, pity, freedom from greed and hypocrisy, sincerity, and humility—all this is taught in simple language as prerequisite and sign of true *bhakti*. They recommend the traditional Vaiṣṇava practices of *nāmajapa, saṁkīrtan, mūrtipūjā*, submission under a guru, and so on.

Simple as their words may be, and understood by everyone, their thoughts reach great depths and their devotion is grounded in philosophical insight. Some samples must suffice. For those who know Indian vernaculars, there are literally hundreds of books to draw from; for English reading students of *bhakti*, an increasingly rich amount of translations and scholarly studies also are becoming available.[37]

Sūrdās (1478-1560?), according to tradition, was blind from birth.[38] Yet, his poetry, aflame with the love of Kṛṣṇa, was so famous all over North India that the Muslim Emperor Akbar invited him to his court to converse with him and listen to his recitation. The *Sūrsagar*, "Sūr's Ocean," a massive work that is still widely read, recreates in contemporary *brājbhāṣā* the tenth canto of the *Bhāgavata Purāṇa*. Besides this, Sūr wrote many couplets that are sung at popular *bhajan* sessions. An English translation cannot bring out the musicality of the original, its clever use of double meanings of words or of closely related sound images, its rhythm, or its color. It will, however, convey some of the content and give an impression of the down-to-earth metaphors used to deliver its transcendental message. For the reader not familiar with this type of poetry, it may be worth mentioning that, as a sort of copyright, the Indian author of a poem usually inserted his or her own name in the last verse.

> Misguided by illusion after illusion
>
> Stuck [like a fly] in the juice of sense objects, [and yet] far from understanding [things]
>
> You have lost the jewel Hari inside your own house.
>
> [You are] like a deer that sees mirages, [which are]
>
> Unable to quench thirst even if approached from ten different directions
>
> Having produced in one life after another

Much *karma* in which you have entangled yourself

[You] resemble the parrot who pinned his hope on the fruit of the silk-cotton tree.

Having set his mind on it day and night,

He took it in its beak [and found] its shell empty—

The cotton had flown up and away.

[You are] like a monkey which is kept tied on a rope

By the juggler who makes him dance for a few grains at every crossroads.

Sūrdās says: without devotion to God you will make yourself into a morsel [to be eaten] by the tiger Time.[39]

In spite of its use of Vaiṣṇava history and scriptures, this kind of *bhakti* is quite transsectarian. At the *bhajan*-gatherings, one may hear poems by *Rāmabhaktas* and *Kṛṣṇabhaktas* recited side by side with those of Kabīr, who did not follow any particular Vaiṣṇava affiliation at all.

What those *bhaktas* search for is true experience.[40] Their basic experience is that God is reality. For Kabīr, the religious experience is a "penetrating to the heart of reality"; for Mīrābāī, Viṣṇu is "the invaluable jewel of reality." Quite often they report about suprasensory phenomena that accompany realization, the most prominent being the hearing of the *anahaṭ-śabda*, the transcendent sound. Kabīr speaks of the "sky-reaching-sound" that breaks forth from the full lake of mellifluous nectar, the means of illumination. Many also describe a taste of sweetness perceived in ecstasy: it is called *Rāmras* or *Hariras* and partaking of it equals immortality. Most *bhaktas* firmly believe that one can have *sākṣātkāra*, a bodily vision of God in this life, that would seal one's love to God with the assurance of final deliverance.

Vaiṣṇavism had and has a deep appeal to women. One of the woman-saint Mīrābāī's songs may help to appreciate the depth of feeling that is *Viṣṇubhakti:*

The Name is gone deep into my mind.

Day and night do I chant it.

O Lord, I am humble and low, can I sing thy praises?

I am encaged in the agony of separation.

I gain solace only by repeating thy name!

Guided by the grace of the *guru* I have turned out

evil thoughts from my mind.

I stretch the arrow of the Name on the bow of Love,
I arm myself with the shield of wisdom
and sing my Lord's praises cheerfully all the time.
Making my body a sound-box
I play on it many notes with the mind
in order to wake up my slumbering soul.
I dance before my Lord
to gain a place in his divine abode. O Giridhāra, confer
thy blessing on me,
Who sing of thy sports,
and let me place the dust of thy lotus-feet on my head,
for *that* boon I cherish the most.
So sings Mīrābāī.[41]

Vaiṣṇavism has not lost its attraction in our time. Not only do the centuries-old *saṁpradāyas* continue and intensify their activities, but new movements have also arisen to reactivate *saṁkīrtan* and regular *pūjā*. Swāmi Rāma Tīrtha has carried the message of Lord Viṣṇu to the West, and Swami Viṣṇupāda Bhakti Vedānta founded in ISKCON a mission to propagate Gauḍīa-Vaiṣṇavism, not only in India but throughout the whole world. An Englishman, who under his Indian name Kṛṣṇa Prem became the guru of Indian as well as Western *bhaktas*, may still be rather exceptional, but there is no denying the fact that Vaiṣṇavism, in its many forms, with its basic message of love, has universal appeal to religiously minded persons.

17. Śiva: The Grace and the Terror of God

Śiva, you have no mercy.
Śiva you have no heart.
Why Why did you bring me to birth
wretch in this world,
exile from the other?

—*Basavanna*[1]

Praise Viśvanātha, the Lord of the City of Benares, whose locks are the charming ripples of the Ganges, adorned on his left by Gaurī, the beloved of Nārāyaṇa, the destroyer of the god of love.

Praise Viśvanātha, the Lord of the City of Benares, beyond speech, the repository of different qualities, whose feet are worshipped by Brahmā, Viṣṇu and the other *devas*, with his wife to the left.

Praise Viśvanātha, the Lord of the City of Benares, the wielder of the trident, adorned by a snake, wearing a tiger skin and matted locks, the Three-eyed one, who keeps in two of his hands the noose and the goad and offers blessing and grace with the two others.

Praise Viśvanātha, the Lord of the City of Benares, wearing a crown with the moon, who burnt the Five-Arrowed-One to ashes with the fire emerging from his third eye on the forehead, whose ears are adorned with the shining rings of *śeṣa*, the king of the snakes.

Praise Viśvanātha, the Lord of the City of Benares, the Five-faced-one, the lion destroying the mad elephant of sin, the Garuḍa destroying the vicious demons, the world fire that burns to ashes the jungle of birth, death and old age.

Praise Viśvanātha, the Lord of the City of Benares, who is effulgent, who is with and without qualities, the One without a second, bliss itself, the unconquerable one, the unknowable one, who is dark and bright and the form of the soul.

Praise Viśvanātha, the Lord of the City of Benares, after you have given up all desires, all reviling of others and all attachment to sinful conduct, enter into *samādhi* and meditate on the Lord, seated in the lotus of the heart.

Praise Viśvanātha, the Lord of the City of Benares, who is free from all emotion such as attachment and others, who is fond of his devotees, the abode of austerities and bliss, the companion of Girija endowed with his throat stained with the poison.

The person who recites this hymn to Śiva, the Lord of the City of Benares, attains in this life learning, prosperity, immense happiness and eternal fame and after death liberation.[2]

To Viśvanātha, Śiva, the Lord of the Universe, the most sacred of all the temples of the holy city of Benares is consecrated; it is off limits to all non-Hindus.

SOURCES OF ŚAIVISM

Śiva worship has been traced back to the Indus civilization, in which it appears to have been an established tradition. *Liṅgas*, the main object of Śiva worship to this day, have been found there as well as figures on seals interpreted as Śiva Mahāyogi and Śiva Paśupati.[3]

The historical homeland of Śiva religion in more recent times, however, has been the Tamiḷ country. Both Śiva's name and his main mythology seem to come from there. The "Red God" was only later given a Sanskrit name, phonetically close to the Tamiḷ one, which is translated as "the graceful one." Tribal religions of northwestern India have contributed other features.

The ambivalence of this Great God, however, owes a great deal to the fusion of Śiva with Rudra, the howler, a deity well known from the *Vedas*. In the *Vedas*, Rudra is regarded as "an apotropäic god of aversion, to be feared, but not adored."[4] He may have been one of the tribal gods as well; too powerful to be suppressed by the official Vedic religion, too alien to be accepted among the *devas*.

This theory gains strength through what may be the oldest and most popular Śiva myth: Śiva coming uninvited to Dakṣa's sacrifice, who had prepared offerings to all the other *devas*, destroying the sacrifice, and after killing Dakṣa, bringing him back to life, converting him into a Śiva worshipper and ensuring for himself a permanent portion of the sacrifice.[5] The myth relating to the destruction of Dakṣa's sacrifice by Śiva, according to all sources the first of Śiva's exploits, may in fact have a historical core: the conquest of Kanakhala, a *tīrtha* close to modern Hardwār, which was of great importance to Śaivites, Vaiṣṇavas, and Śāktas alike and which was linked to an important Vedic settlement associated with the famous patriarch Dakṣa. As a story of the occupation of a holy place beyond the range of

20. Śiva Sadāśiva, Mahārāṣṭra, Heras Institute Bombay

the high Himālayas, the home of Śaivism before it entered the plains of India, it provided legitimacy to the Śaivas, who were originally shunned by the Vedic Āryans.[6]

Śivabhagats are mentioned by Pāṇini and the Indian worshippers of Dionysos, referred to by Megasthenes, may possibly have been Śiva devotees. The oldest Śaivite sect about which we know anything with certainty is that of the *Pāśupatas*, whose teachings are largely identical with the even now flourishing *Śaiva Siddhānta.* Their founder was, according to legend, Śiva himself in the form of Lakuliṣa. Modern research is inclined to see in Lakuliṣa a historical person of the second century C.E.[7] The epics are full of references to Śiva; the *Rāmāyaṇa* usually contains the oldest versions of Śiva myths. The *Mahābhārata* includes several hymns to Śiva and the mention, even at this early stage, of four different Śiva sects.

The *Śiva Purāṇas* and *Āgamas*, the main sources of "modern" Śaivism, seem to be comparatively late compositions, though they contain much ancient material. A good deal of Śiva mythology and theology seems to be an imitation of earlier Vaiṣṇava material.[8] Several powerful kings in the Indian Middle ages were Śaivas who sometimes forced Śaivism on their subjects and built magnificent sanctuaries in honor of Śiva.[9] Between 700 and 1000 C.E., Śaivism appears to have been the dominant religion of India, due largely to the influence of the sixty-three *Nāyanmārs* (leaders) who flourished during this time and propagated Śaivism among the masses in the form of *Śivabhakti.* The greatest among India's theological philosophers, Śaṅkarācārya, according to an ancient tradition, was "an incarnation of Śiva, born for the purpose of consolidating Hindu *dharma* in answer to the implorings of Śaivaguru and Āryandā."[10] In the twelfth century, a powerful reformist Śaiva movement arose in Kaṇṇaḍa, the Liṅgāyats, who still exercise great influence.

The *Ṛgveda* contains but a few hymns to Rudra, mainly imploring him to stay away and not to do harm,[11] occasionally beseeching him as "the great physician who possesses a thousand medicines" to give health and remove sorrow. The *Yajurveda* offers one of the most interesting texts concerning Rudra, the so-called *Śatarudriya.*[12] It displays many features of classical Śaivism. Śiva is described as both terrifying and as gracious. The hymn constantly switches from one Rudra to many Rudras, from praise to earnest prayer not to do any harm. "Innumerable Rudras are on the face of the earth," the text says, but the names given to them are quite often identical with the titles given in later Śaivism to Śiva, the only Lord. Apart from names like Nīlakaṇṭha, Śārva, Paśupati, Nīlagrīva, Bhava, and so on, Rudra is described as the one who stretched out the earth, who is immanent in places and objects, in stones, plants, and animals. There is also the paradoxical ascription of contradictory attributes. After

Figure 17.1 *Dakṣiṇāmūrti*, a Form of Śiva

being praised as the Great Lord of all beings, he is called "cheat" and "Lord of thieves"; he is described as fierce and terrible and also the source of happiness and delight. The singer asks Śiva-Rudra to turn away his fearful form and approach the worshipper in his auspicious, friendly form. The *Vrātya* section of the *Atharvaveda*, again perhaps a remnant of pre-Āryan religion,[13] contains hymns that use the well-known Śiva titles: Bhava, Bharva, Paśupati, Rudra, Mahādeva, and Iśāna.[14] In Vedic ritual, as described in the *Śatapatha Brāhmaṇa*, Rudra is treated differently from the other *devas.* At the end of the sacrifice, a handful of straw is offered to him for propitiation, at the end of a meal the leftovers are placed to the north for Rudra. The *Aitareya Brāhmaṇa* states that "Rudra is an embodiment of all the dread forms of whom *devas* are afraid."[15] The bull that is to be sacrificed to him must be killed outside the village.

We find a fully developed Śiva-Vedānta system in the *Śvetāśvatara Upaniṣad*, a text that plays a part in Śaivism comparable to that of the *Bhagavadgītā* in Vaiṣṇavism.[16] It rejects at length a large number of different theological opinions, surely a sign of its rather late date. Śiva is identified with *brahman.* Thus it teaches: "The immortal and imperishable Hara exercises complete control over the perishable *prakṛti* and the powerless *jīva:* the radiant Hara is one alone." Śiva manifests himself in many forms: as *viśvarūpa* or the universe, as *liṅgaśarīra* in the hearts of all beings, as omnipresent on account of his all-pervasiveness, as *antarātman* of the size of a thumb, to be realized by the *yogis.* (Figure 17.1 shows Śiva in one of his many forms.) It also says that in reality all beings are Śiva and it is due to an illusion that people perceive a difference. "One attains peace on realizing that self-effulgent, adorable Lord, the bestower of blessings, who, though one, presides over all the various aspects of *prakṛti* and into whom this universe dissolves and in whom it appears in manifold forms."[17]

Here we already notice the trend in Śaivism to develop a monistic world view, in contrast to the Vaiṣṇavas, who always maintain an essential difference between Viṣṇu and all other beings.

The *Rāmāyaṇa* of Vālmīki, though pertaining to the Vaiṣṇava tradition, mentions several Śiva myths: Śiva destroying Dakṣa's sacrifice, Śiva's marriage with Umā, Śiva drinking the poison, Śiva killing the demon Andhaka, Śiva destroying Tripura, and Śiva cursing Kaṇḍarpa. All of them have remained vital within Śaivism, and some of them also became the focus of Śaiva theology.

The *Mahābhārata* tells the strange story that Kṛṣṇa was initiated by Śiva, remaining his whole life a *Śivabhakta.* It also explains that Hari (Viṣṇu) and Hara (Śiva) are one and the same, and that among the thousand names of Viṣṇu there also are Śiva, Śārva, Sthānu, Iśāna, and Rudra.[18]

Figure 17.2 Śiva, the Great Yogī

In the *Purāṇas*, Śiva mythology reaches its fullest development and also its exclusivity: Śiva is the Only Lord, Viṣṇu and Brahmā are inferior to him.[19] Śiva is even described as the killer of Yama, the god of death, and the *mantra* that celebrates him as the *mṛtyuñjaya*, the victor over death, is used by his devotees to gain liberation.[20]

The celebrated motif of *Śiva Naṭarāja*, the lord of dance is immortalized in many sculptures and bronzes.[21] The Śiva *avatāras*—twenty-eight of them, the legendary authors of the Śaivite *Āgamas*—were probably conceived after the Vaiṣṇava model and play a relatively minor role.[22]

Though anthropomorphic images of Śiva are very numerous and very often of high artistic quality, the object of veneration in the temples is usually the amorphous *liṅga*, an image of Śiva's formlessness. *Śivarātrī* is the most solemn festivity of the Śaivas, commemorating the graceful appearance of Śiva to a hunter, who inadvertently dropped some dew on a *Śiva-liṅga*.[23]

The Śaiva *Āgamas* detail the mode of worship that has to be followed in Śaiva temples and homes. Largely, the ritual resembles that followed by the Vaiṣṇavas, except for the fact that Śaivas still observe animal—and occasionally human—sacrifices.[24] From very early times Śaivism has been connected with rigorous asceticism. *Yogis* are traditionally Śaivas, seeing in Śiva himself the Mahāyogi (Figure 17.2). Mādhava describes a group called the *Raseśvaris* who had the peculiar habit of consuming mercury in order to build up an immortal and incorruptible body.

ŚAIVA SECTS AND SYSTEMS

The *Pāśupata* sect subdivided into numerous sects, possessing a common philosophy. They consider Lakulin, an *avatāra* of Śiva, their founder and have in their *Pāśupatasūtra* a scripture dealing mainly with ritual. According to this text, Śiva taught five subjects, the knowledge of which is essential for the total annihilation of sorrow: *kārya*, the condition of bondage; *kāraṇa*, the lord and liberator; *yoga*, the means to liberation; *vidhi*, the ritual; and *duḥkhānta*, the final liberation. The person in bondage is also called *paśu*, an ox whose Lord is Śiva, kept in bondage through *pāśa*, a noose formed through illusion, unrighteousness, attachment, and ignorance. In order to free oneself, practices like *japa* and meditation are recommended as well as bathing in ashes, laughing, and dancing like a madman, singing, muttering hum hum "like the bellowing of a bull,"[25] snoring, trembling, limping, in general behaving not quite normally. This theology insists on the complementarity between one's own efforts and Śiva's gracious help.

21. Śiva Bhairava, Mahārāṣṭra, Heras Institute Bombay

The most important of all the Śaiva systems up to the present time is Śaiva Siddhānta, "the final truth of Śiva." It is based upon the recognized twenty-eight *āgamas* and the teachings of the sixty-three *Nāyanmārs*, (leaders) the most famous among whom are Appar, Jñānasaṁbhandar, Sundaramūrti, and Māṇikkavācaka. Meykaṇḍa's *Śivajñānabodham* has acquired high authority and has often been commented upon.[26]

Śaiva Siddhānta acknowledges three principles: *pati, paśu*, and *pāśa*, the Lord, the person, and bondage. In order to gain freedom, four elements are necessary: *vidyā*, knowledge; *kriyā*, ritual actions; *yoga*, austerity; and *caryā*, a virtuous way of life. Śiva is the supreme reality. He is greater than the *trimūrti* of Viṣṇu-Brahmā-Rudra and the only eternal being. He has eight qualities; namely, independence, purity, self-knowledge, omniscience, freedom from sin, benevolence, omnipotence, and blissfulness. The most comprehensive terms to circumscribe the essence of Śiva are *sat* and *cit*, being and consciousness. Śiva is immanent in the five elements, in the sun, the moon, and in sentient beings as *aṣṭamūrti*, his eightfold embodiment. He is male and female and neuter. According to Śaiva Siddhānta, Śiva cannot have any *avatāras*, because this would involve him in both life and death, which contradicts the very nature of Śiva. He appears in a bodily form as the guru out of his great love for humans to save them from *saṁsāra*. "Śiva Is Love" is the most precise description, and Śaiva Siddhānta has only one great theme: the grace of Śiva. Through his form of *Sadāśiva*, often represented in art, Śiva exercises his sixfold activities: *anugraha*, attraction; *tirobhava*, concealment; *ādāna*, taking away; *sthiti*, preservation; *sṛṣṭi*, creation; and *udbhava*, appearance.

Bondage is of three kinds: "*Karma, māyā* and *aṇava*, like sprout, bran and husk hide the real nature of the soul and delude it. They cause enjoyment, embodiment and the state of being the enjoyer."[27] *Māyā* encompasses the whole process of evolution and involution. *Karma* leads to the fruition of heaven and hell, as ordained by Śiva. "Pleasures and pains are the medicines administered by Śiva, the physician, to cure the diseases and delusions caused by *mala*."[28] *Aṇava*, beginningless and eternal, is the primary bondage of the souls. If *aṇava* is removed, the souls would be restored to their esential nature as pure spirits. In the *kevala* state, the soul's cognitive, conative, and affective functions are entirely thwarted by *aṇava;* in the *sakala* state, humans do exert their powers but only under the influence of *moha*, delusion, *mada*, intoxication, *rāga*, passion, *viṣāda*, depression, *śoṣa*, dryness, *vaicitriya*, distraction, and *harṣa*, improper merriness.

The process of liberation itself is a chain of interlinking conditions. *Dīkṣā*, initiation, is the direct cause of liberation; but *dīkṣā* is not possible without knowledge. Knowledge presupposes *yoga; yoga* requires ritual acts, and ritual acts are not possible without proper life. There are three different kinds of knowledge: *paśujñāna* and *pāśajñāna* give only the knowledge of the soul, of words and things; only *patijñāna* gives liberation. The way to it leads through the guru's teaching; Śiva appears in the form of a guru, opens the eyes of the devotee, performs the purificatory rites, and removes the obstacles.

Śaiva Siddhāntins emphasize that only in a human birth and only as a Śaiva has one the possibility of putting an end to the cycle of births and deaths. Only a human being can worship Śiva in the three modes essential to liberation: contemplating him with the mind; praising him with the mouth; exerting the body in different ways in his worship. If a human being does not realize liberation in this life, it might be hard to get another chance. The Siddhāntins claim that only *their* faith is *siddhānta*, that is, final truth. All other beliefs and philosophies lead their followers to one of the thirty-six *tattvas*, below Śiva. Ignoring the *siddhānta* would be a great sin and foolishness, and those despising it have to suffer in hell.

Liberation is but the appearance of the hidden *śivatva* in the soul through *jñāna*. In their free state, humans realize their true and original Śiva nature, which was hidden and curtailed through sin. There can also be *jīvanmukti*, full Śiva realization, while still in this physical body. *Jīvanmuktas* are one with Śiva in their innermost being, while *prārabdha* of different kinds still works itself out in their bodies: "*Śiva-jñānis* may do any good or bad deed—they remain unaffected by the changes and never leave the feet of the Lord. It is difficult to determine the nature of the *jīvanmuktas:* some of them may be short-tempered, some sweet-tempered, some free from desires, some lustful." One of the more famous examples is offered by Saint Sundaramūrti, "who was free from attachment, though outwardly he seemed to live a life of sensual pleasures."

Those who have achieved *jñāna niṣṭha*, "knowledge-establishment," are beyond good and evil. Engaging in activities they do not care for the results. They need not practice austerity nor observe any religious duties nor do they have to engage in meditation or wear external signs of their religion. "Coming to have the qualities of children, of mad people, and people possessed by evil spirits, they may even give themselves up to singing and dancing by reason of their ecstasy."[29]

Śiva resides in the soul always, but only the enlightened will consciously live a Śiva life according to his grace. Whatever the enlightened one does is Śiva's deed, be it good or evil. Śaiva Siddhānta knows of seven different degrees of *jīvanmukti*, liberation while still in a body, likening them in their bliss to the sweetness of sugarcane, fruit, milk, honey, candy, sugar, and nectar. It also knows of a complementarity between the love of God and love of one's neighbor. A person's love for the devotees of Śiva is a sign of love for Śiva. Because Śiva is in all souls, those who love him truly will also love all beings. All the activities of God are ordered toward the liberation of humans. God's essence is it to be "full of grace."

Śrīkaṇṭha's Śaiva-Vedānta, classified with the Vedānta systems as *bhedābheda*, difference and no difference, may be considered as a special form of Śaiva Siddhānta. Śrīkaṇṭha aims at reconciling the *Upaniṣads* with the *Āgamas*, quoting extensively from both sources. For him, Śiva Nīlakaṇṭha is the symbol for God showing care. He differs slightly from classical Śaiva Siddhānta in his assertion that the liberated ones are completely free and enjoy the same bliss and freedom that Śiva himself enjoys. Thus he says:

> The place of the husband of Umā is like millions of suns, the first, full of all objects of desires, pure, eternal, indestructible. Having attained that celestial place they become free from all miseries, omniscient, capable of going everywhere, pure, full. Further they come to have pure sense-organs and become endowed with supreme Lordship. Then again they assume bodies or discard these at will. Those engaged in the pursuit of knowledge and *yoga* concentration who attain this supreme place, do not return to the frightful earthly existence. The liberated ones have Śiva as their souls and shine forth with Śiva in all places at all times.[30]

Despite the similarity in conception to the Vaiṣṇava Vedāntists, Śrīkaṇṭha proves to be a staunch sectarian Śaiva: liberation begins only after the souls have crossed the river *virajā*, the boundary between *Viṣṇuloka* and *Śivaloka*. Viṣṇu's heaven is still within *saṁsāra*. Beyond *Viṣṇuloka* is *Śivaloka*, where the souls find final liberation and fulfillment.

Kāśmīr Śaivism, the most important North-Indian school of Śaivism, also called Śaiva-Advaita, Trika, etc., is represented today by only a few living masters.[31] The earliest writings belong to the eighth or ninth centuries, but the roots of the system may be several centuries older. Its two main branches, Spaṇḍaśāstra and Pratyābhijñā, have much in common. Some of the most respected names in Indian philosophy, like Abhinavagupta, are associated with Kāśmīr Śaivism, which must have been quite popular in former centuries, if the extensive treatment accorded to it in the *Śiva Purāṇa* is any indication.[32]

Whereas in most other systems *adhikāra*, the fulfillment of certain qualifications, is important, here it is stated explicitly that no prerequisites are required of students wanting to enter this school. Since all reality, Śiva, Śakti, and their union, is mirrored in one's own *ātman*, liberation is an introspection and a recognition of this mirrored image—an idea that is expressed in the very name of the system. Since one of the qualities of Śiva is *ānanda*, bliss, one also acquires Śiva's blissfulness by recognizing one's own Śiva nature. The follower of this system aims at becoming a slave of Śiva, "one who is being given everything according to the pleasure of the Lord."[33]

The reason for human unhappiness lies in the five hindrances through which Śiva-nature is restricted: the All becomes an atom; the universal, omniscient, eternal, blissful Śiva becomes a finite, ignorant, limited, and unhappy *puruṣa.* One is bound by *karma, māyā,* and *aṇava,* terms previously encountered. Bondage is a work of *śakti; śakti* also helps to liberate a person. In individuals, *śakti* is present as Kuṇḍalinī, represented as a coiled, dormant snake. The innermost core of a person's being is *caitanya,* consciousness, identical with Śiva. *Śaktipatā,* descent of *śakti,* is the advent of grace. Though under the influence of bondage, the five essential activities of Śiva are at work, developing a person toward "becoming Śiva." The state of awakening while still in the body is called *samaveśa,* a "contemplative experience of unity consciousness, in which the entire universe is experienced as identical with the self." As Abhinavagupta says:

> It is Śiva himself of unimpeded will and pellucid consciousness who is ever sparkling in my heart. It is his highest *Śakti* herself that is ever playing at the edge of my senses. The entire world gleams as the wondrous delight of pure I-consciousness. Indeed I know not what the sound "world" is supposed to refer to.[34]

The stage of consciousness that the *Pratyābhijñā* system claims to achieve is beyond the *turīya* of the *Upaniṣads* and, therefore, called *turyātīta,* divided into "broken" and "unbroken" consciousness. The means to reach this stage is the specific *yoga* of the school that has much in common with later *Kuṇḍalinī-yoga.*

→ The youngest among the major Śaiva schools is Vīraśaivism, "heroic Śiva religion," which is closely connected with the name of Basava.[35] The sect itself seems to go back to a more remote time, about which, however, we have no reliable information. Under Basava's inspiration, Vīraśaivism developed into a vigorous missionary movement. Vīraśaivas are recognizable by the *liṅga* around their neck, which they always wear and which for them is the real presence of Śiva. It is worn in order to make the body a temple of Śiva. As the sources of their religion, they recognize the twenty-eight *Āgamas* and the Tamiḷ *Nāyanmārs,* as well as later writers. They have a *Vedāntasūtra* commentary of their own in Śrīpati's *Śrīkara Bhāṣya.*[36] The system is also called Śaktiviśiṣṭādvaita, the essence of which is: "There is no duality between the soul and the Lord, each qualified by *Śakti.*" The *jīva* is the body of Śiva; *Paraśiva* is both the material and the instrumental cause of the universe. *Śakti* resides eternally in *Paramaśiva:* it is the creative

22. Śiva Taṇḍava, Khajurāho (12th ct.)

principle, also called *māyā.* At creation, all things issue forth from *śakti;* at the time of the destruction of the world, all return into it and remain there in a seminal form. *Jīvas* are in fact part of Śiva. On account of their ignorance, they imagine themselves to be different from the god. *Bhakti,* which is a part of Śiva's own *śakti,* is the means of final deliverance, subdivided into many stages and steps. *Vīraśaivas* lay great stress on rituals, which are considered indispensable.

Pañcācāra, fivefold worship, comprises daily worship of the *liṅga,* a moral and decent life and work, amity toward all Liṅgāyats, humility, and active struggle against those who despise Śiva or maltreat his devotees.[37]

Aṣṭāvaraṇa, the eightfold armour, comprises obeying the *guru,* wearing the *liṅga,* worshipping the Śiva ascetic as an incarnation of Śiva, sipping the water in which the feet of a guru have been bathed, offering food to a guru, smearing ashes on one's body, wearing a string of *rudrākṣa* beads, and reciting the *mantra Śivāya nāmaḥ.*[38] Whereas, for the ordinary *Vīraśaiva,* release is the result of the faithful observance of all these commandments; Śrīpati introduces a Vedāntic element into the faith, teaching that, in the end, full oneness with Śiva is attained through worship and meditation.

Vīraśaivas are social reformers and constitute quite a vigorous community today around Mysore. They have abolished caste differences and are generally quite progressive in economic and social matters. Also, instead of burning their dead, as do most other Hindus, they bury them.

Almost from the beginning of Indian history severe austerity and self-mortification have been connected with Śiva and Śaivism. *Yoga* itself, as expounded by Patañjali, is traced back to the teaching of Śiva, the *mahāyogi.*

ŚAIVA SAINTS AND SINGERS

Śaivism has produced a large number of popular saints, of which the historical sixty-three *Nāyanmārs* of South India are probably the best known.[39] Māṇikavācakar is the author of the celebrated *Tiruvācakam.* He suffered persecution for his faith and Śiva appeared in person to him, an event he celebrates in a song: "O highest Truth, you came to the earth and revealed your feet to me and became the embodiment of grace." His poetry is an ardent appeal for Śiva's grace.

> Madman clad in elephant's skin, Madman with a hide for his garb. Madman that ate the poison, Madman on the burning-ground fire, Madman that chose even me for his own. Whether I adore you or revile you, I crave your forgiveness for my evil deeds which I rue. Leave me not, O you who took mercy on the gods and drank the poison in order to save them. How much more do I stand in need of your loving mercy![40]

In a beautiful stanza, Māṇikavācakar describes the perfection he is hoping for:

> I shall raise my hands in prayer to you; I shall clasp your holy feet and call on your name. I shall melt like wax before the flame, incessantly calling out "My Beloved Father." I shall cast off this body and enter the celestial city of Śivapura. I shall behold your effulgent glory. In joyful bliss shall I join the society of the true devotees. Then I shall look up to hear you say with your beauteous lips: "Fear not!" The assurance of your all-embracing love alone can set my soul at ease and peace.[41]

Appar became a martyr for Śiva's sake. Saṁbandhar vehemently fought the Jainas and Buddhists as enemies of Śiva. Tirumular wanted to reconcile in his songs the *Vedas* and the *Āgamas*.[42]

Sundaramūrti Swāmi is a favourite with the Tamiḷs even today. The metrical translation of one of his hymns[43] may convey something of the emotional appeal of this Śaiva:

> I roamed, a cur, for many days, without a single thought of thee.
>
> Roamed and grew weary, then such grace as none could win,
>
> Thou gavest me Venney-nallur, in "Grace's shrine,"
>
> Where bamboos fringe the Pennai.
>
> There, my shepherd, I became all thine; how could I now myself forswear?
>
> Henceforth for me no birth, no death, no creeping age, bull-rider mine.
>
> Sinful and full of lying breath am I, but do Thou mark me Thine.

From relatively early times, there had also been certain rather unsavory Śaiva sects with "horrible, almost demoniacal practices, which form a ghastly picture of the wild aberrations of the human intellect and spirit."[44] They took their origin from the worship of the Rudra-nature of Śiva; and, though not completely extinct, they play a minor part in today's Śaivism. The most notorious are the Kapālikas and the Kālamukhas. Kapālikas worship Bhairava, the terrible form of Śiva, and eat disgusting stuff; they drink wine and are known to have performed human sacrifices. Kālamukhas believe that they may attain salvation by eating their food from a human skull, smearing their bodies with the ashes of the dead and also eating those ashes. But those extremists should not unduly darken the image of Śaivism, which is generally characterized by serious asceticism and genuine devotion, combined with a high degree of sophisticated speculation.

While the popularity of Śaivism in India was never seriously in doubt since it found acceptance by Vedic orthodoxy and while Śaivism provided the background to much of India's speculative theology, from the *Śvetāśvatara Upaniṣad* to Kāśmīr Śaivism, from Śaṅkara to Śaiva Siddhānta, the intense interest for Śaivism among Western scholars is something new. Śaivism used to be the form of Hinduism upon which most abuse was heaped by early Western observers: imagine the worship of the phallus, the ritual slaughtering of animals, the frenzied dancing! Something must have happened to have made contemporary Western scholars look with so much sympathy and understanding upon this expression of Hinduism. Stella Kramrisch, whose *The Presence of Śiva*[45] is the undisputed masterwork of its genre, a veritable summa of Śaivite mythology and theology, reputedly was initiated into a Śaiva community.[46] Also A. Daniélou, whose *Hindu Polytheism*[47] is a monument of insight, became a member of a Śaivite *saṁpradāya* while in Banaras. Another widely known scholar of Hinduism in the United States, Wendy O'Flaherty has devoted much of her life's work to a study of Śiva.[48] Recently a Śaiva Siddhānta mission began operating in the West; it seems to be quite successful in Australia. Kāśmīr Śaivism has attracted the attention of Western scholars after its more popular teachings were introduced to the West by Gopi Krishna who also aroused the interest of philosopher-scientist C. F. von Weizsäcker.[49]

All this new sympathy for Śiva may have to do with the more liberal attitude toward sexuality that developed in the West in the past twenty years as well as the experience of terror and the dark attraction to horror so evident in contemporary films and TV plays. It is only to be hoped that besides Śiva the Terrible also Śiva the Graceful exert his influence.

18. Devī: The Divine Mother

The Mother is the consciousness and force of the Divine, or, it may be said, she is the Divine in its consciousness-force. The *Īśwara* as Lord of the cosmos does come out of the Mother who takes her place beside him as the cosmic *Śakti*—the cosmic *Īśwara* is one aspect of the Divine.

—Śrī Aurobindo on the Mother (*p. 447*)

By you this universe is borne, by you this world has been created. By you it is protected and you, O Devī, shall consume it at the end. You are the Great Knowledge and the Great Illusion, you are Great Power and Great Memory, Great Delusion, the Great Devī and the Great Asurī. You are Primordial Matter, you are the ground of the three *guṇas*, you are the Great Night of the end of the world and you are the Great Darkness of delusion. You are the goddess of good fortune, the ruler, modesty, intelligence with knowledge, bashfulness, nourishment, contentment, tranquillity and forbearance. Armed with the sword, the spear, the club, the discus, the conch, the bow, with arrows, slings and iron mace you are terrible and also more pleasing than everything else and exceedingly beautiful. Your are above all, the supreme Mistress. You are the *śakti*, the power of all things, sentient and others, you are the soul of everything. Who is capable if praising you, who has given form to all of us, to Viṣṇu, Śiva and myself?[1]

Thus Brahmā implores Devī in a famous text that is recited every year at the great *Durgā Pūjā* festival.

Besides those who worship Viṣṇu as the Lord and those who see in Śiva the Supreme Being, for millions of Hindus Devī, the Great Mother, is all that the word *God* can express.

We have encountered the Goddess before as the consort of Viṣṇu or Śiva; for the Śāktas she is the real Ultimate Power, the other great gods are merely her instruments and servants. This chapter intends to sketch

ॐ जयन्ती मंगला काली भद्रकाली कपालिनी । दुर्गा क्षमा शिवा धात्री स्वाहा स्वधा नमोऽस्तुते ॥
महिषासुरनिर्णाशिनि भक्तानां सुखदे नमः । रूपं देहि जयं देहि यशो देहि द्विषो जहि ॥

Figure 18.1 *Devī Mahiṣāsuramārdiṇī:* The Goddess Slaying the Buffalo Demon

some of the more important myths concerning Devī and to give some idea of the highly technical literature known as *Tantras*, which are considered by the Śāktas as scriptures in addition to the universally accepted *śruti*.[2]

DEVĪ MYTHS AND FEASTS

Devī mythology appears fully developed in the *Purāṇas* associated with Śāktism—all of them *Upapurāṇas*, which indicates their comparatively late origin. The most important one is the *Devī Bhāgavata Purāṇa*, a treasury of Devī lore and speculation.[3] Some of the *Mahāpurāṇas* contain important sections concerning Devī that may be later interpolations, as for example the famous *Devīmāhātmya*, which forms part of the Śaivite *Mārkaṇḍeya Purāṇa*. The Devī *Purāṇas* themselves very often restructure otherwise popular Viṣṇu or Śiva myths in such a way as to show the supremacy of the goddess.[4]

The most prominent and most popular myth connected with Devī is her killing of the buffalo demon (Figure 18.1). It is narrated in several *Purāṇas*, with significant differences, and even in village religion it seems to figure quite prominently.[5] It may in fact constitute an ancient myth connected with an ancient ritual.[6]

The *Mārkaṇḍeya Purāṇa* reports how, for a hundred years, *devas* and *asuras* fought against each other. The *devas* were defeated and *mahiṣa asura*, the buffalo demon, became the lord of heaven. The defeated *devas* approached Śiva and Viṣṇu for help, who had to concede that they were powerless against the Great Demon.

> On hearing the voices of the *devas*, Viṣṇu's anger knew no bounds, nor did Śiva's, and their faces became distorted. A great light sprang from Viṣṇu's countenance, full of anger, and also from the faces of Śiva and Brahmā. This light merged into one, bright as a burning mountain, filling the whole universe with flames. This powerful blast piercing the three worlds took the shape of a woman: Śiva's splendor became her face, Yama's her hair, Viṣṇu's her arms, Candra's her breasts, Indra's her body, Varuṇa's her thighs, the Earth's her hips, Brahmā's her feet, Sūrya's her toes, Vasu's her fingers, Kubera's her nose, Prajāpati's her teeth; through Agni's light her three eyes took form.

Śiva drew out a trident from his own armory, Viṣṇu a discus from his, Varuṇa gave her a conch-shell, Agni a spear, Maruta a bow and quivers filled with arrows, Indra a thunderbolt and a bell, Yama the staff of death, Varuṇa a rope, Brahmā a string of beads and a water vessel, Sūrya the rays of the sun, Kāla a sword and a shield. "The heavens were filled and trembled with her incredibly powerful and terrible roar, all the world was in an

23. Lakṣmī, Khajurāho (12th ct.)

upheaval, the sea was in turmoil."

Devī's "loud roar with a defying laugh" is the sign for the beginning of the battle between Devī and Mahiṣāsura. With her numerous weapons, she kills thousands of demons. Before Mahiṣāsura falls, all the demon generals are killed.

> *Mahiṣāsura* terrified the troops of the goddess with his own buffalo form: some he killed by a blow of his muzzle, some by stamping with his hooves, some by the lashes of his tail, and others by the thrusts of his horns, some by his speed, some by his bellowing and wheeling movement, some by the blast of his breath. Having laid low her army, *Mahiṣāsura* rushed to slay the lion of Mahādevī. This enraged Ambikā. *Mahiṣāsura*, great in valor, pounded the surface of the earth with his hooves in rage, tossed up high mountains with his horns, and bellowed terribly. Crushed by his wheeling, the earth distintegrated, and lashed by his tail, the sea overflowed all around. Pierced by his swaying horns the clouds broke into fragments. Cast up by the blast of his breath, mountains fell down from the sky in hundreds.

This description of the evil embodied in Mahiṣa provides the backdrop for the appreciation of the greatness of Devī's deed, which saved the universe from destruction. First, the goddess uses her noose to capture Mahiṣāsura. He sheds his buffalo form. Devī uses uses her sword to cut down the lion form that he assumes. Then the demon appears as a human being. Devī assails him with bow and arrows. The demon assumes an elephant form, which the goddess atacks with her mace. Finally, the demon assumes again his original buffalo form. Now the final battle takes place.

"Enraged, Caṇḍikā, the Mother of the Universe, quaffed a divine drink again and again and laughed so that her eyes became red." She now kills the buffalo demon, pressing down his neck with her foot and striking him with her spear, finally cutting off his head with her sword. Thus, the salvation of *devas* and humans has been accomplished, and Devī receives due praise as the last resort of all: as Durgā, the boat that carries humans across the ocean of worldly existence; as Vidyā, which is the cause of liberation; as Śrī, who has taken her abode in the heart of Viṣṇu; and as Gaurī, who has established herself with Śiva.

The *devas* ask her to grant delivery from all evil whenever necessary. Devī fulfills her promise by appearing again and again to slay demons who are too powerful to be overcome by Viṣṇu or Śiva. The result of Devī's victory is cosmic relief: "When that evil-natured one was slain the universe became happy and regained perfect peace and the sky grew clear. Flaming portent clouds that were in evidence before became tranquil and the rivers kept within courses. Favorable winds began to blow and the sun became very brilliant."

In the final hymn, the *devas* praise Devī as the mother of the universe, the cause of final emancipation, the bestower of enjoyment and liberation, the one who removes all sufferings, who frees from all fear and from all evils.

Devī then prophesies her repeated incarnations in different ages as Vindhyavāsinī, as Raktadantā, as Śatākṣī, as Śākambharī, Durgādevī, Bhīmadevī, and Bhramaradevī. All these names are titles under which the goddess is still worshipped in India. To those who keep her feasts and praise her, Devī promises protection, riches and victory.

> The chanting and hearing of the story of my manifestations removes sin and grants perfect health and protection from evil spirits. One who is in a lonely spot in a forest or is surrounded by forest fire, or who is encircled by robbers in a desolate spot, or who is captured by enemies, or who under the orders of a wrathful king is sentenced to death, or has been imprisoned, or who is tossed about in a boat by a tempest in the vast sea, or is in the most terrible battle under showers of weapons, or who is amidst all kinds of dreadful troubles, or who is afflicted with pain—such a person, on remembering this story of mine, will be saved from all straits.[7]

This hymn of the greatness of the goddess is recited every year by countless Hindus at the time of the great *Durgā-pūjā*, the major feast of Bengal.[8] It also carries reminiscences of a time in which the structure of society was matriarchal: all the girls who have married away from home, gather at their homes and celebrate *Durgā-pūjā* with their parents. Statues of papier-mâché and plaster, representing Devī in the act of killing Mahiṣāsura are placed in public places and in homes; special local committees are formed for the consecration and worship of these images. Processions and a series of individual feasts are celebrated for eight days; on the ninth day, *Durgā-pūjā* proper commences. It ends with interminable processions to the sea, the Ganges, or another river nearby: the figures of Devī are thrown into the water, after Devī has departed from them.

It is quite impossible to bring all the different names and forms under which the Goddess appears in the *Purāṇas* into one system. By and large, the various names are local varieties of Devī. One text in the *Devī Purāṇa* clearly states the Devī is worshipped as Maṅgalā in the region between the Vindhyas and the Mālayās, as Jayantī in the coastal area between Vindhyas and Kurukṣetra, as Nandā between Kurukṣetra and the Himālayas, as Kālikā, Tārā, and Umā in the Himālaya Mountains, as Kālaratrī in the Sākya Mountains, as Ambā in Candhamadanā, as Ujjainī in Ujjain, and as Bhadrakālī in Vaideha.[9] Similar to Viṣṇu and Śiva *avatāras*, Śāktism has also developed the notion of *Devī-avatāras* for different ages.[10]

The Mātrikās, the divine mothers, especially in the villages, are usually a class apart, worshipped as a group as protectresses against all kinds of ills, particularly those that befall children. The worship of Manasā, the snake-goddess, and Śītalā, the goddess of smallpox, is very widespread in India. The *Kālikā Purāṇa* has a peculiar system of differentiating the goddess according to the different parts of her body. It describes how Satī, without having been invited, attends Dakṣa's (her father's) sacrifice, how she is hurt by Dakṣa's insult of her husband Śiva, and how she voluntarily gives up her life. Śiva then takes Satī's body on his shoulders. Brahmā, Viṣṇu, and Sanaiścara enter into it, cut it into pieces and let these fall to earth. Wherever one of the fifty-one parts of her body touched the earth a sanctuary of Devī would be founded, called *Śākta Pītha*, named after the particular limb of her body.[11]

DEVĪ IN THE *TANTRAS*

It is in the Tantras that the goddess comes to occupy the supreme place: according to the *Tantras*, *brahman*, being neuter and incapable of creation, produced Śiva and Śakti. Śiva is the cause of bondage, Śakti the cause of liberation. She is the life force of the universe; without her, who is symbolized in the letter *i*, Śiva is Śava, a dead corpse.[12] A large number of texts bear the title *Tantras*, and numerous *Purāṇas* also contain sections, probably added after the eighth century C.E., that are unmistakably Tantric. Tantricism is not restricted to Hinduism; the Hindu *Tantras* may owe their development to Buddhist Mahāyāna cults connected with the goddess Tārā. Tārā, the "one who saves," is the personification of Buddha's kindness. According to the *Tantras*, people in our Kali age have become too weak to practice any other kind of religion than the worship of the goddess who offers salvation without demanding austerity.

Tantrikas distinguish three *mārgas*, subdivided into seven stages altogether. The first three stages are identical with practices found among all Hindus: common worship, devotion to Viṣṇu, and meditation on Śiva. From the fourth onward, we have the peculiar Śākta-Tantra forms of worship. *Dakṣiṇācāra*, "right-handed worship," consists of worshipping Devī as the Supreme Goddess with Vedic rites including a *japa* with the name of the goddess on the *Mahaśaṅkha-mālā*. *Vāmācāra*, "left-handed worship," consists of the "worship with *cakras*" in which the "five *m*'s" play a great role.[13] As one author says, "it requires proper training at the hands of a *guru* and the acquisition of the necessary courage to disregard social conventions about sexual purity, to defy taboos about food and drink and to look upon all women as manifestations of Śakti and all males as representatives of Śiva."[14]

The next stage is *Siddhāntācāra*, "perfect worship," in which the

24. Kālī, Bengal, Heras Institute Bombay

practices just mentioned are no longer kept secret because, for the realized one, there is no longer any distinction between pure and impure, good and bad. The highest stage is reached with *Kulācāra*, the "divine way of life," when

> the aspirant transcends the likes and dislikes of earthly life like God himself to whom all things are equal. Pity and cruelty are equally meaningless in an ultimate reference and so too are approved and unapproved conduct. Just as one of the *Upaniṣads* has said that to one who has attained the knowledge of *Brahman* no sin attaches for any kind of antinomian act, so also the *Tantras* place the Kaula above every moral judgement and put no prohibitions and restraints in his way as being unnecessary for one who has pierced the veil of space and time, process and differentiation. A Kaula roams in all *ācāras* at will—being at heart a Śākta, outwardly a Śaiva and in social gatherings a Vaiṣṇava. He sees himself in all things and all things in himself.[15]

Dīkṣā becomes of utmost importance in Tantricism: a special initiation is necessary for anyone who wishes to enter the Tantric way. It is open to all without distinction of caste or sex, but even a Brahmin has to apply for it, otherwise he is not entitled to take part in the Tantric mysteries. Terrible punishment is in store for those who invite anyone not initiated. The purification of the *pañca mākāras* plays a great role. The Tantrikas are aware that the enjoyment of the five *m*'s involves the violation of all moral laws. They are the great temptations of ordinary men. Tantricism is designed as a spiritual homoeopathy; by the very poison of the snake the snakebite is cured. But the administering of this antidote must take place in a controlled way under an expert physician. The *pañca mākāras* have to be purified and are to be taken only under the guidance of a guru, lest they devour the unthinking.[16] The purification takes place by means of *mantras*, whose meaning is clear only to the initiated. Before partaking of any of the *m*'s, the *sādhaka* has to recite the *mantra;* only then is the *mākāra* a sacrament and not a sin.

One of the most conspicuous elements of Tantricism is the use of the *yantra*. The *yantra* is the symbol of the goddess and upon it are inscribed the letters of the alphabet, or short monosyllabic *mantras,* which constitute the *mantra-* or *śabda*-body of the goddess.[17] The design as such is intended to focus on the center point, which is formed by the very essence of the goddess, usually symbolized with a dot and the sign *śrī*. It is situated in a system of interlocking triangles (six to fourteen), forming a polygonal pattern. The △ triangle stands for Śiva, identified with *puruṣa*, the ▽ triangle for Śakti or *prakṛti*. They are encircled by time. On lotus petals within the rims of concentric wheels are inscribed the letters of the alphabet and *bīja-mantras*, "seed spells," identical with certain aspects of the divinity. The whole system is surrounded by two walls with four gates; one at each cardinal point. Again, the gates are connected with major manifestations of the goddess, with seed *mantras* and *mudrās*, that is, gestures accompanying the recitation of *mantras*. The gates, as well as the corners of the walls, are fortified with the *siddhis*, miraculous yogic powers.

The idea behind the *yantra* is that the devotee is supposed to choose one aspect of the goddess as *iṣṭā:* through this "door" one enters the wall that separates the profane world from the realm of worship, using as vehicle the appropriate *mudra* and *mantra* and acquiring the supersensory power through the signs on the lotus petals, as an expression of the deity, until finally realizing the goddess in her own nature as the inmost core of all beings. There one's attention remains fixed, because one's whole search has found its goal.[18] (Fig. 18.2 shows a *yantra*).

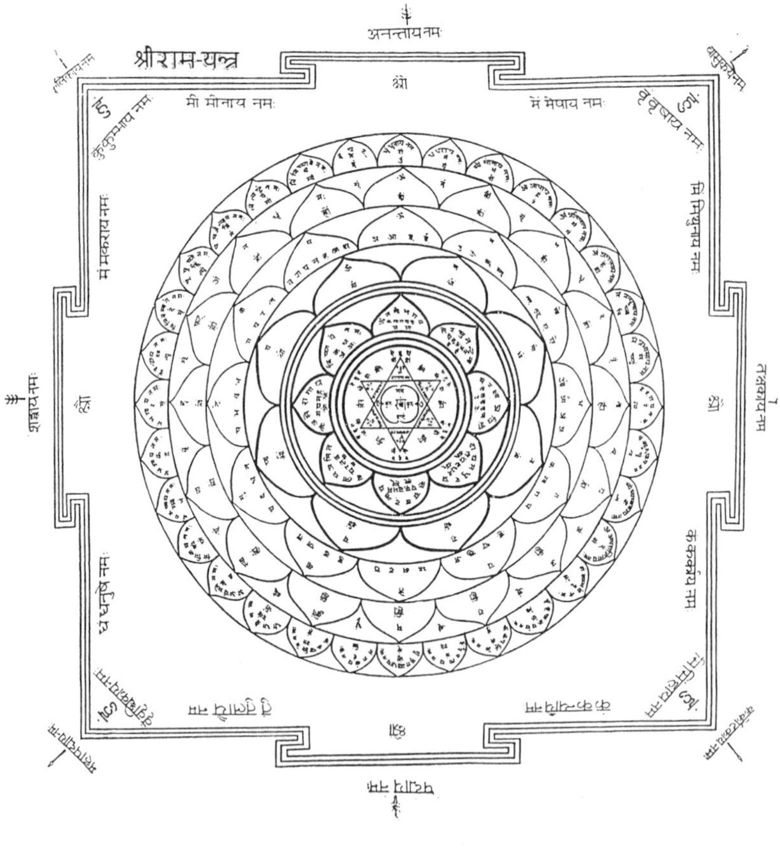

Figure 18.2 Śrī Rāma *yantra*

The identification of Śakti with *prakṛti*, with "matter" rather than "spirit," has one further implication: the body is the seat of the divinity and that, too, expresses itself in the form of worship and meditation. The fifty letters of the alphabet constitute the body of the goddess as well as that of the worshipper. Through *nyāsa*, the worshipper places the letters upon different parts of the body, transforming it, limb by limb, into a divine one. In most forms of Tantric worship, the awakening of the *Kuṇḍalinī śakti* plays a great role—again demonstrating the close connection between physiology and metaphysics in Śāktism. Śakti is supposed to lie dormant, coiled like a snake at the base of the spine: through *yoga* in the Tantric sense she is awakened and sent through the six *cakras* or nerve centers[19] in the spinal cord into the thousand-petalled lotus, situated above the base of the nose, where Śakti meets with Śiva. Their blissful union there is at the same time liberation and supreme joy for the devotee.

According to Tantric physiology, the human body contains 35 million *nāḍīs*, conceived as fine tubular canals through which Śakti is moving. Of these, fourteen are of primary importance. Three of these, Idā, Piṅgalā, and Suṣummā constitute the central complex. Suṣummā runs through the hollow of the spinal cord. Fire, sun and moon are associated with it as its *guṇas*. On its sides lie Idā and Piṅgalā. Idā encircles Suṣummā on the left and ends in the left nostril; Piṅgalā forms its right counterpart. Idā is of a bright hue and contains "the liquid of immortality"; Piṅgalā is red and contains "the liquid of death." The three main *nāḍīs* are also identified with the Gaṅgā, the Yamunā, and the Sarasvatī, the three principal holy rivers of India, identified with forms of Devī.

The *cakras* correspond to *yantras* in all their details. Thus *mūladhāra*, the first of the *cakras*, lying at the base of the spine, the root of *suṣumna* and the resting place of *Kuṇḍalinī*, is depicted as a triangle encircled by an orb with four lotus petals, on which the syllables *vaṁ, śaṁ, ṣaṁ, saṁ* are written. In the center of the lotus lies the *śyambhu liṅga* of a rust-brown color. There is *citranāḍī*, a tube through which Devī descends and closes the Brahman door. Inside the fiery red triangle that encloses the *liṅga* is *kandarpavāyu*, the "wind of the love god" and outside a yellow spot, called *pṛthivī maṇḍala*, the place of the *bīja-mantra laṁ*.

The next *cakra* is *svādhiṣṭhāna*, a six-petalled lotus at the base of the sexual organ; above it is *maṇi-pura*, the jewel-city, a ten-petalled golden lotus in the navel. In the region of the heart is *anahaṭa cakra*, a deep-red lotus with twelve petals; above it, at the base of the throat, is *viśuddha cakra*, the dwelling-place of the goddess of speech, a lotus with sixteen petals. Between the eyebrows is *ājñā-cakra*, a two-petalled lotus, also called *paramakula* or *mukti-triveni*, because here the three main *nāḍīs* separate. This is the place of the *bīja-mantra* OM and the dwelling place of the three main *guṇas*. Here dwell Para-Śiva in the form of a swan and Kālī-Śakti. Brahmā, Viṣṇu, and Śiva are in the three corners of the triangle within the lotus.

Above this is *manas-cakra* and soma-cakra, each with sixteen petals: *kṛpā*, grace; *mṛdutā*, sweetness; *dhairya*, firmness; *vairāgya*, renunciation; *dhṛti*, constancy; *sampat*, wealth; *hasyā*, gaiety; *romāñcā*, enthusiasm; *vinaya*, discipline; *dhyāna*, meditation; *susthiratā*, relaxation; *gambhīrya*, seriousness; *udyamā*, effort; *akṣobhya*, imperturbability; *audārya*, generosity; and *ekāgratā*, one-pointedness. Above this *cakra* is the *nirālaṁbanā purī*, the city without support, wherein the *Yogis* behold the radiant Īśvara. Above it is *praṇava*, luminous as a flame; above this is the white crescent of *nāda;* and above this, the dot *binḍu*, forming the altar for the *paramahaṁsa*, who in turn provides the cushion for the guru's feet.

The body of the swan is *jñāna-māyā*, knowledge and illusion, the wings are *Āgama* and *Nigama*, the scriptures, its feet are Śiva and Śakti, the beak is *praṇava*, the eyes and the throat are *kāma-kāla*. The supreme *cakra* is the thousand-petalled lotus, which is the dwelling place of the First Cause: *Śivasthāna* for the Śaivas, *Devīsthāna* for the Śāktas. Here shine the sun of illumination and the sun of darkness; each petal of the lotus contains all the letters of the alphabet; and whatever appears in the world is represented here in its *avyakta bhava* or unmanifested form.

As the *Kuṇḍalinīśakti* moves upward it assumes all the deities and qualities inherent in the different *cakras*, thus becoming "everything." Devī is ultimately identical with *Brahman—brahman* not conceived as supreme spirit but as supreme matter, or better, as life force. Most of the Tantric literature, including the hymns, is written in *saṁdhyā-bhāsā*, "twilight style," which has a double meaning. Only the initiated are able to grasp the true, spiritual meaning.

DEVĪ WORSHIP AND DEVĪ PHILOSOPHY

Devī worship differs sharply in its two main branches: left-handed and right-handed Śāktism. The latter could be described as *Devībhakti*, differing little from other forms of *bhakti*, except that instead of Viṣṇu or Śiva the name of the Goddess is invoked. Left-hand practices, even today, are surrounded by secrecy: sexual mysteries and human sacrifices are associated with it, a combination not restricted to the barbaric gangs of *thag* but that also found its way into the holy books of Śāktism. The *Kālikā Purāṇa* describes in great detail the ritual of a human sacrifice followed in some temples of Devī as a regular weekly rite.[20] Even now, the Indian daily newspapers report occasional cases of both human sacrifice and self-immolation in honor of the goddess.

In former times, the Śāktas did not attribute any importance to pilgrimages, since the union of Śiva and Śakti was found in one's own body. But later, the fifty-one *Śaktipīṭhas* came to be recognized as centers of pilgrimage, each with its own legends and promises of gain and merit in this world and the next.[21] Assam, whose old name is Kāmarūpa, has been the center of Śāktism as far back as our knowledge of it goes. The most famous Assamese temple, Kāmākhyā near Gauhatī, is the most important of the *Śaktipīṭhas*, being the place where the *yoni* of Devī fell, which is worshipped in the form of a cleft rock under the title Kameśvarī. Reportedly, even now, both right-hand and left-hand rituals are performed in this temple and animals are slaughtered at its altars.

Devī worship intensifies in times of epidemics, which are seen as signs of her wrath for being neglected. She is then appeased by the sacrifice of buffaloes, pigeons, and goats. Devī is also invoked if someone has been bitten by a snake or otherwise shows signs of poisoning.[22]

A good deal of the philosophy of Śāktism forms an integral part of certain schools of Śaivism. Śiva and Pārvatī are considered to be "world parents." Their mutual dependence is so great that one cannot be without the other. In the figure of *Śiva ardhanārī*, Śiva and his consort are combined into one being manifesting a dual aspect. It is often only a matter of emphasis whether a certain philosophy is called Śaiva or Śākta. The roots of this thinking may be traced back to the sources of Vedic religion.[23] Fully developed Tantric philosophy is characterized by its acceptance of the material world as the basic reality and its emphasis on the real existence of *māyā*. Śakti is often called *ādya*, or *mūla prakṛti*, primaeval matter (associating "matter," as the Latin word does, with "mother"!) and *mahāmāyā*, the great illusion. An important Tantric text, the *Tripurā Rahasya*, explicitly says:

> Do not conclude that there is no such thing as the world. Such thinking is imperfect and defective. Such a belief is impossible. One who tries to negate the whole world by the mere act of thought brings it into existence by that very act of negation. Just as a city reflected in a mirror is not a reality but exists as a reflection, so also this world is not a reality in itself but is consciousness all the same. This is self-evident. This is perfect knowledge.[24]

At the same time, it is not possible to classify Śāktism proper under any of the other Vedāntic systems. The *Mahānirvāṇa Tantra* calls it *dvaitādvaita vivarjita*, freed from both dualism and monism. For Śāktism, the fetters that bind humans are neither illusory, as the Advaitins claim, nor are they pure evil to be removed from the *ātman*, as the Dvaitins attempt to do. The imperfections are the very means to perfect freedom. The oneness

25. Durgā, Khajurāho 12th ct.

of *bhukti* and *mukti*, of the enjoyment that binds to the world and the renunciation that frees, of *māyā* and *vidyā*, of illusion and knowledge, are characteristics of Śākta thought. Thus the *Tripurā Rahasya* declares:

> There is no such thing as bondage or liberation. There is no such thing as the seeker and the means for seeking anything. Partless, non-dual conscious energy, *Tripurā* alone pervades everything. She is both knowledge and ignorance, bondage and liberation too. She is also the means for liberation. This is all one has to know.[25]

The metaphysical principle behind this teaching is the realization that the body is not evil, but the incarnation and manifestation of Śiva-Śakti, taking part in this divine play. In poison there are healing qualities, if rightly applied by a wise physician. In the body, seemingly the prison of the spirit, lies the coiled-up energy that enables a person to reach absolute freedom. The awakening of the Kuṇḍalinīśakti, as described earlier, is only partly understandable through theory; it is primarily a practice, requiring the supervision of those already enlightened in order that no harm should come to the *sādhaka*. Certain stages are critical, and more than once, novices have developed serious physical and psychic or mental illnesses as a result of practicing Kuṇḍalinī Yoga without proper guidance. This is not due to any superstitious belief in a magical intervention of the goddess but simply and truly based on experience. The system of Kuṇḍalinī Yoga, as a psycho-physical realization, undoubtedly has repercussions on the nervous system that can be observed clinically.

NEW DEVELOPMENTS IN ŚĀKTISM

Historically, the development of Śāktism, as an organized form of religion with a theology of its own, came after the development of Śaivism and Vaiṣṇavism. Today, almost all schools of Hinduism have strong elements of Śāktism blended with their teaching. Rāmakṛṣṇa Paramahaṁsa, the great Bengali saint whose name is connected with one of the most vigorous neo-Hindu movements, was the priest of Kālī at the Dakṣiṇeśvara Temple near Calcutta. He had frequent visions of the Divine Mother and spent countless hours in trance before her image. Yet, he did not accept the *vāmācāra* as a reputable way. Asked about certain groups of Śāktas, he answered:

> Why should we hate them? Theirs is also a way to God, though it is unclean. A house may have many entrances—the main entrance, the back door and the gate for the *bhaṅgi* who comes to sweep the unclean places of the house.

These cults are like this door. It does not really matter by which door one enters; once inside the house, all reach the same place. Should one imitate these people or mix with them? Certainly not![26]

Today, among the numerous *śāktas*, there are still followers of the left-hand way, who worship the cruel and horrible aspect of the Goddess. But there are also philosophers like Aurobindo Ghose, who find in Śāktism the basis of a religion for our age, in which life and matter are accepted as reality and not shunned as illusion. As V. S. Agrawala writes,

Mother Earth is the deity of the new age. The *kalpa* of Indra-Agni and Śiva-Viṣṇu are no more. The modern age offers its salutations to Mother Earth whom it adores as the super-goddess. The physical boundaries of the Mother Land stretch before our eyes but her real self is her cultural being which has taken shape in the course of centuries through the efforts of her people. Mother Earth is born of contemplation. Let the people devote themselves truthfully to the Mother Land whose legacy they have received from the ancients. Each one of us has to seek refuge with her. Mother Earth is the presiding deity of the age, let us worship her. Mother Earth lives by the achievements of her distinguished sons.[27]

Lately, Western scholars have shown great interest in the various forms of Devī and her worship.[28] This is partly due to the development of feminist perspectives in religion. It is no longer uncommon for Westerners also to speak of God as Mother rather than as Father and to address Her in terms not unlike the prayers Hindus have uttered for centuries to Devī. In addition, the importance of Devī in the practical political sphere of India has been highlighted. The universal name *śakti* given to each and every form of the goddess had not only cosmological and theological overtones but also pragmatic political implications. The king required the sanction of the local temple of the goddess that embodied power. As Gupta and Gombrich express it,

while [*Śakti*] *has* no authority, she *is* authority, concretised or personified as god's *ajñā*. . . . The sign of royal authority is the *mudra* or seal which the king gives to his officers. *Śakti* is called *mudra*. To have god's *mudra* is thus to have his authority, to be empowered to act on his behalf. A person thus empowered is called *ajñādhāra* "bearer of authority," "wielder of the mandate"; the term is common to [tantric] religion and politics.[29]

The relation between *Śakti* and political power does not belong to the past alone. Several *śāktas* like Yogi Dhirendra Brahmacari were associated with top-ranking politicians of post-independence India, and at one point, a Tantrika priest was hired by members of an opposition party to perform a Tantric ritual with a view to killing Prime Minister Indira Gandhi.[30]

19. Mudalvan, Murugan, Māl: The Great Gods of the Tamils

A, as its first of letters, every speech maintains;
The Primal Deity is First through all the world's domains.

—Tirukkuṛaḷ *I, 1, 1*

THE SANSKRITIZATION OF India that took place gradually with the occupation of the subcontinent by the Vedic Āryans brought about a certain measure of uniformity and universality of ritual and belief. As the Vedic *caturvarṇa* organization of society took hold of the entire country, so the celebration of Vedic *yajñas* became a status symbol all over India, from North to South. The systematic expansion of *Āryāvarta* through missionaries like Agastya resulted in the all-Indian acceptance and use of Sanskrit for religious purposes.[1]

Legend associates Ṛṣi Agastya with Śiva. The people from the South, who had gone in great numbers to witness Śiva's marriage to Pārvatī, asked for a sage. Śiva chose Agastya. He was very short but immensely powerful: in a fit of rage he once drunk up the whole ocean. Agastya, keen on familiarizing himself with his mission country asked Śiva to initiate him into Tamil language and literature. He settled in the Podhikai Hills, in today's Tinnevelly District, with his family and a group of northern farmers. Agastya is supposed to have written the *Āgastyam*, a large grammatical work on Tamil, which is lost except for a few fragments. Some, if not most, of the greatest works on Hindu philosophy and religion (such as the numerous treatises by Śaṅkara, Rāmānuja, and Madhva on Vedānta, the *Bhāgavata Purāṇa* and many others) originated in the South. Since Śaṅkara established the four strategic *maṭhs* in the four corners of India, South Indian priests serve in several of the temples of the Kedarnāth complex in the Himālayas.

For long, scholars assumed that, in the religion of the epics and *Purāṇas*, the indigenous traditions and religions mixed with the Vedic-Āryan traditions and that, in the major heroes and heroines of these works, non-Āryan deities, often with Sanskritized names, found entry into Hindu orthodoxy.

In the northern and central parts of India, where people speak Sanskrit-derived languages, it is difficult to identify pre-Sanskritic traditions and cults, except on a local level. In the South, however, where Dravidian languages prevail, and with the renewed pride in their distinct cultural heritage, especially of the Tamils, an impressive case can be stated for the non-Āryan and pre-Sanskritic religions of the area.

Tamilnadu today is the only state of the Indian republic, where the *rāṣṭrabhāṣa* Hindī is not taught as a compulsory subject in schools and the only part of India, where public signs do not indicate the names of localities and buildings in Devanāgarī letters: only Tamil and English are allowed.[2] Some Tamilians have gone so far as to claim the superiority of Tamil culture, in age and sophistication, over Sanskrit culture. Some of the literary documents connected with the so-called Saṅgam period have been assigned dates that would place them in prehistory.[3] Although research is still necessary to fix dates and establish a chronology of South Indian literary documents, it does seem certain that there was not only an Āryanization and Sanskritization of South India but also a penetration of Āryan Vedic religion and culture by Dravidian elements.

The pro-Āryan chauvinism of those who claim that "the south Indian languages are Dravidian only in syntax and the workaday part of the vocabulary," that "all the words which embody cultural notions are Sanskritic," and that "there is not a single element in the culture of any civilized group in South India which is not Āryan Brahmanic,"[4] is countered by the Tamil chauvinists, who derive all of Indian culture from Tamilnadu, and, more important, the work of serious scholars who point out that the *Ṛgveda* already contains twenty words of Dravidian origin and that later classical Sanskrit also borrowed a great many words from Tamil sources.[5]

Tamilnadu, the country of the Tamils, in former times consisted of a much larger area than it does today and included roughly the space where today Dravidian languages are prevalent. That is, the states of Andhra Pradesh, Karnāṭaka, and Keralā,[6] besides the present state of Tamiḷnādu.

The country was inhabited for at least 300,000 years and possesses some of the earliest remnants of late Stone Age flint tools, rock paintings, Neolithic sites, and Megalithic monuments.[7] It is also dotted with a great number of temples and sanctuaries, some of them of all-Indian importance but with roots in the pre-Āryan past of the country. Even the original, and still widely used, names of Indian deities like Śiva and Viṣṇu are different in the South, and the legends associated with them are either quite peculiarly Dravidian or have significant variations as compared to the North Indian versions. In addition, there are many local deities and customs that do not have equivalents in other parts of the country. The feasts celebrated there also have their own distinctive trappings and rituals.[8]

Several lessons can be learned from a brief survey of the major deities of South India. First, they represent a local tradition within Hinduism that is largely intact and quite strong and thus exemplifies a situation that, in other parts of India, is no longer as clearly discernible, suggesting the composition of Hinduism from a mosaic of local cults and traditions. Second, they demonstrate the transformation (Sanskritization) of a formerly independent tradition, the adaptation of a distinct mythological lore to the wider context of Hinduism. Third, they still exhibit elements of indigenous religious traditions, which have resisted absorption into an all-Indian Hinduism.

THE ĀRYANIZATION OF THE TAMIL GODS

Śiva is so powerfully present in Tamilnadu's artistic heritage and literature that one thinks of Tamilnadu predominantly as Śiva country and Śaivism as a South Indian religion. In fact, the name Śiva occurs rather late in Tamil documents, and by then, he is considered to be the same as the indigenous Mudalvan, who had a Tamilian background and a history of his own.[9] A tradition peculiar to the Tamil country—in evidence to this day—is the ritual dance in connection with the worship of Śiva.[10] The Śiva Naṭarāja image, a creation of the South, is admired all over the world especially in the masterful bronzes from the Chola age.[11] Whereas the *liṅga* is associated with Śiva worship throughout India, it seems to have been a tradition in the South long before the emergence of Śaivism as an organized religion. A South Indian representation of a *liṅga* with a bull crouching in front of it has been ascribed to the Neolithic age,[12] and up to the Saṅgam age, stumps of trees known as *kaṇḍu* were worshipped as *liṅgas*.[13] Many of the Śiva myths found, for example, in the *Śiva Purāṇa* have been incorporated into Śiva lore in South India, too. It is significant, however, that major changes took place in the process of adaptation.[14]

Thus, the Dakṣa saga was originally a North Indian Śiva myth dealing with the Śaivite conquest of the famous sub-Himālayan *tīrtha* of Kanakhala. In the Tamil version of the myth, Dakṣa, a Vedic patriarch with Vaiṣṇavite leanings, is represented as a devotee of Śiva whose mind was temporarily clouded.[15] The association of Śiva with burning *ghaṭs*, and death in general, seems to represent a "Śivaization" of the pre-Dravidian *Suḍalaimāḍan*.

Viṣṇu is known in South India as Māl, meaning "great."[16] Kṛṣṇa worship seems also to have been prominent among the shepherds and cowherds of Tamilnadu, and many references to it are found in ancient Tamil literature. It is highly probable, that the *Bhāgavata Purāṇa*, the major text of the Kṛṣṇa worshippers, received its final form in Tamiḻnādu. Viṣṇu is also known as Māyon, Māyan, or Māyavan,[17] references to the dark complexion of the God; the Sanskrit form Kṛṣṇa also means "black." It is hard to say how many of the myths now associated with Viṣṇu in the all-India context of Vaiṣṇavism originated in Tamiḻnādu. There certainly are also peculiar local variants of otherwise commonly known Viṣṇu myths.

Bālarāman, or Bāladevan, in North Indian mythology considered as younger brother of Kṛṣṇa, figures in Tamilnadu as the elder brother of Viṣṇu under the name of Vāliyon.[18] Tirumāl and Vāliyon together are "the two great Gods." Tirumāl's description is entirely South Indian, in spite of his later association with Bālarāma. He was described as of white complexion, resembling the combination of the conch and milk. He had one earring and used a ploughshare as a weapon. His emblem was the palmyra tree.[19]

It is interesting to note that, in South India, Indra retained and even gained prominence at a time when he was supplanted in North India by other deities. Lavish Indra festivals were celebrated by the Chola kings, the so-called *Indraviḷavu* lasting a full lunar month with royal participation.[20]

NON-ĀRYANIZED TAMIL GODS

Whereas the amalgamation of Mudalvan with Śiva and of Tirumāl with Viṣṇu became fairly complete in the course of time, the Tamilians also adopting the Sanskrit names in their own texts, the wholly Tamilian deity Murugan largely resisted this process.[21] Attempts were made in later times to associate him with Śiva and his son and equate him with Skanda, the North Indian god of war, but these were neither fully successful nor did they dislocate Murugan from the prominence he always had. K. K. Pillai states that "Murugan has been doubtless the pre-eminent God of the Tamils through the ages."[22] The name Murugan evokes associations with beauty, youth and divine freedom. According to ancient Tamil texts, Murugan was the lord of all seven worlds. He was the war god of the Tamils; the spear was his favorite weapon. Known also as Śey, Vel, and Neduvel (his priests were known as Velān), he is associated with both the blue-feathered peacock and the elephant. A frenzied form of sacred dance is associated with his cult, the so-called *Veriyadāḷ:*

Figure 19.1 Lakṣmī surrounded by auspicious objects

> It was the dance of the priest in a frenzy, when he was supposed to be under divine inspiration. It took place when the parents of a lovesick girl wanted to know the cause of and remedy for her indisposition. After offering prayers and sacrificing a goat, the priest danced, as if possessed. Invariably under the influence of intoxicating liquor and consequently in a state of delirium, he used to proclaim his diagnosis, prescriptions and predictions.[23]

The Tamils of old also knew a variety of war dances, which were performed by men and women at the beginning of an expedition. War, obviously, played a major role in the life and thought of Tamilians.[24]

The common worship of Murugan consists of offering flowers, paddy, millet, and honey and usually ends with the sacrifice of a goat. During the Saṅgam era, Murugan became Aryanized into Subrahmania and several North Indian legends became associated with him. Murugan's sanctuaries were primarily on hilltops. In Saṅgam works, his name and place of worship is associated with six military camps, which have been largely identified with modern settlements. Two of these sites, now the places of Viṣṇu temples, may have seen transformation from Murugan to Viṣṇu worship.[25] Besides Murugan, the god of war, the Tamilians also worshipped Koṛṛavai, the goddess of war.[26] Being of early Dravidian (and possibly pre-Dravidian) origin, she was later associated with the Hindu deity Mahiṣāsuramārdiṇī. She is also called the younger sister of Māl. The all-Indian Lakṣmī (Figure 19.1), venerated in Tamiḷnādu under the name of Ilakkumi, is also known as Tiru, the exact equivalent of the Sanskrit *Śrī* and used today as Śrī is in the rest of India, as a honorific.

Nature worship as a dimension of Hinduism is much more in evidence in Tamiḷnādu than in most other parts of India. Thus, the sun and moon had, and have, a special place in Tamil worship. Also the worship of trees and of animals, especially the snake, is very prevalent.[27]

The local association of Hindu deities goes beyond the specific Tamilian traditions associated with pan-Indian religions like Vaiṣṇavism, Śaivism, and Śāktism. Within the Tamil country itself, separate regions were assigned to the major Tamilian deities. Thus Śeyon (or Murugan) was the favorite deity of Kuriñchi, Māyon (or Māl, Viṣṇu) of Mullai, Vandan (or Indra) of Maridan, and Varuṇa of Neydal.[28]

As has happened in other countries and in the context of other religions as well, the Tamilians, after being converted to Vedism, became the staunchest and most conservative defenders of Vedic religion. The Tamil kings of the Saṅgam age performed enormously expensive Vedic sacrifices.[29] One of the Chola monarchs, Rājasuyam Vetta Perunarkilli, obtained his title through the performance of the extensive Vedic *rājasuya* sacrifice.[30] Also, the Chera kings were renowned for their orthodox Vedic perform-

26. Virabhadrī, Tanjore, Heras Institute Bombay

ances.[31] In our own day, Kerala Brahmins, in an area formerly part of the Tamil country, performed for Frits Staal and his party of photographers and researchers the ancient Vedic *agnicayana:* a costly and time-consuming Vedic ritual that goes back to ancient times.[32]

Today, South Indian Brahmins are renowned for their tenacious traditionalism; and again, not uncharacteristically, Tamilnadu has brought forth the most articulate organized anti-Brahmin movement. At some time, the movement formed the political party *Draviḍa Munnetra Kazhagam* (DMK), the Dravidian Progress Party, that under the revered Anna held the leadership of Tamilnadu from 1962 to 1968.[33] Several of the South Indian Devasthānams are immensely rich and wield considerable political power as well. State-appointed boards regulate a great deal of the financial transactions taking place in them. Several changes enacted recently have met with resistance from the priesthood.[34]

The typical religiosity of Tamilnadu also manifests itself on the level of folk beliefs and superstitions. As in all such traditions, fate (called Ūḷ or Ūḷ Vinai) plays a major role. The Tamil classic *Tirukkuṛaḷ* devotes an entire chapter to it: "What powers so great as those of Destiny? Man's skill some other thing contrives; but fate's beforehand still."[35]

Also in line with other folk traditions, ghosts and demons play a major role in Tamilnadu. Ghosts were formerly associated primarily with the battlefield: they were supposed to feed on corpses. It is still believed that mustard seed spread around a house and the burning of camphor and incense would keep them away at night.[36] In order to protect children from the malicious actions of goblins, mothers carry a twig of margosa leaves with them when leaving the house.[37] Margosa leaves are also tied to the entrances of houses during epidemics of smallpox. Infectious diseases, especially among children, and in particular smallpox which ravaged India's countryside in previous times, brought on the cult of specific goddesses. Mariamma, associated with smallpox, received many offerings designed to placate her.[38] Belief in auspicious and inauspicious times and places is prevalent throughout Hindu India. Tamils follow a calendar of their own, indicating *Rahukālam*, the inauspicious time, during which all major new ventures and business transactions are avoided.[39]

At some time, roughly from the second century B.C.E. to the eighth century C.E., Buddhism and Jainism were very strong in South India, dominating the cultural life of the country. Major literary and scientific works were created by Jains and Buddhists, and several of the influential rulers are said to have been active in promoting Jainism and Buddhism and persecuting Śaivas and Vaiṣṇavas.[40] The tables were turned during the time of the Āḷvārs and Nāyanmārs, roughly from the sixth century onward, when some quite sensational conversions of royalty to Śaivism took place and when Vaiṣṇavas gained majority status in some districts. Śaivite kings supposedly persecuted Jains.[41] There is a series of gruesome murals in the temple of Madurai, illustrating the impaling and boiling in kettles of Jains. Śaivites also purportedly persecuted Vaiṣṇavas: Rāmānuja had to flee from his see in Śrīrangam because he refused to accept Śiva as his lord, and one of his faithful servants who pretended to be Rāmānuja had his eyes put out. The faithful Viṣṇu devotee got his eyesight miraculously restored through the grace of Viṣṇu when Rāmānuja wept over him.

THE SAINTS OF TAMIḶNĀDU

Tamilnadu is the birthplace of a great many saints and religious scholars of all-Indian repute. In a volume entitled *Ten Saints of India*, T. M. P. Mahadevan,[42] formerly professor of philosophy at the University of Madras, includes nine saints from Tamilnadu; the only "foreigner" is the Bengali Ramakrishna. In addition to the Vedānta *ācāryas* Śaṅkara and Rāmānuja are the Śaivite saints Tirujñāna Saṁbandhar, Tirunāvukkaraśu, Sundaramūrti, and Māṇikavācakar, the author of the famous *Tiruvācagam*, the Vaiṣṇava saints Nammāḷvār and Āṇḍāl, and the twentieth century saint Rāmaṇa Māhārṣi, who inspired a great many Western seekers through his presence and his insistent question Who are you? Śaṅkara and Rāmānuja wrote in Sanskrit and had a large following outside Tamilnadu during their lifetime. Rāmana Māhārṣi knew some English and composed his simple didactic verses in both Sanskrit and English (as well as in Tamil) and obtained international stature. The others composed and preached only in Tamil and are little known outside Tamiḷnādu, except among interested scholars. Their expressions of Śaivism and Vaiṣṇavism are quite peculiarly Tamilian and are apt, even in translation to convey something of the specific religiosity of Tamilnadu. To underscore their importance within the major Hindu communities in Tamilnadu, it must be mentioned that their Tamil devotional hymns did attain canonical status and form part of the officially sanctioned temple worship throughout Tamilnadu.

The legend and poetry of Tiru Jñāna Saṁbandamūrti Swāmi, who flourished in the seventh century C.E., is both typical and instructive.[43] It was a time when Buddhism and Jainism had all but eliminated Śaivism from the Tamil country. One of the few remaining Śiva devotees prayed to Śiva in the temple of his hometown, Śiyālī, that a son be born to him who would win his people back to Śiva. The child of such a prayer uttered his first hymn in praise of Śiva at the age of three, after he was fed milk by Śiva's spouse, from which he derived his name, Sambandar, "the man connected with divine wisdom."

27. Sundara Mūrti, South India, Heras Institute Bombay

When he grew up, he went on pilgrimage to all the Śiva sanctuaries of South India. He was deeply worried by the conversion of the king of Madura to Jainism. The queen-consort and her prime minister, however, had remained Śaivites, and with their help, Sambandar not only reconverted the king but also had him impale 8000 Jains. In another part of Tamiḷnādu, he converted a great number of Buddhists to Śaivism. Sambandar is an example of the formation of sectarian Hinduism in opposition to non-Hindu religions, a process that made Śaivism much more of a dogmatically defined "religion" than it had been through its long history. Still, Sambandar does articulate something of the *bhakti* that knows no boundaries, the generosity of heart and mind that makes Hinduism overall so attractive a faith. Thus does he sing:

> For the Father in Arur
>   Sprinkle ye the blooms of love;
> In your heart will dawn true light,
>   Every bondage will remove.
> Him the holy in Arur
>   Ne'er forget to laud and praise;
> Bonds of birth will severed by,
>   Left behind all worldly ways.
> In Arur, our loved one's gem,
>   Scatter golden blossoms fair.
> Sorrow ye shall wipe away
>   Yours be bliss without compare.[44]

The Vaiṣṇavas were no less fervent in preaching devotion to Viṣṇu, whose sanctuary at Tirupati draws hundreds of thousands of pilgrims every year. Among the āḷvārs, the Viṣṇu-intoxicated singers who were responsible for kindling an all-India Viṣṇu-bhakti, was a woman, Āṇḍāl, whose fame has spread far and wide. Her birth was surrounded by a great many miraculous events and prophecies. She was believed by her father to be the incarnation of Bhū Devī, one of the two consorts of Viṣṇu. Āṇḍāl considered herself the bride of Viṣṇu as he is worshipped in Śrīraṅgam. It is interesting that she began to imitate the ways of the *gopīs* of faraway Vrindāvan and desired to marry the Kṛṣṇa of the *Bhāgavata Purāṇa.*[45]

The lyrics of these God-filled souls not only capture the hearts of the simple people in Tamiḷnādu, but they also shaped the theology of the major centers of Vaiṣṇavism and Śaivism and became part of the ornate worship that has continued to this day. Statues of āḷvārs and nāyanmārs decorate homes and temples in Tamilnadu and receive homage.

Toward the end of the Indian Middle Ages, in the twelfth century, when large parts of India were already under Muslim rule, under the goad of another major religion attacking the flank of Hinduism, the Liṅgāyat movement arose in Karṇāṭaka.[46] In a certain sense, the Liṅgāyat movement represents a monotheistic radicalization of Śaivism, as a parallel to the radical monotheism of Islam. The Liṅgāyats, after initiation, have to wear a *liṅga* at all times and consider themselves the property of Śiva. On the other hand, the Liṅgāyats were reformists. They abolished caste differences, engaged in public works for the benefit of the community, and no longer cremated their dead but buried them, again, perhaps under the influence of Islam. Basavanna, the reputed twelfth century reformer of *Liṅgāytism*, sings:

> The rich will make temples for Śiva
> What shall I, a poor man do?
> My legs are pillars, the body the shrine,
> The head a cupola of gold.
> Listen, O lord of the meeting rivers,
> things standing shall fall,
> but the moving shall ever stay.[47]

SCHOLARSHIP AND FOLK TRADITION

Tamilnadu has brought forth its share of philosophers and theologians, in the past and in the present, such luminaries of modern India as S. Radhakrishnan, T. R. V. Murti, T. M. P. Mahadevan, and many well-known living representatives of Indian philosophy originated from Tamiḷnādu. On the other hand, the religion of Tamilnadu has always had, and still has, a quality of earthiness and joie de vivre. Nothing is better suited to prove this point than the celebration of Pongāl, the great national feast of Tamilnadu.[48] It is a feast in which cattle are honored. Cows and oxen, water buffaloes and goats are decorated, garlanded, and led in processions. Large amounts of rich and varied food is consumed in daylong celebrations, punctuated with the singing of hymns, the exploding of fireworks, and joyous noises day and night. All the gods receive worship and are invoked for blessings, but the central focus of all is life and that which sustains it: the food grown in the fields and the faithful bovines, without whose help humans could not subsist.

Part III

The Structural Supports of Hinduism

This book has emphasized how much Hinduism is a way of life for Hindus and not only a religious or intellectual concern in the more narrow sense of these words. Hinduism is what it is because of the reality of India, the land and its people.

To an incredible degree, Hinduism is identified with the physical landscape of India. It centers around the mountains, the rivers, and the oceans of India: holy mountains, sacred rivers, and mysterious oceans. It has brought forth and requires images for its functioning; the divine is present in India in stone and wood, in metal, and on paper. Hinduism has created and was in turn profoundly shaped by its holy cities and attracts millions each year to the famous temples. Hinduism, finally, has an acute awareness of the qualitative differences in time: of holy and profane days, of auspicious and inauspicious occasions. A great many professionals are employed to interpret the signs of time, an essential ingredient of Hinduism, since all the necessary rites have to be performed in a specific time and since not all times are the same.

While sacred spaces, places, and times are connected with the physical reality of India and provide a sacred structure in its nature, the age-old *caturvarṇāśramadharma* provides a sacred structure to society and to history. By divine fiat, society was divided into functional sections and the life of the individual was structured so as to give room to the realization of all essential values. The caste structure provided Hinduism with a social and political basis strong enough to not only accommodate change and development but also to withstand attacks from outside.

The assignment of a specific function in society provided individuals with a purpose in their lives, ensured on the whole a noncompetitive society, and created a social security net for all its members. Its major failing was not toward those who belonged to it but toward those who did not, the outcastes. Either by expelling from its folds such members who did not conform to the caste regulations or by not accepting outsiders into it, Hindu society created a vast pool of underprivileged, a parallel society of people without social standing and without rights, good to do only the most degrading work and treated worse than cattle. Twenty percent of the total population of India belongs to this category, and the way they were treated by the majority of caste Hindus is not something Hinduism can take pride in.

Hinduism has always reserved the highest respect for those who made religion their profession. The members of the upper castes, toward the end of their lives, are expected to cut off all attachment to the world and concentrate all efforts on *mokṣa*, spiritual liberation. Hinduism also accepted the renunciation of desire and the entrance into the stage of *saṁnyāsa* at an early time in life. *Saṁnyāsis* have been the backbone of Hinduism for many centuries, and they are so today as well. There are millions of them, distributed over hundreds of orders and associations. They include all types of men and women: attractive and repulsive, old and young, learned and illiterate, pious and fanatical, serene and excitable. In more than one way, they provide the ultimate support to Hinduism. They are the living example to the rest of the Hindus of a life dedicated to the activities and ideals which the other Hindus only casually partake in or aspire to. As an ideal, *saṁnyāsa* has enormous attraction also for many modern, educated Hindus, not to mention Westerners, who have joined modern Hindu movements in fair numbers. One can safely predict that Hinduism will flourish as long as *saṁnyāsa* is followed by a significant number of Hindus. There can be no doubt that this is the case today. Equally as important as the physical support and the social structure that Hinduism gave itself is the structure of thought that holds the symbolic world of Hinduism together.

Philosophical speculation and systematic enquiry have been characteristic for Hinduism throughout its long history. The Hindu mind excels in both analytic and systematic thinking and the controversies that erupted periodically, leading to the formation of new schools of thought (the best known and most long lived being Jainism and Buddhism), sharpened concepts and logic to a degree probably not reached anywhere else. The assumption made by some of the greatest exponents of Hinduism, that eternal felicity and release from rebirth depended on a specific kind of knowledge and that wrong notions about the nature of Self and Reality could cause misery and suffering not only in this life but in many lives to come, gave to philosophical debates an urgency that has hardly any parallel in history.

Hindu orthodoxy repeatedly had to define itself against opponents from within and without. Early on, it insisted on membership in one of the four *varṇas* and the observation of the rules governing them, it prescribed public and domestic rituals and it drew boundaries between the *ārya*, insiders, and the *mleccha*, outsiders. It evolved a set of beliefs that included *karma* and rebirth, the existence of gods and demons, the possibility of going to heaven or to hell after death, and many others. As the *Upaniṣads* show, the latitude with regard to the interpretation of the Vedic utterances was considerable and so was the freedom to devise ways of liberation from rebirth.

The *ṣatdarśanas* are often called the six orthodox philosophical systems of Hinduism. To avoid a misunderstanding of the term, a few explanations may be given before dealing with each one in some detail. *Darśana* literally means "seeing" and provides a fairly exact equivalent to the original meaning of the Greek *theoría*. Each of the six *darśanas* has sufficiently different interests and methods to distinguish it from the others. Within certain *darśanas*, for example, those of *Mīmāṁsā* and *Vedānta*, further controversies lead to the emergence of more schools of thought, that, although sharing many more presuppositions, also entered into sharp exchanges and mutual strife.

With the beginning of modern times, the glaring injustices inflicted upon outcastes and on women brought forth reformers who attacked with great zeal and a fair measure of success the ills of Hindu society. Some may have gone too far and may have condemned Hinduism for conditions it could do little about. Others believed that a spiritual regeneration of Hinduism would result almost automatically in a better life for all. We can highlight only a few of the movements that undertook reforms and improvements during the past 150 years, many others of considerable significance had to be left out.

This survey of Hinduism had necessarily to emphasize history and past achievements of the Hindus. Throughout, however, the contemporary scene has been brought in, both to illustrate the continuity of the ancient tradition and its present expression. One of the most prominent features of Hinduism today is its politization. It is linked, quite consciously so by its advocates, with the Hindu tradition, and it may influence the development of India in the years to come in a major way. So we conclude our survey of past and present with a projection into the future.

20. The Divine Presence in Space and Time: *Mūrti, Tīrtha, Kāla*

> A Hindu is he . . . who above all addresses this land, this Sindhusthan, as his *puṇyabhū*, as his Holyland—the land of his prophets and seers, of his godmen and gurus, the land of piety and pilgrimage.
>
> —*Vir Savarkar*, Hindutva[1]

THAT SPACE AND time are permeated with the presence of the supreme is not a mere theological idea with the Hindus; it is a tangible reality in India. Countless temples, many of impressive dimensions, manifest the presence and power of Hinduism in all towns and villages. The intensity of devotion of the Hindus is revealed in numberless images: artistic creations in stone, metal, and wood, and cheap prints on colored paper. A great number of religious centers attract a continuous stream of pilgrims and an unbroken string of festivals impress the foreign visitor as much as the indigenous worshipper with a sense of the sacredness of time.

The Vedic Indians did not know temples and images; the object of worship was the *vedi*, the sacrificial altar, built according to certain specifications on a preselected site, which for the time of the sacrifice became the place where *devas* and *pitṛs* shared with humans the gifts offered for sacrifice. The constantly maintained fire in each home, too, was considered to be a divine presence, as were the more striking natural phenomena like thunderstorms and the heavenly bodies. We do not know whether a deeper conviction that the divine could not be captured in finite forms or inability of artistic expression made the Āryans in the early texts pour contempt on image worshippers and temple builders, who must have been present in

India since times immemorial. The Indus civilization may have known both temples and cult images.

In and around Mathurā, an ancient center, as well as in many other places, terracotta figurines of mother goddesses have been found, dated around 500 B.C.E. Figurative representation reached a first peak in the Indo-Greek art of the golden time of Buddhism.[2] Individual specimens of Hindu sculpture can be traced to pre-Christian times,[3] but the great theoretical development according to which temples and figures had to be fashioned belongs to the post-Christian era. In all probability, there was an early Hindu art and architecture that used wood as the basic material.[4] Even now, a number of temples and statues are fashioned of wood and several famous temples give the impression that they are copies in stone of more ancient wooden models.[5]

With regard to the size and number of temples and images, Hindu India has no equal in the world. Compared with temple cities like Śrīraṅgam, Madurai, Khajurāho, or Bhuvaneśvara, Western religious centers and even cathedrals look modest and poor. And we must not forget that what we admire in India today is largely what the Muslim invaders either did not destroy (an account of the extent of their devastations can be had from Muslim historians themselves) or allowed to be built.[6] A great many temples, also of considerable proportions, are being constructed in our time, temples associated with modern Hindu movements as well as temples funded by pious individuals and families.

MŪRTI: THE EMBODIED GOD

For the Hindu, the most important of all the spatio-temporal manifestations of the divine is the *mūrti*, or image.[7] *Mūrti* means literally "embodiment"; technically, it designates the images of the divinities made of metal, stone, or wood but sometimes also of some perishable material for special purposes. Though the first impression is that of an infinite variety of figures and poses, a more thorough acquaintance with the subject reveals that each artist has to follow very definite rules with regard to proportions, positions, and gestures.

The *Purāṇas*, the *Āgamas*, *Saṁhitās*, and *Tantras* contain many chapters detailing the way in which images to be used in worship have to be made. These rules are supposed to go back to divine revelation and must, therefore, not be violated, if the image is to become an abode of the divine. These works do not constitute the only source for the canons they prescribe; we have old Buddhist texts that specify the proportions of the Buddha images and also other Indian texts, not yet sectarian in their character, that

28. Bhairava, Mahārāṣṭra, Heras Institute Bombay

provide guidelines for architects and sculptors.[8] One of the most important works is the *Viśvakarma Vāstuśāstra*,[9] ascribed to Viśvakarman, the architect and director of all arts of the *devas*, the patron of all the artists and artisans in India. The various *Vāstuśāstras* in existence manifest the variety of different artistic traditions in India. Though one can say that all images that are to be used as cult objects in temples and homes have to conform to definite rules, one cannot reduce these rules to one single canon. We have, in different centers, different canons of art.[10]

The image produced according to the prescribed canons is not yet an object of worship: it has to be consecrated in a formal ceremony of *pratiṣṭhāpana*, the solemn installation. Rituals vary according to religious affiliation and locality, but the consecration of the *mūrti* is an essential requirement and usually marks the formal opening of a new temple. In older temples, one quite often finds so-called *svayamvyaktā mūrtis*, images not fashioned by human hands but miraculously sent by God himself: washed up on the seashore, carried to a place by a river, or found by someone instructed in a dream. Local tradition often tells that a *ṛṣi* received the image of the temple directly from the deity. Depending on the material used and the rite employed, the consecration is limited to a certain time. The clay-and-paper images used, for instance, for *Dūrgā-pūjā* by the *Śāktas* at the time of the Dassera festival, are consecrated only for the duration of the festivities. When the celebrations are over, and the goddess has left them, the images are thrown into the sea or a river.

A worshipper who has no other image may even use a paper image or an image drawn in sand and invoke the divine presence upon it for the time of his or her worship. Images made of stone or metal are usually given a *nitya-abhiṣeka*, a consecration forever, which is terminated only when the image suffers a major injury.[11]

The *Bṛhatsaṁhitā* of Viramitrodaya, one of the most important and interesting texts of early Hindu literature, describes this ceremony in the following way:

> To the south or east [of the new temple], a pavillion furnished with four *toraṇas*, or arches, should be erected, decorated with garlands and banners. Inside, an earthen altar should be raised, sprinkled with sand and covered with *kuśa*-grass upon which the image should be placed. The image should be bathed successively with various kinds of water; first a decoction of *plakṣa, aśvattha, uḍumbara, śirīṣa,* and *vaṭa* should be used; then the auspicious *sarvauṣadhi* water and next the water from *tīrthas*, in which earth raised by elephants and bulls, earth from mountains, anthills, confluences of rivers, lotus ponds, and *pañcagavya*, the five products of the cow[12] are mixed, should be poured. When the image has received this bath and is sprinkled with scented water in which gold and precious gems are put, it should be placed with its head toward the east; during

this ceremony the *tūrya*-trumpet should be blown and *puṇyāhā*, "auspicious day!" and Vedic *mantras* should be uttered. The most respected of the *Brahmans* should then chant *mantras* connected with Indra in the eastern and *mantras* connected with Agni in the southeastern quarter; these *Brahmans* should be honored with handsome fees. The Brahman then should offer *homa* to the fire with the *mantra* peculiar to the enshrined deity. If during the performance of the *homa* the fire becomes full of smoke, or the flames turn from right to left or the burning faggots emit frequent sparks, then it is not auspicious, it is also inauspicious, if the priest forgets his *mantras* or the flames turn backwards. After having bathed the image, decked it with new cloth and ornaments, and worshipped it with flowers and sandalwood paste, the priest should lay it down on a well-spread bed. When the image has rested for its full time it should be aroused from sleep with songs and dances and should be installed at a time fixed by the astrologers. Then, after worshipping the image with flowers, garments, sandalwood paste and the sounds of the conch shell and trumpet, it should be carefully taken inside the sanctum from the pavilion, keeping the temple to the right.

After making profuse offerings, and honoring the Brahmans and the assembly, a piece of gold should be put into the mortise-hole of the base and the image fixed on it. The one who installs the image, honoring specifically the astrologer, the Brahmans, the assembly, the image maker, and the architect, enjoys bliss in this world and heaven hereafter. The installation should take place in the bright fortnight in the period of the summer solstice and during certain particular positions of the planets and asterisms, on days other than *maṅgalavāra* [literally, "auspicious day," our Tuesday] and in a time particularly auspicious to the donor of the image.[13]

Later texts have much more elaborate ceremonies; the interested reader must consult special works, which provide all the details.[14] Whereas the main image of a Vaiṣṇava and Śākta temple is always a figurative image, the object of worship in the *garbha-gṛha*, the central shrine of a Śaiva temple is the aniconic *liṅga*. The older centers boast of *svayambhu liṅgas, liṅgas* that have been revealed by Śiva himself and not fashioned by human hands; indeed, many of them are natural objects and not artifacts. Some of them are oblong stones; the *liṅga* at Kedarnāth in the Himālayas is formed by water dropping from the ceiling of the cave and congealing into a cone of ice. The *svayambhu liṅgas* are surrounded by legends contained in the *sthāla-purāṇas*, the local chronicles of the temples.

The legend connected with Kālahasti in Andhra Pradesh may serve as a typical example. The main *mūrti* of the temple consists of a natural oblong slab of stone. With some imagination, one can find the resemblance of the head of a two-tusked elephant on one side and the head of a five-hooded cobra on the other side, with a small marking that is reminiscent of a spider. Legend has it that these devout animals offered daily *pūjā* to the *liṅga:* the

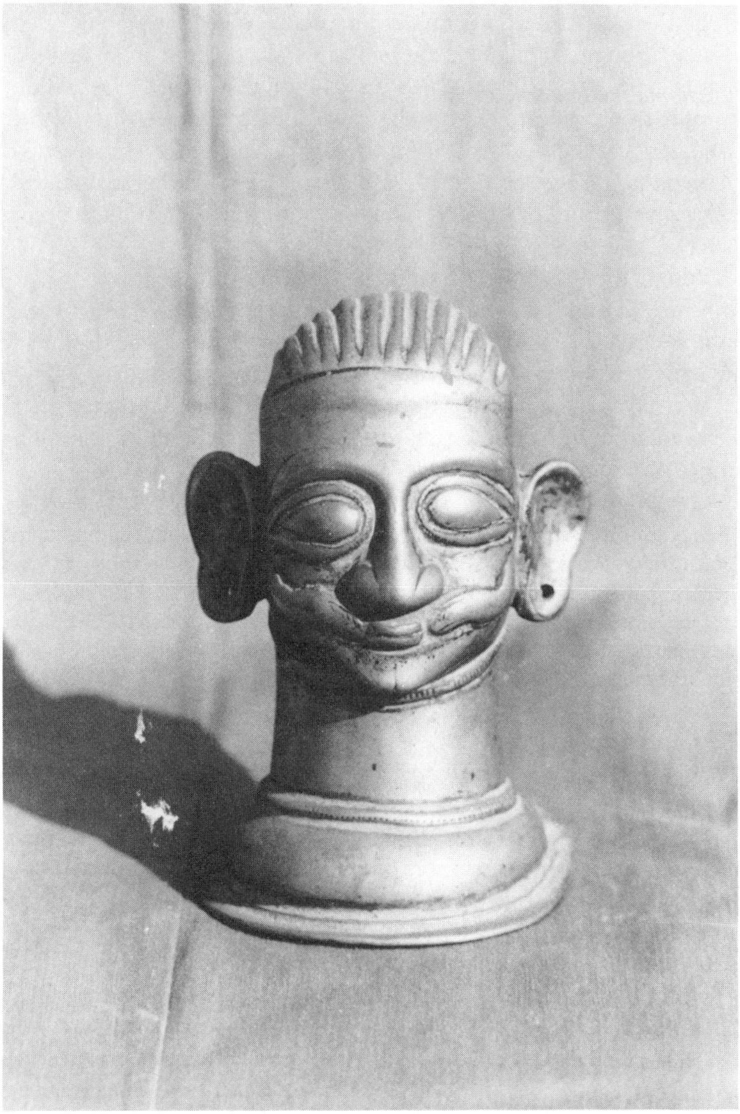

29. Śiva Kānphaṭa, Mahārāṣṭra, Heras Institute Bombay

spider would weave a net to protect it from the sun's rays, the elephant sprayed it with water, and the snake shielded it with its hood. One day the snake, ignorant of the elephant's devotion, noticed that some leaves had fallen on the *liṅga* and this aroused her anger. When the elephant returned, the snake thought him to be the culprit and got hold of his trunk. The elephant, mad with pain, smashed his trunk against the stone, killing both snake and spider and also himself. Śiva pleased with the devotion those animals had shown, granted *mukti* to all of them. This *liṅga* is also one of the *pañcabhūta liṅga*, connected with *vāyu*, the wind, because an oil lamp kept burning in front of the *liṅga* flickers continuously, although no opening is visible anywhere.[15]

Though there is no uniformity as regards the theology of images in Hinduism and though nowadays one can hear Hindus, in a liberal way, explain the images as only symbolizing God, the traditional Hindu still sees in the images a real and physical presence of God and not only a symbolic one. Vaiṣṇavas connect the image worship with their theories of the five different manifestations of Viṣṇu: the *ārcāvatāra* is the Lord himself present in an image. Thus, the *Arthapañcaka* says:

> Although omniscient, [Viṣṇu in his image] appears unknowing; although pure spirit, he appears as a body; although himself the Lord he appears to be at the mercy of men; although all-powerful he appears to be without power; though perfectly free from wants, he seems to be in need; although the protector of all he seems helpless; although invisible, he becomes visibly manifest; although unfathomable, he seems tangible.

Other Vaiṣṇava scriptures speak of the suffering the supreme takes upon himself, making himself present in an image because of his love for humanity.

Mūrti-pūjā, worship of god who is present in the image, is one of the prominent features of contemporary Hinduism both in temples and homes. The rules for it vary greatly from place to place and sect to sect; manuals are available that, in thousands of details, set out the form of worship obligatory in a temple or a *saṁpradāya*.

The *Bhāgavata Purāṇa* offers the following instructions:

> Having purified oneself and having gathered the materials of worship, the devotee should sit on his seat of *darbha* grass facing east or north and conduct the worship with the image in front of him. He should then utter the *mantras* with proper *mudrās* which render his different limbs duly charged with spiritual power.[16] He should then invoke with *mantras* and proper *mudrās* my presence in the image. He should keep in front a vessel of sanctified water and with that water sprinkle thrice the image, the materials of worship, himself and the vessels.

When the devotee's whole being has become pervaded by my form, which is the inner soul of all beings, the devotee shall, having become completely immersed in myself, make my presence overflow into the image established in front of him and then, with all the paraphernalia, conduct my worship. He must first offer me a seat; my seat is made of nine elements: virtue, knowledge, dispassion and mastery as the four feet and the opposite of these as the enclosed plank upon which I sit, the other parts of my seat are the three sheets spread over it representing the three *guṇas* of which my *māyā* is composed; there are also to be established on the seat my nine *śaktis*. With clothes, sacred thread, jewels, garlands and fragrant paste my devotee should decorate my form suitably and with love. With faith my worshipper should then offer me water to wash, sandal, flower, unbroken rice, incense, light and food of different kinds; also attentions like anointing, massage, showing of mirror etc. and entertainments like song and dance; these special entertainments may be done on festive days and even daily. One should engage in singing of me, praising me, dancing with my themes, imitating my exploits and acts, narrating my stories or listening to them. With manifold hymns of praise of me, taken from the *Purāṇas*, or from vernacular collections, the devotee should praise me and pray to me that I bless him and he should prostrate before me. With his hands and head at my feet, he should say: "My Lord, from the clutches of death save me who have taken refuge under you!"

Having consecrated an image of me one should build a firm temple for me and have beautiful flower gardens around for conducting daily worship and festivals. For the maintenance of my worship in special seasons as well as every day, one should bestow fields, bazaars, townships and villages.[17]

THE HINDU TEMPLE

True to the suggestion given in the text just quoted, Hindus over the centuries have built "firm temples" for the god embodied in the *mūrti*. The Hindu temple is not primarily the assembly room of the congregation, like the synagogues and churches of the biblical religions, but the palace of the *mūrta bhagavān*, the embodied lord. The more powerful the *mūrti* of a temple, the larger are the crowds that come for *darśana*, and the richer and bigger, usually, also is the temple. Most temples are the hereditary property of individual families; quite a number of the larger temples are nowadays administered by temple trusts under the control of a government department.[18]

Indian temple architecture lately has attracted the interest of many Western scholars, who have studied the ancient *vāstuśāstra* texts and gained an understanding of the symbolism expressed in it.[19]

[The] structure [of the Hindu Temple] is rooted in Vedic tradition, and primeval modes of building have contributed their shapes. The principles are given in the sacred books of India and the structural rules in the treatises on architecture. They are carried out in the shrines which still stand throughout the country and which were built in many varieties and styles over 1500 years from the fifth century.[20]

The Indian architect worked under the supposition that his creation had to conform to, and be expressive of, the cosmic laws. The cosmos, as he saw it, was the combination of the perfect and the imperfect, the absolute *brahman* and the contingent *jīva*, of the eternal and of time. The eternal is symbolized in the square, the circle is the symbol of time. As the symbol model of the *vāstu-puruṣa* (Figure 20.1) reveals,[21] also in India "the person

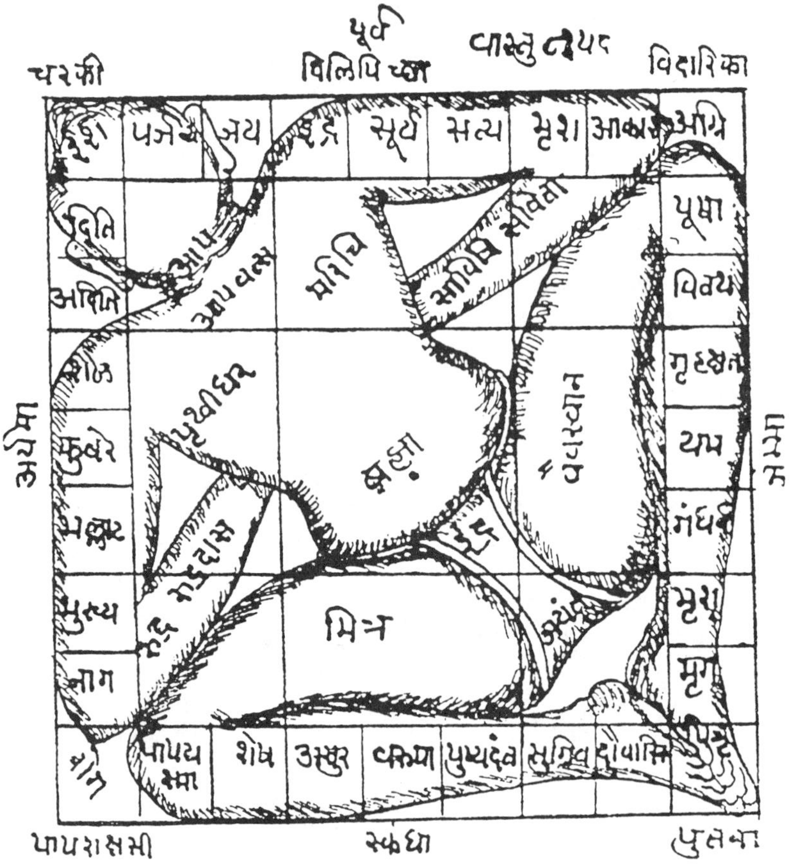

Figure 20.1 *Vāstu-Puruṣa Maṇḍala*

is the measure of all things": the figure of a person enclosed by a square is the basic pattern from which all temple architecture develops. "The gods are settled on the *vāstu-puruṣa.* The fight between the demons and the gods is over, for it is won conjointly. Every building activity means a renewed conquest of disintegration and at the same time a restitution of integrity so that the gods once more are the limbs of a single 'being', of Existence, at peace with itself."[22]

The pattern of a *vāstu-puruṣa maṇḍala* (Figure 20.2) is as follows. The center square (equal to 3 times 3 small squares) is occupied by Brahmā, who gave shape to the world. The inner ring is occupied by the main gods, the outer ring by the thirty-two minor gods, representing at the same time the lunar mansions so that the *vāstu-puruṣa maṇḍala* becomes the instrument to determine both the spatial and temporal components of temple construc-

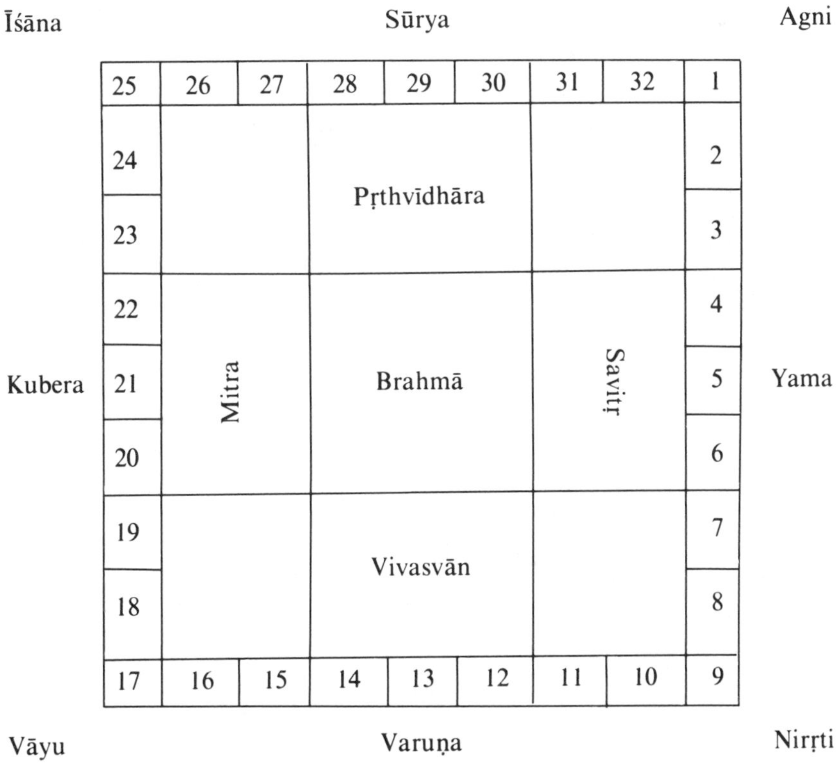

Figure 20.2 The Pattern of a *Vāstu-Puruṣa Maṇḍala*

30. Bhairava, Mahārāṣṭra, Heras Institute Bombay

31. Rādhā Mohan Temple, Vṛndāvan

tion. The gods in the corners and in the middle of each side of the square are the *digpāla*, the guardians of the cardinal points, determining the spatial orientation of the *maṇḍala*.[23]

The *vāstu-puruṣa maṇḍala* serves the town planner as well as the temple builder: ideally, the whole town is structured according to this cosmic model; within the town a certain area is reserved for the temple, which again is patterned according to the laws of the cosmos.[24] The dimensions and proportions of the temple to be built depend on an intricate system of calculations designed to bring the edifice within the framework determined by six prerequisites. Apart from achieving an aesthetically pleasing harmony of proportions among height, length, and width of the building, the actual dimensions must also express the caste of the builder, and the calculations must also determine the spatio-temporal position of the temple.[25] A good example of the application of this scheme is offered by the *Brahmeśvara* temple in Bhuvaneśvara.[26]

In South India, a slightly different ground plan is followed. The *padmagarbha maṇḍala* of the *Bṛhadeśvara* Temple at Tanjore (Figure 20.3) will illustrate these differences.

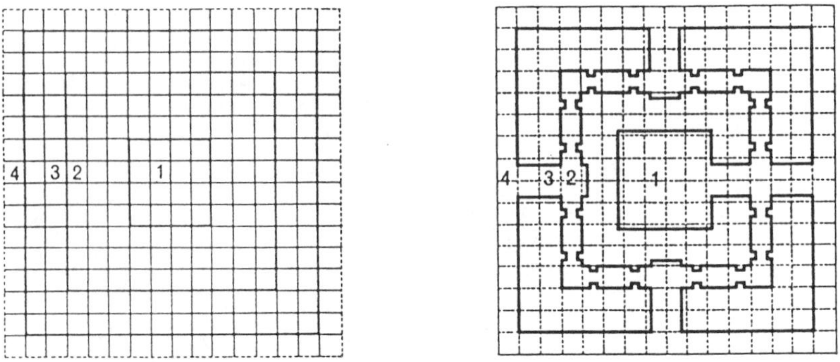

Figure 20.3 Diagram of *Padmagarbha Maṇḍala* of the *Bṛhadeśvara* Temple

1. Brahmā
2. Spheres of the gods
3. Sphere of humans
4. Sphere of demons

1. sanctuary (*garbha-gṛha*) with interior *pradakṣiṇā-patha*.
2. circumambulatory path (exterior *pradakṣiṇā-patha*).
3. circuit wall.
4. terrace.

The center and essence of the cosmos is Brahmā. It is surrounded by an inner ring, the world of the *devas*. Around these, another ring is formed by the world of humans. Still further removed, but within the realm of *jīvas*, and therefore of importance for all the other living beings, are the *asuras*. The *sthaṇḍila maṇḍala* which forms the model for the temple at Tanjore, consists of 16 times 16 fields: sixteen are occupied by the *Brahmā-sthāna*, identical with the *garbha-gṛha;* eighty-four by the world of the *devas*, identical with the *pradakṣiṇā patha;* ninety-six for the world of the humans, identical with the *prakāra*, the outer wall of the sanctuary. The ring of the *asuras*, occupying sixty fields, is situated outside the wall on the terrace that surrounds the temple. Later, the *maṇḍapas* and other shrines within the temple compound were added.

In a grandiose way, the original South Indian *sthaṇḍila maṇḍala* has been realized in the temple city of *Śrīraṅgam*.[27] The central sanctuary of Viṣṇu is surrounded by seven concentric walls, representing the outer spheres. Each wall is broken through at the four quarters. The pilgrims on their way to seeing the supreme have to pass through seven gates, topped by mighty *gopurams*, before reaching their goal. Within the outer enclosures, normal city life goes on: shops and coffee bars run along the huge walls. In the inner enclosures are *maṇḍapas*, places where the pilgrims can rest without being disturbed by worldly traffic. When passing through the last gate they first encounter the *garuḍa-stambha*, the roosting place of Viṣṇu's *vāhana*. Only then do they enter the sanctuary where Viṣṇu's image, representing the Lord of the World resting on Śeṣa, offers itself for worship.

Students of Indian temple architecture have developed a number of classifications for describing the various styles that have developed over the centuries in various parts of India. For details, the reader is referred to specialized works mentioned in the notes and bibliography.

Whereas the oldest extant temples show a basic pattern taken from profane or from Buddhist models, since the seventh century two definite Hindu styles developed, which were modified later in various regions: the so-called *nāgara*, or North Indian style, and the so-called *draviḍa*, or South Indian style.

One of the most interesting sights in India are the five *rathas*, monolithic temples at Mahabalipuram, not far from Madras on the sea coast. King Narasimhavarman apparently founded a school in which the architects and sculptors of his kingdom developed models for temples that would then be built in full size in different parts of the kingdom.[28] Besides imitations of Buddhist Caitya halls and existing wooden structures, the spatial realization of the *yantra*, as shown in the Dharmarāja *ratha*, became the most successful model for the further development of the *draviḍa* style.[29] It can be seen in the famous *Virūpākṣa* Temple at Paṭṭadakal, which in turn served as the model of the *Kailāsa* Temple at Ellora, carved out of the mountain on a previously unheard of scale. The most magnificent specimen of the *draviḍa* model, however, is the previously mentioned *Bṛhadeśvara* Temple at Tanjore: its tower is more than 200 feet tall, topped by a block of granite weighing 80 tons.[30] Situated in flat country, it can be seen from miles away. The *garbha-gṛha* houses the largest *liṅga* in any Indian temple.

The *nāgara* style seems to have developed from bamboo buildings, which gave to the towerlike *śikhara*, the most typical element of this style, its characteristic form. Originally, the *garbha-gṛha*, in the base of the *śikhara*, was the only structure of the North Indian temple; later a place was added for the worshippers to assemble, the *jagamohan* or *mukhaśāla*, also topped by a towerlike structure. In several instances, a *naṭamaṇḍira*, a dancing hall, and an *arthamaṇḍapa*, a place for the sacrificial offerings, were added as well.[31] Some of the best known examples of this style are the *Brahmeśvara* Temple at Bhuvaneśvara,[32] the *Khandārīya Mahādeva* Temple at Khajurāho,[33] and the Sun Temple at Konārkā,[34] all built between the ninth and the twelfth centuries C.E. An interesting fusion of the *nāgara* and the *draviḍa* styles, called *vesara* style, can be seen in the temples built in the thirteenth century by the later Cālukya rulers of Hoyśala in Belur, Halebid, and Somnāthpur.[35] Under Tantric influences, circular temples, imitating the *cakra*, were constructed in several parts of India.[36]

It goes without saying that these models neither exhaust the basic types of temples found in Hindu India nor do they reflect even in a minor way, the extraordinary richness of Indian temple architecture in every detail of the temple structure.[37]

Although Hindus are quite often also truly appreciative of the beauty of the temple, the most important reason for going to the temple is the *darśana* of the *mūrti:* an audience with God.[38]

Besides the chief image, installed in the *garbha-gṛha* of the main temple, the temples usually have a large number of minor images. The second most important is the processional image, the *utsava-bera*, often a replica of the *mūla-bera*, or fixed image. Though the ritual books prescribe the details of *mūrti-pūjā* very strictly, the impression an observer of Hindus worshipping the image in a temple gets is that of a rather informal and very personal style of cult. Some people throw money into the small enclosure where the image is kept, hoping to get a wish fulfilled; others prostrate before it, uttering prayers in a murmur or quite audibly; others again practice meditation with *yoga-āsanas*. People ring the bell before the image to rouse its attention. They get *tilakas* painted on their forehead by the *pūjāris*, receive small morsels of sweets or fruit as *prasāda*, sip holy water. Children play hide and seek, women chatter and giggle, letting their children touch the image. Sick people lie around waiting for a cure, others again sit in a corner and read holy books. At least three times a day, the priests offer worship according to the prescribed ritual, usually with a large crowd participating. Waving lights, ringing bells, and reciting hymns and *mantras* are common ingredients of this worship.

There is no formal obligation for Hindus to visit the temple, but hardly any Hindu will not go to the temple once in a while, and many make it a point to honor the lord through a daily visit and receive *prasāda* as a kind of communion and talisman against misfortune. Many of the larger temples have a fixed order of services, the timing of which can be learned from their notice boards. Temples built in our time often resemble Christian churches in their attempt to create a large hall where people congregate for common worship and regular religious instruction. In large cities, where Sunday is kept as a public holiday, those temples have begun to conduct regular Sunday services with sermons. The Birla temples, built by a member of perhaps the richest Hindu industrial family, in addition to the *maṇḍira*, possess *dharmaśālas* or hostels for pilgrims, parks for recreation, and many other facilities. The number and size of temples recently built or under construction is considerable—another sign of the vitality of Hinduism.

HINDU FESTIVALS

All temples have their feasts, which attract huge crowds. It may be as impossible to describe a Hindu temple festival to someone who has not seen it as it is to describe a surrealist painting to a blind person. The basic structure of the festival is quite simple. Usually, it is a procession in which the *mūrti* is taken through town. But what makes it such an interesting experience is *how* this is done. When the feast of a famous *mūrti* is coming near, many thousands of people gather days ahead. They camp along the roadside, squat together in picturesque groups, cook their curries and bake their *capātīs* on cow-dung fires, roam the streets loudly singing their religious songs—and wait for the great occasion. Usually, too, thousands of *sādhus*, of all denominations, flock together. *Yogis* demonstrate their tricks; all sorts of crippled and deformed people and animals are exhibited; lepers come from far away, sitting in a row on the roads leading to the temple. The streets are lined with peddlers of devotional articles and kitchen carts.

Finally, the great day arrives. If it is a large temple and a big festival, the procession is repeated several times, so as to give all who want to do so the chance to participate. Often a *ratha*, a processional chariot, several stories high, is used. It is a temple on wheels with the *mūrti* as its center. Pulled with thick ropes, often by hundreds of men, it moves along, swaying and creaking, quite often stopped by those whose task it is to keep it on its track. Richly caparisoned elephants, horses, and groups of *sādhus* in festive robes walk in front. Huge crowds move with the procession, throwing flowers, coins, and fruit into the chariot. A silver trumpet gives the sign to stop or to move on again. The *mūrti* is taken to a cooler place at the beginning of summer and returned to its temple when the heat abates or it is simply shown its realms: legally, the *mūrtis* of the big temples are the owners of the temple land, amounting very often to thousands of acres, besides possessing jewels and other valuables.

It is difficult to tell someone following the Western Gregorian calendar the dates of the great Hindu feasts. Apart from the various eras in which Hindus count their years (Vikram, Śaka, Gupta, Harṣa, etc.[39]), their year is slightly longer than the solar year and the months are lunar months, not coinciding with the Western divisions. Each lunar month is divided into a *kṛṣṇapakṣa* and a *śuklapakṣa*, a dark and a bright half, of fifteen *tithis* each; on these are based the dates of the feasts, which always coincide with certain phases of the moon. Usually, new moon and full moon are holidays and several days in between as well. Even a hired worker will not work on a holiday because that would bring ill luck.

The seven days of the week are connected with the planets and special *devatās: Ravivāra* is the day of the Sun; an auspicious day for beginning Vedic studies and journeys. *Somavāra*, the moon day, is consecrated to Śiva. It is auspicious for weddings and births; inauspicious for the purchase of clothing or a journey eastward. *Maṅgalavāra*, the day of Mars, is not auspicious for sowing, shaving, entering a new house, or journeys northward. Whatever is done on *Budhavāra*, Mercury day, brings double fruit; it is a good day for purchases and court cases. *Bṛhaspativāra* is named after the teacher of the *devas:* auspicious for the opening of schools; inauspicious for a journey southward. *Śukravāra* is sacred to Venus and a good day for buying land; inauspicious, however, for journeys westward. *Śanivāra*, the day of Saturn, is inauspicious for practically everything.

The right time is important for every undertaking. Its determination is in the hands of the *jyotiṣi*, the astrologer. In India, astrology is closely linked with scientific mathematics and calendar making. *Jyotiṣa* was cultivated as one of the *Vedāṅgas* from the earliest times to determine the right time for sacrifices; time, *kāla*, also formed one of the most important topics of speculation in the *Upaniṣads.* As the *Maitrī Upaniṣad* says:

> From time are all creatures produced. Through time they grow, through time they fade. There are indeed two kinds of *brahman:* time and timelessness. That which is prior to the sun is timeless, that which begins with the sun is time having parts; the year is the form of time with parts. All beings are produced by the year, they grow by the year and fade by the year. Therefore the year is

> *Prajāpati*, time, nourishment, *brahmā*'s dwelling and *ātman*. It is said: "Time cooks all things in *paramātman*. He who knows in what time is cooked, he is the knower of the *Veda*."[40]

The need to find the right *kairós* is theologically supported by the Vaiṣṇava theory that Viṣṇu's grace waxes and wanes like the moon: he has times of *anugraha* or attraction, and of *nigraha* or rejection. One must seek him when he is "full of grace."[41] As the divine becomes spatially available in the *mūrti*, according to its own will and decision, so it determines its temporal availability in the *utsava*, the feast celebrated at the auspicious and revealed time. Since Hinduism is still very much a cosmic religion, despite its superstructure of mytho-history, the essence of time must be found in the interaction of all the cosmic bodies. Fixing the right time for a religious action depends as little on the will of human beings as does the time for the ripening of a fruit or the course of the year. Grace and merit are insolubly and divinely linked with time. Therefore, it is essential to know about the auspicious time; the astrologer, conversant with the movement of the celestial bodies and their various influences, is indispensable for the average Hindu in all important situations. In many families, the competent *paṇḍit* will draw a child's horoscope immediately after birth; and all the important occasions in the child's life will be determined according to it. There will be very few Hindu weddings for which the astrologer has not selected the *muhūrta*, the auspicious hour, when the marriage is being solemnized.

Public festivals are also determined by the "right time," celebrated at such junctures as to ensure the full benefit of grace to those who participate it it. It is meaningless to try to enumerate all the Hindu festivals.[42] Apart from the more or less universal ones, there are countless local feasts; catalogues count more than a thousand, enough to demonstrate that no Hindu can practice all of Hinduism.

Kṛṣṇajayānti, celebrated all over India, falls on the eighth *kṛṣṇapakṣa* of *Śrāvaṇa:* Kṛṣṇa's birth is celebrated at midnight, after a day of fasting. Midnight is the exact hour in which he was born in the *bandhagṛha*, the prison house, at Mathurā. Through his birth he manifested this hour to be the most auspicious—and so it is.[43]

Rakhi bandhan, on the full-moon day of the same month, has a more social character: girls tie colored threads round their brothers' wrists and make them their protectors, receiving a small gift in return. According to a legend, Indra was saved from the demon Bali through the magical armlet that his wife had tied for him. On this day, Brahmins also usually renew their *janëus*.

Ganeṣa catūrthi is celebrated on the fourth *śuklapakṣa* of *Bhadra;*

32. The Yamunā at Mathurā

business people and students place their books before the image, artisans implore Ganeṣa's blessing upon their tools.

Dassera, in the first half of *Aśvina* is celebrated all over India as a holiday season. It is a string of festivals during the most beautiful time of the year, after the monsoon. The great heat of summer is broken by then and the sun sparkles in a radiantly blue sky. The first nine days, *navarātri* are also the time for *Durgā-pūjā*, the greatest festival of Bengal. The *pūjā* is not limited to the Great Mother: taxi drivers decorate their cars, farmers their cows, and factory workers their machines and perform *pūjā* before them; all worship that by which they live. On the tenth day, the victory of Rāma and his monkey allies over Rāvaṇa is celebrated.

Another series of festivals is connected with *Divālī*, also called *Dīpāvalī*, the feast of the lamps, in the second half of *Aśvina*. Countless little oil lamps, on houses and temples and along the rivers and roads, softly illuminate the darkness of the star-studded tropical sky—a sight which no one who has seen it could ever forget and which every Hindu living abroad remembers nostalgically.

Feasts like the commemoration of Prahlāda's rescue by Nṛsinha, or *Vāmana Dvādaśī*, are celebrated only by small groups.

Nāgapañcamī is still quite popular, especially in the South, where many people regularly feed the cobras in the house with milk, worshipping them as guardians.

At the winter solstice, a kind of harvest festival is celebrated in the North Indian countryside. In February, *vasant*, "spring," is greeted by women and children wearing bright yellow dresses, the color of the *dāl* that flowers at this time.

Śivarātri, on the thirteenth *kṛṣṇapakṣa* in *Magha*, is about as widespread as Kṛṣṇa's birthday. It is the principal feast of the Śaivas and also celebrated by Vaiṣṇavas for whom Śiva is Viṣṇu's first devotee and servant. The *liṅga* is decorated and painted for the occasion, bathed in honey and milk.[44]

Holi, in *śuklapakṣa* of *Phalguṇa*, has much in common with the Western carnival. It is New Year's day for many Hindus, celebrated with gaiety and abandon. According to temperament and upbringing, the festivities are funny to rough. In better circles, people are content to sprinkle each other with colored water and red powder; less civil big and small boys shout indecent words after people and throw dirt from the gutters on everyone. One legend explains the feast thus. Once upon a time there lived a demoness named Holikā who ate a child every day; the place where she had her dwelling had developed a system so that the burden was distributed evenly. One day, the lot fell on a poor widow's only son. A good *sādhu*, seeing the woman's sorrow and despair, advised to gather all the children of the place and receive Holikā with a cannonade of filthy abuse. The advice was followed and Holikā was sensitive enough to die of shame and anger.

These are just a few examples of Hindu festivals that occupy such a prominent place in the life of the ordinary Hindu, even today.

THE IMPORTANCE OF PILGRIMAGE: *TĪRTHA*

As the supreme becomes concretized in space and time through images and festivals, so his grace becomes localized at the *tīrthas* forever, intensified at certain times but always available to the pilgrim.[45] There are thousands of recognized *tīrthas* in India, and millions of Hindus are constantly on pilgrimage. Numerous *saṁnyāsis* spend their lives wandering from one *tīrtha* to another, the most meritorious way of utilizing one's time. Just as worldly globetrotters boast of the many countries and cities they have visited, so one can find *sādhus* competing with each other in enumerating the *tīrthas* visited by each. Places of pilgrimage are not made; they are found. They are what they are by divine manifestation not by human arrangement.

A complex set of rules surrounds the important undertaking of the pilgrimage: fasting, worship of Gaṇeśa, and continence are required before departure; for the pilgrimage itself a certain mode of clothing is prescribed, a copper ring and a brass vessel. Tonsure before or after pilgrimage is still quite common. Ideally, the pilgrim should walk the whole distance; today, most Hindus take public transportation or private cars to the places of grace. Of importance is the *saṁkalpa*, the explicit declaration of intention to undertake a pilgrimage to a certain place. Pilgrimage by proxy is also possible; the *śāstras* lay down in detail what percentage of the merit accrues to the donor and to his or her parents or guru. The rivers are great streams of grace in India; most of the famous *tīrthas*, literally "fords," are situated on the banks of the rivers. All the *tīrthas* have *māhātmyas*, praises of their greatness, sometimes of book length, enumerating all the sacred spots and the merits attached to visits.[46]

Mother Gaṅgā is the first among India's holy rivers, sacred from where she flows through such famous *tīrthas* as Haridvāra, Prayāga, and Kāśī till she reaches the estuary in the Bay of Bengal. The Gaṅgā is considered the supreme *tīrtha* in this *Kaliyuga.* Already, the utterance of her name is supposed to cleanse the sinner and a bath in the Gaṅgā or a drink of her water, said not to putrefy, purifies the families for seven generations back. As long as even a fraction of the bones of a person are lying in the Gaṅgā or touching Gaṅgā water, the deceased person can remain in heaven. Pilgrims carry small bottles of Ganges water home to use it on many occasions; even years later, it is supposed to be fresh and unspoiled.

The three main *tīrthas* on the Gaṅgā, called *tristhalī*, are considered to be superior to any other places in the world. They are Prayāga, renamed Allahābad by the Muslims, on the confluence of Gaṅgā, Yamunā, and the invisible Sarasvatī rivers; Gāyā, sacred also to the Buddhists as Bodhgāyā, the place of enlightenment of Gautama; and Kāśī, also called Vārāṇasī (anglicized into Benares) and for some time renamed Mohammadābad by the Muslim rulers. One of the maxims of pilgrims goes: "One should shave one's head in Prayāga, offer *piṇḍas* in Gāyā, give presents in Kurukṣetra, and end one's life at Kāśī," continuing: "Why offer *piṇḍas* in Gāyā, why die in Kāśī, when one has shaved one's head at Prayāga?"

A question much discussed in the ancient *śāstras* and among Hindu *sādhus* even today is that of religious suicide.[47] For hundreds of years, quite a few famous *tīrthas* were the final goal of many pilgrims, who took their lives there in order to break away from the cycle of rebirths. Generally, Hinduism considers suicide a crime leading to miserable rebirths, but at certain places, it can become the supreme act of liberation. The *śāstras* mention several famous precedents and the *Purāṇas* are definite that whosoever dies in Prayāga, be it naturally or through his or her own hand, is sure to obtain *mokṣa*. Four methods of ending one's life were considered legitimate: burning oneself in a fire fed with dried cow dung; drowning oneself by hanging head downwards in the Gaṅgā; disappearing in the waters where Gaṅgā and Yamunā meet; and cutting off one's flesh to feed the birds. Only a few years ago, a popular Hindu magazine, in an appeal for the ban of cow slaughter, wrote: "Starving oneself to death in a religious cause like the protection of cows is a sort of penance. In the *sanātana dharma* such fasts are recommended as *pāraka* and *sāṅtapana*."[48]

The most famous of all holy cities in India is Kāśī. Although it is first and foremost the holy place of Śiva, who as lord of Kāśī resides in the Golden Temple, all sects, including the Buddhists, consider it a place of pilgrimage. The city must be extremely old, and archeological excavations should reveal much more than has been known so far about this interesting place.[49] The praise showered upon Benares surpasses everything that has been said about other eternal cities of the world. In the *Matsya Purāṇa*, Śiva says:

> Vārāṇasī is always my most secret place; the cause of liberation for all creatures. All sins which a man may have accumulated in thousands of previous lives disappear as soon as he enters Avimuktā. Brahmins, Kṣatriyas, Vaiṣyas, and Śūdras, people of mixed castes, worms, *mlecchas* and other casteless people, insects, ants, birds, all mortal beings find bliss in my auspicious city.

Even today, many old people settle down in Benares toward the end of their lives, others are taken there when dying. One funeral procession after another treks through the narrow lanes of this holy place, and funeral pyres burn constantly at the Maṇikarṇikā *ghāṭ*, which may mark the oldest site of an ancient Āryan settlement. Benares is filled with a peculiar atmosphere: death and life, piety and cynicism, asceticism and abandon, learning and superstition side by side; an illustration of the lord of Kāśī who dispenses grace and terror.[50]

Benares suffered greatly under Muslim rule. Its temples were destroyed repeatedly and what we see today has been rebuilt only since the eighteenth century. Before the Muslim invasion, Benares must have been a splendid city with thousands of temples and sanctuaries. The *liṅgā* of the Viśvanātha Temple is said to have been saved from the invader's fury and reinstalled in its old place, which is now partly occupied by a mosque. Many miraculous cures are said to have happened to people who touched this embodiment of the Lord of the Universe.

For many centuries, Benares has also been the seat of Hindu scholarship, and even today, almost every school and sect has an establishment at Benares. Benares was chosen as the seat of the Hindu University, toward whose foundation the theosophist Madame Besant also contributed her own college. It is also the seat of the Sanskrit University, founded in 1791 by the British Resident Jonathan Duncan, "primarily with a view to appease the restive citizens of Vārāṇasī after the siege of Chet Singh's fort and secondarily to collect ancient texts and carry out research on them and to produce *paṇḍits* who could be readily available to assist the English judges for the correct interpretations of the Hindu personal law."[51] A number of famous Indian and Western scholars taught at this institution, which even now conducts most of its classes in Sanskrit.

Benares is not the only holy city nor the only center of Hindu learning; there are thousands of *tīrthas* and dozens of places famous for scholarship. All of them convey the unique atmosphere of Hinduism, of the supreme being present in different ways and forms in places, images, and temples, approachable at certain times and distributing grace to those who are watchful enough not to miss the occasion of its appearance and to recognize it under its manifold guises.[52]

33. A *ghāṭ* on the Yamunā in Mathurā

21. The Hindu Social Order: *Caturvarṇāśramadharma*

In order to protect this universe He, the most resplendent One, assigned different occupations and duties to those who originated from His mouth, arms, thighs and feet.

—Manusmṛti *I, 87*

CASTE[1] HAS BEEN seen as an essential institution of Hinduism from the very beginning, both by Hindus and by outsiders. A great many studies have been devoted to this phenomenon, either in its entirety or to particular aspects of it. As L. Dumont observed:[2]

> It has often been said that membership in Hinduism is essentially defined as the observance of caste rules and respect for the Brahman. T. Parsons, following Max Weber, is categoric: "Hinduism as a religion is but an aspect of this social system, with no independent status apart from it" (*The Structure of Social Action*, p. 557). More subtle is the following judgement: "In some regards, it [Hinduism] is inseparable from philosophic speculation; in others, it is inseparable from social life." (L. Renou, *L'Hindouisme*, Paris 1951, p. 28).

The historic development and the theory of caste has been expertly described and analyzed in such classics as H. Hutton's *Caste in India*[3] and more recently in L. Dumont's *Homo Hierarchicus*.[4] It has been both defended as the best and most natural functional division of society, a model for the whole world, and attacked as the root of all evil and socio-economic backwardness.

Whatever one's judgement may be, there is no doubt that caste has shaped Indian society throughout the last several thousands of years and that it is still of large practical significance. R. Inden rightly warns against isolating caste from the context of Indian civilization, "substantializing" it and in general conceiving of it as "India's essential institution . . . both the cause and effect of India's low level of political and economic 'development' and of its repeated failure to prevent its conquest by outsiders."[5] Caste in India has lost much of its economic importance, but it has gained immensely in political significance during the past few decades. In contrast to a process of fission, which produced more and more subcastes, who for one reason or another had separated from the major body, a process of fusion has recently been noticed. Clusters of castes unite behind a political candidate, who in turn becomes their spokesman and representative.

These developments have enormous practical consequences that we cannot fully explore in the context of this book. However, it should be clearly understood that (1) the caste structure of Hinduism is much more flexible in many more ways than previously assumed; and (*2*) the meaning of caste in India has changed, but its importance is not diminished.

THE FOUR ORIGINAL CASTES: *CATURVARṆA*

The origin of the caste structure, in the most ancient works is associated with the very act of creation. The *puruṣa-sūkta* of the *Ṛg Veda*[6] dramatically explains the origin of humankind out of the sacrifice of the primaeval *puruṣa* and his dismemberment: out of his mouth originated the *Brahmins*, from his chest came the *kṣatriyas*, from his belly issued the *vaiśyas*, and from his feet the *śūdras*. From as far back as we know, the division of *varṇas*, and later the division of *jātis*, as based upon this, had multiple aspects: the very name *varṇa*, "color" suggests a differentiation between fairer- and darker-skinned people. On the whole, Brahmins even today have a lighter skin color than *śūdras*. As the ordinances of Manu imply, the division was also occupational. The *Brahmins*, as custodians of ritual and sacred word, were to be the teachers and advisors of society. The *kṣatriyas*, as defenders and warriors, were to be the kings and administrators. The *vaiśyas*, composed of farmers and merchants, were the backbone of the economy, the middle class, to introduce a modern term. The *śūdras* were to be the large mass of virtually unpropertied laborers, a class of servants and menials.

The *caturvarṇa* system also embodied a religious hierarchy; combined with the universally accepted dogma of *karma*, it implied merit. Brahmins were born into the highest caste on account of *karma* accumulated over past lives. Lesser *karma* resulted in lower births. Birth as a *śūdra* was designed to atone for sins past. The three upper castes were eligible for initiation and the other *saṁskāras*. They had a degree of purity not to be attained by the *śūdras*. Within the *dvijātis*, the twice-born, again a hierarchy

34. Memorial for *satī*

obtained that was important in the regulation of intermarriage and commensality: on principle, the higher caste was purer and the lower caste member could accept food from a higher without incurring pollution.[7]

In practice, the system is much more complicated and beset with, what appears, like contradictory regulations. In the end, there were more than 3000 *jātis*, arranged hierarchically within the four *varṇas*, regionally diverse. Different locales sometimes follow different ranking and observe different traditions, not always in line with what would follow logically from the *caturvarṇa* scheme which should caution any observer not to draw conclusions too hastily from a superficial knowledge of the principle of how caste works. A number of detailed studies of caste ranking in specific villages or studies of *jātis* (subcastes) over a region can provide some understanding of the intricacies of caste in India.[8]

Every observer of Indian life will attest to the immense importance of caste and caste rules in present independent India. It is not true, as many outsiders believe, that the constitution of the Republic of India abolished caste or intended to. It abolished the notion of "outcasts" and made it a punishable offence to disadvantage a person because of such a status.[9] Within political parties, professional groups, municipalities, in social and economic life, in education, and in government service, caste has remained an important fact of life.

Though, theoretically, the position of one's caste is determined by birth (otherwise it would be meaningless to speak of *svadharma*), a certain upward mobility is found throughout history, as well as the down grading as result of certain offences. Quite a number of *ādivāsis*, the aboriginals of India, have been made Hindus by being associated with one of the three lower castes. According to Indian tradition, Candragupta, the founder of the Maurya dynasty, was a *śūdra* who rose to the rank of a *kṣatriya*.

Many Mahratta princes came from low castes and were helped by Brahmin experts to reconstruct their family tree in such a way as to show *kṣatriya* ancestry, often claiming Rāma as their ancestor. In our own time, quite a number of people from the lower castes have risen to prominence in administration and education. Still, the Brahmins defend their exclusivity: only those who are born Brahmins, are Brahmins; nobody can become a Brahmin. There is a curious ancient tale about King Viśvamitra, a *kṣatriya* who underwent extremely hard *tapasya* in order to compel Brahmā, the creator, to make him a Brahmin. Brahmins, however, contended that not even Brahmā can change someone not born a Brahmin into a Brahmin.

L. Dumont, attempting a structuralist interpretation of the institution of caste comes to the following conclusion:[10]

First Hocart, and still more precisely than Hocart, Dumézil have shown that the hierarchical enumeration of the four *varṇas* was based on a series of oppositions, the principle of which was religious. [Dumont refers here to G. Dumézil's *Mitra-Varuṇa*, Paris: 1940; and A. M. Hocart, *Caste: A Comparative Study*, New York: Russell 1950.] The first three classes, respectively priests, princes and herdsmen-husbandmen, are taken together as twiceborn or as those bestowing gifts, offering sacrifices and studying [the Veda] as opposed to the fourth class, the *śūdra*, who are devoid of any direct relation to religion, and whose sole task is to serve the former without envy. (*Manu* I, 88-91) Among the three kinds of twiceborn, the first two are opposed to the third, for to the latter the lord of creatures has made over only the cattle, to the former all creatures. It is worth noting that this particular opposition is the least frequent of all in the texts. On the contrary, the solidarity of the first two categories, priests and princes, vis-á-vis the rest, and at the same time their distinction and their relative hierarchy are abundantly documented from the *Brāhmaṇas* onward.

THE FOUR STAGES OF LIFE: *CATURĀŚRAMA*

Hindus possess an irresistible urge to classify and organize everything into neat and logical patterns. The number four serves not only to classify the Veda (into four *saṁhitās* and into four classes of books, considered Veda in the wider sense) and to divide humanity into basic sections but also to structure the life of individuals themselves. The successive stages of life of a high-caste person was correlated to another tetrad, the *caturvarga* or the "four aims of life" (*puruṣārtha*): *dharma* (moral law), *artha* (material goods), *kāma* (enjoyment), and *mokṣa* (liberation).[11] During studenthood (*brahmacarya*), the first stage in the life of (mostly) Brahmins—normally about 12 years, beginning after initiation (*upanayana*)—the young Brahmin, in the family of his perceptor, would learn the sacred texts, acquire the necessary skills for the ritual function, get grounded in discipline, and receive his preparation for his future life. The classical writings from the *Upaniṣads* onward are full of descriptions of *āśramas*, training schools for Brahmins, and the routine followed there. The young novice was supposed to serve his teacher in many practical ways in return for what he was taught. Normally, the stage of *brahmacarya* would terminate with the marriage of the student, whereupon he entered the second stage of his life, *gṛhastya*, the life of a householder. This stage is devoted to the enjoyment of life and to the duties associated with the care for a family: the acquisition of *artha*, material wealth. When his children grew to adulthood, or as one text describes it, when his temples started greying, the householder was supposed to hand over his worldly business to his sons and retire to spiritual pursuits.

The term used is *vānaprasthya*, life in the forest. Older literature describes how an elderly couple should set up house outside the village and its bustle and devote themselves to *mokṣa*, liberation, in preparation for the end of life. Ideally, this stage should be followed by an even more radical renunciation—*saṁnyāsa*, the life of a homeless ascetic, who possesses nothing and desires nothing but liberation from the body.[12]

While not all Hindus would follow this sequence of stages in their lives, the structure that the *caturāśrama* scheme suggests and the interests to be pursued according to the *caturvarga* scheme, certainly have deeply influenced the personal and social history of Hindus and Hinduism. Its structure apparently reflects so well what Hindus understand to be the essence of Hinduism that R. N. Dandeker chose it as the schema for his representation of Hinduism in the influential *Sources of Indian Tradition.*[13]

It also appeals to contemporary Hindus, who believe it to have great practical value and to provide orientation to today's India. As Dindayal Upadhyaya, then general secretary of the Bhāratīya Jana Sangh, wrote in 1961: "The ideal of the Hindu life on the basis of the four-fold *puruṣārthas—dharma, artha, kāma and mokṣa*—can take us out of the morass. Hinduism and not socialism is the answer to the world's problems. It alone looks at life as a whole and not in bits."[14]

THE CONTEST BETWEEN *BRAHMINS* AND *KṢATRIYAS*

In many civilizations, we have the phenomenon that the holders of intellectual and spiritual power and those who wield economic and political power vie with each other for supremacy and that this contest, supported by historical and legal arguments on both sides, often breaks out in open rivalry. Hinduism is no exception.

Throughout the history of Hindu India, there has been a contest of supremacy between *Brahmins* and *kṣatriyas*, the religious and the secular powers.[15] Depending on the viewpoint, therefore, Hindu theories of society and state emphasize one or the other as the sovereign power, arriving at quite different schemes of the ideal society.

In a somewhat simplified manner, we may say that the*dharmaśāstra* tradition in classical Hindu literature represents the typical *Brahmin* view of society, whereas the *kṣatriya* views are expressed in the *ārthaśāstra* literature; the very terms express the direction of thought.

The *Manusmṛti*, again a Brahmanic text, takes for granted the division of society into the four *varṇas* and elevates the Brahmin to the position of the preserver and protector of the universe by means of the sacrifice:

> The very birth of a Brahmin is an eternal embodiment of *dharma*; for he is born to fulfill *dharma* and worthy to become *Brahman*. He is born as the highest on earth, the lord of all created beings, for the protection of the treasure of *dharma*. Whatever exists in this world is the property of the Brahmin; on account of the excellence of his origin the Brahmin is entitled to it all. The Brahmin eats but his own food, wears but his own apparel, bestows but his own in alms; other mortals subsist through the benevolence of the *Brāhmaṇa*.[16]

The duties of all the *varṇas* are spelled out in such a way as to strengthen the authority of the Brahmin. The *Brahmins* are to study and to teach the Veda, to sacrifice for themselves and for others, to give and to accept alms. The *kṣatriyas* are to protect the people by means of their arms and to offer gifts to Brahmins. The *vaiṣyas* must tend cattle and devote themselves to agriculture and make gifts to the Brahmins, besides engaging in trade and money lending. The *śūdras* are to serve the three upper classes. This Brahmin's view of society is also repeated in other works. In the *Mahābhārata* and the *Purāṇas*, we find contemporary reflections and a contemplation of the evils of the present age, the *Kaliyuga*, whose corruption consists mainly in the abandonment of the duties of castes, as contained in the brahmanic codes. The need to fulfill *svadharma*, to stick to one's caste duties irrespective of the immediate consequences, for the sake of the world order, is also the central message of the *Bhagavadgītā*.[17]

From the time of Gautama Buddha to the contemporary Draviḍa Munnetra Kazhagam (DMK),[18] anti-Brahmin movements have tried to undermine the claim of the Brahmins to leadership by exposing their theories of superiority as fallacious. Despite all these efforts, the Brahmins have continued to enjoy the most respected positions in society, not only because people in India believe the Brahmin's version of religion but also because of their overall intellectual and educational superiority.

Evidently, quite a number of the ruling *kṣatriyas* in ancient times considered themselves to be superior to the Brahmins. Not only did they possess the actual political power but they also had a theoretical framework that founded this superiority on the divine institution of kingship.[19] All the ancient accounts agree in describing the original political constitution of humankind as close to what we would call today democratic or republican. As the *Mahābhārata* has it:

> Neither kingship nor king was there in the beginning, neither scepter[20] nor the bearer of a scepter. All people protected each other by means of *dharma*. After some time they became lax in it[21] and were overcome by *moha*, a state of mind in which they lost their sense of righteousness. As a consequence of this, *lobha*, greed, developed and desire for each other's property. Then *kāma*, lust, overcame them, along with attachment to things that should be avoided, and

> general moral decay set in. The *devas* in their distress approached Viṣṇu who brought forth from his mind Virajas who became the first king.[22]

According to this *kṣatriya* version of the origin of kingship, the king does not need Brahmin sanction but is divinely appointed. According to the Brahmin's account, he becomes king effectively only through the Brahmin's consecration. That Brahmins did exert considerable influence over the appointment of kings and also their eventual removal, if necessary by violent means, is amply borne out by Indian history. The *Purāṇas* contain an account of a regicide perpetrated by Brahmins, which must have a historical core. Vena, a mythical king, proclaimed himself supreme lord and forbade sacrifices and donations to Brahmins.[23] The *ṛṣis* sent a delegation to him, which politely but strongly urged him to rescind his edict and to restore the rights of the Brahmins "for the preservation of your kingdom and your life and for the benefit of all your subjects." Vena refused to acknowledge anyone superior to himself and maintained the thesis that the king, a *kṣatriya*, is the embodiment of all divinities and, therefore, the supreme being. The first duty also of the Brahmins, he explained, is to obey the king.

The text proceeds: "Then those pious men were filled with wrath and cried out to each other: 'Let this wicked wretch be slain. This impious man who has reviled the Lord of sacrifice is not fit to reign over the earth'. And they fell upon the king, and beat him with blades of holy grass, consecrated by *mantras* and slew him, who had first been destroyed by his impiety towards God." Down with the "wicked king" also meant an end to the firm hand needed to deal with the unruly, and universal chaos broke out, leaving the people at the mercy of large bands of marauders and robbers. Thus, the Brahmins were forced to find another king.

Apparently there were two contenders. According to the story, they arose through the activity of the Brahmins, who rubbed or drilled the right thigh and the right arm of the dead king; thus alluding perhaps to their castes.[24] They rejected Niṣāda and accepted Pṛthu, on whom they conferred universal dominion and who accepted and confirmed the Brahmins' demands and superiority. For the writers of this story, the beginning of true kingship dates from Pṛthu, the Brahmin-appointed ruler, "a speaker of truth, bounteous, an observer of his promises, wise, benevolent, patient, valiant, and a terror to the wicked, knowing his duties, compassionate and with a kind voice, respecting the worthy, performing sacrifices and worshipping Brahmins."[25] The prosperity of his rule is ascribed to his orthodoxy and his submission under the Brahmin's *dharma*. To drive the point of their story home to all, the very name of the earth, *pṛthvī*, is associated with this king, the first to be appointed by Brahmins and in their eyes the first who really and rightfully bore the title *rāja.*

In a different, and perhaps more historical context, the name of India, Bhārata, is associated with king Bharata, the son of Ṛṣabha, who is praised as virtuous and who in recognition of his merits was later reborn as a Brahmin, revealing again the Brahmin claim to superiority over the *kṣatriyas.*

Throughout Indian history, state and religion lived in a symbiotic alliance, more or less happy according to the circumstances and persons involved. The Brahmins served as counsellors and advisors, developing a complex *rājadharma* designed to combine the exigencies of statecraft with brahmanic ideology.[26] In the Brahmins' view, *dharma* was the central point and the source of political power and economic prosperity; in the *kṣatriyas'* opinion, *artha*, statecraft, political power and economic strength, were the basis of *dharma.*

The *ārthaśāstra* works, therefore, are treatises recommending *Realpolitik*, utilizing, if necessary, religious beliefs and customs to strengthen the king's position. Most of these manuals are lost and we know about them only from quotations. The *Kautilīya Ārthaśāstra*, whose full text was recovered and published in 1905 by R. Shamasastry and translated into English ten years later and which is, according to its testimony, a compendium of all its predecessors, gives a fairly typical picture of the style and contents of this type of literature. Ancient Indian tradition identifies Kautilya with Cānakya or Viṣṇugupta, the minister of Candragupta Maurya.[27] Some Western scholars have expressed doubts about this dating and would place the work around the fourth century *C.E.* Historically, Kautilya's work is of great interest, as it gives us a fairly realistic idea of the life in ancient India, of the working of the Mauryan administration, and the economic and social conditions before Aśoka. Not content with wise maxims and theological principles, as are the authors of *dharmaśāstra*, Kautilya offers precise instructions of a very concrete nature concerning all aspects of government. The lip-service he pays to *dharma* in the introductory pages is completely overwhelmed by Machiavellian schemes, designed to make the king an absolute monarch and the state he serves the most powerful one around. *Varta* and *daṇḍa*, economy and law enforcement, constitute the two pillars of the king's power.

However powerful the king's position may be in Kautilya's scheme, he is but one of the elements of the state. The real theme of *arthaśāstra* is the absolutism of the empire; the actual emperor can be exchanged as any other functionary. "The king, the ministers, the country, the fort, the treasury, the army, the friend and the enemy are the elements of sovereignty." These depend so much on each other thay they can stand or fall only together, and the king should never make the fatal mistake of thinking of himself as being the state! Kautilya's ideal ruler is equally removed from any type of altruistic dedication and the world-saving fanaticism of a religious autocrat as he is from the cynicism and power play of a modern self-made dictator.[28] Kautilya demands that the ruler be educated and really competent in the art of ruling a country. In many ways, the *Ārthaśāstra*'s approach may shock a modern democrat, but we must not forget that this book was not supposed to be read by the common man, who is told to follow his traditional *dharma.* It is a royal art—the art of being master. Success in power politics, as history teaches us, does not depend on sensitivity and piety but on determined ruthlessness to acquire power, keep it, and increase it—that is *artha.*[29]

In a broader classification, Kautilya describes his work as belonging to *rāja-nīti. Nīti* is often translated as "ethics"; though the associations most of us have with the term *ethics* would not necessarily coincide with what has just been described. *Nīti* is the art of surviving in a world of enemies, thriving on the folly of others, and making the best out of a given situation.

The Muslim invasion and occupation, the British rule, and modernity in general have made their inroads into Hindu society, for better and for worse. The basic caste structure[30] is still remarkably strong in many areas of life. Though social reformers have attacked it for almost two centuries as the major cause of all social and economic ills in India, it has provided large sections of the population with a minimum of social security and status in society and it also has deep emotional roots that cannot be severed easily without doing great harm.

Much has been written on "tradition and modernity in India" from the sociological viewpoint, and for everyone with even a cursory acquaintance with India, it is clear that Indian society has enormous problems to contend with, problems arising largely out of India's history and not amenable to modern Western solutions (if there are such!). A. D. Moddie, a modern Indian, has written a thoughtful book, *The Brahmanical Culture and Modernity*,[31] in which he analyzes the situation in quite an original way. He writes

> If any country had the problem of two cultures in a bad way, with the leaden weight of dead history and an archaic society behind it, it is India. But here the split is not between anything as simple, as purely intellectual as the literary and the scientific. It is deep and sociological and historical: it is more than an intellectual gap between two quite different types of minds.

He goes on to define the attributes of the brahmanic culture as traditional, caste dominated, hierarchical, authoritarian, village and land based, status oriented, inherently averse to change, essentially undemocratic, accepting as law, life, and reality what is written in the *patra*, the authoritative book.

In contrast to this, the modern, industrial culture is essentially international, not village or caste based in its social motivations, scientific, rational, achievement oriented, with a mobile elite of intellect, skills, and wealth, making material advancement its major objective. Whereas Moddie quite frankly sides with modernity,[32] others, seeing the same dilemma facing Hindu society, try to return to pure Hinduism as the only hope for India's future. Mahātmā Gāndhī's aversion to modern technology and scientific progress had at its source a concern for the masses, who would be left without work and without a frame of moral rules if industrialization and the impersonal, exclusively profit-oriented mentality that goes with it, were to take over in India. Deeper down, however, Gāndhī also felt a concern for Hinduism as a way of life and a religion, which he saw threatened and which he treasured and wanted to see preserved.

THE SHADOW OF THE *CATURVARṆĀŚRAMA* IDEAL: THE OUTCASTES

Theoretical and theological, the *caturvarṇāśrama* scheme may have been but it also translated into Indian reality, so that socially, and quite often also economically and physically, nobody could survive outside his or her caste. Basically, the Brahmins did not develop "human rights" but "caste-rights," which had the side effect that, in the course of time, about one-fifth of the total population, as "outcastes", had virtually no rights. They were treated worse than cattle, which even in legal theory ranked above them.[33] People became casteless by violating the rules of their castes, either by marrying contrary to the caste regulations, by following professions not allowed by caste rules, or by committing other acts that were punished by expulsion from the caste. Some books give them the appellation "fifth caste," but that may leave a wrong impression. They were cut off from all the rights and privileges that caste society extended to its members, ritually impure and ostensibly the product of bad *karma* coming to fruition.

A notorious example of the distance that Brahmins put between themselves and the outcastes was offered by the Nambudiris of Keralā. Whenever a Nambudiri left his house, a Nayar had to precede him to proclaim that the great lord was about to come. All outcastes had to hide, the mere sight of them would make a Nambudiri unclean. If, by any accident, the shadow of a *paria* fell upon a Nambudiri, he had to undergo lengthy purificatory ceremonies. Though the Indian constitution has abolished untouchability, it is still an unpleasant reality in the lives and minds of many Hindus even today. In the villages, the former untouchables still usually live in secluded quarters, do the dirtiest work, and are not allowed to use the village well and other common facilities.[34] The government tries to help them through privileges in schools and offices, but these are often eyed with jealousy and suspicion by the caste Hindus. Mahātmā Gāndhī fought for their rights, especially the right to enter Hindu temples (quite often they are still refused admission!), calling them *Harijan*, God's people. But even he wanted to maintain the caste structure and was extremely angry with Dr. Ambedkar, the leader of the outcastes, who severed all ties with caste society by turning Buddhist and drawing some 3 million of his followers with him.[35] The casteism of the outcastes, however, is highlighted by the fact that, despised and humiliated as they are, they have established among themselves a caste structure analogous to the *caturvarṇa* system and jealousy observe their own ranking within it.

It will have become clear that religion and what we call today politics are very closely allied in Indian society. In modern times, a quite articulate political Hinduism has arisen, and Hindu political parties and organizations have emerged.

22. The Professional Religious: *Saṁnyāsa*

He, who having cut off all desires with the sword of knowledge, boards this boat of Knowledge Supreme and crosses this ocean of relative existence, thereby attaining the Supreme Abode—he indeed is blessed.

—*Śaṅkarācārya*, Vijñānanauka *10*

THE VEDIC SYSTEM of the *caturvarṇāśrama* singled out one of the four great sections of society for professionally practicing religion: studying and teaching the Veda and performing sacrifices for themselves and for others was defined as the foremost social duty of Brahmins.[1] In the course of their individual lives, too, a progressive spiritualization was provided for. After the period of *brahmacarya*, youth spent in studying with a guru, and after the period of *gṛhastya*, family life devoted to fulfilling the duties enjoined by scriptures and offering sacrifices for the benefit of *devas, pitṛs*, and men, the Brahmin was supposed to become a *vānaprastha*, a forest hermit practicing meditation of the Upaniṣadic type, and finally a *saṁnyāsi*, a renouncer, with no fixed abode and no possessions or attachments, solely devoted to the realization of the absolute.

This ideal schema never corresponded in its entirety to the reality of Hindu life, but it institutionalizes a very strong current within Hinduism: the desire to make religion one's whole life rather than just one of the many things in life. Whereas the oldest law books explicitly state that *saṁnyāsa* is only for Brahmins who have passed through the other three stages of life,[2] Hindu practice, for as long as we know it, has been less strict. Many Brahmins chose *saṁnyāsa* right after *brahmacarya*, as its continuance and perfection, and many non-Brahmins took up this mode of life as well.

VARIETIES OF HOLY MEN AND WOMEN

The terms used to identify the "religious" vary, and despite the quite precise definition of some of them, they are used very loosely by the average Hindu.

Sādhu, "holy man," or its feminine form, *sādhvī* or *sant*, "saint," are common designations applied by most people to all categories of religious. *Saṁnyāsi* (female, *saṁnyāsinī*), "renouncer," is a fairly common term, too, though sometimes it is restricted to the members of the order founded by *Śaṅkarācārya, the Daśanāmis* (who do not accept women ascetics). In contrast to these, the Vaiṣṇava religious practitioners are called *Vairāgis*, (its feminine is *vairāginī*), a word that has the same meaning but is used in a more exclusive way. *Yogi* (*yoginī*) as a professional designation can also mean holy men or women in general, or it can designate members of particular groups. Quite often the designation of the *saṁpradāya*, or specific order, is used as a name, particularly in those places where either one *saṁpradāya* is especially prominent or where so many *sādhus* and *sādhvīs* live that people are familiar with the more subtle distinctions among them. Not all the estimated 8-15 million religious practitioners, men and women, of today are formally members of a particular order; many are *svatantra sādhus*, people who, without going through the formalities of initiation through a guru and membership in an order, don the religious garb and follow a way of life within the general frame of Hindu religious life. Quite often English books speak of the *sādhus* as "ascetics" or "monks," terms with associations within the Western Christian religion that do not really apply to Hinduism. The etymology of *sādhu* goes a long way toward clarifying its meaning. It is derived from the root *sādh-*, "to accomplish," and describes someone who follows a certain *sādhana*, a definite way of life designed to accomplish realization of an ultimate ideal, be it the vision of a personal God or the merging with the impersonal *Brahmin*. As long as one has not yet reached the goal one is a *sādhaka*; the perfect one is called *siddha*, having achieved *sādhya*, the goal.

The various groups of religious practitioners differ in their *sādhana*; differences that sometimes concern doctrinal and dogmatic issues, sometimes ways of life and behavior, sometimes rituals and practices. It is hardly possible even to list all the *saṁpradāyas*, numbering three hundred or more. Though there have been efforts on many occasions in the past to organize and classify them, all these attempts have been overtaken by the development of ever new groups and orders.[3] Especially in modern times, there has been a proliferation of new religious orders, often with a reformist or activist character; almost every popular swāmi becomes the founder of a new *saṁpradāya*.

A very impressive demonstration of the variety and strength of Hindu religious orders is offered by the three-yearly *Kumbha melās.* Not only do the many thousands of *sādhus* and *sādhvinīs* assembled form an orderly procession, in which a place is assigned to each group according to a strict canon of precedence, but they also hold their own *saṁpradāya* conferences there and settle disputes concerning teachings and practices.

The forerunners, and quite often still the ideals, of the *saṁnyāsi* of today are the Vedic *ṛṣis*, the sages of the *Upaniṣads*, the ancient *kavīs*, and saints. The history of Hindu *saṁnyāsa* thus goes back into the mythical past. It appears to have been a well-established institution of long standing in the time of Jīna Mahāvīra and Gautama Buddha. Jain and Buddhist sources offer us a detailed account of many different orders.

The Mahābhārata enumerates what may have been the four original and oldest *saṁpradāyas*: *kuṭicakas*, who practiced religious life while living with their families; *bahūdakas*, who lived near settlements and begged their food from Brahmin families only; *haṁsas*, literally, "swans," wandering ascetics, still enjoying a minimum of comfort; *paramahaṁsas*, homeless and divested of everything, including their begging bowl, their staff and their clothes, "a condition that is divested of sorrow and happiness, auspicious and free from decrepitude and death, knowing no change."[4]

The *Mahābhārata* also describes various *vratas* practiced by these people; they very often constitute what was later called *sādhana.* The *Paramahaṁsa Upaniṣad* describes the highest ideal as follows:

> The way of the *paramahaṁsa* is very difficult to find; truly such a one ever rests in pure *brahman*, he is *brahman* as proclaimed in the Vedas, for his spirit always rests in me and I in him. Having left his sons and friends, his wife and relatives behind and having cut off the *śikhā*,[5] put away the sacred thread, given up Vedic studies, all *karma* and the entire world, he may possess only the *kaupina*, the staff and food enough to keep his body alive. He does not need anything beyond that. He experiences neither heat nor cold, neither joy nor sorrow, neither honour nor disdain. Having given up all deceit, untruth, jealousy, arrogance, pride, affection and disdain, lust and anger, selfishness and conceit, envy and avarice, he considers his own body like a corpse, getting altogether rid of the body-idea. Forever liberated from the root of doubt, from false and unfounded knowledge, realizing *brahman*, he lives in the self and knows: "I myself am He, I am That which is ever calm, immutable, undivided, conscious of itself and blissful; this alone is my true nature!" This knowledge alone is his *śikha*, his sacred thread, his *saṁdhyā*. He who has renounced all desire and finds his supreme peace in the One, he who holds the staff of knowledge, he is the true *ekadaṇḍi*. The four quarters of heaven are his clothing, he prostrates before none, he no longer offers sacrifices, he scolds none and praises none. The *saṁnyāsi* is always independent. For him there is no invocation, no ceremony, no *mantra*, no meditation, no worship; this phenomenal world

> does not exist for him, nor the world beyond. He neither sees duality nor unity; he neither sees I nor Thou nor all this. The *saṁnyāsi* has no home. He will not accept gold or disciples, nor any other gift. If asked, why not, he will reply: "Yes, it is harmful!"[6]

THE *SAṀNYĀSI'S* PROGRESS

Very few at any given time have reached this ultimate freedom of the *paramahaṁsa*. For the rest, there are rules that regulate their lives and offer a certain framework within which they can develop. All *smṛtis* have special sections on the rights and duties of *saṁnyāsis*, and later writers have brought these together into the *Yatidharma*, which leaves a certain freedom in quite a few matters but also regulates the basic structure of the life of the religious.[7]

It begins by stating the *adhikāra*, the prerequisite qualification in aspirant and master. Normally, birth as a Brahmin and the performance of the prescribed *saṁskāras* are insisted upon, together with certain physical qualities: a pleasing appearance, certain auspicious marks on hands and feet, unimpeded speech, and absence of physical defects in the limbs. As the *Yatidharma* says:

> A brahmin, after examining those worlds which are reached through Vedic rituals, should become indifferent after seeing that these actions do not result in anything that is eternal. The learned teacher should correctly explain to the disciple, endowed with self-control and a tranquil mind, the knowledge of *brahman*, revealing to him the imperishable and eternal Being.[8]

Moral purity, sincere thirst for ultimate reality and trust in the guru are the basic requirements in practically all schools. Rāmānuja demands in addition a real calling from the side of Viṣṇu.[9] Śrīpati requires the *sādhaka to wear a liṅga* on his body as prerequisite for *sādhana* proper.

The surest sign of a religious vocation for the Hindu is the formal acceptance of the novice by the guru whom he approaches. Also the qualification of the spiritual master must be established. Very often, the guru is well known as an authority and there is no need for further tests. An important factor is the *guru paramparā*, the succession of spiritual masters.[10] It is one of the first things each disciple learns and recites. According to Śaṅkara, only a Brahmin can be a proper guru. The guru must be

> endowed with the power of furnishing arguments pro and con, of understanding questions and remembering them; he must possess tranquility, self-control, compassion; he must have a desire to help others, must be versed in the scriptures, be unattached to enjoyments, a knower of *brahman* and firmly established

in *brahman.* He must never transgress the rules of good behavior, must be free from pride, deceit, cunning, jugglery, jealousy, falsehood, egotism. He must have as his sole aim the wish to help others and the desire to impart *brahmavidyā.*[11]

To some extent the guru must be perfect. This is especially true in Vaiṣṇava *saṁpradāyas*, where the role of the guru becomes all-important as the representative of God on earth and the association of guru and disciple lasts for a lifetime.

After the disciple has been accepted by the guru, there follows a period of training and probation, differing in length and depth from one group to another. Conscientious gurus will see to it that the disciple has made genuine spiritual progress before *dīkṣā*, the official ordination, is imparted. Others, who pride themselves in having a large number of disciples, will undertake it almost without any instruction.

Though they vary from one *saṁpradāya* to another, some elements of initiation are common enough to be mentioned: the body of the novice is completely shaved, including the *śikha*, nails on hands and feet are cut. The novice prepares a pyre and lays down on it for a short while. Then, he gets up and lights it, thus performing his own cremation; from now on the novice is considered dead to the world. When dead, he will be buried and not cremated. The novice strips naked, like a newborn, and remains so until the guru binds the *kaupina*, a strip of cloth, around his waist, and invests him with staff and water bowl. One of the common features is the imparting of the *mantra*, which is whispered into the ear, not to be revealed to anyone, except to one's own disciple. Śaṅkara *Daśanāmis* normally get a *śloka* from the *Upaniṣad*s; and Vaiṣṇavas, a *śloka* from the *Bhāgavata Purāṇa* as a *mantra*.

Usually, a final *upadeśa*, a lesson of religious instruction, is given. According to the classic tradition, maintained by the *Daśanāmis*, the newly ordained religious sets out for a yearlong pilgrimage, traversing the length and breadth of India, and visiting as many *tīrthas* as possible. Vaiṣṇavas continue to stay with their gurus, quite frequently also in a *maṭha*, a kind of monastery, where a large number of monks may live together. Nowadays, many Hindu religious practitioners change from one order to another or return to family life, although in former times, quite heavy penalties had been instituted for such practices.[12] The *saṁpradāya* may also expel members who are found to hold unorthodox views or who commit offences against the rules. Without attempting to offer anything like a complete list of Hindu *saṁpradāyas*, we may give a few details, following the classification in an authoritative Hindu work.[13]

SAṀNYĀSI ORDERS

Vedānta is basically nonsectarian and the main tradition built upon it calls itself *smārta*, claiming to represent the mainstream Vedic religion rather than particular later sects. Its *paramparā* includes all the great Vedāntins mentioned in the *Vedāntasūtra*, beginning with Bādarī, Kārṣṇa, Atreya, Audulomi, and so on to Śaṅkara.[14] Śaṅkara reputedly founded the order of the *Daśanāmi Saṁnyāsis*, so called because they are divided into ten groups, each of which attaches one of the following names to its accepted religious name: Āraṅya, Āśrama, Bhāratī, Giri, Pārvata, Pūrī, Sarasvatī, Sāgara, Tīrtha, and Vāna. The religious names proper usually end with —*ānanda*, bliss: Yogānanda finds his bliss in Yoga, Vivekānanda in discriminatory knowledge, Dāyānanda in mildness, etc.

Śaṅkara wanted his orders to become the vanguard of orthodoxy, the scourge of Buddhism, and the protagonists of the reform of Hinduism. In contrast to the Buddhists, who were somewhat decadent at this time, Śaṅkara insisted on rigorous discipline and intellectual activity. He founded bulwarks of Advaita in the four corners of India. With Govardhana Maṭha, in Puri on the east coast the Āraṇyas and Vānas are associated, who have as their *mantra*, "*prajñānam brahman.*" Jyotiḥ Maṭha, near Badrināṭh in the Himālayas, is the center of the Giri, Pārvata, and Sāgara, with the *mantra*, "*ayam ātman brahman.*" Śārada Maṭha, in Dvāraka on the west coast is home to the Tīrthas and Āśramas, who have as their *mantra*, "*tat tvam asi.*" Śṛṅgeri Maṭha in South India is the base of the Bhāratis, Pūrīs, and Sarasvatīs, with the *mantra*, "*aham brahmāsmi.*" The *ācārya* of the last is considered to be the actual head of the entire order, addressed as *jagadguru*, spiritual master of the whole world.[15] While most *Daśanāmis* identify themselves with the greeting *namaḥ nārāyaṇāya*, the Āśramas, Bhāratis, Sarasvatīs, and Tīrthas say "*namaḥ śivāya.*"[16]

The *Daśanāmis* are the most respected group of religious practitioners in India, usually well versed in Sanskrit learning and Vedānta philosophy and often possessing a modern education. In former times, they had to suffer the attacks of the Bauddhas and Vaiṣṇavas. Being bound to *ahiṁsā*, they recruited armies of *Daśanāmi nāgas*, equipped with heavy iron tridents, who defended the *saṁnyāsis*. As late as the nineteenth century, there were regular battles between these and the Vaiṣṇava *nāgas* in which hundreds were killed.[17] At present, there are six *ākhāḍas*, as the centers of *Daśanāmi nāgas* are called, with several hundred members each. They are often illiterate and their religious program is limited to *Haṭha-yoga*, physical exercises, which are meant to make them insensitive to pain and endow them with supernatural powers.

The Śaṅkarācāryas of the four *maṭhas* trace their *guru paramparā* back through a number of illustrious Vedāntins like Padmapada, Maṇḍanamiśra, Vacaspatimiśra, Vidyārāṇya, Ānandagiri, Appaya Dīkṣita, Sadānanda, and others to Ādiśaṅkarācārya, the founder.

The living Śaṅkarācāryas "represent an institution and are themselves an institution in India's religious life."[18] They are not only almost universally respected in India as successors to the great Śaṅkara, the restorer of Hinduism in the 8th century, but they exert a major influence through the educational institutions they maintain. Each of the five Śaṅkara *maṭhas* has a number of schools attached to it, in which Sanskrit and the traditional subjects of Hindu learning are cultivated. These schools are a major employer of India's traditional paṇḍits and they produce most of today's traditionally trained Hindus. Sanskrit is used as a medium of instruction, and the Śaṅkarācāryas propagate Sanskrit not only as the sacred language of India but also as the lifeblood of Indian culture. These eminent leaders of Hinduism are wholly committed to their tradition, but most are not fanatics. They have their parallel in the institutionalized *saṁnyāsa* of other Hindu denominations, the heads of the Śrīraṅgam *maṭha*, of Uḍipī and other places. There is no doubt at all that, in and through them, *saṁnyāsa* proves to be an institutional support of Hinduism, perhaps the most important one. Their position has gained in strength in the past decades and is likely to increase more so in the future.

Śaṅkara also redefined the idea and ideal of *saṁnyāsa*. Whatever its conception may have been before his time and whatever forms of religious life prevailed after him, the description of *saṁnyāsa* in terms of study and self-consciousness rather than *yoga*, devotional practices or self-mortification, is due to him and his ideas of self-realization. In its intellectuality and outward moderation, its emphasis on introspection and unperturbed serenity of mind, it has created a prototype of universal appeal, free from sectarian fervor and masochistic self-torture.

Vaiṣṇava religious practitioners are usually known as *vairāgis*. A conference in the 18th century affiliated the numerous groups to four *saṁpradāyas* in a rather artificial way; the system has been broken up through many new developments.

The *Śrīvaiṣṇavas* are organized in the *Rāmanujasaṁpradāya*, whose head is the ruling *mahant* of the temple *maṭha* of Śrīraṅgam, endowed since Rāmānuja's time with infallibility in matters of doctrine and ritual. The second *saṁpradāya* is the *Brahmāsaṁpradāya* founded by Madhva, also called Ānanda Tīrtha or Pūrṇa Prajñā. Beginning as a *Daśanāmi*, Madhva became Advaita's bitterest enemy. Madhvites are largely restricted to the South, where they keep custody over the *maṭhas* established by the founder. In former times, they must have been quite numerous. Among their peculiar customs is the adoption of a name of Viṣṇu and the branding of the body with a red-hot iron to imprint upon it forever the *cakra* of Viṣṇu. The third *saṁpradāya* is associated with Nimbārka, a twelfth century Vaiṣṇava. The *Nīmavats*, however, claim to owe their foundation to Viṣṇu himself in the form of the Haṁsa *avatāra*. They have several centers in the district of Mathurā, in Bengal and Rājasthān. Vallabha, the founder of the *Rudrasaṁpradāya*, was a married man; in this order the feasts honoring his two sons and seven grandsons are still celebrated as major events. He taught what became known as *pūṣṭimārga*, which promises salvation to those who unconditionally follow the guru.

Caitanya's followers belong technically to the Madhva *saṁpradāya*, but they are in fact a quite distinct branch, numerous in Bengal and North India, augmented recently by numerous Westerners in the Hare Kṛṣṇa movement.

One of the largest *saṁpradāyas* today is that founded by Rāmānanda, called *Śrīsaṁpradāya*. Its members worship Sītā and Rāma as their divine patrons. Rāmānanda, born around 1300 in Prayāga, accepted into his order people from all castes, including women. His twelve best-known disciples founded subsects, known as *dvāras*. Their main center, called *bara sthāna* is in Ayodhyā, the home town of Rāma. They have several hundred centers today in India, peopled by thousands of fervent, if often uneducated, people. They are said to indulge quite frequently in kidnapping to provide new members for their order. As part of their initiation rites, they burn the name of Rāma into their skins and usually suffix the word *dāsa*, slave to their accepted names. Their form of greeting is "*jay sītārāma*."

As some Kṛṣṇa worshippers take on the role of *gopīs*, thus there are also Rāmānandis who imagine themselves to be Sītā, dressing in women's clothing and walking around laden with jewelry. It is not unusual for Rāmānandis to run *Gośālās*, old-age homes for cows.

The counterpart to the *daśanāmi Nāgas* are the so-called *catursaṁpradāya nāgas*, militant Vaiṣṇavas organized into *ākhāḍas*. They are subdivided into two groups: one carries a banner with the image of Rādhā-Kṛṣṇa, the other one with Sītā-Rāma. Of one Vaiṣṇava *nāga*, it is reliably told that he had taken a vow not to eat one mouthful before he had not killed at least one Śaiva monk. A Śaiva in his turn had sworn never to eat his daily meal unless he had first slain at least one Vaiṣṇava. Bloody clashes, frequent in former centuries, have become rare nowadays, but they are not unknown.[19]

Śiva is the *saṁnyāsi* par excellence; he is described as the great *tyāgi*, the one who renounced to such an extent that he even cut off his member with his own hand, living on burning *ghats* and in mountain recesses. Śaiva *saṁnyāsis* claim to have the oldest tradition of all and in fact predate the writing of the *Mahābhārata*. Śaṅkara knew of several distinct Śaiva schools in his time.

One can classify the numerous sects into those that follow the benevolent, or Śiva, aspect of the deity and those that follow the terrible, or Rudra, aspect. Among the former figure prominently the *Vīraśaivas*, mentioned earlier, and the *Pāśupatas*, reputedly a foundation of Lakuliṣa, a Śiva *avatāra*. Among the latter, the most prominent are the *Kālamukhas* and the *Kāpālikas*, practicing rites and a mode of life that few people in the West would associate with religion.[20] The *Aghoris* are closely associated with them and are quite numerous even today, especially in Benares. According to their rules, they are not allowed to beg nor are they allowed to refuse anything that is offered to them. All their rites are performed on cremation grounds, from which they also get all their belongings. They are reputed to even eat meat from human corpses and spend entire nights dancing around them. They smear their bodies with the ashes from the cremation grounds and are also considered to be masters of the occult arts. They claim to owe their supernatural powers to the *pretas*, the spirits of the departed, whom they worship.

The *samādhi* of their founder, Bābā Kinarām,[21] is a famous place in Benares. Bābā Kinarām is said to have worked many miracles during his lifetime, to have called dead animals back to life, and to have restored the sight of the blind. In a contemporary report about Benares, the following information was offered:

> The *Aghori* leader who now presides over the Baba Kinaram Ashram is Bābā Avadhut Bhagvan Ram. He is, no doubt, a true representative of the Aghori Panth in all its *raudra* and *tamasa* aspects. But he is—what a paradox!—essentially a humanitarian. He has dedicated himself completely to the cause of providing relief for the lepers. He is the moving spirit of the Leper Asylum at Rajghat on the east bank of the Ganga. Indeed, the *Aghoris* are as fond of the living as they are of the dead. Avadhut Bhagvan Ram is a big burly man, full of cleverly concealed contempt for the so-called normal human being. "He bores me," he says with a sinister smile and lapses into silence. Suddenly, after a prolonged pause, he bursts out good-humouredly: "You see, I can't even eat him till he is dead."[22]

Yogis, the next major section, are also divided into numerous subsections, the largest and best known of which are the *Nāthapanthis*, followers of Gorakhnātha.[23] They have a male and a female branch and are subdivided into *Aughara* and *Kānphaṭa*. They wear red and yellow garments and use a vessel without handle for eating and drinking. This vessel used to be a human skull; nowadays, it is usually the blackened half of a coconut shell. Round their neck they wear a thread made of black sheep's wool with a single *rudrākṣa* bead and a goat's horn on a cotton string. The goat's horn is blown before the meals. Often they carry a long pair of iron tongs with a ring. The name of the *Kānphaṭis*, hole-in-the-ear, derives from their initiation ceremony. The guru pierces the ear of the novice with a double-edged knife and inserts an iron ring. Though they also have their centers, most of them are constantly on the move. One of their peculiarities is the circumambulation of the river Narbadā. They begin their pilgrimage in Broach, on the Arabian Sea, go up to the source at Amarakantha, and return along the other bank. In their *maṭhas*, they always keep a fire burning and a bunch of peacock feathers near it.

A more recent foundation are the *Caraṇadāsis*, originating with Śukadeva (1760-1838), who wrote a number of books, dealing with different aspects of *yoga*. In former times, the worshippers of Ganapati and Sūrya formed separate orders; little of these movements remain.[24] A considerable number of *saṁpradāyas*, however, have developed within Śāktism, divided mainly into right-hand Tantrikas and left-hand Tantrikas. Of the 12 *saṁpradāyas* (with subsections) the most important today are the *Lopamudra* and the *Manmatha*.[25]

There are numerous orders that can not be classified under these groups, and Rāmdās Gaur characterizes them as *sudhāraka*, or reformist. Taking their inspiration from the *Bhāgavata Purāṇa*, many saints like Jñāneśvara, Nāmadeva, Nabhajī, etc., founded movements that can be put together loosely under the name of *Bhāgavata saṁpradāya*. Tukārām, born 1665, one of the most popular saints of Mahārāṣṭra, did not really found a new *saṁpradāya*, but out of the groups he led to the sanctuary of Viṭṭal in Pandharpur, there developed the order of the *Vārkarīs*, consisting mostly of householders who follow a certain mode of life.[26] Rāmādāsa Swāmi, born 1865, became the founder of another popular order, that attracted mainly low-caste people.[27] A somewhat less reputable order is the *Dattā saṁpradāya*, also called Mānabhāū, a Vaiṣṇava sect founded in the fourteenth century and proscribed by several rulers. There is also a *Narasinha saṁpradāya*, of unknown origin and date, and a *Rāmavata saṁpradāya*, quite close to the *Rāmadāsis* mentioned earlier. Kabīr, the Muslim weaver who became a Hindu saint and whose hymns have become part of the *Ādi Granth*, the holy book of Sikhs, became the founder of the *Kabīr Panth*, which comes close to being a nonsectarian religious brotherhood, if that is possible.[28] The *Dadu Panth* and the *Lāldāsī Panth* are also popular. The *Satyanāmis* are an interesting group: claiming a very ancient history. They suffered persecution and near extinction at the hands of Aurangzeb. They were revived in the late 18th century by Jagjīvandās and today are found mainly in western India. The Vaiṣṇava suborders of the *Śrīrādhāvallabhis*, the *Śrīharidāsī sampradāya*, the *Śrīsvāmi Narāyaṇī saṁpradāya, the Śrīsatani saṁpradāya*, and the *Paraināmi saṁpradāya* are popular and quite numerous in certain localities.[29]

In our own time numerous new religious movements sprang up around famous living saints like Ānandamāyī or Śrī Satya Sāī Bābā. The disciples of recently departed gurus like Śrī Aurobindo and Śivānanda, as well as numerous others, have begun to develop into independent *quasi saṁpradāyas*.

SĀDHUS AND THE MODERN AGE

Gulzarilal Nanda, a former home affairs minister of the central government in Delhi and a devout Hindu, in 1962, established the Akhil Bhāratīya Sādhu Samāj, the All-India Society for the *Sādhus*, with the aim of organizing and controlling the rather confusing variety of movements and utilizing the moral authority of the *sādhus* for the general uplifting of Indian society. A considerable number of criminals try to escape from the clutches of the police by donning a "holy robe," and numerous vagrants misuse the respect people still have for the *sādhus* to live a relatively easy life without having to work. Generally speaking, the reputation of the *bābājis*, as many people call them (not very respectfully), is rather low. The home affairs minister wanted to enforce registration and issue identity cards for the genuine *sādhus*. He also tried to employ them in the anticorruption campaign started by the government. Only a few thousand enlisted with the *sārkarī sādhus*, the government monks, as they were sarcastically called by the independent *sādhus*. The attempt to establish centers of training for the *sādhus*, with something like a standard theological education, has not produced many results to far.

Nowadays, a number of *sādhus* are also politically active. In the 18th century, they led the famous *saṁnyāsi* revolt in Bengal, aimed at overthrowing the British and re-establishing Hindu rule. The widespread discontent of the populace with the secular government, which has been unable to perform miracles, economic or otherwise, is utilized by many *sādhus* to promise utopia for all, if only they would work for the kingdom of God by faithfully reverting to the observance of the *smṛtis*. Karpātrijī Mahārāj, a Vaiṣṇava *sādhu*, founded the Rāma Rājya Pariṣad, the Kingdom-of-God party, which advocated reactionary right-wing Hinduism. In this kingdom of God, there is no room for Christians or Muslims, Marxists or Democrats.[30] Another *sādhu*, Swāmi Dvijayanātha, was for may years general secretary of the *Hindu Mahāsabhā*, a radically fascist Hindu party, out of whose ranks came the murderer of Mahātmā Gāndhī. Swāmi Rameśvarānanda, a member of parliament on a Jana Sangh ticket, was the instigator of the "black Monday" November 7, 1965, in Delhi, leading a "*sādhus* war for cow-protection" that came dangerously close to a coup d'état on behalf of the right-wing fascists.[31] Swāmi Cinmayānanda, who established a huge enterprise in Bombay to train Hindu missionaries, was the first president of the Viśva Hindu Pariṣad, the Hindu World Fellowship, which was designed to actively propagate Hinduism in India and abroad and which was founded in 1964 to counteract the Eucharistic Congress in Bombay.[32]

Many Westerners have joined Hindu *saṁpradāyas* of all varieties: an Englishman, under the name of Kṛṣṇa Prem, became a recognized Guru of Vaiṣṇavas; the Ramakrishna movement has a number of Western disciples; and people like Mahesh Yogi Maharishi, the founder of the Transcendental Meditation Society, or Swami Bhaktivedanta, the founder of the International Society for Kṛṣṇa Consciousness, have emerged as major figures in the Western counterculture, initiating thousands of young Americans and Europeans. There may be a good deal of faddism in it, which will rub off after a few years, but for many it is more than a fad. It is the discovery of a life-style that is rooted in the ultimate by way of inner experience.

The frustrations of life, its disappointments and sorrows, which thousands of years ago prompted people in India to look for the unchanging and never disappointing Reality, are still with us—and this makes it possible to understand someone like Bhartṛhari, who in his *Vairāgyaśatakam* explains the deeper meaning of *saṁnyāsa* in poetical language.

> I have travelled to inaccessible and perilous places without becoming rich; I have sacrificed self-respect and dignity of birth and position to cater to the wealthy, in vain; like the crows have I fed myself in others' houses hoping for gain—but, you, desire, you prompter of evil deeds, you are not satisfied and keep growing. I have dug into the earth in quest of precious minerals, I have smelted metals from rocks, I crossed the ocean and I sought the favours of Kings, I have spent nights on cremation grounds with my mind occupied with *mantras* and *pūjās*—nothing have I got for it, O desire! In our servile attendance on the filthy rich, their shabby manners and their silly talk we did not mind; suppressing the tears that welled up from our hearts we have smiled out of vacant minds; we have paid homage to idiots spoiled by too much wealth! What more folly would you have me suffer, you desire, never satisfied? We have forgiven, but not out of forgiveness; we have renounced the comforts of the home but not because we were content; we have suffered heat and cold, but not because we wanted to undergo austerities; we have brooded day and night on money, and not on Śiva—we have done what the *munis* do, but we have deprived ourselves of their rewards! We have not enjoyed pleasures, they have eaten us up; we have not practiced asceticism but we have been chastised; time is not gone, but we have lost it. Desire is not reduced, but we are now senile. With the hand as a cup, with food begged on pilgrimages, with the quarters of the sky as the garment and the earth as the bed—blessed are they, who have given up

> all connections with desire and self-contented with a heart fully matured through their acceptance of *saṁnyāsa* root out all *karma*. O earth, my mother; O wind, my father, O fire, my friend, O water, my good relation, O sky, my brother! Here is my last salutation to you! I have cast away illusion with its wonderful power through pure knowledge gained from my association with you, and now I merge into the *parabrahman*![33]

Not all of the many millions who are generically called *sādhus* by the populace are ideal persons—in fact the complaints against them are numerous. Some of them commit criminal acts; others irritate their fellow men through their aggressive begging and their uncivilized behavior. However, even Hindus critical of some of the practices of presentday *sādhus* would defend *saṁnyāsa* as something essential to Indian culture. Thus a writer in *Seminar*, a decidedly progressive and unquestionably secular monthly, after highlighting some of the more common complaints against *sādhus*, goes on defending them against government regulations and public condemnations alike by stating that "the *sādhu* is in our blood and cannot be excised from the total Indian community. . . . So long as the Indian people wish to maintain their *sādhus* the *sādhu* will survive. And so long as India is an India with heart, *sādhus* will be maintained."[34]

More specifically, he protects the *sādhus* from accusations as being useless, unproductive members of society by pointing out that "if he pays no taxes, he costs the government nothing. If he is not gainfully employed, he neither competes for employment nor seeks poor relief. In an over-populated country he practices and preaches sexual abstinence. Where greed and corruption are rife the true *sādhu* demonstrates a life based on honesty, truthfulness, and self-restraint." All this and in addition the engagement of modern *sādhus* in works of charity and education seems, however, to be a rather superficial excuse for the radical challenge that *saṁnyāsa* is to the Hindu. Thus the writer concludes: "Above all, the people look to the man of the spirit to provide them with a meaningful interpretation of existence and from him draw courage to face the tribulations of their lives."

23. Hindu Structures of Thought: The *Ṣaḍdarśanas*

> Thus there are many different opinions, partly based on sound arguments and scripture, partly based on fallacious arguments and scriptural texts misunderstood. If a man would embrace some of these opinions without previous examination, he would bar himself from the highest beatitude and incur grievous loss.
>
> —*Śaṅkara*, Brahma Sūtra Bhāṣya *I, 1*

ALL CULTURES, AS the languages associated with them reveal, have made attempts to transform their life experiences into thoughts and into coherent symbolic world pictures. Indian culture has done so more than most others. Coining words, translating reality into concepts, and elaborating systems of explanation on the basis of universal principles are some of the most prominent features of Indian civilization. The sheer mass of writing it possesses, probably only a fraction of what once existed, is eloquent testimony to this.

In the enormous Indian religious literature, one cluster of words and ideas stands out: words and ideas designing mind, consciousness, thought, *cit, caitanyam, caitta.* Indian religions have been consciousness conscious from a very early date, not all as far as the "consciousness only" school of *Vijñānavāda* Buddhism or the "absolute consciousness alone" school of *Advaita Vedānta.* But the awareness of mind as irreducible reality, a reality different from nature and society, was a very important factor in the history of Hinduism as a whole.

To consider the physical reality of the Hindus' holy land as a support of Hinduism will be quite easily accepted. After all, Hindus live in this sacred geography. To see, in the specific societal arrangements that Hinduism created, a structural support of Hinduism will equally appear quite plausible. All Hindus are, in very important ways, affected by *varṇāśramadharma.* It may need some arguing, however, to prove that the *ṣatdarśana* are structural supports of Hinduism of equal importance.

HINDUISM: A TRADITION OF LEARNING

Hindu tradition has always shown great respect for scholarship. It rested upon a book, the *Veda*, which was memorized and studied, surrounded by other books, which were designed to protect it, explain it, and apply it. Not only had a Brahmin, according to traditional Hindu law, to devote the first part of his life to study, *svādhyāya*, study on his own, was a permanent duty, imposed for life. Although the injunction to devote the first part of one's day to study may not always have been followed literally by all Brahmins, study as a habit certainly characterized them throughout and formed the whole class. Study, according to Manu, was enjoined by the creator himself "in order to protect the universe," and it was also the most effective means to subdue sensual desires and obtain self-control. Manu quotes an ancient verse: "Sacred Learning approached a Brahmaṇa and said to him: 'I am thy treasure, preserve me, deliver me not to a scorner; so preserved I shall become extremely strong'."[1]

The learning a Brahmin acquires is the only claim to eminence: "A man is not considered venerable because his head is grey; him who, though young, has learned the *Vedas*, the gods consider to be venerable."[2] *Veda*-study, Manu says, has been declared the highest form of *tapas* (austerity, self-mortification) of a Brahmin.

Correspondingly, the role of the teacher has always been important. "They call the teacher 'father' because he gives the Veda: for nobody can perform a sacred rite before the investiture with the girdle of Muñja grass."[3]

The teacher was compared to a God, even placed above God, because he could not only convey the sacred knowledge but could also intercede on behalf of his pupils in case of their wrongdoing. The king, according to Kautilya, had the duty to see to it that no student in his realm would be in want for the basic needs.

The prominence of the Brahmins, whose "natural" function was to learn and to teach, is a further indicator of the central place study occupied in Vedic society. The true centers of Hinduism were always centers of study, be they the *āśramas* of classical India or the *pathaśālas* of later times, the private libraries of individual scholars or the large universitylike centers of major denominations.[4]

To the extent to which brahmanic ideas shaped the outlook of Hindu society, and they did so with great effectiveness, scholarship and study occupied a prominent place in it.[5] While much of the brahmanic learning consisted in memorizing the sacred texts and acquiring the skills to perform the rituals, reflection and critical examination of the content of the tradition was also in evidence from very early times. The *Upaniṣads* contain accounts of debates between learned sages and indicate that certain lines of thought had already crystallized into schools associated with prominent names.[6]

The emergence of Buddhism and Jainism—and a host of other movements within Hinduism, critical of certain aspects of it—shows that by the fifth century B.C.E. complete systems of thought had formed, challenged by rival systems, and that is was deemed important to have a clear and correct idea of the intellectual supports of practical life.[7] The fierce polemics carried on among representatives of different schools of thought—polemics not restricted to books and academic retreats but carried out in public with the participation of large numbers of people—is a further fact that corroborates the importance given to thinking and system building. The fully developed Hindu systems of early mediaeval India leave no doubt that they consider it of the highest importance to have correct notions of the key concepts of religion—a person's ultimate felicity depends on it, as Śaṅkara explains.[8]

Contrary to the West, where philosophical and theological discussion, with very few exceptions, was a concern for professional philosophers and theologians only, in India this debate interested all levels of the population. Although not everybody in India is capable of arguing the finer points of *śāstraic* controversies, even today many know about the controversy between the followers of Śaṅkara and Rāmānuja and can discuss the points where Buddhism differs from Hinduism, or are able to marshall arguments for or against *saguṇa* and *nirguṇa brahman* and so on. Many of the most popular *bhajans*, religious lyrics sung at popular gatherings, contain an amazing amount of such highly philosophical thought.[9]

Intellectual penetration of reality, enlightenment, knowledge, and insight are absolutely central in Hinduism. The classical systems are part of the structure of Hinduism as much as anything else. As in the case of the other supports, there is a reality that corresponds to it. The Hindu *darśanas* have provided real insight, have helped people acquire real knowledge, and have been found reliable guides in the search for truth. It is that element of truth realized, that freedom gained, and that transcendence experienced which has prevented Hinduism from becoming an ideology for a power structure, an escape for dreamers, or a merely romantic view of nature.

The close proximity of religious theory and social practice in India through the ages brought with it strong repercussions in "real" life of changes in philosophico-theological orientation. Thus, acceptance of Buddhism or Jainism brought about a loss of caste, with enormous consequences for those concerned. It also, of course, deprived a person of felicity after death. In the context of the practice of *śrāddha*, which was supposed to secure the bliss of the ancestors, this had repercussions not only with regard to one's own fate but with regard to one's entire lineage as well. While Hinduism throughout its history has shown a great fondness for speculation and system building, the need to remain within the socio-cultic context of the Ārya tradition brought up the question of how far one could go with critical thinking. Vedic tradition did not consider itself the result of human thought: it related its content to a revelation received by seers and sages in meditation and trance, it aimed at maintaining and duplicating these states of mind through yogic practices, and it exempted Vedic teaching from criticism by declaring its origin *apauruṣeya*, not man-made but eternally present. Thus, the *Veda* was taken to be the foundation of all thinking and not its object to be analyzed or discussed. No tradition is founded on analytical and critical thought alone, a society needs more than speculative philosophy to flourish and to provide for the needs of its members.

Wide ranging and deep searching as Indian philosophy may be, it had to respect the boundaries set by practical life. Going beyond these boundaries placed one outside society. The *nāstikas*, those who did not accept the *Veda* as authority, did just that.[10] The *āstikas*, those who wished to remain inside tradition had to stay inside the framework of questions permitted by the *Veda*. It appears from the polemics that the difficult task of ascertaining these boundaries has been carried on between the *āstika* systems since the seventh century.

Kumārila Bhaṭṭa, a great authority in *Mīmāṁsā* and a staunch defender of *sanātana dharma* against Buddhism, considers *Sāṁkhya, Yoga, Pāñcarātra*, and *Pāśupata* philosophies as *nāstika*.[11] Some of the followers of Madhva classify Śaṅkara's *Advaita Vedānta* as *pracannabauddha*, crypto-buddhist, and thus unorthodox. Even at the present, this position is taken not only by the Caitanyites and their modern Western exponents but also by some scholarly philosophers.[12] Śaṅkara himself condemns *Sāṁkhya* as non-Vedic and the teaching of *pradhāna* as heretical.[13] S. Radhakrishnan, quite clearly placing himself within the orthodox tradition, explains the rationale for this attitude thus:

> If the unassisted reason of man cannot attain any hold on reality by means of mere speculation, help may be sought from the great writings of the seers who claim to have attained spiritual certainty. Thus strenuous attempts were made to justify by reason what faith implicitly accepts. This is not an irrational

> attitude, since philosophy is only an endeavor to interpret the widening experience of humanity. . . . If we cannot establish through logic the truth of anything, so much the worse for logic.[14]

And "The acceptance of the *Veda* is a practical admission that spiritual experience is a greater light in these matters than intellectual reason. . . . The philosophical character of the systems is not much compromised by the acceptance of the *Veda*."[15] The options that the *Veda* leaves are indeed quite liberal. It did not demand a creed nor a declaration of faith in this or that God.

Vedic tradition embodied the principle of pluralism insofar as a number of family traditions (*śakhas*) were considered as equally authoritative, and it also recognized a variety of valid local traditions. Even the *nāstikas* developed the pluralistic spirit in orthodoxy: it was faced with alternative viewpoints and had to engage in rational argumentation, admitting in the process that many questions had to remain open, questions that permitted a plurality of answers.

Hindu intellectual tradition has dealt in various ways with this pluralistic situation. Some have accepted it as a matter of fact and simply pursued their own paths without looking left or right. Others have taken a defensive stance and polemicized in order to vindicate the truth—often absolute, final, *siddhānta*—of their own school of thought. Still others have made a scholarly study of the whole thing, seeing a kind of complementarity of viewpoints. Among the classical writers, Vācaspati Miśra deserves mentioning. He wrote scholarly commentaries on most of the *darśanas*, entering, as it were, into the spirit of each and clarifying their teachings. Among the modern writers, S. Radhakrishnan comes to mind. His catholicity of thought was able to see the essential unity of Hindu thought behind the diversity of systems.[16]

HINDU PHILOSOPHY OR HINDU THEOLOGY?

Neither *philosophy* nor *theology*, whatever these terms may mean today, are adequate translations of the Indian term *darśana*.[17] *Darśanas* contain psychology and physics, exegesis of Vedic texts and speculation about language, psycho-physical practices as well as meditation, and much more. They demonstrate another type of intellectual approach to the world, alternatives not only to the answers given but to the very questions asked by the Western tradition. We are only slowly beginning to appreciate and to understand them. The reason for dealing with them in this book is that without exception they identify their raison d'être as leading to an ultimate existential ("religious") aim and they represent the cumulative reflection of Hinduism through the ages.

A common characteristic of all *darśanas* is that at some time their basic teachings were condensed into *sūtras*, "leading threads," that helped to express precisely the content of the systems in a technical terminology and also served as texts for students to memorize. Instruction would consist largely of commenting upon the pithy *sūtras* and expanding on the meaning of the terms used in them, pointing out differences between one's own system and others and providing proof for the truth of the *sūtra*. Since many of the *sūtras* are (almost) unintelligible without a commentary and explanation, often the commentary (*bhāṣya*) has become the most important exposition of a system. These *bhāṣyas* in turn have become the object of subcommentaries (*vṛttis* and *ṭīkās*) and further glosses (*ṭippaṇīs*), which constitute the material that an expert in that particular branch of learning has to study. Hindu scholars have invented most peculiar names for their subcommentaries and glosses.[18] The *sūtras* we possess today are not always the oldest texts of the schools and they are not always the work of the authors to whom they are ascribed. But they can be relied upon as containing the gist of the teaching of the systems and providing the technical terminology for each.

And here we encounter another peculiarity. The basic vocabulary is shared by virtually all six *darśanas*. But the meaning given to each term and the place-value accorded to them are very different. This situation has lead to the necessity of specializing in one specific *darśana* rather than studying Hinduism in general, as a philosopher or a theologian. Each *darśana* possesses a highly technical terminology, often new terms are coined or very specific meanings are given to terms used otherwise, a terminology that one does not pick up by learning classical Sanskrit and reading courtly Sanskrit literature. Traditional Indian scholars who specialize in a *darśana* indicate their specialization in their academic title,[19] and they would not consider themselves competent to instruct in other fields. Reading a text of a specific *darśana* in many ways resembles learning a new language: familiar as the sounds of the words may be, their meaning has to be learned anew and must not be confused with that of other systems.

Representatives of "Indian philosophy" in English often restrict themselves to describing those elements from the Hindu *darśanas* that have a parallel in contemporary Western philosophy and leave out the rest.[20] This not only gives a slanted impression of Hindu thought, it often deprives the student of the most valuable lessons to be learned from such a study, the really original and specific contributions to human thought India has made. While restrictions of space and considerations of accessibility do not allow much technical detail of the Hindu *darśanas* in the following chapters, the description attempts to convey the idea that Hindu *darśanas* offer not only parallels to Western thought but contain novel elements for which there are no parallels. Translations of many of the major texts as well as specialized studies are available for a more detailed investigation.[21]

The enumeration and combination of the *darśanas* follows the traditional schema that has been accepted for at least the past 1000 years. In works like Mādhava's *Sarvadarśanasaṁgraha*, many other *darśanas* are mentioned that do not find place among the six described here.[22] Also the designation of the classical *darśanas* has not always remained the same in Indian history. Thus *Nyāya* was used in former times to designate the system today called *Mīmāṁsā, Yoga* was used as a name for *Vaiśeṣika, Anvīkṣikī* designated our *Nyāya*, etc.[23] Information like this may not appear of great significance for a reader who is looking for basic information on the Hindu systems, but it will be of importance for those who consult sources and wish to learn more about the history of each *darśana*. Doing so, they will discover that the description offered here focusses on what might be called the "classical phase" of each *darśana*. Much of the origin and early development has yet to be uncovered, and conflicting views found in older sources have to be reconciled. More recent developments often go off in many different directions and have become much too intricate to permit a nontechnical summary.

This enumeration does not represent an evaluation. Each of the following systems considers itself the best suited to achieving its aim. India's intellectual history over the past millennium, and before, consists of sustained debates between the *āstika* and *nāstika darśanas* as well as between the adherents of the *ṣatdarśanas*, and between rival schools of the same *darśana*. Even texts that are not explicitly polemical—and many are!—contain innumerable references to and attacks against other systems. Precision in expression and incisiveness of thought were qualities aimed at by all professional Hindu thinkers. The English translations of texts do not do full justice to this aspect of Indian systematics, since they have to fill in many words and circumscribe many terms, in order to provide an intelligible text for readers not steeped in the subtleties of an intellectual tradition that enjoyed prestige and renown at a time when Greek thought was only beginning to crystallize. It is not without significance that, in our age, Western scientists of repute like H. Weyl, E. Schrödinger, C. F. von Weizsäcker, D. Bohm, and many others discover parallels between modern scientific thinking and some of the Hindu *darśanas*. Some contemporary Western logicians and linguistic philosophers avidly dig into the intricacies of *Mīmāṁsā* and *Nyāya*. *Yoga*, too, is now studied widely and practiced all over the world. If we can learn from India, it is certainly from the *ṣaḍdarśanas*, which can teach us valuable lessons both in areas in which we feel competent and in areas unknown to us.

The very notion of philosophy, which has acquired in the West the meaning of independent systematic and critical thought, of coherent reflection and sustained argumentation, has to be used with qualifications when applied to "Indian philosophy." As the student of the major histories of Indian philosophy, such as those by S. N. Dasgupta, S. Radhakrishnan, or M. Hiriyanna, will soon discover, Indian philosophy as a whole is not separate from Indian theology: systematic thought in India, throughout its history, has been pursued with the aim of finding salvation. The specializations within Indian philosophy—physics and logic, anthropology and metaphysics, and so on—again do not correspond to the Western notions employed.

Using technical terms coined by the Western cultural tradition to describe the thinking and systemics of Indian traditions is at the same time unavoidable and misleading. Unavoidable because these are the terms we know and understand. Risky, because they have connotations that are not wholly appropriate. Thus, writing on "Logic in the West and in India," Kuppuswami Sastri remarks:

> Those who are familiar with Western logic and desirous of studying Indian logic from a historical and comparative point of view will do well to bear in mind the fact that, while one may find striking parallels in the Indian and Western systems of logic, one would not be misled by such parallels and lose sight of the fundamental differences in respect to scope and method, which Indian logic discloses in its rise and development, as compared with Western logic.[24]

The six "orthodox" systems have been grouped in three pairs from early times. The reason for doing this, in most cases, is quite clear: they complement each other in various ways. However, it should not be overlooked that each of them was developed as a quite independent system, capable of achieving its aims by its own methods.

24. Hindu Logic and Physics: *Nyāya-Vaiśeṣika*

> The Supreme Good results from the knowledge, produced by a particular *dharma*, of the essence of the predicables: substance, attribute, action, genus, species, and combination, by means of their resemblances and differences.
>
> —Vaiśeṣika Sūtra *I, 1, 4*

THE *VAIŚEṢIKA SŪTRAS*, ascribed to Kaṇāda, are, in the words of Dasgupta, "probably the oldest that we have and in all probability are pre-Buddhistic."[1] That does not entitle us, however, to make any statement about the age of the system itself, which is known particularly for its interesting early atomistic theory and its classification of categories. *Vaiśeṣika* may initially have been a school of Vedic thought, as its emphasis on *dharma* and its traditional opinion on *adṛṣṭa* as its fruit would suggest.[2] The book that, besides the *sūtras*, contains the most complete representation of the system, the *Daśapadārtha Śāstra*, is no older than the sixth century C.E.[3]

Several recent works deal with *Nyāya-Vaiśeṣika* as if it were one single system.[4] Though they have much in common and supplement each other in many areas, they began as separate systems with quite different aims. Professor Kuppuswami Sastri has this to say on the conjunction of *Nyāya-Vaiśeṣika:*

> That Indian logic is usually described as the *Nyāya-Vaiśeṣika* system is not because it is the result of the syncretism of the two opposing systems—*Nyāya* realism and Atomistic pluralism; rather it is so described because at a very early stage in the history of Indian logic, the *Vaiśeṣika* stress on the inductive phase of inference came to be synthesised with its deductive phase in the *Nyāya* theory of syllogistic reasoning.[5]

The recent Western philosophical preoccupation with logic, especially under the influence of the Anglo-American school of linguistic analysis, brought about an extensive and intensive study of *Nyāya* texts during the last few decades. Much of it is far too technical and too difficult to summarize in this survey. The interested reader is asked to consult the more specialized books available.[6]

The beginnings of the *Nyāya* systems may go back to the disputations of Vedic scholars; already in the times of the *Upaniṣads* debating was cultivated as an art, following certain rules in which the basic elements of logical proof were contained.[7] The *Nyāya Sūtras*, ascribed to Gautama, the main text of the school, have received very important commentaries. They cannot be assigned to a definite date. All scholars agree that a considerable part of the *sūtras* consists of additions to an original work, additions that suggest early Buddhist interpolations and later Hindu insertions to invalidate the Buddhist arguments. From the probable identification of *nyāya* with the *anvīkṣikī* in Kautilīya's *Ārthaśāstra*,[8] we may assume that the *Nyāya* system already existed in some form in the fourth century B.C.E. Professor Kuppuswami Sastri mentions further references, which prove that "these two schools should have appeared in a fairly definite form with their characteristic methods of reasoning and metaphysics by the middle of the fourth century B.C.E. though the chief doctrines of these schools came to be systematized and redacted in their basic *sūtras* at a relatively later date."[9] Followers of the *Nyāya* system have produced a large amount of important work, and of all the Hindu systems, *Nyāya* enjoys the greatest respect on the part of Western philosophers, who are coming to discover the enormous subtleties and intricacies of Indian logic.

A BRIEF SUMMARY OF *VAIŚEṢIKA*

"Now an explanation of *dharma*," begins the Kaṇāda *Sūtra*. "The means to prosperity and salvation is *dharma*." The attainment of salvation is the result of the cognition of the six categories: substance, quality, action, class concept, particularity, and inherence.[10] The substances are earth, water, fire, air, ether, time, space, *ātman*, and mind. The qualities are taste, color, odor, touch, number, measure, separation, contact, disjoining, prior and posterior, understanding, pleasure and pain, desire and aversion, and volition.

Action (*karma*) is explained as upward movement, downward movement, contraction, expansion, horizontal movement. The feature common to substance, quality, and action is that they are existent, noneternal, and substantive; they effect, cause, and possess generality and particularity. A major part of the *sūtra* consists in a further elucidation of the various terms just mentioned, much in the same way in which the early Greek philosophers of nature analyzed and described the elements, their qualities, and the interrelations. In the third book, the *sūtra* deals with the inference of the existence of the *ātman*, which is impervious to sense-perception, from the fact that there must be some substance in which knowledge, produced by the contact of the senses and their objects, inheres. Thus, the *ātman*'s existence may be inferred from inhalation and exhalation, from the twinkling of the eyes, from life, from movements of the mind, from sense affections, from pleasure and pain, will, antipathy, and effort. It can be proved that the *ātman* is a substance and eternal. Eternal (*nitya*) is that which exists but has no cause for its existence. The noneternal is *avidyā*, ignorance.

In the seventh book, we are told that *dṛṣṭa*, insight based on observation and rationality, is able to explain even natural phenomena only up to a certain point. All the special phenomena of nature are caused by *adṛṣṭa*, an unknown invisible cause. *Adṛṣṭa* is also said to be the cause of the union of body and soul, of rebirth and of liberation. This "invisible fruit," which is the cause of ultimate happiness, is produced by ablutions, fasting, continence, life in the *guru*'s family, life in the forest, sacrifice, gifts and alms, observation of the cosmic cycle, and adherence to the rules of *dharma*. Thus, *Vaiśeṣika* places itself quite explicitly in the tradition of Vedic orthodoxy. The *sūtra* also discusses at some length the means and instruments of valid knowledge, topics that are dealt with more thoroughly in the sister-system of *Nyāya*. The *Vaiśeṣika Sūtras* do not contain any polemics against the Buddhists, although these are opposed to some of their quite fundamental tenets. Buddhism denies the "thing in itself" and explains all phenomena merely as a chain of conditions that ultimately can be reduced to nonexistence; the Vaiśeṣikas, on the contrary, hold fast to the real existence of things.

Later works of the school, the commentaries on the *Sūtra* by Śaṅkara Miśra and Candrakānta, the *Padārthadharmasaṅgraha* by Praśastapāda, and the *Daśapadārthi* by Maticandra (preserved only in a Chinese version) also give a more detailed explanation of Indian atomism. What we hear, feel, see, etc. are not *continua* but *discreta—quanta* we would say today—and these again are not units but compounds of infinitely small indivisible parts (*aṇu*) that clearly differ from one another. Things are products, therefore, and not eternal.

Of the primordial elements, earth, water, fire and air, are partly eternal, partly temporal. Only ether is completely eternal. The first four elements have mass, number, weight, fluidity, viscosity, velocity, characteristic potential color, taste, smell or touch. *Ākāśa*, space or ether, is absolutely inert and structureless, the substratum of *śabda* or sound, which is thought to travel like a wave in the medium of air. Atomic combinations are possible only with the four basic elements. Both in dissolution and before creation, the atoms exist singly; in creation they are always present in combination. Two atoms combine to form a *dvyaṇuka*, a molecule. Also possible are *tryaṇukas, caturaṇukas*, etc., that is, molecules consisting of three or more atoms. Atoms are possessed of an inherent incessant vibratory motion; but they are also under the influence of the *adṛṣṭa*, the will of *Īśvara*, who arranges them into a harmonic universe. Changes in substances, which are limited within the frame of possible atom combinations, are brought about by heat. Under the impact of heat corpuscles, a molecule may disintegrate, and the characters of the atoms composing it may change. The heat particles that continue to impinge on the individually changed atoms also cause them to reunite in different forms so that definite changes are effected through heat.

In many details, the *Vaiśeṣikas* reveal a keen observation of nature and describe in their books a great number of phenomena, which they try to explain with the help of their atom theory. Similar to modern physicists, the ancient *Vaiśeṣikas* explained heat and light rays as consisting of indefinitely small particles that dart forth or radiate in all directions, rectilineally with inconceivable velocity. Heat also penetrates the interatomic space or impinges on the atoms and rebounds, thus explaining the conduction and reflection of heat. All the *paramāṇus* are thought to be spherical. Attempts have been made to link the atomism of the *Vaiśeṣika darśana* with Democritus, so far without any positive evidence.

We shall leave out most of the technicalities of the system that, though of great interest to the specialist, would burden the reader with too much detail. However, a brief description of *viśeṣa*, the term that gave the name to the whole system, may be helpful since it gives us an idea of the subtlety with which the ancient Indian philosophers reasoned and expressed themselves.

Praśastapāda writes:

> *Viśeṣas* are the ultimate specificatives or differentiatives of their substrates. They reside in such beginningless and indestructible eternal substances as the atoms, *ākāśa*, time, space, *ātman* and *manas*—inhering in their entirety in each of these, and serving as the basis of absolute differentiation of specification. Just as we have with regard to the bull as distinguished from the horse, certain distinct cognitions—such, for instance as (a) that is a "bull," which is a cognition based upon its having the shape of other bulls, (b) that it is "white", which is based upon a quality, (c) that it is "running swiftly", which is based upon action, (d) that it has a "fat hump", which is based upon "constituent parts" and (e) that

it carries a "large bell", which is based upon conjunction; so have the Yogis, who are possessed of powers that we do not possess, distinct cognitions based upon similar shapes, similar qualities and similar actions—with regard to the eternal atoms, the liberated selves and minds; and as in this case no other cause is possible, those causes by reason whereof they have such distinct cognitions—as that "this is a peculiar substance", "that a peculiar self" and so forth—and which also lead to the recognition of one atom as being the same that was perceived at a different time and place—are what we call the *viśeṣas.*[11]

According to the teaching of the *Vaiśeṣikas*, there are many different *ātmans* distinguished by their relative and specific *viśeṣas*. The common man, however, is able to recognize their diversity only on account of externally perceptible actions, qualities, and so on. Only the *yogi* has the "insight into the essence of the soul itself and thus into the real cause of their diversity." The *ātman* is eternal and not bound to space and time. But the actions of *ātman*—thought, will, emotions—are limited to the physical organism with which it is united at a given time. *Jñāna*, knowledge, is according to the *Vaiśeṣikas* only an accident of *ātman*, not its nature as such, since in dreamless sleep there is no cognition. Emotions and will are, likewise, mere accidents. The "spiritual" is not substantial but accidental. *Manas*, the mind given to every *ātman*, is merely its instrument and does not produce anything of itself. On the other hand, the cooperation of *manas* is necessary.

The state of *mokṣa*, or freedom, "is neither a state of pure knowledge nor of bliss, but a state of perfect qualitylessness, in which the self remains in itself in its own purity. It is the negative state of absolute painlessness."[12] Concerning the way to reach it, we read in the *Daśapadārtha Śāstra:*

One who seeks eternal emancipation ought to devote himself to *śīla* or morality, *dāna* or liberality, *tapas* or austerities, and *yoga*. From these comes supreme merit which leads to the attainment of emancipation and *tattva-jñāna* or knowledge of ultimate truth.

"Prosperity" is enjoyment of pleasure in *svarga* or heaven. Knowledge of ultimate truth brings *mokṣa* or permanent liberation, when merit and demerit have been completely destroyed and *ātman* and *manas* no longer come in contact with each other, that is when the nine things are no longer produced.[13]

Dharma and *adharma* together form *adṛṣṭa*, which supports the cycle of *samsāra*, of attraction and aversion, and continuously drives the *ātman* back into bodily existence. The activity guided by the feeling of the particular existence depends on *avidyā;* when a person realizes that things as such are only varying combinations of atoms of the particular elements, all affection and aversion ceases. If the right knowledge of the self is achieved, egotism and all selfish activity ceases. When *adṛṣṭa* is no longer produced, the transmigratory cycle comes to an end. On the other hand, *ātman* is never completely without *adṛṣṭa*, because the series of births is beginningless. When the soul has rid itself of its gross body it still is and remains attached to the subtle body, even in *pralaya*, the dissolution of the universe. Time, place, and circumstances of birth, family, and duration of life are all determined by *adṛṣṭa*, and it is not possible ever to destroy it completely.

Kaṇāda's *sūtra* manages without introducing the idea of *Īśvara*. The substances are eternal; movement is due to the impersonal, eternal principle of *adṛṣṭa*. Later authors introduce an eternal, omniscient, and omnipresent *Īśvara*, who is responsible for the universal order of atoms and their movements. This *Vaiśeṣika* God, however, resembles very much the *deus otiosus* of deism. *Ātman* and the *aṇu* do not owe their existence to a creator, they are eternal and independent. *Īśvara* differs from the *ātman* only insofar as he is never entangled in *saṁsāra*. He gives laws to the world but never interferes with it subsequently. He winds up the clockwork and lets it run its course.

NYĀYA AND *NAVYA-NYĀYA*

Nyāya, even in ancient times, was composed of two parts: *adhyātmavidyā* or metaphysics, and *tarkaśāstra*, or science of the rules of debate. Thus, the *Nyāya Sūtra*, famous for its acute analysis of discursive thought, also has substantial sections on suffering, soul, and salvation. It begins with the following aphorism:

> It is the knowledge of the true character of the following sixteen categories that leads to the attainment of the highest good: (1) The Means of Right Cognition; (2) The Objects of Right Cognition; (3) Doubt; (4) Motive; (5) Example; (6) Theory; (7) Factors of Inference; (8) Cogitation; (9) Demonstrated Truth; (10) Discussion; (11) Disputation; (12) Wrangling; (13) Fallacious Reason; (14) Casuistry; (15) Futile Rejoinder and (16) Clinchers.

Logic is practiced here for the sake of salvation. That gives greater weight to the *Nyāya Sūtra* within Hinduism than a book on logic would normally have within a religious tradition. Logic as a way to truth is a means of liberation: "Suffering, birth, activity, mistaken notions, folly—if these factors are cancelled out in reverse order, there will be *mokṣa*."[14]

S. K. Sarma makes an important point when he states: "*Nyāya* is not logic in the strict sense of the word. It is a system of philosophy. It is true that it lays stress on inference or reasoning as a means to correct knowledge, but it is not formal. It is not a mere device for correct thinking, but a well-thought-out and complete metaphysical thesis."[15]

A definite break in the development of *Nyāya* took place in the twelfth century, which marks the rise of *Navya-Nyāya* or the New Logic. Whereas the earlier works had concentrated on the elucidation of the categories, as enumerated in the *Nyāya Sūtra*, the *Tattvacintāmaṇi* by Gaṅgeśa, the major work of the new school emphasized the *pramāṇas*, the means of valid cognition, devoting one chapter each to perception (*pratyakṣa*), inference (*anumāna*) analogy (*upamāna*), and verbal testimony (*śabda*).

In spite of the intention to keep the description nontechnical, it may be remarked that *Navya-Nyāya* not only developed a highly complex epistemology but also created a technical language with the help of newly coined terms and, thus, initiated a quite peculiar style of philosophical writing in India, which stands out for its brevity and precision. The development of *Navya-Nyāya* and the focus upon *pramāṇas* instead of on the *Nyāya Sūtras* did not prevent the continued production of works of the "old school" alongside the flourishing "new logic." Works in both branches keep appearing, even in our day.

The special field of *Navya-Nyāya* is epistemology. It acknowledges four legitimate means of finding truth: *pratyakṣa*, or sense perception; *anumāṇa*, or inference; *upamāna*, or analogy; and *śabda*, or scriptural authority. *Pratyakṣa* is the perception that results from the contact of one of the senses with its proper object: it is definite, uncontradicted and unassociated with names. *Anumāna* is of three kinds: *pūrvavat*, or from cause to effect; *śeṣavat*, or from effect to cause; and *sāmānyato dṛṣṭa*, or from common characteristics. *Upamāna* is the knowledge of anything by its similarity with another well-known thing. *Śabda* is defined as the testimony of reliable authority, which may also transcend one's own experience.

The objects of knowledge are *ātman*, the body, senses, sense objects; *buddhi*, understanding; *manas*, mind; *pravṛtti*, endeavor; rebirths, enjoyment of pleasure, suffering of pain, sorrow, and liberation. Desire, aversion, effort, pleasure, and pain, as well as knowledge, indicate the existence of the *ātman*. Whereas the classical Aristotelian syllogism has three members —major (thesis), minor (antithesis), and conclusion—the Nyāya-syllogism has five:

1. *pratijñā*, or the stating of the point to be proved;
2. *hetu*, or the reason that establishes the proof;
3. *udahāraṇa*, or illustrative example;
4. *upanaya*, or corroboration by the instance;
5. *nigamana*, or inference, identical with the initial assertion.

The standard example of Indian logic for many centuries has been the following:

1. The mountain there in the distance is ablaze;
2. Because it is wreathed in smoke;
3. Whatever is wreathed in smoke is on fire, as for example, a stove;
4. The mountain there is wreathed in smoke in such a manner;
5. Therefore: the mountain there in the distance is ablaze.

The discussion of fallacies and doubt demonstrates the lucidity and sharpness of the Naiyāyikas' intellects. All kinds of fallacies are analyzed and the causes of doubt are explained, but the general scepticism of the Buddhists, who maintained that nothing can be known with certainty, is refuted. The polemics against Buddhism, especially the *Śūnyavādins*, plays a large part in *Nyāya* literature. Naiyāyikas dissolve the extreme scepticism of the Buddhists with their critical realism and take the wind out of the Buddhists' sails by disproving their teaching of emptiness and the impossibility of true cognition with the very arguments that the Buddhists have used. The Naiyāyikas seek to demonstrate that real liberation is possible through true cognition of reality. They largely agree with the *Vaiśeṣika* metaphysics when they define *mokṣa* only in negative terms as "absolute freedom from pain."[16] It is a "condition of immortality, free from fear, imperishable," to be attained only after bodily death—there can be no *jīvanmukta.*[17]

Quite unique in Indian philosophy are the arguments for the existence of *Īśvara*, which are found in *Nyāya* works.[18] The *Nyāya Kusumañjali* states that the experience of contingency, eternity, diversity, activity, and individual existence requires an *adṛṣṭa*, an unseen cause, responsible ultimately for the joys and sorrows of human life. Above the *adṛṣṭa* of the *Vaiśeṣikas*, the Naiyāyikas postulate a lord as the cause of right knowledge, creation, and destruction: "From effects, combination, support, etc. and traditional arts, authority, *śruti* and so on, an everlasting omniscient being must be assumed." The commentary on this text explains:

> The earth etc. must have had a maker, because they have the nature of effects like a jar; by a thing's having a maker we mean that it is produced by some agent who possesses the wish to make, and has also a perceptive knowledge of the material cause out of which it is to be made. "Combination" is an action, and therefore the action which produced the conjunction of two atoms, initiating the *dvyaṇuka* at the beginning of a creation, must have been accompanied by the volition of an intelligent being, because it has the nature of an action like

> the actions of bodies such as ours. "Support" etc.: the world depends upon some being who possesses a volition which hinders it from falling, because it has the nature of being supported. . . . By traditional arts etc.: The traditional arts now current, such as that of making cloth, must have been originated by an independent being, from the very fact that they are traditional usages like the tradition of modern modes of writing. "From authority": The knowledge produced by the *Vedas* is produced by a virtue residing in its cause, because it is right knowledge, just as is the case in the right knowledge produced by perception. "From *śruti*": The *Veda* must have been produced by a person, from its having the nature of a *Veda* like the *Āyur Veda*. . . . At the beginning of creation there must be the number of duality abiding in the atoms, which is the cause of the measure of the *dvyaṇuka*, but this number cannot be produced at that time by the distinguishing perception of beings like ourselves. Therefore we can only assume this distinguishing faculty as then existing in *Īśvara*.[19]

The lord is qualified by absence of *adharma;* of *mithyājñāna*, false knowledge; and of *pramāda*, error and the positive presence of *dharma*, right knowledge, and equanimity. He is omnipotent, though influenced in his actions by the acts of his creatures. He acts only for the good of his creatures and acts toward them like a father toward his children.[20] The Naiyāyikas also develop a theory of grace: "*Īśvara* indeed supports the efforts of people, i.e. if a person tries to attain something special, it is *Īśvara* who attains it; if *Īśvara* does not act, the activity of people is fruitless."

A good deal of Nyāya is so technical that it taxes the understanding even of a specialist in Western logic, not to speak of the general reader. Much of it is of interest mainly against the background of inter-Indian disputes, especially with Buddhist logicians. It is, however, important to note that India, too, has its schools of critical logicians and that, despite the popular opinion of Indian philosophy being merely opaque mysticism, there is also the disciplined reasoning of logic.

Tarkaśāstra, the study of formal logic, is a difficult business and no more popular in India than anywhere else. Keśava Miśra of the fourteenth century, the author of a concise textbook that is still widely used, starts off his course in the following gruff manner: "I am writing this 'Exposition of Reasoning' consisting, as it does, of short and easy explanations of arguments, for the sake of the dull youth who wishes to have to learn as little as possible for the purpose of entering the portals of the Nyaya *darśana*."[21]

The *Nyāya-vaiśeṣika* has remained a living philosophical tradition even in our age. The more it is studied, the more respect it commands for its incisiveness and brilliance of definition. It could also possibly make a substantial contribution to the contemporary philosophy of science, anticipating, often by many centuries, problems that we are only now discovering.

25. Hindu Psychology and Metaphysics: *Sāṁkhya-Yoga*

> Absolute freedom comes when the *guṇas*, becoming devoid of the object of the *puruṣa*, become latent; or the power or consciousness becomes established in its own nature.
>
> —*Pātañjala* Yoga Sūtra *IV, 34*

*Y*OGA IS ONE of the most popular and most ambiguous words in Indian literature, a word with which every Westerner seems to be familiar, as the advertisements of numerous *yoga* schools suggest. Etymologically, the word is derived from the root *yuj-*, "to join, to unite." Pāṇiṇi, the grammarian, explains the meaning of *yoga* as virtually identical with that of the English word *religion*, union with the Supreme. Patañjali, in his *Yoga Sūtra*, defines *yoga* as "cessation of all changes in consciousness." According to the Vedāntins, *yoga* means the return of the *jīvātman*, the individual being, to its union with the *paramātman*, the Supreme Self. In a more general sense, Hindu scriptures use the word *yoga* as a synonym to *mārga*, denoting any system of religion or philosophy, speaking of *karma-yoga, bhaktiyoga, jñānayoga.*

We propose here only to deal with *yoga* in its technical and classical sense; with the *Yoga* system as explained by Patañjali. The system is called *Rāja-yoga*, the "royal way" in contrast to *Haṭha-yoga*, the "tour de force"[1] of most Western *yoga* schools, or the *Kuṇḍalinī-yoga* of the Śāktas, mentioned earlier. It is also called *Sāṁkhya-yoga*, because of its intimate connection with the *darśana* known as Sāṁkhya.[2]

HISTORICAL SURVEY

Sāṁkhya-Yoga is possibly the oldest among the Indian systems.

It has become, in one form or another, part and parcel of most major religions of India. Thus, *Sāmkhya-yoga* is found combined with Vaiṣṇavism, Śaivism, and Śāktism, and most of the *Purāṇas* contain numerous chapters on *Sāṁkhya-yoga* as a path to salvation.[3] If fell into disfavor when Vedānta, in one of its denominational schools, became the predominant theology of Hinduism. The reasons for this development are twofold. First, Sāṃkhya does not base its statements on scripture; it even explicitly rates *śruti* no higher than reasoning. Second, it did not recognize a lord above *puruṣa* and *prakṛti*, an idea that was crucial to the theistic systems of mediaeval Hinduisṃ.

The interpretation of some Indus civilisation seals showing figures in what has been interpreted as *yoga* postures would suggest a prehistoric root of practices, later brought together in the *Yoga* system. The basic idea of the *Sāṁkhya*, the male-female polarity as the source of all development, does not need a specific "inventor," it can easily be considered as "natural." Some of the earlier *Upaniṣads* contain allusions to doctrines that could be termed *Sāṁkhya*, leaving open the question whether the *Upaniṣads* made use of an already developed philosophical system or whether the system developed out of the elements provided in the *Upaniṣads*. In order to explain the name *Sāṁkhya*, in modern Indian languages the word for number, some scholars have resorted to the hypothesis of an original Sāṁkhya that, like the school of Pythagoras, was concerned with numbers, and conceived the world as being constructed from harmonious proportions.[4] S. N. Dasgupta, moreover, sees a close inner relationship between *Sāṁkhya-Yoga* and Buddhism. He writes: "Sāṁkhya and the Yoga, like the Buddhists, hold that experience is sorrowful. *Tamas* represents the pain-substance. As *tamas* must be present in some degree in all combinations, all intellectual operations are fraught with some degree of painful feeling."[5]

The original meaning of Sāṁkhya must have been very general—understanding, reflection, discussion—so that the name came to connote philosophy or system. Kapila, its mythical founder, figures quite often as the father of philosophy as such in the Indian tradition. Later Vedānta, which assumes a different position on many basic issues, polemizes quite frequently against the *Sāṁkhya* system, but there is hardly a book that does not deal with it or that would not betray its influence.

Sāṁkhya ideas may be found already in the cosmogonic hymns of the *Ṛgveda*, in sections of the *Atharvaveda*, in the idea of the evolution of all things from one principle, dividing itself, in the *Upaniṣads* and also in the Upaniṣadic attempts to arrange all phenomena under a limited number of categories. The *Mahābhārata* has sections explaining the full *Sāṁkhya* system, though with significant differences from classical

Sāṁkhya. The Great Epic makes Kapila the son of Brahmā; according to the *Bhāgavata Purāṇa* he is an *avatāra* of Viṣṇu, who teaches *Sāṁkhya,* a system of liberation, through which his mother reaches instant release.[6] There is not much historical evidence for the opinion, found in some works on Indian philosohy, that as a historical person Kapila belongs to the sixth century B.C.E. The oldest traditional textbook of the school is the *Sāṁkhya-kārikā* of Īśvara Kṛṣṇa, dating probably from the third century C.E. This work, which has received numerous important commentaries in later centuries, claims to be the complete summary of the entire *Ṣaṣṭitantra,* perhaps an older work. The *Sāṁkhyakārikā* are a short treatise, containing only seventy aphorisms.[7] The *Sāṁkhya Sūtra,* ascribed to Kapila himself, is a later work, much longer than the *Kārikā* and going into great detail.[8]

Yoga as a system is dealt with quite extensively in some of the later *Upaniṣads,* which in fact sometimes are brief compendia of Yoga.[9] The *Tejobindu Upaniṣad* gives a rather detailed description of *Rāja-yoga.* Many of the teachings found in it can be discovered word for word in Patañjali's *Yoga Sūtra,* which has become the classical textbook, commented upon by great scholars like Vyāsa and Bhoja.[10] This *Upaniṣad* suggests to the *yogi* who is intent on realization to repeat constantly: "I am *Brahman.*" He is advised sometimes to affirm and sometimes to negate the identity of all things with *Brahman.* "Renouncing all the various activities think thus: 'I am *brahman*—I am of the nature of *saccidānanda.*' And then renounce even this!"[11]

Most Indian schools, be they followers of the *Sāṁkhya* or of the Vedānta philosophy, accept *Patañjali yoga* as a practical and indispensable means for purification and concentration. Recently, a commentary to the *Patañjali Yoga Sūtra,* ascribed to Śaṅkara, has come to light. Many scholars assume it to be genuine, in spite of the polemic against *Sāṁkhya-Yoga* in the *Brahmasūtrabhāṣya.*[12]

THE BASIC PHILOSOPHY OF SĀṀKHYA

The *Sāṁkhyakārikās* begin with the aphorism: "From torment by three-fold misery the inquiry into the means of terminating it."[13] Our frustrations and pains, caused by *devas* and *asuras,* fellow humans, beasts, and inanimate objects as well as by ourselves,[14] are the stimulus for the quest for freedom from misery: Sāṁkhya offers the solution. Sāṁkhya neither denies the reality of experience nor the reality of pain accompanying every experience, but it offers a possibility of terminating this pain of experience. Rejecting all other means, the *Kārikās* establish the thesis that "the discriminative knowledge of the evolved, the unevolved and the knower is the means of surpassing all sorrow."[15]

Basically, Sāṁkhya defends, or rather presupposes, a dualistic realism. There are two beginningless realities: *prakṛti* and *puruṣa*, the female and the male principles, matter and spirit. Ideally, before the development of concrete existences, they exist separately in polarity. In actual existence, they are combined and interacting. *Puruṣa*, in himself pure consciousness, experiences the changes that *prakṛti*, on account of her three *guṇas*, is undergoing, as if these were his own. *Puruṣas* are originally many; *prakṛti* is originally one. The association with a *puruṣa* makes *prakṛti*, as the evolved being, manifold and makes *puruṣa* interact with it. Under the influence of *puruṣa*, out of the unevolved primordial *prakṛti*, develop macrocosm and microcosm according to a fixed pattern. Each part of it is characterized in a different measure by the presence of the three *guṇas*.

Originally, the three *guṇas—sattva*, lightness; *rajas*, passion; and *tamas*, darkness—had been in equilibrium in *prakṛti*. Under *puruṣa*'s influence, the equilibrium is disturbed and evolution begins. The first product of this evolutionary process, which simply takes its course without needing a creator or a world soul, is *mahat*, the Great One, also called *buddhi*, the intellect. From *mahat* issues *ahamkāra*, the principle of individuation. Having the *triguṇa* structure, it communicates this structure to the further evolutes, the senses and the elements that form their object. The enumeration of the twenty-four basic elements is intended also to provide a physically correct description of the universe and to prepare the ground for the way back to the source. Against those who assume that there is only one spirit in the universe, the *Kārikās* establish the following argument: "The plurality of *puruṣas* follows from the fact of individual death and individual birth, and from the fact that the organs of cognition and action are individual; moreover not all people are active at the same time and the relationship of the three *guṇas* varies from person to person.[16]

In *devas* and saintly people, *sattva* dominates; in ordinary people, *rajas;* and in animals, *tamas*. To dispel the objection that *prakṛti* is mere fiction because she cannot be seen, heard, touched, etc., the *Kārikās* state: "The non-perception is due to its subtlety, not to its non-existence, since it is cognized from its effects."[17] Knowing *prakṛti* as *prakṛti* is becoming free from her; for *prakṛti* is not only the means to bind *puruṣa* but also the means to free him. A person is free who is able to analyze experience in such a way as to differentiate *puruṣa* from *prakṛti* in consciousness, seeing in *prakṛti* the reason for the contingence of all things and the basis for all change and multiplicity. *Puruṣa*, though free by nature, is incapable of acting and thus unable to become free when united with *prakṛti*. "Certainly no *puruṣa* is in bondage and none is liberated nor has he to undergo any changes; it is *prakṛti*, dwelling in many forms, which is bound, freed and subject to change. *Prakṛti* binds herself sevenfold and through one form she causes liberation for the benefit of *puruṣa*."[18]

The *Kārikās* compare *puruṣa* and *prakṛti* with a lame man being carried by a blind man: the seeing lame man directs the blind walking one and realizes his own purpose. In another simile, the *puruṣa* is compared to a spectator observing a dancer. After the dancer has shown all her skills, she cannot but repeat her performance over and over. When the onlooker becomes aware of the repeat performance, he loses his interest. And the dancer, seeing that the spectator pays no more attention to her, ceases to dance. Although the union still persists, nothing more is produced from it. "*Puruṣa*, because of former impressions, remains united with the body, just like the potter's wheel continues to rotate for a while without being impelled again, due to the impulse received before."[19]

When the separation from the body finally takes place and the aim has been fulfilled, *prakṛti* ceases to be active and *puruṣa* reaches *kaivalya*, aloneness, perfect freedom. By doing away with objective sense perception, by tracing back egoism and discursive reasoning to *prakṛti*, and by coming to know the true nature of *prakṛti, puruṣa* becomes emancipated. Spirit, having been restless in connection with matter, realizes matter to be the cause of his restlessness. By realizing the nature of *prakṛti* as contrary to his own nature and recognizing all objective reality as but evolutes of *prakṛti*, the spirit becomes self-satisfied and self-reliant. The very dissociation of *puruṣa* from *prakṛti* is liberation.

THE THEORY AND PRACTICE OF YOGA

The practical process of discriminative knowledge leading to the actual achievement of the "isolation" of the *puruṣa* is proposed in Patañjali's *Yoga Sūtras*. *Yoga* is not mere theoretical knowledge. It also implies physical training, exertion of will power, and acts of decision, because it wants to deal with the complete human situation and provide real freedom, not just a theory of liberation.

The *Sūtra* itself, a short work of but 194 aphorisms, is clearly structured into four *pādas*, with the subject titles *samādhi, sādhana, vibhuti*, and *kaivalya*. The first *sūtra*, defining the aim and meaning of *Yoga* as *cittavṛttinirodha* goes to the very core of *Sāṁkhya* metaphysics. *Citta* is the same as the *mahat* of the *Sāṁkhya*, the first evolved, whose changes ultimately cause all suffering. For *citta*, the cessation of all changes means merging into *prakṛti*. *Prakṛti* then becomes again undifferentiated and dissociated from *puruṣa:* the *puruṣa* achieves *ekāgratā*, one-pointedness, *kaivalya*, aloneness, solitude, being with oneself only, being nothing but consciousness. The changes that may affect *citta* are fivefold: perception, delusion, imagination, deep sleep, and memory.[20] The means to do away with them is *abhyāsa* and *vairāgya*, the dialectic interaction of positive effort and renunciation.

The *Yoga Sūtras* introduce *Īśvara*, the Lord, as one of the supports of concentration. *Īśvara* is defined as a *puruṣa*, untouched by suffering, activity, and *karma*. He is the teacher of the ancients and is denoted by the sign OM, whose constant repetition is recommended to the *yogi* to attain *kaivalya*.[21] The Lord is also a help in removing the obstacles that hinder self-realization: sickness, suffering, indecision, carelessness, sloth, sensuality, false views, and inconstancy—all of which cause distraction. In the company of these distractions come pain, despair, tremor, and hard, irregular breathing. For the purification of the mind, the *Yoga Sūtra* recommends truthfulness, friendliness, compassion, and contentment, together with indifference toward happiness and unhappiness, virtue and vice. Breath control, too, is recommended.

The second part of the *Yoga Sūtra* dealing with *sādhana*, the means to liberation, begins with the aphorism: "The *yoga* of action is constituted by *tapas*, austerities; *svādhyāya*, scriptural study; and *īśvara praṇidhāna*, meditation with the Lord as object." Its goal is to attain *samādhi*, which may be translated as blissful inner peace, and to terminate the *kleśas*, the frustrations and afflictions. The cause of all suffering is identified as *avidyā*, lack of insight and wisdom. It manifests itself in four principal forms, namely, as *āsmita*, egoism; *rāga*, attachment; *dveṣa*, aversion; and *abhiniveṣa*, love of physical life. *Avidyā* is further explained as mistaking the non-eternal for the eternal, the impure for the pure, the painful for the pleasurable, and the not self for the Self.[22]

To combat these afflictions the *Yoga Sūtras* recommend *dhyāna*, meditation. The actual vehicle of liberation is *viveka*, discrimination, implying understanding of the Self as the only true and worthwhile being and the rest as illusion. This knowledge arises only after the impurities of the mind have been destroyed by the practice of the eight *yogāṅgas*, limbs of *yoga*. These are *yama* and *niyama*, ethical commands and prohibitions; *āsana*, certain bodily postures; *prāṇayama*, breath control; *pratyāhāra*, withdrawal of the senses; *dhāraṇā*, concentration exercises; *dhyāna*, meditation; and *samādhi*, inner composure.

The *Yoga Sūtras* find that the cause of all sin lies in *lobha, moha*, and *krodha*, greed, delusion, and anger, whereas the practice of the virtues produces many side effects that are helpful either for the *yogi's* own realization or for that of his fellows. Thus, when *ahiṁsā*, nonviolence, is firmly established, others, too, will give up their enmity and violence in the presence of the *yogi;* not only people but also animals will live peacefully with each other. When *satya*, the love of truth, is perfected, it enables a person to perform great deeds. When *asteya*, abstention from misappropriation is practiced, the treasures from which the *yogi* runs away will run after him. When *brahmacarya*, perfect continence, is practiced, great strength will come to the *yogi*. The practice of *aparigraha*, of generosity in the widest sense, brings with it a knowledge of the round of births. *Śauca*, disgust with one's own body, is accompanied by the end of the desire to have bodily contact with others. Purity also helps to attain physical well-being, control over one's senses, and concentration. *Santoṣa*, or contentment, brings inner peace and happiness to the *yogi*. *Tapasya*, the practice of austerity, purifies one from sins and makes the *yogi* acquire *siddhis*, supernatural faculties. Through *svādhyāya*, scriptural study, one can reach the *Iṣṭadevatā*. *Īśvara praṇidhāna*, surrender to the Lord, brings about *samādhi*, inner illumination.

Āsana, posture, is defined as a way of sitting that is agreeable and enables the practitioner to sit motionless for a long while without undue strain or falling asleep. It is intended to overcome the distraction caused by the *dvandvas*, the pairs of opposites, like heat and cold, hunger and thirst, comfort and discomfort. While the *Haṭha-yoga* manuals develop a veritable science of the *āsanas*, enumerating altogether eighty-four often extremely difficult body postures for curing or preventing diseases or attaining certain other results, Patañjali is of the opinion that any position will serve, provided that it allows a person to practice continued concentration and meditation. The aim of yoga is neither self-mortification for its own sake nor the cure of bodily ailments but spiritual realization.[23]

In the third *pāda*, Patañjali speaks about the extraordinary or miraculous faculties of the yogi, *siddhis* or *vibhutis* that appear as side effects of *yoga*. Despite Patañjali's warning that they should not be cultivated because they detract from the principal aim of *yoga* as spiritual realization, at all times a number of *yogis* have practiced *yoga* for the sake of those *siddhis:* becoming invisible, reducing one's size to that of a grain of sand or increasing it to the volume of a mountain, adopting a radiant body or leaving the body and re-entering it at will.

Patañjali stresses the moral aspects of the preparation for *kaivalya*. If evil desires and intentions are not completely purged, there is the danger that the increased power a *yogi* wins through concentration may be used for evil purposes rather than for realization of the highest aim.

Dietetic rules are rather prominent in many books on *yoga;* whatever is sour, salty or pungent should be avoided. Nonstimulating food will allow the body to come to rest; milk alone is the ideal food for *yogis*.

THE CORE OF *YOGA*

In the *Yoga Sūtras*, one of the most important topics is *prāṇayama*.

The great significance of *prāṇa*, life breath, in philosophical speculation was mentioned earlier. *Prāṇayama* is one of the most widely practiced disciplines and one of the most ancient methods of purification. Perfect breath control can be carried so far that, to all appearances, a person does not breathe any more and the heart beat becomes imperceptible. Thus, we hear quite frequently about *yogis* who get themselves buried for days or weeks and let themselves be admired on coming out of their graves. According to all indications, there is neither fraud nor miracle involved. The secret lies in the consciously controlled reduction of metabolism to the minimum required for keeping the life processes going and in overcoming fear through concentration, for fear would increase the need for oxygen. The *Yoga Sūtras* end the explanations on *prāṇayama* with the statement: "The mind's ability for concentration." Breath control is the basis of body control and of mental realization.

Pratyāhāra, withdrawal of the senses, is dealt with immediately afterwards: "When the senses do not have any contact with their objects and follow, as it were, the nature of the mind."[24] The senses, in this condition, not only no longer hinder the intellect but the power invested in them actively helps it.

The next section is probably the most crucial one. It deals with three stages of realization. They are briefly explained as follows: "*Dhāraṇa* is the fixation of the intellect on one topic. *Dhyāna* is the one-pointedness in this effort. *Samādhi* is the same [concentration] when the object itself alone appears devoid of form, as it were."[25] The commentaries explain the first stage as a concentration of the mind on certain areas in the body: the navel, the heart, the forehead, the tip of the nose, or the tip of the tongue. In the second stage, all objects are consciously eliminated and the union with the absolute is contemplated. In its perfection, it glides over into the third and last stage. Here, the identification has gone so far that there is no longer a process of contemplation of an object by a subject but an absolute identity between the knower, that which is known, and the process of knowing. Subject-object polarity disappears in a pure "isness," a cessation of the particular in an absolute self-awareness.

The three stages together are called *saṁyama*. They are understood not as something that happens incidentally to someone but as a practice that can be learned and acquired and then exercised at will. It is the specific schooling of the *yogi* to acquire those tools with which one masters the world. Though we must omit the details here, suffice it to say that, as with the mastery of any science, *yoga* requires a certain talent, hard work, and progress through many small steps, avoiding numerous pitfalls on the way, before one can competently use the instruments. If the training is applied to the various objects and the various levels of reality, the *yogi* can win knowledge of the future and the past; obtain a knowledge of all languages and the sounds of all living beings; understand the language of the animals; know about former births; read other people's thought; become invisible; foresee the exact time of death; become full of goodwill toward all creatures; gain the strength of an elephant; have knowledge of what is subtle, distant, and hidden; know the regions of the firmament, the stars and their orbits, and the whole anatomy of the human body; suppress completely hunger and thirst; see the *devas;* have foreknowledge of all that is going to happen; receive extrasensory sight, hearing, and taste; acquire the ability to enter other bodies mentally at will; walk freely on water without even touching it; walk across thorny and muddy ground without getting hurt or dirty; acquire a body that is bright and weightless; leave the body and act without it; become master of all material elements; obtain a body that is beautiful, strong, and as hard as a diamond; have direct knowledge of the *pradhāṇa,* the ground from which all beings come; and have mastery over all conditions of being as well as omniscience.[26]

More than anything else those *vibhutis* have been described and dreamed about in literature about Indian *yogis.* Biographies and autobiographies of *yogis* are full of reports about achievements following the line of the *Yogasūtras.* In actual Indian life, one hardly ever encounters any miracles of this sort. Living for two years in a place where thousands of holy men and women dwelled and where countless rumors of such things circulated, I never witnessed a single incident corresponding to this idea of the miraculous. Not too many years ago, a *yogi* called a press conference in Bombay and announced that he would demonstrate walking on water without wetting even his feet, against a reward of 1 million rupees. The bargain was agreed upon and a tank was filled with water. The *yogi* could choose the auspicious time for his performance. When the hour had come, scores of journalists and hundreds of curious onlookers were present to watch the *yogi* win his million. He lost it, being unable even to swim like an ordinary mortal. Later, "unfavorable circumstances" were blamed for the *yogi's* failure, and another attempt was announced for an undisclosed future date.

According to Patañjali, the purpose of many of these *vibhutis* is fulfilled if the *yogi* in a trance experiences those miraculous happenings as if they were real. In the overall context of *Rāja-yoga,* the *siddhis* are an obstacle on the way to *samādhi.*

The fourth and last *pāda* of the *Yogasūtras* deals with *kaivalya,* the goal of *yoga.* The introductory aphorism states that the *siddhis* mentioned earlier are brought about either by imprints left in the psyche from previous births, by drugs, by *mantras,* or by *samādhi.* The proper thrust of *samādhi,* however, is not backward into the world of objects, from which it is freeing the spirit, but forward into the discrimination of *puruṣa* from the *guṇas* that belong to *prakṛti*. *Viveka*, discriminatory knowledge, means freedom from the influence of the *guṇas:* they return to their source as soon as their task is fulfilled. *Prakṛti* withdraws as soon as *puruṣa* has seen her as *prakṛti*. When the *guṇas* cease to be effective, activity and passivity, action and suffering also cease. "*Kaivalya* is realized when the *guṇas*, annihilated in the objectives of a person, cease to exert influence, or when *citta-śakti*, the power of consciousness, is established in her own proper nature."[27]

Yoga is the reversal of the evolutionary process demonstrated in the Sāṁkhya system, it is the entering into the origins. It is not, however, simply an annihilation of creation. *Sāṁkhya* does not think genetically, in the model of modern science, but phenomenologically. *Prakṛti*, "matter," is not an object of physics but of metaphysics. Her eternity is not the indestructibility of a concrete object but of potentiality.[28] When *puruṣa* combines with her, no additional cause from outside is needed to set evolution going, but an unfolding of primeval matter that, until then, had existed as mere potency and that was always there. *Yoga* comes close to what we today would call psycho-science, that is, a detailed observation of human nature, but with a deep conviction of an ultimate that is missing in modern psychology.

26. Hindu Theology, Old and New: *Pūrva Mīmāṁsā* and *Vedānta*

Dharma is that which is indicated by means of the *Veda* as conducive to the highest good.

—Mīmāṁsāsūtra *I, 1, 2*

Brahman is that from which the origin, subsistence and dissolution of this world proceeds.

—Brahmasūtra *I, 1, 2*

MĪMĀṀSĀ, ENQUIRY, IS the name of two very different systems of Hindu theology that have, however, one thing in common: out of the statements of *śruti* they develop a complete theology.

Pūrva-Mīmāṁsā (often simply called *Mīmāṁsā*), the "earlier enquiry" has *dharma* as its proper subject and the *karmakāṇḍa* of the *Vedas* as its scriptural source. Though, historically, there was a considerable amount of friction between the two systems, they are also complementary in many ways and are considered to be the two most orthodox of the six systems. Certainly, they are the two *darśanas* that come closest to the idea of theology as developed in the West.

THE OLD THEOLOGY

Mīmāṁsā, the "old theology," uses as its basic textbook the *Mīmāṁsā Sūtras* ascribed to Jaimini, dated around 200 B.C.E. The terse *sūtras* have received ample commentary by various writers; the most extensive and famous of these is the *Śābara-bhāṣya*, written probably in the first century

B.C.E.[1] The "old theology" has also produced brilliant philosophers like Prabhākara and Kumārila Bhaṭṭa; the latter is supposed to have been an older contemporary of the great "new theologian," Śaṅkara.[2] Though a good deal of the specific theology of *Mīmāṁsā*, dealing with the Vedic sacrificial ritual, has ceased to command a leading role and has been replaced by the more speculative approach of the Vedāntins, the old theology is still of unquestionably great importance. As Dasgupta writes: "Not only are all Vedic duties to be performed according to its maxims, but even the *smṛti* literatures which regulate the daily duties, ceremonials and rituals of the Hindus even to the present day are all guided and explained by them. The legal side of the *smṛtis* which guide Hindu civil life, . . . is explained according to *Mīmāṁsā* maxims."[3] The principles of Vedic exegesis developed by the Mīmāṁsakas, as well as their epistemology, are accepted by the Vedāntins, too, who otherwise disagree with some of their fundamental tenets.[4]

Athāto dharmajijñāsa, "Now, then, a enquiry into *dharma*," is how the *Jaimini Sūtra* begins. It goes on to explain "*Dharma* is that which is indicated by Vedic injunctions for the attainment of the good."[5] The Mīmāṁsakas took it for granted that the performance of sacrifices was the means to attain everything and that the Veda was meant to serve this end alone. Despite their insistence that the Veda was *apauruṣeya*, not man-made but infallible revelation, they were prepared to drop as nonessential all those parts of the *Veda* that had nothing directly to do with sacrificial ritual. "The purpose of the Veda lying in the enjoining of actions, those parts of the Veda which do not serve that purpose are useless; in these therefore the Veda is declared to be non-eternal."[6]

Classical *Mīmāṁsā* does not admit the existence of any *īśvara* as the creator and destroyer of the universe. Mīmāṁsakas even formulate arguments that positively disprove the existence of God.[7] The world, in their view, has always existed and the only real agent of a permanent nature was the sacrifice, or rather its unseen essence, the *apūrva*. Sacrifice, therefore, is the only topic that really interests the Mīmāṁsakas. The texts concentrate on the eternity of the *Veda*, on the means to its correct understanding, and on the validity of human knowledge as preliminaries to this question.[8]

Many times we read in the *Brāhmaṇas*, "Desiring heaven one should perform sacrifice." Consequently, the Mīmāṁsakas emphasize that "desire for heaven" is the basic presupposition for performing a sacrifice. Besides animals, *devas*, and the Vedic *ṛṣis*, women and *śūdras* are categorically excluded from the performance of sacrifices. So are those who lack sufficient wealth or suffer from a physical disability.[9] The theory of *apūrva* is intended to explain the infallible effect of a sacrifice. The Mīmāṁsakas say that the *apūrva* is related to the verb of the Vedic injunction because this expresses something as yet to be accomplished. More subtly *Mīmāṁsa* distinguishes between principal and secondary *apūrva.*[10]

The *Mīmāṁsāsūtra* is very brief in its description of the state to be achieved through sacrifice, namely, *svarga* or heaven. Mīmāṁsakas are probably convinced that one cannot know much about it. By the very principles that it establishes, *Mīmāṁsa* must come to the conclusion that those passages in the *Vedas* that describe heaven, not enjoining certain acts, cannot be taken as authoritative. One *sūtra* says "That one result would be heaven, as that is equally desirable for all."[11] To which the commentator adds: "Why so? Because heaven is happiness and everyone seeks for happiness." The *Mīmāṁsā Sūtra* does not mention the term *mokṣa* at all. Śabara declared that the statements concerning heaven found in the *Mahābhārata* and the *Purāṇas* can be neglected because these books were composed by men and also that Vedic descriptions of heaven were mere *arthavāda*, that is, without authority.[12]

Later Mīmāṁsakas, perhaps influenced by Vedānta, introduce the term *mokṣa* into their vocabulary and describe it as not having to assume a body after death.[13] They also offer a description of the way to liberation. First of all, a man becomes disgusted with the troubles that he has to undergo during his life on earth. Finding the pleasures of the world to be invariably accompanied by some sort of pain, he comes to lose all interest in and longing for pleasures. He thereupon turns his attention toward liberation, ceases to perform such acts as are prohibited and lead to misfortune, as well as those that are prescribed only to lead to some sort of happiness here or hereafter. He attenuates all previously acquired merit and demerit by undergoing the experiences resulting from them. He destroys the sole receptacle or abode of his experiences by the knowledge of the soul and is aided by such qualities as contentment, self-control, and so forth, all of which are laid down in the scriptures as helping to prevent the further return of the soul into this world. It is only when all this has come about that the soul becomes free, *mukta.*[14]

With their interest in language and analysis, the Mīmāṁsakas are often close to the Grammarians, who developed a philosophical school of their own. Quite important epistemological observations are to be found in the *Śābarabhāṣya*, observations that have prompted contemporary scholars to undertake interesting investigations.[15] The first major commentary on Pāṇini's grammar, the *Mahābhāṣya* by Patañjali (which is ascribed to the second century B.C.E.), contains questions concerning the nature and function of words. The unquestionably most famous name in Indian linguistic philosophy, however, is Bhaṛtrhari (ca. 500 C.E.) whose *Vākyapadīya* has been studied with great interest by Western scholars in recent years. His system is also called *sphoṭavāda* after its most characteristic teaching, which compares the sudden appearance of meaning at the enunciation of a word with the process of the sudden ejection of liquid from a boil.[16]

THE NEW THEOLOGY

Athāto brahmajijñāsa, "Now, then, an enquiry into *brahman*," begins the *Vedānta Sūtra*, which is ascribed to Bādarāyaṇa, and forms the basic text of Vedānta *darśana*. The 550 *sūtras*, purporting to summarize the teaching of the *Upaniṣads*, are usually so short, often consisting of not more than one or two words, that without a commentary they remain incomprehensible. In all probability, there had been a living tradition of Vedāntins in which the meaning of the *Vedānta Sūtra* was passed on from one generation to the next. As the *Upaniṣads* themselves took great care to maintain the *guru paramparā*, the succession of authorized teachers of the *vidyā* contained in them, so did the systematized aphoristic *sūtra* text, and its meaning was preserved in a carefully guarded tradition, the beginning of which we are unable to identify.

According to a very old Indian tradition, there had been other *Brahma Sūtras* before the one composed by Bādarāyaṇa. The most famous of these predecessors must have been an Ācārya Bādarī, who is credited with having written both a *Mīmāṁsā Sūtra* and a *Vedānta Sūtra*.[17] Other *ācāryas*, whose names are found in ancient texts as forerunner to Bādarāyaṇa include Karṣṇajini, Atreya, Audulomi, Asmarāthya, Kasakṛtsna, Kaṣyapa, Vedavyāsa—all mentioned in the extant *Brahma Sūtra*—whose works have not been preserved. In all probability, Bādarāyaṇa's *sūtra* so impressed his contemporaries that in the course of time it completely replaced the others.[18] The *bhāṣyas*, or commentaries to the *Brahma Sūtra*, have gained an authoritative position in the recognized ten branches of Vedānta, combining a textual exegesis with other living traditions, as we saw earlier when dealing with Vaiṣṇavism and Śaivism.[19] The oldest of the extant complete commentaries is that by Śaṅkarācārya, said to have lived from 788 to 820 C.E. We know that there had been earlier commentaries, associated with persons like Bhartṛprapañca, Bhartṛmitra, Bhartṛhari, Upavarṣa, Bodhāyana (whose authority is several times invoked by Rāmānuja against Śaṅkara), Brahmānaṇḍi, Ṭaṅka, Brahmadatta, Bhāruci, Sundarapāṇḍya, Gauḍapāda, and Govinda Bhagavatpāda (the *guru* of Śaṅkārācarya).[20]

As the commentators, expounding the most diverse theological views, demonstrate, the original *Brahma Sūtra* is merely a kind of general frame for a further development of ideas, which are left fairly vague and undetermined. Looking at the bare *sūtras* without a commentary, one can only give a general idea of their structure without discussing their import.

The *Vedānta Sūtra* is divided into four *adhyāyas*, chapters, each subdivided into four *pādas*, literally, "feet" or parts, which again are made up of a varying number of *sūtras* or aphorisms.

The entire first *adhyāya* is devoted to a discussion on *brahman: brahman* is the sole and supreme cause of all things. Systems that teach otherwise are rejected as heretical. The detailed polemic against the Sāṁkhya system is continued into the second *adhyāya*, which also refutes Vaiśeṣika theories. Toward the end of the second *pāda*, the *Bhāgavata* system is mentioned. The comments on this part of the text are a classic example of the wide diversity that exists in the commentaries. Śaṅkara understands the *sūtra* to say that the *Bhāgavata* system is untenable; Rāmānuja sees in it a recognition and justification for the *Bhāgavata* system. The next two *pādas* show the origin of the various phenomena that go into the making of the universe. The third *adhyāya* discusses the *jīvātman*, the individual living being and inquires into the condition and circumstances of the soul after death and the various states of dream, dreamless sleep, etc. A long series of *sūtras* deals with meditation and the types of *brahman* knowledge. The fourth *adhyāya* takes up again the topic of meditation and ends with a description of the *brahman* knower's fate after death.

SCHOOLS OF VEDĀNTA

As it is not possible to expatiate on all the questions broached here, and since complete texts and translations of the most important *bhāṣyas* are available to those interested in Vedānta, this exposition will limit itself to a few essential points and illustrate them with excerpts from the writings of Śaṅkara, the great *Advaitin*, from Rāmānuja, the famous exponent of *Viśiṣṭādaita*, and from Madhva, the illustrious defender of *Dvaita*—thus covering the most important sections of the spectrum of the Vedānta *darśana*.

The specifying terms given to the different systems within Vedānta have as their point of reference the relationship between the absolute supreme *Brahman* and the individual *ātman*. Thus, *advaita* (literally, "nonduality") implies the ultimate identity of *Brahman* and *jīvātman; viśiṣṭādvaita* (literally, "qualified nonduality") maintains a crucial differentiation as well as a fundamental identity; *dvaita* (literally, "duality") opposes *advaita* on almost all points and maintains an ultimate diversity of *Brahman* and *jīvātman*.[21] Translations that explain Advaita as monism and Dvaita as dualism are misleading, because the Western terms have quite different frames of reference and, therefore, quite different implications, which are inapplicable to the Indian systems.

The commentaries to the *Vedānta Sūtra* have become the main works of the *Vedāntācāryas*, whose very recognition as such depends on this as well as the commentaries on the *Upaniṣads* and the *Bhagavadgītā*, constituting the *prasthāna-trayī.* The last one to have done this is S. Radhakrishnan, a former President of India and one of the foremost of twentieth century Indian thinkers.

ADVAITA VEDĀNTA

Śaṅkarācārya (Figure 26.1), according to many the greatest Vedāntin and perhaps the greatest of India's philosophers, born, according to tradition, in 788 C.E. at Kāladī in today's Keralā, became a *saṁnyāsi* at the age of eighteen. He vanquished all his opponents in debate, established four headquarters in the South, East, North, and West of India for the missionaries of his doctrine, the *Daśanāmi Saṁnyāsins*, wrote numerous books, and died at the age of thirty-two.[22] He constructed his *Advaita* Vedānta upon principles set forth by Gauḍapāda in his *Kārikā* to the *Māṇḍukya Upaniṣad.*[23] Gauḍapāda is thought to be Śaṅkara's *prācārya*, that is, his guru's guru. Śaṅkara's commentary on this *Kārikā* may be considered the earliest and most concise statement of his philosophy, which he then expands in his great *Śarīrakabhāṣya.*

As do all Indian philosophical theologians, Śaṅkara clarifies his epistemological position in the introduction to his main work. He offers his own critique of human knowledge and states that all subject-object knowledge is distorted by *adhyāsa*, superimposition, which falsifies knowledge in such a way that the subject is unable to find objective truth. Quoting the familiar example of the traveller mistaking a piece of rope on the road for a snake, or vice versa, he proceeds to call all sense perception into question as possibly misleading, due to preconceived, superimposed ideas. But though all object cognition can be doubted, the existence of the doubter remains a fact. Every perception, be it true, doubtful, or mistaken, presupposes a subject, a perceiver. Even if there were no objective perception at all, there would still be a subject. It cannot be proved, nor does it have to be, because it precedes every proof as its inherent condition. It is distinct from all objects and independent. *Ātman* is pure consciousness that remains even after *manas*, rational thought, has passed away. *Ātman* is ultimately *sat-cit-ānanda.*

Śaṅkara does not regard the world of things as "pure illusion," as is sometimes said of him: the world is neither *abhāva*, nonexistence, nor, as

Figure 26.1 Ādiśaṅkara

Buddhist idealism has it, *śūnyatā*, emptiness. For Śaṅkara, the Buddhists are the archantagonists of *brahman* knowledge. Using Buddhist patterns of thought, which later earned him the title crypto-Buddhist by zealous Vaiṣṇavas, he sets out to re-establish Brahmanism. Sense objects, in his view, are different from fiction, but they also differ from reality in the ultimate sense.

In order to understand Śaṅkara's statements, one must always see them in the frame of reference in which they are made: all his assertions are explicit or implicit comparisons with absolute reality, which alone is of interest to him. The "natural" person does not know how to distinguish between relative and absolute being, between "things" and "being," between *ātman* and non-*ātman*. This is congenital *avidyā*, the nescience that one is not even aware of. It is this ignorance that keeps a person in *saṁsāra*. *Ātman* is *brahman*, which is good Upaniṣadic doctrine; the self of a person is identical with the ground of all being. *Brahman*, however, is invisible, impervious to any sense or mind perception: *brahman* is not identical with any one particular thing. Some Upaniṣadic passages speak of a "lower" and a "higher" brahman,[24] they speak of the immutable supreme *brahman* and also of the *īśvara*, who is creator, lord, and ruler of the world. Śaṅkara takes those passages as the occasion to introduce his most controversial distinction between *brahman saguṇa* and *brahman nirguṇa*, the Supreme with attributes and the Supreme without attributes, the *īśvara* of religious tradition and the absolute and unqualified reality, a no-thing. According to Śaṅkara *īśvara* is only a temporal manifestation of *brahman*, creator for as long as creation lasts.

Śaṅkara is credited with numerous beautiful hymns to the traditional lords of religion: Viṣṇu, Śiva, and Devī.[25] Devotion is a stage that one has to go through but not a stage to remain at: the ultimate goal also is deliverance from God, a complete identification with Reality, which neither develops nor acts, neither loves nor hates, but just *is*. The cleansing process of achieving this complete liberation separates the *ātman* from all untruth, unreality, and temporality. Doing away with *avidyā*, obscuring ignorance, is in itself already *vidyā*, knowledge that is identical with being. In this *vidyā*, the self experiences its identity with *brahman nirguṇa*, the pure and immutable reality.

Commenting on the first *sūtra* of the *Vedānta Sūtra*, Śaṅkara writes:

> The special question with regard to the enquiry into Brahman is whether it presupposes the understanding of *dharma*. To this question we reply: No! Because for a person who has read the Vedānta it is possible to begin the inquiry into the nature of *brahman* before having studied the *dharma*. The study of *dharma* results in transitory heaven and this depends on the performance

of rituals. The inquiry into the nature of *brahman*, however, results in *mokṣa*, lasting liberation. It does not depend upon the performance of ceremonies. A few presuppositions preceding the inquiry into the nature of *brahman* will have to be mentioned. These are:

1. *nityānityavāstuvivekaḥ*, discrimination between the eternal and the non-eternal reality;

2. *ihāmutrārthabhogavirāgaḥ*, giving up the desire to enjoy the fruit of one's actions both here and hereafter;

3. *samadamādisādhanasaṁpat*, the practice of the recognized virtues like peacefulness, self-restraint and so on;

4. *mumukṣutvam*, the strong desire for liberation.

If these conditions are fulfilled, then a person may inquire into *brahman* whether before or after the *dharma*-inquiry; but not if these conditions are not fulfilled. The object of desire is the knowledge of *brahman* and complete understanding of it. Knowledge is therefore the means to perfect *brahman*-cognition. The complete knowledge of *brahman* is the supreme human goal, because it destroys the root of all evil, namely *avidyā*, which is the seed of *saṁsāra*. One may now ask: is *brahman* known or unknown? If *brahman* is known then there is no need for further inquiry; if *brahman* is unknown we cannot begin an inquiry. We answer: *brahman* is known. Brahman, omniscient and omnipotent, whose essential nature is eternal purity, consciousness and freedom, exists. For if we contemplate the derivation of the word *brahman* from the root *bṛh-*, to be great, we understand at once that it is eternal purity, etc. More than that: the existence of *brahman* is known because it is the *ātman*, the self of everyone. For everyone is conscious of the "self" and no one thinks: I am not. *Ātman* is *brahman*. If the existence of the self was not known each one would think: I am not. But if *ātman* is generally known as *brahman*, one does not have to start an inquiry. Our answer is: No. Because there is a diversity of opinions regarding its nature. Uneducated people and the Lokāyatas are of the opinion that the body itself, having *caitanya*, consciousness as an attribute, is the *ātman*. Others believe that the sense-organs, endowed with the potency to experience, are the *ātman*. Others again believe that *cetana*, reasoning, or *manas*, mind, is the *ātman*. Others again believe the self to be simply a momentary idea, or that it is *śūnya*, emptiness. Some others explain that there is besides the body some supernatural being, responsible for the transmigrations, acting and enjoying; others teach that this being enjoys only but does not act. Some believe that besides these there exists an omniscient, omnipotent *īśvara* and others finally declare that the *ātman* is that enjoyer. —Thus there are various opinions, partly founded on reasonable arguments and texts from scripture. If these opinions were accepted without thorough prior investigation and inquiry, one would exclude oneself from liberation and suffer deplorable loss. The *sūtra*, therefore, presents a discussion of the Vedānta texts with the motto: "Inquiry into *brahman*," which proceeds with appropriate arguments and aims at supreme bliss.[26]

His direct disciples and successors considered Śaṅkara a superhuman teacher, the embodiment of divine wisdom, and his words were treated on a par with the words of revelation.[27] Extreme care was taken not only to preserve his written works but also to ensure the succession in the *maṭhas* founded by him.[28] The latter was not always easy. The northernmost, *Jyotirmaṭha* in the high Himālayas, remained vacant for several centuries before being revived in 1941. The southernmost, *Śaradāpīṭha* in Kāñcīpuram near Madras, had to fight for recognition as the fifth *maṭha*, against the claim of others that Śaṅkara had founded only four.[29]

VIŚIṢṬĀDVAITA VEDĀNTA

According to traditional accounts, Rāmānuja (Figure 26.2), after an eventful life of ecclesiastical glory but also some persecution, died in 1137 at age 120 while still the resident head of the great temple-monastery of Śrīraṅgam in South India. He is the greatest among the Vaiṣṇava Vedāntins, offering a theistic interpretation of the *Brahma Sūtra*.[30] For Rāmānuja, too, reality is ultimately one, but reality is tiered. It is composed of three components: the world of material things, the multiplicity of *jīvātmas*, individual living beings, and *brahman*, who is identical with *īśvara*, who is none other than Viṣṇu. Creation is the body of *brahman* but not without qualification.[31]

At the time of Rāmānuja, Hinduism was firmly established. Buddhism had all but disappeared from India and Jainism was concentrated in relatively small areas of western India. The inter-Hindu controversy was taken up again, and Rāmānuja's main opponents were Śaivites, as far as religion was concerned, and Advaitins, in the area of philosophy. Rāmānuja's *Śrībhāṣya* contains many pages of massive polemics against Śaṅkara, finding fault with Śaṅkara's distinction between *nirguṇa* and *saguṇa brahman* and his presupposition of *adhyāsa*.[32] *Īśvara*, as the creator and lord of *prakṛti* and the *jīvas* has an infinite number of supreme and auspicious qualities; this makes him ipso facto *brahman saguṇa*, above whom there is none. He has a most perfect body, which is eternal and immutable. He is radiant, full of beauty, youth, and strength. With his body full of *sattva*, devoid of *rajas* and *tamas*, he is omnipresent; he is the *antaryāmi*, the inner ruler of all. For Rāmānuja, the process of salvation is not just a process of isolation, the elimination of *avidyā*, the disengagement of nonreality, but it is the product of divine grace and human self-surrender.

Figure 26.2 Rāmānuja

His *viśiṣṭa* theory enables him to incorporate into the philosophical system of Vedānta all the traditional Hindu notions of the *bhagavān* from the epic-Purāṇic-Āgamic tradition. Rāmānuja established a detailed code of ceremonial worship at the *maṭha* of Melkote, where he spent the twelve years of his exile and where, according to tradition, the *Draviḍa Prabandham* was recited at his deathbed together with the *Vedas* and the *Upaniṣads.* The passages in the *Upaniṣad* that speak of a *nirguṇa brahman* are interpreted by Rāmānuja as meaning "absence of inauspicious qualities" rather than absolute qualitilessness. *Jīvas*, individual souls, are of three kinds: *nitya-muktas*, who have always been free; *muktas*, those that have become free in time; and *baddhas*, those that are still bound. For these, the "way" is essential.

Despite the prevalent opinion, also held by Western scholars, that Śaṅkara represents Vedānta in its purest form, we must say that it is probably Rāmānuja who can claim to have Hindu tradition on his side and that, on the whole, his interpretation of the *Upaniṣads* may be fairer than Śaṅkara's. This is also the opinion of S. N. Dasgupta, who writes:

> The theistic Vedānta is the dominant view of the *Purāṇas* in general and represents the general Hindu view of life and religion. Compared with this general current of Hindu thought, which flows through the *Purāṇas* and the *Smṛtis* and has been the main source from which the Hindu life has drawn its inspiration, the extreme Sāṁkhya, the extreme Vedānta of Śaṅkara, the extreme Nyāya, and the extreme dualism of Madhva may be regarded as metaphysical formalisms of conventional philosophy.[33]

In his commentary on the first aphorism of the *Brahma Sūtras*, Rāmānuja emphasizes his difference from Śaṅkara's position wherever possible. He adds to the explanation of the four words of the *sūtra* an exposé of his own theology, covering more than a hundred pages of print.

> The word *athā*, now, expresses direct sequence; the word *ata*, then, intimates what has taken place before [namely, the study of *dharma*], which forms the basis [for the *brahman* inquiry]. For it is a fact that the desire to know *brahman* —the fruit of which is infinite and lasting—follows immediately when someone who has read the *Veda* and *Vedāṅgas* realizes that the fruit of rituals is limited and temporary and thus wishes for final release. . . .
>
> The word *brahman* means *puruṣottama*, who is by his very essence free from imperfections and possesses an unlimited number of auspicious qualities of unsurpassable excellence. The term *brahman* applies to all things possessing greatness, but primarily it denotes that which possesses greatness essentially and in unlimited fullness; and such is only the Lord of all. Hence, the word *brahman* primarily denotes him alone and in a secondary sense only those things which possess a small amount of the Lord's qualities. . . . The term is

analogous with the term *bhagavat*. It is the Lord alone who is sought for the sake of immortality by all those who are afflicted by the threefold misery. Hence, the All-Lord (*sarveśvara*) is that *brahman* which according to the *sūtra* constitutes the object of enquiry. . . . The Pūrva-Mīmāṁsā and the Uttara Mīmāṁsā differ only in the material they teach as the two halves of the *Pūrvamīmāṁsāsūtras* differ. The entire *Mīmāṁsāśāstra*, beginning with the *sūtra: Athāto dharmajijñāsa* and ending with the *sūtra: anāvṛttiśśabdāt*[34] has, due to the special character of its contents, a definite order of internal succession.

At this juncture Rāmānuja takes the Advaitins to task, whose main arguments he summarizes in his own words as follows:

Eternal and absolutely immutable consciousness, whose nature is pure undifferentiated reason, shows itself—owing to an error—illusorily as divided into multifarious distinct beings: knower, object of knowledge and acts of knowledge. The discussion of the Vedānta texts aims at completely destroying *avidyā*, which is the root cause of this error, in order to attain a firm knowledge of the unity of *brahman*, whose nature is pure consciousness—free, without stain, and eternal.

Then Rāmānuja introduces his hundred-page counterargument, the *mahāsiddhānta*, or great final statement, as follows:

This entire theory [of the Advaitins] rests on a fictitious foundation of altogether hollow and vicious arguments, incapable of being stated in definite logical alternatives, and devised by men who are destitute of those particular qualities which cause individuals to be chosen by the *puruṣottama* revealed in the Upaniṣads, whose intellects are darkened by the impression of beginningless evil, and who thus have no insight into the meaning of words and sentences, into the real purport conveyed by them, and into the procedure of sound argumentation, with all its methods depending on perception and the other instruments of right knowledge. The theory therefore must needs be rejected by all those who, through texts, perception and the other means of knowledge, assisted by sound reasoning—have an insight into the true nature of things.

In a massive offensive, in the course of which countless passages from the *Upaniṣads*, the *Smṛtis*, and the *Purāṇas* are quoted, Rāmānuja proceeds against the main views of Śaṅkara.

There is, he says, no proof for the acceptance of undifferentiated being. On the contrary, all arguments speak for a differentiation: the use of language, sense perception, and inference. Sense perception does not show us a being in its undifferentiated absoluteness but a being endowed with attributes. The multiplicity of things is not unreal. Being and consciousness can undergo changes. Consciousness is a quality of a conscious self, and it is preposterous to assume that the conscious subject is something unreal. The subject exists even when there is no actual consciousness, as in dreamless sleep. And the conscious subject continues to exist also in the state of perfect liberation.

Rāmānuja quite boldly states that no *śruti* text teaches an undifferentiated *brahman* and that *Smṛtis* and *Purāṇas* were against it as well. The *avidyā* theory cannot be proved because all knowledge relates to what is real. Again, no scripture teaches it. Nor does *śruti* support the teaching that *mokṣa* is realized by the cognition of an unqualified *brahman*. Moreover, ignorance does not simply cease if one understands *brahman* as the universal *ātman*. In this connection, Rāmānuja explains the *mahāvākya* "*tat tvam asi*," one of the core texts of the Advaitins, in his own way:

> In texts such as *tat tvam asi*, the coordination of the constituent parts is not meant to convey the idea of the absolute unity of a non-differentiated substance: on the contrary, the words *tat* and *tvam* denote a *brahman* distinguished by difference. The word *tat* refers to the omniscient etc. *brahman*. . . . The word *tvam*, which stands in coordination to *tat* conveys the idea of *brahman* which has for its body the *jīvātmas* connected with *prakṛti*. If such duality of form were given up there could be no difference of aspects giving rise to the application of different terms, and the entire principle of coordination would thus be given up. And it would further follow that the two words coordinated would have to be taken in an implied sense. There is, however, no need to assume *lakṣana* or implication in sentences such as "this person is Devadatta." . . . Moreover, if the text *tat tvam asi* were meant to express absolute oneness, it would conflict with a previous statement in the same section, namely *tadaikṣata bahu syām*, that is: it thought, may I be many.[35]

We cannot decide here whether Rāmānuja has always been fair to Śaṅkara and whether he does justice to Śaṅkara's rather subtle thinking, but it is very clear that he wished to distinguish his position as sharply as possible from that of the Advaitins.

DVAITA VEDĀNTA

Madhva, the representative of the *Dvaita* Vedānta, lived from 1238 to 1317 C.E. The son of one of his disciples wrote a biography, considered authentic.[36] Madhva was born into a humble Brahmin family in a village not far from Uḍipī, now in Kannaḍa. When he was sixteen, he entered the *Ekadaṇḍi* order of the *Ekānti Vaiṣṇavas* and was given the name *Pūrṇaprajñā*, fullness of wisdom. He quite frequently disagreed with the *Advaita* interpretation of Vedānta given by his teacher, which did not hinder the guru from installing Madhva under the name of *Ānandatīrtha* as the head of his own *maṭha.*

He then went on a missionary tour, engaging Jains, Buddhists, and Advaitins in discussions and defeating them not only by the power of his words but also with the help of a king who, on Madhva's insistence, had thousands of Jains impaled and who exiled other infidels. According to tradition, he wrote his *Brahmasūtrabhāṣya* after a pilgrimage to Vyāsāśrama in the Himālayas. On his North Indian tour, he also met with a Muslim ruler. The Muslim intolerance of Hinduism might have been one of the factors that could explain Madhva's un-Hindu intolerance toward other opinions and some of his stranger views.

The image of Kṛṣṇa Madhva installed at his Uḍipī *maṭha* is still an important focus of pilgrimage and the rotation of the headship of the *maṭha*, taking place every twelve years, is also a major social occasion reported in newspapers. Madhva was the most prolific of all the great Vedāntins. He left more than thirty major works as well as a number of minor ones. In addition to the traditional commentaries on the *Gītā*, the *Upaniṣads*, and the *Brahma Sūtra*, he wrote commentaries on the *Bhāgavata Purāṇa*, the *Ṛgveda*, and portions of the *Mahābhārata*, along with several philosophical monographs and short summaries of his own commentaries, the most famous of which is the *Aṇuvyākhyāna*, a masterful exposition of the *Brahma Sūtra* in eighty-eight verses.[37]

In his arguments, he uses not only traditional *śruti* but also quotes from the *Viṣṇu-* and *Bhāgavata Purāṇa*, from *Pāñcarātra saṁhitās*, and other sectarian writings. All Śaiva literature is taboo for him. He is closer to Rāmānuja than to Śaṅkara, but he goes a decisive step further toward uncompromising *Dvaita.* He develops his whole system upon the presupposition of the *pañca bheda*, the five differences between *īśvara* and *jīvātman*, between *prakṛti* and *īśvara*, between the individual *jīvas* and the various inanimate objects. *Īśvara*, who is Viṣṇu, is absolute: he has an infinite number of excellent qualities and a spiritual body wherewith he shows himself at will in the *vyūhas* and *avatāras.* The world is made through his *līlā*, the free play of his disinterested will; everything depends on his will:

> All knowledge is to be ascribed to the action of Hari, the ties of the world and the release therefrom, rebirth and the unfolding of all things. Hari permeates everything, even the souls, and he lives there as the inner witness, the *sākṣi;* in nature he lives as the *antaryāmin*, the inner ruler. *Prakṛti* is the opposite of Hari, insofar as she is pure dependency, total contingency. It is true, she exists from eternity, but in the hand of Hari she is a mere instrument.[38]

The *jīvas* have, individually, a spiritual self-consciousness. They are of the nature of *sat-cit-ānanda*, even if this is obscured for the duration of bodily life. The *ātman*, therefore, is a mirror image of God. It is completely dependent on God in all its actions. The way to liberation is perfect self-surrender to Viṣṇu through an active love that centers on ritual worship of the image. Vāyu, as the mediator between Viṣṇu and the *jīvas*, plays an important role. It is important to note that Madhva considered himself an *avatāra* of Vāyu. Madhva begins his commentary on the first *sūtra* of the text thus:

> The basis for the inquiry into *brahman* is the grace of the Lord Viṣṇu. Since greater grace can be gained from him only through appropriate cognition, *brahman* inquiry is indispensable as a source of *brahman* knowledge in order to gain his attention. Inquiry into *brahman* itself is to be ascribed to the grace of the Great Lord, for he alone is the mover of our minds. There are three grades of preparedness for the study of Vedānta: an eager person who is devoted to Lord Viṣṇu is in the third grade; a person who has the six-fold moral qualification of self-discipline etc. is in the second grade; and the person who is attached to none but the Lord, who considers the whole world as transitory and is therefore completely indifferent, is in the first grade. The following of the Vedic injunctions can merely give us a claim to the lower grace of the Lord; the listening to the texts of scripture provides us with a somewhat higher grace; but the supreme grace of the Lord, which leads to *mukti* can be secured only through knowledge. Right knowledge can be acquired only through *śravaṇa*, the listening to scripture, *manana*, meditation, *nidhi-dhyāsana*, contemplation, and *bhakti*, devotion; nobody can attain right *jñāna* without these. The term *brahman* designates primarily Viṣṇu, of which some Vedic texts say: "He who dwells in the ocean and is known only to the sages, he who surpasses understanding, who is eternal, who rules all things, from whom issue the great mother of the universe and who brings the *jīvas* into the world, bound to life by their actions and prisoners of the five elements." And another passage: "He is the embodiment of pure wisdom, he is consciously active and is, according to the sages, the one Lord of the universe."[39] From the following sentence: "And may therefore Viṣṇu inspire us" it is clear that only Viṣṇu is meant in the preceding passages. —All the *Vedas* speak of him only; in the *Vedas*, in the *Rāmāyaṇa*, in the *Mahābhārata* and in the *Purāṇas*, in the beginning, in the middle and in the end—everywhere only Viṣṇu is sung of.[40]

TEXTS AND COMMENTARIES

These short extracts from the commentaries to the first four words of the *Vedānta Sūtra* may allow the reader to gauge the great amount of diversity within the one Vedānta *darśana* and also provide a glimpse into the very rich and subtle philosophical tradition drawn upon. These *bhāṣyas*, very often commented upon in *ṭīkās* (subcommentaries) and *ṭippaṇīs* (glosses) by the disciples and followers in later ages, are both difficult and lengthy. The great masters themselves wrote smaller manuals for the laity, in which they provided the gist of their teaching in an abbreviated form without compromising the essentials. Two valuable little works expounding *Advaita* Vedānta, ascribed to Śaṅkarācārya himself, are the *Ātmabodha*, "The Self-Knowledge," and *Upadeśasahasrī*, "The Thousand Teachings."[41] The most widely used and easiest introduction, however, may be Sadānanda's *Vedāntasāra*, a small literary work offering a clear and full explanation of the major terms of Śaṅkara's thought.[42] The greatest among the post-Śaṅkara *Advaita* treatises, however, is the celebrated *Pañcadaśī* of Vidyāraṇya, one of the greatest Hindu scholars of the fourteenth century.[43] The *Vedāntaparibhāṣa*, written by the seventeenth century Advaitin Dharmarāja, is a manual that is still used in Indian universities.[44]

The Viśiṣṭādvaitins also have their shorter compendia. The most famous and most beautifully written is Rāmānuja's *Vedārthasaṁgraha*, with ample quotations from scriptures, despite its brevity.[45] For beginners the most suitable book may be Śrīnivasadāsa's *Yatīndramatadīpikā*.[46] Easy to understand and now easily accessible in an English translation, is also Bucci Venkatācārya's *Vedāntakārikāvalī*.[47]

In addition to the minor works of Madhva himself, the manual by his disciple Jayatīrtha, called *Vādāvalī*, written in the fourteenth century, may offer the most systematic introduction to the thought of *Dvaita* Vedānta.[48]

Vedānta does not belong only to the past but is perhaps the most important contemporary expression of Indian philosophy and theology. An unbroken tradition of scholars and saints leads from the great *ācāryas* into our time; all their major institutions are still centers of living Vedānta. Vedānta is not only speculative, abstract thought but also mysticism, realization, and the way to ultimate freedom. The basic types of this spiritual life thought, as they are represented by the great *ācāryas* briefly examined here, may be representative of basic types of mysticism, for which there are parallels in the Western tradition, too. They are alive in India in numerous gurus, who express their own experiences and convictions in the terminology of Śaṅkara, Rāmānuja, and Madhva, thereby acknowledging the timeless greatness of these thinkers of the absolute.

27. Hindu Reforms and Reformers

> Religion must establish itself as a rational way of living. If ever the spirit is to be at home in this world and not merely a prisoner or a fugitive, secular foundations must be laid deeply and preserved worthily. Religion must express itself in reasonable thought, fruitful actions and right social institutions.
>
> —*S. Radhakrishnan*[1]

THE HISTORY OF Hinduism consists of a series of challenges and responses to challenges, reforms and efforts to resist change, struggle between those who cling tenaciously to tradition and those who wish to go with the times. It took centuries before Hinduism responded as a body to the challenge posed by Buddhism and Jainism—it needed a Maṇḍana Miśra and a Śaṅkara to consolidate and reform Hinduism and to return the initiative to it. While much of this response was creative, advancing the theory and practice of Hindus over the times of Buddha and Mahāvīra, the reaction to the challenge posed by Islam was almost totally negative and defensive. Except for a few movements, which became more or less independent from mainstream Hinduism,[2] the Hindu reaction to Islam was withdrawal, letting the shutters down, hardening customs and beliefs, not admitting any change.[3] That did not prevent Hinduism from decaying and corrupting. The picture eighteenth century visitors to India draw is not only one of a Mughal rule no longer really in control but also of a Hinduism, still the majority religion, beset by cruel customs, superstition, and abysmal ignorance.

Foreign visitors considered Hinduism a hopeless case and expected it to die of degeneration within a century. An example may be found in a book published by the Christian Literature Society for India: *India Hindu and India Christian or, What Hinduism Has Done for India and What Christianity Would Do for It. An Appeal to Thoughtful Hindus.*[4] It enumerates as the fruits of Hinduism ill-health or shortness of life; poverty; national ignorance; intellectual weakness; despotism and religious intolerance; polytheism, animal worship, idolatry, and pantheism; the sanction of robbery, murder, and human sacrifices and promises to India under Christian rule better health and longer life; increase of wealth; diffusion of true knowledge; intellectual strength; national greatness; and the brotherhood of man. For us in 1987, there is some irony in the following remark:

> England is now one of the richest countries in the world. One great cause of this is her commerce. Every sea is traversed by her ships; her merchants are to be found in every land where wealth can be gained. The Parsis have copied their example and have similarly benefitted. Hinduism teaches the people of India to regard all foreigners as impure *mlecchas*. "In their country the twice-born must not even temporarily dwell." The folly of this is now acknowledged by enlightened men; but the above is the doctrine of Hinduism.[5]

Hindus have changed. So has England. History has not been kinder to the following assertion made in the same book under the heading, "Hinduism Incapable of Reform."

> All intelligent Hindus admit that great reforms are needed to purify Hinduism. Many think that this is all that is necessary to render it worthy of retention. Some even affirm that it would then occupy one of the highest places among the religions of the world.
>
> Let the changes necessary to reform Hinduism up to the light of the nineteenth century be considered:
>
> 1. Reformed Hinduism should be neither polytheistic nor pantheistic, but monotheistic. All intelligent men now believe in the existence of only one true God. There are no such beings as Vishnu, Śiva, Sarasvatí, Durgá, or the thirty-three crores of the Hindu Pantheon. The Vishnu *bhakti*, the Śiva *bhakti*, etc., would all come to an end. No sectarial marks would be worn. The blasphemous assertion *aham Brahmásmi*, I am Brahma, would no longer be made.
>
> 2. All idols would be destroyed, and no longer worshipped as giving false and degrading ideas of God. The indecent images on some temples would be broken down. There would no longer be Vaishnava nor Śaiva temples.
>
> 3. The *Vedas*, the Code of Manu, the *Rámáyana, Mahábhárata*, the Puránas, etc., as teaching polytheism, pantheism, containing debasing representations of God, unjust laws, false history, false science, false morals, would no longer be considered sacred books.
>
> 4. Hindu worship in temples would cease. Festivals would no longer be celebrated. Pilgrimages to supposed holy places would come to an end. *Pújá* to idols would not be observed in private families.

5. As Hindu temples contain only small shrines for idols, buildings like churches would require to be erected, in which people might assemble for public worship, and receive instruction in the duties of life.

6. Caste would no longer be recognised, and the brotherhood of man would be acknowledged; all caste distinctions would cease.

Every one of the above changes is necessary to meet the view of enlightened men.

Take away sweetness from sugar, and it is no longer sugar; deprive a man of reason, and he is no longer a human being. Hinduism without its gods, its sacred books, its temples, its worship, its caste, would be no longer Hinduism, but an entirely different religion, like the Sadhárana Brahmo Samáj. It would be simply Theistic.[6]

Hinduism, as we well know now, has been capable of reform. It has not given up its belief in Viṣṇu, Śiva, or Durgā; it has not abandoned its images, has not ceased to worship in temples. Pilgrimages are as popular as ever, *pūjā* continues to be offered in homes.

Contrary to all predictions, Hinduism not only survived but recovered and in many ways may today be stronger than ever. The revival and regeneration of Hinduism is largely the achievement of Hindu reformers who for the past two centuries tirelessly worked for the betterment of their country on the basis of religion. There have been too many of them to mention individually. The issues they concerned themselves with and the institutions they founded to address these concerns are too numerous again to find place within such a short survey.[7] Briefly, one can say that they tried first to rid Hinduism of practices that were perceived to be inhuman and cruel, like the burning of widows and female infanticide. Some felt that the strictures of caste should go, especially the disrespect shown to people who were considered to be outside the caste system altogether. Improving the social standing and education of women became a major issue, too. While it may be admitted that these reforms were effected under the impact of a new social consciousness, sharpened by the contact with representatives of Christianity and often in response to accusations by Western missionaries, the religious reform properly speaking, the intensification of devotion, the purification of ritual, and the new seriousness shown in the study of the religious classics were inter-Hindu phenomena that in the end turned out to be more important for Hinduism.

Reforms and reformers brought new tension to Hindu society, the tension between the secular and the religious beliefs, which in that form was unknown to traditional Hinduism. Western secular civilization became both a fascination and a terror to Hindus. Some found it so attractive that they were able to envision India as a secular society with Hinduism as the private mystical religion of those who had a taste for it, mere interiority and piety. Others considered the onrush of secularism to be a challenge to recapture the *dharmakṣetra*, to re-Hinduize the public life of India.

Swāmi Vivekānanda, one of the foremost of Hindu reformers, expressed it well when he said:

> There are two great obstacles on our path in India: the Scylla of old orthodoxy and the Charybdis of modern European civilization. Of these two I vote for the old orthodoxy and not for the Europeanized system, for, the old orthodox man may be ignorant, he may be crude but he is a man, he has faith, while the Europeanized man has no backbone, he is a mass of heterogeneous ideas picked up at random from every source—and these ideas are unassimilated, undigested, unharmonized.[8]

And: "This is my objection against the reformers. The orthodox have more faith and more strength in themselves, in spite of their crudeness. But the reformers simply play into the hands of the Europeans and pander to their vanity. Our masses are gods as compared with those of other countries. This is the only country where poverty is not a crime."[9]

A NINETEENTH CENTURY HINDU RENAISSANCE

The momentum of Hindu reforms, especially in the area of social customs, gained considerable strength in the early nineteenth century. At this time, several European powers had established themselves in India, welcomed by many Hindus as liberators from the corrupt Muslim rule and admired for their technical achievements. There is an extensive literature in English on these so-called "Hindu-Renaissance movements"; since many of the modern Hindu reformers wrote and spoke English, it is the most easily accessible area of Hinduism for people without a knowledge of Indian languages. The sheer bulk of books available in this area and the captivating attribute "modern" has led many people in the West to believe that these modern Hindu reform movements are identical with contemporary Hinduism, except perhaps for a few remnants of "unreformed" Hinduism that one needed not take seriously. Quite on the contrary, these modern Hindu movements, despite their appeal to Westerners and Westernized Hindus, represent only a small fraction of actual Hinduism, which is still much more rooted in its ancient and mediaeval traditions than inclined toward the modern movements.

The real Hindu Renaissance took place in traditional Hinduism: the traditional *saṁpradāyas* consolidated their influence; generous donations made it possible to restore hundreds of old temples and build thousands of new ones; grass-roots religious organizations gave new life to the religious observations and festivities. This cautionary remark seems necessary for gaining a correct perspective, when we now go on to consider a number of reformers and their work.

The first of the really significant modern Hindu reformers was Rām Mohan Roy (1772-1833), who was called the Father of Modern India by his admirers, a genial man with a multifaceted personality.[10] His father was a Vaiṣṇava, his mother came from a Śākta family, and as a boy he was sent to Patna to study at the Muslim University, learning Arabic and Persian and becoming interested in Sūfism. This turned him against image worship, an issue over which he fell out with his father. He left for Tibet. His father, however, gave in under the condition that he spend twelve years at Benares, the center of Hindu learning, before returning to his home in Bengal.

At Benares, Ram Mohan Roy engaged in a study of Sanskrit and Hindu scriptures; but he also studied English and later entered the service of the East India Company at Calcutta. In 1814, he left its service and devoted himself fully to religious propaganda and reform. He tried to purify Hinduism by returning to the *Upaniṣads* and translated several books. He sought connection with the English missionaries who had opened a college at Serampore, not far from Calcutta, where he studied Greek and Hebrew in order to translate the Bible into Bengalī.

The publication of a little pamphlet, *The Precepts of Jesus: The Guide to Peace and Happiness*, estranged him from both his Hindu friends and the missionaries. The former accused him of canvassing for Christianity; the latter objected to his Hinduizing of Christianity. In the course of quite bitter polemics, Rām Mohan Roy accused the missionaries of having misinterpreted the words of Jesus; a reproach that has been levelled against the Christian missions ever since.

Rām Mohan Roy won a triumph in his battle against the practice of *satī*, the (not always voluntary) burning of widows on their husbands' funeral pyres. As a boy he had witnessed the forced *satī* of a much-liked sister-in-law, which stirred him so profoundly that he vowed to devote his life to the abolition of this cruel custom, allowed by the British officials as part of their policy of noninterference with local religions. Rām Mohan Roy succeeded in convincing the government that *satī* did not form part of original and pure Hindu *dharma* and, thus, against violent opposition, the anti-*satī* law was passed.[11] Interestingly, a number of prominent Englishmen, among them the famous Indologist H. H. Wilson, supported Hindu orthodoxy against Rām Mohan Roy, arguing that *satī* was part of the Hindu religious tradition and that England's policy of not interfering with religious practices should also apply there.[12] It is an ominous sign of the times that more than a century after the abolition of *satī* and the prohibition of infanticide by the British government of India, there is a dramatic rise in the instances of young women burnt to death by their husbands or their husbands' relations in order to obtain dowry, which is officially abolished as well, and thousands of cases of poisoning of baby girls have recently been reported among just one group in South India.[13]

Several times, Rām Mohan Roy tried to organize a group of people to begin a new religious movement, embodying his ideas of religion. He finally succeeded five years before his death with the Brahmo Samāj, somehow combining Hinduism and Christianity. Rām Mohan Roy kept his sacred thread and wanted to remain a faithful Hindu. Hindu orthodoxy, however, excommunicated him. Rām Mohan Roy also became instrumental in establishing English schools in Calcutta, emphasizing the value of modern, scientific education. In its heyday, many Europeans thought the Brahmo Samāj would become the future religion of India; subsequent history has proved the traditional streams of Hinduism stronger than this courageous new attempt.[14]

Rām Mohan Roy's successor was Debendranāth Tagore, called Maharṣi, the father of the more famous Nobel Prize winner for literature, Rabindranath Tagore. Marharṣi founded a Bengalī paper and a school for Brahmo missionaries with the explicit purpose of checking the spread of Christian missions. He also openly broke with orthodox Hinduism by declaring the *Vedas* as neither free from error nor inspired. His book, *Brahmo Dharma*, an anthology from *Upaniṣads* and *Smṛtis*, became the official catechism of the movement.[15]

With the entrance of Keshub Chandra Sen (1838-1884), some explosive issues were brought into the Brahmo Samāj. Since Keshub was not a Brahmin, several members left in protest. The development of peculiar rituals to replace Hindu *saṁskāras* and his close connections with Christians led to a split within the Samāj. Debendranath Tagore remained with the Ādi Samāj whereas Keshub became the leader of the Brahmo Samāj of India, which due to his extravagance suffered another split in later years. Keshub developed a tremendous social activity, collecting funds for victims of famines and floods, founding schools for boys and girls and a workers' association, agitating for literacy and for a civil marriage legislation against the widespread Indian custom of child marriage, pleading for intercaste marriage and widow remarriage. Ironically, he married off his own daughter while she was still a child, an incident that estranged many of his followers. In his youth he lectured enthusiastically on Christ; later he considered himself a superman and expected to be worshipped as such. He preached the New Dispensation, to replace the Old and the New Testaments. While he was becoming increasingly engrossed in ideas like these, the social activities of the Brahmo Samāj declined.[16]

Whereas the largely idealistic Brahmo Samāj is all but defunct as an organized movement, its more radical and often fanatical sister foundation, the Ārya Samāj, not only continues to attract members to its local centers but has spawned a number of notable organizations exerting considerable influence on India's present-day politics.

Swāmi Dāyānanda Sarasvatī (1824-1883), from Morvi in Gujarat, describes how he lost faith in Śiva and image worship while keeping night vigil on *Śivarātrī*, compelled to do so by his father. He saw rats climbing on to the image, which was powerless to defend itself; meanwhile, his pious father was sound asleep. At the age of twenty-four, just before he was to enter a marriage arranged by his parents, he fled from home in search of the means to overcome death. After twelve years of wandering from one guru to another, dissatisfied with all, he met Swāmi Virājānanda Saraswatī of Mathurā. A temperamental man, the blind old swāmi succeeded in completely subduing the restless spirit of Dāyānanda and prophesied that he would become the restorer of Hinduism of his age. His was a strictly orthodox Vedic religion, rejecting the religion of the epics and the *Purāṇas*, the *Saṁhitās* and the *Āgamas*, as corrupt and untrue.

In *Satyārtha Prakāśa*, he lays down the principles of his *sanātana dharma*, quoting *Vedas, Upaniṣads*, the *Manusmṛti*, and some *Dharmasūtras*. The last two chapters are devoted to a refutation of Islam and Christianity. A quotation from the Bible induces the *samīkṣaka* (literally, "inquisitor") to ask for its meaning. The Īsāī, representing Christianity, gives an unsatisfactory answer. A dialogue ensues in which the Ārya Samājist proves his superiority over the man of the Bible. He closes by saying that the Bible is a bunch of lies and that only the *Vedas* teach truth. In practice, the Ārya Samāj, founded in 1875 in Bombay, went further, using persuasion or even moral and physical violence to convert Muslims and Christians. The Ārya Samāj has founded *gurukulas*, training institutions, in which children from the age of four are brought up strictly along Vedic lines.

After initial successes in Punjab, Dāyānanda Saraswatī shifted his headquarters to Lahore and plunged into numerous social and religious activities. After his death, the Ārya Samāj split into a conservative branch, which had its center in the Kaṅgrī Gurukula, now D.A.V. University, and a progressive branch, which kept its headquarters in the D.A.V. College in Lahore. The Mahātmā Party became more and more aggressive and its leader Śraddhānanda was shot dead by a Muslim in 1925. They founded many schools all over India and started many activities with the aim of spreading Vedic culture. They tried to counteract Christian missions by means both fair and foul and performed the *śuddhi* ceremony on thousands of converts.[17]

In a very real sense one can include Mahātmā Gāndhī among the great

Hindu reformers of the Indian Renaissance whose work had considerable impact on the West.[18] He never left any doubt about his Hindu identity. Thus, he declared early on in his Indian career:[19]

> I call myself a *sanātani* Hindu because
>
> 1. I believe in the *Vedas*, the *Upaniṣads*, the *Purāṇas* and all that goes by the name of Hindu Scriptures, and therefore in *avatārs* and rebirth.
> 2. I believe in the *varṇāśrama dharma* in a sense, in my opinion, strictly Vedic, but not in its present popular and crude sense.
> 3. I believe in the protection of the cow in its much larger sense than the popular.
> 4. I do not disbelieve in idol worship.

He qualified and explained all these points in a lengthy commentary:

> I have purposely refrained from using the words "divine origin" in reference to the Vedas or any other scriptures. For I do not believe in the exclusive divinity in the Vedas. I believe the Bible, the Koran and the Zend Avesta to be as much divinely inspired as the Vedas. My belief in the Hindu scriptures does not require me to accept every word and every verse as divinely inspired. . . . I do most emphatically repudiate the claim (if they advance any such) of the present Śankarācāryas and Shastris to give a correct interpretation of the Hindu scriptures.[20]

The great merit of Gāndhī and of his disciples was their tolerance and genuinely religious spirit, which comprises both love of God and service to man. Many Gandhians were engaged in activities designed to overcome the hostility and exclusivity of the various religions, most notably the "Gandhian Patriarch" Kaka Kalelkar, who started a Viśva Samanvaya Saṅgha, working toward a "familyhood of religions."[21]

HINDUISM REACHING OUT FOR THE WORLD

The best known of all the Hindu reform movements is the Ramakrishna Mission, founded by Swāmī Vivekānanda (1863-1902), a disciple of Paramahamsa Rāmakrishna (1836-1886). Rāmakrishna (Figure 27.1), a temple priest at Dakṣineśvar and a mystical devotee of Kālī, became a source of religious renewal for a large number of Bengalis who met him during his lifetime.[22] Totally withdrawn and averse to any organization or reformist activity, after his death, he nevertheless became the central figure

Figure 27.1 Rāmakrishna Paramahaṁsa

in the world movement initiated by his favorite disciple, after the disciple's appearance at the World Parliament of Religions in Chicago in 1893. Touring America and Europe, Swāmī Vivekānanda brought home to India a new consciousness of his Hinduism and a sense of social mission that induced him to work restlessly for the improvement of his countrymen through relief organizations, schools, hospitals, and innumerable other activities. Basically an Advaitin, he was open to the other *mārgas* and also to religions other than Hinduism, though he considered them inferior and spiritually underdeveloped.

The Ramakrishna Mission is a well-organized community today, with some 700 permanent members and a large number of associated workers, maintaining several colleges, high schools, hostels, hospitals, and publishing an impressive amount of religious literature. It also established, with grants from the Indian government and the Ford Foundation, the well-known Institute of Culture in Calcutta.

Swāmi Vivekānanda inspired Hindu-India with immense pride and a sense of mission. He articulated the rationale for the new Hindu religious movements in the West in the following manner: "We Hindus have now been placed, under God's providence, in a very critical and responsible position. The nations of the West are coming to us for spiritual help. A great moral obligation rests on the sons of India to fully equip themselves for the work of enlightening the world on the problems of human existence."[23] And:

> Once more the world must be conquered by India. This is the dream of my life. I am anxiously waiting for the day when mighty minds will arise, gigantic spiritual minds who will be ready to go forth from India to the ends of the world to teach spirituality and renunciation, those ideas which come from the forests of India and belong to Indian soil only. Up India, and conquer the world with your spirituality. . . . Ours is a religion of which Buddhism, with all its greatness is a rebel child and of which Christianity is a very patchy imitation.[24]

The Rāmakrishna Mission, as is well known, not only promotes a nonsectarian (Neo)Hinduism but also a kind of religious universalism. Rāmakrishna is the source of the widely accepted "all religions are the same" theory. Accordingly, the Rāmakrishna Mission not only spreads Hinduism in the West but also invites representatives of other religions to its temples and centers in India to speak about their own traditions.

Swāmi Vivekānanda inspired many young people in India, not only to join his mission and devote themselves to the causes of reform and uplift but also to continue his rearticulation of Hinduism and its application to the modern world, East and West.

Aurobindo Ghose, beginning as a nationalist firebrand, became one of the leading spiritual leaders not only of India but beyond, from his exile-*āśram* in Pondichéry. His followers are not organized in an order but their sense of mission is strong and active, as can be seen in the development of Auroville, a city that tries to realize and put into practice the principles of Aurobindo's spirituality.[25]

In the eyes of the educated Westerner, the most impressive figure of twentieth century Neo-Hinduism is surely Dr. Sarvepalli Radhakrishnan, a former President of India. Educated in Protestant mission schools in South India, well read in Eastern and Western philosophical and religious literature, a successful diplomat and politician, a prolific writer and an excellent speaker, he seems to embody what all are looking for: purified, spiritualized, non-sectarian Hinduism, the "religion of the spirit" and "the world-religion of the future," a valid and final answer to all the great questions of our time. As head of state, he served eminently as the "conscience of the nation," and wherever he spoke, he stressed the importance of spirituality, regardless of his audience. More than any other representative of the Indian intelligentsia, Radhakrishnan has taken up the concrete problems of India, attempting to contribute a religious dimension to their solution.[26]

Universalism and worldwide validity of its principles is claimed by many exponents of Hinduism, both at home and abroad. Few however, would go as far as M. S. Golwalkar, the former leader of the R.S.S., who wrote:

> The mission of reorganizing the Hindu people on the lines of their unique national genius which the Sangh has taken up is not only a process of true national regeneration of Bhārat but also the inevitable precondition to realize the dream of world-unity and human welfare . . . it is the grand world-unifying thought of Hindus alone that can supply the abiding basis for human brotherhood. This knowledge is in the safe custody of the Hindus alone. It is a divine trust, we may say, given to the charge of the Hindus by destiny.[27]

A great many well-known, respected, popular representatives of Hinduism of the more charismatic type, who have their major audience in India, have attracted Western followers, who very often establish centers in their own countries, propagating the words and works of their masters.

Ramaṇa Maharṣi (1879-1950) has been among the greatest and deepest spiritual influences coming from India in recent years (Figure 27.2). He was not educated in the traditional sense but he intuited *Advaita* Vedānta and became something like a Socrates among the Indian *yogis*. He relentlessly asked his visitors Who are You? till they lapsed into silence, arriving finally at some intimation of their true selves. Even after his death, the place

35. Ramaṇa Maharṣi

where he lived, is somehow charged with spiritual power, emanating from him.[28]

Swāmi Śivānanda (died 1964), the founder of the Divine Life Society, with headquarters at Śivānandāśram in Rishikesh, began as a physician before he turned *saṁnyāsi.* His interest, however, continued to be devoted to body and soul. At Rishikesh, his followers collect herbs to produce Ayurvedic medicines, and disciples from many countries are living a religious life that intends to synthetize the great world religions.[29]

J. Krishnamurti, groomed to be the *avatāra* of the twentieth century by Annie Besant, developed into quite an independent man, denouncing his mother-in-God and theosophy. He became known in his own right as a lecturer and writer on spiritual topics.[30]

Among the better known women saints of our time was Mā Ānandamāyī, with establishments in Benares, Vrindāban, and Bombay and quite a considerable following, who consider her a living deity.[31]

Paramahaṁsa Yogānanda, author of the *Autobiography of a Yogi* and founder of the *yoga* fellowship of California,[32] is far better known in the United States than in India. Mahesh Yogi Maharishi became the founder guru of the International Transcendental Meditation Society.[33] Swāmi Bhaktivedānta, at a very advanced age, established the Krishna-Consciousness movement in the United States.[34] Taposwāmi Mahārāj, quite well known in his own right,[35] has become more famous through his world-touring disciple Swāmi Cinmayānanda, who not only gives well-advertised *Gītā*-lectures in large Indian cities but has also founded Sandeepany Sadhanalaya, a training institution for Hindu missionaries in Bombay.[36]

One of the most colorful contemporary saints is easily Śrī Sathya Sāī Bābā, sporting a bright-red silk robe and an Afro hairdo. As a boy of fourteen, he declared that he had no more time for such things as going to school, announcing that he was Sāī Bābā and that his devotees were calling for him. The Sāī Bābā he referred to was a well-known saint living in Śīrdī (Mahārāṣṭra), who is credited with many miracles and who is even now supposed to appear to people and initiate them in their dreams.[37] The first miracle of the now living Sāī Bābā, who is in his fifties, was to create sweets for his playmates and flowers for the villagers of Puttaparthi in Andhra Pradesh. The sacred ashes that he now creates (following the lead of the old Sāī Bābā, on whose images a curious ashlike substance forms) is said to have miraculous properties to cure sickness and to accord mental relief. Modern as he is, he also creates photographs of his own holy person out of nowhere and distributes them, still damp, to his followers. His healing powers are said to be phenomenal, and people come from far that he may help their bodies and their souls. He is said to be able to read thoughts and to have the gifts of prophecy and multilocation. Thus, he speaks: "Trust always in me and lay your burden upon me; I shall do the rest; It is my task to prepare you for the grace of Bhagvān, when you receive it, everything else will be simple." He does not demand any special exercises, only trust: "Sāī is mother and father. Come to him without fear, doubt or hesitation. I am in your heart."[38]

INDIAN "SECULARIST" CRITIQUE OF HINDUISM

The difference between orthodox and reformist Hinduism, so pronounced in the nineteenth century, is no longer easy to make out. Some of the reformist movements have settled into orthodoxies of their own, and some of the staunchest defenders of orthodoxy advocate quite radical reform. K. M. Munshi, a great literary and political figure and the *spiritus rector* behind the establishment of the Bharatīya Vidyā Bhāvan, certainly as articulate a defender of Hinduism in our century as any, declared that the *varṇāśramadharma* was now obsolete, and that "exercises in faith must be satisfying to the modern mind, ceremonies and rituals must be uplifting and religious symbols inspiring. Temples must be clean, set in a sanctified atmosphere, the music accompanying prayers must be soulful and the officiating priests must be men of learning and faith."[39]

The Śaṅkarācārya of Puri, Swami Niranjan Dev, considered the most conservative of the traditional defenders of *sanātana dharma*, is also quoted as having pleaded for the abolition of caste and class differences.

The difference between religious practitioners and secularists, however, has become more pronounced, and it is quite an issue in present-day India. Secularism in India emerged as an ideology with Hindu reform in the nineteenth century. Foreign-educated Indians pressed for a secular India, impressed by what they had seen in the "secular West" and impatient with the obscurantism of traditional religion, the interminable clashes between the religious communities, and their obvious inability to agree on essential matters of importance for Indian society. Thus, in spite of his close association with the devout Hindu Mahātmā Gāndhī, the first Premier of India, Jawaharlal Nehru pushed through his concept of the Indian republic as a "secular democracy" in contrast to the simultaneous emergence of Pakistan as an "Islamic theocracy." A whole generation of modern, educated, highly placed Hindus distanced themselves from religion and worked to transform India into a modern state with a secular outlook. While antireligious movements as such are few, prosecular statements by intellectuals are quite pronounced. M. N. Roy's "radical humanism" is perhaps the best-known formulation of it.[40] Another Bengali philosopher, P. C. Chatterji recently came out with a spirited defence of *Secular Values for Secular India.* He goes into the recent history of communal rioting in India, identifying the narrow factionalism of the representatives of religious communities and pleading for a science-based secularism as the basis of Indian society.[41]

The urban modern educated class, which is more interested in careers and living standards than in traditional loyalties and pieties, is often quite articulate in its critique of Hinduism. A disclaimer, however, is appropriate. Things are changing here again, and more support is coming forth for temples and religious feasts from these groups than one would have suspected. An important Indian weekly, some years ago, invited some prominent Indians to express their ideas on "the role of religion in our lives." One Hindu had the following to say:

> The influence of religion on our lives has been detrimental. The dependence on religion and religious *gurus* has reduced us to a state of helplessness and we are always tempted to look out for an invisible, higher power, which is supposed to solve all our problems. The common people are unable to understand the philosophy of religion and therefore they content themselves with ridiculous ceremonies, making a mockery of everything that is sublime and holy. The impossibility of practicing the lofty commands of religion, the lack of a synthesis between these high values and the daily demands of secular life and the endeavour of every Indian to pretend to live according to these ideals have made us the most hypocritical amongst all the peoples on earth. This hypocrisy pervades every aspect of our life. Also the false emphasis on the "other world" while we are engaged in securing an existence for ourselves here on this earth has made us the most corrupt of all nations—a people which shirks work and is always hoping that something will come, making fate responsible for its misfortune. If our religion, instead of teaching us renunciation could give us guidance in our life and work, to make this world a better place to live in, then we Indians, with all our masses of men and our economic potential could be one of the leading nations of the world. In short—our religion has taught us, instead of "elevating us to the state of spiritual ecstasy" to be hypocrites and like Triśaṅku we have lost touch with both heaven and earth. We have remained behind in the race for a higher living standard because of the queer belief, that we could live in the twentieth century according to ideals that had been proclaimed long, long ago. The result is a hopeless stagnation in our spiritual values.[42]

Another modern Hindu, writing on "Our Changing Values"[43] called the present intellectual situation in India "a world of make-believe," deploring the aspects of hypocrisy and falseness that pervade everything.

> A half-hearted mysticism justifying India's failure to face life squarely leads the Indian intellectual to a sphere where the individual human being loses his

significance in the mumbo-jumbo of a sham mysticism. A deep-rooted apathy towards change and development—born out of frustration and the certificates that the pseudo-intellectuals get from their fellow-travellers in the West have jointly created a world of make-believe. . . . To rub out the rugged edges of their spiritual bankruptcy many Indian intellectuals entertain some make-believe picture of India and use it as a sort of spiritual sand-paper. . . . Power has become the cornerstone of goodness. . . . The ordinary Indian bestows respect on the powerful. Even a cursory survey of the causes for the reverence of the Bābās and Mās and astrologers will convince us that the average Indian does not respect them for any spiritual upliftment. He respects them for very mundane reasons—for getting promotions in his job, for being successful in business, for curing his diseases etc. Today he is finding that he can be more benefitted by the politically powerful and that is why he has developed reverence for them.[44]

A major source of friction between the Hindu reformers and the secularizers are laws that affect Indian society as a whole. A case in point is the Hindu Marriage Act of 1956, which, with amendments of 1978, recently became signed into law by the President of India. While still basically respecting the rights of the religious communities to follow their own traditions, the Indian government drastically secularized Hindu marriage laws and legislated changes that go quite manifestly against the letter and the spirit of the traditional Hindu law.[45] Other points of conflict are the Hindu demand to ban the slaughter of cows all over India,[46] and to prohibit the consumption of alcohol. Further debate arises over the government control of temple boards, and the support of schools maintained by various religious communities.

Hindus, as we have seen, can be very critical of Hinduism, too, but that should not mislead us into thinking that they are waiting for Westerners to solve their problems. Self-righteous as many Westerners still are, the social, psychological, and spiritual problems of the West are of such a magnitude that they should think twice before offering precious advice to India. Even the most critical Indians admit at the end of their devastating self-criticism that they believe in the self-regenerating power of their culture and people and that, if they see any hope, they expect the solution of their difficulties to come from within their own culture rather than from without it. Two world wars, racial and political tensions, flagrant greed and materialism have disillusioned India about the West's role as savior, which it assumed in the nineteenth century. The best we can do is to become partners in a worldwide economic and spiritual community.

28. Hindu Nationalist Politics and Hinduism as World Religion

> Slowly, but surely, like a juggernaut gaining angry momentum, a palpable, resurgent, united and increasingly militant movement of Hindu revivalism—*Hindu Jagaran*—is sweeping across the land. Frenzied in pace, frenetic in character, the religious and communal combat vehicle is freewheeling across the collective Hindu consciousness . . .
>
> —India Today (*31 May 1986*)[1]

THE INDIAN EQUIVALENT of *Time* magazine recently devoted its cover story to the "militant revivalism" of Hinduism in India. It is a phenomenon not entirely new but surprisingly large and potentially frightening. It had been coming for a long time and one can not be sure which way it will go. In the context of the militant revival of religions elsewhere, it cannot but be taken very seriously indeed.[2]

Traditional Hinduism, consisting of a great number of fairly independent and often conflicting denominations, is not yet in a shape to provide the ideology for a unified Hindu political activism. The Hindu Renaissance has spawned all manner of new understanding of Hinduism: from a humanistic, universalistic, tolerant, and generous religiosity to an exclusivistic, fanatical, militant ideology.

Political Hinduism as such does not have a clear identity as far as its strategies and policies are concerned. However, Hinduism always had a political dimension and, in the age of nationalism, which reached Asia in the nineteenth century, Hinduism took a decidedly nationalistic stance.

Terms like Holy Mother India were not meaningless rhetoric for Hindus but signified a living reality, which every Hindu was called upon to defend, protect, and foster. Bankim Chandra Chatterjee, the great Bengalī novelist, whose *Ānandamaṭha* depicted the 1770 Saṁnyāsi uprising as a national war of liberation from foreign rule, made his patriotic ascetics sing a hymn to Mother India, which for some time became the national anthem of the freedom movement, the *Bande Mātaram*, "Mother, I bow to thee," in which India is identified with the Goddess:

> With many strengths who are mighty and stored,
> To thee I call, Mother and Lord!
> Thou who savest, arise and save! . . .
> Thou art wisdom, thou art law,
> Thou our heart, our soul, our breath,
> Thou the love divine, the awe
> In our hearts that conquers death.
> Thine the strength that nerves the arm,
> Thine the beauty, thine the charm.
> Every image made divine
> In our temples is but thine.
> Thou art Durgā, Lady and Queen,
> With her hands that strike and her swords of sheen,
> Thou art Lakṣmī Lotus-throned,
> And the Muse a hundred-toned.
> Pure and Perfect without peer,
> Mother, lend thine ear.[3]

Another Bengalī, Śrī Aurobindo Ghose, who first fought for India's political independence in a terrorist band, according to his own testimony had a vision of Kṛṣṇa through which he was made to understand that his life's work was to be the restoration of the true *dharma*, that is, Hinduism. Bāl Gaṅgādhar Tilak and many others undertook their political agitation against the British *rāj* as a duty imposed on them by their religion; their aim was the restoration of Hindu India on the socio-political level.[4] The most radical advocates of the restoration of Hindu *dharma* on the socio-political level today are the many groups and parties that developed out of the Ārya Samāj, the "Aryan Society" of Swāmi Dāyānanda Saraswatī briefly described in the preceding chapter.

THE RADICAL HINDU POLITICAL MOVEMENTS ON A NATIONAL LEVEL

In 1909, Pandit Mohan Malaviya, who became later the first vice-chancellor of Benares Hindu University, together with other leading Ārya-Samājists founded the Hindu Mahāsabhā, which soon developed into a right-wing militant Hindu political party. It has remained one of the national parties based on a narrow definition of Hindu nationhood. Their election manifesto read:

> Hindustan is the land of the Hindus from time immemorial. The Hindu Mahāsabhā believes that Hindus have a right to live in peace as Hindus, to legislate, to rule, to govern themselves in accordance with Hindu genius and ideals and establish by all lawful and legal means a Hindu state based on Hindu Culture and Tradition, so that Hindu ideology and way of life should have a homeland of its own. The cardinal creed of the Hindu Mahāsabhā is:
>
> 1. Loyalty to the unity and integrity of Hindustan.
>
> 2. The Hindu Mahāsabhā reiterates once again that it is pledged to the re-establishment of Akhaṇḍ Bhārat by all legitimate means.
>
> 3. The Hindu Mahāsabhā again reiterates its clarion call, as given by Vir Savarkar as far back as 1938: "Hinduize Politics and Militarize Hinduism."[5]

The Vīr Savarkar (1883-1966) referred to was the greatest theoretician of the Hindu Mahāsabhā. In countless speeches and publications, he fought under the Hindu banner for the violent liberation of India from everything foreign and a complete restoration of Hindu ideas and Hindu society. India's independence from British rule in 1947 was not enough for him, he bitterly opposed Nehru's concept of a secular state and continued agitating for the total Hinduization of India, which earned him long spells under house arrest in his Bombay-Matunga home. In his essay *Hindutva*, he developed the outlines of the new Hindu India. He distinguished between *Hindu-dharma* (Hinduism as a religion), which is divided into countless *saṁpradāyas*, and *Hindutva* (Hindudom as the unifying socio-cultural background of all Hindus).[6]

One of the members of the Hindu Mahāsabhā, K. V. Hedgewar (1890-1940), a medical doctor who never practiced medicine, founded the Rāṣṭrīya Svayamsevak Saṅgh (R.S.S.) in 1925. He was afraid of Muslim influence over the Indian National Congress. The R.S.S., strictly organized from the very beginning, is the most powerful and most controversial Hindu organization of today: it claims to be a cultural organization and is not registered as a political party.

Nathuram Godse, Gāndhī's murderer, was a member of the R.S.S., which also had been held responsible for a great deal of the communal slaughter around the time of partition.[7] Nehru's reaction to Godse's crime was swift and decisive: he banned the R.S.S. and jailed tens of thousands of its members. About a year later, the ban was lifted and the leaders were freed. Apparently, the movement had friends in high places, so it was declared that no direct involvement of the R.S.S in Gāndhī's death could be proved.

The events connected with partition, which had brought great suffering to many millions of Indians, were perceived by the Hindus in India as inflicting more than an equal share of sacrifice on the Hindus. Differences over Muslim-Hindu policies caused several groups to break away from the monolithic Congress party since 1948.

Events in East Bengal in early 1950 lead to the formation of the Jana Sangh Party, which had a clearly pro-Hindu, anti-Muslim orientation.[8] Millions of Hindus had fled from East Bengal to West Bengal telling about forcible eviction, Muslim brutalities, and large-scale repression. The conciliatory talks between Nehru and Liaquat Ali were considered inadequate by a number of politicians in West Bengal and at New Delhi. The major figures involved were Shyamprasad Mookerjea (minister for industries and supplies), John Mathai (finance minister) and K. C. Neogy, who resigned from the Union Cabinet. They proposed their own set of conditions for Pakistan and, while ostensibly promoting the cause of the Hindus in Pakistan, also articulated an alternative approach to Indian internal and external politics.

The new party called itself Bhāratīya Jana Saṅgh; in Bengal, it first appeared under its English name, People's Party of India. While its origins were rooted in the dissatisfaction with central government policies, the founders of the Jana Sangh pointed out, correctly, that it did not just constitute a break-away Congress party faction.

As Deendayal Upadhyaya wrote:

> The Jana Sangh was founded as an all-India party on 21 October 1951. It was not a disgruntled, dissident or discredited group of Congressmen who formed the nucleus of the party, as is the case with all other political parties. . . . Its inspiration came from those who basically differed from the Congress outlook and policies. It was an expression of the nascent nationalism. It was felt that the ruling party had failed to harness the enthusiasm created by freedom to the task of realization of the great potentialities of the country. It was because of their anxiety to make Bhārat a carbon-copy of the West, that they have ignored and neglected the best in Bhāratīya life and ideals. The Jana Sangh predicted that the Abhāratīya and unrealistic approach to the national problems by the

party in power would create more complications than solve any. Its forebodings have come true.[9]

The leading light in the early years was Dr. Shyamprasad Mookerjea. A man with a distinguished academic record and an early involvement in Bengal politics, he joined the Hindu Mahāsabhā in 1937. In 1946, Nehru offered him a cabinet position. Mookerjea was one of five non-Congress party members of the fourteen member cabinet. Dr. Mookerjea disagreed with the Hindu Mahāsabhā on many issues and demanded, after the assassination of Mahātmā Gāndhī, that it either withdraw from political activities altogether or shed its communal Hindu character. The Hindu Mahāsabhā had not been very successful in the 1946 elections anyhow.

Eventually, Mookerjea left the Hindu Mahāsabhā and also resigned from the Nehru Cabinet in 1950, over the Bengal issue. He established links with R.S.S. leaders Vasantrao Oak and Balraj Madhok. He tried to persuade the R.S.S. to become a political party. The R.S.S. leaders had rejected such an idea since its foundation: the R.S.S. had wider aims.

The Jana Sangh won considerable support in some state elections and became powerful enough on the national level to attract the attention and vituperation of both Congress and leftist parties as being "fascist," "totalitarian," etc. Apart from its overall view to Indianize/Hinduize, Indian politics it kept pleading for a reunification of India, the introduction of Hindī as national language, the recognition of Israel, and the ban of cow slaughter.[10] It merged with a number of other parties, among others the anti-Indira Gandhi wing of the Congress party, to form the Janata party, which after the resignation of Indira Gandhi in 1977 won elections in a landslide victory.

The coalition that was Janata was shaky from the very beginning. Its lack of initiative and its increasing internal quarrels, largely about the relations of former Jana Sangh members with the R.S.S., created widespread disappointment. Eventually, the party split, which brought about the downfall of the Janata government and a return to power of Indira Gandhi's Congress party. The party split further in March 1980 and again in April 1980, when the former Jana Sangh group formed a new party called the Bhāratīya Janatā Party. The leadership was taken over, again, by A. B. Vajpayee, who had been external affairs minister under the Janata government. In a speech on April 6, 1980, he had declared: "We are proud of our association with the R.S.S.". Lately, he has been expressing his disillusionment with the new party as well.[11]

Deen Dayal Upadhyaya, Atal Bihari Vajpayee, Lal Krishna Advani, Nanaji Deshmukh, Balraj Madhok, Lal Hansraj Gupta—men who shaped national politics in the 1960s and 1970s—were all prominent activists of the

R.S.S. The R.S.S. spawned a great number of other front organizations like the Bhāratīya Mazdūr Sabhā, a trade union, and the Viśva Hindu Pariṣad (V.H.P.), a religious organization (founded in 1964), which attempts to articulate a kind of universal Hinduism that would embrace the different sects and at the same time possess a basic common creed and common practice.[12]

It is not always clear where the borderline between the R.S.S. and the V.H.P. lies, if there is one to begin with. Both organizations boast thousands of centers all over India and millions of members, and both are extremely active on behalf of Hindu *jagaran* (Hindu awakening).[13] They organize processions, meetings, and festivities, and they work toward a bridging the differences between different Hindu denominations in the interest of a united, politically strong Hinduism. Membership figures mentioned are impressive, as are the violent confrontations. One of the immediate aims of the Viśva Hindu Pariṣad is to repossess the areas of the Kṛṣṇa Janmabhūmi Temple in Mathurā and of the Viśvanāth Temple in Benares, two of the holiest places of Hinduism, which were occupied and desecrated by the Muslims in the Middle Ages.

Partly cooperating and partly competing with these organizations are others devoted to the same goals of Hindu awakening and Hindu political power: the Virāt Hindu Sammelan, the Hindu Samājotsav, Banjrang Dal, etc. There can be no doubt that the major role in the Hindu revival has been played for quite some time by the R.S.S.

The training of the R.S.S. members is rigorous and purposeful: bodily exercises and indoctrination sessions have to be attended by all members for at least an hour daily. The leaders are usually unmarried, unsalaried, and devote all their time and their energy to the movement.[14]

M. S. Golwalkar, the successor to K. V. Hedgewar, who died in 1973, wrote *Bunch of Thoughts* early in his career. In it, he systematically and openly lays out the ideology and the policies of the R.S.S. He quite frankly declares Muslims, Christians, and communists (in that order) the major enemies of India and promises that they would not be citizens of a Hindu India shaped according to R.S.S. principles. According to Golwarkar, the Hindu nation has been given the divine mandate to spiritualize the world and this mandate has fallen on the R.S.S. in our time. With genuinely religious fervor, Golwarkar exhorts his followers to do their utmost for the re-establishment of this Hindu order not only in India but worldwide. Thus he writes: "The R.S.S. has resolved to fulfill that age-old national mission by forging, as the first step, the present-day scattered elements of the Hindu Society into an organised and invincible force both on the plane of the Spirit and on the plane of material life. Verily this is the one real practical world-mission if ever there was one."[15]

After Golwalkar's death, Madhukar Dattatreya, known as Balasaheb Deoras (also a bachelor and a member of the R.S.S. since his twelfth year) became *Sarsanghachalak*, the supreme leader of the R.S.S. He echoes Sarvarkar when stating:

> We do believe in the one-culture and one-nation Hindu *rāṣṭra*. But our definition of Hindu is not limited to any particular kind of faith. Our definition of Hindu includes those who believe in the one-culture and one-nation theory of this country. They can all form part of the *Hindu-rāṣṭra*. So by Hindu we do not mean any particular type of faith. We use the word Hindu in a broader sense.[16]

Many Indians, who subscribe to the idea of a secular democratic state with equal rights for all its members, regardless of race, creed, or sex, consider the R.S.S. to be a threat to this state—the biggest and most serious threat considering its membership (upwards of 5 million) and the calibre of its organization. While the R.S.S. and its front organizations may be the most visible manifestation of extremist and radical political Hinduism on the national level, it is not the only one. Thus, in the late 1940s, Swāmi Karpātrījī Mahārāj founded the Rām Rājya Pariṣad (Kingdom of God party), which also contended in national elections, objecting to Nehru's secular democracy.[17] It is not very influential but it has attracted a number of Swāmis, who campaign on its behalf for seats in the Lok Sabhā.

REGIONAL HINDU POLITICAL MOVEMENTS

In the 1960s, numerous regional organizations developed in India, with the aim to either establish language- or religion-based separate states or to protect the natives of a particular state from the competition of out-of-state migrants. Regional interests and Hindu interests very often overlap; however, they are too numerous to be examined within the context of this book.[18] One example, the earliest, most active, and exclusive Hindu organization of this type, may suffice to make the point.[19]

The Shiv Sena (Shivajī's Army) was founded in 1966 in Bombay by Val Thakkeray, a former cartoonist for a local paper. It was to protect the rights and jobs of Mahārāṣṭrians, especially in Bombay, which had become a metropolis with large contingents of Indians from almost all parts of the country. It demanded, among other things, that 80 per cent of government jobs be reserved for native Mahārāṣṭrians. By 1969, it had become powerful enough to call a general strike in Bombay, paralyzing the entire huge city for three days, burning buses and trains, terrorizing non-Mahārāṣṭrians. Many South Indian coffee shops were burned down, many non-Mahārāṣṭrian businesses were vandalized. Not long afterwards, the Shiv Sena won the majority of seats in Bombay's municipal election and became a major factor in Mahārāṣṭrian state politics.[20]

Hindu interests and regional interests overlap in the Shiv Sena. While the organization is Hindu, it demonstrated hostility to all non-Mahārāṣṭrians, Hindu as well as non-Hindu. During the past few years, the Shiv Sena has expanded to other Indian states, especially to Uttar Pradesh and Punjab. It claims to have hundreds of thousands of followers there.

Although the Shiv Sena may have arisen as a rightist Hindu movement counterbalancing leftist forces, its rise has occasioned the emergence of a great number of regional communal "defense organizations." A Muslim Sena and a Christian Sena emerged with the aim to protect the interests of these minorities. It is often difficult to arrange the *senas* within the Indian political spectrum: Kanada Sena, Gopala Sena, Tamil Army, Lachit Sena, Bhim Sena, etc. Whereas many of them may not have a significant following and no more than local importance, they certainly have helped to polarize the Indian political scene and to weaken any sense of unity on the basis of a common Indianness that had developed over the years. While not all of them are Hindu, several of them are increasingly becoming the instruments of politically active and often extreme Hinduism, which throughout history has considered regional loyalties of greater importance than all-Indian interests.

POLITICAL HINDUISM ON A SECTARIAN BASIS

The Ānand Mārg (Path of Bliss) was founded in 1955 by Anand Murti alias P. R. Sarkar, who after several stints with newspapers found employment with the railways in Jamalpur/Bihar. For his followers, Anand Murti is "the great Preceptor, the harbinger of a new civilization and the loving guru." He was born in 1921 and claims to be the third incarnation of God after Śiva and Kṛṣṇa. The movement has many front organizations, including a national political party, the Proutist Block of India. Some years ago, it claimed to have 2000 centers and 5 million members. Its declared aim is to "establish the dictatorship of Bābā." The Ānand Mārg was linked to a number of acts of violence in India and abroad, and P. R. Sarkar was arrested when his wife denounced him to the police as responsible for thirty-five murders, mostly of former Ānandmārgis who had become disloyal to the movement. While the number of followers is not large enough to make any impact on the Indian political scene, the violence perpetrated by some of its members aroused the Indian public.[21]

HINDU COMMUNALISM

In its forty years of independence, India so far has successfully upheld its ideal of a secular democracy on the national level. This did not prevent extremist political Hindu groups from putting pressure on non-Hindu minorities in a number of states like Madhya Pradesh, Uttar Pradesh, Bihar, and Orissa. Although documents such as the Niyogi report purport to attack only foreign Christian missionaries, the Indian Christians rightly interpreted it as an attack on Christianity in India. Again, although it was India at war with Pakistan, and not Hindus with Muslims, in the several wars that eventually lead to the establishment of Bangladesh, during these wars, Muslims experienced harassment from fanatical Hindus, who saw them as "enemies of India." At numerous occasions in the past forty years, the potential for violence that political Hinduism possesses translated into provocation of Muslims and subsequent large-scale rioting along communal lines.[22]

"Communalism," of course, is not only a Hindu problem.[23] It is a vast and complex phenomenon with which many social and political scientists have dealt and that seems to develop ever new forms, although its basic structure remains the same. Moin Shakir, an Indian political scientist calls communalism "the most intractable problem of the Indian polity and society." It is, he says, "a many faced phenomenon with diverse causes and reveals itself in difficult [sic] forms under different sets of circumstances." His own view is that "under the mask of religion, culture and tradition the communal leaders have been aiming at protecting the interests of the lower middle class and urban intelligentsia."[24]

All are agreed that religious identities are a major factor in communalism and that it constitutes a misapplication of religious principles. For several decades, it appeared as if communalism were largely a Hindu-Muslim problem. Lately, the Sikh communalists have raised their voices and the regional chauvinisms that find expression in the various *senas* described earlier are not only promoting intrareligious but also intraregional hatred.

Many analysts interpret the increasing communal wave as caused by a weakening of the central government's power.[25] That may be so, but it does not explain much either. The Indian socio-political landscape is still forming. The most pressing economic needs have been satisfied, which provided a certain measure of cohesion among all groups, and national independence has been achieved, which also united people in spite of differences. Now, the normalization of life includes the development of political factions and societal groups that have to arrange themselves vis-á-vis each other on matters other than nationality and bare survival.

It was a symbol of things to come, when, at the celebrations marking the fortieth anniversary of India's independence in Delhi, on August 15, 1987, a group of people described as the Revolutionary Hindu movement protested loudly against Rajiv Gandhi and his concept of a secularist India. "Hindus will be like lions and they will dominate the country," one of their representatives declared.

A PRELIMINARY ASSESSMENT

A long history of foreign occupations has given an extra edge to political Hinduism: it almost always contains an element of rejection of foreign institutions, customs, and authorities. Considering the high sophistication of traditional Indian thought in the area of government, the detailed provisions made for the bearers of political authority from the ancient *smṛtis* onward, it is understandable that traditional Hindus want to see these provisions once more in place. Such a suggestion gains even more weight when one compares a glorified Indian past with the disenchanting and problematic Indian present.

Political Hinduism is not a homogenous "movement." It is the result of a reinterpretation of Hinduism along many different lines. Neither are all Hindus agreed that Hinduism or its professional representatives ought to be involved in power politics at all. The traditional *yatidharma*, as explained before, forbids involvement of *saṁnyāsis* in political or economic affairs. There are many voices in today's India who demand a separation of religion and state and many view the influence of Hindu authorities on party politics with disapproval.

Political Hinduism is right wing. Its major support comes from landowners and industrialists, shopowners, high school and college teachers and students, and small entrepreneurs. The potential power of the Hindu political parties, however, does not only lie in the as yet pervasive traditionalism of the large masses (especially in rural and small-town India) but also in the correct perception of a widespread lack of social, ethical, and personal values in Western-style party politics. Indians, who have become aware of the lack of values in the formal democratic process, frequently fall back on Hinduism (often somewhat modernized, desectarianized, and enlightened in Sarvepalli Radhakrishnan's way) as the only acceptable basis. Hinduism, after all, is indigenous; it has shaped Indian society and mentality for thousands of years; it is flexible and is, in the opinion of most Hindus, far superior in its philosophy to any other religion or philosophy.

The standard Western sociological and economic investigation, which leads to the compilation of statistics of election results, distribution of incomes, family size, etc., leaves out important factors. It seems to presuppose tacitly U.S. society and politics as a standard model that contains all the relevant parameters. It also seems to presuppose that developments can go only in one direction, the direction of what the West calls modernity. One indication that things are still different in India are the widespread and frequent large-scale defections from parties, the "crossing over" of large groups of elected representatives from one party to another, the splitting of existing parties, and the formation of new ones. Personal loyalties have priority over party tradition; personal rifts override party discipline. Matters of conviction and principle, however questionable and shallow, very easily win out against an economic or voting calculus.

Contrary to the commonly held belief that ideological parties are obsolete and that modern politics boils down to a distribution of shares in the economy of a given country, I would maintain that we are in for a new wave of ideological politics on all levels.[26] Issues with highly emotional content become anew the focus of world and national politics. The peace issue is one of these; reunification of divided nations (the favorite recipe for peace in the 1940s and 1950s) is another. Language issues become still another source of political ferment. In the process, the structures of political parties, built upon the rationalization of societal needs, seem to become irrelevant. Grass-roots movements arise and become decisive, cutting across the classical political spectrum, mobilizing people who would never join an existing political party. Such movements are usually not wholly spontaneous; they develop out of issues that for a long time had been neglected by the official parties but were cultivated by interest groups.

All these elements are present in political Hinduism. By declaring its contempt for the institution of Western-style political parties, it attracts all those who find distasteful the spectacle of party bickering and horse trading. By promoting Akhaṇḍ Bhārat, undivided India, it appeals not only to those who have suffered directly under the partition and its continued aftereffects but also to all those for whom Mother India is a reality—and they are many. By its emphasis on Indianization, it again appeals to vast numbers who feel that the present élite is much too Western oriented and forgetful of India's own cultural and spiritual heritage. And, last but not least, by emphasizing Hindudom, it speaks to many shades of religiosity alive in present-day India.

The majority of Indian political scientists and sociologists are Marxist oriented. They try to find emerging "classes" in India as the major political agents and a class struggle, of sorts, as the key to political dynamics. I fear this is too simple a solution, and too Western a view, too. Of course, there are "new classes," of course, there is "class struggle," but the Indian socio-political scene has dimensions not covered by these categories.

The Indian Freedom movement was not a class struggle; political

Hinduism is not a matter of class, although some of its interpreters try to make it out as reactionary middle-class movement. The age-old fascination with renunciation, selfless service, worship of an absolute incarnate in a person, a place, a tradition is still alive. It was sufficiently alive to attract hundreds of dedicated coworkers to Gāndhī, who had renounced all property, title, and class affiliations. It is alive in the R.S.S., which demands from its leaders rigorous self-control, renunciation of private property, of pleasure, and of status, and not only insists on classlessness but also on castelessness.

Political Hinduism, I hold, cannot be understood by applying either a Western-party democratic gauge or a Marxist-socialist pattern. Its potential has much to do with the temper of Hinduism, which was able throughout the ages to rally people around causes that were perceived to be of transcendent importance and in whose pursuit ordinary human values and considerations had to be abandoned. Whether one considers this good or bad will depend on one's standpoint. The fact remains, however; and a student of Indian politics will be able to ignore this only to his or her detriment.

HINDUISM AS WORLD RELIGION

The picture of Hindu communalism and narrowly focussed Hindu politics has to be balanced by pointing toward the profound ambivalence of present-day Hinduism.

Side by side with the most intense nationalistic fervor shown by Hindus, as pointed out earlier, is a rejection of the "Western" concept of nation-state in the writings of such spokesmen of modern Hinduism as Rabindranath Tagore, Aurobindo Ghose, and Sarvepalli Radhakrishnan.

Alongside the reaffirmation of the *varṇāśramadharma* as the basis of India are also statements from representatives of orthodoxy and of political Hinduism that advocate a casteless and classless society. The wholesale condemnation of modernization and secularization by some is counterbalanced by the advocacy of a militarily strong, industrially modern India by others.

While all along there had been Hindu resistance against all changes introduced in society and legislation, it must also be pointed out that virtually all the progressive moves have been initiated by Hindus, too. Parallel to, and in stark contrast with, the tendency to provincialize and sectarianize Hinduism are strong countermoves to universalize and spiritualize Hinduism and to regard it as the home of all genuine religiosity.

Hinduism has brought forth in the modern era not only a Dāyānanda and a Tilak but also a Gāndhī and a Sarvepalli Radhakrishnan, an Aurobindo Ghose and a Krishnamurti, true citizens of the world and prophets of a universal religion. What we see happening with Hinduism today may be the formation of a truly new world religion. Hinduism, of course, already is a world religion on account of the large number of its adherents. But its strong ties to the geographic entity of India and the social structure of native castes has prevented it from reaching out into the world at large. Also, its internal dissensions, its uncertainty with regard to its own essentials, its history of sectarianism has worked against its status as a truly universal religion.

All this is changing. In our century, Hinduism has produced high-profile exponents who downplayed sectarianism, emphasized the common foundations of all its branches, and modernized and revitalized Hinduism. Hinduism has proved much more open than any other religion to new ideas, to scientific thought, and to social experimentation. Many beliefs, basic to Hinduism and initially strange to the West, like reincarnation, polydevatism, meditation, and guruship have found worldwide acceptance. Also Hinduism's traditional fuzziness with regard to doctrinal boundaries is becoming a fairly universal feature of religion worldwide. Its living tradition of *yoga* and methods of interiorization give it an edge over other traditional religions, which stress the absolute authority of an official or the ultimate truth of a scripture.

Hinduism is organizing itself, it is articulating its own essentials, it is modernizing, and it is carried by a great many people with strong faith. It would not be surprising to find Hinduism the dominant religion of the twenty-first century. It would be a religion that doctrinally is less clear-cut than mainstream Christianity, politically less determined than Islam, ethically less heroic than Buddhism; but it would offer something to everybody, it would delight by its richness and depth, it would address people at a level that has not been plumbed for a long time by other religions or prevailing ideologies. It will appear idealistic to those who look for idealism, pragmatic to the pragmatists, spiritual to the seekers, sensual to the here-and-now generation. Hinduism, by virtue of its lack of an ideology and its reliance on intuition, will appear to be much more plausible than those religions whose doctrinal positions petrified a thousand years ago or whose social structures remain governed by tribal mores.

That is how an open-minded, scholarly Hindu like A. S. Altekar sees it:

> Hindu religion, philosophy and social structure are nothing but the records of a glorious and instructive struggle of the human mind to free itself from limitations that have become meaningless in the course of time, and to attain to more and more glorious heights that are revealed by man's ever expanding

> vision. There is no doubt that Hinduism will become once more a great world force, the moment this consciousness becomes a part and parcel of the modern Hindu mind and begins to mold and influence its activities in the different spheres of life.[27]

Hinduism will spread not so much through the gurus and *swāmis*, who attract a certain number of people looking for a new commitment and a quasi-monastic life-style, but it will spread mainly through the work of intellectuals and writers, who have found certain Hindu ideas convincing and who identify them with their personal beliefs. A fair number of leading physicists and biologists have found parallels between modern science and Hindu ideas. An increasing number of creative scientists will come from a Hindu background and will consciously and unconsciously blend their scientific and their religious ideas. All of us may be already much more Hindu than we think.

29. Chronology

DATES CONCERNING INDIAN prehistory and protohistory are very questionable as yet. So far, the earliest signs of human activity in India, Paleolithic sites in Tamilnadu and Punjab, are dated at ca. 470,000 B.C.E. The so-called Soan culture, in its different phases,[1] flourished between 400,000 and 200,000 B.C.E. The so-called Indus civilization, which according to recent finds reached far into today's Gujarat and Punjab as well as western Uttar Pradesh, reached its peak between 2700 and 1700 B.C.E. Western authors generally connect the decline of the Indus civilization with the invasion of the Vedic Aryans ca. 1500-1200 B.C.E.[2]

India's traditional chronology, supported by astronomical calculations,[3] gives precise dates for prehistoric events, too. Thus, the creation of the present world is dated at 1,972,947,101 B.C.E. and the beginning of the *Kaliyuga* at 3102 B.C.E., which is the date of the end of the Bhārata War according to one school. Historians accepting the historicity of the Purāṇic materials[4] also take this to be the date of Manu. Rāmacandra is said to have flourished around 1950 B.C.E. and Kṛṣṇa around 1400 B.C.E. According to this school, that is the date for the Bhārata War, too.

According to P. C. Sengupta[5] July 25, 3928 B.C.E. is the date of the earliest solar eclipse mentioned in the *Ṛgveda,* He fixed the birthdate of Kṛṣṇa on July 21, 2501 B.C.E. and the date of the Bhārata War at 2449 B.C.E. S. B. Roy, using astronomical observations recorded in the *ṚgVeda* and working with the list of Purāṇic kings and *ṛṣis* established by Pargiter, comes to fairly precise dating of most of the major events of early Indian history.[6] By cross-referencing Indian events and names with exactly dated events and names of Babylonia and Persia, he appears to provide a fairly good foundation for his dates. He points out that Max Müller, whom most Western scholars followed in dating Vedic literature and events of early Indian history, had based his calculations only "on the ghost story of *Kathāsaritasāgara* composed in about 1200 A.D. i.e. nearly three thousand five hundred years after the event." He also assumed that certain events mentioned in the *Ṛgveda* took place in Iran, where the Vedic Indians had lived before the invasion of India. He provides a list of basic dates according to "high chronology" and "low chronology".

Manu Vaivasvata, the first of the kings in the Purāṇic list, was born in 3167 B.C.E. according to the high chronology (h.c.) and in 2851 B.C.E. according to the low chronology (l.c.). On the assumption that Bharata (number 44 in the Purāṇic list) was a contemporary of Sargon of Accad, his birthdate would either be 2393 B.C.E. (h.c.) or 2077 B.C.E. (l.c.). The major portion of the Vedic hymns was composed at the time of Viśvamitra I (2609 B.C.E. h.c.; 2293 B.C.E. l.c.), whereas the invasion of India took place under the Divodāsa dynasty (2051-1961 B.C.E. h.c.; 1735-1645 B.C.E. l.c.). The Āryans spread thoughout northern India during the next five centuries. The Bhārata battle took place in 1424 B.C.E. (h.c.) or 1088 B.C.E. (l.c.). The early Upaniṣads were composed between 1450 and 1350 B.C.E. (h.c.) or 1100 and 1000 B.C.E. (l.c.). *Vedāṅga* and *Sūtra* literature is assumed to be of similar age. The *Aṣṭādhyāyī* of Pāṇini was composed in 1320 B.C.E. (h.c.) or 1000 B.C.E. (l.c.). By the end of the eighth century B.C.E., Sanskrit ceased to be a spoken tongue.

Many of these dates appear surprisingly high compared to the dates found in most Indological literature. Although it may be premature to endorse S. B. Roy's chronology without further study, it should be kept in mind that the chronology provided by Max Müller and accepted uncritically by most Western scholars is based on very shaky ground indeed. Given the paucity of clues for the chronologies established in the West a century ago, we should not be surprised if these have to be revised drastically with the application of more sophisticated and more precise methods of dating archeological finds.

As regards the date of composition of the Vedic *Saṁhitās*, there is a wide difference of opinion among modern scholars. Leaving aside the opinion of Dāyānanda Saraswatī, who claims prehistoric antiquity for the Vedas, there is still a wide divergence. P. V. Kane assumes that the bulk of the *Saṁhitās, Brāhmaṇas*, and *Upaniṣads* were composed between 4000 and 1000 B.C.E. and thinks that some hymns of *Ṛgveda* and *Atharvaveda* and parts of the *Taittirīya Saṁhitā* and *Brāhmaṇa* go back to the time before 4000 B.C.E. B. G. Tilak arrives at 4500 B.C.E. as the date of the Vedas, M. Winternitz at 2500 B.C.E., and M. Bloomfield at 2000 B.C.E. Indian chronology reaches comparatively firmer ground with the life of Gautama Buddha, whose traditional dates and the dates as established by Western scholars differ by only about half a century. From then on numerous dated inscriptions and monuments ensure a fairly commonly accepted chronology.

Indians who do not use the Western (Gregorian) calendar have several other systems of dating. The most common are *samvat* (beginning 57 B.C.E.)

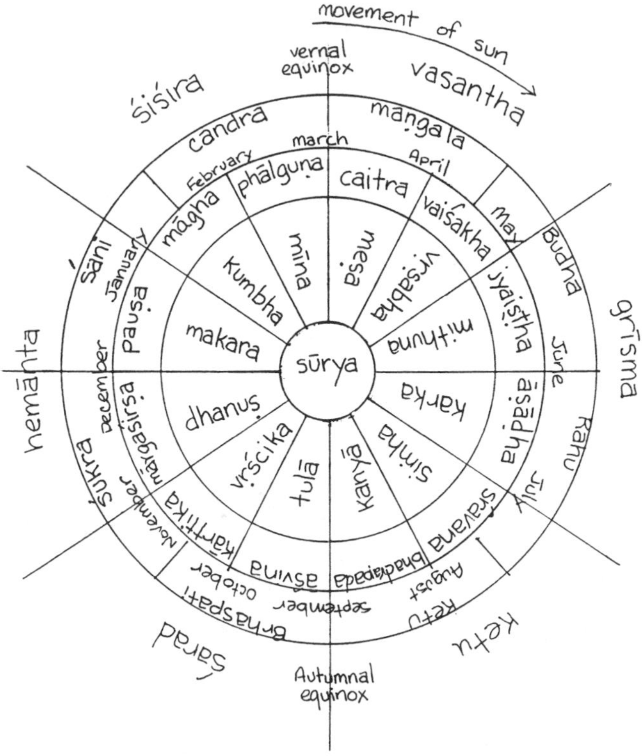

Figure 29.1 The Hindu Calendar

Notes:

Inner circle: signs of the zodiac (solar).
Second circle: names of months (lunar-solar).
Third circle: corresponding months of Julian calendar; planets.
Outer circle: names of seasons.

The coincidence of vernal equinox and the beginning of month *caitra/meṣa*, upon which the calendar was based in the sixth century C.E. has since moved, due to an inexact calculation.

The days of the week are *ravivāra*, Sunday (day of the Sun); *somavara*, Monday (day of the Moon); *maṅgalavāra*, Tuesday (day of Mars); *budhavāra*, Wednesday (day of Mercury); *guruvāra*, Thursday (day of Jupiter); *śukravāra*, Friday (day of Venus); *śanivāra*, Saturday (day of Saturn).

The names of the fifteen moon days in each half month are 1. *prathamā;* 2. *dvitīyā;* 3. *tṛtīyā;* 4. *caturthī;* 5. *pañcamī;* 6. *ṣaṣṭhī;* 7. *saptamī;* 8. *aṣṭamī;* 9. *navamī;* 10. *daśamī;* 11. *ekādaśī;* 12. *dvadaśī;* 13. *trayodaśī;* 14. *caturdaśī;* 15. *pañcadaśī* (a) in *śuklapakṣa: pūrṇimā;* (b) in *kṛṣṇapakṣa: amāvāsyā, darśa.*

and *śaka* (beginning 78 C.E.).[7] Figure 29.1 shows the Hindu calendar used today.

The majority of Indologists following Max Müller still accept more or less the following chronology:

ca. 1500-1200 B.C.E.	Āryan invasion of India; early Vedic hymns
ca. 1200-900 B.C.E.	Composition of the Vedic *Saṁhitās*
ca. 900-500 B.C.E.	Composition of later parts of the *Saṁhitās*, of the *Brāhmaṇas*, and the early *Upaniṣads*
ca. 900 B.C.E.	The great Bhārata War
817 B.C.E.	Birth of Parśvanātha (twenty-third Tīrthāṅkāra)
ca. 600 B.C.E.	Early *Smṛtis*
624-544 B.C.E.	Life of Gautama Buddha according to traditional Śrī Laṅka reckoning (563-483 according to most Western scholars)
527 B.C.E.	End of Mahāvīra's earthly life according to Jain tradition
518 B.C.E.	Persian invasion under Skylax and conquest of the Indian satrapy for Darius I
ca. 500 B.C.E.-500 C.E.	Composition of *Śrautasūtras, Gṛhyasūtras, Dharmasūtras, Vedāṅgas;* the basis of the orthodox systems; composition of the epics and the original *Purāṇas*
ca. 500-200 B.C.E.	Composition of the *Bhagavadgītā* (according to P. V. Kane; others date it ca. 100 B.C.E.-100 C.E.)
ca. 500-200 B.C.E.	Bādarāyaṇa's *Vedāntasūtra* (according to P. V. Kane)
ca. 490-458 B.C.E.	Reign of Ajātaśatru, king of Magadha
ca. 400 B.C.E.	Paninis *Aṣṭādhyāyī* (Grammar)
ca. 400-200 B.C.E.	Jaimini's *Pūrvamīmāṁsāsūtra*
327-325 B.C.E.	Alexander of Macedonia's invasion of India
ca. 322-298 B.C.E.	Reign of Candragupta of Magadha
ca. 300 B.C.E.	Megasthenes, Greek ambassador to Magadha

ca. 300 B.C.E.	Kautilīya's *Ārthaśāstra* (according to some scholars, 100 C.E.); Gautama's *Nyāyasūtra;* and Kaṇāda's *Vaiśeṣikasūtra*
ca. 273-237 B.C.E.	Reign of Aśoka
ca. 200 B.C.E.-100 C.E.	*Manusmṛti*
ca. 200 B.C.E.-100 C.E.	Invasions of Śūngas, Iranians, Śākas, and Kuśānas, who founded kingdoms in India
ca. 200 B.C.E.-200 C.E.	Peak period of Buddhist and Jain influence
ca. 150 B.C.E.-100 C.E.	Patañjali's *Mahābhāṣya*
ca. 115 B.C.E.	Besnagar inscription of Heliodorus with a mention of Kṛṣṇa worship
ca. 100 B.C.E.-500 C.E.	Patañjali's *Yogasūtra*
ca. 100 B.C.E.-100 C.E.	Upavarṣa's commentary to *Pūrvamīmāṁsāsūtra* and *Vedāntasūtra* (according to P. V. Kane)
ca. 100 B.C.E.-400 C.E.	*Śābarabhāṣya* on Jaimini Sūtras
ca. 100 B.C.E.-800 C.E.	Composition of *Tirukkuṛaḷ*
ca. 100 B.C.E.	Early Mathurā sculpture; images of gods in temples
ca. 25 B.C.E.	Indian embassy to Emperor Augustus of Rome
ca. 50 C.E.	First documentation of images of gods with several pairs of arms
ca. 100	Indian embassy to Emperor Trajan of Rome
ca. 100-500	Expansion of Hinduism in Southeast Asia
ca. 100-200	*Yājñavalkyasmṛti*
ca. 100-300	*Viṣṇudharmasūtra*
ca. 100-400	*Nāradasmṛti*
ca. 200-500	Composition of *Viṣṇupurāṇa*
ca. 250-325	*Sāṁkhyakārikā* of *Īśvarakṛṣṇa*
ca. 300-600	Composition of some of the older *Purāṇas* in their present form
ca. 300-888	Paḷḷava rulers in South India (Kāñcīpuram)

ca. 319-415	Gupta Empire of Mathurā
ca. 400-500	Vatsyāyana's *Kāmasūtra*
ca. 400	Composition of *Harivaṁśapurāṇa, Ahirbudhnya-saṁhitā;* age of Kalidāsa, the greatest Indian dramatist; spread of Vaiṣṇavism, especially Kṛṣṇa cult; beginning of Tantricism
ca. 400-500	Vyāsa's *Yogabhāṣya*
ca. 450-500	Huna invasions
ca. 500	*Devīmāhātmya* (in *Mārkaṇḍeyapurāṇa*); spread of Śāktism into larger areas
ca. 500-800	Composition of *Kūrmapurāṇa*
547	Kosmas Indikopleustes travels to India
ca. 600-650	Age of poet Bāṇa, author of *Kādāṁbarī* and *Harṣacaritā*
ca. 600-800	Peak of Pāñcarātra Vaiṣṇavism
ca. 600-900	Late (metrical) *smṛtis;* composition of *Agnipurāṇa* and *Garuḍapurāṇa*
after 600	Strong development of Vedānta
ca. 600-800	Brahmanical renaissance; successful fight against strongly Tantric Buddhism
ca. 640	King Harṣa of Kanauj sends embassy to China
ca. 650-1200	Several independent kingdoms in West, Central, East, and South India
ca. 650-700	Life of Kumārilabhaṭṭa and Māṇikavācaka
since ca. 700	Prevalence of *bhakti* religions
ca. 700-750	Gauḍapāda, author of a *kārikā* on the *Māṇḍukya Upaniṣad* and Paramaguru of Śaṅkarācārya
since ca. 700	Flourishing of Kaśmīr Śaivism
ca. 788-820	Life of Śaṅkarācārya
ca. 800-900	Composition of the *Bhāgavata Purāṇa* in its present form; *Śukranītisāra*
ca. 800-1250	Chola dynasty in Tamiḷnādu

ca. 825-900	Age of Medāthiti, writer of a commentary on *Manusmṛti*
ca. 900	Udāyana's *Nyāyakusumañjalī*
ca. 900-1100	*Śivapurāṇa;* Śaivite Tantricism in Indonesia
ca. 900-1100	Composition of *Yogavāsiṣṭharāmāyaṇa* and *Bhaktisūtra*
999-1026	Mahmud of Ghazni repeatedly raids India
1026	Muslims loot temple of Somnāth
1025-1137	Life of Rāmānuja
ca. 1100	Buddhism virtually extinct in India; life of Abhinavagupta; composition of Hindu Tantras
ca. 1100-1400	Composition of *Śākta Upaniṣads;* rise of Vīra-śaivism in South India
ca. 1150-1160	Composition of Kalhana's *Rājataraṅginī*, recording the history of Kaśmīr
ca. 1150	*Śrīkaṇṭhabhāṣya;* building of Jagannath Temple at Puri
ca. 1197-1276	Life of Madhvācārya
ca. 1250	Beginning of *Śaivasiddhānta;* building of Sun Temple in Konārkā
1211-1236	Reign of Iltutmish, first sultan of Delhi; beginning of Muslim rule over large parts of India
ca. 1216-1327	Rule of Pāṇḍyas at Madurai; foundation of the famous Mīnākṣī and Śiva Temple of Madurai
ca. 1275-1675	Jñāneśvara of Mahārāṣṭra and other *bhakti* mystics
1288	Marco Polo at Kalyan
ca. 1300-1386	Life of Sāyaṇa, famous commentator of the Vedic *Saṁhitās* and *Brāhmaṇas*
1327	Muslims loot temple at Śrīraṅgam
ca. 1333	Ibn Battuta's travels in India
ca. 1340	Life of Mādhava, author of *Sarvadarśana-*

	saṁgraha and *Pañcadaśī*
1336-1565	Kingdom of Vijāyanāgara, last Hindu empire in India extending as far as Malaysia, Indonesia, and the Philippines
ca. 1350-1610	Vīraśaivism becomes state religion of Mysore
ca. 1350-1650	Composition of many works of the *Pūrva-mīmāṁsakas*
ca. 1360	Life of Vedāntadeśika
ca. 1400-1470	Life of Rāmānanda
ca. 1420	Life of Mīrābāī
1440-1518	Life of Kabīr
ca. 1449-1568	Life of Śaṅkaradeva, great Vaiṣṇava preacher in Assam
ca. 1475-1531	Life of Vallabha
ca. 1469	Birth of Gurū Nānak, founder of Sikhism
ca. 1485-1533	Life of Caitanya
1498	Vasco da Gama, having rounded the Cape of Good Hope, lands on the Malabar coast
ca. 1500	Composition of *Adhyātmarāmāyaṇa* and of Sadānanda's *Vedāntasāra*
ca. 1500-1800	Peak of Durgā worship in Bengal
ca. 1500-1600	Life of Sūrdās of Agra
ca. 1550	Life of Brahmānanda Giri, author of a famous commentary on Śaṅkara's *Śarīrakabhāṣya*
1510	Portugese occupy Goa
ca. 1526-1757	Moghul rule in India, destruction of most Hindu temples in North and Central India
ca. 1532-1623	Life of Tulasīdāsa
ca. 1542	Jesuit missionary Francis Xavier lands in Goa
ca. 1548-1598	Life of Ekanātha
1580	Akbar the Great invites some Jesuit missionaries

	from Goa to his court for religious discussions
ca. 1585	Life of Harivaṁśa, founder of the Rādhā-Vāllabhis
1608-1649	Life of Tukārāma
1608-1681	Life of Rāmdās
1610-1640	Composition of Mitramiśra's *Vīramitrodaya*, famous digests of the *dharmaśāstras*
ca. 1630	Composition of Śrīnivāsadāsa's *Yatīndramata-dīpikā*
1631	Death of Mumtaz, in whose honor Shah Jahan built the famous Tāj Mahal at Agra
1651	East India Company opens first factory on the Hugli (Bengal)
1657	Dara Shikoh translates the Upaniṣads into Persian
1661	Bombay becomes a British possession
1664	Śivajī declares himself king of Mahārāṣṭra
1675	Founding of the French colony of Pondichéry
ca. 1670-1750	Life of Nagojībhaṭṭa, author of numerous works on grammar, *dharmaśāstra*, yoga, etc.
1690	Founding of Calcutta through East India Company (Fort St. George)
ca. 1700-1800	Life of Baladeva, author of *Govindabhāṣya*
ca. 1750	Composition of the (reformist) *Mahānirvāṇatantra*
1757	Battle of Plassey; Clive becomes master of India
1784	Asiatic Society founded in Calcutta by Sir William Jones
1818	Defeat of the last Maratha Peshwa
1828	Ram Mohan Roy founds Brahmo Samāj
1829	Law against *satī*
1829-1837	Suppression of the *thags*
1834-1886	Life of Ramakrishna Paramahamsa

1835	Introduction of English school system in India
1842-1901	Life of M. D. Ranade, great social reformer
1857	The so-called Mutiny (First Indian War of Independence in more recent history books)
1858	The British Crown takes over the administration of India from the East India Company
1875	Founding of Ārya Samāj by Swami Dāyānanda Sarasvatī
1885	Founding of Indian National Congress in Bombay
1913	Nobel prize in literature for Rabindranath Tagore
1920	Mahātmā Gāndhī begins first All-India Civil Disobedience Movement
1942	Founding of Rāṣṭrīa Svayamsevak Sangh
1947	Partition of India and creation of the Indian Union and Pakistan as independent nations
1948	Assassination of Mahātmā Gāndhī; founding of Rām Rājya Pariṣad; Pandit Nehru Prime Minister of the Indian Union; Śrī Cakravarti Rajagopalacari appointed governor general
1950	India declared a republic within the commonwealth; acceptance of the constitution; death of Sri Aurobindo Ghose and Ramaṇa Maharṣi
1951	Beginning of the first Five Year Plan; inauguration of the *Bhūdān* movement; founding of the Bhāratīya Jana Sangh
1955	The Hindu Marriage Act passed in parliament
1956	Reorganization of states (provinces) according to linguistic principles; inauguration of the second Five Year Plan
1961	Goa, Damão, and Diu, Portuguese colonies in India, liberated in a military action
1962	Dr. Rajendra Prasad, the first president of the Republic of India (since 1950), dies; Dr. Sarvepalli Radhakrishnan, vice-president, succeeds him;

	Chinese attack on India.
1964	Death of Jawaharlal Nehru; Lal Bahadur Shastri succeeds as prime minister
1965	Conflict with Pakistan (West)
1966	Tashkent Conference and death of Lal Bahadur Shastri; Indira Gandhi succeeds as prime minister
1967	In general elections, Congress loses most of the state governments to coalitions of rightist parties; unprecedented droughts precipitate severe crisis
1971	India takes action against West Pakistan over the East Bengal issue and is instrumental in creating independent Bangladesh; Indira Gandhi wins overwhelming victory in general elections
1975	In wake of massive demonstrations by the opposition parties, the president of India, at the request of Prime Minister Indira Gandhi, declares a National Emergency and the suspension of many civil rights: mass arrests of opposition leaders, censorship of newspapers, promulgation of a twenty-point programme, etc.
1977	As a result of free elections, Indira Gandhi's government is replaced by a Janata government, a coalition of a number of political parties with a wide spectrum; Morarji Desai, aged 80, a member of the Old Congress, heads the government as prime minister and minister for foreign affairs
1979	Resignation of Morarji Desai as prime minister; Indira Gandhi wins election with a landslide victory
1984	Sikh agitation for an independent Khalistan; central government forcefully evicts Sikh extremists from Golden Temple in Amritsar/Punjab; Indira Gandhi assassinated by two of her Sikh guards.
1985	Rajiv Gandhi, Indira's oldest son, elected prime minister

Notes

INTRODUCTION

1. W. Crooke, *The Popular Religion and Folklore of Northern India.* (Oxford: Oxford University Press,[2] 1896; reprint Delhi: Manoharlal 1968), vol. I, 1.
2. Bibhuti S. Yadav, "Vaiṣṇavism on Hans Küng: A Hindu Theology of Religious Pluralism," *Religion and Society* (Bangalore) 27, no. 2 (June 1980): 45.
3. Cf. W. Halbfass, "Indien und die Geschichtsschreibung der Philosophie," *Philosophische Rundschau* 23, no. 1-2: 104-131.
4. L. Dumont, "A Fundamental Problem," in *Religion/Politics and History in India* (The Hague: Mouton, 1970) [École Pratique des Hautes Études; Sorbonne, VIe section: sciences économiques et sociales: "Le Monde d'Outre-Mêr-Passè et Présent" Première Série, Études XXXXIV], 160.
5. Malati J. Shendge, an Indian scholar who also had studied in the West, made a strong plea for "The Interdisciplinary Approach in Indian Studies" in *ABORI* 63 (1982): 63-98.
6. Agehananda Bharati, a Western scholar who spent years in India noted in "Psychological Approaches to Indian Studies: More Cons than Pros" (*Indian Review* 1, no. 1 [1978]: 71-75): "I strongly believe that psychological models are infertile and quite inadequate for Indian studies, particularly for antiquarian research."
7. L. Dumont, op. cit., 161. The emphases are L. Dumont's.
8. K. Klostermaier, *In the Paradise of Kṛṣṇa* (Philadelphia: Westminster, 1971) and "Remembering Vrindaban," in *Vignettes of Vrindaban* (New Delhi: Books & Books, 1987), A. McDowall and A. Sharma, eds., 45-61.
9. K. Klostermaier, "Hinduism in Bombay," *Religion* (U.K.) 1, no. 2 (1972).
10. According to the 1981 census of India, Hindus constituted 82.64 percent of the population, Muslims 11.43 percent, and Christians 2.43 percent.

11. See Alexandra George, *Social Ferment in India* (London: Athlone Press 1986), Chapter 9: "The tribes of India," 233-55. Also, Nirmal Minz, "Anthropology and the Deprived," *Religion and Society* 32, no. 4 (1985): 3-19.

12. George, ibid., "The Scheduled Castes," 202-32. An interesting document shedding light on the life of an untouchable community is the so-called Kahar Chronicle by Tarashankar Banerjee. See Raja Kanta Ray, "The Kahar Chronicle" in *Modern Asian Studies*, 21/4 (1987), 711-749.

13. A. Bharati, *The Ochre Robe* (Seattle: University of Washington Press, 1962), 17.

14. R. Inden, "Orientalist Constructions of India," *Modern Asian Studies* 20, no. 3 (1986): 401-46.

15. As far as sociology goes, this has been acknowledged by L. Dumont in the lead essay of the first issue of the *Journal of Indian Sociology*, "For An Indian Sociology." The theme has been taken up by one of his prominent Indian students, T. N. Madan. Madan concluded his festschrift for L. Dumont edited by him with "Towards an Indian Sociology," in which he quotes L. Dumont, who stated: "From a comparative point of view, modern thought is exceptional in that, starting from Kant, it separates 'is' and 'ought to be', fact and value. The fact has two consequences: on the one hand, this specific feature requires to be respected in its domain, and one cannot without serious consequences presume to transcend it within modern culture; on the other hand, there is no need to impose this complication or distinction on cultures which do not recognise it: in the comparative study one will be considering value ideas" (Quoted in T. N. Madan "For a Sociology of India," in *Way of Life: King. Householder. Renouncer. Essays in honour of L. Dumont*, T. N. Madan, ed. [New Delhi: Vikas 1982], 406. The reference is to L. Dumont 1979: 814. More likely it is from L. Dumont, "The Anthropological Community and Ideology," *Social Sciences Information* 18, no. 6 (1978): 785-817). A similar comment was made by McKim Marriott: "In the course of our work we have developed an increasing respect for the indigenous social sciences and other conceptual systems of South Asia" (*Journal of the Asian Society* [Ann Arbor] 36, no. 1 [November 1976]: 195). "Interpreting Indian Society: A Monistic Alternative to Dumont's Dualism," pp. 119-195.

1. INDIA AND THE WEST

1. G. W. F. Hegel, *Vorlesungen über die Philosophie der Weltgeschichte*, G. Larsson, ed., vol. II, p. 344 (Hamburg:[3] 1968, my translation).

2. See R. C. Majumdar, *The Classical Accounts of India* (Calcutta: K. L. Mukhopadhyay 1960), for translations of all passages relating to India found in Diodorus, Herodotus, Megasthenes, Arrian, Strabo, Quintus, Justin, Plutarch, Pliny, Ptolemy, and others. W. Halbfass, *Indien und Europa: Perspektiven ihrer geistigen Begegnung* (Basel-Stuttgart: Schwabe & Co., 1981) offers a great deal of material relevant to this chapter. See also J. Schwab, *La Renaissance*

Orientale (1950); English translation: *The Oriental Renaissance: Europe's Rediscovery of India and the East, 1680-1880*, G. Patterson-Black and V. Reinking, trans. (New York: Columbia University Press, 1984).

3. Plutarch, *Life of Alexander*, Chapter 64. The standard work on this period is W. W. Tarn, *The Greeks in Bactria and India* (Cambridge: Cambridge University Press, 1951; reprint 1966).

4. Diodorus Siculus, *Historical Library*, vol. 17, 107.

5. *Alisaunder. Alexander and Dindimus*, ed. W. W. Skeat (Early English Text Society, Extra Series No. XXXI, 1876; reprint Oxford University Press 1930). Latin text 10 ff., my translation.

6. I. K. K. Menon, "Kerala's Early Foreign Contacts," *Indian and Foreign Review* 15 (July 1980): 13 f.

7. A famous Pāli work, *Milindapañha*, whose historical character is still a matter of dispute among scholars, describes the questions put to the Buddhist sage Nāgasena by Menander of Sagala in northwestern India. The English translation is by T. W. Rhys Davids, *The Questions of King Milinda*, Sacred Books of the East, vols. 25 and 26 (Oxford: Oxford University Press, 1890).

8. For more details see E. Benz, *Indische Einflüsse auf die frühchristliche Theologie* (Mainz: Mainzer Akademie der Wissenschaften 1951).

9. A great many interesting articles on this subject are contained in R. Baine Harris, ed., *Neoplatonism and Indian Thought: Studies in Neoplatonism Ancient and Modern*, vol. 2 (International Society for Neoplatonic Studies, Norfolk, Virginia, 1982). Albany, SUNY Press 1982. See also E. Elintoff, "Pyrrho and India," *Phronesis* 1980/1: 88-108. An attempt to prove the independent origin of Greek philosophy against the arguments of those who assume Indian influence is undertaken by H. J. Krämer, *Der Ursprung der Geistmetaphysik* (Amsterdam: B. R. Bruner[2] 1967).

10. For more details, see J. Filliozat, *Les rélations extèrieures de l'Inde*. 1. Les échanges de l'Inde et de l'Empire Romain aux premiérs siécles de l'ère chrêtienne. 2. La doctrine brahmanique a Rome au IIlême siécle (Pondichéry: Institut Français d'Indologie 1956).

11. The legend itself is of uncertain age. It found its expression in Nicolas Novotitch' *Life of Issa*, which is supposed to be the translation of a manuscript in a Tibetan monastery containing the life story of Jesus. Quite a few Indians have accepted it. See, for instance, Pundit Shunker Nath, *Christ: Who and What He Was:* Part 1. *Christ a Hindu Disciple, Nay a Buddhist Saint:* Part 2. *Christ a Pure Vedantist* (Calcutta: Dayamoy Printing Works 1927-1928).

12. Tertullian, *Apologia versus gentes*, in *Migne Patrologia Latina*, vol. 1, 1080 ff.

13. *Migne Patrologia Latina*, vol. 17, 1167 ff.

14. Evidence of lively exchange between India and the Arab countries is collected in J. Duncan M. Derett "Greece and India Again: The Jaimini-Aśvamedha, the Alexander Romance and the Gospels," *Zeitschrift für Religions—und Geistesgeschichte* 22, no. 1 (1970): 19-44.

15. Edward C. Sachau, trans., *Alberuni's India: An Account of the Religion, Philosophy, Literature, Geography, Chronology, Astronomy, Customs, Laws and Astrology of India about A.D. 1030*, Trübner's Oriental Series (reprint Delhi: S. Chand & Co. 1964).

16. R. E. Latham, trans., *The Travels of Marco Polo* (Harmondsworth, U.K.: Penguin Classics 1958), on India, see p. 233-68. See also Heimo Rau, "The Image of India in European Antiquity and the Middle Ages," in *India and the West: Proceedings of a Seminar Dedicated to the Memory of Hermann Goetz*, J. Deppert, ed. (New Delhi: Manohar 1983), 197-208.

17. One of the most interesting accounts of South Indian Hinduism in the early eighteenth century is the recently discovered work by the Lutheran missionary Bartholomaeus Ziegenbalg (1682-1719), *Traktat vom Malabarischen Heidentum* (1711), which was never printed. See Hans-Werner Gensichen, "Abominable Heathenism—A Rediscovered Tract by Bartholomaeus Ziegenbalg," *Indian Church History Review* 1, no. 1 (1967): 29-40.
The work of Abbé Dubois (1770-1848) *Hindu Manners, Customs and Ceremonies*, first published by the East India Company in 1816, has become a classic in its own right and has been reprinted many times by the Oxford University Press.

18. W. Leifer, *Indien und die Deutschen: 500 Jahre Begegnung und Partnerschaft* (Tübingen und Basel: Horst Erdmann Verlag 1969). Gita Dharampal compiled a bibliography of early German writing about India: "Frühe deutsche Indien-Berichte (1477-1750)," *ZDMG* 134, no. 2 (1984): 23-67.

19. *Systema Brahmanicum* (Rome: 1792); *Reise nach Ostindien* (Berlin: 1798).

20. P. J. Marshall, ed., *The British Discovery of Hinduism in the 18th Century*, The European Understanding of India Series (Cambridge: Cambridge University Press 1970).

21. *Asiatic Researches* 8: 369-476. For details on the *Ezour Vedam*, used as a source for Indian traditions by Voltaire, see M. Winternitz, *Geschichte der indischen Literatur*, vol. 1, 12, n. 1 (1905); reprint (Stuttgart: K. F. Kohler Verlag, 1968). See also L. Rocher, *Ezourvedam: A French Veda of the Eighteenth Century*, University of Pennsylvania Studies on South Asia, Vol. 1 (Amsterdam and Philadelphia: John Benjamin Publication Company, 1984).

22. A brief history of French Indology is given in P. S. Filliozat, "The French Institute of Indology in Pondichéry," *WZKSA* 28 (1984): 133-47. A major contribution to Indian studies was also made by Russian and Polish scholars. In Russia especially, the study of Indian languages still flourishes today. Italian, Dutch, Belgian, and Finnish scholarship in Indian studies is alive, too; as, to a lesser degree perhaps, in Spain and Latin American, from where, however, some very good work has come out recently.

23. At the age of twenty-five, he wrote his epoch-making work: *Über das Conjugationsystem der Sanskrit Sprache in Vergleichung mit jenen der griechischen, lateinischen, persischen und germanischen Sprache. Nebst Episoden des Ramajan und Mahabharat in genau metrischen Übersetzungen aus dem Originaltexte und einigen Abschnitten aus den Vedas.* F. Staal, *A Reader on the Sanskrit Grammarians*, Cambridge, Mass: M.I.T. Press 1972 has assembled many valuable documents and comments on the history of Western Sanskrit scholarship.

24. The first complete translation of the Bible into Sanskrit seems to have been published by W. Carey from Serampore between 1808 and 1818. It was later improved upon by W. Yates and J. Wenger. For further details, see J. S. M. Hooper, *Bible Translation in India, Pakistan, Ceylon*, 2d ed. revised by W. J. Culshaw (Oxford: Oxford University Press, 1963).

25. Published originally by Oxford University Press and reprinted by other publishers, the *Sacred Books of the East* have not yet been replaced as a standard work.

26. For more complete information, consult P. J. Chinmulgund and V. V. Mirashi, eds., *Review of Indological Research in the Last 75 Years* (Poona: Bharatiya Charitrakosha Mandal 1967).

27. Hindu scholars like R. G. Bhandarkar, S. N. Dasgupta, S. Radhakrishnan, T. M. P. Mahadevan, T. R. V. Murti to name just a few, have spent considerable time lecturing in the West.

28. For more details, see Dale Riepe, *The Philosophy of India and Its Impact on American Thought* (Springfield, Ill.: Charles C Thomas 1970). See also C. T. Jackson, *The Oriental Religions and American Thought, Nineteenth-Century Explorations* (Westport, Conn.: Greenwood Press 1981).

29. The journal *East and West*, published by the University of Hawaii, has remained one of the principal instruments for the continued discussion of the conferences' issues.

30. Dale Riepe, op. cit., 275 f.: "If the American empire meets with the fate of the British, if Americans cannot resolve their life-and-death struggle with the intelligent use of technology, if the alienation in American society cannot be alleviated, then a new attitude may gradually replace the 300 year reign of optimism. Such eventualities may lead to more philosophers turning to contemplation, meditation and increased pouring over the Hindu and Buddhist scriptures."

31. Ibid.

32. The case is well stated in Malati J. Shendge, "The Interdisciplinary Approach to Indian Studies," *ABORI* 62 (1982): 63-98.

33. Ananda Coomaraswamy, *Transformation of Nature in Art*, p. 4 (New York: Dover 1956).

34. *Indian and Western Philosophy: A Study in Contrasts* (London: Allen & Unwin 1937). *Facets of Indian Thought* (London: Allen & Unwin 1964).

35. *Philosophies of India*, J. Campbell, ed. (Princeton: Bollingen Foundation 1951). *Myths and Symbols in Indian Art and Civilization* (Princeton: Bollingen Foundation 1946).

36. *Nāma-Rūpa and Dharma-Rūpa: Origin and Aspects of an Ancient Indian Conception* (Calcutta: University of Calcutta 1943).

37. *Introduction génerale a l'étude des doctrines hindoues* (Paris: Les editions Véga [5]1964).

38. *The Hindu Temple* (Calcutta: University of Calcutta 1946). *The Presence of Śiva* (Princeton: Princeton University Press 1981).

39. *Asceticism and Eroticism in the Mythology of Śiva* (London: Oxford University Press 1973). *The Origins of Evil in Hindu Mythology* (Berkeley: University of California Press 1976).

40. For those who need a proof the case is convincingly stated in Jaideva Singh's edition and translation of the *Pratyābhijñāhṛdayam* in the numerous references to the earlier translation of the text by K. F. Leidecker.

2. THE HISTORY AND DEVELOPMENT OF HINDUISM

1. Jawaharlal Nehru *The Discovery of India* (London: Meridian Books, 1960), 55.

2. J. C. Heesterman, *The Inner Conflict of Tradition* (Chicago: University of Chicago Press 1985), 2.

3. The greatest authority in Indian archaeology and prehistory today is H. D. Sankalia. Besides numerous reports on his own excavations and papers in learned journals, he has written two general books for wider circles: *Indian Archeology Today*, (New York: Asia Publishing House 1962); and *Prehistory and Protohistory in India and Pakistan* (Bombay: Asia Publishing House 1961). D. D. Kosambi draws very interesting connections between prehistoric, tribal, and present popular Indian culture in his two major works: *An Introduction to the Study of Indian History* (Bombay: Popular Book Depot 1956); and *Myth and Reality: A Study in the Foundations of Indian Culture* (Bombay: Popular Book Depot 1961). Still of some interest is B. Hronzny, *Über die älteste Völkerwanderung und über das Problem der proto-indischen Zivilisation* (Prague: Orientalischen Institut 1939). Cf. also S. K. Chatterji, "Contributions from Different Language-Culture Groups," in *The Cultural Heritage of India* (CHI), H. Battacharya, general ed., (Calcutta: Ramakrishna Mission Institute of Culture [2]1958), vol. 1, 76-90; N. K. Bose and D. Sen, "The Stone Age in India," ibid., 93-109.

4. One of the most comprehensive treatments of the position of tribal cultures in India is provided by Alexandra George, *The Social Ferment in India*, Chapter 9,

"The Tribes of India," 235-55 (London and Atlantic Highlands, N.J.: Athlone Press 1986).

5. First reported by Sir J. Marshall in his *Mohenjo Daro and the Indus Civilization* 3 vols. (London: University of Oxford Press 1931). For more recent work, consult V. N. Mishra, "Prehistory and Protohistory," in *Review of Indological Research in the Last 75 Years*, P. J. Chinmulgund and V. V. Mirashi, eds. (Poona: Bharatiya Charitrakosha Mandal 1967), 353-415, with detailed bibliography. For a short account, M. Wheeler, *The Indus Civilization* (London: Cambridge University Press 1962); and S. Piggott, *Prehistoric India* (Baltimore: Penguin 1950).

6. Cf. K. A. Nilakanta Sastri, *The History and Culture of the Tamils* (Calcutta: Firma K. L. Mukhopadhay 1964); S. K. Aiyangar, *Some Contributions of South India to Indian Culture* (Calcutta: Calcutta University 1942). T. Balakrishnan Nayar, *The Problem of Dravidian Origins—A Linguistic, Anthropological and Archeological Approach* (Madras: University of Madras 1977).

7. R. C. Majumdar, general ed., *The Vedic Age*, volume 1 of *The History and Culture of the Indian People* (*HCIP*) (Bombay: [4]1965). Also, C. Kunhan Raja, "Vedic Culture," in *CHI*, op. cit., vol. 1, 199-220.

8. D. D. Kosambi, *An Introduction to the Study of Indian History*, p. 20 (Bombay: Popular Book Depot, 1956).

9. Swami Bharati Krishna Tirtha, *Sanātana Dharma*, pp. 8-38 (Bombay: Bharatiya Vidya Bhavan 1964), gives various interesting meanings of this term. *Dharmāṅk* (Gorakhpur: Gita Press 1966) contains contributions by all four living Śaṅkarāchāryas on the topic of *Sanātana Dharma. Viśva Hindu*, special issue (January 1966), has contributions in English and Hindī by leading Hindus on the topic What Is Hinduism?

10. *Essentials of Hinduism* (Allahabad: The Leader, no date). In the Preface, we are informed: "The articles collected together in this volume appeared originally as a symposium in the columns of the *Leader* in Allahabad. They have been brought under one cover in the hope that an authoritative declaration as to the 'Essentials of Hindusim' by leading Hindus may be read with interest."

11. "Essentials of Hindutva," in *Samagra Savarkar Wangmaya, Hindu Rastra Darshan*, vol. 6, 64 (Poona: Maharastra Prantik Hindusabha 1964).

12. *Bunch of Thoughts* (Bangalore: Vikrama Prakashan 1966), 47.

13. *Viśva Hindu Viśeṣāṅk* (Bombay: World Council of Hindus 1966).

14. Kosambi, op. cit., p. 20 f.

15. The most complete representation and summary of research is found in E. Neumayer, *Prehistoric Indian Rock Paintings* (Delhi: Oxford University Press 1983). Attempts at interpretation are made by Kapila Vatsyayan, "Pre-

historic Paintings," *Sangeet Natak, Journal of the Sangeet Natak Akademi* (October-December 1981): 5-18.

16. On recent attempts to decipher the Indus civilization script, see S. R. Rao, "Deciphering the Indus Valley Script," *Indian and Foreign Review* (15 November 1979): 13-18, with samples; and *The Decipherment of the Indus Script* (Bombay: Asia Publishing House 1982). See also the review of this work by B. B. Lal "Reading the Indus Script," *Indian and Foreign Review* (15 April 1983): 33-36; and "The Indus Script: Some Observations Based on Archaeology," *JRAS* (1975): 173-209, with a very extensive bibliography. See also the interesting work by Asko Parpola, *The Sky Garment: A Study of the Harappan Religion and the Relation to the Mesopotamian and Later Indian Religions*, Studia Orientalia 57 (Helsinki: Finnish Oriental Society 1985).

17. A. D. Pusalker, "The Indus Valley Civilization," *in HCIP*, op. cit., vol. 1, pp. 172-202. Interesting anthropological information is provided in an article by G. D. Kumar (director, Anthropological Survey of India) in "The Ethnic Components of the Builders of the Indus Civilization and the Advent of the Aryans," *Journal of Indo-European Studies* 1, no. 1 (Spring 1973): 66-80. Also D. P. Agrawal, "The Technology of the Indus Civilization" in *Indian Archeology, New Perspectives*, R. K. Sharma, ed., 83-91 (Delhi: Agam Kala Prakashan, 1982). On the question of the relation between Aryans and early Indian civilizations, see K. C. Varma, "The Iron Age, the Veda and the Historical Urbanization," ibid., pp. 155-83.

18. Cf. *Ṛgveda* 1, 32, and many other sources.

19. K. A. Nilakantha Sastri, *op. cit.*, p. 5 f. A convenient summary of research concerning Indian prehistory can be found in C. Maloney's *Peoples of South Asia*, Ch. 4, "Prehistory," 63-80, and Chapter 5, "The Rise of Village and Urban Life," 81-113, (New York: Holt, Rinehart and Winston 1974).

20. Cf. B. K. Ghosh, "The Āryan Problem," in *HCIP*, op. cit., vol. 1, 205-21; and A. D. Pusalker, "Āryan Settlements in India," ibid., 245-67.

21. *Ancient Indian Historical Tradition*, (Oxford: 1922); reprint (Delhi: Motilal Banarsidass 1962).

22. Cf. B. K. Ghosh, "The Origin of the Indo-Aryans," in *CHI*, op. cit., vol. 1, 129-43.

23. Apart from the commonly followed methods to establish chronology through archeological, epigraphical, and literary documents, astronomical methods are utilized by several scholars. Cf. P. C. Sengupta, *Ancient Indian Chronology: Illustrating Some of the Most Important Astronomical Methods* (Calcutta: University of Calcutta 1947).

24. Indian scholars like P. V. Kane, *History of Dharmaśāstra*, (Poona: 1935-1962), point quite frequently toward this attitude of Western scholars to underestimate Indian tradition as regards its age and its own historiography. The increasing importance given to Purāṇic accounts is reflected in the contribution

of A. D. Pusalker, "Historical Traditions," in *HCIP*, op cit., vol. 1, 271-323. Evidence for the historicity of some of the detail of the Kṛṣṇa tradition seems to emerge from archeological excavations done at Dwarka in 1979. See S. R. Rao, "Krishna's Dwarka," *Indian and Foreign Review* (15 March 1980): 15-19.

25. Pargiter, op. cit., p. 308 ff: "it appears that the original brahmans were not so much priests as 'adepts' in matters supernatural, 'masters' of magico-religious force, wizards, medicine men. . . . The Ailas Āryanized the brahmans as they did the other peoples, and then the new brahmanism became the stronghold of Āryanism."

26. This is also the opinion expressed by Om Prakash in *Political Ideas in the Purāṇas* (Allahabad: Panchanda Publications 1977), who furthermore maintains that it was not the Purāṇas who took over passages from the Smṛtis but that the Purāṇa sections dealing with *dharma*, representing the consensus of the people at large, were incorporated by the *Śāstrakāras* into their own codes.

27. Dev Raj, *L'ésclavage dans l'Inde ancienne d'après les textes Pālis et Sanskrits* (Pondichery: Institute Français d'Indologie 1957).

28. Cf. S. N. Dasgupta, *History of Indian Philosophy*, (1922); reprint Cambridge: Cambridge University Press 1963), vol. 1, 10 ff.: "Even at this day all the obligatory duties of the Hindus at birth, marriage, death etc. are performed according to the old Vedic ritual. The prayers that a Brahmin now says three times a day are the same selections of Vedic verses as were used as prayer verses two thousand years ago. . . . Even at this day there are persons who bestow immense sums of money for the performance and teaching of Vedic sacrifices and rituals."

29. Cf. R. C. Majumdar: "Colonial and Cultural Expansion," in *The Age of Imperial Kanauj*, *HCIP*, vol. 4, 412-53; *The Classical Age*, *HCIP*, vol. 3, 642-55; *The Age of Imperial Unity*, *HCIP*, vol. 2, 634-58; *The Struggle for Empire*, *HCIP*, vol. 5, 730-74. R. C. Majumdar, *Hindu Colonies in the Far East* (Calcutta: K. L. Mukhopadhyay [2]1963). Somewhat more daring reconstructions of history may be found in works like Swami Sankarananda's *Hindu States of Sumeria*, When India Ruled the West, no. 1 (Calcutta: Firma K. L. Mukhopadhyay 1962); and Chaman Lal's *Hindu America* (Bombay: Bharatiya Vidya Bhavan 1960).

30. Cf. R. C. Majumdar, H. C. Raycaudhuri, and K. Datta, *An Advanced History of India* (London: Macmillan 1960), 199-210.

31. "The Chola King Koluttunga I, a Śaiva, put out the eyes of Mahāpūrṇa and Kureśa, the Vaiṣṇava disciples of Rāmānuja, who refused to be converted to Śaivism." (Dasgupta, op. cit., vol. 5, 45).

    Kingsbury and G. E. Philips, trans., *Hymns of the Tamil Śaivite Saints*, (Calcutta: Association Press 1921), 10 f: "The cause [Sambandhar] loved suffered a severe blow when the great King of Madura, with many of his subjects, went over to the Jaina religion. The queen consort and her prime minister remained faithful to Śaivism and sent for Sambandhar. The lonely saint faced a vast multitude of Jains in the royal presence, conquered them with arguments and reconverted the king. Eight thousand of the stubborn Jains, with Sambandhar's consent, were impaled alive . . ."

32. In the *Bhāgavata Purāṇa*, those who do not follow Kṛṣṇa are called dogs, etc.

33. They come out very markedly in the different *senas* that have developed over the last years in India. Cf. "The Private Armies," and "Secret Societies," *Illustrated Weekly of India* 91, no. 11 (15, March 1970); and "Secret Societies," *Seminar* 151 (March 1972).

34. N. K. Bose, "The Geographical Background of Indian Culture," *CHI*, op. cit., vol. 1, 3-15. The best work on physical geography is O. H. K. Spate, *India and Pakistan; A General and Regional Geography*, (London: Methuen ^{2}1960).

35. Cf. *Tīrthāṅk* (*Kalyāṇ*) (Gorakhpur: Gītā Press 1957). The most popular may be Brājbhūmī, the land connected with Kṛṣṇa's birth and youthful exploits. Cf. K. Klostermaier, *In the Paradise of Krishna*, (Philadelphia: Westminster 1971).

36. Cf. the beautiful illustrated report of a voyage along the Ganges by John J. Putnam in *National Geographic Magazine* (October 1971): 445-83.

37. O. Viennot, *Le culte de l'arbre dans l'Inde ancienne* (Paris: Presses universitaire de France 1954).

38. The ideas of men like Swami Vivekananda, Sri Aurobindo, B. G. Tilak, and others are represented in V. P. Varma, *Modern Indian Political Thought* (Agra: Agrawala ^{2}1964).

39. (Bombay: Asia Publishing House 1968), 9 ff.

40. Kushwant Singh offers a striking proof for this in *India: A Mirror for Its Monsters and Monstrosities* (Bombay: Pearl Books 1969). After describing the fanatical behavior of certain religious leaders that finally led to Delhi's "Bloody Monday" on November 7, 1967, he continues: "I left the sands of the Jumna and drove to the home of my friend Cyrus Jhabwalla, a Parsi architect, and his novelist wife Ruth, who is Jewish. There were other friends present. I was among my own type—Anglicized Indian sahibs. I narrated my experiences of the day. We defied our traditions. We drank Scotch. We ate beef sandwiches ('Not-so-holy-cow; imported beef,' explained my host. Someone stretched his hand across the table: 'Ruth, can I have one of your kosher pork sausages, please?'). And so it went on until we felt we had liquidated all the *sadhus* and freed our countrymen of the Hindus' silly food fads. Then our host spoilt it all with a short speech: 'Listen, chaps! When the chips are down, you know very well that however Westernized the Indian and whatever religion he may have or not have, whenever he eats beef he has a sense of guilt—a teeny-weeny bit of a bad conscience. And not one Indian will bandy words with a *sadhu* for fear of arousing his wrath. It is like our attitude to *sati*. We condemn it but we cannot help admiring a woman who becomes a *sati*. These

things have been with us for over 4000 years. They are in our blood and in our bones. We cannot fight them with reason. They are stronger than reason." (p. 126).

41. *The Times of India* reported on 11 December 1965 about an appeal made by Dr. S. Radhakrishnan to the *Hindu Viśva Dharma Sammelan* then in session at Delhi: "The President emphasised that all roads lead to the same God. Men of religion should not quarrel about the road one should take. There was nothing sectarian or dogmatic about Hindu philosophy." See also S. Radhakrishnan's last work; *Religion in a Changing World* (London: Allen & Unwin 1967).

42. J. B. Segal. "White and Black Jews at Cochin, the Story of a Controversy," *JRAS* 1983, no. 2: 228-52. See also B. J. Israel, *The Bene Israel of India* (Bombay: Orient Longman 1984). T. A. Timberg, ed., *Jews in India* (New York: Advent Books, 1986).

43. The most scholarly account of the interaction between early Christianity and Hinduism is found in Stephen Neill, *A History of Christianity: The Beginnings to AD 1707* (Cambridge: Cambridge University Press 1984). For an Indian Christian view, see A. M. Mundaden, *The Traditions of St. Thomas Christians* (Bangalore: Dharmaram Studies 1972).

44. See literature quoted in Chinmulgund and Mirashi, eds., op. cit., 601 ff.

45. J. Duncan M. Derret, "Greece and India: The Milindapañha, the Alexander Romance and the Gospels," *Zeitschrift für Religions- und Geistesgeschichte* 19 (1967): 33-64.

46. See A. M. Mundaden, *St. Thomas Christians and the Portuguese*, (Bangalore: Dharmaram Studies 1970).

47. See, for instance, the examples quoted in M. M. Thomas, *The Acknowledged Christ of the Indian Renaissance* (London: SCM Press 1969), and Stanley J. Samartha, *Hindus vor dem universalen Christus*, (Stuttgart: Evangelisches Verlagswerk 1970).

48. See R. Boyd, *An Introduction to Indian Christian Theology* (Madras: Christian Literature Society [2]1977).

3. HINDU *DHARMA:* ORTHODOXY AND HERESY IN HINDUISM

1. *Manusmṛti* II, 6; cf. also *Yājñavalkyasmṛti* I, 7.

2. Ibid., II, 9.

3. Ibid. II, 11.

4. Ibid., II, 17-24.

5. Ibid., I, 111-18.

6. "Sanātan dharm hi sārvabhaum dharm yā mānav dharm hai," *Dharmāṅk* (*Kalyāṇ*) 30, no. 1 (January 1966): Gorakhpur, 242-49 [Hindī], my own translation.

7. *Bhagavadgītā*, III, 35.

8. *Manusmṛti*, VIII, 15.

9. From *Gautama's Nyāyasūtras with Vātsyāyana Bhāṣya*, Ganganatha Jha, Sanskṛt ed. and English trans., 2 vols (Poona: Oriental Book Depot 1939).

10. *Yogasūtras* II, 30-32.

11. Vaikunthavāsī Śrī Bābū Sādhucaraṇprasād, *Dharmaśāstrasaṅgraha* (Bombay: Venkateśvar Press 1913), a digest of Hindu law for practical use, with selections from forty-six *smṛtis* according to topics, gives a good idea of the range of *dharmaśāstra*.

12. The best known and best documented case is that of Rājā Rām Mohan Roy, who successfully fought for the abolition of *satī* (burning of widows with their husbands).

13. "Hinduism: A Static Structure or a Dynamic Force," in *Nehru Abhinandan Granth* (Calcutta: N.A.G. Committee 1949), 421-25. The author was formerly head of the department of ancient Indian history and culture, Banares Hindu University.

14. "Moral Foundations of Indian Society," in ibid., 464-69. The author is the editor of the multivolume *Dharmakośa* (Wai: Dharmakośa Mandala 1937-1961), and one of the most outstanding paṇḍits of contemporary India.

15. Apart from the countless instances one encounters in daily life in India itself, Indian daily newspapers quite frequently carry "letters to the editor" with massive complaints like the following from *Times of India* (8 March 1968): "At the national integration conference held at Delhi in September last a code of conduct was prescribed to be observed by political leaders. The code required them not to exploit communal and caste feelings for political purposes. Hardly six months later, during the recent general elections, one saw in Poona the sorry spectacle of the code of conduct being flagrantly violated by the political leaders in general and the Congress leaders in particular. In each of the six constituencies in Poona the Congress candidate nominated was of the same caste that was in overwhelming majority in that constituency. The election speeches of the leaders conveyed the impression that they were totally unaware of the existence of the code of conduct. Every candidate openly preached caste hatred and exhorted the electorate to vote for him as he belonged to their caste. Perhaps never before were caste and communal feelings so deeply aroused as they were during the recent general elections in Poona" (V. D. Mahajan).

Another reader complained that "even after twenty years of freedom untouchability in the villages is still as virulent as ever. The social justice said to have been done to the Scheduled Castes and Tribes has just not been adequate" (Raja Sekhara Rao).

16. "Sādhana," *Religion and Society* 16, no. 2 (June 1969): 36-50.

17. The most complete and systematic description is to be found in Ramdas Gaur, *Hindutva* [Hindī] (Kāśī: Saṁvat 1995). H. H. Wilson's *Religious Sects of the Hindus* (originally published in 1861; reprint, Calcutta: Punthi Pustak, 1958) is incomplete, unsystematic, and in quite a few instances, incorrect.

18. G. S. Ghurye, *Indian Sādhus*, pp. 110 ff and 177 ff (Bombay: Popular Prakashan [2]1964). The latest major incident occurred in Hardwar in spring 1986.

19. *Liṅgapurāṇa* I, 107, 41 f.

20. We have to interpret some of these as a reaction against persecution on the part of non-Vaiṣṇavas such as Citrasena, who at the instigation of Śaiva monks prohibited the worship of Viṣṇu in his realm, ordered his officers to persecute the Vaiṣṇavas, and had the images of Viṣṇu thrown into the ocean. Cf. R. C. Hazra, *Studies in the Upapurāṇas* (Calcutta: Sanskrit College 1963), vol. 2, 362 f.

21. W. O'Flaherty "The Origin of Heresy in Hindu Mythology," *History of Religion* (*HR*) 10 (May 1971): 271-333; S. N. Dasgupta, *History of Indian Philosophy* (Cambridge: Cambridge University Press [3]1963), vol. 3, 19. Cf. *Kūrma-purāṇa* XV.

22. For a more extensive treatment of this topic, see K. Klostermaier, "Hindu Views of Buddhism," in R. Amore, ed., *Canadian Contributions to Buddhist Studies* (Waterloo, Ont.: Wilfrid Laurier University Press, 1980), 60-82.

23. Cf. *HCIP*, Majumdar, general ed., vol. 3, p. 437; S. N. Dasgupta, op. cit., vol. 5, 45; M. Winternitz, *Geschichte der Indischen Literatur* (1922; reprint Stuttgart: K. F. Koehler Verlag 1960), vol. 3, 426 ff.; Alkondavilli Govindacharya, *The Divine Wisdom of the Draviḍa Saints* (Madras: C. N. Press 1902), 78 f., etc.

24. *Viṣṇupurāṇa*, III, 18, 15 ff. (Gorakhpur: Gītā Press 1954). My translation.

25. P. V. Kane, *History of Dharmaśāstra* (Poona: Bhandarkar Oriental Research Institute (B.O.R.I.) 1941), Vol. 2, part 2, 716 f.

26. Nārāyaṇa Bhatta's *Maṇimañjarī* as summarized by S. N. Dasgupta, op. cit., vol. 4, 52.

27. The English translation by E. B. Cowell and A. E. Gough is incomplete, it leaves out the last chapter on Advaita Vedānta.

28. *Brahma-sūtra Bhāṣya* I, 1, 2: Thibaut's translation part I, 15.

29. W. Ruben, "Materialismus im Leben des Alten Indien," *Acta Orientalia* 13, (Leiden: 1935); Dale Riepe describes himself in *The Philosophy of India and*

Its Impact on American Thought (Springfield, Ill.: Charles C Thomas 1970) as "interested in the naturalistic and materialistic philosophy in India" mentioning his thesis *The Naturalistic Tradition of Indian Thought.* In India, M. N. Roy (*Materialism*, written in 1934, published 1940; reprint Calcutta: Renaissance Publishers, [2]1951), on his way toward radical humanism via Marxism-Leninism, drew attention to the often underplayed materialistic stream of the Indian tradition.

30. II, 4, 12.

31. *Sarvadarśanasaṁgraha* I.

32. This has been proposed, for example, by Raymond Panikkar in *Kerygma und Indien: Zur heilsgeschichtlichen Problematik der christlichen Begegnung mit Indien* (Hamburg: Evangelischer Verlag, 1967), 84 f.

33. They also quite often claim personal infallibility!

34. "No Hold Barred Battle," *India Today* (11 March 1987): 56 f.

4. REVELATION AND SCRIPTURE IN HINDUISM

1. Those who have no opportunity to observe the actual recitation of a Hindu scripture, may get an idea of it from the description given in "Procedure of Reciting *Śrīmad Bhāgavata*," *Kalyāṇa Kalpatāru* 18, no. 1 (August 1952): 6-8. The details given there apply, with appropriate modification, to other scriptures, too.

2. Almost all the important popular scriptures have been supplied with a *Māhātmya*, a praise of the greatness (of the work concerned) that contains profuse descriptions of promises attached to the reading of the scripture.

3. See, e.g., K. Sivaraman, "The Word as a Category of Revelation," in *Revelation in Indian Thought, A Festschrift in Honour of Professor T. R. V. Murti*, H. Coward and K. Sivaraman, eds., (Emeryville: Dharma Publishing 1977), 45-64.

4. Some interesting details are mentioned by A. Esteller in "The Quest for the Original *Ṛgveda*," *Annals of the Bhandarkar Oriental Research Institute*, (ABORI) 50 (1969): 1-40; and "The *Ṛgveda Saṁhitā* as a 'Palimpsest'," *Indian Antiquary* (Third Series) 4, no. 1 (January 1967): 1-23.

5. The *guru-paramparā*, the succession of teachers, had to be memorized by each student as legitimation of his knowledge. In *Bṛhadāraṇyaka Upaniṣad* IV, 6, sixty links of this chain of tradition are mentioned, going back through mythical figures to Brahmā, the creator himself, who revealed it.

6. P. V. Kane, *History of Dharmaśāstra* (*HDhS*), vol. 1, 70-75 (Poona: B.O.R.I. 1930).

7. Cf. G. Srinivasa Murti's introduction to *Śrī Pañcarātra Rakṣa of Śrī Vedānta*

Deśika, M. D. Aiyangar and T. Venugopalacharya, eds., pp. ix-xiii (Madras: Adyar Library 1942).

8. The most exhaustive account is given in J. Gonda, *Vedic Literature (Saṁhitās and Brāhmaṇas)*, History of Indian Literature, vol. 1 (Wiesbaden: Harrassowitz 1975). On the Vedic schools, see L. Renou, *Les Écoles védiques et la formation du Veda*, (Paris: 1947).

9. For annotated text, see T. Aufrecht, *Die Hymnen des Ṛgveda*, (Bonn: A. Marcus [2]1877; and *Ṛgveda with the Commentary of Sāyaṇa*, M. Müller, ed., 6 vols., (London [2]1892; reprint Varanasi: Chowkhambha Sanskrit Office 1966). The best complete translation is H. F. Geldner's *Ṛgveda deutsch*, 5 vols. (Cambridge, Mass.: Harvard University Press, 1951-57). A complete English translation is R. T. H. Griffith, *Hymns of the Ṛgveda*, 2 vols. (reprint Varanasi: Chowkhambha Sanskrit Office [4]1963).

10. For text, see Ram Sarma Acarya, *Sāmaveda* (Bareilly: Sanskrit Samsthana [2]1962). For a translation, see R. T. H. Griffith, *Hymns of the Sāmaveda* (reprint Varanasi: Chowkhambha Sanskrit Office 1963).

11. For text, see A. Weber, *Yajurveda Vajaseyasaṁhitā*, 2 vols. (Berlin: Dümmler 1871 ff.). For translations, see T. R. H. Griffith, *Hymns of the Yajurveda* (reprint Varanasi: Chowkhambha Sanskrit Office 1957).

12. For text, see R. Roth and W. D. Whitney, *The Atharvaveda Saṁhitā* (Berlin: Dümmler 1856). For a translation, see W. D. Whitney, *Atharvaveda Saṁhitā*, 2 vols. Harvard Oriental Series (1902; reprint Varanasi: Chowkhambha Sanskrit Office 1962).

13. L. Renou, *Vedic India* (Calcutta: Susil Gupta 1957).

14. Ramdas Gaur, *Hindutva*, [Hindī] (Kasi: Śivaprasād Gupta, Samvat, 1995). (=C.E.: 1938) 81 ff.

15. For text, see Pandurang Jawaji, *Śīkṣādivedaṣadaṅgāni* (loose leaf) (Bombay: Nirṇaya Sagar Press 1934).

16. In later times, all these auxiliary sciences developed into independent scholarly disciplines, each with a voluminous literature of its own.

17. I, 6, 3, 10. The story and the precise wording of the fatal formula are repeated often in the epics and *Purāṇas*.

18. As for instance in the *Bṛhadāraṇyaka Upaniṣad*.

19. For text, see W. C. Sastri Pancikar, ed. *One Hundred and Eight Upaniṣads* (Bombay: Nirṇaya Sagar Press [4]1932). Most of these have been translated in several volumes in the Adyar Library Series. A good English translation of the major early Upaniṣads with Sanskṛt text and copious notes in S. Radhakrishnan, *The Principal Upaniṣads* (London: Allen & Unwin 1953; numerous reprints).

20. Thus, a *Ramakrishna Upaniṣad* has been published by the Ramakrishna

Mission. Dhanjibhai Fakirbhai, an Indian Christian, recently composed a *Khristopaniṣad* (Bangalore: The Christian Institute for the Study of Religion and Society 1965).

21. For details consult L. Renou, *Vedic India*, op. cit., p. 50 f.

22. One of the most important Vaiṣṇava Saṁhitās is the *Ahirbhudhnyasaṁhitā*, 2 vols. M. D. Ramanujacarya, ed. (2 rev. ed., V. Krishnamacharya, ed.) (Adyar: Adyar Library, [2]1966). There is no translation available in any Western language. An important Śaivite Āgama is the *Ajitāgama*, 2 vols., N. R. Bhatt, ed. (Pondichéry: Institut Français d'Indologie 1964-1967), no translation available in any Western language. An important Śākta Tantra is the *Tripurarāhasya*, Swami Sanatanadevaji Maharaja, ed. [*Jñānakhaṇḍa* only] (Varanasi: 1967); Chowkhamba Sanskrit Series English translation by A. U. Vasaveda, (Varanasi: Chowkhambha Sanskrit Office 1965).

23. F. O. Schrader, *Introduction to the Pāñcarātra and the Ahirbudhnya Saṁhitā* (Adyar: Adyar Library, 1916). Quite useful also the brief introduction by Jean Filliozat, "Les Āgamas Çivaites," in *Rauravāgama*, N. R. Bhatt ed. (Pondichéry: Institut Français d'Indologie, 1961). Lately F. H. Daniel Smith has done extensive research in the literature (largely still in manuscript) of Vaiṣṇava *āgamas*.

24. *Pañcarātra Rakṣa of Śrī Vedānta Deśika*, critically edited with notes and variant readings by Pdt. M. Duraiswami Aiyangar and Pdt. T. Venugopalacharya, with an introduction by G. Srinivasa Murti (Adyar: Adyar Library, 1942).

25. Cf. "Purāṇas and Their Authority in Religious Matters," *Kalyāṇa Kalpatāru* 18, no. 1 (August 1952): 5 f.

26. For details, consult L. Renou, *Vedic India*, op. cit., pp. 41 ff. Texts and translations are too numerous to be mentionded here; this type of literature has been extensively studied by nineteenth century European Indologists. For a fairly representative section of translated texts, see *Sacred Books of the East* (*SBE*), vols. 29 and 30. First published: Oxford: The Clarendon Press 1875-1901, Reprint Varanasi: Motilal Banarsidass 1962-66. Ed. by F. M. Müller.

27. The unquestioned authority in this field is P. V. Kane, with his seven volume *History of Dharmaśāstra* (op. cit.), which offers an unrivalled wealth of details about works, their authors, and materials pertaining to *smṛti*. The major Western authorities in this field are Duncan M. Derrett, professor of Oriental law at the School of African and Oriental Studies in London, and Ludo Rocher, professor of Indian studies at the University of Pennsylvania.

28. For text, see J. Jolly, *Mānava Dharma Śāstra* (London: 1887); English translation by G. Bühler, *The Laws of Manu, SBE*, vol. 25.

29. For a brief discussion of historical problems related to it cf. Kane, *HDhS*, *op. cit.*, pp. 79-85 as well as Bühler's introduction to his translation, ibid.

30. Cf. Kane, *HDhS, op. cit.*, pp. 60-70.

31. Ramdas Gaur, *Hindutva, op. cit.*, p. 755.

32. The greatest authority on Purāṇas is R. C. Hazra, who wrote numerous books and papers on Purāṇas and Upapurāṇas. Cf. his two contributions on Purāṇas and Upapurāṇas in *CHI*, vol. 2, pp 240-86. The latest comprehensive work on the subject is L. Rocher, "The Purāṇas," in *A History of Indian Literature* (*HIL*), Jan Gonda, ed., vol. 3, fasc. 3 (Wiesbaden: Otto Harrassowitz 1986).

33. Kane, *HDhS, op. cit.*, vol. 5, pp. 973-80 with ample references to original sources.

34. Cf. A. D. Pusalker, "Puranic Studies," in *Review of Indological Research in the Last 75 Years* (op. cit.), pp. 689-773.

35. Poona: Bhandarkar Oriental Research Institute, 1927-1966.

36. Published in seven volumes (*Baroda: Oriental Institute, 1960-1975*).

37. For details, see next chapter.

38. Most Purāṇas are now available in English translation. For details see next chapter.

39. Its main texts are the *Nyāya-sūtras* by Gautama. More about this in Chapter 23.

40. H. G. Coward, ed., *Studies in Indian Thought. Collected Papers of Prof. T. R. V. Murti* (Delhi: Motilal Banarsidass, 1983), 357-76. See also "Revelation and Reason," in ibid., 57-71.

41. Ibid., viii.

42. Ganganatha Jha, *Pūrva-Mīmāṁsā in Its Sources*, p. 146 (Benares: Benares Hindu University 1942). A very good recent study of this issue is Othmar Gächter, *Hermeneutics and Language in Pūrvamīmāṁsā: A Study in Śābara Bhāṣya* (Delhi: Motilal Banarsidass, 1983).

43. Mādhava, *Sarvadarśanasaṁgraha*, XIII, 6. An excellent introduction to this school is provided by Harold G. Coward in *Sphoṭa Theory of Language* (Delhi: Motilal Banarsidass, 1980). See also Coward's *Bhartṛhari*, Twayne World Authors Series (Boston: Twayne Publishers 1976).

44. Mādhava, *ibid.*, XIII, 13.

45. There are numerous editions, e.g., by Devaprakasa Patanjala Sastri (Delhi: Motilal Banarsidass 1954). A complete English translation (with text and notes) was done by Srisa Chandra Vasu, 2 vols. (reprint Delhi: Motilal Banarsidass 1961).

46. V. S. Agrawala, *India as Known to Pāṇini* (Varanasi: Prithvi Prakasan, [2]1963), 3: "Pāṇini, unlike Sakatayana did not carry to extremes the theory of treating all nouns as verbal derivatives, but also recognized the formation of fortuitous

words in the languages for which no certain derivation could be vouchsafed."

47. A complete edition of Patañjali's *Mahābhāṣya* with Kayyaṭa's and several other glosses was published in 10 volumes by Harayāṇā Sāhitya Saṁsthānam, Gurukul Jhajjar (Rohtak), 1961.

48. K. A. Nilakanta Sastri, *The Culture and History of the Tamils*, (Calcutta: Firma K. L. Mukhopadhyay, 1964), 10.

49. *Devanāgarī* is the name of the characters in which Sanskṛt is usually written, though in various parts of the country other characters also have been used.

50. The famous *Vāk-Sūkta* in *Ṛveda* X, 125. The tenth book of the *Ṛgveda* is considered to be its most recent part.

51. J. Woodroffe, *Introduction to Tantra Śāstra*, (Madras: Ganesa 1963).

52. H. H. Wilson, *The Viṣṇupurāṇa*, 1, n. (1840) Reprint: Calcutta: Punthi Pustak 1961 with an Introduction by R. C. Hazra.

53. II, 23, 3.

54. *Taittirīya Upaniṣad*, I, 8.

55. *Māṇḍukya Upaniṣad.*

56. *Skandapurāṇa*, Viṣṇukhaṇḍa XVI, 30 ff.

57. *Times of India*, (9 October 1963).

58. S. K. Belvalkar, *Lectures on Vedānta Philosophy* (Poona: Bilvakunja, 1929). The individual *śākhās* try to expurgate the contradictions in their literatures. The existing *Brahmasūtra* is essentially a (Sāmavedi) Chāṇḍogya Sūtra with later revisions and additions.

5. *ITIHĀSA* AND *PURĀṆA:* THE HEART OF HINDUISM

1. For a general orientation, see M. Winternitz, "The Popular Epics and the Purāṇas," *A History of Indian Literature*, Vol. 1, Part 2, (Calcutta: University of Calcutta 1963). Among modern Western studies of the *Mahābhārata* the following stand out: B. A. van Nooten, *The Mahābhārata* (New York: Twayne 1971); A. Hiltebeitel, *Ritual of Battle: Krishna in the Mahābhārata* (Ithaca: Cornell University Press, 1976). Among older studies, E. W. Hopkins, *The Great Epic of India* (New York: 1901; reprint Calcutta: Punthi Pustak 1969); and H. Oldenberg, *Das Mahābhārata* (Göttingen: Vandenhoeck & Ruprecht 1922) are still often referred to . On the *Rāmāyaṇa*, H. Jacobi's *Das Rāmāyaṇa* (originally published Bonn: 1893, new ed. with foreword by E. Frauwallner and additional literature, Darmstadt: Wissenschaftliche Buchgesellschaft 1970) is still indispensable. A new English translation of the *Rāmāyaṇa, Critical Edition* has begun to appear (Princeton: Princeton University Press, 1984). Goldman's Introduction to the first volume, *Bālakāṇḍa*, (3-59) deals both

with the history of the *Rāmāyaṇa* text and the literature connected with it.

2. For details, consult P. J. Chinmulgund and V. V. Mirashi, eds., *Review of Indological Research in the Last 75 Years*, (Poona: Bharatiya Charitrakosha Mandal, 1967); 670 ff. as well as V. S. Sukhtankar, "Introduction," in *Critical Edition, Mahābhārata*, (Poona: Bhandarkar Oriental Research Institute, 1933), *Ādiparvan*, i-cx and G. H. Bhatt, "Introduction" in *Rāmāyaṇa, Critical Edition* (Baroda: Oriental Institute 1960), Bālakāṇḍa, xiii-xxxv, i-xviii. Cf. also S. M. Katre, *Introduction to Textual Criticism*, with an appendix by P. K. Gode (Poona: Deccan College, 1954).

3. Vishnu S. Sukthankar writes in his "Prolegomena to the Critical Edition of the *Mahābhārata*," in ibid., vol. 1, *Ādiparvan:* "Next to the Vedas [the *Mahābhārata*] is the most valuable product of the entire literature of ancient India, so rich in notable works. Venerable for its very antiquity, it is one of the most inspiring monuments of the world and an inexhaustible mine for the investigation of the religion, mythology, legend, philosophy, law, custom, and political and social institutions of ancient India" (p. iii).

4. N. Sen, "The Influence of the Epics on Indian Life and Literature," in *CHI*, vol. 2, 117. For details of the immense influence on drama, poetry, and fine arts in India and in all of Southeast Asia see this paper as well as B. R. Chatterjee, "The *Rāmāyaṇa* and the *Mahābhārata* in South-East Asia," in ibid., pp. 119 ff.

5. H. Raychaudhuri, "The *Mahābhārata:* Some Aspects of its Culture," in *CHI*, vol. 2, 71 ff. See also J. L. Fitzgerald, "The Great Epic of India as Religious Rhetoric: A Fresh Look at the *Mahābhārata*," *Journal of the American Academy of Religion* (*JAAR*), 51, no. 4 (1986): 611-29.

6. The names connected with the former theory are Lassen, Sørenson, Winternitz, and Meyer; with the latter, especially J. Dahlmann. About the theories and their criticism, cf. A. D. Pusalker, "The *Mahābhārata:* Its History and Character," in *CHI:* Vol. 2, 51 ff. See also Fitzgerald, op. cit., 611-30.

7. *Mahābhārata, Critical Edition*, 20 vols. (Poona: Bhandarkar Oriental Research Institute, 1927-1966). Several vulgate editions are available, e.g., one in four volumes from the Gītāpress, Gorakhpur.

8. I, 1, 50. See also M. Mehta, "The Problem of the Double Introduction to the Mahābhārata," *JAOS* 93, no. 4 (1973): 547-50.

9. The Bhandarkar Oriental Research Institute has published a critical edition in two volumes. A vulgate edition is available from several publishers; among others, Gītāpress, Gorakhpur (n.d.), with Hindī translation. (The same publisher has also brought out a vulgate edition of the entire *Mahābhārata* in four volumes with a *Nāmanukramāṇikā*.)

10. *Yad ihāsti tad anyatra yad nehāsti na tat kva cit.*

11. In *Mahābhāratātparyanirṇaya*

12. V. S. Sukhtankar, *On the Meaning of the Mahābhārata*, (Bombay: Asiatic Society of Bombay, 1957), 128 ff.

13. A complete English translation of the *Mahābhārata* was prepared by Pratap Chandra Roy toward the end of the last century; it has been reprinted in twelve volumes by Oriental Publishing Co., Calcutta, in the late fifties. A new English translation, following the critical edition was begun by J. A. B. van Buitenen (Chicago: University of Chicago Press, 1973-1978); so far three volumes have appeared. C. Rajagopalachari has compiled a one-volume rendering of some of the most important stories of the *Mahābhārata* (Bombay: Bharatiya Vidya Bhavan 1958), which has become very popular.

14. *Āraṇyakaparvan*, Chapters 295-98, condensed.

15. The present introduction to the Rāma story contains the story of Vālmīki, who according to legend started out as a brigand, was converted into a Rāma-bhakta, did penance for his sins in a forest by remaining seated in meditation even while ants began building an anthill (Sanskṛt; *valmīkaḥ*) on his body, covering it completely.

16. *Jātaka* 461; about *Rāmāyaṇa* criticism, cf. Pusalker, op. cit., 14 ff. C. Bulcke, *Rāmakathā* [Hindī] (Prayāg: Hindi Pariṣad, Viśvavidyālaya 1950).

17. Cf. G. H. Bhatt, "Introduction," in *Mahābhārata, Critical Edition*, op. cit.

18. In the *Hindustan Times* (29 July 1972), a note appeared saying that the original manuscript of the *Rāmacaritamānasa* had been found in the house of a Pathan landlord in Malihabad, near Lucknow. There are countless editions of this work in India. The Gītāpress brought out the full text with an English translation in 1968.

19. Cf. A. D. Pusalker, *Studies in Epics and Purāṇas of India* (Bombay: Bharatiya Vidya Bhavan, 1955), 174 ff.

20. The Oriental Institute Baroda has published the *Rāmāyaṇa, Critical Edition*, 7 vols. (1960-1975). Vulgate editions are numerous and easily available, e.g., from the Gītāpress.

21. Pusalker, in *CHI*, op. cit., 27 f.

22. R. T. H. Griffith has brought out a complete English translation of the *Rāmāyaṇa* in verse (Benares: 1915; reprint Varanasi: Chowkhamba Sanskrit Studies No. 29, 1963). A prose translation, together with the Sanskrit text began to appear from Gītāpress Gorakhpur, *Kalyāṇa Kalpataru*, in 1960; so far, ten fascicles have come out (up to VII, 41). C. Rajagopalachari has summarized the stories of the *Rāmāyaṇa* in one volume (Bombay: Bharatiya Vidya Bhavan 1962), which also has become very popular.

23. *Bālakāṇḍa*, Chapter 67.

24. Laṅka is often identified with Śrī Laṅka; scholars are in disagreement, however,

about the identity of Laṅka, and many are inclined to look for it not far from eastern central India, where the rest of the Rāma story takes place.

25. *Uttarakāṇḍa*, 111, 21 f.

26. Cf. A. P. Karmarkar, "Religion and Philosophy of the Epics," in *CHI*, vol. 2, 80 ff.

27. Thus Swami Dayananda Sarasvati, the founder of the *Ārya Samāj*.

28. In 1986, as part of the multivolume *History of Indian Literature*, Jan Gonda, ed., Ludo Rocher wrote a monograph on the *Purāṇas*, which for many years to come will be the most authoritative study of the subject. It would be meaningless to attempt to summarize the work here. It goes into the history of *Purāṇa* studies, the question of the number of *Purāṇas*, the controversies surrounding the division between *Mahāpurāṇas* and *Upapurāṇas*, the debate about the "*Ur-purāṇa*" and eventually lists all *Purāṇas*, giving a short summary, indicating text editions, translations, and studies. For all detail concerning either the *Purāṇas* themselves or scholarship about them, the reader is referred to this work.

29. R. C. Hazra, "The Purāṇas," in *CHI*, vol. 2, 240 f.

30. *Atharva Veda*, XI, 7, 24; *Bṛhadāraṇyaka Upaniṣad* IV, 5, 11, etc.

31. R. C. Hazra, op. cit.

32. Sixth century C.E.

33. Cf. F. E. Pargiter, *Ancient Indian Historical Tradition* (Oxford: Oxford University Press, 1922; reprint Delhi: Motilal Banarsidass, 1962).

34. See "Preface," in ibid. Critizised by P. V. Kane in *HDhS*, vol. 5, part 2, 850 ff.

35. M. A. Mehendale, "Purāṇas," in *HCIP*, vol. 3, 296.

36. Thus the *Devībhāgavata Purāṇa* of the Śāktas claims to be the real *Bhāgavata Purāṇa* and is accepted as such by the Śāktas. Cf. C. Mackenzie Brown, "The Origin and Transmission of the Two *Bhāgavata Purāṇas:* A Canonical and Theological Dilemma," *JAAR* 51, no. 4 (1983): 551-67.

37. As does the *Bhaviṣya Purāṇa*, which claims to be an ancient prophetical book about the future (*bhaviṣyam*).

38. All the *Mahāpurānas* have been published, most of them by different publishers; Motilal Banarsidass has started a fifty-volume series, *Ancient Indian Tradition and Mythology*, which aims at providing a complete translation of all the *Mahāpurāṇas*. So far thirty-six volumes have appeared, including *Śiva, Liṅga, Bhāgavata, Garuḍa, Nārada, Kūrma, Brahmāṇḍa, Agni, Varāha, Brahmā Purāṇas*. Older translations are available of the *Mārkaṇḍeya*, the *Bhāgavata, Matsya*, the *Viṣṇu*, the *Agni* and the *Garuḍa Purāṇas*. For the *Upapurāṇas*, consult R. C. Hazra, *Studies in the Upapurāṇas*, 2 vols. (Calcutta: Sanskrit College, 1958) 63 and L. Rocher, "The Purāṇas," in *History of Indian Literature*,

Jan Gonda, ed. (Wiesbaden: Harrassowitz, 1986).

39. *Viṣṇu Purāṇa* VI, 8, 40 ff.

40. *Skanda Purāṇa*, Viṣṇukhaṇḍa Margaśirṣamāhātmya XVI, 30 ff.

41. *Newsweek*, (21 September 1987): 74 ff. reviewed a performance of Peter Brook's *The Mahābhārata*, a nine-hour long re-creation of the Indian Epic. He and his coworkers had been preparing this modern dramatization for twelve years. *India Today* (15 February 1987): 84, reported: "Britain's most influential body—the Inner London Education Authority is to stage a £100,000 spectacular based on the *Rāmāyaṇa* to be performed by school children in London's Battersea Park in June this year." *India Today* (30 April 1987), under the title "Ramayan: Divine Sensation," reported the unexpected success of a current TV dramatization of the *Rāmāyaṇa* in India.

6. THE *BHAGAVADGĪTĀ*

1. E. J. Sharpe, *The Universal Gita: Western Images of the Bhagavadgita*, A Bicentenary Survey. (Lasalle, Ill.: Open Court 1985). R. Minor, ed., *Modern Indian Interpreters of the Bhagavadgita* (Albany: State University of New York Press, 1986).

2. The *Mahābhārata* contains also an *Aṇugītā* and many of the *Purāṇas* have *Gītās*, summarizing in a popular form their main ideas.

3. A Kashmirian text of the *Gītā* with quite considerable variants was discovered about fifty years ago. *Mahābhārata, Critical Edition* vol. 7, *Bhīṣmaparvan*, (Poona: Bhandarkar Oriental Research Institute, 1947), 114-18 with critical notes (pp. 769-86) contains a wealth of precise information about the text and the commentaries as well as major studies on the *Bhagavadgītā*.

4. Bombay: Bharatiya Vidya Bhavan 1965.

5. *Ibid.*, p. 83 f.

6. *Die Bhagavadgītā* (Leipzig: H. Haessel [2]1921), 32.

7. N. C. Chaudhuri, *Hinduism* (London: Chatto & Windus 1979), however, accepts the *Gītā*'s dependence on Christian ideas.

8. S. Buddhiraja, *The Bhagavadgītā: A Study* (Madras: Ganesh & Co. 1927).

9. English translation, in two vols. (Poona: 1935).

10. Mahadev Desai, *The Gītā According to Gandhi* (Ahmedabad: Navajivan 1946).

11. Sri Aurobindo, *Essays on the Gītā* (Pondichéry: Sri Aurobindo Ashram 1928).

12. S. Radhakrishnan, *The Bhagavadgītā* (London: Allen & Unwin 1948).

13. S. K. Belvalkar, "Vedānta in the *Bhagavadgītā*," *Lectures on Vedānta Philosophy* (Poona: Bilvakunja, 1929).

14. Ibid., p. 118 f., slightly revised.

15. Quoted in M. Winternitz, *A History of Indian Literature*, vol. 1, part 2 (Calcutta: University of Calcutta, 1963), 375.

16. W. M. Callewaert and S. Hemraj, *Bhagavadgītānuvāda: A Study in Transcultural Translation* (Ranchi: Sathya Bharati Publication, 1983).

17. The term is *adhikāra*, qualification or prerequisite.

18. Despite the often advocated spirit of tolerance in the *Gītā*, the teaching is solidly Kṛṣṇaitic and would not admit that any other religion would yield the same results.

19. *Bhagavadgītā* (*B.G.*) IX, 4-8.

20. Ibid., 16-19.

21. Ibid., 26-34, condensed.

22. The titles given at the end of the chapters are not found in many manuscripts and, in those in which they are found, they are not uniform; the critical edition leaves them out.

23. *BG* XI, 3.

24. *BG* XVIII, 51-55.

25. *BG* XVIII, 64-66; the term is *pāpam*, the Vedic technical word for sin, not evil in the general sense, as Radhakrishnan translates.

26. Thomas McCarthy in the Introduction (p. xxv) to his translation of Jürgen Habermas, *The Theory of Communicative Action*, vol. 1. *Reason and the Rationalization of Society* (Boston: Beacon Press, 1984), 4: "Sociology became the science of crisis par excellence; it concerned itself above all with the anomic aspects of the dissolution of traditional social systems and the development of modern ones."

27. Heiner Kipphardt, "In the Matter of J. Robert Oppenheimer," *Stücke*, vol. 1, 309.

28. Published in the *Indian and Foreign Review* (1 March 1981), 27.

7. THE WORLD OF THE HINDU

1. The best work on the Vedic creation myths is still A. A. Macdonell's *Vedic Mythology*, originally published in 1897 in the *Encyclopedia of Indo-Aryan Research*, G. Bühler, ed., vol. 3, part 1 a, (*reprint Varanasi: Indological Book*-house, 1963). See also R. N. Dandekar, "Vṛtraha Indra," *ABORI* 30, no.1 (1951): 1-55. On creation myths in general, see D. Maclagan, *Creation Myths: Man's Introduction to the World*, (London: Thames and Hudson, 1977).

2. *Ṛgveda* I, 185.

3. S. Kramrisch, "The Triple Structure of Creation in the *ṚgVeda*," *HR* 2, no. 1 (1962): 141.

4. *Ṛgveda* X, 82.

5. Ibid., verses 2, 3, 7.

6. *Ṛgveda* X, 90.

7. Ibid., verse 16.

8. *Ṛgveda* X, 129.

9. Kramrisch, op. cit., 147.

10. *Bṛhadāraṇyaka Upaniṣad* I, 1, 4.

11. *Kaṭha Upaniṣad* 3, 10 f.; *Ṛgveda* X, 121, 1; *Manusmṛti* I, 9.

12. *Manas* cannot be exactly translated, the nearest concept is the mediaeval *sensus communis*, the coordinating faculty of the senses, not intellect itself.

13. *Ahaṁkāra* is sometimes translated "egoism" (G. Bühler, repeated by M. Eliade, *From Primitives to Zen* [New York: Harper & Row, 1967], 112), which gives a wrong idea.

14. *Manusmṛti* I, 1 ff.

15. Ibid., I, 64 f.

16. Ibid., 65-74.

17. Ibid., 81-86.

18. The best work on the subject is S. M. Ali, *The Geography of the Purāṇas* (New Delhi: People's Publishing House 1966), which offers, as well as exhaustive references to the sources, many serious suggestions concerning the identity of ancient names with contemporary geography.

19. Ali, ibid., 32 and figure 2.

20. *Viṣṇu Purāṇa* II, 4, and many parallels in other *Purāṇas.*

21. One *yojana* is approximately nine miles.

22. *Viṣṇu Purāṇa*, II, 2, and parallels.

23. Ibid., II, 3, and parallels.

24. Ibid., II, 3, 24-26.

25. The account is taken from a Vaiṣṇava scripture.

26. *Viṣṇu Purāṇa* II, 4, 87.

27. Ibid., verse 98.

28. Ibid., II, 5-8.

29. Ibid., II, 5, 5.

30. Ibid., verse 13 ff.

31. Ibid., II, 7, 11.

32. Ibid., verse 15 ff.

33. Ibid., II, 7, 22 ff.

34. Concerning the discussion of this date see P. V. Kane, *History of Dharmaśāstra*, vol. 5, part 1, 648 f. (Poona: B.O.R.I. 1962).

35. A. D. Pusalker, "Historical Traditions," in *HCIP*, R. C. Majumdar, general ed., vol. 1, 271-333.

36. According to Purāṇic accounts, before the present creation, the Creator produced several kinds of creatures who, because produced from Brahmā's mind in meditation, did not multiply themselves. He created "mind-born sons, like Himself," the nine Brahmarṣis, celebrated in Indian mythology, all absorbed in meditation and without desire of progeny. Brahmā's anger produced Rudra, half male and half female, who began multiplying into various beings. Finally, he created Manu Svayambhu "born of, and identical with his original self," and the female part of himself he constituted as *Śatarūpā*. *Viṣṇu Purāṇa* I, 7.

37. *Viṣṇu Purāṇa* I, 13 and parallels.

38. *Śatapatha Brāhmaṇa* I, 8, 1, 1-6 seems to be the oldest account. Also see *Bhāgavata Purāṇa* VIII, 24 ff.

39. To forestall a popular confusion, *Kali-yuga* comes from *kali*, "strife, fight" and has nothing to do with *Kālī*, "The Black One," the name of Devī, the Goddess, in her terrible form.

40. Cf. *Viṣṇu Purāṇa* IV, 21 ff., and parallels.

41. Ibid., IV, 20.

42. Ibid., IV, 24 128 ff.

43. Ibid., verse 1121 ff.

44. The representatives of the Ārya Samāj have been most prominent in this regard.

45. In a talk given on December 10, 1965.

8. THE MANY GODS AND THE ONE GOD OF HINDUISM

1. E.g., A. A. Macdonell, *Vedic Mythology* (reprint Varanasi: Indological Bookhouse, 1963).

2. K. C. Bhattacharya, *Studies in Philosophy* (Calcutta: Progressive Publishers,

1956). vol. 1, 35, connects the *devatās* with Plato's *ideas* and the concept of *universalia ante rem.* Through *upāsana* ("worship") man ascends from the concrete individual things to their *adhyātma* ("spiritual") and *adibhūta* ("primeval") aspect, their absoluteness. *Devatā* would correspond to the *noumenon* of Kant.

3. R. N. Dandekar, "God in Hindu Thought," lecture at Bharatiya Vidya Bhavan, 13 January 1968.

4. See the research of A. Esteller, e.g., "The Quest for the Original *Ṛgveda,*" *ABORI* 50 (1969): 1-40.

5. R. N. Dandekar, "Vṛtraha Indra," *ABORI* 30, no. 1 (1951): 1-55. The etymology of Indra is not clear as yet. A. A. Macdonell derives it from *indu*, "drop" (*A History of Sanscrit Literature* [reprint Delhi: Motilal Banarsidass [2]1961], 44); J. Gonda, from *intoi*, "pushing" (*Die Religionen Indiens* [Stuttgart: Kohlhammer, 1960], vol. 1, 60); R. N. Dandekar from *indu*, bringing it in connection with "virile power" ("Vṛtraha Indra," ibid.); S. S. Sastri connects it with *in, inva*, "to rule," and *ina*, "sun," "lord," ("Vṛṣakapi," *Bhāratīya Vidyā* 10: 159). A very thorough and insightful study of Indra is provided by Hertha Krick, "Der Vaniṣṭusava und Indras Offenbarung," *WZKSA* 19 (1975): 25-74.

6. R. N. Dandekar, "Vṛtraha Indra."

7. It is important to note that the Vedic *devas* are in constant conflict with the *asuras*, the demons, and that their high position is due precisely to their power to subjugate the hostile forces. Of interest in this context is H. v. Stietencron, "Dämonen und Gegengötter: Überlegungen zur Typologie von Antagonismen," *Saeculum* 34, nos. 3-4 (1983): 372-83.

8. The exact number is 1028 (divided into ten *maṇḍalas*), from which 11 Vālakhilya hymns are usually subtracted, because neither the great Sāyaṇa (fourteenth century) had commented upon them nor are they mentioned in the list (considered authoritative) ascribed to Śaunaka.

9. *Ṛgveda* I, 164, 46.

10. *Ṛgveda* II, 12. From R. T. H. Griffith's trans. (with modifications), *Hymns of the Ṛgveda*, 2 vols. (Benares: Chowkhamba [4]1963).

11. *Ṛgveda* I, 1.

12. *Ṛgveda* I, 35.

13. E.g., *Ṛgveda* VII, 86.

14. *Bṛhadāraṇyaka Upaniṣad* III, 9, 1, 9.

15. *Viṣṇu Purāṇa* I, 2, 66 f.: "The only God, *Janardana* takes the designation Brahmā, Viṣṇu and Śiva accordingly as he creates, preserves or destroys. Viṣṇu as creator creates himself, as preserver preserves himself, as destroyer, destroys himself at the end of all things."

16. Thus, the celebrated Maheśa (Śiva) *mūrti* in the main cave of Gharapurī (Elephanta). See S. Kramrisch, "The Image of Mahādeva in the Cave Temple on Elephanta Island," *Ancient India* 2 (1946): 4-8.

17. According to this legend, Viṣṇu and Brahmā had been arguing about their supremacy when a huge fiery column appeared before them. To find out about its nature, Viṣṇu, in the form of a boar, dived down to find its lower end and Brahmā, in the form of a swan, flew up to discover its upper extremity. After some time they met again. Viṣṇu admitted that he had not found an end; Brahmā asserted that he had found the upper end and was hence greater than Viṣṇu and therefore the universal Lord. Just then the sides of the column opened and out stepped Śiva, the infinite, praising Viṣṇu for his truthfulness and establishing him second to Himself, severely chiding Brahmā for his lie and condemning him to remain without worship henceforth.

18. *Ṛgveda* III, 62, 10.

19. *Kūrma Purāṇa* 20.

20. R. C. Hazra, *Studies in the Upapurāṇas* 2 vol. (Calcutta: Sanskrit College, 1958), vol. 1, 29 f. H. v. Stietencron has assembled much interesting information on sun worship in India and its possible connection with Iran in his monograph on Sūrya, *Indische Sonnenpriester: Sāmba und die Śākasdiśpīya Brāhmaṇa* (Wiesbaden: Otto Harrassowitz, 1966).

21. Cf. Sir Mortimer Wheeler, *The Indus Civilization*, (Cambridge: Cambridge University Press, 1953).

22. *Ibid.*, 83 and 95. Wheeler speaks of a "likelihood that both Śiva and Liṅga worship have been inherited by the Hindus from the Harappans."

23. S. K. Chatterji, "Race Movements and Prehistoric Culture," *HCIP*, 164 ff.. Cf. also C. V. Narayana Ayyar, *Origin and Early History of Śaivism in South India* (Madras: University of Madras, 1936), 10.

24. A. D. Pusalker, "Aryan Settlements in India," *HCIP*, R. C. Majumdar, general ed., vol. 1, 258 ff.

25. Chatterji, op. cit.

26. *Yajurveda Vajasaneyasaṁhitā*, Chapter 16.

27. *Śvetāśvatara Upaniṣad*, VI, 1.

28. *Mahābhārata, Śāntiparvan* 274 and Appendix I, 8; *Droṇaparvan*, 201, 64-68; and *Sauptikaparvan* 18.

29. The myth is told in both the epics and most of the *Purāṇas*. The oldest version is probably in *Vāyu Purāṇa* I, 30.

30. E.g., *Vālmīki Rāmāyaṇa* I, 45.

31. Cf. V. Paranjoti, *Śaiva Siddhānta* (London: Luzac 1964), 54 ff.

32. Cf. Ananda Coomaraswamy, *The Dance of Śiva* (Bombay: Asia, 1948), 83.

33. *Śiva Purāṇa, Śatarudrasaṁhitā* 3.

34. Ibid., *Umāsaṁhitā.*

35. Ibid., *Rudrasaṁhitā, Sātīkhaṇḍa* 38, 34.

36. A whole *Liṅga Purāṇa* is devoted to this.

37. Cf. the collection of hymns with English translation, F.Kingsbury and G. E. Philips, trans., *Hymns of the Tamil Śaivite Saints* (Calcutta: Association Press 1921).

38. *Śatapatha Brāhmaṇa* I, 1, 2, 13; I, 9, 3, 9; III, 6, 3, 3.

39. Chatterji, op. cit., 165.

40. Cf. A. D. Pusalker, "Historicity of Kṛṣṇa," in *Studies in Epics and Purāṇas*, (Bombay: Bharatiya Vidya Bhavan 1955), 49-81.

41. On the underlying theoretical basis of the *avatāra* doctrine, cf. P. Hacker, "Zur Entwicklung der Avatāralehre," *WZKSA* 4 (1960): 47-70.

42. The *Viṣṇusahasranāma* is contained in the *Mahābhārata* and in all *Vaiṣṇava Purāṇas* and has been printed separately many times. It has also been commented upon by several authorities.

43. Cf. N. Macnicol, *Psalms of the Maratha Saints* (Calcutta: Association Press 1919). There are countless collections of such hymns in Indian vernaculars, most of them as yet untranslated.

44. E. Neuman, *An Analysis of the Archetype the Great Mother*, (Princeton: Princeton University Press, 1955), 120 ff.

45. Hazra, op. cit., vol. 2, 16.

46. H. Whitehead, *The Village Gods of South India* (Calcutta: [2]1921), 11.

47. *Mahābhārata, Sauptikaparvan* 8, 64 ff., describes a vision of "Death-Night in her embodied form" just before the great war begins!

48. A. P. Karmarkar, *The Religions of India*, (Lonavla: Mira Publishing House 1950), 99.

49. H. v. Stietencron, *Gaṅgā und Yamunā* (Wiesbaden: Otto Harrassowitz, 1972).

50. Examples are found in A. Daniélou, *Hindu Polytheism* (London: Routledge & Kegan Paul, 1964), 350 ff.

51. Ibid., 291 ff.

52. *Viṣṇu Purāṇa* I, 8 ff.; *Śiva Purāṇa, Rudrasaṁhitā* III, etc.

53. See J. Gonda, "The Historical Background of the Name *Satya* Assigned to

the Highest Being," *ABORI* 48 (1968): 83-93.

54. On this whole issue, see K. Klostermaier, *Mythologies and Philosophies of Salvation in the Theistic Traditions of India* (Waterloo: Wilfrid Laurier University Press, 1984.).

9. THE PATH OF WORKS: *KARMAMĀRGA*

1. A brief analysis is given by L. A. Ravi Varma, "Rituals of Worship," in *CHI*, vol. 4, 445-63.
2. This is done with reference to *Manusmṛti* VI, 35 f.
3. *Ṛgveda* X, 90.
4. A. A. Macdonell, "Vedic Religion," in *Encyclopedia of Religion and Ethics*, E. Hastings, ed., [3]1954), vol. 12, 601-18.
5. About the technical aspects of the *yajña*, see: P. V. Kane, *HDhS*, vol. 2 (part 2), 983 ff.
6. *Taittirīya Saṁhitā* I, 8, 4, 1.
7. In the same report: "In the West, people talk of peace; they hold an atom bomb in one hand and a peace-dove in the other. Thus peace was destroyed. But in the East the guiding principle is *pañca śila*, which has its deep roots in the moral and spiritual tradition of the East. This is the true way to peace."
8. *Blitz, India's Greatest Weekly* (11 April 1970) reported that the Brahmin who was hired to do it died through electrocution while performing the *yajña*.
9. F. Staal, *AGNI: The Vedic Ritual of the Fire Altar*, 2 vols., with many plates (Berkeley: University of California Press, 1983).
10. F. Staal has dealt with Vedic ritual by itself and in a comparative fashion in many other important publications, e.g., *The Science of Ritual*, (Poona: Deccan Institute 1982); "The Meaninglessness of Ritual," *Numen* 26 (1979): 2-22; "The Sound of Religion," *Numen* 33 (1986): 33-64, 185-224. See also his exchange with a reviewer of *AGNI in JAS* 46, no. 1 (1987): 105-10.
11. *Chāṇḍogya Upaniṣad* V, 3-10, contains the *pañcāgni vidyā*.
12. Cf. C. M. Carstairs, *The Twice-Born* (London: Hogarth Press 1951), which describes in meticulous detail the rituals performed by a Brahmin family in Poona.
13. From *Śaiva Upaniṣads*, T. R. Srinivasa Ayyangar and G. Srinivasa Murti, trans. (Adyar Library, 1953), 165 ff.
14. Ibid., 203 f.
15. It is quite typical that even a former leader of the Communist Party in Kerala, N. Nambudiripad, belonged to the Brahmin caste. In Tamilnādu, the *Draviḍa*

Munnetra Kazhagam (DMK), staged a kind of anti-Brahmin revolt.

16. *Manu* II, 176, already prescribes daily *tarpaṇa.*

17. *Caṇḍālas*, the offspring of a Brahmin father and a *śūdra* mother, were considered the lowest in the social hierarchy.

18. In the *Kaṭha-Upaniṣad*, Yama, the god of death himself, apologizes to Naciketas, a Brahmin youth who has come to him, for not having served him due to his absence.

19. *Taittirīya Upaniṣad* II, 2, 1.

20. *Chāṇḍogya Upaniṣad* VII, 26, 2.

21. Details may be found under the heading *bhojana*, in Kane, op. cit., 757-800.

22. Vedic ritual has been a major preoccupation of Western Indology for more than a hundred years. Part of the fascination this type of study held for Western scholars may have to do with the age of the texts concerned, the quest for origins was a widely shared concern of nineteenth century scholars, as well as with the formalism of the texts themselves. Rituals are designed to bring order into the cosmos, and ritual literature is characterized by the meticulousness with which it regulates every movement and every sound. In this respect, it resembles scholarship: it leaves nothing unexplained, leaves nothing to chance, or to the layman's inexpert handling of things.

    Modern scholars dealing with Vedic sacrifice range from early comprehensive reconstructions from texts like J. Schwab's *Das indische Tieropfer* (Erlangen: Deichert 1886), and Sylvain Lévi's still often referred to *La doctrine du sacrifice dans le Brāhmaṇas* (Paris: 1898; reprint Paris: Presses Universitaires de France, 1966), to specialized studies like those of F. Staal, op. cit., and J. Gonda's *Vedic Ritual: The Non-solemn Rites* (Amsterdam: North-Holland Publ. 1980) and J. C. Heesterman's *The Inner Conflict of Tradition: Essays in Indian Ritual, Kingship and Society* (Chicago: University of Chicago Press, 1985). In addition to these, the following works are of interest: W. Caland and V. Henry, *L'Agniṣṭoma: description complète de la forme normal du sacrifice de Soma dans le culte védique*, 2 vols. (Paris: E. Léroux 1907); C. G. Diehl, *Instrument and Purpose: Studies on Rites and Rituals in South India* (Lund: C. W. K. Gleerup 1956); L. Dumont, *Homo hierarchicus: Essai sur le systéme des castes* (Paris: Gallimard 1966); L. Renou, *The Destiny of the Veda in India*, (Delhi: Motilal Banarsidass 1965); M. Strickmann, ed., *Classical Asian Rituals and the Theory of Ritual* (Berlin: Springer 1986); and Ria Kloppenborg, ed., *Selected Studies on Ritual in the Indian Religions: Essays to D. J. Hoens*, Studies in History of Religions: *Supplements to Numen* 45 (Leiden: Brill, 1983). How detailed this kind of study can become is shown in the most recent work of the doyen of European Indology, J. Gonda, *The Ritual Functions and Significance of Grasses in the Religion of the Veda* (Amsterdam: North-Holland Publ. 1985) with thousands of textual references.

23. Interesting economic details are supplied by D. D. Kosambi, *An Introduction*

to the Study of Indian History (Bombay: Popular Book Depot 1956), 94 ff.

24. A. Weber, "Über das Menschenopfer bei den Indern der vedischen Zeit," in *Indische Streifen*, (Berlin: 1886), vol. 1, 54-89, has a collection of all the Vedic evidences concerning human sacrifice. See, *Aitareya Brāhmaṇa* VII, 13-18; II, 8; VI, 8; *Śatapatha Brāhmaṇa* I, 2, 3, 6; VI, 2, 2, 18, etc.

25. *Bhāgavata Purāṇa* IX, 7, 20, describes a human sacrifice according to a Vedic ritual.

26. Cf. P. E. Dumont, *L'Aśvamedha* (Paris: P. Geuthner 1927).

27. The last seems to have been performed in the eighteenth century, as described in P. K. Gode's interesting article "The Aśvamedha Performed by Sevai Jayasingh of Amber 1699-1744 A.D.," in *Studies in Indian Literary History*, (Bombay: Bharatiya Vidya Bhavan 1954), 292-306.

28. *Aitareya Brāhmaṇa* II, 18. According to the same text, the *medha* went from the goat into the earth and from the earth into rice. "All those animals from which the *medha* had gone [e.g., camel, ass, mule] are unfit to be sacrificed." See also *Śatapatha Brāhmaṇa* I, 2, 3, 6.

29. R. Gordon Wasson: "The Soma of the Rig Veda: What Was It? *Journal of the American Oriental Society* (*JAOS*) 91, no. 2 (1971): 169-91.

30. *Ṛgveda* VIII, 48, 3.

31. *Bhagavadgītā* IX, 26 f.

32. The ritual is minutely described in the *kriyā-pāda* of the *Āgamas, Saṁhitās*, and *Tantras*, the most elaborate of the four traditional parts of each of those scriptures.

33. The ritual of the famous Viṣṇu temple at Śrīraṅgam, as detailed in the *Śrīparameśvara Saṁhitā*, Sri Govindacarya, ed. (Śrīraṅgam: Kodaṇḍarāmasannidhi 1953), is said to have been revealed to Yamunācārya by Lord Viṣṇu himself. Similarly, the ritual of South Indian Śaivite temples, as outlined in the *Somaśambhupaddhatī* with French translation and notes by H. Brunner-Lachaux, (Pondichéry: Institute Français d'Indologie, 1963), is associated with a Śiva revelation to its author.

34. A good example is R. V. Joshi, *Le Rituel de la dévotion Kṛṣṇaite*, (Pondichéry: Institute Français d'Indologie, 1959).

35. The most famous is that of Ajamila, as reported in the *Bhāgavata Purāṇa*.

36. Cf. M. Strickman, op. cit. See also A. J. Blasi, "Ritual as a Form of the Religious Mentality," *Sociological Analysis* 46, no. 1 (1985): 59-72.

37. See note 9; also J. F. Staal, "Language and Ritual," in *Prof. Kuppuswamy Sastri Birth-Centenary Volume*, part II, (Madras: Kuppuswamy Research Institute 1985), 51-62.

10. PURITY AND MERIT: THE TWIN CONCERNS OF *KARMAMĀRGA*

1. W. Cenkner, *A Tradition of Teachers. Śaṅkara and the Jagadgurus Today* (Delhi: Motilal Banarsidass, 1983), 150.

2. The importance of such activities in contemporary India cannot only be gauged from the increasing crowds at such events like the *Kumbhamelā*, attendance of up to 7 million pilgrims, but also by the attention given it even by a liberal secular news magazine. "Kumbh Mela: Nectar of the Gods, Photofeature by Raghu Rai," *India Today* (15 May 1986): 74-85. See also J. B. Carman and A. Marglin, eds., *Purity and Auspiciousness in Indian Society* (Leiden: Brill, 1985).

3. P. V. Kane's *History of Dharmaśāstra* is the most complete work on the subject, an inexhaustible source of information on all aspects of *dharma*.

4. A good account of it is given in S. K. Maitra, *The Ethics of the Hindus* (Calcutta: University of Calcutta, [3]1963), 81 ff.

5. Ibid., 83: "Thus for the Nyāya-Vaiśeṣikas righteousness is a quality of the *Ātman* or Self, i.e., is a subjective category to be distinguished from the objective act (*karma*) as well as from any impersonal transcendental category (*apūrva*) which may be generated by it. Nor is it any objective quality of an act which has any such supersensuous category in its aid or support (*apūrvaprakṛti-karmaguṇa*)."

6. Ibid., 117 ff.

7. Ibid., 119.

8. S. N. Dasgupta, *HIPh* (Cambridge: Cambridge University Press 1955) vol. 5, 134.

9. *Bhagavadgītā* III, 47. *Niṣkāma Karma*, Special Volume of *Kalyāṇ* 54 (1980) contains over a hundred articles (in Hindī) on this topic.

10. *Bhagavadgītā*, XVI, 21.

11. Jayanta uses the triad *moha* ("delusion"), *rāga* ("attraction") and *dveṣa* ("aversion"), which materially is exactly the same; he utilizes *lobha* and *krodha* as derivations of *rāga* and *dveṣa*.

12. This is a typical Vaiṣṇava injunction.

13. *Viṣṇu Purāṇa* III, 12.

14. *Cārakasaṁhitā*, T. Yadava Sarma, ed. (Bombay: Nirnaya Sagara Press, [3]1963), 45-51, *Sūtrasthānam* 8.

15. *The Tirukkuṛaḷ* [in Tamil] with translations in English by G. U. Pope, W. H. Drew, J. Lazarus, and F. W. Ellis (Tinnevelly: South India Śaiva Siddhānta Works Publishing Society, 1962), quotations: nos. 72, 101, 156, 160, 203.

16. One of the most complete may be the Sādhucāraṇa Prasād, *Dharmaśāstra-saṅgraha* (Bombay: Śrī Venkateśvar Press, 1970 Samvat); *Prayaścittas* form Chapter 21, the longest of all.

17. The *Manusmṛti*, as well as other *dharmaśāstras*, are quite up to date as regards protection of the environment. They punish by loss of caste the injuring of living plants, cutting down green trees for firewood, mining and all mechanical engineering that does damage to the environment, etc. See *Manusmṛti* XI, 64 f.

18. Ibid., XI, 53. In XII, 54 ff. (a later addition perhaps) Manu points out the various animal rebirths persons have to go through in consequence of their sins: "Those who committed *mahāpātakas*, having passed during large numbers of years through dreadful hells, obtain after that the following births: the slayer of a brahmin enters the womb of a dog, a pig, an ass, a camel, a cow, a goat, a sheep, a deer, a bird, a Caṇḍāla, a Pukkasa; a brahmin who drinks *surā* shall enter the bodies of small and large insects, of moths, of birds feeding on ordure . . . the violator of the *guru*'s bed enters a hundred times grasses, shrubs and creepers."

19. Cf. *Devībhāgavata Purāṇa* VIII, 22 ff.

20. *Manusmṛti* XI, 45 f.

21. Ibid., 73-87. Note, however, that this applies only to a Brahmin; a man from a lower caste who kills a Brahmin has no such means available.

22. Ibid., 228-231.

23. Ibid., 31-33.

24. Thus in Viśvanātha Cakravartti, "*Bhaktirasāmṛtasindhubinduḥ*," *JAOS* 1 (1974). For Śaivite rules regarding violation of worship cf. *Somaśambhu-paddhati*, H. Brunner-Lachaux, ed. and trans. [French] (Pondichéry: Institut Français d'Indologie, 1963-68), vol. I, 102 f. For the means of expiation, see *Śaiva-upaniṣads*, ed. by A. Mahadeva Sastri, (Madras: The Adyar Library 1950), trans. by T. R. Srinivasa Ayyangar, (Madras: The Adyar Library 1955), 142 and 149, where *bhasma*, sacred ashes, is praised as the great remover of sins: "This *bhasma* alone is possessed of the special virtue of bestowing the knowledge of Hari and Śaṅkara, of destroying the most heinous sins resulting from the murder of a *brahmana* and the like and of bestowing great power and glory."

11. THE HINDU SACRAMENTS: THE *SAṀSKĀRAS*

1. On *saṁskāras* in general, the most exhaustive source is again P. V. Kane, *History of Dharmaśāstra*, vol. 2 (part 1) (Poona: B.O.R.I. ²1978.). See also R. B. Pandey, *Hindu Saṁskāras: Socio-religious Study of the Hindu Sacraments* (Delhi: Motilal Banarsidass 1969).

2. *Manusmṛti* II, 26.

3. *Dvija*, twice-born, is the designation of the upper three castes (*Brahmins, kṣatriyas*, and *vaiśyas*), whose initiation is considered to be a second, spiritual, birth.

4. *Manusmṛti* II, 27f.

5. The child gets a "secret name" immediately after birth, which is known only to the parents. *Manusmṛti* II, 30, says that the official name giving should take place "on the tenth or twelfth on a lucky *tithi*, in an auspicious *muhūrta*, under an auspicious constellation."

6. *Viṣṇu Purāṇa* III, 10.

7. *Manusmṛti* II, 33.

8. Hindus calculate their years of life from the day of conception, not from the day of birth. This must be kept in mind when mentioning age. A good study of the implication of *upanayana* is provided by B. K. Smith, "Ritual, Knowledge, and Being: Initiation and Veda Study in Ancient India," *Numen* 33, no. 1 (1986): 65-89, with a good bibliography.

9. *Viṣṇu Purāṇa* III, 10, says: "If he does not propose to enter into the married state, he may remain as a student with his teacher, first making a vow to that effect, and employ himself in the service of his guru and the *guru*'s descendants; or he may become at once a hermit or adopt the order of the religious mendicant according to his original determination."

10. *Manusmṛti* III, 20-42 mentions *brahmā, daiva, ārṣa, prājānatya, āsura, gāndharva, rākṣasa*, and *paiśaca*. It explains them and says that some of these are "blamable," though valid, e.g., forcible abduction of the bride (*rākṣasa*), seduction (*paiśaca*), love marriage (*gāndharva*), or bride buying (*āsura*).

11. J. Duncan M. Derret, *The Death of a Marriage Law: Epitaph for the Rishis* (Delhi: Vikas, 1978). Derret has written extensively on Hindu law and teaches Oriental law at the London School of Oriental and African Studies. Among his well known publications are *Hindu Law, Past and Present* (Calcutta: A. Mukherjee 1958); *Introduction to Modern Hindu Law* (Calcutta: A. Mukherjee 1963); *Critique of Modern Hindu Law* (Bombay: H. M. Tripathi 1970); *History of Indian Law* (Dharmasastra) (Leiden: Brill 1973); *Essays in Classical and Modern Hindu Law*, 4 vols. (Leiden: Brill 1976-79).

12. *Viṣṇu Purāṇa* III, 10; *Garuḍa Purāṇa* 62 f.

13. The most complete source for all details and variations of ritual is again Kane's *HDhS*, op. cit., vol. 2.

14. *Ṛgveda* X, 85, 36.

15. Ursa major.

16. Manu, however, also has a verse that would weaken this argument, when he says: "Many thousands of *brāhmaṇas* who were chaste from their youth,

have gone to heaven without continuing their race" (V, 159).

17. Ibid., III, 56.

18. Ibid., 58 f.

19. Ibid., VIII, 68.

20. Ibid., V, 154.

21. Ibid., 150.

22. *Ṛgveda* X, 14-18.

23. E.g., *Viṣṇu Purāṇa* III, 13.

24. The *Pretakalpa* of the *Garuḍapurāṇa* contains a wealth of information on beliefs concerning the afterlife.

12. THE PATH OF KNOWLEDGE: *JÑĀNAMĀRGA*

1. *Muktikā Upaniṣad* I, 30, 39, gives the list of the acknowledged 108 *Upaniṣads* and their classification with regard to the four Vedas.

2. The Samskṛti Samsthān Bareli (Uttar Pradesh) brought out in 1967 a complete edition of the 108 *Upaniṣads* (with Hindī paraphrase) divided into three volumes, *Jñāna Khaṇḍa, Sādhana Khaṇḍa*, and *Brahma Vidyā Khaṇḍa.*

3. A survey of recent work done in this area is given in P. J. Chinmulgund and V. V. Mirashi, eds., *Review of Indiological Research in the Last 75 Years* (Poona: Bharatiya Charitrakosha Mandal, 1967), 40 ff.

4. This is the chronology given by R. D. Ranade in his excellent and comprehensive study, *A Constructive Survey of Upanishadic Philosophy: Being an Introduction to the Thought of the Upaniṣads*, (1926; reprint Bombay: Bharatiya Vidya Bhavan, 1968).

5. Thus, P. V. Kane.

6. Thus, e.g., J. Gonda and the majority of Indologists today.

7. Cf. R. D. Ranade, op. cit., 30-40.

8. *Muṇḍaka* II, 1, 1 ff.

9. *Chāṇḍogya* III, 19.

10. *Praśna* IV, 1.

11. *Chāṇḍogya* III, 14.

12. *Bṛhadāraṇyaka* II.

13. *Chāṇḍogya* VII, 17 ff.

14. Ellison Banks Findly, "Gārgī at the King's Court: Women and Philosophic Innovation in Ancient India," in *Women, Religion and Social Change*, Y. Y. Haddad and E. B. Findly, eds. (Albany: State University of New York Press, 1985), 37-85.

15. E.g., *Śvetāśvatara* IX.

16. E.g., the *Māṇḍūkya*, which reduces everything to OM.

17. *Bṛhadāraṇyaka* IV, 5, 15.

18. E.g., *Chāṇḍogya* VIII, 9 ff.

19. *Taittirīya* I, 7.

20. Meister Eckhart in one of his sermons states: "Why does my eye recognize the sky, and why do not my feet recognize it? Because my eye is more akin to heaven than my feet. Therefore my soul must be divine if it is to recognize God!" Platonic and the later Stoic philosophy with their ideas of cosmic harmony and correspondence between man and universe have kept those ideas alive even in the West.

21. *Chāṇḍogya* II.

22. *Bṛhadāraṇyaka* I, 2.

23. Ibid., III, 7.

24. *Māṇḍūkya* 3 ff.

25. *Muṇḍaka* I, 1, 4 ff.

26. Neo-Platonism, possibly under Indian influence, is the one Western intellectual tradition that comes closest to Vedānta. Plotinus, Proclus, Jamblichus, and others also speak of stages of ascent of the soul, of the need to turn inward and to dissociate consciousness from the senses.

27. *Īśa* 9.

28. *Upadeśasahasrī*, ascribed to Śaṅkara, no. 6.

29. End of *Chāṇḍogya*.

13. *ĀTMAN* AND *BRAHMAN:* SELF AND ALL

1. *Bṛhadāraṇyaka Upaniṣad* III, 8.

2. Ibid., III, 9, 1, 9.

3. *Taittirīya Upaniṣad* II, 1 f.

4. *Chāṇḍogya Upaniṣad* VI, 8 ff.

5. Ibid., VIII, 7.

6. *Muṇḍaka Upaniṣad* II, 2, 10 ff.
7. *Bṛhadāraṇyaka Upaniṣad* I, 4.
8. *Chāṇḍogya Upaniṣad* VI, 8, 7.
9. *Bṛhadāraṇyaka Upaniṣad* II, 5, 19.
10. *Aitareya Upaniṣad* III, 1, 3.

14. *KARMA, VIDYĀ, MOKṢA:* LIBERATION FROM REBIRTH

1. *Bṛhadāraṇyaka Upaniṣad* IV, 4, 1-7.
2. Ibid., I, 2, 7; III, 2, 10, etc. It should be emphasized that the frightening factor is not so much rebirth but the repeated painful experience of death!
3. *Kaṭha Upaniṣad.*
4. *Muṇḍaka Upaniṣad* III, 1, 10.
5. *Kaṭha Upaniṣad* I, 5 ff.
6. This is a reference to the *pañcāgni vidyā*, discussed immediately before this passage.
7. *Bṛhadāraṇyaka Upaniṣad* VI, 2, 15. Cf. also *Chāṇḍogya Upaniṣad* V, 10, 5.
8. A comprehensive coverage of the understanding of *karma* in various schools is given in W. D. O'Flaherty, ed., *Karma and Rebirth in Classical Indian Traditions* (Berkeley: University of California Press, 1980) and in R. Neufeldt, ed., *Karma and Rebirth: Post-Classical Developments* (Albany: State University of New York Press, 1986).
9. There are other expressions in Sanskrit for *fate*, such as *daivam, bhāgyam, niyati*, etc.
10. *Muṇḍaka Upaniṣad* I, 2, 7 ff.
11. *Chāṇḍogya Upaniṣad* IV, 11, 3.
12. *Muṇḍaka Upaniṣad* II, 2, 9.
13. One of the varieties of the Śiva *naṭarāja* image, in which Śiva is shown with his right leg thrown high up is interpreted as showing how Śiva accepts into himself all the *karma* of his devotees, so as to offer them instant liberation.
14. The term *mukti* occurs only once in the principal *Upaniṣads*, namely, in *Bṛhadāraṇyaka* III, 1, 3. The term *mokṣa* is used several times in the *Maitrī Upaniṣad* VI, 30.
15. S. N. Dasgupta, *HIPh*, vol. 1, 48.
16. *Muṇḍaka Upaniṣad* III, 2, 6.

17. *Praśna Upaniṣad* IV, 11.

18. *Muṇḍaka Upaniṣad* III, 3, 8 f.

19. *Bṛhadāraṇyaka Upaniṣad* III, 8.

20. *Kaṭha Upaniṣad* II, 3, 8 f.

21. *Taittirīya Upaniṣad* II, 9.

22. Ibid., I, 2, 1 f.

23. *Muṇḍaka Upaniṣad* III, 2, 8.

15. THE PATH OF LOVING DEVOTION: *BHAKTIMĀRGA*

1. The *Śabdakalpadruma* III, 463b f. offers the following etymology under the entry *bhaktiḥ:* "*Vibhāga* [division, separation] *sevā* [worship, service] and refers to the two roots *bhañj-* [to split, to disappoint] and *bhā-* [to serve, to honor]."

2. That they were not considered as of equal importance even within *bhakta*-circles is demonstrated by the fact that they have not been commented upon as extensively as the *Brahmasūtras.* The real textbooks of *bhakti* are the *Purāṇas* and the special compendia of the various *saṁpradāyas: Saṁhitās, Āgamas,* and *Tantras.*

3. *Bhaktidarśana,* with Hindī paraphrase, Swami Jnanandaji Maharaj, ed. (Bombay: Sake 1844), 23 ff.

4. Swami Tyagisananda, ed., *Aphorisms on the Gospel of Divine Love or Nārada Bhakti Sūtras,* Sanskrit text with English translation and copious notes, (Madras: Ramakrishna Math Mylapore, 1955). The notes offer numerous other definitions and descriptions of *bhakti.*

5. *Bhagavadgītā* XII, 6 ff.

6. P. V. Kane, *HDhS,* vol. 5 (part 2), 950 f.

7. *Kaṭha Upaniṣad* II, 22; *Muṇḍaka Upaniṣad* III, 2, 3.

8. Another striking instance is offered by the *puruṣa-sūkta,* which contains the Vaiṣṇava cosmogony *in nucleo:* everything owes its existence to a transformation of a part of the body of the *puruṣottama.*

9. A good survey of literature in English on *bhakti* (up to 1975) is provided by Eleanor Zelliot, "The Mediaeval Bhakti Movement in History. An Essay on the Literature in English," in *Hinduism: New Essays in the History of Religions,* B. L. Smith, ed. (Leiden: Brill, 1976).

10. *Sad-nām* is the key term in this religion, meaning the most profound revelation of God.

11. A famous collection is the *Bṛhatstotraratnakaraḥ* (Bombay: Sri Venkatesvar Press) containing 224 hymns, in many editions, with old illustrations. The Ramakrishna Mission has also brought out small collections of hymns with translations.

12. *Bhāgavata Purāṇa.*

13. Ibid., VI, 2, 14; XII, 12, 46.

14. Each crore equals 10 million.

15. *Kalyāṇa Kalpataru* 18, no. 1 (August 1952): 3 f.

16. Cf. Swami Rupa Gosvami, *Bhaktirasāmṛtasindhu*, V. Snataka, ed. I, 2, 90 f.

17. *Varāha Purāṇa*, Chapter 68.

18. *Padma Purāna* IV, 263.

19. *Bhagavadgītā* VII, 15.

20. Tyagisananda, ed., op. cit., 82 f.

21. *Bhāgavata Purāna*, VII, 5, 23 f.

22. *Rāmānuja's Vedārthasaṁgraha*, S. S. Raghavchar, ed. and trans. (Mysore: Ramakrishna Ashrama, 1956), 23.

23. Cf. *Sarvadarśanasaṁgraha* of Mādhava, V. S. Abhyankar, ed. (Poona: B.O.R.I. [3]1978), Chapter 5, the Pūrṇaprajñā system.

24. An important reference work is S. K. De, *Early History of the Vaiṣṇava Faith and Movement in Bengal* (Calcutta: Firma K. L. Mukhopadhyay 1961). Recently possibly under the influence of *bhakti* missions in the West, much scholarly literature devoted to the study of *bhakti* literature has come out. Jayadeva's *Gītāgoviṇḍa* received a large amount of attention. Cf. B. Stoler-Miller, *Love Song of the Dark Lord* (New York: Columbia University Press, 1977); G. Kuppuswami and M. Hariharan, eds. *Jaya-deva and Gītāgoviṇḍa: A Study*, (Trivandrum: College Book House 1980), with a contribution by B. Stoler-Miller "Rādhā: Consort of Kṛṣṇa's Vernal Passion," earlier published in *JAOS* 95, no. 4 (1975): 655-71; L. Siegel, *Sacred and Profane Dimensions of Love in Indian Traditions as Exemplified in the Gītāgoviṇḍa of Jayadeva* (Oxford: Oxford University Press, 1978). See also Basanti Choudhury, "Love Sentiment and Its Spiritual Implications in Gauḍīa Vaiṣṇavism," in *Bengal Vaiṣṇavsm, Orientalism, Society and the Arts*, D. T. O'Connel, ed., South Asia Series Occasional Papers No. 35. (East Lansing: Asian Studies Center, Michigan State University, 1985).

25. Cf. Krishna Chaitanya, *Sanskrit Poetics* (Bombay: Asia Publishing House 1965). Cf. P. V. Kane, *History of Sanskrit Poetics* (Delhi: Motilal Banarsidass, [3]1961), 355 ff.; the Rasa School: "*Rasa* primarily means 'taste' or 'flavour' or 'savour' or 'relish' but metaphorically it means 'emotional experience of

beauty in poetry and drama'." By contrast Swami Bon Maharaj, *Bhaktirasāmṛtasindhu* (Vrindaban: Institute of Oriental Philosophy 1964) vol. 1 n. 2: "There is no English equivalent for *rasa.* It is a purely spiritual expression which may be explained like this. When the heart is perfectly purified of all the possible dirts of the three *guṇas* or attributes of *Māyā*, the Deluding Energy of the Godhead, viz., *rajas, tamas* and *sattvas*, and when the unalloyed soul as distinct from the physical body of flesh and blood and the subtle body of mind-intelligence-ego far transcends the realm of imagination and mental thought-world, the fourfold ingredients called *Vibhāva, Anu-bhāva, Sāttvika-bhāva* and *Sañcari-bhāva* of mellow-sweetness of the sentiment of the innate normal nature of the *cit*-soul combine with *Sthāyī-bhāva* or permanent and eternal as also unconditional relation that exists between God and the individual soul, in manifold shades and forms, it gives rise to an inexplicably wondrous flow of charm, which is *Rasa.*"

26. Cf. Viśvanātha Cakravartti, "*Bhaktirasāmṛtasindhubinduḥ*," K. Klostermaier, trans., *JOAS* 94, no. 1 (1974): 96-107.

27. Kṛṣṇadāsa Goswāmī, *Caitanyacaritāmṛta*, Mādhyalīlā XIX and XXII.

28. *Vedāntaratnamañjuṣa* VI.

29. *Sarvadarśanasaṁgraha of Mādhava*, op. cit., Chapter 7, "The Paśupata System." An example of what Hindus call the *pagala* (mad-type) of *bhakti* is available in Anne Feldhaus, trans. and annot., *The Deeds of God in Ṛddhipur*, with introductory essays by Anne Feldhaus and E. Zelliot (New York: Oxford University Press, 1984).

30. V. A. Devasenapathi, *Śaiva Siddhānta as Expounded in the Śivajñāna Siddhiyar and Its Six Commentaries* (Madras: University of Madras 1960), 250 ff. On Śiva *bhakti* in South India, Carl A. Keller, "Aspiration collective et éxperience individuelle dans la bhakti shivaite de l'Inde du sud," *Numen*, 31, no. 1 (July 1984): 1-12, with an ample bibliography.

31. Translation from E. J. Thompson and A. M. Spencer, *Bengali Religious Lyrics, Śākta.* The Heritage of India Series, No. 47. (Calcutta: Association Press 1923), 60. Cf. also Lupsa, M. *Chants á Kali de Rāmprasād*, with introduction, trans. and notes. (Pondichéry: Institute Français d'Indologie, 1967).

32. *Words of Godrealization*, (Sarnath: Rama Tirtha Pratisthan, 1956) 415.

33. *Paramārtha Sopāna*, R. D. Ranade, ed. (Allahabad: Adhyatma Vidya Mandir Sangli 1954).

34. Tyagisananda, ed., op. cit., 5 ff.

16. LORD VIṢṆU AND HIS DEVOTEES

1. *Viṣṇu Purāṇa* I, 19, 64 ff.

2. The most complete survey is offered in Ramdas Gaur, *Hindutva*, (Kāśī: Visva-

prasad Gupta, 1995), Chapter 17, "Bhāgavata yā vaiṣṇava mata." The doctrinal side is well covered in S. N. Dasgupta, *HIPh*, vols. 3 and 4.

3. *Ṛgveda* I, 22; I, 154: VII, 100.

4. *Ṛgveda* X, 90.

5. "Śāntiparvan," in *Mahābhārata, Critical Edition* (Poona: Bhandarkar Oriental Research Institute, 1954), vol. 16, Chapter 321 ff.

6. *Bhagavadgītā* IV, 7 f. One of the most extensive studies was done by Brajendranath Seal, in 1899, under the title *Comparative Studies in Vaishnavism and Christianity with an Examination of the Mahābhārata Legend about Nārada's Pilgrimage to Śvetadvīpa and an Introduction on the Historico-Comparative Method.* In articles in the *Journal of the Royal Asiatic Society of Bengal* in 1907, J. Kennedy tried to prove Christian influence on the development of Viṣṇu-*bhakti.* His claims were refuted by B. D. Basu, trans., *Balarāma Vedāntasūtrabhāṣya* Sacred Books of the Hindus, vol. 5 (Allahabad: Panini Office, 1934), Appendix 1, "The Origin of Bhakti Doctrine." N. Chaudhuri in his *Hinduism* (London: Methuen, 1979), 256 ff. again suggests Christian influence on the development of Kṛṣṇa *bhakti.*

7. The most comprehensive discussion of the theory of avatārahood may be R. Seemann, "Versuch zu einer Theorie des Avatāra. Mensch gewordener Gott oder Gott gewordener Mensch?" *Numen*, 33, no. 1 (July 1986): 90-140.

8. D. C. Sirkar, "Viṣṇu," *Quarterly Journal of the Mythological Society* 25 (1935): 120 ff.

9. For details consult, e.g., A. Daniélou, *Hindu Polytheism* (London: Routledge & Kegan Paul 1964) besides the sources, *Mahābhārata* and *Vaiṣṇava Purāṇas*, that deal extensively with several or all *avatāras.*

10. More about these in K. Klostermaier, *Mythologies* (Waterloo: Wilfrid Laurier University Press, 1984).

11. Ibid., pp. 73 ff.

12. *Bhāgavata Purāṇa* VI, 8.

13. A. George, in *Social Ferment in India* (London: Althone Press, 1986), advances the theory that "The Rāma tradition probably goes much further back into remote layers of pre-Āryan folklore from the days of tribal struggles between Austric groups in the Gangetic valley. The word Gaṅgā itself has been identified linguistically with a non-Āryan Austric word signifying merely a river. All this may account for the seeming paradox whereby the suffix 'Rām', which ought to denote a blue-blooded Kshatriya prince, tends in modern India to be that of the lower castes" (p. 236).

14. *Bālakāṇḍa* I, 1, of the *Adhyātma Rāmāyaṇa*, which was written probably in the fifteenth century. Of great importance is the *Yogavāsiṣṭha Rāmāyaṇa*,

pertaining to the ninth to twelfth centuries, in which the Rāma story serves as frame for the exposition of Advaita Vedānta. The most popular of all books on Rāma, however, is the Hindī *Rāmacaritamānasa* by Tulasīdāsa, praised by Mahātmā Gāndhī as "the greatest religious book in the world." See the critical study by C. Bulcke, *Rāmakathā* (Prayag: Hindī Pariṣad, Viśvavidyālaya 1950).

15. Literature on Kṛṣṇa by Indian authors fills bibliographies. Critical-historical writing by Western scholars is growing steadily. Most of it is devoted to studying certain aspects of the Kṛṣṇa tradition. Thus, John Stratton Hawley, *Kṛṣṇa the Butter Thief* (Princeton: Princeton University Press, 1983). Cf. S. J. White, "Kṛṣṇa as Divine Child," *HR* 12, no. 2 (1972): 156-77; Norvin Hein, "A Revolution in Kṛṣṇaism: The Cult of Gopāla," *HR* 26, no. 3 (1986): 296-317; U. Schneider, "Kṛṣṇa's postumer Aufstieg. Zur Frühgeschichte der Bhaktibewegung," *Saeculum* 33, no. 1 (1982); 38-49. Many books on Indian Art, especially on Indian painting, are dealing with Kṛṣṇa as well; e.g., W. G. Archer, *The Loves of Krishna in Indian Painting and Poetry* (London: Allen & Unwin, 1957).

16. For more detail, see Klostermaier, op. cit.

17. The most thorough attempt to establish the historicity of Kṛṣṇa has been made by A. D. Pusalker. See his "Historicity of Kṛṣṇa," in *Epics and Purāṇas of India* (Bombay: Bharatiya Vidya Bhavan, 1955), 49-81; and "Traditional History from the Earliest Time to the Accession of Parīkshit," in *The Vedic Age*, vol. 1 of *HCIP* (Bombay: Bharatiya Vidya Bhavan, ^{4}1965), 271-322. Pusalker places the Kṛṣṇa period ca. 1950-1400 B.C.E. Recent archeological excavations in Dwāraka, the reputed capital city of Kṛṣṇa are supposed to have confirmed these assumptions.

18. The most complete Kṛṣṇa scripture is the *Bhāgavata Purāṇa.*

19. Cf. K. Klostermaier, *In the Paradise of Kṛṣṇa*, (Philadelphia: Westminster Press, 1971).

20. Several recent theses have devoted substantial attention to the position of Śrī. E. T. Hardy, *Emotional Kṛṣṇa Bhakti*, (London: London School of Oriental and African Studies, 1978); V. Rajagopalan, "The Śrī Vaiṣṇava Understanding of Bhakti and Prapatti" (Thesis, University of Bombay, 1978); M. R. Paramesvaran "The Twofold Vedānta of Śrīvaiṣṇavism" (Thesis, University of Manitoba, 1981).

21. See J. A. B. van Buitenen, "The Name Pāñcarātra," *HR* 1, no. 2 (1961): 291-99, with numerous references to other literature.

22. *Yatīndramatadīpikā of Śrīnivāsadāsa*, Swami Adidevananda, ed., and trans. (Madras: Ramakrishna Math Mylapore, 1949).

23. III, 26, 12.

24. J. B. Carman in *The Theology of Rāmānuja. An Essay in Interreligious Under-*

standing (New Haven and London: Yale University Press, 1974), deals only with some aspects of Rāmānuja's theology but provides extensive background and full information on the sources of Śrīvaiṣṇavism. A systematic exposition of the thought of Rāmānuja is given in Krishna Datta Bharadwaj, *The Philosophy of Rāmānuja*, (New Delhi: Sir Sankar Lall Charitable Trust Society, 1958).

25. *Vedārthasaṁgraha*, S. S. Raghavachar, ed. and trans. (Mysore: Ramakrishna Ashrama, 1956).

26. *Śrībhāṣya* II, 1, 3.

27. Ibid., II, 3, 41.

28. *Vedārthasaṁgraha*, 126, a slightly condensed rendering.

29. *Śrībhāṣya* I, 1, 4.

30. A good comparison of the main points of difference is given in Narasinha Iyengar, ed., and trans., *Mumukṣupadi of Lokācārya* (Madras: Adyar Library 1962), Introduction.

31. Cf. B. N. K. Sharma, *Madhva's Teaching in His Own Words*, (Bombay: Bhavan's Book University, 1961). A very thorough study of Madhva's theology was recently made by I. Puthiadan, an Indian Jesuit, *Viṣṇu the Ever Free: A Study of the Madhva Concept of God*, Dialogue Series No. 5 (Madurai: Dialogue Series 1985).

32. Roma Chaudhuri, "The Nimbārka School of Vedānta," in *CHI*, vol. 3, 333.

33. Rāmdās Gaur (op. cit., 674 ff., "*Puṣṭimārga*") enumerates also the successors to Vallabha and the main points of doctrine. See M. V. Joshi, "The Concept of Brahman in Vallabha Vedānta," *JBOI* 22, no. 4 (June 1973): 474-83; and, with a polemical twist, B. S. Yadav, "Vaiṣṇavism on Hans Küng: A Hindu Theology of Religious Pluralism," *Religion and Society* 27, no. 2 (June 1980): 32-64.

34. The best work, with substantial translations from many sources, is W. Eidlitz, *Kṛṣṇa-Caitanya, Sein Leben und Seine Lehre*, Stockholm Studies in Comparative Religion 7 (Stockholm: Almquist and Wiksell 1968). A good historical survey is offered by R. C. Majumdar, *Caitanya: His Life and Doctrine* (Bombay: 1969).

35. The "*Śīkṣāṣṭaka*" in *Caitanya Caritāmṛtam* III, 20, 3-45, is considered to be his own formulation of the essence of Vaiṣṇavism.

36. *The Vedāntasūtras of Bādarāyaṇa with the Commentary of Bāladeva*, Srisa Candra Vasu Vidyarnava, trans., vol. 5 *SBH* (Allahabad: Panini Office, 1934).

37. Among Indian scholars writing in English on this subject are R. D. Ranade *Pathway to God in Hindi Literature* (Bombay: Bharatiya Vidya Bhavan 1959); *Pathway to God in Marathi Literature* (Bombay: Bharatiya Vidya

Bhavan 1961); and *Pathway to God in Kannada Literature* (Bombay: Bharatiya Vidya Bhavan 1960); and Bankey Bihari, *Sufis, Mystics, and Yogis of India* (Bombay: Bharatiya Vidya Bhavan 1962) and *Bhakta Mīrā*, (Bombay: Bharatiya Vidya Bhavan 1961), who deserve special mention. See also V. Raghavan, *The Great Integrators: The Saint Singers of India*, (Delhi: Ministry of Information and Broadcasting 1966), a good selection of mediaeval religious poetry in translation. Among Western writers C. Vaudeville deserves special credit for her scholarly monographs and translations (in French and English) dealing with Kabīr, Tulasīdāsa, and others. See also M. Neog, *Early History of the Vaiṣṇava Faith and Movement in Assam: Śaṅkaradeva and His Time* (Delhi: Motilal Banarsidass, [2]1985).

38. J. S. Hawley has recently brought out a very attractive monograph on Sūrdās with beautifully translated texts. *Sūrdās: Poet, Singer, Saint* (Seattle: University of Washington Press, 1984).

39. My own translation, following the text in R. D. Ranade, *Paramārtha Sopāna* (Sourcebook of Pathway to God in Hindi Literature) (Allahabad: Adhyatma Vidya Mandir Sangli, Nimbal (R.S.) 1954), 2 (part I, Chapter 1, 1). J. S. Hawley offers a translation in *Sūrdās*, ibid., 173, which differs quite substantially from mine. He probably followed a different edition. While not claiming to be as knowledgeable on Sūrdās as Hawley or as poetically gifted, I decided to give my own translation because it conveys—or so I believe—better the simplicity and earthiness of the original. I have made a number of translations of the texts in *Paramārtha Sopāna* which I hope to have published at some later date.

40. A good contemporary example is Swami Ramdas, *God-Experience*, (Bombay: Bharatiya Vidya Bhavan, 1963).

41. Bankey Bihari, *Bhakta Mira*, op. cit., 109.

17. ŚIVA: THE GRACE AND THE TERROR OF GOD

1. A. K. Ramanujan, *Speaking of Śiva* (Harmondsworth, U.K.: Penguin Books, 1973), 71.

2. Stotra 53 in *Bṛhatstotraratnakāra* (96 f.), ascribed to Vyāsa.

3. Sir Mortimer Wheeler, *The Indus Civilization* (Cambridge: Cambridge University Press, 1953). Doris Srinivasan, "Unhinging Śiva from the Indus Civilization," *Journal of the Royal Asiatic Society of Great Britain and Ireland* 1 (1984): 77-89, tries to prove that the *liṅgams* found in remnants of the Indus civilization do not present a case for an origin of Śaivism in that civilization. Tribal-prehistoric origin of *liṅgam* worship is widely accepted today.

4. B. K. Ghosh, "*The Aryan Problem*," in *HCIP*, vol. 1, 207. In the oldest ritual texts, care is taken not to mention the name of this "terrible god" directly.

5. Cf. *Mahābhārata Śāntiparvan* 274: *Droṇaparvan* 201, 64-82; *Sauptikaparvan*

18; *VāyuPurāṇa* I, 30; *Śiva Purāṇa, Vāyavīyasaṁhitā* , 23, and numerous other places.

6. I have developed the argument more fully in "The Original Dakṣa Saga," *Journal of South Asian Literature* 20, no. 1 (1985): 93-107.

7. T. M. P. Mahadevan, *"Śaivism" in HCIP* vol. 2, 454.

8. This is the source of the *Śiva-avatāras,* which never gained an importance in actual Śiva worship. Among the Vaiṣṇava Purāṇas, the *Vāmana Purāṇa* also has Śaivite materials and the *Viṣṇu Purāṇa* explains the origin of the eight Rudras in I, 8.

9. Kumara Gupta (415-455 C.E.) was a Śaiva king. The Huna king Mīhirakula seems to have been Śaiva, as were many of his contemporary rulers in Bengal and the Deccan. Mahendra Varman I (600-630), a convert from Jainism, made his capital, Kāñcī, into a stronghold of Śaivism, embellishing it with temples and statues of Śiva.

10. *HCIP,* vol. 4, 300 f.

11. *Ṛgveda* I, 114; II, 33; VII, 46.

12. It forms the sixteenth chapter of the *Yajurveda* according to the *Vajasaneya-saṁhitā.* English translations in J. Eggeling, *Śaṭapathabrāhmaṇa,* vol. 4 (*SBE,* vol. 43), 150 ff.; and in R. T. H. Griffith, *The Texts of the White Yajurveda* (Benares: E. J. Lazarus [3]1957), 168.

13. It forms Chapter 15 of the *Atharvaveda,* W. D. Whitney, trans. (HOS, 1902; reprint Varanasi: Motilal Banarsidass 1962), Introduction, 769 ff. See also J. W. Hauer, *Der Vrātya: Untersuchungen über die nichtbrahmanische Religion Altindiens* (Stuttgart: Kohlhammer, 1927).

14. *Atharvaveda* XV, 5, 1 ff.

15. *Aitareya Brāhmaṇa* I, 3, 9 f.

16. Text and translation in S. Radhakrishnan, *The Principal Upaniṣads* (London: Allen & Unwin 1953), 707-50.

17. *Śvetāśvatara Upaniṣad* VI, 11.

18. *Anuśāsanaparvan,* 135.

19. The oldest among the Śaiva Purāṇas is probably the *Vāyu Purāṇa,* which was written before the second century C.E. according to R. C. Hazra, *CHI,* vol. 2, 240 f. The *Śiva Purāṇa,* a very important source for many features of later Śaivism, belongs to the class of *Upapurāṇas.* For more detailed information, consult L. Rocher, "The Purāṇas," in *HIL,* vol. 2 (part 3) (Wiesbaden: Otto Harrassowitz 1986).

20. *Śiva Purāṇa, Rudrasaṁhitā Sātīkhaṇḍa* 38, 34 f.

21. V. Paranjoti, *Śaiva Siddhānta* (London: Luzac 1954), 53 ff.: "The importance attached to the dance of Śiva is due to the fact that it symbolizes in graphic, concrete and dynamic form the religion and philosophy of Śaiva Siddhānta. Hence the dance cannot be understood without the philosophy which it adumbrates in its movements. Love is the motif of the dance; the dance is love in practical form." On Śaivasiddhānta, see also V. A. Devasenapathi, *Śaiva Siddhānta as Expounded in the Śivajñāna Siddhiyār and Its Six Commentaries* (Madras: University of Madras, 1960); and K. Sivaraman, *Śaivism in Philosophical Perspective* (Delhi: Motilal Banarsidass, 1973).

22. *Śiva Purāṇa, Śatarudrasaṁhitā*, 1 ff.; and *Vāyavīyasaṁhitā* II, 9.

23. *Śiva Purāṅa, Kotirudrasaṁhitā* 38 ff.

24. Several *Āgamas* have been published recently by the Institute Français d'Indologie at Pondichéry, containing the *padas* on *kriyā* (ritual) and *caryā* (mode of life). E.g., *Rauravāgama* (with an important introduction by J. Filliozat, "Les Āgamas çivaites," in vol. 1), *Mṛgendrāgama, Ajitāgama, Mataṅgaparameśvarāgama*, all edited by N. R. Bhatt.

25. *Sarvadarśanasaṁgraha of Mādhava*, Chapter 6, quoting from the *Gaṇakarikā*, an ancient *Pāśupata* textbook.

26. Cf. V. A. Devasenapathi, op. cit.

27. Ibid., 192.

28. Ibid., 175.

29. Ibid., 257.

30. Śrīkaṇṭha *Brahmasūtrabhāṣya* IV, 4, 22. English translation by Roma Chaudhuri, 2 vols. (Calcutta: Pracyavani 1959-62).

31. Jaideva Singh, in his edition and translation of the *Pratyabhijñāhṛdayam* (Delhi: Motilal Banarsidass 1963), mentions his guru, Lakṣman Joo, as "practically the sole surviving exponent of this system in Kashmir." Recently, however, Gopī Kṛṣṇa, a layman who describes his own realization more or less according to classical Kaśmīr-Śaivism has written a number of publications that might gain more adherents and students to the system.

32. *Śiva Purāṇa, Kailāsasaṁhitā* 17-19.

33. *Sarvadarśanasaṁgraha of Mādhava*, Chapter 8.

34. Quoted by Jaideva Singh, op. cit., 21.

35. Cf. S. C. Nandimath, *A Handbook of Vīraśaivism* (Dharwar: Lingayat Educational Association 1942). A very attractive introduction to Vīraśaivism is provided by A. K. Ramanujan in *Speaking of Śiva* (Hammondsworth, U.K.: Penguin Classics, 1973). Besides artistic renderings in English of numerous *vacanas*, lyrics by Liṅgāyat poet-saints, the book also contains valuable intro-

ductions by A. K. Ramanujan and an essay on "Lingāyat Culture" by William McCormack.

36. Hayavadana Rao, ed., (Bangalore: Bangalore Press 1936). Not all *Vīraśaivas*, however, accept Śrīpati's interpretation.

37. Sri Kumaraswamiji, "*Vīraśaivism*," in *CHI*, vol. 4, 101.

38. Ibid.

39. Cf. S. Satchidanandam Pillai, "The Śaiva Saints of South India," in *CHI*, vol. 4, 339 ff. See also C. V. Narayana Ayyar, *Origin and Early History of Śaivism in South India* (Madras: 1936).

40. *Tiruvācakam* VI, 50, Ratna Navaratnam, trans. (Bombay: Bharatiya Vidya Bhavan 1963), 126. The most celebrated complete translation of the *Tiruvācakam* was made by the Rev. G. V. Pope in 1903, reprinted 1970 by the University of Madras in a Jubilee edition.

41. *Tiruvācakam* XXV, 8-10; ibid., 181.

42. Cf. T. M. P. Mahadevan, "Śaivism," in *HCIP*, vol. 3, 433 ff.

43. F. Kingsbury and G. E. Philips, *Hymns of the Tamil Śaivite Saints*, Heritage of India Series (Calcutta: Association Press), 77.

44. R. M. P. Mahadevan, *HCIP*, vol. 2, 458 ff.

45. With photography by P. C. Patel (Princeton: Princeton University Press, 1981).

46. See the biographical sketch of Kramrisch by B. Stoler-Miller in *Exploring India's Sacred Art*, (Philadelphia: University of Pennsylvania, 1983), 3-33.

47. Bollingen Series (New York: 1964).

48. Besides her widely known monograph *Asceticism and Eroticism in the Mythology of Śiva* (London: Oxford University Press, 1973), she has written a number of scholarly articles on Śiva symbols and myths.

49. Besides the numerous books by Gopī Kṛṣṇa expounding Kuṇḍalinī Yoga the remarkable book of C. F. von Weizsäcker and Gopi Kṛṣṇa, *Biologische Basis Religiöser Erfahrung* (Weilheim: Otto Wilhelm Barth Verlag, 1971) deserves mention.

18. DEVĪ: THE DIVINE MOTHER

1. *Devīmāhātmya* I, 75, ff. (from *Mārkaṇḍeya Purāṇa* 81).

2. John Woodroffe, under the pen-name Arthur Avalon, did much to make the *Tantras* known in the West. See his translation of the *Mahānirvāṇatantra: The Great Liberation* (Madras: Ganesh & Co. [4]1963). For Tantric doctrines in general, his *Principles of Tantra*, a translation of the *Tantratattva* of Śivacandra Vidyāraṇya, may be recommended (Madras: Ganesh & Co. [3]1960).

For beginners, the *Introduction to Tantra Śāstra* (Madras: Ganesh & Co. 1963), provides the explanation of the technical terms. More recent scholarly writing on *Tantra* includes H. V. Günther, *Yuganādha: The Tantric View of Life* (Benares: 1952; Reprint: Boulder, Colo.: Shambala, 1976); and A. Bharati, *The Tantric Tradition* (London: Rider and Co., 1965). See also the richly illustrated volume by Ajit Mookerjee and Madhu Kanna, *The Tantric Way. Art-Science-Ritual*, (London: Thames & Hudson, 1977), with bibliography.

3. Sanskrit edition (Kāśī: Paṇḍit Pustakālāya, Saṁvat 2016); English translation by Swami Vijñānanda, *SBH*. For a fuller treatment, consult R. C. Hazra, *Studies in the Upapurāṇas*, vol. 2: *The Śākta Upapurāṇas* (Calcutta: Sanskrit College, 1963), 1-361.

4. For more details on Devī mythology, Śākta systems, and iconography of the goddess, see *Mythologies*, Part IV.

5. R. C. Hazra, op. cit., 19 f.: "The story of Devī's killing of the demon Mahiṣa in a previous *kalpa* and the tradition that whenever Devī kills the demons she has a lion as her mount seem to be based on the aboriginal concept of Devī as a spirit controlling wild beasts. The bell which is said to be carried by Devī might have been originally meant for scaring away wild beasts." Cf. also H. Whitehead, *The Village Gods of South India*, Religious Life of India Series, (Calcutta: Association Press 1921), passim.

6. The most recent comprehensive study is by H. von Stietencron, "Die Göttin Durgā Mahiṣāsuramārdinī: Mythos, Darstellung und geschichtliche Rolle bei der Hinduisierung Indiens," in *Visible Religion, Annual for Religious Iconography*, vol. 2: *Representations of Gods.* (Leiden: Brill, 1983), 11-166, with illustrations.

7. *Devīmāhātmya* X, 1 ff.

8. See P. V. Kane, *HDhS*, vol. 5 (part 1), 154 ff.

9. *Devī Purāṇa* 38.

10. *Devī Bhāgavata* passim; *Śiva Purāṇa Umāsaṁhitā* 28-45.

11. *Kālikā Purāṇa* 15.

12. Śiva without the *i* is Śava, a corpse.

13. The five *m*'s are *maṁsa* (meat), *matsya* (fish), *mudra* (fried rice), *mada* (intoxicants), and *maithuna* (intercourse).

14. H. D. Bhattacharya, "Tantrik Religion," in *HCIP*, vol. 4, 320.

15. Ibid., 321.

16. *Mahānirvāṇa Tantra* XVIII, 154 ff.

17. Cf. D. N. Bose, *Tantras: Their Philosophy and Occult Secrets* (Calcutta: Oriental

Publishing Co. 1956), Chapter 10, "Tantric Symbols and Practices," explains a number of basic *yantras.*

18. For details see R. Fonseca, "Constructive Geometry and the Śrī-Cakra Diagram," *Religion* 16, no. 1 (1986): 33-49. A very professional study of Devī iconography is Om Prakash Misra's *Mother Goddess in Central India* (Delhi: Agam Kala Prakashan, 1985).

19. Cf. John Woodroffe, *Introduction to Tantra Śāstra,* op. cit., 42 ff.

20. "Kālikā Purāṇa," Chapter 14, is called the *rudhirādhyāya* or "blood chapter." A. P. Karmarkar, "Religion and Philosophy of the Epics," in *CHI,* cites many historical instances of human sacrifices in honor of Kālī. Volunteers were offered every Friday at the Kālī temple in Tanjore up to the nineteenth century. The head of the victims was placed on a golden plate before Kālī, the lungs were cooked and eaten by Kandra Yogis, the royal family ate rice cooked in the blood of the victim.

21. D. C. Sirkar, *Śākta Pīṭhas* rev. ed. (Delhi: Motilal Banarsidass, n.d.).

22. Beni Kanta Kakati, *The Mother Goddess Kāmākhyā* (Gauhati: Lawyers Book Stall 1948). The snake goddess Manasā is widely worshipped especially in South India.

23. Cf. Maryla Falk, *Nāma-Rūpa and Dharma-Rūpa; Origin and Aspects of an Ancient Indian Conception* (Calcutta: University of Calcutta, 1943), 2 ff.

24. *Tripurā Rahasya, Jñānakāṇḍa,* A. U. Vasavada, English trans. (Varanasi: Chowkhamba 1965), 156 f.

25. Ibid.

26. A description of *vāmācāri* practices is given in H. Wilson, *The Religious Sects of the Hindus* (reprint Calcutta: Punthi Pustak, 1958), 142 f. He also gives the translation of the *Śakti Sudhāna.*

27. V. S. Agrawala, "Mother Earth," in *Nehru Abhinandan Granth,* (Calcutta: Nehru Abhinandan Granth Committee 1949), 490 ff.

28. Some of the recent books are D. R. Kinsley, *The Sword and the Flute: Kālī and Kṛṣṇa, Dark Visions of the Terrible and the Sublime in Hindu Mythology* (Berkeley: University of California Press, 1975); C. M. Brown, *God as Mother: A Feminine Theology in India* (Hartford, Vt.: Claude Stark, 1974). D. Jacobsen and S. Wadley, eds., *Women in India: Two Perspectives* (Delhi: Manohar Book Service 1977); J. S. Hawley and D. M. Wulff, eds., *The Divine Consort: Rādhā and the Goddesses of India, Berkeley Religious Studies Series* (Berkeley: University of California Press, 1982); L. E. Gatwood, *Devī and the Spouse Goddess: Women, Sexuality and Marriage in India* (Delhi: Manohar, 1985).

29. Sanjukta Gupta and Richard Gombrich, "Kings, Power and the Goddess," *South Asia Research,* 6, no. 2 (November 1986): 127.

30. *BLITZ—"India's Greatest Weekly"* reported on its front page: "Tantrik priest dies half-way through *havan* to kill Indira" (11 April 1970).

19. MUDALVAN, MURUGAN, MĀL: THE GREAT GODS OF THE TAMILS

1. On Agastya, see the entry in John Dowson, *A Classical Dictionary of Hindu Mythology* (London: Routledge & Kegan Paul [10]1961), 4 ff., which provides the major references for Agastya in *Ṛgveda, Mahābhārata*, and *Rāmāyaṇa* and specifically says: "The name of Agastya holds a great place in Tamil literature, and he is venerated in the south as the first teacher of science and literature to the primitive Dravidian tribes." The authority of Dr. Caldwell is cited who thinks that "we shall not greatly err in placing the era of Agastya in the seventh, or at least in the sixth century B.C.". See also information on the Agastaya tradition in volume 2 of *HCIP*, 290 ff.
2. For several years secessionist movements in Tamiḷnādu were agitating for an independent Tamiḷnādu outside the Republic of India.
3. On dates concerning the *Saṅgam* (*Cankam*) see *HCIP*, op. cit., vol. 2, 291 ff., and K. A. Nilakanta Sastri, *The Culture and History of the Tamils* (Calcutta: Firma K. L. Mukhopadhyay, 1964), 127 ff. See also C. Jesudason and H. Jesudason, *A History of Tamil Literature*, Heritage of India Series (Calcutta: Y.M.C.A. Publishing House 1961).
4. N. Chaudhuri, *Hinduism* (London: Methuen, 1979), 64 f.
5. T. Burrow, *The Sanskrit Language* (London: Faber & Faber [2]1965).
6. Together, these areas are home to about 120 million people.
7. For details, see K. K. Pillai, *A Social History of the Tamils* (Madras: University of Madras, [2]1973), vol. 1, Chapter 3, "Pre-History;" and F. W. Clothey, *The Many Faces of Murukan*, The Hague: Mouton, 1978, 4-37.
8. See the instructive article by F. W. Clothey, "Tamil Religion," in *Encyclopedia of Religions*, M. Eliade, ed., vol. 12, 260 ff.
9. K. K. Pillai, op. cit., 480 ff.
10. The solemn ritual of Cidāmbaran, a major Śaivite center of Tamiḷnādu, consists of the daily ritual dance.
11. C. Sivaramamurti, *South Indian Bronzes* (New Delhi: Lalit Kala Akademi 1963).
12. Pillai, *op. cit.*, 476, referring to Bruce Foote.
13. Ibid., 477.
14. See D. D. Shulman, *Tamil Temple Myths* (Princeton: Princeton University Press 1980). See also B. Oguibenine, "Cosmic Tree in Vedic and Tamil Mythology: Contrastive Analysis," *Journal of Indo-European Studies* 12, nos. 3-4

(1984): 367-74; G. Kuppuswamy and M. Hariharan, "Bhajana Tradition in South India," *Sangeet Natak* 64-65 (April-September 1982): 32-50.

15. K. Klostermaier, "The Original Dakṣa Saga," *Journal of South Asian Literature* 20, no. 1 (1985): 93-107.

16. Pillai, op. cit., 488 ff.

17. Ibid., 489. The Tamil name of *Kṛṣṇa* is *Kannan.*

18. Ibid., 492, with references to Tamil sources.

19. Ibid.

20. F. W. Clothey, *The Many Faces of Murugan: The History and Meaning of a South Indian God* (The Hague: Mouton, 1978); K. Zvelebil, *Tiru Murugan* (Madras: International Institute of Tamil Studies 1982).

21. Pillai, op. cit., 484.

22. Ibid.

23. Ibid., 485.

24. Ibid.

25. Ibid., 487 f.

26. Ibid., 497.

27. A peculiarity of Tamiḷnādu are the *nadukal* (memorial stones) and *vīrakal* (hero stones), which were erected with religious solemnities to commemorate, especially, warriors who had died in battle.

28. This division goes back to the *Tolkappiam*, an ancient Tamil grammar and reputedly the oldest document of Tamil literature, ascribed to the second century B.C.E.

29. Cf. Pillai, op. cit., 504 ff.

30. Ibid., with references to Tamil sources.

31. Ibid. Pillai emphasizes that during these sacrifices live animals were sacrificed, a practice that continues to this day in certain forms of Śiva worship.

32. F. Staal, *Agni: The Vedic Ritual of the Fire Altar* (Berkeley: University of California Press, 1983).

33. Meanwhile, the DMK has split several times. While officially "atheistic" and pronouncedly anti-Brahmin, DMK followers have transformed the tomb of Anna at the shore of the Bay of Bengal into a veritable *samādhi:* people bring flowers and other gifts and expect blessings to come from the visit.

34. Cf. also F. A. Presler, "The Structure and Consequences of Temple Policy in Tamiḷnādu, 1967-81," *Pacific Affairs* (Summer 1983): 232-46. See also, "Priestly

Protest," *India Today* (15 December 1986): 111.

35. *Tirukkural*, G. U. Pope, W. H. Drew, J. Lazarus, and F. W. Ellis, trans. (Tinnevelly: South India Saiva Siddhanta Works Publishing Society, 1962).

36. Pillai, op. cit., 524 ff.

37. Ibid., 426.

38. H. Whitehead, *The Village Gods of South India*, Religious Life of India Series (Calcutta: Association Press 1921), with illustrations.

39. The author obtained a chart from his Madras landlord, who was not only a modern, educated, successful industrialist but also a staunch believer in *rahukālam*, during which time he refused to conduct any business.

40. K. A. Nilakanta Sastri, *The Culture and History of the Tamils* (Calcutta: K. L. Mukhopadhyay), 108 ff. belives that many of the accounts of religious persecution in Tamiḷnādu are exaggerated. But there is no doubt that violence did occur and that the various religious communities denounced each other.

41. Sastri reports that "even now Madura conducts an annual festival in the temple commemorating the incredible impalement of 8000 Jainas at the instance of the gentle boy saint" ibid., 110.

42. Bombay: Bharatiya Vidya Bhavan, 1961.

43. Cf. F. Kingsbury and G. E. Philips, trans. *Hymns of the Tamil Śaivite Saints*, Heritage of India Series (Calcutta: Association Press 1921), 10-33.

44. Ibid., 25.

45. Bankey Bihari, *Minstrels of God*, Part 1 (Bombay: Bharatiya Vidya Bhavan, 1956), 118-27.

46. See literature mentioned in Chapter 17 (notes 35-37) and A. K. Ramanujan, *Speaking of Śiva* (Hammondsworth, U. K.: Penguin Classics, 1973).

47. In ibid., 88 (Basavanna No. 820).

48. From my own observations.

20. THE DIVINE PRESENCE IN SPACE AND TIME: *MŪRTI, TĪRTHA, KĀLA*

1. "Essentials of Hindutva," *Hindu Rastra Darshan* (Poona: Maharastra Prantik Hindu Sabha, 1964), vol. 6, 74.

2. For details see J. N. Banerjea, *The Development of Hindu Iconography* (Calcutta: University of Calcutta, [2]1956), Chapters 1-6.

3. See N. R. Roy in *HCIP*, vol. 2, 506 ff.

4. Cf. H. Zimmer, *The Art of Indian Asia* (New York: Bollingen Foundation 1955),

vol. 1, 259 ff, plates on 268 ff.

5. As, e.g., the famous group of temples at Belur, Mysore.

6. Lively accounts are found in Elliot and Dowson, eds., *The History of India as Told by Its Own Historians: The Mohammedan Period*, 8 vols., (reprint Allahabad: Kitab Mahal, 1964). Some doubt has been expressed as to the truth of these reports, whose writers evidently wanted to impress their readers.

7. J. P. Waghorne and N. Cutler, eds., *Gods of Flesh/Gods of Stone: The Embodiment of Divinity in India* (Chambersburg: Anima Publications, 1985).

8. Cf. J. N. Banerjea, op. cit., Chapter 8. A seminal work is S. Kramrisch, *Indian Sculpture* (1933; reprint Delhi: Motilal Banarsidass, 1981). Of great interest is also H. Zimmer, *Kunstform und Yoga im indischen Kultbild* (Berlin: Frankfurter Verlagsanstalt, 1926).

9. K. Vasudeva Sastri and N. B. Gadre, eds., Tanjore Sarasvati Mahal Series No. 85, in 1958. Two complete manuals of Hindu architecture are available in Western language translations: *Manasāra*, P. K. Acharya, English trans. (1934; reprint New Delhi: 1980) and *Māyāmata*, 2 vols. ed and trans. B. Dagens, French (Pondichéry: Institut Français d'Indologie 1970-1976).

10. For details, see T. Bhattacharya, *The Canons of Indian Art*, (Calcutta: [2]1963), Chapters XIV to XX.

11. There are special works giving rules for restoration of images and special rites for its reconsecration.

12. That is, milk, curds, *ghī*, dung, and urine.

13. *Bṛhatsaṁhitā of Varāhamihira*, published with a Hindī translation by Paṇḍit Acutyānanda Jhā Śarmanā, Chaukhambha Vidyābhavan Sanskṛt Granthamālā No. 49 (Varanasi: 1959), Chapter 60, slightly condensed.

14. The ritual of Viṣṇu worship as followed at Śrīraṅgam is described in *Śrī Parameśvara Saṁhitā*, (Śrīraṅgam: Kodandarāma Sannidhi 1953). No translation in a Western language is available. The ritual of Śiva worship as followed in South Indian Siva temples is detailed in *Somaśambhupaddhatī*, 3 vols., H. Brunner-Lachaux, ed., French trans. and notator (Pondichéry: Institut Français d'Indologie, 1963-1968). A very detailed study, with illustrations, of Kṛṣṇa worship in the Caitanyite tradition, relying mainly on the *Haribhaktivilāsa* by Gopala Bhaṭṭa, the authoritative work for it, is R. V. Joshi, *Le Rituel de la Dévotion Kṛṣṇaite* (Pondichéry: Institut Français d'Indologie, 1959).

15. Cf. N. Ramesan, *Temples and Legends of Andhra Pradesh* (Bombay: Bharatiya Vidya Bhavan 1962), 70 ff.

16. The technical expression for this is *nyāsa:* see R. V. Joshi, op. cit., 87 ff.

17. *Bhāgavata Purāṇa* XI, 27, 20 ff.

18. One of the earliest such government-appointed boards was established to regulate the affairs of one of the most famous and richest temples in India, the *Tirupati Devasthānam.* Largely unknown outside India, the former Kacheri Nammalvar Temple within the Tirupati compound has been transformed into the S. V. Museum on Temple Art, the most complete museum of its kind, with a large number of well-described exhibits explaining all aspects of temple worship, from the planning stage to the completion of the building, from the daily routine of *pūjās* to the musical instruments used, etc. It is well worth a visit.

19. The merit of having pioneered this study goes to Stella Kramrisch who, in the early 1920s made the first attempt to study Hindu temples with the aid of ancient manuscripts on architecture. See her magnum opus, *The Hindu Temple*, 2 vols. (Calcutta: University of Calcutta Press, 1946). Barbara Stoler-Miller has selected and edited essays by S. Kramrisch covering a span of almost fifty years and touching upon virtually all aspects of Hindu art, under the title *Exploring India's Sacred Art* (Philadelphia: University of Pennsylvania Press, 1983). The book also contains a brief biography of Kramrisch and a full bibliography. Much recent work has been done by the Indologist-architect W. Meister. He is editor of the *Encyclopedia of Indian Temple Architecture* and author of several important articles in scholarly journals, such as "Maṇḍala and Practice in Nāgara Architecture in North India," *JAOS* 99 (1979): 204-19; "Measurement and Proportion in Hindu Architecture," *Interdisciplinary Science Reviews* 10 (1985): 248-58. See also his informative "Hindu Temples," in *Encyclopedia of Religion*, M. Eliade, ed., vol. 10, 368-73.

20. S. Kramrisch, op. cit., vol. 1, Preface.

21. For an interpretation see A. Volwahsen, *Living Architecture: Indian* (New York: Grosset & Dunlap 1969), 43 ff.

22. S. Kramrisch, op. cit., vol. 1, 97.

23. A very informative article dealing with this issue is R. Kulkarni, "Vāstupāda-maṇḍala," *JOIB* 28, nos. 3-4 (March-June 1979): 107-38, with many diagrams and tables.

24. The most perfect application of this scheme can be seen in the city of Jaipur. On city planning in general, the *Viśvakarman Vāstusśāstra* (op. cit in note 9), an authoritative work, can be consulted. The most systematic work is D. Schlingloff, *Die altindische Stadt* (Wiesbaden: Harrassowitz, 1969).

25. The details of the calculation are given in A. Volwahsen, op. cit., 50-55.

26. Ibid., 51.

27. Cf. O. Fischer, *Die Kunst Indiens* (Berlin: Propyläen ^{2}1928), plate 253 f.

28. B. Rowland, *The Art and Architecture of India* (Baltimore: The Pelican History of Art 1967), plate 112.

29. Ibid., plates 101 and 118.

30. Placing the capstone on top of such a tall structure was a marvelous engineering feat of the time. According to tradition, a four-mile-long ramp was built, upon which it was inched up. A different theory is held by some Western authors. See A. Volwahsen, op. cit., 180 f.; cf. B. Rowland, op. cit., plate 121b.

31. Cf. A. Volwahsen, ibid., 145.

32. Cf. B. Rowland, op. cit., plate 103a.

33. Cf. ibid., plate 106; S. Kramrisch, *The Hindu Temple*, op. cit.

34. Ibid., plate 104; A. Boner.

35. Cf. Rowland, ibid., plate 124.

36. Cf. ibid., plate 120a.

37. Cf. B. Rowland, op. cit., Chapters 15-17. Much fascinating detail on the technicalities of temple building, the tools used, and the organization of the trades employed can be gathered from A. Boner, S. R. Sarma, and R. P. Das, *New Light on the Sun Temple of Konārka: Four Unpublished Manuscripts Relating to Construction History and Ritual of This Temple* (Varanasi: Chowkhambha Sanskrit Series Office, 1972). The work also contains reproductions of the late-mediaeval palm leaf manuscripts with the complete "blueprint" of the temple and appropriate annotations.

38. D. L. Eck, *Darśan: Seeing the Divine Image in India*, (Chambersburg: Anima Books, [2]1985).

39. For details, consult P. V. Kane, *HDhS*, vol. 5 (part 1), 463 ff.

40. *Maitrī Upaniṣad*, VI, 14 ff.

41. Kane, *HDhS*, vol. 5 (part 1), 253-452, offers a list of *vratas* containing more than a thousand individual feasts and observances.

42. *Dharmayuga* brought out an issue dedicated to this feast on August 30, 1964. Cf. Kane, *HDhS*, op. cit., 124 ff.

43. For details, see Kane, ibid., 154-87.

44. For details, see Kane, *ibid.*, 227 f. *The Illustrated Weekly of India* brought out a Special *Mahāśivarātri* issue 87, no. 8 (20 February 1966). See also the very detailed and interesting study by J. B. Long, "Festival of Repentance: A Study of Mahāśivarātri," *JBOI* 22, no. 1-2 (September-December 1972): 15-38.

45. The Gītāpress brought out a special volume, *Tīrthāṅka* [in Hindī] in 1956, describing thousands of *tīrthas* on more than 700 pages with numerous illustrations. See also M. Jha, ed., *Dimensions of Pilgrimage* (New Delhi: Inter-Indian Publication, 1985); R. Salomon, ed. and trans., *The Bridge to the Three Holy Cities, The Samāyaṇa-Praghattaka of Nārāyaṇa Bhaṭṭa's Tristhalisetu*

(Delhi: Motilal Banarsidass, 1985). E. A. Morinis, *Pilgrimage in the Hindu Tradition: A Case Study of West Bengal*, South Asian Studies Series (New York and New Delhi: Oxford University Press 1984).

46. The *Padma Purāṇa* contains a great number of *tīrtha māhātmyas* as does the *Matsya* and *Agni.* The *Padma Purāṇa* has a long *khaṇḍa* in honour of Kāśī, perhaps the *sthāla purāṇa* itself.

47. Cf. H. von Stietencron, "Suicide as a Religious Institution," *Bharatiya Vidya* 27 (1967) pp. 7-24.

48. *Kalyāṇa Kalpataru* 39, no. 12 (March 1966).

49. Cf. E. B. Havell, *Benares, The Sacred City: Sketches of Hindu Life and Religion* (London: [2]1905). Also Diana Eck, *Benares, the City of Light* (Princeton: Princeton University Press, 1983). Valuable information is also found in Kane, *HDhS*, vol. 4, 618-42.

50. Quite instructive are the two special Homage to Varanasi issues brought out by the *Illustrated Weekly of India* 85, nos. 6-7 (9 and 16 February 1984), with numerous illustrations.

51. *Varanasi at a Glance*, a souvenir issued on the eve of the twenty-fourth session of the All India Oriental Conference, (Varanasi: Varanaseya Sanskrit Vishwavidyalaya, October 1968), 17.

52. Cf. the section "Tīrthayātra" in Kane, *HDhS*, vol. 4, 552-827, including a list of *tīrthas* over 100 pages long with thousands of names and indications of further information. A visit to a *Kumbhamelā*, which is held in turn every three years in Allahābad (Prayāga), Hardwār, Ujjain, and Nāsik gives a good impression of the fervor with which millions of Hindus today engage in *tīrthayātra* and the observance of holy times. See also the report on the last *Kumbhamelā*, in Hardwar in 1986, in *India Today* (15 May 1986): 74-85.

21. THE HINDU SOCIAL ORDER: *CATURVARṆĀŚRAMADHARMA*

1. The word *caste* is usually derived from the Portuguese *casta*, "race, species, lineage." It serves as a rather inadequate translation for two Indian words: *varṇa* (originally "color"), the four "original divisions of mankind" into *Brahmins, kṣatriyas, vaiśyas*, and *śūdras*, and *jāti* (originally "birth"), the actual "castes" which number over 3000. Each *varṇa* is divided into a great many *jātis* that, among themselves, again are hierarchically ordered, although not uniformly so over India.

2. L. Dumont, *Religion/Politics and History in India: Collected Papers in Indian Sociology* (The Hague: Mouton, 1970), 38, n. 10.

3. J. H. Hutton, *Caste in India: Its Nature, Function and Origins* (1946; Oxford: Oxford University Press, [3]1961).

4. *Homo Hierarchicus*, English translation, (Chicago: University of Chicago Press, 1970). A very valuable work is also P. H. Prabhu, *Hindu Social Organization: A Study in Socio-Psychological and Ideological Foundations* (Bombay: Popular Prakashan [4]1963). Very worthwhile is the work of an Indian anthropologist, Irawati Karve, *Hindu Society: An Interpretation* (Poona: Deshmukh Prakashan 1961), highlighting especially the great diversity of Indian society and its customs in the various parts of India.

5. "Orientalist Constructions of India," *Modern Asian Studies* 20, no. 3 (1986): 401-46. Inden writes: "Indological discourse, I argue, holds (or simply assumes) that the essence of Indian civilization is just the opposite of the West's. It is the irrational (but rationalizable) institution of 'caste' and the Indological religion that accompanies it, Hinduism. Human agency in India is displaced by Indological discourse not onto a reified State or Market but onto a substantialized caste" (p. 402). To set the record straight. Although I agree with much of Inden's criticism of the "Orientalist Constructions of India," let it be understood that caste is essential and has been understood as such not only by Indologists but by Indians themselves, high and low.

6. *Ṛg Veda* X, 190.

7. An important issue became the question of intercaste marriages and the position of the "mixed castes." See *Manusmṛti* X, 6-73.

8. Apart from encyclopedic works like E. Thurston and K. Rangachari, *Tribes and Castes of South India*, 4 vols. (Madras: Government Press 1929), and parallels in other parts of India, village or regional studies like M. N. Srinivas, *Religion and Society among the Coorgs of South India* (Reprint: Bombay: Asia Publishing House 1965) and books inspired by this seminal work give a good idea of the actual working of caste.

9. *Article 17:* "Untouchability is abolished and its practice in any form is forbidden. The enforcement of any disability arising out of Untouchability shall be an offence punishable in accordance with law."

10. "The Conception of Kingship in Ancient India," in *Religion/Politics*, op. cit., 62 f.

11. Cf. Arvind Sharma, *The Puruṣārthas: A Study in Hindu Axiology* (East Lansing: Asian Studies Center, Michigan State University, 1982). See also C. Malamoud, "On the Rhetoric and Semantics of *Purusartha*," in *Way of Life*, T. N. Madan, ed. (Delhi: Vikas Publishing House 1982), 33-52.

12. A rich source of information on these matters is P. V. Kane, *HDhS*, vol. 2 (part 2).

13. "Hinduism," in W. Theodore de Bary, general ed., *Sources of Indian Tradition* (reprint New York: Columbia University Press, 1958), vol. 1, 200-361.

14. "Another Path," *Seminar* 17 (January 1961): 41.

15. For an overall view, see U. N. Ghosal, *A History of Indian Political Ideas:*

The Ancient Period and the Period of Transition to the Middle Ages (Oxford: Oxford University Press, 1959). For the question of Brahmanic vs. *Kṣatriya* views, see the excellent article by R. N. Dandekar, "Ancient Indian Polity," *Indo-Asian Culture* 11, no. 4 (April 1963): 323-32.

16. *Manusmṛti* I, 98-101.

17. See especially *Bhagavadgītā*, III, 35.

18. The DMK, the ruling party of Tamiḷnādu for more than a decade, began as an anti-Brahmin movement and declared itself "Atheistic." It continues with vociferous, if not always credible, propaganda for modernization and secularization.

19. "Sacred kingship" in India and in other cultures has been the topic of a recent Congress of the International Association for the History of Religion. Cf. *Numen* Supplement no. 4, with C. M. Edsman's introductory essay "Zum sakralen Königtum in der Forschung der letzten hundert Jahre," pp. 3-17. Important essays on this topic by M. Biardeau, R. Inden, and A. C. Mayer are also contained in T. N. Madan, ed., *Way of Life. King, Householder, Renouncer. Essays in Honor of Louis Dumont* (Delhi: Vikas Publishing House, 1982). The relationship between kingship and local temple cults is explored by R. Inden, "Hierarchies of Kings in Early Mediaeval India" in this work (pp. 99-125); and S. Gupta and R. Gombrich, "Kings, Power and the Goddess," *South Asia Research* 6, no. 2 (November 1986): 123-38.

20. The term is *daṇḍa*, literally, "a stick," an instrument of punishment, as the scepter has to be understood throughout in this tradition.

21. The term is *kheda*, meaning "exhaustion"; other Mss. have *dhainya.*

22. *Śāntiparvan* 59, 12 ff.

23. *Viṣṇu Purāṇa* I, 13; *Bhāgavata Purāṇa* IV, 14.

24. According to Brahmanic lore the *vaiśyas* originated from the thigh, the *kṣatrias* from the arms of the *puruṣa.*

25. *Viṣṇu Purāṇa* I, 13, 61-63.

26. One of the best examples is the *Rājadharma* section in the *Mahābhārata Śāntiparvan* 1-128.

27. See *The Kautilīya Ārthaśāstra*, R. P. Kangle, ed. and trans., 3 parts (reprint Bombay: University of Bombay, 1960), containing the Critical Text, a translation and a study. See also U. N. Ghosal, "Kautilīya," in *Encyclopedia of Social Sciences.* ([10] 1953), vol. 3, 473 ff.

28. The difference between the Kautilīyan idea of kingship and European absolutism is explored in N. P. Sil, "Political Morality vs. Political Necessity: Kautilya and Machiavelli Revisited," *Journal of Asian History* 19, no. 2 (1985): 101-42.

29. The *Ārthaśāstra* concludes with the maxim "What mankind lives by that is *artha*, the science that deals with the means of conquering and possessing the earth is *ārthaśāstra*."

30. *Jāti* is derived from *jā-*, "being born" and is usually translated as "subcaste". In fact, the *jātis* determine the real place of the Hindu in society, since every *varṇa* (literally "color") has within itself a hierarchy of *jātis*.

31. Bombay: Asia Publishing House, 1968.

32. Which he defines as not necessarily Westernization, as he shows when he writes: "Modernity, in that sense, is not new; it is a recurring historical force, a recurring opportunity 'which, taken at the flood, leads on to fortune, omitted, all the voyage of your life is bound in shallows and miseries'. Ultimately, we today are striving for the most strategic thing in our time, a new identity for ourselves and for the world. It is no less than an identity with the spirit of the age, the fulfillment of a new *karma*, and here the responsibility has lain squarely on the elites of history" (p. 4).

33. See, e.g., the *prayaścittas* for killing a cow and for killing a *caṇḍāla*.

34. The following letter to the editor of the *Times of* (Bombay) *India* (20 March 1968) on "Harijan's plight" by Rajaram P. Mukane from Thana is quite telling: "Millions of untouchables in this country continue to suffer shameful humiliations twenty years after independence. Almost every aspect of our life is infested with casteism and communalism. The Chief Minister of Andhra Pradesh disclosed in the Assembly last week that a Harijan youth was roasted alive on a charge of theft. The committee on untouchability constituted by the Union Government recently revealed that three untouchables were shot dead by caste Hindus for growing their moustaches upward instead of downward, in keeping with the local Hindu tradition, and that an untouchable youth was killed in Mysore for walking along the street wearing chappals. Everyone remembers how in Maharastra three Harijan women were stripped naked and made to walk before the public on the roads. These are not isolated incidents. Such atrocities are perpetrated everywhere in our country due to the virus of casteism and untouchability, although the practice of the latter has been banned by law. The law against untouchability is almost inoperative because of the indifferent attitude of the so-called upper caste Hindus holding key positions. For Hinduism the cow and other such things seem to occupy a more significant position than human dignity." More recent examples of injustices committed against the former outcastes can be found in A. George, *Social Ferment in India*, (London: The Athlone Press, 1986), Chapter 7, "The Scheduled Castes," 202 ff.

35. See B. R. Ambedkar, *What Congress and Gandhi Have Done to the Untouchables* (Bombay: Thacker and Co., [1945] [2]1946).

22. THE PROFESSIONAL RELIGIOUS: *SAṀNYĀSA*

1. *Manusmṛti*, X, 74 ff.

2. Ibid., VI, 37, threatens those with hell who take *samnyāsa* without having begotten a son and performed the proper rites. Cf. also *Viṣṇusmṛti* V, 13.

3. Some of the works that could be mentioned in this context are I. C. Oman, *The Mystics, Ascetics and Saints of India* (Reprint: Delhi: Oriental Publishers 1973); H. H. Wilson, *Religious Sects of the Hindus*, first published in *Asiatick Researches* XVI (1828) and XVII (1832); (reprint Calcutta: Punthi Pustak, 1958); S. Chattopadhyaya, *The Evolution of Theistic Sects in Ancient India* (Calcutta: Progressive Publishers 1962); G. S. Ghurye, *Indian Sādhus* (Bombay: Asia, [2]1964).

4. *Mahābhārata Anuśāsanaparvan* 141.

5. The *śikhā*, also called *choṭī* is the little wisp of hair left at the place of the *brahmārandra*, the place where according to Vedic belief, the *ātman* leaves the body. It is never cut, while the rest of the head is shaved ritually quite often. It is, even today, a sign of Brahmanic orthodoxy and is cut off only if someone takes *saṁnyāsa*, whereby he technically ceases to belong to the community that observes *dharma*.

6. *Paramahaṁsa Upaniṣad*, condensed rendering from *108 Upaniṣadẽ, Brahmā Vidyā Khaṇḍa*, No. 33, pp. 526 ff.

7. A classical text relating to *saṁnyāsa* has recently been translated into English. *Vasudevāśrama's Yatidharmaprakāśa. A Treatise on World Renunciation*, P. Olivelle, ed. and trans., 2 vols. *DeNobili Research Library, No. 5* (Wien: 1977). Also P. Olivelle, *Renunciation in Hinduism: A Mediaeval Debate*, 2 vol. Publications of the De Nobili Research Library, Vol. 13 (Vienna: Institute for Indology, University of Vienna, 1986/87).

8. *Viśveśvarasarasvati Yatidharmasaṅgraha*, V. G. Apte, ed., (Poona: Ānandāśrama, 1928), 154.

9. *Vedārthasaṃgraha* No. 251.

10. An early example is *Bṛhadāraṇyaka Upaniṣad* II, 6, mentioning fifty-eight generations of gurus ending with "Parameṣṭhin from Brahman." Later sectarian *sūtras* carry lengthy lists of names, too.

11. *Upadeśasahasrī* No. 6.

12. For many details concerning the legal aspects of *saṁnyāsa*, see P. V. Kane, *HDhS*, vol. 2 (part 2), 933 ff.

13. Rāmdās Gaur, *Hindutva* [in Hindī] (Kasi: Samvat 1995), "*saṁpradāya khaṇḍa*," Chapters 67-75.

14. On the life and work of Śaṅkara and the order founded by him, see W. Cenkner, *A Tradition of Teachers. Śaṅkara and the Jagadgurus Today* (Delhi: Motilal

Banarsidass, 1983). Cf. also Yoshitsugu Sawai, "Śaṅkara's Theology of Saṁnyāsa," *Journal of Indian Philosophy* 14 (1986): 371-87.

15. Also other ancient establishments claim to be founded by Śaṅkarācārya and to posses his *guru paramparā*, expressed in the titles *jagadguru* and Śaṅkarācārya given to the resident chief ascetic. See e.g., T. M. P. Mahadevan, *The Sage of Kanchi*, (Secunderabad: Sri Kanchi Kamakothi Sankara Mandir 1967) describing the life of Śrī Jagadguru Śaṅkarācārya of Kāmakothi Pīṭha, His Holiness Śrī Chandrasekharendra Sarasvatī on the completion of sixty years of spiritual rulership as the sixty-eighth head of the Pīṭha.

16. In order to enhance their prestige non-Śaṅkarite *sādhus*, as, e.g., the neo-Caitanyites also adopt these titles.

17. Cf. S. G. Ghurye, op. cit., Chapter 6.

18. W. Cenkner, op. cit., 134.

19. Ibid., Chapter 10.

20. Cf. T. M. P. Mahadevan, in *HCIP*, vol. 5, 458. See also H. H. Wilson, op. cit., 131 ff. and 142 ff. Rāmānuja, *Śrībhāṣya*, II, 2, 36; S. G. Ghurye, op. cit., 48 ff.

21. This group, founded in the early seventeenth century with centers in Benares, Gazipur, and Jaunpur is classified as *sudhārak* (reformist) in Rāmdās Gaur op. cit., 739. The traditional *Aghoris* are unapproachable to outsiders.

22. A. S. Raman, "Homage to Varanasi," *Illustrated Weekly of India* 85, no. 6-7.

23. For a full-length monograph, see A. K. Banerjea, *Philosophy of Gorakhnāth* (Gorakhpur: Mahant Dig Vijai Nath Trust, Gorakhnath Temple, 1962).

24. Besides the information offered by Rāmdās Gaur, see H. H. Wilson, op. cit., 148 f.

25. Paṇḍit Śrīnarāyan Śāstrī Khiste, "Śrīvidyā," in *Kalyāṇa Devībhāgavatam Aṅgka* (Gorakhpur: Gita Press 1960), 689-96.

26. Rāmdās Gaur, op. cit., 730 f.

27. W. S. Deming, *Rāmdās and the Rāmdāsīs*, Religious Life of India Series, (Oxford: Oxford University Press, 1928).

28. Besides the text editions, translations, and works mentioned by C. Vaudeville in *Kabīr Granthavālī* (*Doha*) (Pondichéry: Institute Français d'Indologie, 1957), G. H. Westcott, *Kabīr and the Kabīr Panth* (first published in Kanpur 1907; reprint Calcutta: YMCA Press 1953), is still highly recommended.

29. Details in Rāmdās Gaur, op. cit., 735 ff.

30. Karpatrijī Mahārāj, *Rāmrājya aur Marksvāda* [in Hindī] (Gorakhpur: Gītā Press, 1964).

31. It was interesting to see the comments and reports in the daily and weekly newspapers of India, in the days following the incident, especially the rather interesting opposite versions offered by the left-wing *Blitz* and the right-wing *Organiser*.

32. Cf. the Viśva Hindu Pariṣad publication, *Hindu Viśva*, started in Bombay in 1964; special edition in January 1966, on occasion of a conference at the *Kumbha Melā* at Allahabad.

33. D. D. Kosambi has critically edited *The Epigrams Attributed to Bhartṛhari Including the Three Centuries*, Singhi Jain Series No. 23 (Bombay: Bharatiya Vidya Bhavan 1948). The Advaita Āśrama Calcutta has brought out the text with translation of the *Vairāgya Śatakam* (1963) according to the rather heavily interpolated "vulgate" text. The extract here is from Nos. 2-7 and 99-100.

34. Madhava Ashish, "The *Sādhu* in Our Life," *Seminar* 200 (April 1976): 12-18.

23. HINDU STRUCTURES OF THOUGHT: THE *ṢAḌDARŚANAS*

1. *Manusmṛti* II, 114 (Bühler's translation in *SBE*, vol. 25).

2. *Manusmṛti* II, 156.

3. *Manusmṛti* II, 171.

4. Some interesting details are presented in a lighthearted manner by Kuppuswami Sastri in a contribution to "the library movement," under the title "*Kośavan ācāryaḥ*" (i.e., one who has a library is a teacher or a teacher is one who has a library). Reprinted in S. S. Janaki, ed., *Kuppuswami Sastri Birth Centenary Commemoration Volume* (*KSBCCV*), Part 1 (Madras: 1981). This claim is also supported by the information on the scholastic engagement of the Śaṅkarācāryas past and present, in W. Cenkner, *A Tradition of Teachers* (Delhi: Motilal Banarsidass, 1983), especially Chapter 4, "The Teaching Heritage after Śaṅkara," 84-106.

5. A popular maxim is *Svadeśe pūjyate rājā vidvān sarvatra pūjyate* ("while a king is honored in his own realm [only], a scholar is honored everywhere").

6. The many (thirty-two) different *vidyās* mentioned in the *Upaniṣads* can be seen as the beginning of different school traditions of Hinduism.

7. *Vādavāda*, a study of different viewpoints and polemics, became an integral part of traditional Indian learning. As T. R. V. Murti says, "polemic (*parapakṣa-nirākaraṇa*) is an integral part of each system" ("The Rise of the Philosophical Schools," *CHI*, vol. 3, 32).

8. The text used as motto for this chapter provides the rationale for Śaṅkara to develop his extensive commentary on the *Brahmasūtra*.

9. Not only are a number of highly philosophical *stotras* ascribed to Śaṅkarācārya, hymns to different deities that are recited by ordinary Hindus in their daily worship, the vernacular religious poetry of such favorites of contemporary Hindus like Tulasīdāsa, Kabīr, Sūrdāsa, Tukārām, and others also are highly speculative.

10. *Manusmṛti* II, 11.

11. *Tantravārttika* I, 3, 4.

12. S. Radhakrishnan mentions in *Indian Philosophy* (London: Allen & Unwin [2]1948), vol. 2, 20, n. 4, that Bhīmācārya in his *Nyāyakośa* included Sāṁkhya and Advaita Vedānta under the *nāstika*, i.e., unorthodox systems. He specifically quotes the sentence: *Māyāvādivedānti api nāstika eva paryavasāna sampadyate* ("In the end also the Vedāntin holding the opinion of illusionism [*māyāvāda*] turns out to be a *nāstika*, i.e., a nonbeliever in the Veda"). This sentence is not found in the fourth edition, revised by V. S. Abhyankar, (Poona: Bhandarkar Oriental Research Institute, 1978).

13. *Brahmasūtrabhāṣya* I, 1, 5.

14. S. Radhakrishnan, op. cit., vol. 2, 19.

15. Ibid., 20 f.

16. Ibid., 24: "The six systems agree on certain essentials." In a footnote, Radhakrishnan quotes Max Müller, who [with reference to Vijñānabhikṣu, who had (in the fourteenth century) attempted to bring about a unified *darśana*] had stated "that there is behind the variety of the six systems a common fund of what may be called national or popular philosophy, a large *manasa* lake of philosophical thought and language far away in the distant North and in the distant past, from which each thinker was allowed to draw for his own purposes." (Max Müller, *The Six Systems of Indian Philosophy*, [reprint Varanasi: Chowkhambha 1962), xvii). Radhakrishnan made a bold statement of the unity of Hindu philosophy in his popular *The Hindu View of Life* (New York: 1962).

17. The term *darśana* has been common in India since the second century. Before that, the term *anvīkṣikī*, later restricted to "logic," seems to have served. This issue is competently discussed by W. Halbfass in "Indien und die Geschichtsschreibung der Philosophie," *Philosophische Rundschau* 23 (1976): 104-31.

18. Thus the commentaries on Gangeṣa's *Tattvacintāmaṇi* were called *Didhiti, Gangadhārī, Kārṣikā, Candrakālā, Nakṣatramālikā*, etc. See R. Thangasami Sarma, *Darśanamañjarī*, Part 1 (Madras: University of Madras, 1985), 64 f.

19. Thus, Thangasami uses the titles *Nyāya, Vyākāraṇa, Vedānta Śiromaṇī*, showing that he is qualified in logic, grammar, and Vedānta.

20. Thus, K. H. Potter, in his otherwise indispensable and much valued *Encyclopedia of Indian Philosophies*, restricts selection of text extracts to those portions that have a parallel in contemporary analytic Western philosophy.

21. K. Potter has assembled a very extensive *Bibliography of Indian Philosophies* (Delhi: Motilal Banarsidass 1970), with additions published in the *Journal of Indian Philosophy*. For professional Indologists, the as yet incomplete *New Catalogus Catalogorum*, which is appearing from the University of Madras (eleven volumes so far), is the most valuable bibliographic resource, listing

not only published editions and translations but also manuscripts and their location.

22. The text has been published several times (e.g.. Poona: Bhandarkar Oriental Research Institute) and was translated into English, without *Śaṅkaradarśana*, more than a century ago, by Cowell and Gough. It has been reprinted many times.

23. See Kuppuswami Sastri's Introduction to his *Primer of Indian Logic*, (Madras: Kuppuswami Sastri Research Institute, 1932; reprints 1951, 1961), reprinted in *KSBCCV*, vol. 1, 104-18.

24. Ibid., 104.

24. HINDU LOGIC AND PHYSICS: *NYĀYA-VAIŚEṢIKA*

1. S. N. Dasgupta, *History of Indian Philosophy* (*HIPh*) (Cambridge: Cambridge University Press 1961), vol. 1, 282.

2. See the evidence offered by S. N. Dasgupta, ibid.

3. It has only been preserved in a Chinese translation; this has been edited and translated and commented upon by H. Ui (1917; reprint Varanasi: Chowkhambha Sanskrit Series, 1962).

4. The best known may be the *Bhāṣāpariccheda* with *Siddhānta Muktavalī* by Viśvanātha Nyāyapañcānana; there is an edition with English translation by Swami Madhavananda (Calcutta: Advaita Ashrama, [2]1954).

5. K. Sastri, "Nyāya-Vaiśeṣika—Origin and Development," Introduction to Kuppuswami Sastri, *Primer of Indian Logic* (1932; reprinted in *KSBCCV*, vol. 1, 104.

6. In addition to sections on Nyāya and Vaiśeṣika in the major handbooks on Indian philosophy (besides the English language works by S. N. Dasgupta and S. Radhakrishnan, the French works by Renou and Filliozat as well as Biardeau and Siauve, the German works by P. Deussen and E. Frauwallner, and the Sanskrit survey by Thiru Thanghasamy deserve consultation), the following specialized works are recommended. D. H. H. Ingalls, *Materials for the Study of Navya-Nyāya Logic* Harvard Oriental Series No. 40 (Cambridge, Mass.: Harvard University Press, 1968); B. K. Matilal, *The Navya-Nyāya Doctrine of Negation*, Harvard Oriental Series no. 46 (Cambridge, Mass.: Harvard University Press, 1972); S. C. Chatterjee, *The Nyāya Theory of Knowledge* (Calcutta: University of Calcutta, [3]1965); U. Mishra, *The Conception of Matter According to Nyāya-Vaiśeṣika* (Allahabad: 1936; reprint Delhi: Gian Publ. 1983). Some important and very informative essays on Nyāya-Vaiśeṣika in S. K. Maitra, *Fundamental Questions of Indian Metaphysics and Logic* (Calcutta: Chuckervertty, Chatterjee & Co., 1956). An indispensable source is Sati Chandra Vidyabhusana, *A History of Indian Logic*, (1920; reprint Delhi: Motilal Banarsidass, 1971). The most authentic repre-

sentation of *Nyāya* and *Vaiśeṣika*, historically and doctrinally, is found in R. Thangaswami Sarma, *Darśanamañjarī*, Part 1 [in Sanskrit] (Madras: University of Madras, 1985), which not only contains abundant information on the literature of *Nyāya* and *Vaiśeṣika* and their authors but also has many charts and diagrams illustrating the interconnection of works and concepts.

7. Early writers use the word *Nyāya* as a synonym with *Mīmāṁsā*.

8. *Ārthaśāstra* 2, 30, a text often referred to in this connection. So far, I have not seen reference made to *Viṣṇu Purāṇa* I, 9, 121, which has the same enumeration of sciences. In this text, the goddess (after churning the Milk Ocean) is addressed as the embodiment of all knowledge (*vidyā*), specifically of *anvīkṣikī, trayī, vārtā*, and *daṇḍanīti*.

9. Kuppuswami Sastri, op. cit., 107.

10. *Vaiśeṣikardarśana*, Anatalal Thakur, ed., (Darbhanga: Mithila Institute 1957) N. Sinha, trans. (Allahabad: Panini Office 1911).

11. *Padārthadharmasaṅgraha* No. 156, Ganganatha Jha, trans. (Allahabad: Lazarus 1916).

12. Dasgupta, *HIPh*, vol. 1, 363.

13. These "nine things" are *buddhi, sukha, duḥkha, icchā, dveṣa, prayatna, dharma, adharma*, and *saṁskāra*.

14. *Nyāyasutra with Vātsyāyana Bhāṣya*, Ganganatha Jha, ed., trans. and commentator, 2 vols. (Poona: Oriental Book Agency, 1939).

15. *Maṇikaṇa, A Navya-Nyāya Manual*, E. R. Sreekrishna Sarma, ed. and trans. (Adyar: Adyar Library, 1960), Introduction, xvii.

16. *Nyāyasūtra* I, 1, 22.

17. Ibid., VI, 1, 66.

18. For details see G. Chemparathy, *An Indian Rational Theology. Introduction to Udayana's Nyāyakusumañjalī* (Vienna: De Nobili Research Library 1972).

19. *Nyāyakusumañjalī of Udayana*, with the commentary of Haridasa Bhattacarya, E. B. Cowell, trans. (Calcutta: 1864), vol. 5, 1.

20. *Nyāya-bhāṣya* IV, 1, 21 f.

21. *Tarkabhāṣa of Keśava Misra*, Ganganatha Jha, ed. and trans. (Poona: Oriental Book Agency, 1949).

25. HINDU PSYCHOLOGY AND METAPHYSICS: *SĀṀKHYA-YOGA*

1. The best known text of *Haṭha-yoga* is the *Haṭhayogapradīpikā* by Svātmārāma Yogindra, (Adyar: Theosophical Publishing House, 1933).

2. See Chapter 23.

3. E.g., *Bhāgavata Purāṇa* II, 25, 13 ff.; III, 28, etc.

4. A. B. Keith, *The Sāṁkhya System*, The Heritage of India Series (Calutta: YMCA Publishing House [2]1949), 18. The most comprehensive recent study of Sāṁkhya is G. J. Larsen, *Classical Sāṁkhya* (Delhi: Motilal Banarsidass, 1969). Cf. also H. Bakker, "On the Origin of the Sāṁkhya Psychology," *WZKSA* 26 (1982): 117-48, with an extensive bibliography. Larsen also makes an important point in his essay, "The Format of Technical Philosophical Writing in Ancient India: Inadequacies of Conventional Translations," *Philosophy East and West* 30, no. 3 (1980): 375-80. Comprehensive information on the development of Sāṁkhya is contained in E. Frauwallner, *Geschichte der Indischen Philosophie* (Salzburg: Otto Müller Verlag, (1953), vol. 1, 228 ff. and 472 ff.

5. S. N. Dasgupta, *History of Indian Philosophy* (*HIPh*), vol. 1, 264.

6. *Bhāgavata Purāṇa* III, 28.

7. The best edition and translation with ample comments is by S. S. Suryanarayana Sastri, trans. (Madras: University of Madras, 1948). *Sāṁkhya Kārika of Mahāmuni Śrī Īśvarakṛṣṇa*, with the commentary of Paṇḍit Śivanarāyaṇa Śāstrī with *Sāṁkhya Tattvakaumudī* of Vācaspati Miśra (Bombay: Nirṇaya Sagar Press 1940).

8. *Sāṁkhyadarśana*, Pyarelal Prabhu Dayal, ed., [Sanskrit and Hindī] (Bombay: 1943); J. R. Ballantyne, English trans. (London: [3]1885).

9. They have been edited and translated under the title *The Yoga Upaniṣads* (Adyar: Adyar Library, 1920 and 1952).

10. A good edition is that by Swami Vijñāna Āśrama (Ajmer: 1961). In English is J. H. Woods trans., *Pātañjali's Yogasūtra with Vyāsa's Bhāṣya and Vācaspati Miśra's Tattva Vaiśāradī*, Harvard Oriental Series 17 (Cambridge, Mass.: Harvard University Press, 1914). Students may find I. K. Taimni's *The Science of Yoga* (Wheaton: Theosophical Publishing House, [3]1972) useful; it offers the text and the translation of the *Yogasūtra* and a good running commentary that avoids the technicalities of the classical commentaries. Valuable recent treatments of *yoga* are S. N. Dasgupta, *Yoga as Philosophy and Religion* (1924; reprint Delhi: Motilal Banarsidass, 1973); J. W. Hauer, *Der Yoga als Heilsweg* (Stuttgart: Kohlhammer, 1932); G. Feuerstein, *The Philosophy of Classical Yoga* (Manchester: University of Manchester Press, 1982); G. M. Koelman, *Pātañjala Yoga. From Related Ego to Absolute Self* (Poona: Papal Athenaeum, 1970). Special problems connected with *Sāṁkhya-yoga* are addressed in these recent papers: Swami Ranganathananda, "The Science of Consciousness in the Light of Vedānta and Yoga," *Prabuddha Bharata* (June 1982): 257-63; Mohan Singh, "Yoga and Yoga Symbolism," *Symbolon: Jahrbuch für Symbolforschung*, Band 2 (1959): 121-43; S. Bhattacharya, "The Concept of *Bideha* and *Prakṛti-Laya* in the Sāṁkhya-Yoga System," *ABORI*

48-49 (1968): 305-12; C. T. Kenghe, "The Problem of the Pratyayasarga in Sāṁkhya and Its Relation with Yoga," *ABORI* 48-49 (1968): 365-73; K. Werner, "Religious Practice and Yoga in the Time of the Vedas, Upaniṣads and Early Buddhism," *ABORI* 56 (1975): 179-94; G. Oberhammer, "Das Transzendenzverständnis des Sāṁkhyistischen Yoga als Strukturprinzip seiner Mystik," in *Transzendenzerfahrung, Vollzugshorizont des Heils*, G. Oberhammer, ed., (Vienna: De Nobili Research Library, 1978), 15-28; idem., "Die Gotteserfahrung in der yogischen Meditation," in *Offenbarung als Heilserfahrung im Christentum, Hinduismus und Buddhismus*, W. Strolz and S. Ueda, eds. (Freiburg-Basel-Vienna: Herder), 146-66; M. Eliade's *Yoga: Immortality and Freedom*, Bollingen Series 56 (Princeton: Princeton University Press, 1958 and [2]1969) has become a classic in its own right: it not only describes Pātañjala Yoga but compares it to other phenomena and has an exhaustive bibliography of works up to 1964. Controversial new ideas on classical Yoga are advanced in G. Oberhammer, *Strukturen Yogischer Meditation* (Vienna: Österreichische Akademie der Wissenschaften, 1977).

11. *Tejobindu Upaniṣad*, VI, 107.

12. P. Hacker, "Śaṅkara der Yogin und Śaṅkara der Advaitin: Einige Beobachtungen," *WZKSA* 12-13 (1968): 119-48.

13. *Sāṁkhya Kārika* 1.

14. This is the traditional interpretation given to *duḥkhatraya.*

15. *Sāṁkhya Kārikā* 2.

16. Ibid., 18.

17. Ibid., 8.

18. Ibid., 63.

19. Ibid., 67.

20. *Yogasūtra* I, 5 ff.

21. Ibid., I, 23 ff.

22. Ibid., II, 5 f.

23. According to *Haṭha-yoga*, the *utthita padmāsana* confers superhuman vision and cures troubles of the respiratory tract; *śupta padmāsana* cures illnesses of the digestive organs; *bhadrāsana* activates the mind; *dhastricāsana* regulated body temperature, cures fever, and purifies the blood; *guptāṅgāsana* cures venereal diseases, etc. There are centers in India, like the Yoga Research Institute at Lonavla, in which medical research is done on the effects of *yoga* on body and mind.

24. *Yogasūtra* II, 54.

25. Ibid., III, 1-3.

26. Ibid., III, 16 ff.

27. Ibid., IV, 34: *puruṣārthaśūnyānām guṇānām pratisprasavaḥ kaivalyam svarūpa-pratiṣḥhā vā citiśaktiriti*

28. These notions find a surprising parallel in contemporary scientific thought. See I. Prigogine's *Order Out of Chaos* (New York: Bantam Books, 1948).

26. HINDU THEOLOGY, OLD AND NEW: *PŪRVA MĪMĀṀSĀ* AND *VEDĀNTA*

1. The best edition, with a contemporary Sanskrit commentary, is B. G. Apte, *Śābarabhāṣya*, 6 vols. (Poona: Ānandāśrama, 1931-1934). In English, see Ganganatha Jha, trans., 3 vols., Gaekwad Oriental Series (Baroda: 1933-1936; reprint 1973-1974.).

2. Prabhākara Miśra wrote a voluminous subcommentary to the *Śābarabhāṣya* called *Bṛhatī.* S. K. Ramanatha Sastri, ed., 3 vols. (Madras: 1931-). Kumārila Bhaṭṭa's main work is the *Ślokavārtika*, another subcommentary, S. K. Ramanatha Sastri, ed. (Madras: 1940) and Ganganatha Jha, trans. (Calcutta: 1909).

3. S. N. Dasgupta, *History of Indian Philosophy* (*HIPh*), Vol. 1, 371. Concerning the influence of *Mīmāṁsā*, the very useful book by Ganganatha Jha, *Pūrva Mīmāṁsā in Its Sources* (Benares: Benares Hindu University, 1942), Chapter 33, has some interesting things to say. An important source for *Mīmāṁsā* studies is the 7 volume *Mīmāṁsākośa*, Kevalanda Sarasvati, ed. and published by the Dharmakośa Mandala (Wāī: from 1952-1966).

4. As W. Cenkner in *A Tradition of Teachers* (Delhi: Motilal Banarsidass, 1983) reports, the study of *Mīmāṁsā* is one of the subjects that students in the schools associated with the present Śaṅkaramaṭhas have to take. See also F. Staal, ed., *A Reader on the Sanskrit Grammarians* (Cambridge Mass.: 1972) and K. Kunjunni Raja, *Indian Theories of Meaning* (Adyar: Theosophical Institute, 1963).

5. *Jaiminī Sūtras* I, 1, 2: *codanalakṣano'artho dharmah.*

6. Ibid., I, 2, 1.

7. *Śābarabhāṣya* I, 1, 22: "There can be no creator of this relation because no soul is cognized as such by any of the means of cognition. If there had been such a creator, he could not have been forgotten." Cf. also Kumārila Bhaṭṭa, *Ślokavārtika*, XVI, 41 ff.

8. Ganganatha Jha, *Pūrva Mīmāṁsa in Its Sources*, op. cit., 178 ff.

9. *Jaimini Sūtras* VI, 1, 6 ff.

10. Ganganatha Jha, *Pūrva Mīmāṁsā*, 264 f.

11. *Jaimini Sūtras* IV, 3, 15.

12. *Śābarabhāṣya* on VI, 1, 1.

13. *Nyāyaratnakāra:* "Liberation must consist in the destruction of the present body and the non-production of the future body." Quoted by G. Jha, *Pūrva Mīmāṁsā*, op. cit., 38.

14. *Prakāraṇapañcikā, Tattvāloka*, p. 156.

15. Cf. O. Gächter, *Hermeneutics and Language in Pūrvamīmāṁsā, A Study in Śābara Bhāṣya* (Delhi: Motilal Banarsidass, 1983), with bibliographic references to both Eastern and Western authors.

16. The best introduction is H. G. Coward, *The Sphoṭa Theory of Language. A Philosophical Analysis* (Delhi: Motilal Banarsidass, 1980), with an extensive bibliography. The complete text has been edited by K. V. Abhyankar and Acharya V. P. Limaye in the University of Poona Sanskrit and Prakrit Series (Poona: University of Poona, 1965). No good complete translation is available as yet.

17. Rāmdās Gaur, *Hindutva*, 589.

18. According to S. K. Belvalkar, *Shree Gopal Basu Mallik Lectures on Vedānta Philosophy* (Poona: Bilvakunja, 1929), Part 1, Chapter 4, "Vedānta in the Brahmasūtras," 142, Jaimini, the author of the *Mīmāṁsāsūtra* wrote a *Śarīraka-sūtra*, which sought to harmonize the teaching of the *Sāmaveda Upaniṣads* particularly the *Chāṇḍogya Upaniṣad*, and this *sūtra* was incorporated within and forms the main part of the present text of the *Brahmasūtra*.

19. The ten recognized *Vedāntācāryas* are Śaṅkara, Rāmānuja, Madhva, Vallabha, Bhāskara, Yadavaprakāśa, Keśava, Nīlakaṇṭha, Vijñānabhikṣu, and Baladeva. They are the founders of separate branches of Vedānta philosophy. There are several comparative studies of the different schools of Vedānta, such as V. S. Ghate, *The Vedānta* (Poona: 1926; reprint 1960); O. Lacombe, *L'absolu sélon le Vedānta* (Paris: Geuthner 1957; reprint 1966). The major histories of Indian philosophy present information about all the schools. B. N. K. Sharma, *A Comparative Study of Ten Commentaries on the Brahmasūtras* (Delhi: Motilal Banarsidass 1984).

20. Cf. Rāmdās Gaur, op. cit., 591 ff.

21. Other commentaries interpret, as we have seen, Vedānta in the light of sectarian dogma under the names of Dvaitādvaita (Nimbārka), Śuddhādvaita (Vallabha), Acintyabhedābheda (Baladeva), etc.

22. A complete list of these books, with a critical analysis, is given in S. K. Belvarkar, op. cit., 218 ff. See also R. T. Vyas, "Roots of Śaṅkara's Thought," *JOIB* 32, nos. 1-2 (September-December 1982): 35-49.

23. Swami Nikhilananda has brought out an English paraphrase of the *Māṇḍukyopaniṣad with Gaudapāda's Kārikā and Śaṅkara's Commentary*, (Mysore: Sri Ramakrishna Ashrama, [4]1955). T. Vetter, "Die Gauḍapadīya-Kārikās: Zur

Entstehung und zur Bedeutung von [A]dvaita," *WZKSA* 22(1978): 95-131.

24. E.g., *Maitrī Upaniṣad* VI, 15; *Muṇḍaka* II, 2, 8.

25. Contained in H. R. Bhagavat, ed., *Minor Works of Śrī Śaṅkara-ācārya*, Poona Oriental Series No. 8 (Poona: Oriental Book Agency, [2]1952), 374-402.

26. Several complete English translations of the *Śaṅkarabhāṣya* are available: G. Thibaut, *SBE*, vols. 34 and 38 1904); Swami Gambhirananda (Calcutta: Advaita Ashrama, 1965) makes use of some major classical commentaries. P. Deussen's German translation is still of importance. Out of the numerous publications dealing with Śaṅkara and his *Advaita* Vedānta, a few may be mentioned: S. G. Mudgal, *Advaita of Śaṅkara: A Reappraisal* (on the impact of Buddhism and Sāṁkhya on Śaṅkara's thought) (Delhi: Motilal Banarsidass, 1975). Haripada Chakraborti, "Śaṅkarācārya," in *Asceticism in Ancient India* (Calcutta: Punthi Pustak, 1973); D. N. Lorenzen, "The Life of Śaṅkarācārya," in *Experiencing Śiva*, F. Clothey and J. B. Long, eds., (Columbia, MO: South Asia Books, 1983); P. Hacker, "Eigentümlichkeiten der Lehre und Terminologie Śaṅkaras: *Avidyā, Nāmarūpa, Māyā, Īśvara*," *ZDMG* 100(1950): 246-86; idem. *Vivarta: Studien zur Geschichte der illusionistischen Kosmologie und Erkenntnistheorie der Inder* (Wiesbaden: Akademie der Wissenschaften Mainz, 1953). Every American student of Hinduism will be familiar with E. Deutsch, *Advaita Vedānta: A Philosophical Reconstruction* (Honolulu: University of Hawaii, 1969); and E. Deutsch and J. A. B. van Buitenen, *A Source Book of Advaita Vedānta* (Honolulu: University of Hawaii, 1971). See also R. V. Das, *Introduction to Śaṅkara* (Calcutta: Firma K. L. M. Mukhopadhyay, 1968); K. S. Murty, *Revelation and Reason in Advaita Vedānta* (Waltair: Waltair University, 1959). Authoritative and important studies on various aspects of *Advaita* Vedānta are also contained in the collections of essays by S. K. Maitra, *Fundamental Questions of Indian Metaphysics and Logic* (Calcutta: Chuckervertty, Chatterjee & Co., 1959-1961) and H. G. Coward, ed., *Studies in Indian Thought. Collected Papers of Prof. T. R. V. Murti* (Delhi: Motilal Banarsidass, 1984). The most exhaustive survey of the source literature for *Advaita* Vedānta is R. Thangaswami, *A Bibliographical Survey of Advaita Vedānta Literature* [Sanskrit] (Madras: University of Madras, 1980).

27. Sureśvara, in his *Naiṣkarmyasiddhi*, refers to Śaṅkara as "the source of pure knowledge . . . and of illumination." He calls him "omniscient," "the guru of gurus," and compares him to Śiva himself. Śaṅkara, as is well known, is one of the names of Śiva. The *Naiṣkarmyasiddhi* has been edited and translated by K. K. Venkatachari (Adyar: Adyar Library, 1982). For Sureśvara's teaching and his relationship to Śaṅkara, cf. the Introduction to R. Balasubramanian, ed. and trans., *The Taittirīyopaniṣad Bhāṣya-Vārtika of Sureśvara* (Madras: Radhakrishnan Institute for the Advanced Study of Philosophy, University of Madras, [2]1984).

28. A. Nataraja Aiyer and S. Lakshminarasimha Sastri, the authors of *The Traditional Age of Śrī Śaṅkarāchārya and the Maṭhs* (Madras: private publication,

1962) not only provide the lists of all the successors to Śaṅkārācarya relying on eminent scholars who "have already proved that the date of Śaṅkara is 509-477 B.C." (Preface) but also bring excerpts from court cases initiated in our century in order to settle the claims of candidates and countercandidates to some *gaddis* (headships of *mathas*).

29. A very informative account of the Śaṅkarite tradition, including its present condition, is given in W. Cenkner, *A Tradition of Teachers. Śaṅkara and the Jagadgurus Today.* (Delhi: Motilal Banarsidass, 1983).

30. For biographical details, see M. Yamunacarya, *Rāmānuja's Teachings in His Own Words* (Bombay: Bharatiya Vidya Bhavan, 1963), 1-39; also J. B. Carman, *The Theology of Rāmānuja. An Essay in Inter-religious Understanding*, Yale Publications in Religion 18 (New Haven and London: Yale University Press, 1974), Chapter 2, "Rāmānuja's Life."

31. See Krishna Datta Bharadwaj, *The Philosophy of Rāmānuja,* (New Delhi: Sir Sankar Lall Charitable Trust Society, 1958). Also Arvind Sharma, *Viśiṣṭādvaita Vedānta: A Study* (New Delhi: Heritage Press, 1978).

32. R. Balasubramanian, a contemporary Indian scholar, is associated with the Radhakrishnan Institute for the Advanced Study in Philosophy at the University of Madras, which under T. M. P. Mahadevan's leadership had become the leading modern scholarly center for *Advaita.* Balasubramanian responds to this criticism in *Some Problems in the Epistemology and Metaphysics of Rāmānuja*, Professor L. Venkataraman Endowment Lectures 1975-1979 (Madras: University of Madras, 1978).

33. S. N. Dasgupta, *HIPh*, op. cit., vol. 3, 471.

34. This is the last verse of the *Vedāntasūtra* meaning "no return, on account of the scripture words."

35. In English, see *Rāmānujabhāṣya* G. Thibaut, trans., in *SBE*, vol. 48, 1904. The edition that has been used here is *Śrī Bhagavad Rāmānuja Granthamālā*, P. B. Annangaracharya Swami, ed. (Kancheepuram: Granthamala Office, 1956).

36. For details, see B. N. K. Sarma, *Madhva's Teachings in His Own Words* (Bombay: Bharatiya Vidya Bhavan, 1961), 1-26; and also the major works of the same author: *Philosophy of Śrī Madhvācārya* (Bombay: 1961); *A History of the Dvaita School of Vedānta and Its Literature*, 2 vols. (Bombay: 1960-1961). S. Siauve, *La doctrine de Madhva,* (Pondichéry: 1968).

37. Text and French translation with introduction and notes in Suzanne Siauve, *La voie vers la connaissance de Dieu sélon l'Aṇuvyākhyāna de Madhva* (Pondichéry: Institue Français d'Indologie, 1957).

38. *Aṇuvyākhyāna*, 13.

39. *Mahānārāyaṇopaniṣad* 1 f.

40. Complete text edition (Bombay: Nirṇāyasāgara Press). Complete English translation, S. S. Rao (Tirupati: [2]1936).

41. Sanskrit text and English translation of *Ātmabhodha*, Swami Nikhilananda, trans. (Mylapore: Ramakrishna Math, [2]1962); of *Upadeśasahasrī*, Swami Jagadananda, ed. and trans. (Madras: Ramakrishna Math, [3]1961); of *Viveka-cudāmaṇī*, Swami Madhavananda, trans. (Calcutta: Ramakrishna Math, [7]1966).

42. Sanskrit text and English translation, Swami Nikhilananda, ed. and trans. (Calcutta: Ramakrishna Math, [4]1959).

43. Sanskrit text and English translation, Swami Swahananda, ed. and trans. (Madras: Ramakrishna Math, 1967). Vidyāraṇya Swāmi is supposed to be identical with Mādhavācārya, the author of the famous *Sarvadarśanasaṁgraha* and head of the Śṛṅgerī Math from 1377 to 1386. In India, the Hindī *Vedānta-sāgara* by Swami Niścaldās of the nineteenth century enjoys a very great reputation. A Sanskrit version of this work has also been published.

44. Sanskrit text, English translation, and notes, S. S. Suryanarayana Sastri, ed. and trans. (Adyar: Adyar Library, 1942).

45. Sanskrit text and English translation, S. S. Raghavacar, ed. and trans. (Mysore: Ramakrishna Ashrama, 1956).

46. Sanskrit text, English translation and notes by Swami Adidevananda, ed. and trans. (Mylapore: Ramakrishna Math, 1949).

47. Sanskrit text and English translation, V. Krsnamacarya, ed. and trans. (Adyar: Adyar Library, 1950).

48. Sanskrit text and English translation, P. Nagaraja Rao, ed. and trans. (Adyar: Adyar Library, 1943).

27. HINDU REFORMS AND REFORMERS

1. S. Radhakrishnan, *My Search for Truth* (Agra: Agrawala, 1946), 6 f.

2. I am thinking specifically of the "Nātha movements," such as the Gorakhnāta and the Kabīr Panths, the Sikh community founded by Gurū Nānak, and similar groups. See G. H. Westcott, *Kabīr and the Kabīrpanth* (Calcutta: YMCA Publishing House, [2]1953); M. A. Macauliffe, *The Sikh Religion: Its Gurūs, Sacred Writings and Authors*, 6 vols. (Oxford: Oxford University Press; reprinted in 3 vols., Delhi: S. Chand, 1963); and more recent works by H. McLeod.

3. In "Hinduism a Static Structure or a Dynamic Force," in *Nehru Abhinandan Granth* (Calcutta: Nehru Abhinandan Granth Committee, 1949) A. S. Altekar, a highly respected scholar, wrote: "It was an evil day when the non-official change-sanctioning authority, the *Daśāvara pariṣad* of the *Smṛti* was replaced by a government department presided over by the Minister for Religion. For,

when Hindu rule came to an end by the thirteenth century, this department also disappeared, and during the last 600 years Hinduism has remained more or less static. With no authoritative and intelligent agency to guide him, the average Hindu believes that religious beliefs, philosophical theories and social practices, current in the twelfth century, are of hoary antiquity, it is his conviction that they are all sanctioned by the scriptures (which he does not understand), and that to depart from them is unpardonable sin" (pp. 421 f.).

4. Second edition (Madras: Christian Literary Society for India, 1900).

5. Ibid., 12.

6. Ibid., 40 ff. See also C. T. Jackson, *The Oriental Religions and American Thought* (Westport, Conn.: Greenwood Press, 1981), Chapter 5, "The Missionary View."

7. The first major study was J. N. Farquar, *Modern Religious Movements in India* (Oxford: Oxford University Press, 1914). Since then, countless studies have been produced by Indian and foreign scholars. See N. S. Sarma, *Hindu Renaissance* (Benares: Benares Hindu University, 1944).

8. *Complete Works of Swami Vivekananda*, 8 vols. (Calcutta: Advaita Ashrama, 1970-1971), vol. 3, 151.

9. Ibid., vol. 5, 152.

10. The most recent work is S. C. Crawford, *Ram Mohan Roy: Social, Political and Religious Reform in Nineteenth Century India* (New York: Paragon House, 1987). A source still indispensable is M. C. Parekh, *The Brahmo Samāj* (Calcutta: Brahmo Samaj, 1922).

11. A party of orthodox Brahmins, in an attempt to get the law rescinded, travelled to London to state their case; Ram Mohan Roy also journeyed there, dying in Birmingham in 1833.

12. Important contemporary documents are collected in J. K. Majumdar, *Raja Rammohun Roy and Progressive Movements in India, Volume I. A Selection from Records (1775-1845)* (Calcutta: Brahmo Mission Press, n.d.), 19, reproduces the list of names who voted for or against the abolition of *satī*.

13. The cover story of *India Today* (15 June 1986): 26-33: "Female Infanticide: Born to Die." Also child marriages are still quite common in India as a feature article, "Wedding of the Dolls," (pp. 74-77) in the same magazine demonstrates.

14. See M. C. Parekh, op. cit.

15. The text with English translation by Hem Chandra Sarkar appeared as a Centenary Edition (Calcutta: Brahmo Samaj, 1928).

16. See M. C. Parekh, *Brahmarṣi Keshub Chander Sen* (Rajkot: Oriental Christ House, 1926).

17. See Lala Lajpat Rai, *The Ārya Samāj* (London: Longmans, 1932). Major work on Dāyānanda Saraswatī and the Ārya Samāj has recently been done by J. Jordens, whose findings are apt to revise the prevailing impressions. Dāyānanda's main work is *Satyārtha Prakāśa*, published first in the Āryan-era year of 1972949060 and reprinted many times (English translation Allahabad: Kal Press, 1947).

18. D. G. Tendulkar, *Mahatma*, 8 vols. (Bombay: V. K. Jhaveri, 1952-1958), with numerous illustrations; Suresh Ram, *Vinoba and His Mission* (Kasi: Akhil Bharata Sarva Seva Sangh, Rajghat, [3]1962).

19. *Young India* (6 October 1921).

20. Ibid.

21. Modhi Prasad, *A Gandhian Patriarch. A Political and Spiritual Biography of Kaka Kalelkar*, foreword by Lal Bahadur Shastri (Bombay: Popular Prakashan, 1965).

22. The source of all books about Ramakrishna is the voluminous *Gospel of Ramakrishna*, an English rendering of the transcript of all the utterances of Ramakrishna over many years. See Swami Nirvedananda, "Sri Ramakrishna and Spiritual Renaissance" in *CHI*, vol. 4, 653-728 (Calcutta: Ramakrishna Mission Institute of Culture). A large amount of literature about the main figures of the Ramakrishna Mission and its activities are published by this movement.

23. *Complete Works* op. cit., vol. 3, 139.

24. Ibid., 27-29.

25. The Sri Aurobindo Ashram Pondichery is bringing out all the writings of Sri Aurobindo and, through numerous magazines, films, etc., also reports its present activities.

26. See the Bibliography for the works of S. Radhakrishnan. An informative survey, with an autobiographical sketch, is given in P. Schilpp, ed., *The Philosophy of Sarvepalli Radhakrishnan*, Library of Living Philosophers (New York: Tudor Publishing Co., 1952).

27. *Bunch of Thoughts,* (Bangalore: Vikrama Prakashan, [2]1966), 123.

28. *The Collected Works of Śrī Ramaṇa Mahārṣi*, A. Osborne, ed., (New York: S. Leites, 1959); A. Osborne, *Ramaṇa Mahārṣi and the Path of Self-knowledge* (Bombay: Jaico, [2]1962). The Also, *Śrī Mahārṣi: A Short Lifesketch*, with many photographs (Tiruvannamalai: Ramaṇāśramam, [4]1965).

29. Consult the Bibliography for his own works. About him, see the brief biography of his successor, Swami Cidānanda, *Light Fountain* (Rishikesh: 1967); K. S. Ramaswami Sastri, *Śivānanda: The Modern World Prophet* (Rishikesh: 1953).

30. The numerous and often reprinted books by Jiddu Krishnamurti are transcripts

of his public addresses and questions and answers noted down by his numerous followers. One of the most popular is Krishnamurti's *The First and Last Freedom* with a foreword by Aldous Huxley (London: V. Gollancz, 1967). One of the last, his *The Awakening of Intelligence* (New York: Avon Books, 1976), contains a by-now famous interview with physicist David Bohm. About him, see Pupul Jayakar, *J. Krishnamurti: A Biography* (Delhi: Penguin India, 1987).

31. C. Das Gupta, *Mother as Revealed to Me* (Benares: Shree Shree Anandamayi Sangha, 1954); Bhaiji, transl.

32. See *Autobiography of a Yogi* (*Bombay: 1960*) and the magazines of the Yoga Fellowship.

33. Martin Eban, ed., *Maharishi the Guru. The Story of Maharishi Mahesh Yogi* (Bombay: Pearl Publications, 1968). See also the numerous periodical publications of this movement.

34. See *Back to Godhead*, the magazine of the Hare Krishna movement, which gives in each issue several times complete lists of the works of the founder guru.

35. His works have been collected under the title *Wanderings in the Himalayas* (Madras: Ganesh, 1960).

36. See his twelve-volume commentary on the *Bhagavadgītā* and his monthly publication, *Tapovan Prasād*, as well as the pamphlets issued in connection with the Sandeepany Sadhanalaya.

37. See *Satya Sāī Speaks*, 6 vols. (Sri Sathya Sai Education and Publications Foundation, Kadugodi, 1974-75).

38. H. Sunder Rao, "The Two Babas," *Illustrated Weekly of India* (21 November 1965).

39. "Call to Revive Hinduism: Viswa Sammelan," *Times of India* (10 December 1977).

40. Cf. M. N. Roy, *Materialism* (Calcutta: Renaissance Publishers, ^{2}1951). In the Foreword to the second edition, he wrote: "Since this book was written in 1934 and first published in 1940 religious revivalism has gained ground in philosophical thought. Mystic and irrationalistic tendencies have become more and more pronounced even in social philosophy and political theories. These developments are the symptoms of an intellectual crisis." See also his *New Humanism*, 2d rev. ed. (Calcutta: Renaissance Publishers, 1953).

41. P. C. Chatterji, *Secular Values for Secular India* (Delhi: 1986).

42. *Illustrated Weekly of India* (5 February 1965). It must be kept in mind that this English-language weekly does not necessarily reflect the opinion of the traditional non-English-speaking Hindus.

43. *Seminar* 64(December 1964).

44. S. K. Haldar, Ibid., 20 ff.

45. J. Duncan M. Derret, *The Death of a Marriage Law. Epitaph for the Rishis,* (New Delhi: Vikas, 1978). A. S. Altekar (see note 3) blames the opposition on a misunderstanding: "This utter and pitiable ignorance of the real nature of Hinduism is at the root of the amazing opposition which measures like the Hindu Code have evoked in the recent past even in educated circles. . . . Our ancient *rishis* never expected that the rules that they had laid down would be regarded as binding for ever by their descendants. They themselves have pointed out the necessity of making periodical changes in them." Altekar refers here to *Manusmṛti* IV, 60.

    One of the major symptoms of "secularism" in India is the rapidly increasing divorce rate. See *India Today* (31 December 1986), "Divorce Getting Common," 86-93. The New Hindu Marriage Act allows Hindu women to file for divorce and to expect alimony from their former husbands.

46. As Peter Robb, "The Challenge of Gau Mata: British Policy and Religious Change in India, 1880-1916," *Modern Asian Studies* 20, no. 2(1986): 285-319, has shown, the agitation against cow slaughter, which is a major political issue in today's India, has a rather long history.

28. HINDU NATIONALIST POLITICS AND HINDUISM AS WORLD RELIGION

1. Cover story *India Today* (31 May 1986): 76-85.

2. H. J. Klimkeit, *Der politische Hinduismus. Indische Denker zwischen religiöser Reform und politischem Erwachen* (Wiesbaden: Harrassowitz, 1984). Important source material is utilized, much of it for the first time, in Jürgen Lütt, *Hindu-Nationalismus in Uttar Pradeś 1867-1900* (Stuttgart: Ernst Klett Verlag, 1970). A good analysis of the decisions facing Hindu society after Independence, and still quite relevant, is K. M. Panikkar, *Hindu Society at Cross Roads* (Bombay: Asia Publishing House, 1955). From a Western viewpoint, see W. H. Morris-Jones, *The Government and Politics of India* (London: Hutchinson University Library, 1964).

3. An extract (in translation) from *Ānanadamaṭha* with the full text of the *Bande Mātaram* is provided in W. T. de Bary, general ed., *Sources of Indian Tradition* (New York and London: Columbia University Press, 1958), vol. 2, 156 ff.

4. See M. J. Harvey, "The Secular as Sacred? The Religio-Political Rationalization of B. G. Tilak," *Modern Asian Studies* 20, no. 2(1986): 321-31.

5. The full text of the manifesto is reproduced in M. Pattabhiram, ed., *General Elections in India in 1967. An Exhaustive Study of Main Political Trends* (Bombay: Allied Publishers, 1967), 217 ff.

6. Samagra Savarkar Wangmaya, *Hindu Rastra Darsan*, 6 vols. (Poona: Maharastra Prantik Hindu Sabha, 1964).

7. A very well-researched account of the background of N. Godse and the events up to and including Gandhi's assassination is given in L. Collins and D. Lapierre, *Freedom at Midnight* (New York: Simon and Shuster, 1975; reprint New York: Avon Books, 1980).

8. M. A. Jhangiani, *Jana Sangh and Swatantra: A Profile of the Rightist Parties in India* (Bombay: Manaktala, 1967). Also see V. P. Varma, *Modern Indian Political Thought* (Agra: L. N. Agrawala, [4]1968) and S. Ghose, *Modern Indian Political Thought* (New Delhi: Allied Publishers, 1984).

9. Quoted in M. A. Jhangiani, ibid., 10.

10. See the "election manifesto" in Pattabhiram, op. cit., 204 ff.; also Deendayal Upadhyaya, "Jana sangh," *Seminar* 89(January 1967): 34-37 and "A Democratic Alternative," *Seminar* 80(April 1966): 21-24.

11. See K. Saxena, "The Janata Party Politics in Uttar Pradesh (1977-79)," *Indian Political Science Review* (July 1983): 172-87. The vindictiveness of the Janata government vis-á-vis the former Congress leaders is quite vividly described in Chapter 15 of the biography of the present President of India, *Giani Zail Singh*, by Surinder Singh Johar (New Delhi: Gaurav Publishing House, 1984).

12. The Viśva Hindu Pariṣad publishes a monthly, *Hindu Viśva.* In a special issue, brought out before the Prayaga Sammelan January 1966, a number of prominent leaders spelled out the essence of the movement in Hindī and English articles: e.g., S. S. Apte, "Viśva Hindu Pariṣad. Confluence of Hindu Society," *Hindu Viśva* (January 1966): 87-89.

13. The article in *India Today* quoted at the beginning of this chapter calls the Viśva Hindu Pariṣad "the intellectual arm of the R.S.S., with a million dedicated workers in 2500 branches all over India."

14. Information on the origin and structure of the R.S.S. is contained in literature mentioned in note 7. *Seminar* 151(March 1972) had a major article on the R.S.S. by D. R. Goyal and provided a fairly extensive bibliography. More recent publications are referred to in P. Dixit, "Hindu Nationalism," *Seminar* 216(August 1977): 27-36. *The Illustrated Weekly of India's* cover story on its March 12, 1978 was "How Powerful is the R.S.S.?" It also carried an interview with Balasaheb Deoras. The R.S.S. publishes a weekly magazine, *The Organiser.* See also C. P. Barthwal, "Rashtriya Swayamsevak Sangh: Origin, Structure and Ideology," *Indian Political Science Review* (December 1983): 23-37.

15. *Bunch of Thoughts* (Bangalore: Vikrama Prakashan, 1966), Chapter 1, "Our World Mission," 9 f.

16. *Illustrated Weekly of India* (12 March 1978): 11.

17. His principles are laid down in *Rām Rājya aur Marxvād* (Gorakhpur: Gītā Press, 1956).

18. Cf. K. P. Karunakaran, "Regionalism," *Seminar* 87(November 1966): 21-25.

19. The *Illustrated Weekly of India* devoted its March 15, 1970, issue to the theme "Private Armies." Meanwhile, much has been written on them.

20. See, e.g., A. George, *Social Ferment in India* (London: Athlone Press, 1986); Also K. K. Gangadharan, "Shiv Sena," *Seminar* 151(March 1972): 26-32.

21. N. K. Singh, "Ānand Mārg," *Seminar* 151(March 1972): 21-25, with a bibliography. Also see "Anand Marg's Lust for Blood," *Illustrated Weekly of India* (30 October 1977).

22. P. C. Chatterji, "Secularism: Problems and Prospects," Chapter 7 in *Secular Values for Secular India* (New Delhi: Lala Chatterji, 1984), gives a fairly detailed account of some of the major recent communal riots and their genesis. See also S. P. Aiyar, *The Politics of Mass Violence in India* (Bombay: Manaktalas, 1967).

23. Louis Dumont, in a very incisive study, "Nationalism and Communalism," in *Religion/Politics and History in India* (The Hague: Mouton, 1970), 89-110, operates with a definition of communalism provided by W. C. Smith in *Modern Islam in India,* (Lahore: Mohammed Ashraf, ^{3}1963), 185, as "that ideology which emphasizes as the social, political and economic unit the group of adherents of each religion, and emphasizes the distinction, even the antagonism, between such groups." Communalism is, in a certain sense, a specifically Indian phenomenon, large enough to make sure that the routine Western sociology and political science approach to Indian society is inadequate. Nirmal Mukarji, "The Hindu Problem," *Seminar* 269(January 1982): 37-40.

24. Moin Shakir, "Social Roots of Communalism," *Religion and Society* 31, no. 4(December 1984): 24-44.

25. Ajit Roy, "Communalism—Its Political Roots," *Religion and Society* 31, no. 4(December 1984): 14-23. Ajit Roy is editor of *Marxist Review*.

26. Upadhyaya, "A democratic alternative," op. cit., 23: "Ideology-based parties and policy-oriented politics are desirable, for they alone can sublimate politics and distinguish it from the game of self-aggrandizing power-hunting . . . an education of the people on an ideological and programmatic basis is necessary so that they are freed of casteism, communalism and regionalism."

27. A. S. Altekar, "Hinduism; A Static Structure or a Dynamic Force," p. 425.

29. CHRONOLOGY

1. See H. D. Sankalia, "Paleolithic, Neolithic and Copper Ages," in *HCIP*, R. C. Majumdar, general ed., vol. I, pp. 125-42.

2. F. E. Pargiter, *Ancient Indian Historical Tradition* (reprint Delhi: Motilal Banarsidass, 1952), starting from Puranic records takes a notably different departure and assumes that the Aryans entered India from the mid-ranges of the Himalayas and settled around Benares ca. 2300 B.C.E. before spreading

westward and eastward, so that the decline of the Indus civilization would not have any causal connection with the Aryan invasion.

3. See P. C. Sengupta, *Ancient Indian Chronology* (Calcutta: University of Calcutta, 1947), illustrating some of the most important astronomical methods.

4. See A. D. Pusalker, "Historical Traditions," in *HCIP*, vol. 1, pp. 271-336.

5. Sengupta, *op.cit.*, pp. 101 f.

6. S. B. Roy, "Chronological Infrastructure of Indian Protohistory," *Journal of the Bihar Research Society* (JBRS) 58 (1972): 44-78; and "Chronological Framework of Indian Protohistory—The Lower Limit," *Journal of the Baroda Oriental Institute* (JBOI) 32, nos. 3-4 (March-June 1983): 254-74.

7. About these and other eras used in India, see L. Renou and Jean Filliozat, eds. *L'Inde Classique*, vol. 2. (Paris-Hanoi: Imprimerie National, 1953), Appendix 3, "Notions de chronologie," 720-38.

Glossary

abhāva	Nonperception (in the Nyāya system); nonbeing (in the Vaiśeṣika system).
abhaya	fearlessness; in iconology, *abhaya mudra* is the hand pose of deity, inspiring confidence and trust.
abhiniveśa	desire; in the *yoga* system; instinctive craving for life.
abhiṣeka	anointment, part of installation ceremony of a king and an image of the deity.
abhyāsa	exercise, practice, exertion.
abhyudaya	rise of sun or other heavenly bodies; festival
ācamana	rinsing of mouth with water before worship and before meals.
acara	immobile (used as an attribute of the Supreme Being).
ācārya	master (also used as equivalent to M.A.).
acetana	without consciousness (used as attribute of matter).
acintya	beyond intellectual understanding.
ādāna	taking away.
adbhuta	marvelous, miraculous.
adharma	unrighteousness, evil.
adhikāra	qualification (especially of students of religion).
adhikāraṇa	section of a textbook.
adhyāsa	superimposition; misidentification.

adhyātma	supreme; spiritual; relating to the Supreme Being.
adhyaya	chapter (of a treatise).
aditi	Vedic goddess, "Mother Earth," mother of *ādityas*
ādivāsi	original inhabitants; appellation adopted by the tribals of India.
adṛṣṭa	invisible; important technical term in the Nyāya and Vaiśeṣika systems as well as in linguistic speculation.
advaita	nonduality; name of a school of Vedānta.
ādya prakṛti	primeval matter.
āgama	source, beginning; name of a class of writings considered as revealed by the Śaivas.
aghora	horrible; name of a sect of Saivites.
agni	fire; one of the foremost Vedic gods.
agnicayana	a particular kind of Vedic fire sacrifice.
agnihotra	a Vedic fire sacrifice.
agniṣṭoma	fire sacrifice.
ahaṁkāra	principle of individuation; egotism.
ahiṁsā	not killing; nonviolence.
ahita	improper, unwholesome, not propitious.
aiśvarya	lordliness.
aja	unborn (masc.); attribute of the Supreme Being; billygoat.
ajā	unborn (fem.); attribute of primordial matter; nannygoat.
akala	without parts; attribute of Supreme Being.
akāma	without desire.
ākāśa	ether (one of the five elements of Indian cosmology); space.

ākhyāna bhāga	narrative part of a sacred text.
akhāḍā	place of assembly; proper name of establishment of some sects.
akhila	undivided; complete.
akṛti	uncreated; eternal principle underlying words, etc.
akṣara	imperishable; syllable (letter); name of Supreme Being.
alaṁkāra	ornament; technical term for ornate literature.
amara	immortal.
amarṣa	impatience; anger; passion.
aṁbikā	mother; Mother Goddess.
amṛta	nectar; draught of immortality.
aṁśa	part, fragment.
anādhāra	without support.
anādi	without beginning; eternal.
ānanda	bliss; used as last part of the proper name of many *saṁnyāsis*.
ananta	without end; proper name of the world-snake upon which Viṣṇu rests.
aṇava	veil; congenital ignorance concerning the ultimate; stain.
aṅga	member; constituent part, e.g., of a major work.
aṇimā	smallness; in *yoga* the faculty to diminish one's size.
aniruddha	free, without hindrance; proper name of one of the *vyūhas* of Viṣṇu.
anitya	not permanent; transient.
añjali	a handful (e.g., of flowers).
aṅkuśa	goad; one of the divine weapons.

anna	food, especially rice; formerly, sixteenth part of a rupee.
anṛta	against the (moral) law.
anta	end, death.
antarātman	conscience.
antaryāmin	the "inner ruler," the Supreme Being as present in the heart (literally understood).
antyeṣṭi	last rites.
aṇu	atom.
anubhava	experience.
anugraha	attraction; grace of God.
anumāna	inference.
apara	unsurpassed; attribute of the Supreme Being.
aparādha	fault, sin.
aparādha kṣamāpañca	prayer for forgiveness of faults.
aparigraha	without having (or wanting) possessions.
aparokṣa	immediate, present.
apas	water.
apāśraya	supportless.
apauruṣeya	not man-made; technical term to describe the supernatural origin of the Veda in the Mīmāṁsā system.
āpsara	nymph.
apūrva	technical term in the Mīmāṁsā system to denote the not-yet realized effect of a sacrifice.
araṇya	forest.
arcā	rites of worship of an image.
arcāvatāra	image of God, who took on this form in order to become an object of worship for the devotees.

ardha	half.
ardhanarīśvara	figurative representation of Śiva, in which one half shows a male figure, the other half a female one.
arghya	water to rinse hands before worship or before meals.
arjuna	bright; proper name of the hero of the *Bhagavadgītā*.
arka	sun.
artha	object; meaning; wealth.
arthāpatti	inference, presumption.
ārya	noble (man); self-designation of the "Āryans."
asaṁbaddha	unfettered; incoherent (talk).
āsana	seat, sitting posture.
asat	not true; "not real"
āśīrvādam	(ritual) blessing.
āsmitā	egoism; from *asmi*, "I am."
aspṛha	without desire.
āśrama	hermitage; stage in life; proper name of a group of *saṁnyāsis*.
aṣṭāgraha	a certain constellation of sun, moon, earth, and the five major planets.
aṣṭāvaraṇa	eight concealing (clouding) veils of the Self.
asteya	not stealing.
āstika	someone who accepts the authority of the Veda; orthodox.
aśubha	inauspicious.
asuras	demons; class of superhuman beings.
asūyā	indignation; envy, jealousy.
aśvamedha	horse sacrifice.

aśvattha	a tree (ficus sacra).
aśvins	Vedic gods, a pair of brothers; astronomy, Castor and Pollux.
ātmakūta	self-deceit.
ātman	self.
ātmanastuṣṭi	contentment.
audarya	being in the womb.
audārya	generosity
āvāhana	invitation of the deity at worship.
avatāra	descent (of god in a bodily form).
avidyā	ignorance (of reality).
avyakta	unmanifest.
āyurveda	traditional Indian medicine; literally, "life knowledge."
bābā(jī)	"little father"; affectionate nickname for ascetics.
bala	strength, power.
bandha	bondage.
bhadra	well, happy; blessing.
bhāga	luck, fortune.
bhagavan	lord; most general title of god.
bhāī [Hindī]	brother; most common appellation.
bhajana	devotional recitation.
bhakti	love, devotion.
bhasma	(sacred) ashes.
bhāṣya	commentary.
bhāva	condition; emotion; nature.
bhaviṣya	future.

bhaya	fear, terror.
bheda	difference.
bhikṣu	mendicant; proper name of Buddhist monks.
bhoga	enjoyment.
bhū, bhūmī	earth; proper name of Viṣṇu's second consort.
bhukti	enjoyment.
bhūta	a being, a spirit.
bibhatsa	trembling.
bīja	seed.
biṇḍu	crescent.
brahmā	(personal) creator-god.
brahmacari	student; celibate.
brahmacarya	first period in life, celibate studenthood.
brahmaloka	world of Brahma; highest abode.
brahman	(impersonal) absolute.
brāhmaṇa	member of the highest caste; class of ritual texts.
brahmārandra	the place from where the soul departs at death (the back of the cranium).
buddhi	intelligence; in the Sāṁkhya system, name of the first product of the union of *puruṣa* and *prakṛti*.
caitanya	spirit, also proper name for the Supreme; proper name of a Bengali saint of the sixteenth century.
cakra	circle, disc; centers in the body; one of Viṣṇu's weapons; discus.
cakravartin	universal ruler.
caṇḍa	moon; silver.
caṇḍāla	wild; bad; proper name of lowest caste; outcaste.

caṇḍana	sandalwood.
caṇḍī	fierce woman; proper name of Devī.
capātī	bread; flat unleavened wheat breads.
carita	biography.
caryā	activity; mode of behavior.
caturmukha	four-faced; proper name of Brahmā.
caturvarṇāśrama	the four *varṇas* ("castes") and stages of life.
chāyā	shadow.
choṭī	the wisp of hair left on the top of the head.
cit	consciousness; spirit.
citta	thought.
daitya	a goblin, a slave, a demon.
dakṣiṇā	sacrificial fees.
dakṣiṇācāra	right-handed path.
dāna	gift; charity.
darśana	view; audience; theory; philosophical system.
dāsa	servant; often part of proper name.
daśanāmi	ten-named; proper name of a religious order.
dasyu	slave; name for non-Āryans in *Ṛg Veda*.
dayā	compassion.
deva, devatā	divine (superior) being.
devayāna	path of the gods.
devī	goddess.
dhairya	firmness.
dhāma	area; body.
dhāraṇa	support.

dharma	"law," religion, support, etc.
dharmakṣetra	"the field of righteousness."
dharmaśāstra	law book.
dhatṛ	giver; proper name for God.
dhātu	root (in grammar).
dhṛti	firmness.
dhūpa	incense.
dhyāna	meditation; concentration in *yoga.*
digvijaya	conquest of the four quarters; appellation of the successful competition of a religious teacher.
dīkṣā	initiation.
dīpa	lamp.
dohā	a couplet in Hindī poetics.
dravya	substance; material (for sacrifice).
droha	malice.
duḥkha	sorrow, suffering.
dvaita	duality; name of a school of Vedānta.
dvaitādvaita vivarjita	beyond duality and monism.
dvandva	pair of opposites (hot-cold, etc.).
dvāpara yuga	second era of each *kalpa.*
dveśa	hatred.
dvija	twice-born; appellation of the three upper castes, whose initiation is considered a second birth.
dvīpa	island; continent.
dyaus	resplendent; sky; Vedic high god.
ekādaśī	eleventh day (of each half-month); sacred to Vaiṣṇavas.

ekāgratā	one-pointedness, single-mindedness.
ekoddiṣṭa	funeral ceremony for one deceased.
ekaśṛṅga	one-horn (unicorn); the fish descent (of Viṣṇu) with one horn, on which Manu fastened his raft and thus was saved in the great flood.
gaddi	throne, seat, headship (as of a *matha*).
gambhīrya	serenity; seriousness.
gandharva	celestial musician.
Gaṇeśa	lord of the celestial armies; elephant-headed son of Śiva and Pārvatī.
garbha	womb; *garbha-gṛha*; innermost santuary of the temples.
garuḍa	Viṣṇu's vehicle; gryphius.
gāyatrī	the Vedic formula that a Brahmin is supposed to recite three times a day.
ghāṭ(a)	steps; especially flight of steps leading to a river.
ghī	liquified butter.
gopī	milk maid.
gopuram	towerlike structure over entrance into (South) Indian temple compounds.
gośālā	old-age home for cows, maintained for religious reasons.
gosvāmi	lord of cows; title for high-ranking Vaiṣṇavas of certain communities.
gotra	stable; family, descent.
grantha	(sacred) book; an ancient Indian script.
gṛhasta	house father, male head of household.
gṛhastya	second stage in the life of a Hindu (as householder).
gṛhyasūtras	scriptures setting down the rituals to be performed in the home.

guṇa	quality.
guru	elder; spiritual master; teacher, in general.
gurukula	school according to the ancient Indian pattern.
hala	plough.
halāhala	poison churned up from the Milk Ocean, consumed by Śiva in order to save the world.
hara	literally, the one who takes away; name of Śiva.
hari	literally, the yellowish green one; name of Viṣṇu.
harṣa	joy.
hasyā	laughter.
haṭha-yoga	literally, forced or violent *yoga*; physical exercises.
hetu	cause.
hiṁsā	violence, killing.
hiraṇyagarbha	literally, golden womb; in cosmology the first being.
hita	beneficial, good.
hitavācana	well-intentioned speaking.
hlādinī	enjoyment.
holi	popular festival (Indian carnival); New Year.
homa	fire oblation.
hotṛ	class of Vedic priests.
hṛdaya	heart; core of something.
icchā	wish, desire.
iḍā	name of one of the main vessels in the body according to traditional Indian physiology.
indriya	sense organs.
īrṣyā	envy, jealousy.

iṣṭa	preferred, wished for; *iṣṭa-deva*, the god of one's choice.
īśvara	Lord; God.
itihāsa	history; technical term for the epics; historical proof.
jāgarita (*sthāna*)	waking consciousness.
jagat	world; e.g., *jagadguru* is the world preceptor.
jāl(*a*)	net (symbol for the world entangling the spirit).
jana sangha	literally, people, community; name of (rightist) political party.
janëu	sacred thread worn by the three upper castes.
japa	repetition of the name of God or a *mantra*.
jātakarma	rites performed at time of birth.
jātī	birth; race, family, "subcaste."
jaya	victory; also as greeting; "hail."
jīva(*-ātman*)	life; individual living being.
jñāna	knowledge; *jñānaniṣṭha* is the state of being firmly and irrevocably established in ultimate knowledge.
jñāni	a knower (of the absolute).
jyotiṣa	one of the auxiliary sciences of the Veda: astronomy and astrology.
jyotiṣṭoma	a seasonal sacrifice for the departed.
kaivalya	"aloneness"; ultimate aim of *yoga*.
kāla	time; black color; fate; death.
kālamukha	black mouth; name of Śiva; name of a Śaivite sect.
kālī	the "black one"; name of the terrible form of the goddess.
kaliyuga	age of strife; last period in each world era (*kalpa*).

kalki	the future (last) *avatāra* of Viṣṇu, in the form of a white horse.
kalpa	world era, day of Brahmā (432 million years); ritual; one of the auxiliary sciences of Veda, e.g., *kalpasūtras* is the texts describing sacrificial rituals.
kāma	desire, lust, love; name of god of love.
kāmadhenu	"wishfulfilling cow."
kāṇḍa	part (of a text).
kāpālin	literally, one with a skull; name of followers of certain Śaivite groups.
kāraṇa	cause; title of the Supreme Being; God.
karma	work; action; result of an action.
karyā	worship of an image through various acts.
kaṣṭa	evil; wrong; harsh.
kaupina	small strip of cloth to cover the private parts; the only garment worn by many ascetics.
kavi	poet, wise man, omniscient.
khadga	sword.
khila-bhāga	supplement (of texts).
kīrtana	congregational religious singing.
kleśa	suffering; pain.
kośa	sheath; cover; treasury; lexicon.
kriyā	activity; skill; exercises.
krodha	anger.
kṛpā	favor; grace.
kṛṣṇa	black; proper name of the most famous *avatāra* of Viṣṇu.
kṛtayuga	the first age in each world era; the golden age.

kṣamā	forgiveness.
kṣaṇa	moment; shortest time measure.
kṣatriya	warrior; the second caste.
kṣetra	field, also metaphorical.
kubera	god of wealth, king of the *yakṣas*, friend of Śiva.
kumbha	waterpot; astronomically, the sign of Aquarius.
kumbha-melā	a great gathering at specific holy places every twelfth year.
kuṇḍalinī	serpent; in Tantricism, life force.
kūrma	tortoise; one of the *avatāras* of Viṣṇu.
kuśa	a kind of grass required in Vedic rites.
lajjā	modesty; shame.
lakṣaṇa	characteristic; attribute; sign.
līlā	play.
liṅga	characteristic sign; subtle nature; phallic symbol of Śiva.
lobha	greed.
loka	world; sphere, e.g., *loka-nātha* is the Lord of the world.
lokasaṅgraha	universal welfare.
mada	intoxication; dementia.
mādhava	sweet like honey (*madhu*); proper name of Kṛṣṇa; proper name of several famous philosophers.
madhurasa	literally, honey sentiment; highest love and affection.
madhuvidyā	literally, honey knowledge; see, *Upaniṣads.*
mahā	great.
mahant(*a*)	head of a monastic establishment.

maharṣi	great sage, honorific title.
mahat	great; in the Sāṁkhya system, first evolute (intellect).
mahātmā	great soul, honorific title.
maheśvara	great lord; proper name of Śiva.
mahiṣa	buffalo; proper name of a demon killed by Devī.
maithuna	copulation; pair; astronomically, Gemini.
makara	crocodile; alligator.
mala	stain.
mālā	garland; chain; "rosary" of beads.
maṁsa	meat.
mānasa	mind borne.
māna	pride; idea, concept; honor.
manas	mind.
mānava	relating to Manu; human, e.g., *mānava-dharma* is the laws given by Manu, laws valid for the entire humankind.
maṇḍala	circle; section of *Ṛgveda.*
maṇḍapa	covered hall; tent.
maṇḍira	palace; temple.
maṅgala	auspicious, lucky.
maṅgalaśloka	an opening verse or prayer of a text to ensure that the undertaking is auspicious.
maṇi	jewel.
mantra	word, formula (especially from scriptures).
manu	ancestor of humankind.
manvantara	an age of one (of fourteen) Manu (432 million years); according to Hindu tradition, we live now in the

	seventh *manvantara* (seven more are to follow before the end).
mārga	way; street; especially in metaphor, path of salvation.
mārjāra	cat.
markaṭa	monkey.
marut(a)	wind; wind god.
maṭha	monastic establishment.
mātsara	jealous; selfish.
matsya	fish.
māyā	fiction.
melā	fair, assembly.
mīmāṁsā	inquisition; system; proper name of one *darśana.*
mithyā	futile, false; e.g., *mithyā-jñāna* is false knowledge.
mleccha	"barbarian," somebody who does not belong to Hindu culture.
moha	delusion.
mokṣa	liberation.
mṛtyu	death.
mudrā	(hand) pose.
muhūrta	thirtieth part of day, about forty-five minutes, "hour."
mukta	one who is liberated; e.g., *jīvanmukta* is one liberated while still living in the body.
mukti	liberation; e.g., *mukti-dātā* is the giver of liberation.
mūla	root; *mūla prakṛti* is primary matter ("Urmaterie").
mūla-bera	the firmly installed image in a temple.
mūla-saṁhitā	original text.
mulayahan	name of demon, personification of evil, subdued by Śiva.

mumukṣutva	desire for liberation.
muñja	a kind of grass.
mūrti	literally, embodiment; figure; image.
muśala	hammer.
nāda	(loud) sound.
nāḍī	(body) vessel, nerve.
nāga	superior being; snake; naked, heretic.
nagna	naked.
naivedya	food offered to the image of God (prepared under certain conditions to ensure its purity).
nāmakīrtana	congregational singing whereby the name of God is repeated.
nāma-rūpa	name and form; individuality.
namaskāra	greeting in a spirit of worship.
nandi	Śiva's vehicle; a bull.
naraka	hell.
nāsadīya	title of a famous Ṛgveda hymn beginning with *nāsad* ("there was not").
nāstika	heretic; someone who denies the authority of the Veda.
nāstikya	irreligiosity.
naṭarāja	king of dance, title of Śiva.
nātha	lord; e.g., *Viśvanātha* is the Lord of the Universe.
nigama	*Veda;* authoritative scripture.
nigamana	quotation (from *Veda*); in logics, deduction, conclusion.
nīla	dark blue, e.g., *Śiva nīlakaṇṭha* is Śiva with a dark blue throat.

nimeṣa	moment (shortest measure of time).
nimitta	cause.
nirguṇa	without qualities or attributes.
nirukta	classical work of etymology.
niṣkala	without part; undivided, complete.
niṣkāma	without desire; e.g., *niṣkāma karma* is action done without selfish motive.
nīti	"ethics," rules for living.
nitya	eternal.
nivṛtti	withdrawal.
niyama	(negative) commandment.
nṛsinha	man-lion; one of the *avatāras* of Viṣṇu.
nyāya	rule, method; motto; logics; syllogism.
pada	foot; verse.
pāda	part of a text.
padārtha	category (in Vaiśeṣika system).
padma	lotus.
pādya	water for washing feet in ritual.
pañca	five; e.g., *pañcāgni* is five fires.
pañcāṅga	the traditional Indian calendar.
pañcagavya	the five products of the cow.
pāñcarātra	branch of Vaiṣṇavism.
pañcatantra	famous collection of allegorical animal stories.
pañcāyat(a)	"council of five," the traditional caste or village authority.
pañcāyātanapūjā	worship of five gods.

paṇḍa	pale; proper name of father of the Pāṇḍavas.
pāṇḍa	family Brahmin who performs the traditional rituals.
paṇḍit(a)	learned man; honorific title.
pantha	path, way; e.g., *Kabīr-pantha* is the religious sect founded by Kabīr.
pāpa	sin.
para	beyond; supreme; liberation.
paradravyābhīpsā	desiring another's property.
paradroha	injurious in speech or deed.
paramārthika	that which concerns ultimate reality.
paramparā	tradition.
paraśurāma	Rāma with the battle-ax; one of the *avatāras* of Viṣṇu.
paricaraṇa	attending; rendering service.
parikrama	circumambulation.
paritrāṇa	deliverance.
paruṣa	harsh speech.
pārvatī	daughter of the mountains; name of Śiva's consort.
pāśa	fetter.
pāṣaṇḍa	heretic; unbeliever; hypocrite.
paśu	animal; cattle; in Śaivasiddhānta: unliberated men.
paśupati	lord of the animals; name of Śiva.
paṭṭiśa	spear.
pāvana	purifying; holy; fire.
pavitra	ritually pure; holy.
phala	fruit; result of an action.
piṇḍa	small ball of rice offered to ancestors as oblation.

piṅgalā	one of the major vessels in the body.
piśāca	imp; ogre.
pitāmahā	grandfather, often used as proper name of Brahmā.
pitṛ	ancestor, forefather; *pitṛyāna* is the path of the ancestors.
plakṣa	a tree (ficus Indica).
prabhā	splendor.
pradākṣiṇā	respect shown through certain actions.
pradhāna	head; source; in Sāṁkhya system, ground from which everything develops.
prajāpati	lord of creatures; creator.
prakāśa	splendor.
prakṛti	matter; nature.
pralaya	dissolution of the world.
pramāda	error.
pramāṇa	logical proof; means of cognition.
prāṇa	life breath.
praṇava	the mantra OM.
prāṇayama	breath control.
prārabdha	remainder (or karma of former births).
prārthana	prayer.
prasthāna trayī	triad of authorities (*Upaniṣads, Bhagavadgītā, Brahmasūtras*).
pratibiṁba	reflection; mirror image.
pratijñā	recognition; proposition.
pratisarga	dissolution of the universe.
pratisiddha maithuna	unlawful liaison.

pratyabhijñā	recognition.
pratyakṣa	immediate (sense) perception.
pravṛtti	inclination; active liberation.
prayaścitta	atonement (through certain prescribed acts).
prayatna	effort.
preta	soul of a deceased who has not (yet) received offerings.
prīti	amity; love.
priyavācana	gentle of speech.
pṛthivī	earth.
pūjā	worship.
punarjanma	rebirth.
punarmṛtyu	redeath.
pundarikākṣa	lotus eyed.
puṇya	merit.
pura	fort.
purāṇa	old; proper name of class of authoritative scriptures.
pūrṇimā	full moon.
purohita	class of Vedic priests.
puruṣa	man; person; supreme being; spirit.
puruṣārtha	aim of human life.
puruṣottama	supreme person.
puṣpa	flower.
puṣṭimārga	special form of *bhakti*.
putra	son.
rāga	passion; in music, basic tune.

rāgānuga bhakti	"passionate love"; special form of *bhakti.*
rājanīti	statecraft.
rajas	excitement; one of the basic three *guṇas.*
rājayoga	"royal way"; name of Patañjali's *yoga* system.
rajñī	splendor.
rakṣasa	goblin.
raktāmbara	red clothed, a name for Buddhist monks.
rāma	main hero of the *Rāmāyaṇa;* general name for God.
rāmarājya	Rāma's rule; "kingdom of God."
rasa	juice; sentiment.
rathamelā	chariot feast.
rati	pleasure; proper name of consort of god of love.
ratna	jewel; pearl; often used as honorific title.
ratrī	night.
romāñcā	horripilation; gooseflesh; enthusiasm.
ṛk	hymn.
ṛṣi	seer; wise man.
ṛta	(Vedic) law of the world (moral and cosmic).
ṛtvik	class of Vedic priests.
rudra	reddish; name of Vedic god; name of Śiva, especially in his frightful aspect.
rudrākṣa	"Rudra's eye"; rough-round seed of an Indian shrub, used in garlands of Śaivites.
rukminī	Kṛṣṇa's spouse.
śabda	sound; word; scriptural authority.
saccidānanda	the Supreme Being (being, consciousness, bliss).

sadācāra	morality; good behavior.
ṣaḍdarśana	the six orthodox systems.
sādhana	means (to gain liberation).
sādhaka	one who practices a *sādhana.*
sādhāraṇadharma	common law; religion common to humankind.
sādhu	"holy man"; mendicant.
sadhvī	a female ascetic.
sāgara	sea; great mass of things.
saguṇa	with qualities; e.g., *saguṇa brahman* is *brahman* with attributes.
sahajā	natural; in-born.
sahāmārga	one of the practices of Śaivasiddhānta.
śākhā	branch; a school of thought or practice.
sākṣātkāra	bodily vision of the supreme.
sākṣī	witness; the Supreme as present in humans.
śākta	follower of Śakti cult.
śakti	power; name of Śiva's consort.
śālagrāma	ammonite; symbol under which Viṣṇu is present.
sālokya	sharing the same world; one of the stages of liberation.
samādhi	deep concentration; death; memorial.
sāman	Vedic tune.
sāmānya	equality; category in *Vaiśeṣika.*
samāvāya	similarity.
samāveśa	togetherness.
saṁbhoga	enjoyment.
saṁdhyā	twilight; dusk and dawn; prayers recited at dawn.

saṁdhyā-bhāṣā	words with double meaning.
saṁhitā	collection; name of class of authoritative scriptures.
samīpa	nearness; stage of liberation.
samjñā	understanding.
sāṁkhya	figure, number; proper name of philosophical system.
samkīrtaṇa	congregational singing.
saṁnyāsa	renunciation.
saṁnyāsin	ascetic, homeless mendicant.
sampat	wealth.
saṁpradāya	a religious order or sect.
saṁsāra	world; connoting constant cyclic change.
saṁskāra	rites; "sacraments."
samskṛtam	artfully composed, refined; name of an old Indian high language.
samyama	concentration.
sanātana dharma	eternal law; "Hinduism."
śaṅkha	conch shell.
sanmārga	"the true way"; highest stage in Śaivasiddhānta.
saṅskṛti	culture.
śānta	sentiment of peacefulness.
santāpa	heat; compunction; atonement.
śanti	peace.
santoṣa	contentment.
śaraṇāgatī	seeking refuge.
sarga	creation; emanation.
sāraṅga	bowstring.

śarīra	body.
sarūpa	of equal form.
sarvauṣadi	mixture of all (healing) herbs.
śāstra	doctrine; treatise.
śāstri	one who knows the traditional doctrine; B.A.
sat	being, truth.
śatasāhasrasaṁhitā	collection of 100,000 verses; proper name for the *Mahābhārata*.
sattva	being; nature; virtue; one of the three *guṇas*.
satya	truth; reality.
sauca	purity.
saulabhya	benevolence.
sauśilya	kindness.
śava	corpse; Śiva with out *i* (*śakti*) is *śava*.
savitṛ	sun God.
sāyujya	togetherness.
śeṣa	the endless, immortal world-serpent upon which Viṣṇu rests.
seva	service.
siddha	accomplished; saint.
siddhi	accomplishment; in *yoga*, extraordinary faculties.
śikhā	tuft on the crown of the head, tonsure.
śikhara	spirelike elevation over central sanctuary.
śīkṣā	instruction.
śīla	good behavior; morality.
śirīṣa	a tree (acacia).

sītā	furrow; proper name of Rāma's consort.
śloka	double verse.
smāsana	cremation ground.
smṛti	what has been committed to memory; proper name for a certain class of scriptures.
snāna	(ritual) bath.
śoka	sorrow.
soma	intoxicating drink used in Vedic sacrifices.
spaṇḍaśāstra	part of Kaśmīr Śaivism; treatise of vibrations.
sphoṭa	boil; idea; connection between letter and meaning.
spṛha	worldliness.
śraddhā	faith.
śrāddha	last rites.
śrautasūtra	ritual text dealing with public Vedic sacrifices.
śravaṇa	listening to the recitation of religious texts.
śrī	fortune; proper name of Viṣṇu's consort; Sir.
śrīvatsa	mark on Viṣṇu's body signifying Lakṣmī's presence.
śṛṅgāra	feeling of erotic love.
sṛṣṭhi	creation; emanation.
śruti	what has been revealed and heard.
steya	stealing.
sthūla	gross material.
stithi	maintenance.
stotra	hymn in praise of God.
strīdhāna	marriage.
śubha	auspicious.

sūcanā	calumny.
śuddha	pure.
śuddhi	ritual of purification (for readmission into caste).
śukla	bright.
sūkṣma	subtle.
sūkta	Vedic hymn.
sūnā	activity (or place) where life is harmed.
śūṇya	zero; nothing; emptiness.
sura	divine being.
surā	intoxicating drink.
sūrya	sun.
suṣumnā	one of the main vessels in the body.
suṣupti	dreamless deep sleep.
sūtra	aphoristic textbook; thread.
svadharma	one's own duties.
svādhyāya	study of Vedic texts.
svāhā	invocation at offering to *devas.*
svāmin	Lord; today usually "Reverend."
svapna	dream.
svarga	heaven.
svārtha	self-contained.
svāstika	sign of auspiciousness.
svatantra	free.
svayambhu	being of itself; name for Supreme Being.
śyāma	black; name of Kṛṣṇa.
tamas	darkness; dullness; one of the three *guṇas.*

tantra	loom; system of practices; main branch of Hinduism.
tapas	heat; energy.
tapasvin	ascetic; one who has accumulated much merit through self-mortification.
tarka	logic; debate.
tarpaṇa	offering of water to ancestors.
tat	that; name of the Supreme Being.
tatetat	this is that; identity of Self and Supreme.
tattva	principle; nature; reality, element.
tejas	splendor; light; heat.
ṭīkā	subcommentary.
tīlaka	mark on forehead.
tirobhāva	disappearance.
ṭippaṇī	gloss.
tīrtha	fording place; place of pilgrimage (on holy river).
tīrthayātra	pilgrimage.
tiru (Tamil)	holy; e.g., *tiru-kuṛaḷ* is the *Tamiḷveda.*
tithi	moon day.
traividyā	knowledge of the three *Vedas.*
tretayuga	third world age.
trilocana	three-eyed; name of Śiva.
triloka	the three worlds.
trimārga	literally, "three ways"; the collective name for the paths of works, devotion, and knowledge.
tripuṇḍra	Śiva's trident; sign on the forehead.
triśaṅku	name of a constellation halfway between heaven and earth; name of a mythical king of Ayodhyā.

tristhalī	the three most important places of pilgrimage, viz., Prayāga (Allahābad), Kāśī (Benares), and Gāyā.
trivarga	the triad of *dharma, artha*, and *kāma.*
tṛṣṇa	thirst; greed for life.
tulasī	a small tree (holy basil), sacred to Viṣṇu.
turīya	the fourth; designation of highest stage of consciousness.
turyātīta	beyond the fourth; highest stage in some Hindu schools who claim to transcend the Vedantic *turīya.*
tyāgi	renouncer; ascetic.
udāharaṇa	example, illustration; part of Nyāya syllogism.
udbhava	appearance.
uḍumbara	Indian fig-tree, sacred to Śiva.
udyama	exertion; rising or lifting up.
upadeśa	advice; religious instruction.
upādhi	attribute; title; deceit.
upa-Gītā	"lesser Gītā."
upamāna	analogy
upamśū	prayer uttered in a whisper.
upanayana	initiation; investiture with sacred thread.
upāṅga	auxiliary sciences or texts in addition to Vedāṅgas.
upaniṣad	class of authoritative scriptures; secret doctrine.
upapurāṇa	lesser *Purāṇa.*
upāsana	worship.
upavāsa	(religious) fasting.
ūrdhva	upward.
utsava bera	processional image.

vācika	uttered audibly.
vahana	conveyance.
vaicitriya	manifoldness; distraction.
vaidhibhakti	devotion expressing itself through ritual worship.
vaikunṭha	Viṣṇu's heaven.
vairāgi(ṇī)	ascetic (fem.).
vairāgya	renunciation.
vaiśeṣika	name of a philosophical system.
vaiśya	member of third caste; businessman, artisan.
vajra	diamond; thunderbolt.
vāk	voice; word.
vālmīka	an ant's hill.
vāmācāra	left-handed way (in Tantra).
vāmana	dwarf; one of the *avatāras* of Viṣṇu.
vaṁśa	genealogy.
vānaprastha	forest dweller; third stage in a Brahmin's life.
varāha	boar; one of the *avatāras* of Viṣṇu.
varṇāśramadharma	social system of Hindu based on a partition into four classes and four stages of life.
vāstuvidyā	architecture.
vaṭa	the fig tree.
vātsalya	love toward a child.
vāyu	wind; wind god.
veda	knowledge; sacred knowledge: revelation; scripture.
vedāṅga	limb of *Veda;* auxiliary sciences.
Vedānta	end of *Veda; Upaniṣads;* name of a system.

vedī	altar for Vedic sacrifices.
vibhava	emanation.
vibhuti	supernatural power.
videha	without a body.
vidhi	ritual.
vidyā	knowledge.
vijñānamaya	made of knowledge.
vinaya	discipline.
vipra	Brahmin.
vīra	hero.
virajā	purity.
virāṭ	first product of Brahman; the universe.
vīrya	heroism.
viṣāda	despair.
viśeṣa	propriety.
viśiṣṭa	qualification.
viśvarūpa	all form.
vitarka	debate; logical argument.
viveka	descrimination.
vrata	vow; celebration.
vrātya	mendicant; a class of people; Supreme Being.
vṛddhi	growth.
vṛtti	being; condition; fluctuation; activity, means of subsistence.
vyākaraṇa	grammar.
vyakta	manifest; revealed.

vyāpāra	function.
vyāsa	arranger; proper name of a Vedic sage credited with the compilation of the *Vedas*, the *Mahābhārata*, and the *Purāṇas*.
vyavahāra	livelihood; the world of senses.
vyūha	part; special manifestation of Viṣṇu.
yajña	Vedic sacrifice.
yajñopavīta	sacred thread.
yajus	rites.
yakṣa	goblin; tree spirit.
yama	god of the netherworld; restraint (yoga).
yantra	machine; meditational device.
yatanīya	something to be accomplished.
yati	wandering ascetic.
yatidharma	rules for ascetics.
yātra	pilgrimage.
yoga	yoke; name of a system.
yojana	"mile" (either four, five, or nine miles).
yoni	source; womb.
yuga	world era.

Abbreviations Used

ABORI	*Annals of the Bhandarkar Oriental Research Institute* (Poona)
CHI	*The Cultural Heritage of India* (H. Bhattacharya, general ed.)
HCIP	*The History and Culture of the Indian People* (R. C. Majumdar, general ed.)
HDhS	*History of Dharmaśāstra* (P. V. Kane)
HIL	*A History of Indian Literature* (Jan Gonda, ed. Wiesbaden: Harrassowitz)
HIPh	*History of Indian Philosophy* (S. N. Dasgupta)
HOS	*Harvard Oriental Series* (Cambridge, Mass.)
HR	*History of Religion* (Chicago)
IFR	*Indian and Foreign Review*
JAAR	*Journal of the American Academy of Religion*
JAOS	*Journal of the American Oriental Society* (New Haven)
JAS	*Journal of the Asian Society* (Ann Arbor)
JBRS	*Journal of the Bihar Research Society* (Patna)
JIPH	*Journal of Indian Philosophy*
JOIB	*Journal of the Oriental Institute* (Baroda)
JRAS	*Journal of the Royal Asiatic Society*

KSBCCV	*Kuppuswami Sastri Birth Centenary Commemoration Volume* (Madras: Kuppuswami Research Institute)
RS	*Religion and Society* (Bangalore/Delhi)
SBE	*Sacred Books of the East* (Oxford University Press)
SBH	*Sacred Books of the Hindus* (Allahabad: Panini Office)
WZKSA	*Wiener Zeitschrift für die Kunde Südasiens*
ZMDG	*Zeitschrift der Deutschen Morgenländischen Gesellschaft*

Bibliography

Abbot, J. E. ed. and trans. *The Poet Saints of Mahārāṣṭra*, 12 vols., Poona: Scottish Mission Industries, 1926-1941.

Agni Purāṇa. Poona: Anandashram, 1957.

Agni Purāṇa, M. N. Dutt, trans., 2 vols. Reprint Varanasi: Chowkhambha, 1967.

Agrawal, D. P. "The Technology of the Indus Civilization." In *Indian Archeology, New Perspectives*, R. K. Sharma, ed., Delhi: Agam Kala Prakashan, 1982, 83-91.

Agrawala, V. S., *India as Known to Pāṇini.* Varanasi: Prithvi Prakasan, [2]1963.

———. *Matsya-Purāṇa: A Study.* Varanasi: All-India Kashiraj Trust, 1963.

———. "Mother Earth." In *Nehru Abhinandan Granth.* Calcutta: Nehru Abhinandan Granth Committee, 1949, 490 ff.

Ahirbhudhnyasaṁhitā, 2 vols., M. D. Ramanujacarya, ed.; 2d rev. ed. V. Krishnamacharya, ed., Adyar: Adyar Library, [2]1966.

Aiyangar, S. K. *Some Contributions of South India to Indian Culture.* Calcutta: Calcutta University, 1942.

Aiyar, C. P. Ramaswamy. *Fundamentals of Hindu Faith.* Trivandrum: Govt. Press, 1944.

Aiyar, S. P. *The Politics of Mass Violence in India.* Bombay: Manaktalas, 1967.

Aiyer, A. Nataraja, and S. Lakshminarasimha Sastri. *The Traditional Age of Śrī Śaṅkārācharya and the Maṭhs.* Madras: private publication, 1962.

Aiyer, V. G. Ramakrishna. *The Economy of a South Indian Temple.* Annamalai: Annamalai University, 1946.

Ajitāgama, N. R. Bhatt, ed., 2 vols. Pondichery: Institut Français d'Indologie, 1964-67.

Ali, S. *The Congress Ideology and Programme.* New Delhi: People's Publishing House, 1958.

Ali, S. M. *The Geography of the Purāṇas.* New Delhi: People's Publishing House, 1966.

Alisaunder. Alexander and Dindimus, ed. by W. W. Skeat, Latin text. Early English Text Society, Extra Series No. 31. 1876; reprint 1930.

Alper, H. P. "Śiva and the Ubiquity of Consciousness," *JIPH* (1976): 345-407.

Altekar, A. D. "Hinduism, A Static Structure or a Dynamic Force?" In *Nehru Abhinandan Granth.* Calcutta: 1949, 421-25.

———. *The Position of Women in Hindu Civilization from Prehistoric Times to the Present Day.* Benares: Motilal Banarsidass, 1956.

———. *Sources of Hindu Dharma in its Socio-Religious Aspect.* Sholapur: Institute of Public Administration, 1952.

———. *State and Government in Ancient India.* Delhi: Motilal Banarsidass, ⁴1962.

Ambedkar, B. R. *What Congress and Gandhi Have Done to the Untouchables.* Bombay: Thacker and Co., ²1946.

Amore, Roy C., and Larry D. Shinn. *Lustful Maidens and Ascetic Kings: Buddhist and Hindu Stories of Life.* New York: Oxford University Press, 1981.

Anand, Mulk Raj. *The Hindu View of Art.* Bombay: Popular, 1957.

———. *Coolie.* Bombay: Kutub, 1957.

———. *Untouchable.* Bombay: Jaico, 1956.

Sri Anandamurti. *Ānandamārga.* Anandanagar: private publ., ²1967.

Ancient Indian Tradition and Mythology (English translation of all the *Mahāpurāṇas*), 50 vols. Delhi: Motilal Banarsidass, n.d.

Anderson, W. K. and S. D. Dhamle, *The Brotherhood in Saffron: The*

Rastriya Swayamsevak Sangh and Hindu Revivalism Boulder CO: Westview Press, 1987.

Animananda, B. *The Blade: Life and Work of Brahmabhandav Upadhyaya.* Calcutta: Roy and Son, n.d.

Aṇuvākhyāna of Madhva. Bombay: Nirnaya Sagara Press, 1932. S. S. Rao, trans. Tirupati: ²1936.

Aparokṣānubhūti. Swami Vimuktananda, trans., Calcutta: Ramakrishna Math, ²1955.

Appadorai, A. *Economic Conditions in Southern India 1000-1500* A.D., 2 vols. Madras: University of Madras, 1936.

Apte, S. S. "Viśva Hindu Pariṣad. Confluence of Hindu Society," *Hindu Viśva* (January 1966): 87-89.

Apte, V. M. *Ṛgvedic Mantras in Their Ritual Setting in the Gṛhyasutras.* Poona: Deccan College Research Institute, 1950.

Arapura, J. G. *Hermeneutical Essays on Vedāntic Topics.* Delhi: Motilal Banarsidass, 1986.

Archer, W. G. *India and Modern Art.* London: Allan & Unwin, 1959.

———. *Indian Miniatures.* Greenwich: New York Graphic Society, 1960.

———. *The Loves of Krishna in Indian Painting and Poetry.* London: Allen & Unwin, 1957. New York: Grove Press (pb), 1957.

Arthasaṅgraha of Laugākṣi Bhāskara, D. V. Gokhale, trans. Poona: Oriental Book Agency, 1932.

Ashish, Madhava. "The *Sādhu* in Our Life," *Seminar* 200 (April 1976): 12-18.

Athalye, D. *Life of Lokamanya Tilak.* Poona: A. Chiploonkar, 1921.

———. *Neo-Hinduism.* Bombay: Tareporevala, 1932.

Atharvaveda, W. D. Whitney, trans., 2 vols. HOS, 1902; reprint Varanasi: Chowkhamba, 1962.

The Atharvaveda Saṁhitā, R. Roth and W. D. Whitney, (eds.) Berlin: 1856.

Ātmabodha, Swami Nikhilananda, trans. Mylapore: Ramakrishna Math, ²1962.

Atreya, B. L. *The Philosophy of the Yogavāsiṣṭha.* Adyar: Adyar Library, 1936.

Auboyer, J. *Daily Life in Ancient India from Approximately 200* B.C. to A.D. 700. New York: Macmillan, 1965.

Aufrecht, T. *Die Hymnen des Ṛgveda.* Bonn: A. Marcus, ²1877.

Ayrookuzhiel, A. M. Abraham. *The Sacred in Popular Hinduism: An Empirical Study in Chirakkal, North Malabar.* Madras: Christian Literature Society, 1983.

Ayyar, C. V. Narayana, *Origin and Early History of Śaivism in South India.* Madras: University of Madras, 1936.

Ayyar, P. V. Jagadissa. *South Indian Festivities.* Madras: Higginbothams, 1921.

Baden-Powell, B. H. *The Indian Village Community.* Reprint New Haven: Yale University Press, 1958.

———. *Land Systems of British India*, 3 vols. Oxford: Oxford University Press, 1892.

Bailey, G. M. "Brahmā, Pṛthu and the Theme of the Earth-Milker in Hindu Mythology," *Indo-Iranian Journal* 23 (1981): 105-16.

———. "Notes on the Worship of Brahmā in Ancient India," *Annali dell' Istituto Orientale di Napoli* 39 (1979): 1-170.

Baird, Robert D., ed. *Religion in Modern India.* Delhi: Manohar, 1981.

Bakker, H. "On the Origin of the Sāṁkhya Psychology," *WZKSA* 26 (1982): 117-48.

Balarāma Vedāntasūtrabhāṣya, B. D. Basu, trans. *Sacred Books of the Hindus*, vol. 5. Allahabad: Panini Office, 1934.

Balasubramanian, R. *Advaita Vedānta.* Madras: University of Madras, 1976.

———. *The Mysticism of Poygai Alvar.* Madras: Vedanta Publications, 1976.

———. *Some Problems in the Epistemology and Metaphysics of Rāmānuja*, Professor L. Venkataraman Endowment Lectures 1975-1976. Madras: University of Madras, 1978.

———, ed. and trans. *The Taittirīyopaniṣad Bhāṣya-Vārtika of Sureśvara.* Madras: Radhakrishnan Institute for the Advanced Study of Philosophy, University of Madras, [2]1984.

Balasundaram, T. S. *The Golden Anthology of Ancient Tamil Literature,* 3 vols. Madras: South India Saiva Siddhanta Book Publishing Society, 1959-1960.

Balsara, J. F. *Problems of Rapid Urbanisation in India.* Bombay: Manaktala, 1964.

Banerjea, A. K. *Philosophy of Gorakhnāth.* Gorakhpur: Mahant Dig Vijai Nath Trust, Gorakhnath Temple, 1962.

Banerjea, J. N. *The Development of Hindu Iconography.* Calcutta: University of Calcutta, [2]1956.

Banerjea, S. C. *Dharma Sūtras: A Study of Their Origin and Development.* Calcutta: Punthi Pustak, 1962.

Banerjee, G. N. *Hellenism in Ancient India.* Delhi: Munshi Ram Manoharlal, 1961.

Bannerjee, N. V. *The Spirit of Indian Philosophy,* New Delhi: Arnold-Heinemann, 1958.

Barthwal, C. P. "Rashtriya Swayamsevak Sangh: Origin, Structure and Ideology," *Indian Political Science Review* (December 1983): 23-37.

Barua, B. M. *History of Pre-Buddhistic Indian Philosophy.* Calcutta: Calcutta University, 1921.

de Bary, W. T., general ed. *Sources of Indian Tradition.* New York: Columbia University Press, 1958.

Basham, A. L. *History and Doctrines of the Ajīvikas.* London: Luzac, 1951.

———. *The Wonder that Was India.* New York: Grove Press, 1959.

Beal, S. *Si-Yu-Ki: Buddhist Records of the Western World.* London: 1884; reprint Delhi: Oriental Books Reprint Corporation, 1969.

Beals, A. R. *Gopalpur, a South Indian Village.* New York: Holt Rinehart & Winston, 1965.

Beane, W. C. *Myth, Cult and Symbols in Śākta Hinduism: A Study of the Indian Mother Goddess.* Leiden: Brill, 1977.

Bechert, H., & G. von Simson. *Einführung in die Indologie.* Darmstadt: Wissenschaftliche Buchgesellschaft, 1979.

Beck, B. (ed.) *Folktales of India*, Chicago: University of Chicago Press, 1987.

Belvalkar, S. K. *Shree Gopal Basu Malik Lectures on Vedānta Philosophy.* Poona: Bilvakunja, 1929.

Belvalkar, S. K., and R. D. Ranade. *History of Indian Philosophy. Volume II. The Creative Period. Volume III. Mysticism in Maharastra.* Poona: Bilvakunja, 1927 and 1932.

Bengali Religious Lyrics: Śākta, E. J. Thompson and A. M. Spencer, trans. Calcutta: Association Press, 1923.

Benz, E. *Indische Einflüsse auf die frühchristliche Theologie.* Mainz: Mainzer Akademie der Wissenschaften, 1951.

Bernard, T., *Haṭha Yoga.* New York: S. Weiser, 1944.

Berreman, G. D. *Hindus of the Himālayas.* Berkeley: University of California Press, 1963.

Besant, A. *Hindu Ideals.* Adyar: Theosophical Publishing House, 1904.

———. *Wake Up, India.* Adyar: Theosophical Publishing House, 1913.

———. *Theosophy and World Problems.* Adyar: Theosophical Publishing House, 1922.

Beteille, A. *Caste, Class and Power: Changing Patterns of Stratification in a Tanjore Village.* Berkeley: University of California Press, 1965.

———. *Castes, Old and New.* New York: Asia Publishing House, 1969.

Betty L. Stafford, trans. *Vādirāja's Refutation of Śaṅkara's Non-Dualism: Clearing the Way for Theism.* Delhi: Motilal Banarsidass, 1978.

Bhagavadgīta, F. Edgerton, trans. Cambridge, Mass.: Harvard University Press, 1944.

Bhagavadgītā, S. Radhakrishnan, trans. London: Allen & Unwin, 1956.

Bhagavadgītā, R. C. Zaehner, trans. Oxford: Oxford University Press, 1969.

Bhagavat, H. R., ed. *Minor Works of Śaṅkarācārya*, Poona Oriental Series No. 8. Poona: Oriental Book Agency, ^{2}1952.

Bhāgavata-Purāṇa, 2 vols. text & transl. Gorakhpur: Gītā-Press, 1952-60.

Bhaktirasāmṛtasindhu, Vijendra Snataka, ed. Delhi: Dilli Viśvavidyālaya, 1963; Swami Bon Maharaj, trans., 3 vols. Vrindaban: Institute of Oriental Philosophy, 1964-78.

The Bhāmatī of Vācaspati on Śaṅkara's Brahmasūtrabhāṣya, S. S. Suryanarayana Sastri and C. Kunhan Raja, eds. and trans. Adyar: Theosophical Publishing House, 1933.

Bhandarkar, R. G. *Vaiṣṇavism, Śaivism and Minor Religious Systems*. Reprint Varanasi: Indological Book House, 1965.

Bharadwaj, Krishna Datta. *The Philosophy of Rāmānuja*. New Delhi: Sir Sankar Lall Charitable Trust Society, 1958.

Bharati, Agehananda (L. Fischer). *The Ochre Robe*. Seattle: University of Washington Press, 1962.

———. "Psychological Approaches to Indian Studies: More Cons than Pros," *Indian Review* 1, no. 1 (1978): 71-75.

———. *The Tantric Tradition*. London: Rider and Company, 1965.

Bhardwaj, Surinder Mohan. *Hindu Places of Pilgrimage in India: A Study in Cultural Geography*. Berkeley: University of California Press, 1973.

Bhartṛhari: Vākyapādīya, K. V. Abhyankar and Acharya V. P. Limaye, eds., University of Poona Sanskrit and Prakrit Series. Poona: University of Poona, 1965.

Bhāṣapariccheda with Siddhānta Muktāvalī of Viśvanātha Nyāyapañcanana, Swami Madhavananda, trans. Calcutta: Advaita Ashrama, 1954.

Bhatt, G. P. *The Epistemology of the Bhatta School of Pūrva Mīmāṁsā*. Benares: Chowkhamba, 1954.

Bhattacharji, Sukumari. *The Indian Theogony: A Comparative Study of Indian Mythology from the Vedas to the Purāṇas*. Cambridge: Cambridge University Press, 1970.

Bhattacharya, H., general ed. *The Cultural Heritage of India*, 4 vols. Calcutta: Ramakrishna Mission Institute of Culture, ²1957-1962.

Bhattacharya, H. D. "Tantrik Religion." In *HCIP*, vol. 4.

Bhattacharya, K. C. *Studies in Vedāntism*. Calcutta: University of Calcutta, 1909.

———. *Studies in Philosophy*, vol. 1. Calcutta: Progressive Publishers, 1956.

Bhattacharya, S., "The Concept of *Bideha* and *Prakṛti-Laya* in the Sāṁkhya-System," *ABORI* 48-49 (1968): 305-12.

Bhattacharya, T. *The Canons of Indian Art: A Study of Vāstuvidyā.* Calcutta: Firma K. L. Mukhopadhyay, [2]1963.

———. *The Cult of Brahmā.* Patna: C. Bhatacarya, 1957.

Bhattacharyya, N. N. *History of the Tantric Religion.* Delhi: Manohar, 1982.

Bhaṭṭojī-Dīkṣita: Siddhānta Kaumudī, Srisa Candra Vasu, ed. and trans. 2 vols. Reprint Delhi: Motilal Banarsidass, 1962.

Bhave, Vinoba. *Bhoodan-Yajña.* Ahmedabad: Navajivan, 1954.

———. *Sarvodaya and Communism.* Tanjore: Sarvodaya Prachuralaya, 1957.

Bihari Bankey. *Minstrels of God*, 2 vols. Bombay: Bharatiya Vidya Bhavan, 1956.

———. *Bhakta Mīrā.* Bombay: Bharatiya Vidya Bhavan, 1961.

———. *Sufis, Mystics and Yogis of India.* Bombay: Bharatiya Vidya Bhavan, 1962.

Bishop, Donald H., ed. *Indian Thought: An Introduction.* New York: John Wiley & Sons, 1975.

———, (ed.), *Thinkers of the Indian Renaissance.* New York: Wiley Eastern, 1982.

Blasi, A. J. "Ritual as a Form of Religious Mentality," *Sociological Analysis* 46, no. 1 (1985): 59-72.

Bloomfield, M. *The Religion of the Veda.* New York: G. B. Putnam's, 1908.

———. *Vedic Concordance.* Reprint Delhi: Motilal Banarsidass, n.d.

Bolle, Kees W., trans. *The Bhagavadgītā, a New Translation.* Berkeley: University of California Press, 1979.

Boner, A., S. R. Sarma, and R. P. Das. *New Light on the Sun Temple of Konārak: Four Unpublished Manuscripts relating to Construction*

History and Ritual of This Temple. Varanasi: Chowkhamba Sanskrit Series Office, 1972.

Bose, D. N. *Tantras: Their Philosophy and Occult Secrets.* Calcutta: Oriental Publishing Co., [3]1956.

Bose, N. K. "The Geographical Background of Indian Culture." In *CHI*, vol. 1, 3-16.

———. *Peasant Life in India: A Study in Indian Unity and Diversity.* Calcutta: Anthropological Survey of India, 1961.

Bose, N. K. and D. Sen. "The Stone Age in India." In *CHI*, vol. 1, 93-109.

Boyd, R. *An Introduction to Indian Christian Theology.* Madras: Christian Literature Society, [2]1977.

Brahma, N. K. *Philosophy of Hindu Sādhana.* London: Trübner, 1932.

Brecher, M. *Nehru: A Political Biography*, London: Oxford University Press, 1959.

Bṛhaddevatā, A. A. Macdonell, ed. and trans. Reprint Delhi: Motilal Banarasidass, 1965.

Bṛhatī, Prabhākara Miśra's Sub-commentary to the Śābarabhāṣya. S. K. Ramanatha Sastri, ed. 3 vols. Madras: University of Madras, 1931-.

Bṛhatsaṁhitā of Varāhamihira, Pandit Acutyananda Jha Sarmana, ed. and Hindī trans. Varanasi: Motilal Banarsidass, 1959.

Briggs, G. W. *The Chamars.* Calcutta: Association Press, 1920.

———. *Gorakhanātha and Kānphaṭa Yogis.* Calcutta: Association Press, 1938.

Brown, C. M. *God as Mother: A Feminine Theology in India: An Historical and Theological Study of the Brahmavaivarta Purāṇa.* Hartford, Vt.: Claude Stark, 1974.

———. "The Origin and Transmission of the Two *Bhāgavata Purāṇas:* A Canonical and Theological Dilemma," *JAAR*, 51, no. 4 (1983): 551-67.

Brown, L. W. *The Indian Christians of St. Thomas.* London: Cambridge University Press, 1956.

Brown, P. *Indian Painting.* Calcutta: YMCA Publishing House, 1960.

———. *Indian Architecture,* 2 vols. Bombay: Taraporevala, [4]1964.

Brown, W. N. *Man in the Universe: Some Continuities in Indian Thought.* Berkeley: University of California Press, 1966.

———. *The United States and India and Pakistan.* Cambridge: Harvard University Press, 1963.

———. *India and Indology: Selected Articles.* Rosane Rocher, ed. Delhi: Motilal Banarsidass, 1978.

Brunton, P. *Maharṣi and His Message.* London: Rider & Co., 1952.

Buck, Harry M. and Glenn E. Yocum, eds. *Structural Approaches to South Indian Studies.* Chambersburg: Wilson Books, 1974.

Buddhiraja, S. *The Bhagavadgītā: A Study.* Madras: Ganesh & Co., 1927.

Bühler, G., ed. *Encyclopedia of Indo-Aryan Research.* 1897; reprint Varanasi: Indological Bookhouse, 1963.

———. *The Sacred Laws of the Āryas.* In *SBE,* vols. 2 and 14. Reprint Delhi: Motilal Banarsidass, 1964.

van Buitenen, J. A. B. *Tales of Ancient India.* New York: Bantam Books, 1961.

———. "The Name Pāñcarātra." *HR* 1, no. 2 (1961): 291-99.

———. *Rāmānuja on the Bhagavadgītā.* Delhi: Motilal Banarsidass, 1965.

Bulcke, C., *Rāmakathā*[Hindī]. Prayāg: Hindī Pariṣad Viśvavidyālaya, 1956.

Burrow, T. *The Sanskrit Language.* London: Faber & Faber, 1965.

Bussabarger, R. F., and B. D. Robins. *The Everyday Art of India.* New York: Dover, 1968.

Sri Caitanyacaritāmṛtam, S. K. Chaudhuri, trans., 3 vols. Calcutta: Gauḍia-Math, [2]1959.

Cakravartti, Viśvanātha. "*Bhaktirasāmṛtasindhubinduḥ,*" K. Klostermaier, trans., *JAOS* 1 (1974): 96-107.

Caland, W., and V. Henry. *L'Agniṣṭoma: description complète de la forme normal du sacrifice de Soma dans le culte védique,* 2 vols. Paris: E. Leroux, 1906-1907.

Callewaert, W. M., and S. Hemraj. *Bhagavadgītānuvāda: A Study in Transcultural Translation.* Ranchi: Sathya Bharati Publication, 1983.

Campbell, A. *The Heart of India.* New York: Knopf, 1958.

Candidasa, Baru. *Singing the Glory of Lord Krishna.* M. H. Klaiman, trans. Chico: Scholars Press, 1984.

Cārakasaṁhitā, T. Yadava Sarma, ed. Bombay: Nirṇaya Sāgara Press, [3]1933.

Carman, J. B. *The Theology of Rāmānuja. An Essay in Interreligious Understanding.* New Haven and London: Yale University Press, 1974.

———, and A. Marglin, eds. *Purity and Auspiciousness in Indian Society.* Leiden: Brill, 1985.

Carpenter, J. E. *Theism in Mediaeval India.* London: Constable & Co., 1921.

Carstairs, G. M. *The Twice-Born.* London: Hogarth Press, 1957.

Cenkner, W. *A Tradition of Teachers: Śaṅkara and the Jagadgurus Today.* Delhi: Motilal Banarsidass, 1983.

Chaitanya, Krishna. *Sanskrit Poetics.* Bombay: Asia, 1965.

Chakladar, H. C. *Social Life in Ancient India.* Calcutta: Greater India Society, 1929.

Chakraborti, Karipada. "Śaṅkarācārya." In *Asceticism in Ancient India.* Calcutta: Punthi Pustak, 1973.

Chakravarti, C. *Tantras: Studies on Their Religion and Literature.* Calcutta: Punthi Pustak, 1963.

Chakravarti, S. C. *The Philosophy of the Upaniṣads.* Calcutta: University of Calcutta, 1935.

Chand, T. *Influence of Islam on Indian Culture.* Allahabad: The Indian Press, 1963.

Chandavarkar, B. D. *A Manual of Hindu Ethics.* Poona: Oriental Book Agency, [3]1965.

Chatterji, J. C. *The Hindu Realism.* Allahabad: The Indian Press, 1912.

Chatterjee, B. R. "The *Rāmāyaṇa* and the *Mahābhārata* in South-East Asia." *CHI*, vol. 2, 119 ff.

Chatterjee, M., *Gandhi's Religious Thought*. South Bend: University of Notre Dame Press, 1983.

Chatterjee, S. *The Nyāya Theory of Knowledge*. Calcutta: University of Calcutta, [3]1965.

Chatterji, P. C. *Secular Values for Secular India*. New Delhi: Lola Chatterji, 1984.

Chatterji, S. and D. M. Datta. *An Introduction to Indian Philosophy*. Calcutta: University of Calcutta, [7]1968.

Chatterji, S. K. "Contributions from Different Language-Culture Groups." In *CHI* vol. 1, 76-90.

———. *Languages and Literatures of Modern India*. Calcutta: 1963.

———. "Race Movements and Prehistoric Culture." In *HCIP*, vol. 1, 164 ff.

Chattopadhyaya, S. *Reflections on the Tantras*. Delhi: Motilal Banarsidass, 1978.

———. *Some Early Dynasties of South India*. Delhi: Motilal Banarsidass, 1974.

Chattopadyaya, S. *The Evolution of Theistic Sects in Ancient India*. Calcutta: Progressive Publishers, 1963.

Chaudhuri, N. C. *Autobiography of an Unknown Indian*. London: Macmillan, 1951.

———. *The Continent of Circe*. Bombay: Jaico, 1966.

———. *The Intellectual in India*. New Delhi: Vir Publishing House, 1967.

———. *Hinduism*. London: Chatto & Windus, 1979.

Chaudhuri, Roma. "The Nimbārka School of Vedānta." In *CHI*, vol. 3, 333 ff.

———. *Doctrine of Śrīkantha*, 2 vols. Calcutta: Pracyavani, 1959-1960.

Chemparathy, G. *An Indian Rational Theology. Introduction to Udāyana's Nyāyakusumañjalī*. Vienna: De Nobili Research Library, 1972.

Chethimattam, J. B. *Consciousness and Reality. An Indian Approach to Metaphysics*. Bangalore: Dharmaram Publications, 1967.

Chethimattam, J. B., ed. *Unique and Universal: Fundamental Problems of an Indian Theology*. Bangalore: Dharmaram Publications, 1972.

Chinmulgund, P. J., and V. V. Mirashi, eds. *Review of Indological Research in the Last Seventy-five Years*. Poona: Bharayita Charitrakosha Mandal, 1967.

Choudhuri, D. C. Roy. *Temples and Legends of Bihar*. Bombay: Bharatiya Vidya Bhavan, 1965.

Choudhury, Basanti. "Love Sentiment and Its Spiritual Implications in Gauḍīa Vaiṣṇavism." In *Bengal Vaiṣṇavism, Orientalism, Society and the Arts*, D. T. O'Connel, ed. South Asia Series Occasional Papers No. 35. East Lansing: Asian Studies Center, Michigan State University, 1985.

Cidananda, Swami. *Light Fountain*. Rishikesh: Divine Light Society, 1967.

Clothey, F. W. *The Many Faces of Murukan: The History and Meaning of a South Indian God*, Religion and Society, No. 6. The Hague: Mouton, 1978.

———. "Tamil Religions." In *Encyclopedia of Religions*, M. Eliade, ed. Vol. 12, 260 ff.

———. "Pilgrimage Centers in the Tamil Cultus of Murukan," *JAAR*, 40 (1972): 79-95.

Clothey, F. M. and J. B. Long (eds.) *Experiencing Śiva*, Columbia MO: South Asia Books, 1983.

Coburn, T. B. *Devī Mahātmya: The Crystallization of the Goddess Tradition*. Delhi: Motilal Banarsidass, 1984.

Cohn, B. *India: The Social Anthropology of a Civilization*. Englewood Cliffs, N.Y.: Prentice Hall, 1971.

Colebrook, Thomas. "On the Vedas, or Sacred Writings of the Hindus," *Asiatic Researches* 8: 369-476.

Collins, L., and D. Lapierre. *Freedom at Midnight*. New York: Simon and Schuster, 1975; reprint New York: Avon Books, 1980.

Coomaraswamy, Ananda. *The Dance of Śiva*. Bombay: Asia Publishing House, ^{3}1956.

———. *History of Indian and Indonesian Art.* Reprint New York: Dover, 1965.

———. *The Transformation of Nature in Art.* Reprint New York: Dover, 1956.

Coomaraswamy, Ananda, and Sister Nivedita. *Myths of the Hindus and Buddhists.* Reprint New York: Dover, 1967.

Cormack, M. L. *She Who Rides a Peacock: Indian Students and Social Change.* New York: Praeger, 1962.

Courtright, Paul B. *Ganeṣa: Lord of Obstacles, Lord of Beginnings.* New York: Oxford University Press, 1985.

Coward, Harold G. *Bhartṛhari*, Boston: Twayne Publishers, 1976.

———. *Jung and Eastern Thought.* Albany: State University of New York Press, 1985.

———, ed. *"Language" in Indian Philosophy and Religion*, SR Supplements. Waterloo, Ont.: Wilfrid Laurier University Press, 1978.

———. *The Sphoṭa Theory of Language: A Philosophical Analysis.* Delhi: Motilal Banarsidass, 1981.

———, ed., *Studies in Indian Thought. Collected Papers of Prof. T. R. V. Murti.* Delhi: Motilal Banarsidass, 1984.

Crawford, S. Cromwell. *The Evolution of Hindu Ethical Ideals*, rev. ed. Honolulu: University of Hawaii Press, 1982.

———. *Ram Mohan Roy: Social, Political and Religious Reform in Nineteenth Century India.* New York: Paragon House, 1987.

Creel, A. B. *Dharma in Hindu Ethics.* Columbia, Mo.: South Asia Books, 1977.

Cronin, V. A. *Pearl to India: The Life of Roberto de Nobili*, London: Darton, Longman & Todd, 1966.

Crooke, W. *Popular Religion and Folklore in Northern India*, 2 vols. 1896; reprint Delhi: Munshiram Manoharlal, 1968.

Cunningham, A. *Ancient Geography of India.* Calcutta: Archeological Survey of India, 1924.

Cuttat, J. A. *Encounter of Religions.* New York: Desclee & Co., 1962.

Dandekar, R. N. "Ancient Indian Polity," *Indo-Asia Culture*, 11, no. 4 (April 1963): 323-32.

———. *Some Aspects of the History of Hinduism.* Poona: University of Poona, 1967.

———. *Universe in Hindu Thought.* Bangalore: University of Bangalore, 1972.

———. *Vedic Bibliography.* vol. 1, Bombay: Karnatak Publ. House, 1946; vol. 2, Poona: University of Poona, 1967.

———. "Vṛtraha Indra," *ABORI* 30, no. 1 (1951): 1-55.

Daniélou, A. *Hindu Polytheism.* London: Rutledge & Kegan Paul, 1963.

———. *Yoga: The Method of Re-Integration.* New York: University Books, 1956.

Danielson, H., trans. *Adiśeṣa: The Essence of Supreme Truth (Paramārthasāra).* Nisaba, Religious Texts Translation Series. Leiden: Brill, 1980.

Das, Bhagwan. *Kṛṣṇa: A Study in the Theory of Avatāras.* Bombay: Bharatiya Vidya Bhavan, 1962.

Das, R. V. *Introduction to Śaṅkara.* Calcutta: Punthi Pustak, 1968.

Daśapadārtha Śāstra, H. Ui, ed. and trans. 1917; reprint, Chowkhambha Sanskrit Series, Varanasi: Chowkhamba, 1962.

Dasgupta, G. *Mother As Revealed to Me.* Benares: 1954.

Dasgupta, S. H. *Obscure Religious Cults.* Calcutta: Firma K. L. Mukhopadhyay, [2]1962.

Dasgupta, S. N. *Development of Moral Philosophy in India.* Bombay: 1961.

———. *Hindu Mysticism.* New York: 1960.

———. *History of Indian Philosophy*, 5 vols. Cambridge: Cambridge University Press, [3]1961-1962.

———. *Natural Science of the Ancient Hindus.* Delhi: 1986.

———. *A Study of Patañjali.* Calcutta: 1930.

———. *Yoga as Philosophy and Religion.* 1924; reprint Delhi: Motilal Banarsidass, 1973.

Dass, A. C. "The Origin of Brahmanical Image Worship and the Icono-Genic Properties in *RgVeda*," *JOIB* 34, nos. 1-2 (1984): 1-11.

Dave, J. H., *Immortal India*, 4 parts. Bombay: Bharatiya Vidya Bhavan, [2]1959-1962.

Davis, K. *The Population of India and Pakistan.* Princeton: Princeton University Press, 1951.

Day, Terence P. *The Conception of Punishment in Early Indian Literature.* Waterloo, Ont.: Wilfrid Laurier University Press, 1982.

De, S. K. *Early History of the Vaiṣṇava Faith and Movement in Bengal.* Calcutta: Firma K. L. Mukhopadhyay, [2]1961.

———. *Sanskrit Poetics as a Study of Aesthetic.* Berkeley: University of California Press, 1963.

Deming, W. S. *Rāmdās and Rāmdāsis*, Religious Life of India Series. Oxford: Oxford University Press, 1928.

Derret, J. D. M., *Critique of Modern Hindu Law.* Bombay: N. M. Tripathi, 1970.

———. *The Death of a Marriage Law: Epitaph for the Rishis.* Durham, NC: Academic Press, 1978.

———. *Essays in Classical and Modern Hindu Law*, 3 vols. Leiden: Brill, 1976-1977.

———. "Greece and India: The Milindapañha, the Alexander-Romance and the Gospels," *ZRGG* 19 (1967): 33-64.

———. "Greece and India Again: The Jaimini-Aśvamedha, the Alexander Romance and the Gospels," *ZRGG* 22, no. 1 (1970): 19-44.

———. *Hindu Law, Past and Present.* Calcutta: A. Mukherjee, 1957.

———. *History of Indian Law* (*Dharmaśāstra*). Leiden: Brill, 1973.

———. *Introduction to Modern Hindu Law.* Calcutta: A. Mukherjee, 1963.

Desai, Mahadev. *The Gita According to Gandhi.* Amhedabad: Navajivan, 1946.

Deussen, P. *The Philosophy of the Upaniṣads.* 1905; reprint New York: Dover, 1966.

———. *The Philosophy of the Veda.* Edinburgh: Clark, 1908.

Deutsch, E. *Advaita Vedānta: A Philosophical Reconstruction.* Honolulu: University of Hawaii, 1969.

Deutsch, E., and J. A. B. van Buitenen. *A Source Book of Advaita Vedānta.* Honolulu: University of Hawaii, 1971.

Devanandan, P. D. *The Concept of Māyā.* Calcutta: YMCA Publishing House, 1954.

Devasenapathi, V. A. *Śaiva Siddhānta as Expounded in the Śivajñāna Siddhiyar and Its Six Commentaries.* Madras: University of Madras, 1960.

Devī Bhāgavata Purāṇa, (Varanasi: Swami Vijñananda 1962), Pandit Pustakalaya, trans., 2 vols. in SBH. Allahabad: Panini Office, 1923.

Dharampal, Gita. "Frühe deutsche Indien Berichte (1477-1750)," *ZDMG* 134, no. 2 (1984): 23-67.

Dhatta, A. K. *Bhaktiyoga.* Bombay: Bharatiya Vidya Bhavan, 1959.

Dhavamony, M. *Classical Hinduism*, Rome: Universitá Gregoriana Editrice, 1982.

———. *Love of God According to Śaiva Siddhānta: A Study in the Mysticism and Theology of Śaivism.* Oxford: Clarendon Press, 1971.

Dhingra, B. *Asia Through Asian Eyes.* Bombay: Asia Publishing House, 1959.

Diehl, C. G. *Instrument and Purpose: Studies on Rites and Rituals in South India.* Lund: 1956.

Diksitar, V. R. *Studies in Tamil Literature and History.* London: Luzac, 1930.

Dimmit, C., and J. A. B. van Buitenen, eds. and trans. *Classical Hindu Mythology: A Reader in the Sanskrit Puranas.* Philadelphia: Temple University Press, 1978.

Dimock, E. C., trans. *The Thief of Love: Bengali Tales.* Chicago: University of Chicago Press, 1963.

Dixit, P. "Hindu Nationalism," *Seminar* 216 (August 1977): 27-36.

Dowson, J. *A Classical Dictionary of Hindu Mythology and Religion, Geography, History and Literature.* London: Routledge & Kegan Paul, 1961.

Dube, S. C. *India's Changing Villages.* London: Routledge & Kegan Paul, 1958.

———. *Indian Village.* New York: Harper & Row, 1967.

Dubois, Abbé. *Hindu Manners, Customs and Ceremonies.* Oxford: Oxford University Press, [3]1959.

Dumont, L. *Homo hierarchicus: Essai sur le systéme des castes.* Paris: Gallimard 1966; English translation Chicago: University of Chicago Press, 1970.

———. *Religion/Politics and History in India: Collected Papers in Indian Sociology.* The Hague: Mouton, 1970.

Dumont, P. E. *L'Aśvamedha.* Paris: Geuthner, 1927.

Dutt, R. P., *India Today and Tomorrow.* Delhi: People's Publishing House, 1955.

Dutt, R. C. *Economic History of India 1757-1900*, 2 vols. Reprint Delhi: Publications Division, Govt. of India, 1960.

Dutt, S. *Buddhist Monks and Monasteries in India: Their History and Their Contribution to Indian Culture.* London: Allen & Unwin, 1962.

Eban, Martin, ed. *Maharishi the Guru. The Story of Maharishi Mahesh Yogi.* Bombay: Pear Publications, 1968.

Eck, Diana L. *Banaras: City of Light.* Princeton: Princeton University Press, 1983.

——. *Darśan: Seeing the Divine Image in India.* Chambersburg: Anima Books, [2]1985.

Edsman, C. M. "Zum sakralen Königtum in der Forschung der letzten hundert Jahre," *Numen Supplement* no. 4: 3-17.

Edwardes, S. M., and H. O. O. Garrett. *Mughal Rule in India.* Reprint Delhi: S. Chand, 1962.

Eidlitz, W. *Kṛṣṇa-Caitanya, Sein Leben und Seine Lehre.* Stockholm Studies in Comparative Religion 7. Stockholm: Almquist & Wiksell, 1968.

Eisenstadt, S. N., R. Kahane, and D. Shulman, eds. *Orthodoxy, Heterodoxy and Dissent in India.* Leiden: Walter de Gruyter, 1984.

Elder, J. W. ed. *Lectures in Indian Civilization.* Dubuque: Kendall Hunt Publ. Co., 1970.

Eliade, M. *From Primitives to Zen.* New York: Harper & Row, 1967.

———. *Yoga: Immortality and Freedom*, Bollingen Series 41. Princeton: Princeton University Press, ²1969.

Elintoff, E. "Pyrrho and India," *Phronesis* 1980, no. 1: 88-108.

Elkman, S. M. *Jīva Goswāmi's Tattvasandarbha.* Delhi: Motilal Banarsidass, 1986.

Elliot, H. M., and J. Dowson. *The History of India as Told by Its Own Historians: The Mohammedan Period*, 8 vols. Reprint Allahabad: Kitab Mahal, 1964.

Elmore, W. R. "Dravidian Gods in Modern Hinduism," *University Studies* 15, no. 1 (January 1915).

Elwin, V. *The Religion of an Indian Tribe.* London: Oxford University Press, 1955.

Erikson, E. H. *Gandhi's Truth.* New York: W. W. Norton, 1970.

Essentials of Hinduism. Allahabad: The Leader, n.d.

Esteller, A. "The Quest for the Original *Ṛgveda,*" *ABORI* 507 (1969): 1-40.

———. *"The Ṛgveda Saṁhitā* as a 'Palimpsest'," *Indian Antiquary* (Third Series) 4, no. 1 (January 1967): 1-23.

Falk, H. "Die Legende von Sunaḥśepa vor ihrem rituellen Hintergrund," *ZDMG* 134, no. 1 (1984): 115-35.

Falk, M. *Nāma-Rūpa and Dharma-Rūpa; Origin and Aspects of an Ancient Indian Conception.* Calcutta: University of Calcutta, 1943.

Fakirbhai, D. *Khristopaniṣad.* Bangalore: C.I.S.R.S., 1966.

Farquar, J. N. *Modern Religious Movements in India.* Oxford: Oxford University Press, 1914; reprint Varanasi: 1967.

———. *An Outline of the Religious Literature of India.* Reprint Varanasi: Motilal Banarsidass, 1967.

Feldhaus, A. trans. and annotator *The Deeds of God in Ṛddhipur.* New York: Oxford University Press, 1984.

Fergusson, J. *Tree and Serpent Worship.* London: W. H. Allen, 1868.

Feuerstein, G. *The Philosophy of Classical Yoga.* Manchester: University of Manchester Press, 1982.

Feuerstein, G., and Jeanine Miller. *Yoga and Beyond: Essays in Indian Philosophy.* New York: Schocken Books, 1972.

Filliozat, J. "Les Āgamas Çivaites," Introduction in *Rauravāgama*, R. Bhatt, ed. Pondichéry: Institut Français d'Indologie, 1961.

———. *The Classical Doctrine of Indian Medicine: Its Origins and Its Greek Parallels*, D. R. Chanama, trans. Delhi: Munshiram Manoharlal, 1964.

———. "The French Institute of Indology in Pondichery," *WZKSA* XXVIII (1984) pp. 133-147.

———. *Les rélations éxterieures de l'Inde.* Pondichéry: Institut Français d'Indologie, 1956.

Findly, E. B. "Gārgī at the King's Court: Women and Philosophic Innovation in Ancient India." In *Women, Religion and Social Change*, V. V. Haddad and E. B. Findly, eds. Albany: State University of New York Press, 1985, 37-85.

Fischer, L. *The Life of Mahatma Gandhi.* Reprint Bombay: Bharatiya Vidya Bhavan, 1959.

Fitzgerald, James L. "The Great Epic of India as Religious Rhetoric. A Fresh Look at the *Mahābhārata*," *JAAR* 51, no. 4 (1986): 611-30.

Fonseca, R. "Constructive Geometry and the Śrī-Cakra Diagram," *Religion* 16, no. 1 (1986): 33-49.

Frauwallner, E. *Geschichte der Indischen Philosophie*, 2 vols. Salzburg: Otto Müller Verlag, 1953.

———. *History of Indian Philosophy*, V. M. Bedekar, trans., 2 vols. Delhi: Motilal Banarsidass, 1983-1984.

Frekmeier, C. *Kingship and Community in Early India.* Stanford: Stanford University Press, 1962.

French, H. W., and A. Sharma. *Religious Ferment in Modern India.* New York: St. Martin's Press, 1981.

Frykenberg, R. E., ed. *Land Control and Social Structure in Indian History.* Madison: University of Wisconsin Press, 1969.

Gächter, O. *Hermeneutics and Language in Pūrvamīmāṁsā, A Study in Śābara Bhāṣya.* Delhi: Motilal Banarsidass, 1983.

Gandhi, M. K. *Collected Works.* 90 vols. Delhi: Government of India, 1958-1984.

Gangadharan, K. K. "Shiv Sena," *Seminar* 151 (March 1972): 26-32.

Gangadharan, N. *Liṅgapurāṇa: A Study.* Delhi: Ajanta Books International, 1980.

Garbe, R. *Die Bhagavadgītā.* Leipzig: H. Haessel, [2]1921.

Gatwood, L. E. *Devī and the Spouse Goddess: Women, Sexuality and Marriage in India.* Delhi: Manohar, 1985.

Gaur, Ramdas. *Hindutva* [Hindī] Kaśi: Viśvaprasad Gupta, 1995 (samvat).

Gaur, R. C. *Excavations in Atranjikhera. Early Civilization of the Upper Ganga Basin.* Delhi: Archeological Survey of India, 1983.

Gautama's Nyāyasūtras with Vātsyāyana Bhāṣya, Ganganatha Jha, Sanskrit ed. and English trans. 2 vols. Poona: Oriental Book Depot, 1939.

Gayal, S. R. *A History of the Imperial Guptas.* Allahabad: Kitab Mahal, 1967.

Gazetteer of India. Reprint, 4 vols., Delhi: Ministry for Information and Broadcasting, 1965.

Gelberg, S. J., ed. *Hare Krishna, Hare Krishna: Five Distinguished Scholars on the Krishna Movement in the West.* New York: Grove Press, 1983.

Geldner, H. F., *Ṛgveda deutsch,* 5 vols. Cambridge, Mass.: Harvard University Press, 1951-1957 (English translation in progress).

Gensichen, Hans-Werner. "Abominable Heathenism—A Rediscovered Tract by Bartholomaeus Ziegenbalg," *Indian Church History Review* 1, no. 1 (1967): 29-40.

George, A. *Social Ferment in India.* London: Athlone Press, 1986.

Getty, A. *Gaṇeśa.* Oxford: Oxford University Press, 1936.

Ghate, V. S. *The Vedānta.* Poona: B.O.R.I., 1926, reprint 1960.

Gheraṇasaṁhitā, S. C. Vasu, trans. Allahabad: Panini Office, 1914.

Ghose, Aurobindo. *Sri Aurobindo.* Birth Centenary Library 30 vols. Pondichéry: Sri Aurobindo Ashram, 1972-1975.

Ghose, S. K. *Lord Gaurāṅga.* Bombay: 1961.

———. *Modern Indian Political Thought.* New Delhi: Allied Publishers, 1984.

Gosh, B. K. "The Āryan Problem." In *HCIP*, vol. 1, 205-21.

———. "The Origin of the Indo-Āryans." In *CHI*, vol. 1, 129-43.

Ghoshal, U. N. *A History of Indian Political Ideas: The Ancient Period and the Period of Transition to the Middle Ages.* Oxford: Oxford University Press, [3]1959.

———. "Kautilīya." In *Encyclopedia of Social Sciences.* [10]1953, vol. 3, 473 ff.

Ghurye, G. S. *Caste, Class and Occupation.* Bombay: Popular Book Depot, [3]1961.

———. *Gods and Men.* Bombay: Popular Book Depot, 1962.

———. *Indian Sādhus.* Bombay: Popular Prakashan, [2]1964.

Gibb, H. A. R., ed. *Ibn Battuta: Travels in Asia and Africa.* London: Routledge & Kegan Paul, [2]1957.

Glucklich, A. "Karma and Pollution in the Dharmasastra," *JOIB* 35, nos. 1-2 (1985): 49-60.

Gode, P. K. "The Aśvamedha Performed by Sevai Jayasingh of Amber 1699-1744 A.D.," in *Studies in Indian Literary History.* Bombay: Bharatiya Vidya Bhavan, 1954, 292-306.

Godman, D. (ed.) *Be as you are: The Teachings of Ramana Maharsi.* Boston: Arkana, 1985.

Goetz, H. *The Art of India.* New York: Crown Publishers, 1964.

Goldman, Robert P., trans. *The Rāmāyaṇa of Vālmīki: An Epic of Ancient India. Volume 1: Bālakāṇḍa.* Princeton: Princeton University Press, 1984.

Golwalkar, M. S. *Bunch of Thoughts.* Bangalore: [2]1966.

Gonda, J. *Aspects of Early Viṣṇuism.* Utrecht: 1954. Reprint Delhi: Motilal Banarsidass, 1965.

———. "The Historical Background of the Name *Satya* Assigned to the Highest Being," *ABORI* 48-49 (1968): 83-93.

———. *Die Religionen Indiens* 2 vols. Stuttgart: Kohlhammer, 1960-1963.

———. *The Ritual Functions and Significance of Grasses in the Religion of the Veda.* Amsterdam: North-Holland Publ., 1985.

———. *Vedic Ritual: The Non-Solemn Rites.* Amsterdam: North-Holland Publ., 1980.

Gopal, R. *British Rule in India: An Assessment.* New York: Asia Publ. House, 1963.

———. *Indian Muslims.* New York: 1959.

Gopi, Krishna. *The Biological Basis of Religion and Genius,* Religious Perspectives, New York: Harper and Row, 1972.

Gordon, D. H. *The Prehistoric Background of Indian Culture.* Bombay: N. M. Tripathi, 1960.

Goudriaan, T. *Māyā Divine and Human: A Study of Magic and Its Religious Foundations in Sanskrit Texts, with Particular Attention to a Fragment on Viṣṇu's Māyā Preserved in Bali.* Delhi: Motilal Banarsidass, 1978.

Govindacharya, Alkondavilli. *The Divine Wisdom of the Draviḍa Saints.* Madras: C. N. Press, 1902.

———. *The Life of Rāmānuja.* Madras: C. N. Press, 1906.

Griffith, R. T. H. *The Texts of the White Yajurveda.* Reprint Benares: Chowkhamba, [3]1957.

———, trans. *Hymns of the Ṛgveda,* 2 vols. Reprint Benares: [4]1963.

———, trans. *Hymns of the Yajurveda.* Reprint Benares: 1957.

Grihyasūtras, H. Oldenberg and F. Müller, trans. in *SBE,* vols. 29 and 30.

Griswold, H. D. *Religion of the Rigveda.* Delhi: Motilal Banarsidass, n.d.

Guénon, Rene. *Introduction génerale a l'étude des doctrines hindoues.* Paris: Les editions Vega, [5]1964.

Günther, H. V. *Yuganādha: The Tantric View of Life.* Benares: 1952; reprint Boulder: Shambhala, 1976.

Gupta, S., and R. Gombrich. "Kings, Power and the Goddess," *South Asia Research* 6, no. 2 (1986): 123-38.

Gupta, S., D. J. Hoens, and T. Goudriaan. *Hindu Tantrism. Handbuch der Orientalistik.* B. Spuler, general ed. Leiden: Brill, 1979.

Gyani, S. J., *Agni Purāṇa: A Study.* Benares: Chowkhamba, [2]1966.

Hacker, P. "Eigentümlichkeiten der Lehre und Terminologie Śaíkaras: *Avidyā, Nāmarūpa, Māyā, Īśvara,*" *ZDMG* 100 (1950): 246-86.

———. "Śaṅkara der Yogin und Śaṅkara der Advaitin: Einige Beobachtungen," *WZKSA* 12-13 (1968): 119-48.

———. *Vivarta: Studien zur Geschichte der illusionistischen Kosmologie und Erkenntnistheorie der Inder.* Wiesbaden: Akademie der Wissenschaften Mainz, 1953.

———. "Zur Entwicklung der Avatāralehre," *WZKSA* 4 (1960): 47-70.

Halbfass, W. "Indien und die Geschichtsschreibung der Philosophie," *Philosophische Rundschau* 23, no. 1-2 (1976): 104-31.

———. *Indien und Europa: Perspektiven ihrer geistigen Begegnung.* Basel-Stuttgart: Schwabe & Co., 1981.

Hardgrave, R. L. *The Dravidian Movement.* Bombay: Popular Prakashan, 1965.

Hardy, E. T. *Viraha Bhakti.* Delhi: Oxford University Press, 1983.

Harper, E. B., ed. *Religion in South Asia.* Seattle: University of Washington Press, 1964.

Harper, M. H. *Gurus, Swamis, and Avatāras: Spiritual Masters and Their American Disciples.* Philadelphia: Westminster Press, 1972.

Harris, I. C. *Radhakrishnan: The Profile of a Universalist.* Columbia, Mo.: South Asia Books, 1982.

Harris, R. B., ed. *Neoplatonism and Indian Thought: Studies in Neoplatonism Ancient and Modern*, vol. 2. Albany, SUNY Press, 1982.

Harrison, S. S., *India: The Most Dangerous Decade*. Oxford: Oxford University Press, 1960.

Harvey, M. J. "The Secular as Sacred? The Religio-Political Rationalization of B. G. Tilak," *Modern Asian Studies* 20, no. 2 (1986): 321-31.

Haṭhayogapradīpikā, Svatmarama Yogindra. Adyar: Theosophical Publishing House, 1933. Srinivasa Iyengar, Eng. trans. Adyar: Theosophical Publ. House, ^{2}1933.

Hauer, J. W. *Der Vrātya: Untersuchungen über die nichtbrahmanische Religion Altindiens*. Stuttgart: Kohlhammer, 1927.

———. *Der Yoga als Heilsweg*. Stuttgart: Kohlhammer, 1932.

Havell, E. B. *Benares, The Sacred City: Sketches of Hindu Life and Religion*. London: W. Thacker & Co., 1905.

Hawley, J. S. *Kṛṣṇa the Butter Thief*. Princeton: Princeton University Press, 1983.

———. *At Play with Krishna: Pilgrimage Dramas from Brindavan*. Princeton: Princeton University Press, 1981.

———. *Sūrdās: Poet, Singer, Saint*. Seattle: University of Washington Press, 1985.

Hawley, J. S., and D. M. Wulff, eds. *The Divine Consort: Rādhā and the Goddesses of India*. Berkeley: University of California Press, 1982.

Hazra, R. C. "The Purāṇas." In *CHI*, vol. 2, 240 ff.

———. *Studies in the Puranic Records of Hindu Rites and Customs*. Dacca: University of Dacca, 1940; reprint Delhi: 1968.

———. *Studies in the Upapurāṇas*, 2 vols. Calcutta: Sanskrit College, 1958-63.

Hedayetullah, M. *Kabīr: The Apostle of Hindu-Muslim Unity*. Delhi: Motilal Banarsidass, 1978.

Heesterman, J. C. *The Inner Conflict of Tradition: Essays in Indian Ritual, Kingship and Society*. Chicago: University of Chicago Press, 1985.

Heimann, B. *Facets of Indian Thought*. London: Allen & Unwin, 1964.

———. *Indian and Western Philosophy: A Study in Contrasts.* London: Allen & Unwin, 1937.

Heimsath, C. H. *Indian Nationalism and Hindu Social Reform.* Princeton: Princeton University Press, 1968.

Hein, N. *The Miracle Plays of Mathura.* New Haven: Yale University Press, 1972.

———. "A Revolution in Kṛṣṇaism: The Cult of Gopāla." *HR* 26, no. 3 (1986): 296-317.

Hellman, S. *Rādhā: Diary of a Woman's Search.* Porthill: Timeless Books, 1981.

Hiltebeitel, A. *The Ritual of Battle: Krishna in the Mahābhārata.* Ithaca: Cornell University Press, 1976.

Hiriyanna, M. *Outlines of Indian Philosophy.* London: George Allen & Unwin, [4]1958.

———. *Indian Conception of Values.* Mysore: Kavyalaya Publishers, 1975.

Hocart, A. M. *Caste: A Comparative Study.* New York: Russell, 1950.

Holland, B., compiler. *Popular Hinduism and Hindu Mythology: An Annotated Bibliography.* Westport: Greenwood Press, 1979.

Hooper, J. S. M. *Bible Translation in India, Pakistan and Ceylon,* 2d ed. revised by [2]. J. Culshaw. Oxford: Oxford University Press, 1963.

———. *Hymns of the Āḷvārs.* Calcutta: Association Press, 1929.

Hopkins, E. W. *Epic Mythology.* Strassburg: Trübner, 1915.

———. *Ethics of India.* New Haven: Yale University Press, 1924.

———. *The Great Epic of India.* New York: 1902; reprint Calcutta: Punthi Pustak, 1969.

Hopkins, T. J. *The Hindu Religious Tradition.* Belmont: Dickenson, 1971.

Hronzny, B. *Über die älteste Völkerwanderung und über das Problem der Proto-indischen Zivilisation.* Prague: Orientalisches Institut, 1939.

Hume, R., trans. *Principal Upaniṣads.* Oxford: Oxford University Press, 1921.

Hunashal, S. M. *The Vīraśaiva Social Philosophy.* Raichur: Amaravani Printing Press, 1957.

Hutton, J. H. *Caste in India: Its Nature, Function and Origins.* Oxford: Oxford University Press, [3]1961.

Inden, R. "Hierarchies of Kings in Early Mediaeval India." In *Way of Life, King, Householder, Renouncer. Essays in Honour of Louis Dumont,* T. N. Madan, ed. Delhi: Vikas Publishing House, 1982, 99-125.

———. "Orientalist Constructions of India," *Modern Asian Studies,* 20, no. 3 (1986): 401-46.

Indich, W. M. *Consciousness in Advaita Vedānta.* Delhi: Motilal Banarsidass, 1980.

Indradeva, S. "Cultural Interaction Between Ancient India and Iran," *Diogenes* 111 (1980): 83-109.

Ingalls, D. H. H. *Materials for the Study of Navya-Nyāya Logic,* Harvard Oriental Series No. 40. Cambridge, Mass.: Harvard University Press, 1968.

Ions, V. *Indian Mythology.* London: Paul Hamlyn, 1967.

Isaacs, H. R. *India's Ex-Untouchables.* New York: John Day, 1965.

Isacco, E., and A. L. Dallapiccola, eds. *Krishna, the Divine Lover: Myth and Legend Through Indian Art.* Boston: Serindia Publications and David R. Godine, 1982.

Israel, B. J. *The Bene Israel of India, Some Studies.* Bombay: Orient Longman, 1984.

Iyengar, N., ed. and trans. *Mumukṣupadī of Lokācārya.* Madras: 1962.

Iyer, L. K. Anantakrishna. *The Mysore Tribes and Castes.* 4 vol. Mysore: Mysore University, 1928-1935.

Iyer, M. K. Venkatarama. *Advaita Vedānta.* Bombay: Asia Publishing House, 1964.

Jacobi, H. *Das Rāmāyaṇa.* Bonn: 1983; revised edition Darmstadt: Wissenschaftliche Buchgesellschaft, 1970.

Jacobsen, D., and S. Wadley, eds. *Women in India: Two Perspectives.* Delhi: Manohar Book Service, 1974.

Jackson, C. T. *The Oriental Religions and American Thought. Nineteenth-Century Explorations.* Westport: Greenwood Press, 1981.

Jaiminimīmāṁsāsūtra with Śabara's Commentary and Notes, Ganganatha Jha, trans., 3 vols., Gaekwad Oriental Series. Baroda: 1933-1936; reprint Oriental Institute, 1973-1974.

Jarrell, Howard R. *International Yoga Bibliography, 1950-1980.* Metuchen: Scarecrow Press, n.d.

Jayakar, P. *J. Krishnamurthi: a Biography*, Delhi: Penguin India, 1987.

Jesudason, C. S. H. *A History of Tamil Literature*, Heritage of India Series. Calcutta: Y.M.C.A. Publishing House, 1961.

Jha, Ganganatha. *Pūrva Mīmāṁsā in Its Sources.* Benares: Benares Hindu University, 1942; reprint Delhi: 1981.

Jha, M., ed. *Dimensions of Pilgrimage.* New Delhi: Inter-Indian Publications, 1985.

Jhangiani, M. A. *Jana Sangh and Swatantra: A Profile of the Rightist Parties in India.* Bombay: Manaktalas, 1969.

Jindal, K. B. *A History of Hindi Literature.* Allahabad: Kitab Mahal, 1955.

Johar, Surinder Singh. *Giani Zail Singh.* New Delhi: Gaurav Publishing House, 1984.

Johnson, Clive, ed. *Vedānta: An Anthology of Hindu Scripture, Commentary, and Poetry.* New York: Harper & Row, 1971.

Johnston, E. H. *Early Sāṁkhya.* Delhi: Motilal Banarsidass, 1969.

Jolly, J. *Hindu Law and Custom.* Calcutta: Greater India Society, 1928.

Joshi, Laxman Shastri. "Moral Foundations of Indian Society," in *Nehru Abhinandan Granth.* Calcutta: Nehru Abhinandan Granth Committee, 1949, 464-69.

Joshi, M. V. "The Concept of Brahman in Vallabha Vedānta," *JBOI* 22, no. 4 (June 1973): 474-83.

Joshi, R. V. *Le Rituel de la Dévotion Kṛṣṇaite*, Pondichéry: Institut Français d'Indologie, 1959.

Kakati, B. K. *The Mother Goddess Kāmākhyā.* Gauhati: Lawyers' Book Stall, 1948.

Kale, M. R. *A Higher Sanskrit Grammar.* Reprint Delhi: Motilal Banarsidass, 1961.

Kane, P. V. *History of Dharmaśāstra*, 5 vols. (7 parts). Poona: Bhandarkar Oriental Research Institute, 1930-1962.

———. *History of Sanskrit Poetics.* Delhi: Motilal Banarsidass, [3]1961.

Kapadia, K. M. *Marriage and Family in India.* Oxford: Oxford University Press, [2]1959.

Karmarkar, A. P. "Religion and Philosophy of the Epics." In *CHI*, vol. 2, 80 ff.

———. *The Religions of India.* Lonavla: Mira Publ. House, 1950.

Kārpatrījī Mahārāj. *Rāmrājya aur Marksvāda* [in Hindī] Gorakhpur: Gītā Press, 1964.

Karunakaran, K. P. "Regionalism," *Seminar* 87 (November 1966): 21-25.

Karve, I. *Hindu Society: an Interpretation.* Poona: Deshmukh Prakashan, 1961.

———. *Kinship Organisation in India.* New York: Asia Publishing House, 1965.

Katre, S. M. *Introduction to Textual Criticism.* Poona: Deccan College, 1954.

Kautilīya's Ārthaśāstra, R. P. Kangle, ed. and trans., 3 parts. Bombay: University of Bombay, 1960-1961.

Kaylor, R. D. "The Concept of Grace in the Hymns of Nammāḷvār," *JAAR* 44 (1976): 649-60.

Keay, F. E. *Hindi Literature.* Calcutta: YMCA Publishing House, [3]1960.

———. *Kabīr and His Followers.* London: 1931.

Keith, A. B. *The Age of the Ṛgveda.* Cambridge, Mass.: Harvard University Press, 1922.

———. *A History of Sanskrit Literature.* London: Oxford University Press, 1920.

———. *Indian Logic and Atomism.* Oxford: Clarendon Press, 1921.

———. *The Karma Mīmāṁsā.* Calcutta: Association Press, 1921.

———. *The Religion and Philosophy of the Veda and Upaniṣads*, Cambridge, Mass.: Harvard University Press, 1925.

———. *The Sāṁkhya System*, Heritage of India Series. Calcutta: YMCA Publ. House, ³1949.

———. *The Sanskrit Drama.* Reprint Oxford: Oxford University Press, 1924.

Keller, C. A. "Aspiration collective et éxperience individuelle dans la bhakti shivaite de l'Inde du sud," *Numen* 31, no. 1 (July 1984): 1-21.

Kenghe, C. T. "The Problem of Pratyayasarga in Sāṁkhya and Its Relation to Yoga," *ABORI* 48-49 (1968): 365-73.

Kennedy, M.T. *The Chaitanya Movement.* Calcutta: Association Press, 1925.

Khiste, Paṇḍit S. S. "Śrīvidyā." in *Kalyāṇa Devībhāgavatam Aṅgka.* Gorakhpur: Gita Press, 1960, 689-96.

Kingsbury, F., and G. E. Philips, trans. *Hymns of the Tamil Śaivite Saints.* Calcutta: Association Press, 1921.

Kinsley, D. *Hindu Goddesses*, Berkeley: University of California Press, 1986.

———. *Hinduism: A Cultural Perspective.* Englewood Cliffs: Prentice-Hall, 1982.

———. *The Sword and the Flute: Kālī and Kṛṣṇa, Dark Visions of the Terrible and the Sublime in Hindu Mythology.* Berkeley: University of California Press, 1975.

Kirfel, W. D. *Purāṇa Pañcalakṣana.* Benares: Motilal Banarsidass, 1963.

Klaiman, M. H., trans. "Singing the Glory of Lord Krishna." In *The Śrī Kṛṣṇa Kīrtana of Baṛu Cāṇḍīdāsa.* Chico: Scholars Press, n.d.

Klimkeit, H. J. *Der politische Hinduismus. Indische Denker zwischen religiöser Reform und politischem Erwachen.* Wiesbaden: Harrassowitz, 1984.

Kloppenborg, Ria, ed. *Selected Studies on Ritual in the Indian Religions: Essays to D. J. Hoens. Supplements to Numen 45.* Leiden: Brill, 1983.

Klostermaier, K. "Hindu Views of Buddhism." In *Canadian Contributions to Buddhist Studies*, R. Amore, ed. Waterloo, Ont.: Wilfrid Laurier University Press, 1980, 60-82.

———. *Hinduism in Bombay," Religion* (U.K.) 1, no. 2 (1972): 83-91.

———. *Hinduismus.* Cologne: Bachem, 1965.

———. *In the Paradise of Kṛṣṇa.* Philadelphia: Westminster, 1971.

———. *Mythologies and Philosophies of Salvation in the Theistic Traditions of India.* Waterloo, Ont.: Wilfrid Laurier University Press, 1984.

———. "The Original Dakṣa Saga," *Journal of South Asian Literature* 20, no. 1 (1985): 93-107.

———. *"Sādhana," Religion and Society* 16, no. 2 (1969): 36-50.

Knipe, D. M. *In the Image of Fire: Vedic Experiences of Heat.* Delhi: Motilal Banarsidass, 1975.

Koelman, G. M. *Pātañjala Yoga. From Related Ego to Absolute Self.* Poona: Papal Athenaeum, 1970.

Koestler, A. *The Lotus and the Robot.* New York: Harper & Row, 1961.

Kölver, B. "Stages in the Evolution of a World Picture," *Numen* 32, no. 2: 131-68.

van Kooij, K. R. "Protective Covering (*Kavaca*)." In *Selected Studies on Ritual in the Indian Religions*, R. Kloppenburg, ed. Leiden: Brill, 1983, 118-29.

Kopf, D. *The Brahmo Samāj and the Shaping of the Modern Indian Mind.* Princeton: Princeton University Press, 1979.

Kosambi, D. D., ed. *The Epigrams Attributed to Bhartṛhari Including the Three Centuries*, Singhi Jain Series. Bombay: Bharatiya Vidya Bhavan, 1948.

———. *An Introduction to the Study of Indian History.* Bombay: Popular Book Depot, 1956.

———. *Myth and Reality: A Study in the Foundations of Indian Culture.* Bombay: Popular Prakashan, 1961.

Kothari, R. *Caste in Indian Politics.* New Delhi: Orient Longman, 1970.

Krämer, H. J. *Der Ursprung der Geistmetaphysik.* Amsterdam: B. R. Bruner, [2]1967.

Kramrisch, S. *The Art of India: Traditions of Indian Sculpture, Painting and Architecture*. London: Phaidon, 1954.

———. *The Hindu Temple*, 2 vols. Calcutta: University of Calcutta 1946; reprint Delhi: Motilal Banarsidass, 1977.

———. "The Image of Mahādeva in the Cave Temple on Elephanta Island," *Ancient India* 2 (1946): 4-8.

———. *Indian Sculpture*. 1933; reprint Delhi: Motilal Banarsidass, 1981.

———. *The Presence of Śiva*, Princeton: Princeton University Press, 1981.

———. "The Triple Structure of Creation in the *ṚgVeda*," *HR* 2, nos. 1-2 (1962): 140-75, 256-85.

Krick, H. "Der Vaniṣṭutsava und Indras Offenbarung," *WZKSA* 19 (1975): 25-74.

Krishna, G. *The Awakening of Kuṇḍalinī*. New York: E. P. Dutton, 1975.

Krishnamurti, J. *The Awakening of Intelligence*. New York: Avon Books, 1976.

———. *The First and Last Freedom*. London: V. Gollancz, 1967 [1954].

Kṛṣṇakarṇāmṛta of Līlāsūka, M. A. Acharya, ed. and trans. Madras: V. Ramaswamy Sastrulu, 1958.

Kulkarni, R. "Vāstupadamaṇḍala," *JOIB* 28, nos. 3-4 (March-June 1979): 107-38.

Kumar, G. D. "The Ethnic Components of the Builders of the Indus Civilization and the Advent of the Aryans," *Journal of Indo-European Studies* 1, no. 1 (1973): 66-80.

Kumarappa, B. *The Hindu Conception of the Deity*. London: Luzac, 1934.

Kumari, V., trans. *The Nīlamata Purāṇa*. Srinagar: J & K Academy of Art, Culture and Language, 1968.

Kuppuswamy, B. *Dharma and Society: A Study in Social Values*. Columbia, Mo.: South Asia Books, 1977.

Kuppuswamy, G., and M. Hariharan. "Bhajana Tradition in South India," *Sangeet Natak* 64-65 (April-September 1982): 32-50.

———, eds. *Jayadeva and Gītāgovinda: A Study*. Trivandrum: College Book House, 1980.

Lacombe, O., *L'absolu sélon le Védānta*. Paris: 1957; reprint Geuthner, 1966.

Laghusiddhāntakaumudī of Vāradarāja, J. R. Ballantyne, ed. and trans. Reprint Delhi: Motilal Banarsidass, 1961.

Lal, B. B. "The Indus Script: Some Observations Based on Archaeology," *JRAS* 1975, no. 2: 173-209.

———. "Reading the Indus Script," *IFR* (15 April 1983): 33-36.

Lal, C. *Hindu America*. Bombay: Bharatiya Vidya Bhavan, 1961.

Lal, K. *Holy Cities of India*. Delhi: Asia Press, 1961.

Lamb, B. P. *India: A World in Transition*. New York: Praeger, [3]1968.

Lannoy, R. *The Speaking Tree*. Oxford: Oxford University Press, 1971.

Larson, G. J. "The *Bhagavad-Gītā* as Cross-Cultural Process: Toward an Analysis of the Social Locations of a Religious Text," *JAAR*, 43 (1975): 651-69.

———. *Classical Sāṁkhya*. Delhi: Motilal Banarsidass, [2]1969.

———. "The Format of Technical Philosophical Writing in Ancient India: Inadequacies of Conventional Translations," *Philosophy East and West* 30, no. 3 (1980): 375-80.

Latham, R. E., trans. *The Travels of Marco Polo*. Penguin, Harmondsworth, U.K., 1958.

Laws of Manu, G. Bühler, trans. In *SBE*, vol. 25.

Leifer, W. *Indien und die Deutschen: 500 Jahre Begegnung und Partnerschaft*, Tübingen and Basel: Horst Erdmann Verlag, 1969.

LeMay, R. *The Culture of South-East Asia: The Heritage of India*. London: Allen & Unwin, 1954.

Lester, R. C. *Rāmānuja on the Yoga*. Madras: Adyar Library and Research Centre, 1976.

Lévi, S. *La doctrine du sacrifice dans le Brāhmaṇas*. Paris: 1898; reprint Presses Universitaires de France, 1966.

Liebert, G. *Iconographic Dictionary of the Indian Religions: Hinduism, Buddhism, Jainism.* Leiden: Brill, 1976.

Long, J. B. "Festival of Repentance: A Study of Mahāśivarātrī," *JBOI* 22, no. 1-2 (September-December 1972): 15-38.

Lorenzen, D. N. *The Kāpālika and Kālamukhas: Two Lost Śaivite Sects.* Berkeley: University of California Press, 1972.

———. "The Life of Śaṅkarācārya." In *Experiencing Śiva*, F. Clothey and J. B. Long, eds. Columbia, Mo.: South Asia Books, 1983.

Lott, E. J. *God and the Universe in the Vedāntic Theology of Rāmānuja: A Study in His Use of the Self-Body Analogy.* Madras: Ramanuja Research Society, 1976.

Lupsa, M. *Chants a Kālī de Rāmprasād.* Pondichery: Institute Français d'Indologie, 1967.

Lütt, Jürgen. *Hindu-Nationalismus in Uttar Prades 1867-1900.* Stuttgart: Ernst Klett Verlag, 1970.

Macauliffe, M. A. *The Sikh Religion: Its Gurūs, Sacred Writings and Authors*, 3 vols. Reprint Delhi: S. Chand, 1963.

Macdonnell, A. A. *A History of Sanskrit Literature.* Reprint Delhi: Motilal Banarsidass, [2]1961.

———. *Vedic Mythology.* Reprint Varanasi: Indological Bookhouse, 1963.

———. "Vedic Religion." In *Encyclopedia of Religion and Ethics*, E. Hastings, ed. [3]1954, vol. 12, 601-18.

———, and A. B. Keith. *Vedic Index of Names and Subjects*, 2 vols. Reprint Delhi: Motilal Banarsidass, 1958.

Maclagan, D. *Creation Myths: Man's Introduction to the World.* London: Thames and Hudson, 1977.

Macnicol, N. *Indian Theism.* London: Oxford University Press, 1915.

———. *Psalms of the Maratha Saints*, Heritage of India Series. Calcutta: Association Press, 1919.

Madan, T. N., ed. *Way of Life. King, Householder, Renouncer. Essays in Honor of Louis Dumont.* Delhi: Vikas Publishing House, 1982.

———, and G. Sarana. *Indian Anthropology.* New York: Asia Publishing House, 1962.

Mahābhārata (short summary), C. Rajogopalachari, ed. Bombay: Bharatiya Vidya Bhavan, 1958.

Mahābhārata, P. C. Roy, trans. Calcutta: 1884-1896 (several reprints: Calcutta Oriental without date).

Mahābhārata, Books 1-5. J. A. B. van Buitenen, trans. 3 vols. Chicago: University of Chicago Press, 1973-1978.

Mahābhārata, Critical Edition, 22 vols. Poona: Bhandarkar Oriental Research Institute, 1933-1966.

Mahadevan, T. M. P., *Outline of Hinduism.* Bombay: Cetana, [2]1960.

———. *Ramaṇa Maharṣi and His Philosophy of Existence.* Annamalai: 1951.

———. *The Sage of Kāñchī.* Secunderabad: 1967.

———. "Śaivism." In *HCIP,* vol. 2, 433 ff.

———. *Ten Saints of India.* Bombay: Bharatiya Vidya Bhavan, 1961.

———, ed. and trans. *Hymns of Śaṅkara.* Madras: 1970.

Mahadevananda, Swami, trans. *Devotional Songs of Narsi Mehta.* Delhi: Motilal Banarsidass, 1985.

Maitra, S. K. *The Ethics of the Hindus.* Calcutta: University of Calcutta, [3]1963.

———. *Fundamental Questions of Indian Metaphysics and Logics,* 2 vols. Calcutta: Chuckervertty, Chatterjee & Co., 1956-1961.

Maitra, S. *An Introduction to the Philosophy of Sri Aurobindo.* Benares: Benares Hindu University, [2]1945.

Majumdar, A. K. *Caitanya: His Life and Doctrine.* Bombay: Bharatiya Vidya Bhavan, 1969.

Majumdar, D. N. *Caste and Communication in an Indian Village.* Bombay: Asia Publishing House, [3]1962.

———. *Races and Cultures of India.* Bombay: Asia Publishing House, 1964.

Majumdar, J. K. *Raja Rammohan Roy and Progressive Movements in India, Volume I. A Selection from Records (1774-1845).* Calcutta: Brahmo Mission Press, n.d.

Majumdar, R. C. *The Classical Accounts of India.* Calcutta: Firma K. L. Mukhopadhyay, 1960.

———. *Hindu Colonies in the Far East.* Calcutta: Firma K. L. Mukhopadhyay, [2]1963.

———, general ed. *The History and Culture of the Indian People.* Bombay: Bharatiya Vidya Bhavan, 1945-1978.

Majumdar, R. C., H. C. Raychaudhuri, and K. Datta. *An Advanced History of India.* London: Macmillan, [3]1965.

Malamoud, C. "On the Rhetoric and Semantics of *Puruṣārtha.*" In *Way of Life*, T. N. Madan, ed. Delhi: Vikas Publishing House, 33-52.

Maloney, C. *Peoples of South Asia.* New York: Holt, Rhinehart and Winston, 1974.

Mānameyodaya, C. Kunhan Raja, trans. Adyar: Theosophical Publishing House, 1933.

Manasāra, P. K. Acharya, trans. 1934; reprint New Delhi: Motilal Banarsidass, 1980.

Mānava Dharma Śāstra, J. Jolly, trans. London: 1887.

Mānava Śrauta Sūtra, J. M. van Gelder, trans. New Delhi: International Academy of Indian Culture, 1963.

Māṇḍukyopaniṣad with Gauḍapāda's Kārikā and Śaṅkara's Commentary, Swami Nikhilananda, trans. Mysore: Ramakrishna Math, [4]1955.

Manickam, V. S. *The Tamil Concept of Love.* Madras: South Indian Saiva Siddhanta Works Publishing Society, 1962.

Maṇikana, A Navya-Nyāya Manual, E. R. Sreekrishna Sarma, ed. and trans. Adyar: Adyar Library, 1960.

Mārkaṇḍeya-Purāṇa. Bombay: Venkatesvar Steam Press, [3]1910; F. E. Pargiter, trans., reprint Delhi: Indological Book House, 1969.

Marriott, McKim, ed. *Village India: Studies in the Little Community.* Chicago: University of Chicago Press, 1963.

Marshall, J. *Mohenjo Daro and the Indus Civilization.* 3 vols. London: University of Oxford Press, 1931.

Marshall, P. J. ed. *The British Discovery of Hinduism in the Eighteenth Century*, European Understanding of India Series. Cambridge: 1971.

Masani, M. R. *The Communist Party of India.* London: Derek Versdroyle, 1954.

Mate, M. S. *Temples and Legends of Maharastra.* Bombay: Bharatiya Vidya Bhavan, 1962.

Mathur, S. K. *Caste and Ritual in a Malwa Village.* New York: Asia Publishing House, 1964.

Matilal, B. K. *Logic, Language and Reality.* Delhi: Motilal Banarsidass, 1985.

———. *The Navya Nyāya Doctrine of Negation*, Harvard Oriental Series No. 46. Cambridge, Mass.: Harvard University Press, 1972.

Māyāmata, B. Dagens, French trans. 2 vols. Pondichéry: Institut Français d'Indologie, 1970-1976.

Mayer, A. C. *Caste and Kinship in Central India: A Village and Its Religion.* Berkeley: University of California Press, 1965.

McDowall, A., and A. Sharma, eds. *Vignettes of Vrindaban.* New Delhi: Books & Books, 1987.

McKenzie, J. *Hindu Ethics.* Oxford: Oxford University Press, 1922.

Meenaksisundaram, T. P. *A History of Tamil Literature.* Annamalainagar: Annamalai University, 1965.

Mehendale, M. A. "Purāṇas." In *HCIP*, vol. 3, 291-99.

Mehta, M. "The Evolution of the Suparṇa Saga in the *Mahābhārata*," *JOIB* 1971: 41-65.

———. "The Problem of the Double Introduction to the *Mahābhārata*," *JAOS* 93, no. 4 (1973): 547-50.

Meister, W. "Hindu Temples." In *Encyclopedia of Religion*, M. Eliade, ed., vol. 10, 368-73.

———. "Maṇḍala and Practice in Nāgara Architecture in North India," *JAOS* 99 (1979): 204-19.

———. "Measurement and Proportion in Hindu Architecture," *Interdisciplinary Science Reviews* 10 (1985): 248-58.

Meister, M. W. (ed.) *Discourses on Śiva*, Philadelphia: University of Pennsylvania Press, 1984.

Menon, I. K. K. "Keralā's Early Foreign Contacts," *IFR* (15 July 1980): 13 f.

Miller, D. M., and Dorothy C. Wertz. *Hindu Monastic Life: The Monks and Monasteries of Bhubaneśwar*. Montreal: McGill-Queen's University Press, 1976.

Mīmāṁsākośa, Kevalananda Sarasvati, ed. 7 vols. Wai: Dharmakośa-mandala, 1952-1966.

Mīmāṁsāparibhāṣa of Kṛṣṇa Yajvan, Swami Madhavanand, ed. and trans. Belur Math: The Ramakrishna Mission Sarada Pitha, 1948.

Minor Lawbooks, J. Jolly, trans. In *SBE*, vol. 33.

Minor, R., ed. *Modern Indian Interpreters of the Bhagavadgītā*. Albany: State University of New York Press, 1986.

Minor, R. *Bhagavad-Gītā: An Exegetical Commentary*. Columbia, Mo.: South Asia Books, 1982.

Minz, N. "Anthropology and the Deprived," *Religion and Society* 32, no. 4 (1985): 3-19.

Mishra, V. *The Conception of Matter According to Nyāya-Vaiśeṣika*. Reprint Delhi: Gian Publishers, 1983.

———. *Hinduism and Economic Growth*. Oxford: Oxford University Press, 1963.

———. "Prehistory and Protohistory." In *Review of Indological Research in Last Seventy-five Years*, P. J. Chinmulgund and V. V. Mirashi, eds. Poona: Bharatiya Caritra Kosha Mandal, 1967, 353-415.

Misra, Om Prakash. *Mother Goddess in Central India*. Delhi: Agam Kala Prakashan, 1985.

Mitra, A. M. *India as Seen in the Brihatsaṁhitā of Varāhamihira*. Delhi: Motilal Banarsidass, n.d.

Mollat, M. "The Importance of Maritime Traffic to Cultural Contacts in the Indian Ocean," *Diogenes* 3 (1980): 1-18.

Mookerjee, A., and M. Khanna. *The Tantric Way: Art-Science-Ritual.* London: Thames & Hudson, 1977.

Morinis, E. A. *Pilgrimage in the Hindu Tradition: A Case Study of West Bengal,* South Asian Studies Series. New York and New Delhi: Oxford University Press, 1984.

Morris-Jones, W. H. *The Government and Politics of India.* London: Hutchinson University Library, 1964.

Mudgal, S. G. *Advaita of Śaṅkara: A Reappraisal.* Delhi: Motilal Banarsidass, 1975.

Mukarji, Nirmal. "The Hindu Problem," *Seminar* 269 (January 1982): 37-40.

Müller, M., ed., *Ṛgveda with the Commentary of Śayaṇa* 4 vols. London: [2]1892; reprint Varanasi: Chowkhambha Sanskrit Office, 1966.

———. *The Six Systems of Indian Philosophy.* Reprint Varanasi: Chowkhamba, 1962.

Mundaden, A. M. *St. Thomas Christians and the Portuguese.* Bangalore: Dharmaram Studies, 1970.

———. *The Traditions of St. Thomas Christians.* Bangalore: Dharmaram Studies, 1972.

Murti, T. R. V. "The Rise of the Philosophical Schools." In *CHI,* vol. 3, 32.

Murty, K. S. *Revelation and Reason in Advaita Vedānta.* Waltair: Waltair University, 1959.

Nagendra, D. *Indian Literature.* Agra: Lakshmi Narain Agarwal, 1959.

Nair, K. *Blossoms in the Dust.* London: Duckworth, [2]1962.

Naiṣkarmyasiddhi, K. K. Venkatachari, ed. and trans. Adyar: Adyar Library, 1982.

Nāḷadiyār, G. U. Pope, trans. Oxford: Oxford University Press, 1893.

Nandimath, S. C. *Handbook of Vīraśaivism.* Dharwar: L. E. Association, 1941.

Nārada Bhakti Sūtras. Aphorisms on the Gospel of Divine Love, Swami Tyagisananda, trans. Mylapore: Ramakrishna Math, [3]1955.

Narayan, J. *From Socialism to Sarvodaya.* Kashi: Sarva Seva Sangh Prakashan, n.d.

Nath, Pundit Shunker, *Christ: Who and What He Was:* Part 1. *Christ a Hindu Disciple, Nay a Buddhist Saint;* Part 2. *Christ a Pure Vedantist.* Calcutta: Calcutta Dayamoy Printing Works, 1927-1928.

Nayar, T. Balakrishnan. *The Problem of Dravidian Origins—A Linguistic, Anthropological and Archeological Approach.* Madras: University of Madras, 1977.

Neevel, Walter G., Jr. *Yamuna's Vedānta and Pāñcarātra: Integrating the Classical and the Popular.* Chico: Scholars Press, 1977.

Nehru, J. *Autobiography.* London 1936; Indian Ed. New Delhi: Allied Publishers, 1962.

———. *The Discovery of India.* London: 1946; reprint Meridian Books, 1960.

Neill, S. *A History of Christianity in India: The Beginnings to* A.D. 1707. Cambridge: Cambridge University Press, 1984.

Neog, M. *Early History of the Vaiṣṇava Faith and Movement in Assam: Śaṅkaradeva and His Time.* Delhi: Motilal Banarsidass, [2]1985.

Neufeldt, R. *F. Max Müller and the Ṛg-Veda: A Study of its Role in His Work and Thought.* Columbia, Mo.: South Asia Books, 1980.

———, ed. *Karma and Rebirth: Post-Classical Developments.* Albany: State University of New York Press, 1986.

Neuman, E. *An Analysis of the Archetype The Great Mother*, R. Manheim, trans. Princeton: Bollingen, 1955.

Neumayer, E. *Prehistoric India Rock Paintings.* Delhi: Oxford University Press, 1983.

de Nicolás, A. T. *Avatāra: The Humanization of Philosophy Through the Bhagavad Gītā.* New York: Nicholas Hays, 1976.

Swami Nikhilananda, trans. *Gospel of Sri Ramakrishna.* Calcutta: 1930.

Nimbārka. Vedānta Parijāta Saurabha and Vedānta Kausthubha of Śrīnivāsa, R. Bose, trans., 3 vols. Calcutta: Royal Asiatic Society of Bengal, 1940-1943.

Nirvedananda, Swami. "Sri Ramakrishna and Spiritual Renaissance." In *CHI*, vol. 4, 653-728.

Nooten, B. A. van. *The Mahābhārata.* New York: 1971.

Nyāyakusumañjalī of Udāyana, E. G. Cowell, ed. and trans. Calcutta: 1864.

Oberhammer, G. "Die Gotterserfahrung in der yogischen Meditation." In *Offenbarung als Heilserfahrung in Christentum, Hinduismus and Buddhismus,* W. Strolz and S. Ueda, eds. Freiburg-Basel-Vienna: Herder, 1982, 146-66.

———. *Strukturen Yogischer Meditation.* Vienna: Österreichische Akademie der Wissenschaften, 1977.

———. "Das Transzendenzverständis des Sāṁkhyistischen Yoga als Strukturprinzip seiner Mystik." In *Transzendenzerfahrung, Vollzugshorizont des Heils,* G. Oberhammer, ed. Vienna: De Nobili Research Library, 1978, pp. 15-28.

O'Flaherty, W. D., *Asceticism and Eroticism in the Mythology of Śiva,* London: Oxford University Press, 1973.

———. *The Origins of Evil in Hindu Mythology,* Berkeley: University of California Press, 1976.

———. "The Origin of Heresy in Hindu Mythology." *HR* 10 (May 1971): 271-333.

———. *Śiva: The Erotic Ascetic.* New York: Oxford University Press, 1981.

———, ed. *Karma and Rebirth in Classical Indian Traditions.* Berkeley: University of California Press, 1980.

Oguibenine, B. "Cosmic Tree in Vedic and Tamil Mythology: Contrastive Analysis," *Journal of Indo-European Studies* 12, no. 3-4 (1984): 367-74.

Oldenberg, H. *Das Mahābhārata.* Göttingen: Vandenhoeck & Ruprecht, 1922.

Olivelle, P., ed. and trans. *Vasudevāśrama's Yatidharmaprakāśa. A Treatise on World Renunciation,* 2 vols. Vienna: De Nobili Library, 1977.

Olivelle, P., "Contributions to the Semantic History of Saṁnyāsa", in *JAOS* 101 (1981), 265-274.

O'Malley, L. S. *Popular Hinduism: The Religion of the Masses.* Oxford: Oxford University Press, 1941.

Oman, J. C. *The Mystics, Ascetics and Saints of India.* Reprint Delhi: Oriental Publishers, 1973.

O'Neil, L. T. *Māyā in Śaṅkara: Measuring the Immeasurable.* Delhi: Motilal Banarsidass, 1980.

Osborne, A. *Ramana Maharshi and the Path of Self-Knowledge.* Bombay: Jaico, [2]1962.

———, ed. *The Collected Works of Ramana Maharshi,* New York: S. Weiser, 1959.

Ostor, Akos. *The Play of the Gods: Locality, Ideology, Structure and Time in the Festivals of a Bengali Town.* Chicago: University of Chicago Press, 1980.

Otto, R. *Mysticism East and West.* New York: Macmillan, 1957.

Overstreet, L., and M. Windmiller. *Communism in India.* Berkeley: University of California Press, 1959.

Pañcadaśī of Vidyāraṇya, Swami Swahananda, ed. and trans. Madras: Ramakrishna Math, 1967.

Pāñcarātra Rakṣa of Śrī Vedānta Deśika, M. Duraiswami Aiyanjar and T. Venugopalacharya, critical eds. with notes and variant readings, introduction by G. Srinivasa Murti. Adyar: Adyar Library, 1942.

Pañcatantra, A. W. Ryder, trans. Reprint Bombay: Jaico, [2]1962.

Pañcaviṁśa Brāhmaṇa, W. Caland, trans. Calcutta: Asiatic Society of Bengal, 1931.

Pancikar, W. C.. ed. *One Hundred and Eight Upaniṣads.* Bombay: Nirnaya Sāgar Press, [4]1932.

Pandey, R. B. *Hindu Saṁskāras: A Socio-Religious Study of the Hindu Sacraments.* Benares: Vikrama Publications, 1949.

Pandeya, L. P. *Sun Worship in Ancient India.* Delhi: Motilal Banarsidass, 1972.

Panikkar, K. M. *Asia and Western Dominance.* London: Allen & Unwin, [3]1955.

———. *Geographical Factors in Indian History.* Bombay: Bharatiya Vidya Bhavan, 1955.

———. *Hindu Society at Cross-Roads.* Bombay: Asia Publishing House, 1956.

———. *Hinduism and the Modern World.* Bombay: Bharatiya Vidya Bhavan, 1956.

———. *A Survey of Indian History.* Bombay: Asia Publishing House, 1947.

Panikkar, Raymond. *Kerygma und Indien: Zur heilsgeschichtlichen Problematik der christlichen Begegnung mit Indien,* Hamburg: Evangelischer Verlag, 1967.

———, ed. and trans. *The Vedic Experience: Mantramañjarī—An Anthology of the Vedas for Modern Man and Contemporary Celebration.* Berkeley: University of California Press, 1977.

Pāṇini's Aṣṭādhyāyī, Srisa Candra Vasu, ed. and trans. 2 vols. Reprint Delhi: Motilal Banarsidass, 1961.

Paramārtha Sopāna, R. D. Ranade. Allahabad: Adhyatma Vidya Mandir Sangli, Nimbal (R.S.), 1954.

Paramesvaran, M. R. "The Twofold Vedanta of Śrīvaiṣṇavism." Thesis, University of Manitoba, 1981.

Paranjoti, V. *Śaiva Siddhānta.* London: Luzac, [2]1954.

Pareckh, M. C. *Brahmarshi Keshub Chander Sen.* Rajkot: Bhagavat Dharma Mission, 1926.

———. *The Brahmo Samāj.* Calcutta: Brahmo Samaj, 1922.

———. *A Hindu's Portrait of Jesus Christ,* Rajkot: Bhagavat Dharma Mission, 1953.

———. *Sri Swami Narayana,* Rajkot: Bhagavat Dharma Mission, 1936.

———. *Vallabhācārya.* Rajkot: Bhagavat Dharma Mission, 1936.

Pargiter, F. E. *Ancient Indian Historical Tradition.* Reprint Delhi: Motilal Banarsidass, 1962.

———. *The Purāṇa Text of the Dynasties of the Kaliage.* Oxford: Oxford University Press, 1913.

Parpola, A. *The Sky Garment: A Study of the Harappan Religion and the Relation to the Mesopotamian and Later Indian Religions.* Helsinki: Finnish Oriental Society, 1985.

Parvathamma, C. *Politics and Religion.* New Delhi: Sterling Publishers, 1971.

Pātañjali Mahābhāṣya, Vedavrata Snataka, ed. 10 vols. Gurukul Jhajjar (Rohtak): Haryana Sahitya Samsthan, 1961-1964.

Patañjali's Yogasūtra, Swami Vijanana Asrama, ed. and trans. Ajmer: Sri Madanlal Laksminivas Chandak, 1961.

Pathak, P. V. "Tectonic Upheavals in the Indus Region and Some Rgvedic Hymns," *ABORI* 64 (1983): 227-32.

Patil, D. R. *Cultural History of Vāyu Purāṇa*. Delhi: Motilal Banarsidass, n.d.

Patthabhiram, M., ed. *General Elections in India 1967. An Exhaustive Study of Main Political Trends*. Bombay: Allied Publishers, 1967.

Payne, A. A. *The Śāktas*. Calcutta: YMCA Publishing House, 1933.

Pereira, José, ed. *Hindu Theology: A Reader*. Garden City: Doubleday, 1976.

Piggott, S. *Prehistoric India*. Baltimore: Penguin Books, 1961.

Pillai, G. S. *Introduction and History of Śaiva Siddhānta*. Annamalai: Annamalai University, 1948.

Pillai, K. K. "The Caste System in Tamil Nadu," *Journal of the Madras University* 49, no. 2 (1977): 1-89.

———. *A Social History of the Tamils*, vol. 1. Madras: University of Madras, ^{2}1973.

Pillai, S. Satchidanandam. "The Saiva Saints of South India," in *CHI*, vol. 4, 339 ff.

Podgorski, F. R. *Hinduism: A Beautiful Mosaic*. South Bend: Foundations Press of Notre Dame, 1983.

Popley, H. A. *The Music of India*. Calcutta: YMCA Publishing House, 1950.

Potter, K. *Bibliography of Indian Philosophies*. Delhi: Motilal Banarsidass, 1970.

———. *The Encyclopedia of Indian Philosophies*. Varanasi: Motilal Banarsidass, 1970-.

———. *Presuppositions of India's Philosophies*. Englewood Cliffs: Prentice Hall, 1963.

Powell-Price, J. C. *A History of India*. London: T. Nelson, 1955.

Prabhananda, Swami. "Who Gave the Name Ramakrishna and When? *The Vedanta Kesari* 74 (1987): 107-12.

Prabhu, P. H. *Hindu Social Organisation: A Study in Socio-Psychological and Ideological Foundations*. Bombay: Popular Prakashan, ⁴1963.

Prabhupada, A. C. Bhaktivedanta Swami, *Sri Caitanya-Caritamrta of Krsnadasa Kaviraja Gosvami: Antya-lila*, vol. 7. New York: Bhaktivedanta Book Trust, 1975.

Prakash, Om. *Political Ideas in the Puranas*. Allahabad: Panchanda Publications, 1977.

Prasad, Modhi. *Kaka Kalelkar: A Gandhian Patriarch*. Bombay: Popular Prakashan, 1965.

Pratyābhijñāhṛdayam, Jaideva Singh, ed. and trans. Delhi: Motilal Banarsidass, 1963.

Presler, F. A. "The Structure and Consequences of Temple Policy in Tamilnadu, 1967-81," *Pacific Affairs* (Summer 1983): 232-46.

Pusalker, A. D. "Aryan Settlements in India." In *HCIP*, vol. 1, 245-67.

———. "Historical Traditions." In *HCIP*, vol. 1, 271-336.

———. "Historicity of Kṛṣṇa." In *Studies in Epics and Purāṇas of India*. Bombay: Bharatiya Vidya Bhavan, 1955, 49-81.

———. "The Indus Valley Civilization." In *HCIP*, vol. 1, 172-202.

———. "The *Mahābhārata:* Its History and Character." In *CHI*, vol. 2, 51 ff.

———. "Puranic Studies," *Review:* 689-773.

———. "The *Rāmāyaṇa:* Its History and Character." In *CHI*, vol. 2, 14 ff.

———. *Studies in Epics and Purāṇas of India*. Bombay: Bharatiya Vidya Bhavan, 1955.

———. "Traditional History from the Earliest Time to the Accession of Parikshit." In *The Vedic Age*, vol. 1 of *HCIP*, 271-322.

Puthiadan, I. *Viṣṇu the Ever Free: A Study of the Madhva Concept of God*. Dialogue Series No. 5., Madurai: Dialogue Publications, 1985.

Putnam, John J. "The Ganges, River of Faith" with photography by Raghubir Singh. *National Geographic Magazine* (October 1971): 445-83.

Radhakrishnan, S. *The Bhagavadgītā.* London: Allen & Unwin, 1948.

———. *The Brahmasūtra.* London: Allen & Unwin, 1961.

———. *Eastern Religions and Western Thought.* New York: Oxford University Press, 1964.

———. *The Hindu View of Life.* New York: Macmillan, 1962.

———. *Indian Philosophy*, 2 vols. London: Allen & Unwin, ²1948.

———. *My Search for Truth.* Agra: Agrawala, 1946.

———. *The Principal Upaniṣads*, London: Allen & Unwin, 1953.

———. *Religion and Society.* London: Allen & Unwin, 1947.

———. *Religion in a Changing World.* London: Allen & Unwin, 1967.

———, and C. A. Moore, *A Sourcebook in Indian Philosophy.* Princeton: Princeton University Press, 1957.

Raghavan, V. *The Great Integrators: The Saint Singers of India.* Delhi: Ministry of Information and Broadcasting, 1966.

———. *The Indian Heritage.* Bangalore: Indian Institute of Culture, 1956.

Rai, L. *The Ārya Samāj.* London: Longmann, 1915.

Raj, D. *l'ésclavage dans l'Inde ancienne d'apres les textes Palis et Sanskrits.* Pondichéry: Institut Françcais d'Indologie, 1957.

Raja C. Kunhan. "Vedic Culture." In *CHI*, vol. 1, 199-220.

Raja, K. Kunjunni. *Indian Theories of Meaning.* Adyar: The Adyar Library and Research Center, 1963.

Rajagopalachari, R. C. *Hinduism: Doctrine and Way of Life.* Bombay: Bharatiya Vidya Bhavan, 1959.

Rajagopalan, V. "The Srī Vaiṣṇava Understanding of Bhakti and Prapatti." Thesis, University of Bombay, 1978.

Raju, T. T. *The Philosophical Traditions of India:* London: Allen & Unwin, 1971.

———. *Idealistic Thought of India* London: Allen & Unwin, 1953.

Raju, P. T. *Structural Depths of Indian Thought.* Albany: State University of New York Press, 1985.

Ram, S. *Vinoba and his Mission.* Kāśī: Akhil Bharat Sarva Seva Sangh, Rajghat, [3]1962.

Rāmacaritamānasa by Tulsīdās. Gorakhpur: Gita Press, 1968.

Rāmānuja's Vedārthasaṅgraha, S. S. Raghavachar, ed. and trans. Mysore: Ramakrishna Ashrama, 1956.

Ramanujan, A. K., trans. *Speaking of Śiva.* Harmondsworth: Penguin Books, 1973.

Rāmāyaṇa (brief summary), C. Rajagopalachari, ed. Bombay: Bharatiya Vidya Bhavan, [4]1962.

The Rāmāyaṇa, M. N. Dutt, trans., 3 vols. Reprint Calcutta: Oriental Publishing Co., 1960.

Rāmāyaṇ of Vālmīki, R. T. H. Griffith, trans. Reprint Varanasi: Chowkhamba, [3]1963.

Rāmāyaṇa, Critical Edition, 7 vols. Baroda: Oriental Institute, 1960-1975.

Rāmdās, Swāmi. *God-Experience.* Bombay: Bharatiya Vidya Bhavan, 1963.

Ramesan, N. *Temples and Legends of Andhra Pradesh.* Bombay: Bharatiya Vidya Bhavan, 1962.

Ranade, R. D. *The Bhagavadgītā as a Philosophy of God-Realization, Being a Clue Through the Labyrinth of Modern Interpretations.* Bombay: Bharatiya Vidya Bhavan, [2]1965.

———. *A Constructive Survey of Upaniṣadic Philosophy.* Reprint Bombay: Bharatiya Vidya Bhavan, 1968.

———. *Pathway to God in Hindī Literature.* Bombay: Bharatiya Vidya Bhavan, 1959.

———. *Pathway to God in Kaṇṇaḍa Literature.* Bombay: Bharatiya Vidya Bhavan, 1960.

———. *Pathway to God in Marathi Literature.* Bombay: Bharatiya Vidya Bhavan, 1961.

Ranganathananda, Swami. "The Science of Consciousness in the Light of Vedanta and Yoga," *Prabuddha Bharata* (June 1982): 257-63.

Rao, H. S. "The Two Bābās," *Illustrated Weekly of India* (21 November 1965).

Rao, S. R. "Deciphering the Indus Valley Script," *Indian and Foreign Review* (15 November 1979): 13-18.

———. *The Decipherment of the Indus Script*. Bombay: Asia Publishing House, 1982.

———. "Krishna's Dwarka," *Indian and Foreign Review* (15 March 1980): 15-19.

Rao, T. A. G., *Elements of Hindu Iconography*, 4 vols. Reprint New York: Paragon, 1968.

Rapson, E. I., general ed. *Cambridge History of India*, 6 vols. Reprint Delhi: S. Chand, 1964.

Rau, C. V. Sankar. *A Glossary of Philosophical Terms* [Sanskrit-English]. Madras: University of Madras, 1941.

Rau, H. "The Image of India in European Antiquity and the Middle Ages." In *India and the West: Proceedings of a Seminar Dedicated to the Memory of Hermann Goetz*, J. Deppert, ed. New Delhi: Monohar, 1983, 197-208.

Raychaudhuri, "The *Mahābhārata:* Some Aspects of its Culture." In *CHI*, vol. 2, 71 ff.

Reddy, Y. G. "The Svargabrahma Temple of Alampur: Iconographical Study," *Journal of Indian History* 55, nos. 1-2 (1977): 103-17.

Renou, L. *Le déstin du Veda dans l'Inde*. Paris: Adrien Maisouneuve, 1960.

———. *Destiny of the Veda in India*, Delhi: Motilal Banarsidass, 1968.

———. *Les écoles védiques et la formation du Veda*. Paris: Adrien Maisonneuve, 1947.

———. *Hinduism*. New York: Washington Square Press, 1964.

———. *Indian Literature*. New York: Praeger, 1965.

———. *Religions of Ancient India*. London: Athlone Press, 1953.

———. *Vedic India.* Calcutta: Sunil Gupta, 1957.

———, and J. Filliozat, eds. *L'Inde Classique*, 2 vols. Paris-Hanoi: Imprimerie Nationale, 1953.

Rhys Davids, T. W. *The Questions of King Milinda.* In *SBE*, vols. 25 and 26.

Rice, E. P. *Kanarese Literature.* Calcutta: Association Press, 1921.

Riepe, D. *The Naturalistic Tradition in Indian Thought.* Seattle: University of Washington Press, 1961.

———. *The Philosophy of India and its Impact on American Thought.* Springfield, Ill.: Charles C Thomas, 1970.

Risely, H. H. *The Peoples of India.* London: W. Thacker, ^{2}1915.

Roach, J. R., ed. *India 2000: The Next Fifteen Years.* Riverdale: Riverdale Publ., 1986.

Robb, Peter. "The Challenge of Gau Mata: British Policy and Religious Change in India, 1880-1916," *Modern Asian Studies* 20, no. 2 (1986): 285-319.

Robins, R. H. "The Evolution of Historical Linguistics," *JRAS* 1986, no. 1: 5-20.

Rocher, L. "The Purāṇas." In *HIL*, vol. 2, 3.

Ross, A. D. *The Hindu Family in Its Urban Setting.* Toronto: University of Toronto Press, 1962.

Rowland, B. *The Art and Architecture of India: Buddhist, Hindu, Jain.* Baltimore: Penguin Books, ^{2}1967.

Roy, Ajit. "Communalism—Its Political Roots," *Religion and Society*, 31, no. 4 (1984): 14-23.

Roy, D. K., and J. Devi. *Kumbha: India's Ageless Festival.* Bombay: Bharatiya Vidya Bhavan, 1955.

Roy, M. N. *India's Message.* Calcutta: Renaissance Publishers, 1950.

———. *Materialism.* Calcutta: Renaissance Publishers, ^{2}1951.

———. *New Humanism*, 2d rev. ed. Calcutta: Renaissance Publishers, 1953.

Roy, S. B. "Chronological Framework of Indian Protohistory—The Lower

Limit," *JBOI* 32, nos. 3-4 (March-June 1983): 254-74.

———. "Chronological Infrastructure of Indian Protohistory" *JBRS* 32 (1972): 44-78.

Ruben, W. *Materialismus im Leben des Alten Indien*, Acta Orientalia 13. Leiden: Brill, 1935.

Rudolph, L. I., and S. H. Rudolph. *The Modernity of Tradition*. Chicago: Chicago University Press, 1967.

Ruhela, S. P., and D. Robinson, eds. *Sai Baba and His Message*. Delhi: Vikas, 1976.

Śābarabhāṣya, with contemporary Sanskrit commentary by B. G. Apte, 6 vols. Poona: Anandasrama, 1931-1934.

Sachau, Edward C., trans. *Alberuni's India: An Account of the Religion, Philosophy, Literature, Geography, Chronology, Astronomy, Customs, Laws and Astrology of India about* ffi.⅛. *1030*, Trübner's Oriental Series. Reprint Delhi: 1964.

Sadhucaranprasad, Vaikunthavasi Sri Babu. *Dharmaśāstrasaṅgraha*. Bombay: Sri Venkateśvar Stīm Mudranayantrālaya, 1913.

Sāī Bābā (Śrī Sathya). *Satya Sāī Speaks*, 7 vols. Kadugodi: Sri Sathya Sai Education and Publication Foundation, 1972-76.

Sakhare, M. R. *History and Philosophy of the Lingayata Religion*. Belgaum: Publ. by the author, 1942.

Śākta, Vaiṣṇava, Yoga, Śaiva, Samānyavedānta, and Minor Upaniṣads. P. Mahadev Sastri, ed. and trans. Adyar: Adyar Library, 1912-1938.

Saletore, B. A. *Ancient Indian Political Thought and Institutions*. Bombay: Asia Publishing House, 1963.

Salomon, R. ed. and trans. *The Bridge to the Three Holy Cities, The Samāyaṇa-Praghaiṭṭaka of Nārāyana Bhaṭṭa's Tristhalisetu*. Delhi: Motilal Banarsidass, 1985.

Sāmaveda, Ram Sarma Acarya, ed., Bareilly: Saṁskṛti Samsthāna [2]1962; R. T. H. Griffith, trans., reprint Varanasi: Chowkhamba, 1963.

Sāṁkhyakārikā, S. S. Suryanarayana Sastri, trans. Madras: University of Madras, [4]1948.

Sāṁkhya Kārikā of Mahāmuni Śrī Īśvarakṛṣṇa, with the commentary of Pandit Swanarayana Sastri and *Sāṅkhya Tattvakaumudī of Vācaspati Miśra*. Bombay: Nirnaya Sagar Press, 1940.

Sangani, N. P. "*Sanātan dharm hi sarvabhaum dharm yā mānav dharm hai*," *Dharmaṅk, Kalyān* 30, no. 1 (1966): 242-49.

Sankalia, H. D. *Indian Archeology Today*. New York: Asia Publishing House, 1962.

———. "Paleolithic, Neolithic and Copper Ages." In *HCIP*, vol. 1, 125-42.

———. *Prehistoric Art in India*. Delhi: Vikas Publishing House, 1978.

———. *Prehistory and Protohistory in Indian and Pakistan*. Bombay: University of Bombay, 1961.

Śaṅkarabhāṣya, Swami Gambhirananda, trans. Calcutta: Advaita Ashrama, 1965.

Sankarananda, Swami. *Hindu States of Sumeria*. Calcutta: Firma K. L. Mukhopadhyay, 1962.

Sankaranarayan, P. *The Call of the Jagadguru*. Madras: Akhila Bharata Śaṅkara Seva Samiti, 1958.

Sankhāyana Śrautaśūtra, S. W. Caland, trans. Nagpur: The International Academy of Indian Culture, 1953.

Santucci, J. A. *An Outline of Vedic Literature*, American Academy of Religion Aids to the Study of Religion Series, Missoula: Scholars Press, 1977.

Saraswati, Dayananda. *Satyārtha Prakāśa*. Allahabad: Kal Press, 1947.

Sarkar, B. K. *The Positive Background of Hindu Sociology*, 3 vols. In *SBH*. vols. 18, 25, 32; Allahabad: Panini Press, 1914-37.

Sarkar, S. *The Aboriginal Races of India*. Calcutta: Bookland, 1954.

Sarma, D. S. *Hinduism Through the Ages*, rev. ed. Bombay: Bharatiya Vidya Bhavan, 1958.

———. *The Renaissance of Hinduism*. Benares: 1958.

Sarma, N. S. *Hindu Renaissance*. Benares: 1944.

Sarma, R. Thangasami. *Darśanamañjarī*, part 1. Madras: University of Madras, 1985.

Sarvadarśanasaṁgraha of Mādhava, V. S. Abhyankar, ed. Poona: B.O.R.I. [3]1978; E. B. Cowell and A. E. Gough, trans. (incomplete), 1892; reprint Varanasi: Chowkhamba, 1960.

Sarvarkar, V. "Essentials of Hindutva." In *Samagra Savarkar Wangmaya, Hindu Rastra Darshan*, vol. 6. Poona: Maharashtra Prantik Hindusabha, 1964.

Sastri, G. *A Study in the Dialectics of Sphoṭa.* Delhi: Motilal Banarsidass, 1981.

Sastri, K. A. Nilakantha. *The Colas.* 3 vols. Madras: University of Madras, 1935.

———. *The Culture and History of the Tamils.* Calcutta: Firma K. L. Mukhopadhyay, 1964.

———. *History of South India.* Madras: Oxford University Press, 1955.

Sastri, K. S. Ramaswami. *Sivananda: The Modern World Prophet.* Rishikesh: Divine Light Society, 1953.

Sastri, Kuppuswami. "*Kośavan ācāryaḥ.*" Reprinted in *Kuppuswami Sastri Birth Centenary Commemoration Volume*, S. S. Janaki, ed. Madras: Kuppuswami Research Institute, 1981, Part 1.

———. "Nyāya-Vaiśeṣika—Origin and Development." Introduction to K. Sastri, *Primer of Indian Logic.* 1932; reprinted in *Kuppuswami Birth Centenary Commemoration Volume*, S. S. Janaki, ed. Madras: 1981.

Sastri, P. D. *The Doctrine of Māyā in Vedānta.* London: 1911.

Sastry, R. A., trans. *Viṣṇusahasranāma: With the Bhāṣya of Śrī Śaṁkarācārya.* Adyar Library General Series. Adyar: Adyar Library and Research Centre, 1980.

Śatapatha Brāhmaṇa, J. Eggeling, ed. and trans., 5 vols. In *SBE*, vols. 12, 26, 41, 43 and 44.

Sawai, Yoshitsugu. "Śaṅkaras Theology of Saṁnyāsa," *Journal of Indian Philosophy* 14 (1986): 371-87.

Saxena, K. "The Janata Party Politics in Uttar Pradesh (1977-79),"

Indian Political Science Review (July 1983): 172-87.

Schilpp, P. A., ed. *The Philosophy of Sarvepalli Radhakrishnan.* New York: Tudor Publ. Co., 1952.

Schlingloff, D. *Die altindische Stadt.* Wiesbaden: Harrassowitz, 1969.

Schneider, U. "Kṛṣṇa's postumer Aufstieg; zur Frühgeschichte der Bhakti-bewegung." *Saeculum* 33, no. 1 (1982): 38-49.

Schrader, F. O. *Introduction to the Pāñcarātra and the Ahirbudhnya Saṁhitā.* Adyar: Adyar Library and Research Centre, 1916.

Schwab, J. *Le Renaissance Orientale,* 1950. English translation: *The Oriental Renaissance: Europe's Rediscovery of India and the East, 1680-1880,* G. Patterson-Black and V. Reinking, trans. New York: Columbia University Press, 1984.

Schwartzberg, J. E. ed. *Historical Atlas of India.* Chicago: University of Chicago Press, 1978.

Seal, A. *The Emergence of Indian Nationalism.* Cambridge: 1968.

Seal, B. N. *Comparative Studies in Vaishnavism and Christianity with an Examination of the Mahābhārata Legend about Nārada's Pilgrimage to Śvetadvīpa and an Introduction on the Historico-Comparative Method.* Calcutta: Private publication, 1899.

———. *The Positive Sciences of the Hindus.* Reprint Delhi: Motilal Banarsidass, 1958.

"Secret Societies," *Seminar* 151 (March 1972).

Seemann, R. "Versuch zu einer Theorie des Avatāra. Mensch gewordener Gott oder Gott gewordener Mensch?" *Numen* 33, no. 1 (1986): 90-140.

Segal, J. G. "White and Black Jews at Cochin, the Story of a Controversy," *JRAS* 1983, no. 2: 228-52.

Segal, R. *The Crisis of India.* Penguin: Harmondsworth, 1965.

Sen, N. "The Influence of the Epics on Indian Life and Literature," In *CHI,* vol. 2, 117.

Sengupta, N. C. *Evolution of Ancient Indian Law.* London: Probsthain, 1953.

Sengupta, P. C. *Ancient Indian Chronology.* Calcutta: University of Calcutta, 1947.

Shankar, M. "Social Roots of Communalism," *Religion and Society*, 31, no. 4 (December 1984): 24-44.

Sharma, A. *The Puruṣārthas: A Study in Hindu Axiology.* East Lansing: Asian Studies Center, Michigan State University, 1982.

———. *Viśiṣṭādvaita Vedānta: A Study.* New Delhi: Heritage Press, 1978.

Sharma, B. N. K. *A Comparative Study of Ten Commentaries on the Brahmasūtras.* Delhi: Motilal Banarsidass, 1984.

———. *A History of Dvaita School of Vedānta and its Literature*, 2 vols. Bombay: Booksellers Publishing Co., 1960-1961.

———. *Madhva's Teaching in His Own Words.* Bombay: Bhavan's Book University, 1961.

———. *Philosophy of Śrī Madhvācārya.* Bombay: Bharatiya Vidya Bhavan, 1962.

Sharma, H. D. *Brahmanical Asceticism.* Poona: Oriental Book Agency, 1939.

Sharma, R. K. (ed.) *Indian Archeology. New Perspectives.* Delhi: Agam Kala Prakashan, 1982.

Sharma, R. S. *Sudras in Ancient India.* Delhi: Motilal Banarsidass, 1958.

Sharma, S. R. *Swami Rama Tirtha.* Bombay: Bharatiya Vidya Bhavan, 1961.

Sharpe, E. J. *The Universal Gītā: Western Images of the Bhagavadgītā*, A Bicentenary Survey. La Salle: Open Court, 1985.

Shastri, A. M. *India as Seen in the Bṛhatsaṁhitā of Varāhamihira.* Delhi: Motilal Banarsidass, 1969.

Shastri, D. R. *Short History of Indian Materialism.* Calcutta: The Book Company, 1930.

Shendge, M. J. "The Interdisciplinary Approach to Indian Studies," *ABORI* 63 (1982): 63-98.

Sheth, Noel. *The Divinity of Krishna.* Delhi: Munshiram Manoharlal Publishers, 1984.

Shils, E. A. *The Intellectual Between Tradition and Modernity: The Indian*

Situation. The Hague: Mouton, 1961.

Shourie, A. *Hinduism: Essence and Consequence—A Study of the Upaniṣads, the Gītā and the Brahma-Sūtras*. New Delhi: Vikas Publishing House, 1980.

Shulman, D. D. *Tamil Temple Myths: Sacrifice and Divine Marriage in the South Indian Śaiva Tradition*. Princeton: Princeton University Press, 1980.

Siauve, S. *La doctrine de Madhva*. Pondichéry: Institut Français d'Indologie, 1968.

———. *La voie vers la connaissance de Dieu sélon l'Aṇuvyākhyāna de Madhva*. Pondichéry: Institut Français d'Indologie, 1957.

Siegel, L. *Fires of Love—Waters of Peace: Passion and Renunciation in Indian Culture*. Honolulu: University of Hawaii Press, 1983.

———. *Sacred and Profane Dimensions of Love in Indian Traditions as Exemplified in the Gītāgoviṇḍa of Jayadeva*. Oxford: Oxford University Press, 1978.

Śīkṣādivedaṣadaṅgāṇi, Pandurang Jawaji (loose leaf). Bombay: Venkatesvara Steam Press, 1934.

Sil, N. P. "Political Morality vs. Political Necessity: Kautilya and Machiavelli Revisited," *Journal of Asian History* 19, no. 2 (1985): 101-42.

Singer, M. ed. *Krishna: Myths, Rites and Attitudes*. Chicago: University of Chicago Press, 1969.

———, ed. *Traditional India: Structure and Change*. Philadelphia: American Folklore Society, 1959.

Singh, Kushwant. *India: A Mirror for its Monsters and Monstrosities*. Bombay: Pearl, 1970.

Singh, Mohan. "Yoga and Yoga Symbolism," *Symbolon: Jahrbuch für Symbolforschung*, Band 2 (1959): 121-43.

Singh, N. K. "Anand Marg," *Seminar* 151 (March 1972): 21-25.

Singh, S. *Vedāntadeśika*. Varanasi: Chowkhamba, 1958.

Sinha, J. *History of Indian Philosophy*, 2 vols. Calcutta: Sinha Publishing House, 1956-1961.

———. *Indian Psychology*, 2 vols. Calcutta: Sinha Publishing House, 1958-1960.

———. *Indian Realism*. London: K. Paul, French, Trübner & Co., 1938.

Sinha, P. N. *A Study of the Bhāgavata Purāṇa*. Madras: Theosophical Society, [2]1950.

Sirkar, D. C. *The Śākta Pīthas*, rev. ed. Delhi: Motilal Banarsidass, 1948.

———. "Viṣṇu." *Quarterly Journal of the Mythological Society* 25 (1935): 120 ff.

Sivapadasundaram, S. *The Śaivaschool of Hinduism*. London: Allen & Unwin, 1934.

Śiva-Purāṇa, Benares: Pandit Pustakalaya, 1962; J. L. Shastri, trans. 4 vols., Delhi: Motilal Banarsidass, 1970-1971.

Sivaramamurti, C. *Indian Bronzes*. Bombay: Taraporevala, 1960.

Sivaraman, K. *Śaivism in Philosophical Perspective*. Delhi etc.: Motilal Banarsidass, 1973.

———. "The Word as a Category of Revelation." In *Revelation in Indian Thought, A Festschrift in Honour of Professor T. R. V. Murti*, H. Coward and K. Sivaraman, eds., Emeryville: Dharma Publishing, 1977, 45-64.

Śivasaṁhitā, S. C. Vasu, trans. Allahabad: Panini Office, 1923.

Ślokavārtika of Kumārila Bhaṭṭa's with the commentary Nyāyaratnakāra of Parthasarathi Miśra. Swami Drāṅkasāsa Sastri, ed. Varanasi: Tara Publications, 1978. Ganganatha Jha, trans. Calcutta: Asiatic Society, 1907.

Smart, N. *Doctrine and Argument in Indian Philosophy*. London: Allen & Unwin, 1964.

Smith, B. K. "Ritual, Knowledge, and Being: Initiation and Veda Study in Ancient India," *Numen* 33, no. 1 (1986): 65-89.

Smith, B. L., ed. *Religion and the Legitimation of Power in South Asia*, International Studies in Sociology and Social Anthropology. Leiden: Brill, 1978.

Smith, B. L. (ed.) *Hinduism: New Essays on the History of Religions* Leiden: Brill, 1976.

Smith, D. E., *India as a Secular State.* Princeton: Princeton University Press, 1967.

Smith, V. *History of India.* Oxford: Oxford University Press, 1955.

Smith, W. C. *Modern Islam in India.* Lahore: Mohammed Ashraf, ³1963.

Somaśambhupaddhatī, H. Brunner-Lachaux, ed. French trans. and notator, 2 vols. Pondichéry: Institut Français d'Indologie, 1963-1968.

Sørenson, M. *Index of Subjects in the Mahābhārata.* Reprint Delhi: Motilal Banarsidass, 1962.

Spate, O. H. K. *India and Pakistan: A General and Regional Geography.* New York: Dutton, rev. ed. 1963.

Spear, T. G. P. *India: A Modern History.* Ann Arbor: University of Michigan Press, 1961.

Spellman, J. W. *Political Theory of Ancient India.* New York: Oxford University Press, 1964.

Śrī Bhagavad Rāmānuja Granthamālā, P. B. Annangaracharya Swami, ed. Kanchipuram: Granthamala Office, 1956.

Srinivas, M. N. *Caste and Other Esays.* Bombay: Asia Publishing House, ²1965.

———. *India's Villages.* Bombay: Asia Publishing House, 1960.

———. *Religion and Society Among the Coorgs.* Bombay: Asia Publishing House, ²1965.

Srinivasacari, P. *The Philosophy of Viśiṣṭādvaita.* Adyar: Theosophical Society, 1946.

Srinivasan, D. "Unhinging Śiva from the Indus Civilization," *JRAS* 1 (1984): 77-89.

Śrī Parameśvara Saṁhitā, Sri Govindacarya, ed. Srirangam: Kodaṇḍarāmasannidhi, 1953.

Śrīpati's Śrīkara Bhāṣya, Hayavadana Rao, ed. Bangalore: 1936.

Staal, J. F. *Advaita and Neoplatonism.* Madras: University of Madras, 1961.

———. *AGNI: The Vedic Ritual of the Fire Altar*, 2 vols. Berkeley: University of California Press, 1983.

———. "Exchange with a Reviewer of Agni," *JAS* 46, no. 1 (1987): 105-10.

———. "Language and Ritual." In *Prof. Kuppuswamy Sastri Birth Centenary Volume*. Madras: Kuppuswami Research Institute, 1985, part 2, 51-62.

———. "The Meaninglessness of Ritual," *Numen* 26 (1979): 2-22.

———. *The Science of Ritual*. Poona: Deccan Institute, 1982.

———. "The Sound of Religion," *Numen* 33 (1986): 33-64, 185-224.

———, ed. *A Reader on the Sanskrit Grammarians*. Cambridge, Mass.: MIT Press, 1972.

Stevenson, M. *The Rites of the Twice Born*. Oxford: Oxford University Press, 1920.

von Stietencron, H. "Dämonen und Gegengötter: Überlegungen zur Typologie von Antagonismen," *Saeculum* 34, nos. 3-4 (1983): 372-83.

———. "Die Göttin Durgā Mahiṣāsuramārdiṇī: Mythos, Darstellung und geschichtliche Rolle bei der Hinduisierung Indiens," *Visible Religion, Annual for Religious Iconography*. Leiden: Brill, 1983, vol. 23, 11-166.

———. *Gaṅgā und Yamunā*. Wiesbaden: Harrassowitz, 1972.

———. *Indische Sonnenpriester: Sāmba und die Śākasdiśpīya Brāhmaṇa*. Wiesbaden: Harrassowitz, 1966.

———. "Suicide as a Religious Institution," *Bharatiya Vidya* 27 (1967): 7-24.

Stoler-Miller, B. *Love Song of the Dark Lord*. New York: Columbia University Press, 1977.

———. "Rādhā: Consort of Kṛṣṇa's Vernal Passion," *JAOS* 95, no. 4 (1975): 655-71.

———. "Stella Kramrisch: A Biographical Essay." In *Exploring India's Sacred Art*, B. Stoler-Miller, ed. Philadelphia: University of Pennsylvania, 1983, 3-33.

Subbarao, B. *The Personality of India*. Baroda: University of Baroda, 1959.

Śukra Nītisāra, B. K. Sarkar, trans. Allahabad: Panini Office, ^{2}1923.

Sukthankar, V. S. *On the Meaning of the Mahābhārata*. Bombay: Asiatic Society, 1957.

Sundaram, P. K. *Advaita Epistemology.* Madras: University of Madras, 1968.

Swarup, B. *Theory of Indian Music.* Allahabad: Swamy Brothers, [2]1958.

Tagore, R. *Sādhana.* Calcutta: Macmillan, 1950.

———. *Creative Unity.* Calcutta: Macmillan, 1959.

Taimni, I. K. *The Science of Yoga.* Wheaton: Theosophical Publishing House, [3]1972.

Talbot, P. and S. L. Poplai. *India and America: A Study of Their Relations.* New York: Harper and Row, 1959.

Tandon, P. *Punjabi Century.* Berkeley: University of California, 1968.

Taposwami Maharaj, Swami. *Wanderings in the Himalayas,* Madras: Ganesh, 1960.

Tarkabhāṣa of Keśava Miśra, G. Jha, ed. and trans. Poona: Oriental Book Agency, [2]1949.

Tarn, W. W. *The Greeks in Bactria and India.* Cambridge: Cambridge University Press, 1951; reprint 1966.

Tendulkar, D. G. *Mahātmā: Life and Work of M. K. Gandhi.* 8 vols. Bombay: V. K. Jhaveri, 1952-1958.

Thangaswami, R. *A Bibliographical Survey of Advaita Vedānta Literature* [in Sanskrit]. Madras: University of Madras, 1980.

———. *Darśanamañjarī.* Madras: University of Madras, 1985.

Thapar, R. *A History of India.* Baltimore: Penguin Books, 2 vols. 1966.

———. *India in Transition.* Bombay: Asia Publishing House, 1956.

Thomas, M. M. *The Acknowledged Christ of the Indian Renaissance.* London: SCM Press, 1969.

Thomas, P. *Epics, Myths and Legends of India.* Bombay: Taraporevala, 1961.

———. *Hindu Religion, Custom and Manners.* Bombay: 1961.

Thompson, E. J., and A. M. Spencer. *Bengali Religious Lyrics, Śākta.* Calcutta: Association Press, 1923.

Thurston, E., and K. Rangachari. *Tribes and Castes of South India*, 4 vols. Madras: Government Press, 1929.

Tilak, B. G. *The Arctic Home in the Vedas*. Reprint Poona: Tilak Bros., 1956.

———. *Gītā Rahasya*, 2 vols. Reprint Poona: Tilak Bros., 1956.

———. *Orion or Researches into the Antiquity of the Veda*. Bombay: Sagoon, 1893. Reprint Poona: Tilak Bros., 1955.

———. *Vedic Chronology*. Poona: 1909.

Timberg, T. A., ed. *Jews in India*. New York: Advent Books, 1986.

Tirtha, Swami Bharati Krishna. *Sanātana Dharma*. Bombay: Bharatiya Vidya Bhavan, 1964.

The Tirukkural [in Tamil] G. U. Pope, W. H. Drew, J. Lazarus, and F. W. Ellis, trans. Tinnelvelly: South India Saiva Siddhanta Works Publishing Society, 1962.

Tiruvācagam, G. U. Pope, ed. and trans. 1900; reprint Madras: University of Madras, 1970.

Tiruvācakam, Ratna Navaratnam, trans. Bombay: Bharatiya Vidya Bhavan, 1963.

Tod, J. *Annals and Antiquities of Rajasthan*, William Crooke, ed., 3 vols. Delhi: Motilal Banarsidass, n.d.

Tripurā Rahasya, A. U. Vasavada, trans. Varanasi: Chowkhamba, 1965.

Tripurārahasyam, Swami Sanatanadevaji Maharaja, ed. Varanasi: Chowkhamba, 1967.

Trivedi, M. M., "Citsukha's View on Self-Luminosity," *JIPh* 15 (1987): 115-23.

Tyagisananda, Swami, ed. *Aphorisms on the Gospel of Divine Love or Nārada Bhaktisūtras*. Madras: Ramakrishna Math, [5]1972.

Underhill, M. M. *The Hindu Religious Year*. Calcutta: Association Press, 1921.

Upadaśasahasrī of Śaṅkarācārya, Swami Jagadananda, ed. and trans. Madras: Ramakrishna Math, [3]1962.

Upadhyaya, Deendayal. "A Democratic Alternative," *Seminar* 80 (April 1966):21-24.

———. "Jana Sangh," *Seminar* 89 (January 1967): 34-37.

Upadhyaya, K. D. *Studies in Indian Folk Culture*. Calcutta: Indian Publications, 1964.

Upadhye, P. M. "Manusmrti—Its Relevance in Modern India," in *JOIB* 35, no. 1-2 (1985): 43-48.

Vadāvalī of Nagojī Bhaṭṭa, Nagaraja Rao, ed. and trans. Adyar: Adyar Library, 1943.

Vaidyanathan, K. R. *Sri Krishna, the Lord of Guruvayur*. Bombay: Bharatiya Vidya Bhavan, 1974.

Vaiśeṣikardarśana, Anantalal Thakur ed. and trans. Darbhanga: Mithila Institute, 1957.

Vaiśeṣikasūtras of Kanāḍa, N. Sinha, trans. Allahabad: Panini Office, 1911.

Varma, K. C. "The Iron Age, the Veda and the Historical Urbanization." In *Indian Archeology, New Perspectives*, R. K. Sharma, ed. New Delhi: Indian Archeological Survey, 1982, 155-183.

Varma, L. A. Ravi. "Rituals of Worship." In *CHI*, vol. 4, 445-63.

Varma, V. P. *Modern Indian Political Thought*. Agra: Laksmi Narain Agarwala, ^{4}1968.

Vasudevāśrama: Yatidharmaprakāśa. A Treatise on World Renunciation, P. Olivelle, ed. and trans., 2 vols. Vienna: De Nobili Research Library, 1977.

Vatsyayan, Kapila. "Prehistoric Paintings," *Sangeet Natak, Journal of the Sangeet Natak Akademi* 66 (October-December): 5-18.

Vaudeville, C. *Kabīr Granthavālī* (Doha). Pondichery: Institut Français d'Indologie, 1957.

Vedāntakarikāvalī of Venkatācārya, V. Krisnamacarya, ed. and trans. Adyar: Adyar Library, 1950.

Vedāntaparibhāṣa by Dharmarāja (Sanskrit text, English translation and notes), S. S. Suryanarayana Sastri, ed. and trans. Adyar: Adyar Library, 1942.

Vedāntasāra of Sādānanda Yogīndra, Swami Nikhilananda, ed. and trans. Calcutta: Ramakrishna Math, ^{4}1959.

Vedāntasūtras with the Commentary of Baladeva, S. C. Vasu Vidyaranava, trans., *SBH*. Allahabad: Panini Office, [2]1934.

Vedāntasūtras with the Commentary of Madhva, S. S. Rao, trans. Tirupati: Sri Vyasa Press, [2]1936.

Vedāntasūtras with Rāmānuja's Commentary, G. Thibaut, trans. In *SBE*, vol. 48.

Vedāntasūtras with Śaṅkarācārya's Commentary, G. Thibaut, trans., 2 vols. In *SBE*, vols. 34 and 38.

Vedārthasaṁgraha, S. S. Ragavachar, ed. and trans. Mysore: Ramakrishna Ashrama, 1956.

Venkatācārya's Vedāntakarikāvalī (Sanskṛt text and English translation), V. Krsnamacarya, trans. Adyar: Adyar Library, 1950.

Vetter, T. "Die Gaudapadīya-Kārikās: Zur Entstehung und zur Bedeutung von [A]dvaita," *WZKSA* 22 (1978): 95-131.

Vidyabhusana, S. C. *A History of Indian Logic*. Calcutta: University of Calcutta, 1921.

Vidyarthi, L. P. *Aspects of Religion in Indian Society*. Meerut: Vedant Nath Ramnath, 1962.

Vidyarthi, P. B. *Knowledge, Self and God in Rāmānuja*. New Delhi: Motilal Banarsidass, 1978.

Viennot, O. *Le culte de l'arbre dans l'Inde ancienne*. Paris: 1954.

Viṣṇu Purāṇa, H. H. Wilson, trans. Reprint Calcutta: Punthi Pustak, 1961.

Viśva Hindu Viśeṣāṅk Bombay: World Council of Hindus, 1966.

Viśvakarma Vāstuśāstra, K. Vasudeva Sastri and N. B. Gadre, eds., Tanjore Sarasvati Mahal Series No. 85, 1958.

Viśveśvarasarasvatī Yatidharmasaṅgraha, V. G. Apte, ed. Poona: Anandasrama, 1928.

Vivekacudāmanī of Śaṅkarācārya, Swami Madhavananda, ed. and trans. Calcutta: Ramakrishna Math, [6]1957.

Vivekananda, Swami. *Complete Works of Swami Vivekananda*, 8 vols. Calcutta: Advaita Ashrama, 1970-1971.

Vogel, J. P. *Indian Serpent Lore.* London: Probsthain, 1926.

Volwahsen, A. *Living Architecture: Indian.* New York: Grosset & Dunlap, 1969.

Vyas, K. C. *The Social Renaissance in India.* Bombay: Asia Publishing House, 1957.

Vyas, R. T. "Roots of Śaṅkara's Thought," *JBOI* 32, nos. 1-2 (September-December 1982): 35-49.

Vyas, S. N. *India in the Rāmāyaṇa Age.* Delhi: Atura Ram & Sons, 1967.

Waghorne, J. P., and N. Cutler, ed. *Gods of Flesh/Gods of Stone: The Embodiment of Divinity in India.* Chambersburg: Anima Publications, 1985.

Walker, B. *The Hindu World: An Encyclopedic Survey of Hinduism,* 2 vols. New York: Praeger, 1968.

Warder, A. K. *Outline of Indian Philosophy,* Delhi: Motilal Banarsidass, 1968.

Wasson, R. Gordon. "The Soma of the Rig Veda: What Was It?" *JAOS* 91, no. 2 (1971): 169-91.

Weber, A. "Über das Menschenopfer bei den Indern der vedischen Zeit." *Indische Streifen* I Berlin: Nicolai, 1868, vol. 1, 54-89.

Weber, M. *The Religion of India: The Sociology of Hinduism and Buddhism.* Reprint New York: Free Press, 1967.

Weiss, B. "Meditations in the Myth of Savitri," *JAAR* 53, no. 2: 259-70.

von Weizsäcker, C. F. and Gopi Kṛṣṇ a. *Biologische Basis Religiöser Erfahrung.* Weilheim: Otto Wilhelm Barth Verlag, 1971.

Welborn, G. and G. E. Yocum (eds.) *Religious Festivals in South India and Sri Lanka,* Delhi: Manohar, 1985.

Werner, K. "A Note on Karma and Rebirth in the Vedas," *Hinduism* 83 (1978): 1-4.

———. "Religious Practice and Yoga in the Time of the Vedas, Upaniṣads and Early Buddhism," *ABORI* 56 (1975): 179-94.

———. "The Vedic Concept of Human Personality and Its Destiny," *JIPh* 5 (1978): 275-89.

Westcott, G. H. *Kabir and the Kabir Panth.* Reprint Calcutta: Susil Gupta, ^{2}1953.

Whaling, F. *The Rise of the Religious Significance of Rama.* Delhi: Motilal Banarsidass, 1980.

Wheeler, M. *The Indus Civilization.* Cambridge: Cambridge University Press, 1953.

Wheelock, W. T. "Patterns of Mantra Use in a Vedic Ritual," *Numen* 32, no. 2 (1986): 169-93.

White, S. J. "Kṛṣṇa as Divine Child." *HR* 12, no. 2 (1972): 156-77.

Whitehead, H. *The Village Gods of South India*, Religious Life of India Series. Calcutta: Association Press, ^{2}1921.

Williams, R. B. *A New Face of Hinduism: The Swaminarayan Religion.* Cambridge: Cambridge University Press, 1984.

Wilson, H. H. *Essays and Lectures on the Religion of the Hindus.* 2 vol. London: Trübner, 1862.

———. *Religious Sects of the Hindus.* 1861; reprint Calcutta: Punthi Pustak, 1958.

Winternitz, M. *A History of Indian Literature*, S. Ketkar and H. Kohn, tran., 3 vols. Reprint Calcutta: University of Calcutta, 1927-1967.

Wiser, W. H. *Behind Mud Walls 1930-60.* Berkeley: University of California, 1963.

———. *The Hindu Jajmani System.* Lucknow: Lucknow Publishing House, 1958.

Woodroffe, J. (Arthur Avalon). *Introduction to Tantra Śāstra.* Madras: Ganesh & Co., ^{4}1963.

———. *Mahānirvāṇatantra: The Great Liberation.* Madras: Ganesh & Co., ^{4}1963.

———. *Principles of Tantra.* Madras: Ganesh & Co., ^{3}1960.

Woods, J. H., trans. *Patañjali's Yogasūtra, with Vyāsa's Bhāṣya and Vācaspati Miśra's Tattva Vaiśāradī*, Harvard Oriental Series 17. Cambridge, Mass.: Harvard University Press, 1914.

Yadav, B. S. "Vaiṣṇavism on Hans Küng: A Hindu Theology of Religious Pluralism," *Religion and Society* 27, no. 2 (June 1980): 32-64.

Yajurveda Vajasaneyasaṁhitā, ed. A. Weber, 2 vols. Leipzig: Indische Studien, 1871-1872.

Yamunacarya, M. *Rāmānuja's Teachings in His Own Words.* Bombay: Bharatiya Vidya Bhavan, 1963.

Yatidharmasaṅgraha of Viśvesvarasaraswati, by V. G. Apte, ed. Poona: Anandasrama, 1928.

Yatīndramatadīpikā of Śrīnivāsadāsa, Swami Adidevananda, ed. and trans. Madras: Ramakrishna Math, 1949.

Yatiswaranda, Swami. *The Divine Life.* Mylapore: 1964.

———, ed. *Universal Prayers.* Mylapore: Ramakrishna Math, 1956.

Yocum, G. E. "The Goddess in a Tamil Śaiva Devotional Text, Manikkavācakar's Tiruvācakam," *JAAR* Supplement 45 (1977): 367-88.

———. *Hymns to the Dancing Śiva: A Study of Manikkavācakar's Tiruvācakam.* Columbia, Mo.: South Asia Books, 1982.

———. "Shrines, Shamanism, and Love Poetry: Elements in the Emergence of Popular Tamil Bhakti," *JAAR*, 41 (1973): 3-17.

Yogananda, Paramahamsa. *Autobiography of a Yogi.* Bombay: Jaico, 1960.

Yogavāsiṣṭha Rāmāyaṇa, D. N. Bose, trans., 2 vols. Calcutta: Oriental Publishing Co., 1958.

Young, K., and A. Sharma. *Images of the Feminine—Mythic, Philosophic and Human—in the Buddhist, Hindu and Islamic Traditions: A Biography of Women in India.* Chico: New Horizons Press, 1974.

Young, R. F. *Resistant Hinduism: Sanskrit Sources on Anti-Christian Apologetics in Early Nineteenth-Century India.* Vienna: Indologisches Institut der Universität Wien, 1981.

Younger, P. "A Temple Festival of Mariyamman," *JAAR*, 48 (1980): 493-517.

———. *Introduction to Indian Religious Thought.* Philadelphia: Westminster Press, 1972.

Zaehner, H. *Hinduism*. Oxford: Oxford University Press, 1962.

Zelliot, E. "The Mediaeval Bhakti Movement in History. An Essay on the Literature in English." In *Hinduism: New Essays in the History of Religions*, B. L. Smith, ed. Leiden: Brill, 1976.

Zimmer, H. *The Art of Indian Asia*, 2 vols. New York: Bollingen Foundation, 1955.

———. *Artistic Form and Yoga in the Sacred Images of India*, Gerald Chapple and James B. Lawson, trans. Princeton: Princeton University Press, 1984.

———. *The King and the Corpse*. New York: Pantheon, 1947.

———. *Myths and Symbols in Indian Art and Civilization*. New York: Harper & Row, ^{4}1963.

———. *Philosophies of India*, J. Campbell, ed. Princeton: Bollingen Foundation, 1951.

Zvelebil, K. *Tiru Murugan*. Madras: International Institute of Tamil Studies, 1982.

Index